The Sounds of Language

Linguistics in the World

Linguistics in the World is a textbook series focusing on the study of language in the real world, enriching students' understanding of how language works through a balance of theoretical insights and empirical findings. Presupposing no or only minimal background knowledge, each of these titles is intended to lay the foundation for students' future work, whether in language science, applied linguistics, language teaching, or speech sciences.

What Is Sociolinguistics?, by Gerard van Herk
The Sounds of Language, by Elizabeth Zsiga

Forthcoming

Second Language Acquisition, by Kirsten Hummel
An Introduction to Language, by Kirk Hazen
The Nature of Language, by Gary Libben
Sociolinguistics in Language Teaching, by Gary Barkhuizen

The Sounds of Language

An Introduction to Phonetics and Phonology

Elizabeth C. Zsiga

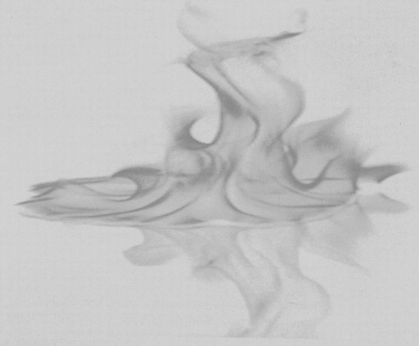

WILEY-BLACKWELL

A John Wiley & Sons, Ltd., Publication

This edition first published 2013
© 2013 Elizabeth C. Zsiga

Blackwell Publishing was acquired by John Wiley & Sons in February 2007. Blackwell's
publishing program has been merged with Wiley's global Scientific, Technical, and Medical
business to form Wiley-Blackwell.

Registered Office
John Wiley & Sons Ltd, The Atrium, Southern Gate, Chichester, West Sussex, PO19 8SQ, UK

Editorial Offices
350 Main Street, Malden, MA 02148-5020, USA
9600 Garsington Road, Oxford, OX4 2DQ, UK
The Atrium, Southern Gate, Chichester, West Sussex, PO19 8SQ, UK

For details of our global editorial offices, for customer services, and for information about how
to apply for permission to reuse the copyright material in this book please see our website at
www.wiley.com/wiley-blackwell.

Library of Congress Cataloging-in-Publication Data
Zsiga, Elizabeth C.
  The sounds of language : an introduction to phonetics and phonology / Elizabeth C. Zsiga.
      p. cm. – (Linguistics in the world)
  Includes bibliographical references and index.
  ISBN 978-1-4051-9103-6 (pbk. : alk. paper) – ISBN 978-1-4051-9104-3 (hbk. : alk. paper)
1. Grammar, Comparative and general–Phonology.   2. Phonetics.   I. Title.
  P217.Z75 2013
  414–dc23
                                                                            2012026660

A catalogue record for this book is available from the British Library.

Cover image: © Andrejs Pidjass / iStockphoto
Cover design by Nicki Averill

Set in Minion 9.5/11.5 pt by Toppan Best-set Premedia Ltd
Printed and bound in Singapore by Markono Print Media Pte Ltd

3   2014

Contents

4 A Map of the Vowels 55

5 Anatomy, Physiology, and Gestural Coordination 76

19 Variation 426

20 Acquisition and Learning 447

Preface

to the student: what this book is about

This book is about the sounds of speech. Communication sometimes takes place without sound, of course: with a smile or a raised fist, a nod or a wave, a photograph or a drawing. There can even be language without sound: those who cannot hear use languages based on gestures instead. Yet for most of us most of the time, getting our message across involves encoding it in sounds. Even when we write, we use symbols that are based on speech (though, in English, sometimes not very directly).

The study of the sounds of speech is often divided into the disciplines of *phonetics* and *phonology*. *Phonetics* studies speech sounds as physical objects. Phoneticians ask questions such as:

- How are speech sounds made?
- How many different sounds do languages use?
- How does sound travel through the air?
- How is it registered by the ears?
- How can we measure speech?

Questions concerning how sounds are made fall under the domain of *articulatory phonetics*; questions concerning how sound propagates and how it can be measured fall under the domain of *acoustic phonetics*.

Phonology studies how languages organize sounds into different patterns. Phonologists ask questions such as:

- How do languages organize sounds to distinguish different words?
- What sorts of restrictions, or constraints, do languages put on sequences of sounds?
- What sorts of changes (alternations) do sounds undergo if illicit sequences arise?
- How are sounds organized into larger constituents (syllables, stress feet, words, phrases)?

Patterns relating to linear strings of segments are the concern of *segmental phonology*; patterns relating to larger hierarchically-organized constituents are the concern of *suprasegmental* phonology.

In addition, phonologists and phoneticians may study how sound patterns arise, change, and vary, asking questions such as:

- How do languages change over time?
- Why are there different dialects?
- How do children learn to speak?
- Why is it hard to learn a second language as an adult?

This book begins to address each of these questions, providing a basic introduction to what the linguistic study of sounds is about. While the book follows the traditional divisions of phonology and phonetics, it is hoped that this overview will help students to see the sub-disciplines in relation to each other, identifying areas of overlap and mutual concern.

to the teacher: how to use this book

This book is designed as an introduction to the linguistic study of speech sounds, that is, the disciplines of phonetics and phonology, in either undergraduate or beginning graduate classes. The book is divided into five sections, each of which deals with one of the traditionally-recognized divisions of the discipline: Articulatory phonetics, Acoustic phonetics, Segmental phonology, Suprasegmental phonology, and Variation and change. As noted above, while the divisions are traditional, the approach seeks to present the linguistic study of sound patterns as a unified endeavor, with different sub-disciplines approaching the object of study from different points of view, asking different kinds of questions about the same subject. Phonetics and phonology inform one another, but are not conflated.

Though the topics and presentation are theoretically grounded, it is not a goal of the book to present the details of particular theories. Rather, the goal is to present: (1) the range of data that any theory must account for; (2) important concepts and constructs that emerge from the data; and (3) some critical overviews of different approaches that have been taken to tackling the issues, with opportunities for the students to practice data analysis and hypothesis testing. Many examples will be from English (as the one language accessible to all readers), and several sections are devoted to the detailed description of English phenomena (as this is of particular interest to many), but there is also broad coverage of typologically diverse systems.

The book follows a modular design, allowing maximum freedom for the instructor. There is enough material for a two-semester course, covering both phonetics and phonology. It will be an advantage that the two subjects are covered from a consistent point of view with consistent terminology, avoiding the gaps and contradictions often encountered when different texts are used.

The book can also be used, however, in a one-semester course that covers both. The first two chapters of each section present a generally non-technical, data-oriented overview, with emphasis on English, raising topics which the following chapters treat in more detail or more formally. Chapter 2, for example, describes the sounds of English, while Chapters 3 and 4 delve into the full IPA. Chapter 11 surveys the types of alternations common in the languages of the world, with a rich set of examples, and Chapters 12–14 discuss more formal theoretical approaches to accounting for them. A one-semester class covering both phonetics and phonology might be created using the first two chapters of each section, with the instructor choosing other chapters according to the topics deemed most important. The final section of the book discusses historical change, first and second language acquisition, and sociolinguistic variation, topics that are often of great interest to students of speech, but are not often covered in introductory texts.

Finally, fresh exercises are included at the end of every chapter.

ad majorem dei gloriam

1 The Vocal Tract

In all things of nature there is something of the marvelous.

Aristotle, *Parts of Animals*

Parts is parts.

Wendy's commercial

Chapter outline

The Sounds of Language: An Introduction to Phonetics and Phonology, First Edition. Elizabeth C. Zsiga.
© 2013 Elizabeth C. Zsiga. Published 2013 by Blackwell Publishing Ltd.

We begin our study of the sounds of speech by surveying the parts of the body used to make speech sounds: *the vocal tract*. An understanding of how these parts fit and act together, the topic of Section 1.2, is crucial for everything that comes later in the book. Before we dive into the study of human anatomy, however, Section 1.1 considers some of the tools that speech scientists have used or currently use to do their work: How can we "see" inside the body to know what our vocal tracts are doing?

1.1 seeing the vocal tract: tools for speech research

The vocal tract is comprised of all the parts of the body that are used in the creation of speech sounds, from the abdominal muscles that contract to push air out of the lungs, to the lips and nostrils from which the sound emerges. We sometimes call this collection of parts "the organs of speech," but there really is no such thing. Every body part that is used for speech has some other biological function – the lungs for breathing, the tongue and teeth for eating, the larynx to close off the lungs and keep the two systems separate – and is only secondarily adapted for speech.

We're not sure at what point in time the human vocal tract developed its present form, making speech as we know it possible; some scientists estimate it may have been 50,000 to 100,000 years ago. And we don't know which came first, the development of a complex brain that enables linguistic encoding, or the development of the vocal structures to realize the code in sound. While hominid fossils provide some clues about brain size and head shape, neither brains nor tongues are well preserved in the fossil record. We do know that no other animal has the biological structure needed to make the full range of human speech sounds. Even apes and chimpanzees, whose anatomy is generally similar to ours, have jaws and skulls of very different shape from ours, and could only manage one or two consonants and vowels. That's why scientists who try to teach language to chimps or apes use manual sign language instead: chimps are much better at manipulating their fingers than their mouths. There are birds that are excellent mimics of human speech sounds, but their "talking" is really a complex whistling, bearing little resemblance to the way that humans create speech. (The exact mechanism used by these birds is discussed in Chapter 9.)

But probably for as long as people have been talking, people have been interested in describing how speech sounds get made. Linguistic descriptions are found among the oldest records of civilization. In Ancient India, as early as 500 BCE, scribes (the most famous of whom was known as Pāṇini) were making careful notes of the exact articulatory configurations required to pronounce the Vedic Scriptures, and creating detailed anatomical descriptions and rules for Sanskrit pronunciation and grammar. (The younger generation, apparently, was getting the pronunciation all wrong.) Arab phoneticians, working several centuries later but with many of the same motivations as the Indian Grammarians, produced extensive descriptions of Classical Arabic. Al-Khalil, working in Basra around 100 CE, produced a 4,000-page dictionary entitled *Kitab al ʻayn*, "The Book of the Letter ʻAyn." The ancient Greeks and Romans seemed to be more interested in syntax and logic than in phonetics or phonology, but they also conducted anatomical experiments, engaging in an ongoing debate over the origin of speech in the body. Zeno the Stoic argued that speech must come from the heart, which he understood to be the source of reason and emotion, while Aristotle deduced the sound-producing function of the larynx. The Greek physician Galen seems to have settled the argument in favor of the Aristotelian view by noting that pigs stop squealing when their throats are cut. Medieval European linguists continued in the Greek tradition, further developing Greek ideas on logic and grammar, as well as continuing to study anatomy through dissection.

The main obstacle in studying speech is that the object of study is for the most part invisible. Absent modern tools, studies of speech production had to be based on either introspection or dissection. (According to one history of speech science, it didn't occur to anyone until 1854 that one could use mirrors to view the living larynx in motion.) Of course some speech movements are visible, especially the lips and jaw and sometimes the front of the tongue, so that "lip reading" is possible, though difficult. But most of speech cannot be seen: the movement of the tongue in the throat, the opening of the passage between nose and mouth, sound waves as they travel through the air, the vibration of the fluid in the inner ear. The experimental techniques of modern speech science almost all involve ways of making these invisible movements visible, and thus measurable.

One obvious way is to take the pieces out, at autopsy. Dissection studies have been done since antiquity, and much important information has been gained this way, such as our knowledge of where muscles and cartilages are located, and how they attach to each other. But the dead patient doesn't speak. Autopsy can tell us about the *anatomy* of the vocal tract, that is, the shape and structure of its parts, but it cannot tell us much about *physiology*, that is, the way the parts work together to produce a specific sound or sound sequence.

The discovery of the X-ray in 1895 was a major advance in speech science, enabling researchers to "see" inside the body. (The mysterious "X" ray was discovered by physicist Wilhem Conrad Röntgen, who received the first Nobel Prize in physics for his work.) X-rays are not necessarily great tools for visualizing the organs of speech, however, for two reasons. X-rays work because they pass through less dense, water-based soft tissue like skin, but are absorbed by denser materials like bone, teeth, and lead. Thus, if an X-ray is passed through the body, the bones cast a white "shadow" on a photographic film placed behind the subject.

The first problem with the use of X-rays in speech science is that muscles, like the tongue, are more like skin than like bones. The tongue is visible on an X-ray, but only as a faint cloud, not a definite sharp outline.

Figure 1.1 shows the results of one experiment where researchers tried to get around this problem in an ingenious way. These images were made by the British phonetician Daniel Jones, in 1917. Jones was very interested in vowel sounds, and is famous (among other achievements) for devising a system for describing the sound of any vowel in any language (the "cardinal vowel" system, which is discussed in Chapter 4). But nobody really knew exactly how the tongue moved to make these different sounds, since we cannot see most of the tongue, and we do not have a very good sense of even where our own tongues are as we speak.

To create these images, Jones swallowed one end of a small lead chain, holding on to the other end, so that the chain lay across his tongue. He then allowed himself to be X-rayed while articulating different vowel sounds, and these pictures are the result. The images, beginning at the upper left and going clockwise, show vowels similar to those in the words "heed," "who'd," "hod," and "had." ("Hod" rhymes with "rod", and was a common word in 1917. It refers to a bucket or shovel for carrying coal.) The tongue itself does not image well, but the lead chain shows up beautifully, indicating how the tongue is higher

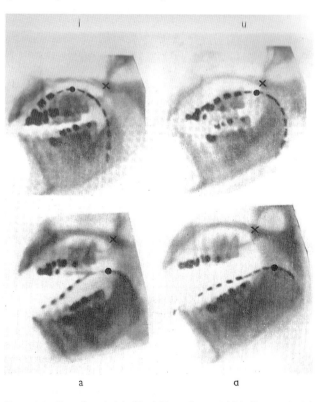

Figure 1.1 X-rays from the lab of Daniel Jones. Source: Published in Jones (1966) *The Pronunciation of English.*

and more towards the front of the mouth for the vowel in "heed" than the vowel in "hod." (The large dot showing the high point of the tongue was drawn in by hand, and the other black dots are lead fillings in the subject's teeth.)

The second problem with X-ray technology, of course, is that we eventually learned that absorbing X-rays into your bones, not to mention swallowing lead, is dangerous for the subject. Prof. Jones' experiments would never make it past the review committees that every university now has in place to protect subjects' health.

A safe way to get pictures of parts of the vocal tract is through *sonography*. This technology, based on the reflection of sound waves, was developed in World War II, to allow ships to "see" submarines under the water. Most of us are familiar with this technology as it is used to create images of a fetus *in utero*. The technology works because sound waves pass harmlessly and easily through materials of different kinds, but bounce back when they hit a surface of different density from what they are traveling through. (Transmission of sound waves is covered in detail in Chapter 6.) So sound waves travel through the air, but bounce back when they hit a mountainside, creating an echo. They travel through the water, but bounce back when they hit the ocean bottom (or a submarine), creating a sonar image. They travel through the amniotic fluid, but bounce back when they hit a body part. A transducer receives the echoed signal and calculates the time delay between transmission and reception. The time measurement is converted into distance between the transducer and the reflecting object. Graphing these distances creates an outline, resulting in an image of the object being studied.

In speech science, the sonar probe is held under the chin, so that the sound waves travel up through the tongue. They bounce back when they hit the border between the tongue and the air in the mouth, creating an image of tongue shape. Such an image is seen in Figure 1.2: The shape of the tongue for the vowel similar to the one in "heed" is seen as a bright line. (In this image, the subject is facing to the right.)

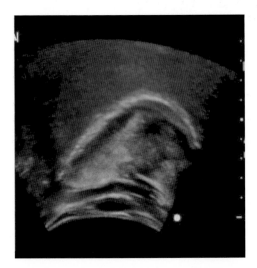

Figure 1.2   Ultrasound image of tongue shape for a vowel similar to the one in "heed." Image courtesy of the author.

Finally, Figures 1.3 and 1.4 show images of the head made by *magnetic resonance imaging* (MRI). The phenomenon of magnetic resonance was discovered in 1946 by Felix Bloch and Edward Purcell (working independently). (As with X-rays, the discovery resulted in a Nobel Prize.) Applications for imaging the body began to be used around 1977. This technology is in some ways the reverse of an X-ray: because it is based on the response of hydrogen atoms to a magnetic field, it works best on soft tissue that is mostly H_2O. For MRI imaging, the subject is placed in a very large electro-magnet. If you've ever had an MRI scan, you know this is like being slid into a small plastic tunnel. When the magnet is turned on, all the hydrogen atoms in the watery parts of the body line up with the direction of the magnetic field. Then a radiowave pulse of energy is sent to a specific part of the body, and this pulse knocks the atoms out of their alignment. When the pulse passes, the atoms snap back into position, but they give off energy as they do so. This energy is detected and measured by the MRI technology. Depending on the density of the hydrogen atoms in a given material, more or less energy is given off, and thus the presence and shape of different kinds of tissue can be detected. The technology is excellent, for example, at differentiating a tumor from normal brain tissue. It

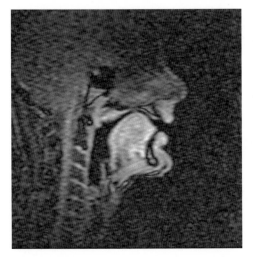

Figure 1.3   MRI mid-sagittal section of the tongue, showing the same vowel as in Figure 1.2. Source: Courtesy of Maureen Stone, Vocal Tract Visualization Laboratory, University of Maryland. http://speech.umaryland.edu/MICSR.html.

also creates beautiful, crisp pictures of the inside of a subject's head. It's especially useful because it can image a "slice" at any depth into the body. Image acquisition is rather slow in speech terms, however: while MRI "movies" are possible, at this writing, the technology is mostly used for still pictures.

The image in Figure 1.3, a view that's often used in speech science, is called a *mid-sagittal section* – that is, cutting halfway through, and looking from the side. It's basically a profile, but cut down the middle of the head. You can clearly see the nose and chin in outline, as well as the spinal cord. Our interest will be in the structures in the mouth. The mid-sagittal section is especially useful because the different parts of the vocal tract are clearly outlined. Over-reliance on this way of picturing the vocal tract, however, can give a false impression that our mouths are two-dimensional and that the only differences that matter are front-to-back. Figure 1.4 shows a different MRI view, called a *coronal section*: this is a view from the front, again slicing the head in half, this time from ear to ear. The coronal section in Figure 1.4 shows the whole head: the brain and eyes are unmistakable. The dark open spaces are the sinus cavities. The solid gray structure under the nose is the tongue. Notice how the top of the tongue is high and arched from side to side, while the muscle mass fills the floor of the mouth and extends down to the jawbone. (While the source does not indicate what, if any, sound was being pronounced when this picture was taken, the high position of the tongue looks consistent with that of the previous figures.)

While the coronal section reminds us not to be trapped in two dimensions, the mid-sagittal section is the most useful view to begin our discussion of the names and locations of the different parts of the vocal tract.

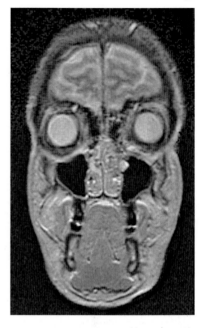

Figure 1.4   MRI coronal section of the head. Source: Image by Patrick J. Lynch, medical illustrator; C. Carl Jaffe, MD, cardiologist. http://en.wikipedia.org/wiki/File:Head_mri_coronal_section.jpg.   Creative Commons.

1.2 the parts of the vocal tract

As stated above, the vocal tract comprises all the structures of the body that are used to create speech sounds, from the lungs to the nose. It is useful, however, to divide the overall structure into a number of sub-systems, which are diagrammed in Figure 1.5. (This view, which is not actually biologically possible, might be called "Egyptian": The head is in profile, but the shoulders are square to the reader.)

The dividing point of the subsystems is the larynx, a valve of cartilage and muscle in the throat that sits on top of the trachea (windpipe) at the point where the passage to the lungs separates from the passage to the stomach, and that can be felt in the front of the neck as the "Adam's apple." The parts are the *sub-glottal* or *sub-laryngeal system* (everything below the larynx), the *laryngeal system* (the larynx itself), and the *supra-laryngeal system* (everything above the larynx). The supra-laryngeal system can be further divided into the *oral tract* (the mouth) and the *nasal tract* (the nose). In this section, we'll consider each of these systems in turn, describing each of the structures and the role they play in speech production, starting at the bottom, with the lungs, and working our way out. In this chapter, the perspective is functional: The structures and systems are described in just enough detail that the job that they play in making speech sounds can be understood. Further details of anatomy and physiology are covered in Chapter 5.

1.2.1 the sub-laryngeal vocal tract

Breathing is generally pretty quiet, snoring aside. The act of speaking is the act of making the movement of air out of the mouth and nose audible, using a code that associates different

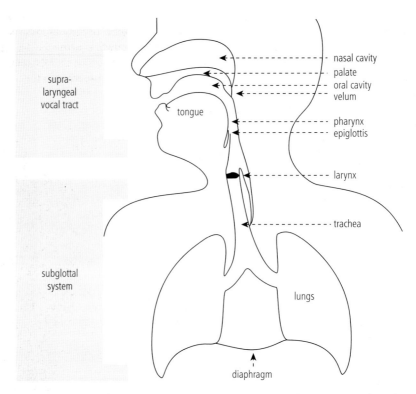

supra-
laryngeal
vocal tract

tongue

subglottal
system

nasal cavity
palate
oral cavity
velum

pharynx
epiglottis

larynx

trachea

lungs

diaphragm

Figure 1.5   The sub-systems of the vocal tract. Source: Philip Rubin and Eric Vatikiotis-Bateson, Haskins Laboratories. http://www.haskins.yale.edu/featured/heads/MMSP/figure1.html.

sound combinations with different meanings. The movement of air can be made audible by making it fast and turbulent, like water rushing through rapids. It can be made audible by building up pressure that is suddenly released, like the pop of a champagne cork. Or air can be made audible by making the air molecules vibrate (or *resonate*), like a bell or like the air inside the body of a guitar or clarinet. Each of these methods, alone and in combination, are used in making speech sounds. And all involve first getting the air moving, and then shaping that movement either by making a narrow channel, by closing off the airflow momentarily so that pressure builds up, or by changing the shape of the resonating chamber.

In most cases, the movement of the air is powered by the lungs: the *pulmonic airstream mechanism*. It is possible to get air moving in other ways, by movements of the tongue and larynx, and many languages use speech sounds created in these ways. These other airstream mechanisms are covered in Chapter 3. But all languages use the pulmonic airstream mechanism, some (like English) exclusively, so we begin with that.

Speech begins when air is drawn into the lungs, and then forced out. The lungs, of course, are air-filled sponges, covered with a membrane, that fill the ribcage. The lungs have no muscles of their own, but expand or contract as the muscles of the abdomen and ribcage squeeze or pull on them.

The largest muscle used in speech is the *diaphragm*, which is a large dome-shaped muscle that runs through the middle of the body and separates the chest cavity from the stomach. When the diaphragm contracts, the dome flattens out, causing the chest cavity, and thus the lungs, to enlarge. Remember Boyle's law from high-school physics? When the volume of an enclosed space increases, air pressure decreases. So when the volume of the lungs is increased the air pressure goes down, and air rushes in from outside the body to equalize the difference. Then, as the diaphragm is slowly relaxed, and the muscles running inside the ribcage slowly contract, the lungs are squeezed, and air is forced out in a measured stream, up the trachea, through the larynx, and into the mouth and nose.

Note that, generally, speech takes place on the exhalation only. That is, the airstream is pulmonic *egressive*. It is possible to speak on the indrawn breath – in gasps, for example, or when children want to count quickly to 100 for a game of hide and seek – but no language uses the pulmonic *ingressive* airstream in any systematic way.

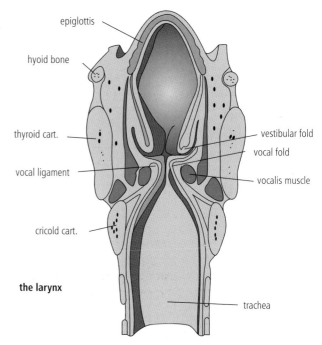

Figure 1.6   The vocal folds, coronal section.

1.2.2 the larynx

The *trachea*, or windpipe, is the tube that connects the mouth and lungs. It consists of rings of cartilage (horseshoes, really, open to the back) connected by muscle fibers and lined with smooth moist tissue. The top ring of the trachea, the *cricoid cartilage*, is thickened, and instead of being open at the back is closed with a flat plate: the shape is often compared to a signet ring, with the plate of the ring toward the back of the neck. (*Cricos* is Greek for ring.) Just above the cricoid cartilage, the tissue inside the trachea thickens into two folds or flaps: the *vocal folds*, which can potentially cover the opening to the trachea. (They were erroneously called the vocal cords by a Medieval anatomist, and the term stuck, but they are not strings.) The folds are actually composed of multiple layers of tissue: they are thin and somewhat stiff on their inside edge, at the *vocal ligament*, thick and muscular at the sides. The muscle running inside the vocal folds is called the *vocalis muscle*. Figure 1.6 shows a diagram of the vocal folds and surrounding structures (in coronal section). Note that above the true vocal folds is another set of flaps of tissue, the *vestibular folds*, often called the *false vocal folds*. Vibration of the false vocal chords may play a role in various forms of "throat singing," but they are not active for speech.

A set of cartilages surrounds, protects, and manipulates the vocal folds. Figure 1.7 shows the cartilages of the larynx as viewed from the side; other views are shown in Chapter 5 (Figures 5.2 and 5.3).

In Figure 1.7, one can see the thickened cricoid cartilage sitting on top of the trachea, with its signet-like plate in the back. The large *thyroid* cartilage sits over the front of the cricoid like a shield, folded in the middle. On top of the cricoid plate, hidden behind the thyroid and thus not visible in Figure 1.7, are the two *arytenoid cartilages*, shaped approximately like triangular pyramids. The vocal folds are attached to the thyroid cartilage in the front and the arytenoid cartilages in the back. These four cartilages – the cricoid, the thyroid, and the two arytenoids – along with the vocal folds and the muscles that connect them all make up the *larynx*.

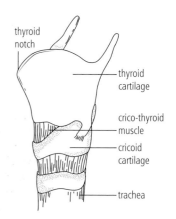

Figure 1.7   The cartilages of the larynx, viewed from the side.

You can locate your own larynx by tilting your chin up and running your finger down the underside of your chin to your throat. You should be able to feel the forward point of the thyroid cartilage as a bump under the skin, with a small notch at the top. (This thyroid notch is usually called the "Adam's apple," and it is larger in men than in women; more on sex-specific characteristics of the larynx in Chapter 5.) The whole larynx will move up and down if you swallow. You should also be able to feel some of the other tracheal rings below the larynx along the front of your throat.

During speech, the positions of the vocal folds can be changed in various ways by adjusting the position of the thryoid and arytenoid cartilages, and by increasing or decreasing the tension in the vocalis and other muscles. (Details are given in Chapter 5.) The vocal folds can be pulled together tightly and clamped down to temporarily stop the airflow, or they can be pulled apart to allow air to flow freely. If they are held in an intermediate position with just the right tension, touching but not tightly closed, the vocal folds will vibrate as the air passes over them, with a movement similar to a flag undulating in the breeze. This vibration produces a hum called *voicing*, and the vibration of voicing is the basis of many of the sounds of speech.

You can feel this vibration by placing your fingers on the side of your larynx, and alternately pronouncing a sustained [zzzzzz] and [ssssss]. The vibration you feel during the *voiced* [z] will cease during *voiceless* [s]. (Conventionally, symbols for sounds are written within square brackets. There will be much more information on symbols for sounds in the coming chapters.)

The faster the vibration of the vocal folds, the higher the pitch of the voice. To some extent, the pitch of your voice is determined biologically: large vocal folds vibrate more slowly than small vocal folds, producing a lower range of sound. Men, on average, have vocal folds 50% longer than women's (hence the more prominent Adam's apple); male vocal folds are also thicker. Thus, men tend to have lower voices. The average rate of vocal fold vibration for adult males is about 120 times per second, for adult females, about 220 times per second, and for small children, as high as 300 to 400 times per second. Part of this difference is due to the fact that men on average have larger bodies than women, and both of course are larger than children. But males will tend to have larger vocal folds even when matched with females for overall body size. In adolescence, young males undergo a hormone-driven laryngeal growth spurt, during which the size of the vocal folds and thyroid cartilage rapidly increase. They may find that their voice "cracks" until they become used to manipulating their newly-found deeper voices. The growth of female vocal folds is steady and proportional to body size, with no disproportional growth spurt in adolescence. There is presumably a selective advantage for males, but not females, to sound bigger (and thus stronger and more fearsome) than they actually are.

So the overall range of your voice – whether you'll be a soprano, alto, tenor, or bass – is a biological given. (Modulo human intervention, of course. In seventeenth- and eighteenth-century Italy, there was a tradition of male *castrati* undergoing surgery to maintain their operatic high voices throughout life.) But within the biologically-given range, the actual note that is sung is under individual speaker control. Pitch is adjusted by changing the tension of the vocal folds. Pulling forward on the thyroid cartilage stretches the folds and raises the pitch. Contraction of the vocalis and other muscles can also be directly controlled. You can feel the laryngeal control of pitch if you once again place your finger lightly on your larynx and then hum a series of notes from the lowest in your range to the highest. Can you feel the thyroid cartilage move up in your throat as pitch rises? Such speaker-controlled changes in pitch can be very important to the linguistic message.

Thus, the linguistic function of the larynx is (mainly) to control pitch and voice. Its biological, non-speech, function is to serve as a valve that separates the lungs and the stomach. Other animals that use their mouths to both breathe and eat have valves that serve the same non-speech function as the human larynx, but no other animal has such fine-tuned laryngeal control.

The human larynx is also nearly unique in being placed so low in the throat. In adult humans, the trachea (the passage to the lungs) and esophagus (the passage to the stomach) do not split off until halfway down the throat. In addition, the trachea is in front of the esophagus, so that food and water must pass over the top of the trachea in order to get to the stomach – a surprisingly dangerous arrangement. (Your mother was right – don't try to talk and eat at the same time.) In other primates and almost all other mammals the trachea extends much higher, up through the back of the mouth so that the trachea can connect directly to the nasal passages.

Thus a deer can drink and breathe at the same time: the air going through the nose and down the trachea, with water going around the sides of the trachea rather than over the top. Humans cannot.

In order to be able to eat at all without getting food into the lungs, the human must close off the trachea by tightly closing the larynx when food or drink is being swallowed. The closure is aided by the *epiglottis*, a flap of tissue attached to the base of the tongue, which folds down over the top of the larynx, which rises to meet it, during swallowing. Try swallowing a few times, paying attention to the muscular sensations. Can you feel the larynx rising up, and the tension in the throat that corresponds to the lowering of the epiglottis?

1.1   In Focus

Human infants, who have very poor muscle control and spend a lot of time drinking while lying down, are born with the larynx high in the throat, similar to the arrangement typical of other primates. Thus, the liquid the baby ingests passes around the sides of the trachea rather than over the top, preventing choking. The larynx lowers to the normal human position over the first months of life, as the child gains control over the muscles of the neck and head, learns to sit up, and begins to eat solid food and to babble.

The tradeoff for the lowered larynx position in the human is significant, however. With the trachea down and out of the way, humans have an open space, the *pharynx*, at the back of the mouth behind the tongue. This open space allows greater freedom for movement of the tongue, making a wide range of vowel and consonant sounds, and thus human language, possible.

1.2.3 the supra-laryngeal vocal tract

Thus far, we've seen that the lungs provide the moving air on which speech is based, and the larynx adds (or not) the vibration of voicing and control of pitch. It is the structures above the larynx that move to further shape and constrict the air as it moves out from the lungs, creating distinctions between individual speech sounds. It is useful to divide the structures of the mouth into the *active articulators* and *passive articulators*. The active articulators move toward the passive articulators in order to constrict and shape the airstream. The labels for the active and passive articulators are shown in Figure 1.8. In this chapter, we concentrate just on the names, relationships, and basic functions of the

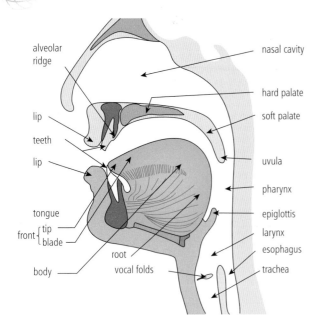

alveolar ridge

nasal cavity

hard palate

lip

soft palate

teeth

lip

uvula

pharynx

tongue

epiglottis

front { tip
       blade

larynx

root

esophagus

body

vocal folds

trachea

Figure 1.8 The supralaryngeal vocal tract.

different parts. Chapter 2 begins the discussion of how each is involved in creating specific distinct speech sounds.

The active articulators are the lips and tongue. The movement of the lips, being visible, is obvious. In speech, the lips may be closed or open, pursed or spread. Both lips move to some degree, but the lower lip moves more, so it receives the active label.

All that we usually see of the tongue is the small, pink tip, but it is in fact a large mass of interconnected muscles that fills the floor of the mouth. The tongue is all muscle: it has no bones or cartilage, thus no definite shape, though it maintains a constant volume. The technical term for this kind of organ is a *muscular hydrostat*: the closest biological analogs are an elephant's trunk or the tentacle of an octopus. The various muscles of the tongue are discussed in detail in Chapter 5. At this point it suffices to know that three different regions of the tongue can move relatively independently: the *tongue front*, the *tongue body*, and the *tongue root*. The tongue front is made up of the very *tip* of the tongue and the *tongue blade*, which extends a few centimeters behind the tip. The tongue front can be raised or lowered, stuck forward or curled back. The tongue body, or *dorsum*, is the main mass of the tongue. It can move up and down, back and forward. The tongue root is the very back part of the tongue, extending down into the pharynx to the epiglottis. The tongue root can be pulled forward or back, enlarging or constricting the pharynx.

Each of these four active articulators – the lower lip, tongue front, tongue body, and tongue root – can move to create a constriction, that is, a narrowing of the vocal tract, against one or more of the passive articulators that lie along the top of the vocal tract.

1.2   In Focus

The jaw, of course, and the lower teeth embedded in the jaw, also move during speech, but the jaw is not counted as a separate active articulator because the jaw and lower teeth are never the parts that actually make the constriction. It is always the lips or tongue riding on the movement of the jaw: no language makes any speech sounds by grinding the teeth together.

The easily visible passive articulators are the *upper lip* and *upper teeth*. Right behind the upper teeth is the *alveolar ridge*: you can feel this raised ridge with your tongue. If you continue to run your tongue along the top of your mouth, you'll feel the *post-alveolar region* arching from the alveolar ridge toward the *hard palate*, the very roof of the mouth. If you curl your tongue very far back in your mouth, you can feel that the bony structure of the hard palate gives way to softer tissue, which is known as the *soft palate*, or *velum*. The velum is a muscular flap, like a trap door, that regulates the *velar port*, the opening in the back of the mouth that connects the mouth and nose. At the very end of the velum is the *uvula*, the little pink pendulum you can see hanging down in the back of your mouth when you open wide and say "ah." The final passive articulator is the *pharyngeal wall*, the back of the throat, toward which the tongue root and epiglottis may move to constrict the passage of air.

The velum has something of a dual status. When the tongue body moves up and back to make a constriction in the velar region, the velum is serving as a passive articulator. But it also has an active status as a valve that regulates airflow between the oral tract and nasal tract. The velum is lowered during quiet breathing, and air flows freely through the open port (so that you can breathe with your mouth closed). For most speech sounds, however, the velum is raised, closing off the velar port and thus directing all the airflow through the mouth. When the velum is opened during speech, as it is for some sounds such as [m] and [n], the diversion of air through the nose gives these sounds their distinctive nasal quality. There are, of course, no moving articulators within the nasal tract itself, though the unique shape of an individual's sinus cavities help determine the particular quality of an individual voice.

chapter summary

- People throughout recorded history have been interested in describing the structure and function of the organs of speech, but this was difficult to do with precision until the advent of tools such as the X-ray, sonography, and MRI that allow us to "see" inside the body. In this chapter we recall the basics of how each technology works, with its strengths and limitations.
- There are no parts of the body used exclusively for speech. All the parts of the vocal tract have another, non-speech use.
- Speech is the movement of air made audible. Air can be made audible by making a narrow turbulent channel, by building up pressure behind a constriction, or by making the body of air resonate.
- The vocal tract can be divided into three sub-sections: sub-laryngeal, laryngeal, and supra-laryngeal.
- Most speech sounds are made with air exiting the lungs: the pulmonic egressive airstream.
- The larynx is made up (in part) of the cricoid cartilage, thyroid cartilage, arytenoid cartilages, and vocal folds. This chapter shows us the approximate shape and position of each. The primary linguistic function of the larynx is the control of vocal fold vibration (pitch and voicing).
- The supralayrngeal tract can be divided into active and passive articulators. The active articulators are the lower lip, tongue front (tip and blade), tongue body, and tongue root. The passive articulators are the upper lip, upper teeth, alveolar ridge, post-alveolar region, hard palate, soft palate (velum), uvula, and pharyngeal wall.
- In addition to its status as a passive articulator, the velum is a valve that opens and closes to regulate airflow between oral and nasal cavities.

further reading

Well, you might want to start with the rest of this book. Chapters 2 and 5 in particular have more details on anatomy and physiology, and further in-depth readings are listed at the ends of those chapters.

Language Evolution (2003, Oxford: Oxford University Press), edited by Morten Christiansen and Simon Kirby, provides a number of perspectives on the theories and controversies surrounding the evolution of language.

A Short History of Linguistics (1979, London: Longmans) by R.H. Robins, surveys linguistic studies from antiquity through the twentieth century.

The first section of *The Handbook of the Phonetic Sciences* (1999, Oxford: Blackwell), edited by William Hardcastle and John Laver, discusses other means of visualizing the vocal tract and measuring speech articulation.

Peter Ladefoged's *Phonetic Data Analysis* (2000, Oxford: Blackwell) also describes ways of measuring speech, along with anecdotes from his fieldwork experiences.

review exercises

1. Review the definitions of the following terms: active articulator, coronal section, mid-sagittal section, muscular hydrostat, nasal tract, oral tract, passive articulator, pulmonic egressive airstream mechanism, vestibular folds.
2. Review the pros and cons of each method of "seeing" the vocal tract. What kind of information can we get from each? What drawbacks does each have?

   dissection
   X-ray
   sonography
   MRI

3. Make your own mid-sagittal diagram of the upper vocal tract, and label the active and passive articulators. Base your drawing on Figure 1.3, but make it face the opposite way.
4. Label each anatomical structure as belonging to the surpralaryngeal, sublaryngeal, or laryngeal system:

   alveolar ridge
   arytenoid cartilages
   cricoid cartilage
   diaphragm
   epiglottis
   lungs
   pharynx
   nasal cavity
   thyroid cartilage
   tongue root
   trachea
   uvula
   upper teeth
   velum
   vocalis muscle

5. What is the function of the diaphragm as an organ of speech?
6. What is the function of the velar port?
7. Why is the pharynx important for human speech?
8. The chief linguistic functions of the larynx are to control_____and_____.
9. Why are men's voices, on average, lower than women's?

further analysis and discussion

10. Try speaking on an ingressive airstream. Why is it hard to do so?

further research

11. Read one or more articles in the book *Language Evolution*, edited by Christiansen and Kirby. What are some of the different theories of where and when language began? What sorts of evidence do scientists use to support these theories?
12. Beginning with the *Handbook of Phonetic Sciences* or *Phonetic Data Analysis* (and references therein), investigate and report on other ways of "seeing" the vocal tract.

Go online Visit the book's companion website for additional resources related to this chapter at:http://www.wiley.com/go/zsiga.

references

Stemple, J., Glaze, L., and Gerdeman, B. 2000. *Clinical Voice Pathology: Theory and Management.* San Diego: Singular Publishing Group.

Parts of this chapter were adapted from
Zsiga, E. 2006. "The Sounds of Speech." In Ralph Fasold and Jeff Connor-Linton (eds), *An Introduction to Language and Linguistics.* Cambridge: Cambridge University Press.

2

Basics of Articulation
Manner and Place in English

Don't speak of *letters* when you mean *sounds*. Languages are made up of sounds.
Daniel Jones, *The Sechuana Reader*, 1916, p. xxxvi (emphases original)

Daniel Jones is correct: (Spoken) languages are made up of sounds. In this chapter, we consider first how sounds combine to create linguistic messages, and then how articulator movements combine to create specific sounds. Section 2.2 considers the tricky problem of how to write down sounds in a systematic and unambiguous way. Section 2.3, the bulk of the chapter, describes the vocal tract movements and configurations that act as "building blocks" to create the sounds of English.

2.1 the dance of the articulators

It is a basic tenet of linguistics that human language is *discrete*, *combinatorial*, and *unbounded*. That is, the stream of language can be broken down into smaller, individual pieces, and these pieces (which may in themselves mean nothing) can be combined in different ways to create an infinite number of messages. Thus, human language is like a set of Lego bricks that can be combined into a boat or a barn or a starship, depending on the plan of the builder. At the level of sentence structure, every language user knows a set of individual words that can be combined in new and different ways to create an infinite number of sentences. Or, through the property of *recursion*, which permits embedding one sentence inside another, a speaker can create sentences that are indefinitely long, with no limits except the practical ones of memory and patience: "Mary said that John said that Sally said that her mother said . . . that Robin likes Joey."

At the level of sound structure, a dictionary full of words is made up of different combinations of discrete sounds, chosen from a limited inventory of vowels and consonants, which by themselves mean nothing. The set of words known by any individual is large but not infinite (usually estimated between about 40,000 and 300,000, depending on experience and education.) However, recursion can sometimes apply at the word level as well, as in great-great-great-great-grandmother or re-re-re-re-re-apply. In addition, the set of words is open-ended: new words are created every day. If I told you about a delicious new fruit that combined the tastes of a mango and banana, you'd have no problem adding "mananas" to your grocery list, and thus your vocabulary.

Finally, we will see that every vowel and consonant is made up of a combination of vocal tract movements we will call *articulatory gestures*, which combine to create a particular sound.

These properties (discrete, combinatorial, unbounded, recursive) set human language apart from every other animal communication system. While birdsongs or dolphin calls may be complex and meaningful, they do not, so far as we know, combine individual meaningless pieces in different ways to create an open-ended number of messages, and no clear example of recursion has been discovered in animal communication.

Those of us familiar with English spelling probably accept the ideas of "speech sound" or "vowel" and "consonant" without thinking, because we are used to seeing words represented as a sequence of letters. However, the idea that speech can be broken down into discrete elements is far from obvious. As a physical object in the world, speech exists as a continuous stream. As a person is speaking, the lips, tongue, larynx, lungs – all the vocal organs – are in constant, continuous motion. The lips open and close, the tongue body slides forward and back, the tongue tip flips up and down, all without stopping. Words, and the vowels and consonants that make them up, are run together and overlapped. We don't pause between sounds as though each one was a letter in a spelling bee. This running together is especially obvious when you're listening to a language you don't know. When you're not able to associate meanings with the different chunks of speech, you cannot tell where one word stops and the next begins.

You might think of speech movements as a dance of the articulators. As you watch a skilled dancer move across the floor, you see her feet, legs, arms, and head constantly and fluidly moving: dancing does not consist of jumping from one pose to the next. An unskilled onlooker would have trouble picking out the individual steps. Only if you saw the dance being choreographed would you know that you were watching a sequence of discrete steps that were learned separately and then put together. The sounds of speech are like the steps in a dance. Just as each dance step may combine movements of different parts of the body, so each sound of speech combines movements of different parts of the vocal tract. Just as dancing combines a set of steps in a sequence, but does not consist of holding one pose and then jumping to the next, so speech combines a set of sounds in sequence, but does so fluidly, with no obvious breaks between. And just as a dancer who knows his dance well can execute the movements from "muscle memory" without thinking "left foot here, right foot there" at every step, so humans who are proficient language users execute the movements of speech without any conscious thought at all about the vocal tract movements they are executing.

The movements that create each step of the dance of the articulators are articulatory gestures. In order to define a dance step, you would specify which part of the body to move (left foot, right arm, etc.) and then specify the position to which it moves (left foot slides back, right arm raised over head). In the same way, to define a vocal tract gesture, you choose the articulator, and specify the position, or goal, toward which it moves. In most cases, for speech, this goal is a constriction in some part of the vocal tract, which will result in some particular sound. When we define the position to which the articulator moves (the combination of active articulator and passive articulator), we are defining the *place of articulation*. When we define the type of constriction that is made (complete stoppage of air vs. narrow channel, for instance) we are defining the *manner of articulation*. In addition to the place and manner of articulation of a vocal tract constriction, the definition of a speech sound will also include the states of the velum and larynx, as well as the method of getting the air to move.

Every speech sound, then, is defined by a particular combination of the following components:

- airstream mechanism
- state of the larynx
- state of the velar port
- combination of active and passive articulator (= place of articulation)
- manner of articulation

This chapter discusses each of these in turn. Before we can begin to talk about specific sounds, however, we need to deal with an important problem: how can sounds be written down?

2.2 phonetic transcription

As students of speech, we need to consider how we can most simply and effectively symbolize the sounds that are the object of our study. A system of symbols for sounds is a *phonetic alphabet*. Writing down sounds using a phonetic alphabet is called *phonetic transcription*. Since this is a textbook, I need to be able to communicate to you which speech sound I am describing, without having the opportunity to actually pronounce it for you. So far, I have been able to get away with using example sounds for which the sound–spelling correspondence is reasonably unambiguous: we all know what sound the letter "m" makes, or "b." Or I can cite English words, and say "the sound at the beginning of the word 'mall,'" and you can say it to yourself and know what I mean. But this won't get us very far.

> 2.1   The relationship between language and writing would be a course in itself. Some writing systems do not represent sounds at all: Chinese logograms, for example, represent word meanings rather than pronunciations. This is a very useful property, given that many of the language varieties that we group under the label "Chinese" are so different as to be mutually unintelligible. But residents of Hong Kong in the south and Beijing in the north, for example, who might not be able to understand each other speak, can all read the same newspaper. Many other writing systems (such as Japanese and Korean) use symbols that correspond to syllables. For languages that use an alphabet (English, Spanish, Greek, Russian, Arabic, etc.), the correspondence between sounds and letters may be more or less straightforward (as in Spanish), or to a large extent arbitrary (English).

When English dictionaries first began to appear about 500 years ago, the dictionary writers did their best to write words the way they sounded, and thus there was a much better correspondence between sound and spelling than there is now. For example, "made" really was pronounced "ma-deh" and there really was a "k"-sound and "gh"-sound in "knight." But pronunciation has changed a lot in half a millennium, and spelling has not kept up. What with "silent" letters like "e" in "made" and "k" in "knight," words like "read" that can be pronounced either "red" or "reed," and incomprehensible sets like "through," "though," "thought," and "tough," English spelling is almost as much a matter of memorization as it is sound–letter correspondence. If English words were spelled the way they sound, elementary school children would not have to study lists of spelling words every week, and spelling bees would be no challenge at all.

Even if we pick "easy" spelling words, however, another problem is that different people pronounce words in different ways. In English, this is especially problematic for the pronunciation of vowels. If I wanted to talk about "the vowel in the word 'bite,'" you would have to ask if the bite occurred in Atlanta, Baltimore or Seattle (not to mention London or Perth) before you could know which vowel was meant. (Variation between dialects can become a real political issue for languages that are being written down for the first time. Even if the sound–letter correspondence is transparent, which group's pronunciation gets to be the "official" one?)

Finally, a complete system of phonetic transcription cannot be limited to the sounds of any one language. We do not have unambiguous letters in the Roman alphabet for the clicks in some Southern African languages or the sounds that are made in the back of the throat in Arabic. For the purpose of spelling foreign names, we use the closest English equivalent, or letters that are not much used otherwise, like q and x. But sometimes it is not clear which letter is the closest: is it Peking or Beijing, Bombay or Mumbai? (Answer: neither, really: it's a non-English sound for which we do not have an obvious spelling.) The sound spelled with an X in the name of the African language Xhosa is nothing like the sound spelled with an X in the Chinese family name Xu. (The former is a click, the latter, a sound similar to "sh." If you are limited to English spelling, it is hard to be any more specific.)

In 1887, a group of phoneticians, the International Phonetic Association, tackled the problem of how to describe precisely and unambiguously any sound they might encounter in their efforts to describe all the languages of the world. They decided to create a new alphabet, the *International Phonetic Alphabet (IPA)*, based on a set of principles, two of the most central being:

1. *The alphabet would be universal.* There would be enough symbols so that every sound in every human language could be represented.
2. *The alphabet would be unambiguous.* There would be a one-to-one correspondence between sounds and symbols: every sound would have one symbol, and every symbol would stand for only one sound.

English spelling frequently falls short on both these principles. It was noted above that there are many sounds for which we do not have symbols. The IPA currently contains 83 unique symbols for consonants and 28 symbols for vowels. The Roman alphabet, of course, has 21 and 5. (Don't worry too much about memorizing every symbol in the IPA right away. That is why there is a chart in this book to look them up (Figure 3.1). Plus, there are regularities that make learning the IPA somewhat easier than you think.) As new sounds have been discovered, the IPA has been revised to include new symbols for them. The latest revision, as of this writing, took place in 2005. The new sound that prompted the revision is described in Chapter 3.

 2.2   In Focus

In English spelling, the one sound/one symbol correspondence is constantly violated. There are, for example, at least four different ways to pronounce the letter "c," as in "each vicious circle" (five if you count "silent c" as in "back"). The "s-sound" can be spelled with either "s" as in "sent" or "c" as in "cent," a combination of the two, as in "scent," or with a double "s" ("assent"). The letter "x" stands for a sequence of two sounds, [k] followed by [s] ("box" rhymes with "locks"), while the sequence of letters "ph" stands for one sound, the same as "f."

The English system is not *totally* chaotic. Various rules can be used to figure out whether a "c" should be "hard" or "soft," for example. And it can be useful to have different spellings for words that sound the same: the sentence "I was looking for a big sail" is ambiguous in speech but not in writing. But the level of ambiguity, randomness, and mismatches is high enough to keep the system of English spelling from being useful as a clear way to refer to sounds, even for English alone, or even if only one dialect was being considered.

Numerous different phonetic alphabets have been developed, with different purposes in mind. Some were developed for a single language, with the goal of writing the language down and teaching people to read. For this goal, simplicity is probably the most important criterion. At the time when many of these systems were created, the set of symbols was constrained to those available on typewriter keys. Other systems are meant to be used in dictionaries, or for the purpose of teaching a foreign language, for which purposes keeping the phonetic alphabet close to the "spelling alphabet" might be most important. Tradition often plays an important role. If you grew up learning about "long e" and "short e," or if scholars have written words a certain way for hundreds of years, a phonetic alphabet that represents sounds in the same ways may be preferred. There is no one correct system to use for every case.

However, for the purposes of the general description of all the sounds of the many languages of the world, the principles of the International Phonetic Alphabet best meet the need and are most widely accepted in the linguistic community, and thus this book will use IPA. Where symbols from other transcription systems are commonly in use, these will be noted. We begin, in this chapter, with the sounds of English. This is not because English has some special linguistic status among the languages of the world – like every other language, English has some properties that are pretty common and some others that are more unusual – but because it is the one language that every reader of this book is familiar with. You will find that most, if not quite all, of the IPA symbols for English sounds are already familiar, being based on their most common values in the Roman alphabet. Table 2.1 gives the IPA symbols for the consonants of English, along with example words.

Note that only the basic symbols, enough to distinguish different English words, are given in Table 2.1. This basic style of transcription is known as *broad transcription*. Various additional articulatory details or modifications, which are often indicated by diacritical marks added to the basic symbol, are discussed in the text. A style of transcription that includes

Table 2.1   IPA symbols for the consonants of English.

	Initial				*Final*	*Medial*	*Alternate symbol*
p	pat	pie	pen	pin	whip	upper	
b	bat	buy	Ben	bin	bib	rubber	
m	mat	my	men	minion	whim	summer	
f	fat	fight	fen	fin	whiff	suffer	
v	vat	vie	vendor	vintage	wave	ever	
θ		thigh	thin		with	Ethel	
ð	that	thy	then		bathe	weather	
t	tat	tie	ten	tin	wit	retool	
d	data	dye	den	din	mid	redo	
n	Nat	night		ninja	win	renew	
s	sat	sigh	sensor	sin	miss	presser	
z	zap		zen	zip	wiz	buzzer	
l	lateral	lie	lentil	lip	will	filler	
r	rat	rye	rent	rip	where	terror	
ʃ	shack	shy	shell	ship	wish	pressure	š
ʒ					beige	measure	ž
tʃ	chat	chai	check	chip	witch	etcher	č
dʒ	jack	giant	gender	gin	wedge	edger	ǰ
k	cat	kite	Ken	kin	wick	wrecker	
g	gap	guy	gecko		wig	mugger	
ŋ					wing	singer	
h	hat	high	hen	hip		ahead	
w	whack	why	when	win		away	
j	yak		yen	yip			y

Table 2.2   A simplified IPA chart for the consonants of English.

	bilabial	labio-dental	dental	alveolar	post-alveolar	palatal	velar	glottal
plosive	p b			t d			k g	ʔ
fricative		f v	θ ð	s z	ʃ ʒ			h
affricate					tʃ dʒ			
nasal	m			n			ŋ	
approximant	(w)			l	r	j	(w)	

these additional details is known as *narrow transcription*. Neither narrow nor broad transcription is better or more correct; they are just more or less detailed. Broad transcription focuses on aspects of pronunciation that are *contrastive*: that is, that make a difference in the meaning of a word (like the difference between [p] and [b] in "pit" vs. "bit." Narrow transcription includes both contrastive and non-contrastive details.

Table 2.2 provides the same symbols in the form of a chart. In an *IPA chart*, place of articulation is written across the top, manner down the side. Thus you can see that any given sound is a combination of a certain place and a certain manner, and place and manner combine relatively freely. (Additional place and manner combinations are shown in the full IPA chart in Figure 3.1.) If there are two symbols in a cell, the one on the left is voiceless, the one on the right is voiced. All these symbols may seem like a lot to learn at first, but in the long run it's a lot easier than trying to describe sounds using English spelling or description. As you learn the definitions of the different places and manners of articulation, you should be able to combine them to figure out the pronunciations of unfamiliar symbols in the chart, even if you cannot yet produce them perfectly.

The next section of the chapter now turns to describing the sounds in the chart, based on their articulatory characteristics. Section 2.3.1 addresses airstream mechanism, laryngeal state, and nasality. Section 2.3.2 discusses manner, and Section 2.3.3, the longest and most detailed, describes place.

2.3 the building blocks of speech

2.3.1 airstream, larynx, and velum

All speech sound is the movement of air made audible. Therefore, the first defining component of a speech sound is that of airstream mechanism: How will we get the air moving in the first place? As noted in Chapter 1, for English, this choice is invariably pulmonic egressive, that is, air moving out from the lungs. All the sounds in Table 2.1 are pulmonic egressive. Even in languages that use other airstream mechanisms for certain consonants, pulmonic egressive will be used for the majority of consonants, and for all the vowels. Because this is the most common state of affairs, it generally goes without saying: Unless otherwise stipulated, assume the airsteam is pulmonic egressive. In linguistics, when we can assume one state of affairs holds generally, although an alternative may be specified in a more limited set of cases, we call the general case the *default* or *unmarked* state. The limited case is the *marked* option. Pulmonic egressive is the unmarked airstream mechanism.

The second defining characteristic of a sound is the state of the vocal folds. In English, the folds may be held in the airstream at the correct tension to produce vibration, or they may be pulled out of the way so that the air passes freely between them, or they may be clamped down tight to close off the airflow completely. As was noted in Chapter 1, sounds produced with vocal fold vibration are *voiced*; sounds produced without vocal fold vibration are *voiceless*. Again, if you place your finger on your larynx and produce a sustained [z], you should be able to feel the vibration. If you switch to [s], a voiceless sound, the vibration ceases. Another pair of sounds that illustrate the voiced/voiceless distinction is [v] and [f]. Can you feel which is which?

If a sound is produced as voiceless, the speaker must control how long and large the vocal fold opening will be. For some sounds, as in the initial [p] in "pat," the vocal folds are held apart far enough and long enough to allow an extra "puff of air" to exit the mouth at the end of the [p]. This extra voicelessness is called *aspiration*. You can feel the extra release of air if you hold your fingertips an inch or so in front of your lips as you say "pat" or "pill," but not as you say "bat" or "bill." Another test for aspiration is to hold a piece of notebook paper flat and level in front of your lips, holding it a few inches from the end so that one edge of the paper hangs down. Saying "pat" will make the edge of the paper move. However, the paper will not move, and you will not feel any aspiration, for a [p] that occurs after [s] as in "spot" or "spill." For these non-initial consonants, the vocal folds resume a position of voicing more quickly. Aspiration is indicated by a superscript "h" following the consonant [p^h], though this detail is indicated for English only in narrow transcription.

Voicing and aspiration are the two most important systematic laryngeal distinctions for English vowels and consonants, but speakers have control over various other laryngeal configurations. English uses these distinctions mostly on the periphery of its vocabulary, in a small set of expressions or exclamations, though they play a more central role in other languages. Shutting the folds down very tight, completely cutting off the airflow at the larynx produces a *glottal stop* (IPA [ʔ]). A glottal stop occurs in the middle of the word (or expression) usually written "uh-oh." If you say this slowly, stopping after the first syllable, you should be able to feel the tension in your throat, and note that you are also holding your breath. Some English speakers produce glottal stops in place of [t] in certain positions (which positions vary by dialect). In American English, this is often at the end of the word or before an [n]. For example, many American English speakers pronounce [ʔ] instead of [t] in "button," or in a not-too-careful pronunciation of the word "important" (IPA [ɪmporʔnʔ]). Adjusting the tension on the vocal folds changes the quality of voicing, making it *creaky* (more tense) or *breathy* (more relaxed). A narrow IPA transcription indicates these differences with subscripts: a tilde for creaky and a double dot for breathy. Voice quality may be the only difference between affirmative, breathy [m̤hm̤], and negative, creaky [m̰ʔm̰].

The third defining characteristic is whether the velum will be open or not. If the velum is open, so that air flows through the nasal cavity, the sound is *nasal* (like [m]). If the velum is closed, the sound is *oral*.

2.3.2 manner of articulation

Manner of articulation defines the kind or degree of constriction that is made, independent of where in the vocal tract. As was noted in Chapter 1, there are three ways of making moving air audible: making it pop, making it turbulent, or making it resonate. The first two ways involve creating some obstruction to the flow of air, and sounds made in this way are called *obstruents*. Sounds that resonate are *sonorants*. The set of obstruent consonants includes *plosives*, *fricatives*, and *affricates*. The set of sonorant consonants includes *nasal stops* and *approximants*. Vowels are always sonorant. The consonantal manners of articulation are seen in the leftmost column of Table 2.2.

Plosives may also be called *oral stops*. As the name implies, a *stop* manner of articulation brings the active and passive articulators together to make a complete closure that stops air from exiting the mouth. Try saying the word "poppa" very slowly, and note that there is complete silence, with no air exiting the mouth, while the lips are closed for [p] in the middle of the word. You may even feel pressure building up behind the lips, as air continues flowing from the lungs and has nowhere to go. This pressure is released with a slight pop, or *burst*, when the lips are opened. The sounds [p], [t], and [k] are plosives. Can you the feel the closure between the different active and passive articulators in the syllables [pɑ] (lower and upper lips), [tɑ] (tongue front to alveolar ridge), and kɑ (tongue body to velum)?

For a *fricative*, the articulators are brought close together but not quite closed completely, creating a narrow slit or groove through which the stream of air is forced. Just as a river will flow smoothly and noiselessly when its channel is wide, but will become faster, turbulent and noisy when forced to flow through a narrow channel, so the flow of air becomes turbulent and noisy when channeled through a narrow gap in the vocal tract. The sounds [f] and [s] are fricatives. Try drawing out each sound. You should both be able to hear the characteristic hissing noise, and to feel where the constriction is made. For [f], air is forced between the upper teeth and lower lip. For [s], air shoots down a groove in the center of the tongue, like water out of a pipe, and crashes into the teeth. If you think about the splash that can be created with water shooting out of a hose and splashing into a wall, you'll understand why [s] is so loud.

An *affricate* combines a sequence of stop plus fricative in a single sound. The sound usually written "ch" in English is an affricate. The IPA symbol is [tʃ]: the two letters symbolize the stop and the fricative, combined into a single symbol that counts as one sound. Say the word "achoo" as slowly as possible, paying attention to what your tongue is doing in between the "a" and "oo" sounds. You should feel that you first make a closure of the tongue front at or just behind the alveolar ridge, and then lower the tongue front to let the air out through a narrow constriction.

As you can see from the IPA chart, plosives, fricatives, and affricates (that is, the class of obstruents) can be voiced or voiceless. For [p, t, k, f, θ, s, ʃ], the vocal folds are pulled apart during the time the oral constriction is made, making them voiceless. For the voiced stops [b, d, g] and voiced fricatives [v, ð, z, ʒ] the vocal folds are held together throughout, and voicing may continue through the constriction. There is, however, something of a contradiction between voicing and obstruents. Voicing requires airflow over the vocal folds to produce the vibration, but obstruents, by definition, block this flow to a greater or lesser extent. Pressure builds up behind the constriction in the oral cavity, and when air pressure in the mouth and lungs becomes equal, airflow stops. When airflow stops, vibration of the vocal folds stops. Therefore, while voiced stops and fricatives are possible, they are relatively difficult. The voiced plosives of English tend to *devoice* as vocal fold vibration dies out, and some languages (such as Finnish, Hawai'ian, Mandarin, and Nootka, to name a few) skip voiced obstruents altogether. Because they are both more difficult and rarer, voiced obstruents are marked. Because they are both easier and more common, voiceless obstruents are unmarked.

Sonorants, on the other hand, are almost always voiced. You will see only a single sound in each sonorant block in the IPA chart. That is, for sonorants the reverse holds: voiced sonorants are unmarked. The definition of a sonorant is a sound in which there is *no* build-up of pressure in the supralaryngeal vocal tract. By definition, they allow the free flow of air, so there is no hissing or popping involved. Sonorants make audible sound not by obstructing the airflow, but by making the air resonate, that is, causing it to vibrate at different frequencies. Chapters 6 through 8 discuss vocal tract resonance in detail, including formulas for deriving different vowel sounds; here a few words on how resonance works in general should suffice to understand how sonorants are made.

A sonorant speech sound is very much like the note of a clarinet. To play a clarinet, the musician blows air over the reed, causing it to vibrate. The vibration of the reed causes the air inside the body of the instrument to vibrate as well, producing a particular note. When the musician changes his fingering, opening and closing the valves on the body of the instrument, he effectively is changing the size of the column of air inside, which changes the note. The vocal tract works in a similar way. In the vocal tract, air passing over the vocal folds causes them to vibrate. The vibration of the folds then causes the air in the supralaryngeal vocal tract to resonate. When the speaker moves her tongue, lips, and other articulators, she changes the shape of the vibrating body of air, and this changes the quality of sound that is produced. The shape of the vocal tract is more complex than the shape of the clarinet, so the sound that is produced is more complex as well. (Details can be found in Chapter 8.) Because vibration is the basis of resonance, sonorants are almost always voiced. It is possible to get sound without vocal fold vibration out of a vocal tract configured for resonance, but it requires a lot of airflow, as in whispering, which is both very effortful and not very loud.

Sonorant consonants include the *nasal stops*, such as [m]. An [m] counts as a stop because the lips are completely closed, exactly as they are for [p] or [b]. No air exits the mouth. If you observe your lips in a mirror, or just feel their position, as you say phrases such as [ama] or [aba], you will see and feel the same lip position in both. The difference between a plosive and a nasal stop, however, is that for a nasal stop the velum is open and air flows freely out of the nose. There is thus no build-up of pressure, and no burst noise on release. The vibration of the air in the mouth and nasal cavity produces the sound. You can probably feel this vibration by articulating a sustained [m] (humming). Now, while you're humming, try pinching your nose closed for a moment. What happens?

You can also make a voiceless nasal: try producing an [m], then making it voiceless. The only sound you'll make is that of quiet breathing. You can make the voiceless nasal louder by forcing a lot of air through the nose (but proceed with caution if you have a cold).

The next set of sonorants is the approximants. In an *approximant*, the active articulator moves to narrow the vocal tract, but not so much that fricative noise is created. *Glides*, such as the sounds at the beginning of the words "yell" and "well," are approximants, as are the sounds [r] and [l]. There are many different r-sounds, called *rhotics*, in the languages of the world, and l-sounds, called *laterals*. Rhotics and laterals together are sometimes called *liquids*.

The [r] sound in American English is one of those aspects that is unusual cross-linguistically: The body of the tongue is bunched up high, and the tongue tip may be raised or curled backwards, without touching any other surface of the vocal tract. (Try saying [rrrrr].) It is no surprise that non-native speakers of English have trouble with this sound. In narrow transcription, the symbol for the specific configuration of the English rhotic is [ɹ]. Since English has only one rhotic, however, in broad transcription the basic symbol [r] can be used, and that practice will be followed in this chapter. Chapter 3 discusses some other rhotic variants.

The l-sounds are called laterals because air flows out over the sides of the tongue. Try drawing out the initial sound in the word "lateral": [llllllll…]. You should be able to feel the contact between tongue tip and upper teeth or alveolar ridge. But [l] is not a stop: air continues to flow, exiting not through the center of the mouth but at the side. Without moving your tongue, take a deep breath in and out. Can you feel the air moving over the sides of the tongue? (For some people, air flows over the right side of the tongue only, for others only the left, and for others both. Which are you?)

The final class of sounds to be considered is the class of vowels. For a vowel, the vocal tract is relatively wide open, with no significant constriction at any point. Different vowel sounds are made by changing the position of the tongue and lips, changing the shape of the resonating body of air. Different vocal tract shapes for different vowel sounds are discussed in Section 2.3.4 below.

To summarize the manners of articulation covered so far:

- Stop: complete closure cutting off airflow in the oral cavity:
  - Oral stops (plosives) have a closed velum, and build-up of pressure behind the oral closure.
  - Nasal stops have an open velum, with air escaping through the nose.
- Fricative: narrow constriction causing turbulent, noisy airflow.
- Affricate: sequence of stop + fricative in one sound.
- Approximant: some constriction in the vocal tract, more so than for vowels, but not so much as to produce frication:
  - Glides.
  - Laterals (l-sounds).
  - Rhotics (r-sounds).
- Vowel: open vocal tract.

2.3.3 place of articulation for consonants

Having covered airstream, nasality, voicing and manner of articulation, we move on in this section to place of articulation. With all of these descriptive tools in place, we are now able to work systematically through the IPA chart of English consonants in Table 2.2, covering each of the sounds represented. Table 2.1 provides example words for each sound.

As noted above, the term "place of articulation" combines both the articulator that moves to make the constriction, the *active articulator*, and the location to which it moves, the *passive articulator*. We will organize our discussion of the consonants grouped by active articulator first, and passive articulator second. Generally, each active articulator can move to more than one location. The combinations of active and passive articulator that make up the places of articulation for English are shown in Table 2.3.

Any sound made with the lower lip as an active articulator is termed *labial*. The lower lip can make constrictions at two different places. If the lower and upper lips come together, the sound is *bilabial*. The sounds [p], [b], and [m] are bilabials. Note that [p] is voiceless and [b] (and [m]) are voiced. Alternatively, the lower lip can make contact with the upper teeth to produce a *labiodental* sound. The fricatives [f] and [v] are labiodentals. English makes its labial stops at the bilabial place of articulation and its labial fricatives at the labiodental place.

The lower lip is rather limited in the places at which it can make a constriction. The next articulator, the tongue front, is the most versatile of the active articulators, moving to at least four different places of articulation. All sounds made with the tongue front are *coronal*. The tongue tip moves forward to the upper teeth for the sounds at the beginning of "thin" and "then." These *dental* fricatives are written [θ] (voiceless) and [ð] (voiced) in IPA. Some English speakers protrude the tip of the tongue between the teeth in producing these sounds (making them *interdental*); other speakers are more circumspect and keep the tongue behind the teeth. (Which are you?)

Sounds made with the tongue front against the alveolar ridge comprise the *alveolar* place of articulation. The alveolar sounds of English include the plosives [t] and [d], fricatives [s] and [z], the nasal stop [n], and the lateral [l]. There is some interesting variation in the way [s] and [z] are made. Some English speakers raise the tip

Table 2.3   Active articulators, passive articulators, and place of articulation.

Active Articulator	+ Passive Articulator	= Place of Articulation
lower lip	upper lip	bilabial
	upper teeth	labio-dental
tongue front	upper teeth	dental
	alveolar ridge	alveolar
	post-alveolar region	retroflex (tip)
	post-alveolar region	post-alveolar (blade)
tongue body	hard palate	palatal
	soft palate	velar
larynx		laryngeal

of the tongue to the alveolar ridge for [s] and [z]; others tuck the tip of the tongue behind the lower teeth and make the alveolar constriction using the blade of the tongue, a centimeter or so further back. In either case, for the alveolar fricatives, the tongue forms a narrow groove like a spout that shoots a stream of air against the teeth, producing a very high-pitched hissing sound. Though the point of narrowest constriction for these fricatives is alveolar, the front teeth are necessary to create the proper high-pitched hiss, as every child discovers when she loses her baby teeth.

The fricatives [ʃ] and [ʒ] (as in the middle of "pressure" and "pleasure," or the beginning of "ship") are made further back, with the blade of the tongue making a constriction at the point where the roof of the mouth is steeply rising behind the alveolar ridge. This place of articulation is variably known as *palato-alveolar*, *alveo-palatal*, or *post-alveolar*. Here, we will follow the IPA chart and use post-alveolar. (If you produce an alternating sequence of [s – ʃ – s – ʃ] you'll feel how the constriction moves: [ʃ] is further back both on the tongue and on the roof of the mouth.) These fricatives also involve a grooved tongue shape that channels the air. Interestingly, [ʒ] never occurs in initial position in English, except in obvious borrowings, such as "genre" from French, or in names such as "Zsa Zsa" or "Zhivago." (For the record, my own family name was pronounced with initial [ʒ] in the original Hungarian, like Zsa Zsa, but was Americanized to [z] three generations ago.)

The affricates in "church" [tʃ] and "judge" [dʒ] are also post-alveolar. In other transcription systems commonly used in linguistics books and dictionaries, such as the American Phonetic Alphabet (APA), [ʃ], [ʒ], [tʃ], and [dʒ] are written [š], [ž], [č], and [ǰ]. The IPA convention for affricates, with its double symbols, emphasizes the sequenced aspect of the sound. The APA convention emphasizes the affricate's unity. This book will follow IPA convention, but the APA convention is also common, and every student of linguistics should be familiar with it.

Usually a post-alveolar constriction is made with the blade of the tongue. It is also possible, however, for the tip of the tongue to curl back to make a constriction in this area. If the tip of the tongue curls back, the sound is called *retroflex*. For some English speakers (but not all), [r] is a retroflex approximant ([ɻ] in narrow transcription). You can determine whether your own tongue tip curls back in a word like "road" by drawing out the initial [r], then (gently!) inserting a toothpick between your teeth until it touches the surface of the tongue. If you feel the point of the toothpick on the underside of your tongue, then your [r] is a retroflex approximant. If you feel the point on the upper side of the tongue, then your [r] is more likely an alveolar or post-alveolar approximant.

Moving further back in the vocal tract, the next place of articulation is *palatal*. The glide at the beginning of the words "you" and "yacht" is palatal. To make a palatal constriction, the whole middle section of the tongue, including blade and body, is pushed straight up to narrow the space between the tongue and hard palate. The IPA symbol for a palatal glide is [j]. (Think Scandinavian "ja.") The IPA reserves the symbol [y] for a particular, comparatively rare, vowel sound, and linguists describing languages that don't have that vowel sound often use [y] for the palatal glide instead. Here, however, we'll stick to IPA.

Sounds for which the tongue body makes the primary constriction are termed *dorsal*. If the tongue body moves further back to make a constriction against the velum, high in the back of the mouth, the place of articulation is *velar*. The English sounds [k] and [g] are velar stops. The sequence of letters "ng," as at the end of "song" or "ring," usually indicates a velar nasal. If you pay attention to what your tongue is doing in the word "song," you'll realize you're not making a sequence of alveolar nasal followed by velar stop (n-g), but a single nasal sound at the same place as [k] or [g]. (Notice how little your tongue moves in the word "king": the tongue tip is not involved at all.) The IPA symbol for a velar nasal stop is [ŋ]. As with [ʒ], English uses [ŋ] only at the end of words ("song") or in the middle ("singer"), never at the beginning, though other languages use [ŋ] as freely as [n] or [m], as in Thai [ŋa:] *tusk*, [ma:] *come*, [na:] *rice paddy*. (The colon indicates a long vowel.)

The glide [w], as in "well" combines a narrowing of the vocal tract at the velar place of articulation with rounding of the lips. It is thus a *double-articulation*, a *labio-velar* glide: in the chart, it is entered under both bilabial and velar place. The sound [h] is made with the larynx as the only articulator. An [h] consists of the noise of air rushing through the open vocal folds, and may be considered a *glottal* fricative. As was noted in Section 2.3, it is also possible to produce a glottal stop (IPA [ʔ]), by closing the vocal folds up tight, stopping the airflow at the larynx.

It is perfectly possible to make consonantal constrictions in between velar place and laryngeal place: The tongue body can move to make constrictions against the uvula (*uvular* place), and the tongue root can move back to constrict the pharynx (*pharyngeal* place). Consonants at these places of articulation are not used in English, however. Uvular and pharyngeal consonants are discussed in Chapter 3.

In summary, there are nine places of articulation used for English consonants: bilabial, labiodental, dental, alveolar, post-alveolar, retroflex, palatal, velar, and laryngeal. Keep in mind that each symbol refers to a specific combination of place, manner, voicing, and nasality. For example, [m] = bilabial nasal (voiced) stop, and [s] = alveolar (oral) voiceless fricative. Predictable values are listed in parentheses: one can leave out "voiced" in the description of [m] because all English nasals are voiced, and leave out "oral" in the description of [s] because no English fricatives are nasal. In most cases, however, exchanging one term for another creates a different sound: changing "bilabial nasal stop" to "*alveolar* nasal stop" changes [m] to [n]. Changing "alveolar voiceless fricative" to "alveolar voiced fricative" changes [s] to [z]. It is a useful exercise to keep these relationships in mind.

The articulatory information provided in the preceding sections provides enough information to identify and distinguish the consonants of English. Much more can be said about the details of their articulation, relationships with each other, and distinctions from the consonants of other languages, and these topics will be covered in the following chapters. First, however, Section 2.3.4 turns to the (large) set of English vowels.

2.3.4 vowels

Vowels are harder to describe than consonants. By definition, vowels have an open vocal tract, so the tongue does not make contact at any particular place. If you slowly repeat the sequence of words "he, who, ha," drawing out the vowel sounds, you can feel that your tongue and lips move to different positions, but it is very difficult to feel exactly what position the tongue has taken. It was not until the advent of devices such as X-rays, which could actually image the whole of the tongue inside the vocal tract, that phoneticians had a very accurate idea of the exact articulatory positions for vowels. We are much more sensitive to the variations in sound quality that these movements produce. Nonetheless, vowels are described in terms of the relative position of the tongue body – high, low, front, back – and of the lips – pursed, (that is, rounded) or not.

If describing vowel systems in general is a difficult task, describing the vowels of English is even more so. As noted above, the vowel system of English is marked compared to that of most other languages. The most common number of vowels for a language to have is five. Spanish, Hawai'ian, Swahili, and Modern Standard Arabic, to name a few, use just five different vowel qualities. Though English writers use just five letters to encode them (relics of an older system!), the English language uses more than a dozen different vowel sounds. The exact number depends on the dialect.

Table 2.4 gives the IPA symbols, with example words, for the vowels of "General American" English, that is, English as it is more or less spoken in the central United States, or on national

2.3   Another reason the English vowel system is difficult to describe: vowel qualities differ a lot from dialect to dialect, much more so than for the consonants. For example, the word "mate" as pronounced by a speaker from Perth sounds a lot (though not exactly) like the word "might" as pronounced by a speaker from Baltimore. The word "my" spoken by a native of Atlanta sounds similar to "mar" as pronounced in Boston, and "ma" as pronounced in Seattle. For most speakers on the East Coast of the United States, the words "caught" and "cot" have two different vowel sounds; for most speakers on the West Coast, the two words are pronounced the same.

TV. (I say "more or less" since every dialect of English has particular regional characteristics, and the ideal speaker of pure "General American" doesn't exist.) Your pronunciation of the example words may well differ from the one described. For example, if you're from California, you probably use a vowel in between [ɔ] and [ɑ] instead of two distinct vowels. If you speak a British variety of English, you may have an additional low vowel, a round version of [ɑ], in words like "lot." (For more discussion of dialect variation in English vowels, see Chapters 4 and 19; Table 19.1 compares vowel pronunciation in General American and in "BBC" English.)

Table 2.4 (and Figure 2.1) use broad transcription, so certain details are left out. For example, the vowels in "bade" and "bode" actually change in quality during the pronunciation of the word: For both vowels the tongue body moves up towards the end of the vowel, and in a narrower transcription they would be represented as [beɪd] and [boʊd]. While this "off-glide" is a salient aspect of the pronunciation of these vowels in American English, pronouncing [e] or [o] without the offglide does not make a different word: it just makes you sound like you have a foreign accent.

In contrast, for the vowels in "bide," "bout," and "boy," the movement upward at the end of the vowel is contrastive: "find" [aɪ] is distinct from "found" [aʊ], which is distinct from "fond;" and "soy" [ɔɪ] is distinct from "saw." Thus a separate symbol for the offglide is included in the transcription. These two-part sequenced vowels (the vocalic counterparts of affricates) are called *diphthongs*. (Vowels like [eɪ] and [oʊ] that have a non-contrastive offglide may be described as *diphthongized*.)

As with the consonants, vowels can be described in terms of a set of choices made by the speaker. Vowels are almost always voiced; they may be nasalized or not. All vowels use the tongue body and lips, and sometimes the tongue root, as active articulators. By definition, all vowels have an open manner of articulation. Because the tongue does not actually touch the upper surface of the vocal tract anywhere, the term *place of articulation* is not really appropriate, but different vowels may be described

Table 2.4   IPA symbols for the vowels of General American English.

i	bead	key	he
ɪ	bid	kit	
e	bade	kate	hey
ɛ	bed	ketchup	
æ	bad	cat	
u	booed	coot	who
ʊ	book	cook	
o	bode	coat	hoe
ɔ	baud	caught	haw
ɑ	body	cot	ha
ʌ	bud	cut	
aɪ	bide	kite	high
aʊ	bout	count	how
ɔɪ	boy	coy	ahoy

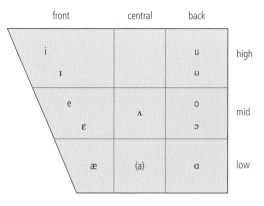

Figure 2.1   Chart of the vowels of General American English. Example words are given in Table 2.4. The vowel [a] is shown in parentheses because it occurs in GA only in the first half of diphthongs. Source: Based on a similar chart in Zsiga (2006).

2.4   In Focus

Note that the IPA symbols for the vowels do not correspond to their usual values in English spelling, nor to the names of the letters as they are taught to children. (Once I became used to phonetic transcription, I became absolutely useless in helping my kids with their spelling words.) The word "see," for example, with its "long e" is transcribed as [si]. (The pronunciation of IPA [i] and [u] are actually much closer to their values in Spanish spelling, if that's a help to you.) The reason for the discrepancy lies in the history of English. Five hundred years ago, when English spelling was getting established, the sounds of the English vowels were much closer to their mainland European counterparts: "see," for example, was pronounced similarly to a long version of Spanish "se" (similar to present-day English "say"), and the difference between "made" (long "a") and "mad" (short "a") really was one of length. Over the next 500 years, however, "The Great Vowel Shift" moved the vowel qualities of English around like the tiles in those plastic puzzles where you have to put all the numbers in order: See Chapter 18 for more details.

in terms of the ways in which the tongue body and lips move. Figure 2.1 charts the positions of the vowels relative to each other, based roughly on the position of the highest point of the tongue during that vowel.

The terms we use to classify different vowels refer to this position. Vowels may differ with respect to the height of the tongue: the tongue body moves up for the *high* vowels [i, ɪ, u, ʊ], down for the *low* vowels [æ, a, ɑ], and stays in the middle for the *mid* vowels [e, ɛ, ʌ, o, ɔ]. The tongue moves forward in the mouth for the *front* vowels [i, ɪ, e, ɛ, æ] and backward for the *back* vowels [u, ʊ, o, ɔ, ɑ]. The vowels [ʌ] and [a] are *central*. In General American English, [a] occurs only as the first part of a diphthong: [aɪ] begins in a low central position and moves to high front, [aʊ] begins from the same low central position and moves to high back.

Vowels also differ with respect to lip rounding. In General American, the back vowels [u, ʊ, o, ɔ] are *round*, all other vowels are *unround*. Finally, English divides its vowels into two sets, *tense* and *lax*. The tense vowels [i, e, o, u] are longer, slightly higher, and produced with greater stiffening of the tongue root than their lax counterparts [ɪ, ɛ, ɔ, ʊ]. (Linguists disagree over which set the low vowels belong to.)

All these descriptive terms can be combined to pick out a specific vowel: [ɪ] is high, front, lax, unround; [o] is mid, back, tense, round. Can you write the symbol for the mid, front, lax, unround vowel? High, front, unround, tense?

One more English vowel should be mentioned here: the reduced vowel [ə], called *schwa*. This symbol is used to mark the vowel quality in short, unstressed syllables, such as first syllable of "about" [əbaʊt] or the last syllable of "panda" [pændə]. Because it is a short, mid, central vowel, the symbol [ə] means that the mouth is open for a vowel sound, but the tongue basically stays in a neutral position: neither high nor low, front nor back. For a mid, central vowel in a stressed syllable, the symbol [ʌ] ("wedge") is used. Thus the word "abut" is transcribed [əbʌt].

More details on describing, and more narrowly transcribing, English consonants and vowels are given in Chapters 3 and 4 respectively. But the symbols discussed here should be sufficient to unambiguously transcribe any word of English. Just as important as getting the symbols correct, however, is understanding the different articulatory choices that a speaker combines to create each sound.

chapter summary

- Human language is discrete, combinatorial, unbounded, and recursive. Utterances are made up of words, which are made up of sounds, which are made up of articulatory gestures.
- English spelling is ill-suited for a general representation of the sounds of language. The International Phonetic Alphabet aims to provide one unambiguous symbol for any sound used in the languages of the world.
- A speaker makes choices to produce a speech sound. These include:
  - How should I get the air moving? Generally, this will be pulmonic egressive: air forced out of the lungs.
  - Which active articulator should I use: lips, tongue front, tongue body, tongue root, or larynx?
  - What kind of constriction should I make: stop, fricative, affricate, approximant, vowel?
  - Where should I make the constriction? For consonants, the choices are bilabial, labio-dental, dental, alveolar, postalveolar, retroflex, palatal, velar, uvular, pharyngeal, and laryngeal; for vowels, the choices are high/mid/low, front/central/back, tense/lax, and round/unround.
  - Should the velum be open or closed?
  - What should I do with the larynx: voiced or voiceless, aspirated or unaspirated?

The figures and charts provided should help in keeping these straight. The best way to learn the symbols and descriptions is to practice!

further reading

Any introductory phonology or phonetics book will cover place and manner in English. If you'd like to read about the topic from another source, I recommend:

Ladefoged, Peter (2006). *A Course in Phonetics*. 5th edition. Independence, KY: Thomson Wadsworth.

For more on writing systems:
Rogers, Henry (2005). *Writing Systems: A Linguistic Approach*. Oxford: Blackwell.

The idea of speech as a "dance of the articulators" is due to Louis Goldstein. The centrality of the articulatory gesture as the basic building block of speech is based on the joint work of Louis Goldstein and Cathe Browman (see Chapter 5 for more details on their theory of "Articulatory Phonology").

review exercises

1. What does it mean to say that "that human language is *discrete, combinatorial, unbounded,* and *recursive*? Illustrate each property with examples.
2. Review the definitions of the following terms:

   marked/unmarked
   aspiration
   glottal stop
   creaky voice
   breathy voice
   obstruent/sonorant
   rhotic
   lateral
   liquid
   labial
   coronal
   dorsal
   double articulation
   advanced/retracted tongue root
   schwa

3. What are the two central principles of IPA transcription? How does English fall short in meeting these standards?
4. Explain the difference between broad and narrow transcription.
5. Explain the physical reason (having to do with airflow) why voiced obstruents are more marked than voiceless ones.
6. Choose the words in each list that fit the description, and add three more of your own. Pay attention to pronunciation, not spelling!
   a. contain a nasal consonant

      plain map bring wrap camper those

   b. begin with an approximant

      ram max lute shoot vat when

   c. have a voiceless consonant in the middle

      assure attend believe upper defend over

   d. end with a fricative

      believe max laugh right rush cool

   e. contain an affricate

      rich joy please those chat rage

   f. end with a voiced consonant

      lax voiced fold tag ram pose

   g. begin with an alveolar consonant

      ship sand talk caught free dawn

h. end with a velar consonant

   trip   sang   rag   page   walk   spoke

i. contain a high vowel

   pool   beat   sun   pin   seen   cook

j. contain a back vowel

   rose   loft   tab   top   room   led

k. contain a round vowel

   cup   rope   cough   sob   soon   look

l. contain a diphthong

   bite   bread   noise   caught laugh   house

7. Transcribe the following English words (broad transcription):

freezing	mud
thoughtful	cruise
children	thanks
tasks	budget
shaped	coal
pitched	crow
football	crowd
regime	unite
yearbook	enjoy
eyes	food
afraid	them
yes	linguistics

8. Write the following words in English spelling:

[tim]
[ʃɪp]
[wʊdnʔ]
[mɛt]
[kɔt]
[kræʃt]
[jus]
[ritʃt]
[plɛʒər]
[haʊs]
[jɛlo]
[rezd]
[sun]
[praɪs]
[rɑk]

(Continued)

further analysis and discussion

9. Fill in the descriptions for each of the following English consonants.

	Place	Manner	Voiced?	Nasal?	Lateral
g					
r					
n					
d					
f					
ð					
z					
ʃ					
j					
p					

10. Fill in the descriptions for each of the following English vowels.

	Height	Backness	Rounding	Tense or lax
ɑ				n/a
ʊ				
ɛ				
o				
i				

further research

11. Find a passage in a favorite poem or novel, and transcribe it using IPA.
12. Find a speaker of English whom you perceive to have an accent different from your own and ask them to read the words in Table 2.4. How would you transcribe their vowel sounds?

Go online Visit the book's companion website for additional resources related to this chapter at: http://www.wiley.com/go/zsiga.

3 A Tour of the Consonants

The art of writing phonetically does not come of itself any more than the art of painting. The average English person can't paint his own portrait, nor can he write his own language phonetically or anything approaching it . . . he is always thinking he says one thing when he really says something else; besides which . . . he is always wanting to write down what he thinks people ought to say (which has nothing to do with the case).

Daniel Jones, *The Sechuana Reader*, 1916, p. 18.

Chapter outline

The Sounds of Language: An Introduction to Phonetics and Phonology, First Edition. Elizabeth C. Zsiga.
© 2013 Elizabeth C. Zsiga. Published 2013 by Blackwell Publishing Ltd.

This chapter provides a whirlwind tour of the consonants of the world. The full IPA chart is introduced in Section 3.1, and Sections 3.2 and 3.3 work through it systematically, discussing the factors that combine to create each sound, as well as the combinations of factors that do not work. We begin with place and manner of pulmonic consonants, and then discuss non-pulmonic consonants, with notes on diacritics and other symbols included along the way. For most readers, most of the symbols in this chart will be unfamiliar, and the sounds they represent may seem strange. It might be tempting to call some these sounds "exotic," to be found, like rare orchids, only in the dense rainforests or remote mountaintops. Our tour of these sounds will in fact take us to every inhabited continent, and to some remote places. You may be surprised, however, to discover how many of these sounds are lurking in common English pronunciations, given the right environments. We finish the chapter, Section 3.4, with a discussion of some details of the pronunciation of English.

3.1 "exotic" sounds and the phonetic environment

Figures 3.1 and 3.2 provide the IPA symbols for consonants. These cover all the consonants of the languages of the world – at least it is the goal of the International Phonetic Association

the international phonetic alphabet (revised to 2005)

consonants (pulmonic)   © 2005 ipa

	bilabial	labiodental	dental	alveolar	post alveolar	retroflex	palatal	velar	uvular	pharyngeal	glottal
plosive	p b			t d		ʈ ɖ	c ɟ	k ɡ	q ɢ		ʔ
nasal	m	ɱ		n		ɳ	ɲ	ŋ	N		
trill	ʙ			r					ʀ		
tap or flap		ⱱ		ɾ		ɽ					
fricative	ɸ β	f v	θ ð	s z	ʃ ʒ	ʂ ʐ	ç ʝ	x ɣ	χ ʁ	ħ ʕ	h ɦ
lateral fricative				ɬ ɮ							
approximant		ʋ		ɹ		ɻ	j	ɰ			
lateral approximant				l		ɭ	ʎ	ʟ			

where symbols appear in pairs, the one to the right represents a voiced consonant. shaded areas denote articulations judged impossible.

Figure 3.1   IPA symbols for pulmonic consonants. Source: International Phonetic Association (Department of Theoretical and Applied Linguistics, School of English, Aristotle University of Thessaloniki, Thessaloniki 54124, Greece).

consonants (non-pulmonic)

clicks		voiced implosives		ejectives	
ʘ	bilabial	ɓ	bilabial	ʼ	examples:
ǀ	dental	ɗ	dental/alveolar	pʼ	bilabial
ǃ	(post)alveolar	ʄ	palatal	tʼ	dental/alveolar
ǂ	palatoalveolar	ɠ	velar	kʼ	velar
ǁ	alveolar lateral	ʛ	uvular	sʼ	alveolar fricative

other symbols

ʍ	voiceless labial-velar fricative	ɕ ʑ	alveolo-palatal fricatives
w	voiced labial-velar approximant	ɺ	voiced alveolar lateral flap
ɥ	voiced labial-palatal approximant	ɧ	simultaneous ʃ and x
ʜ	voiceless epiglottal fricative		
ʢ	voiced epiglottal fricative	affricates and double articulations	
ʡ	epiglottal plosive	can be represented by two symbols joined by a tie bar if necessary. k͡p t͡s	

diacritics diacritics may be placed above a symbol with a descender, e.g. ŋ̊

̥	voiceless	n̥ d̥	̤	breathy voiced	b̤ a̤	̪	dental	t̪ d̪
̬	voiced	s̬ t̬	̰	creaky voiced	b̰ a̰	̺	apical	t̺ d̺
ʰ	aspirated	tʰ dʰ	̼	linguolabial	t̼ d̼	̻	laminal	t̻ d̻
̹	more rounded	ɔ̹	ʷ	labialized	tʷ dʷ	̃	nasalized	ẽ
̜	less rounded	ɔ̜	ʲ	palatalized	tʲ dʲ	ⁿ	nasal release	dⁿ
̟	advanced	u̟	ˠ	velarized	tˠ dˠ	ˡ	lateral release	dˡ
̠	retracted	e̠	ˤ	pharyngealized	tˤ dˤ	̚	no audible release	d̚
̈	centralized	ë	̴ velarized or pharyngealized ɫ					
̽	mid-centralized	e̽	̝	raised	e̝	(ɹ̝ = voiced alveolar fricative)		
̩	syllabic	n̩	̞	lowered	e̞	(β̞ = voiced bilabial approximant)		
̯	non-syllabic	e̯	̘	advanced tongue root	e̘			
˞	rhoticity	ɚ a˞	̙	retracted tongue root	e̙			

Figure 3.2 Other IPA consonant symbols.
Source: International Phonetic Association (Department of Theoretical and Applied Linguistics, School of English, Aristotle University of Thessaloniki, Thessaloniki 54124, Greece).

that they do so. The chart has several different parts: pulmonic consonants (Figure 3.1) and non-pulmonic consonants, other symbols, and diacritics (Figure 3.2). (Vowels, suprasegmentals, and tone are covered in Chapter 4.) The most extensive is the chart of pulmonic consonants. Again, place of articulation runs across the top of the chart, and manner down the side, so each block represents a particular combination of place and manner. Where there are two symbols in a block, the one on the left is voiceless. Empty blocks indicate combinations that have not been found in any language; shaded empty blocks indicate combinations "deemed impossible." The goal of this chapter is to explain what all of the symbols stand for, and why the shaded blocks are shaded.

Learning the IPA symbols is an important skill for anyone hoping to do linguistics. With these symbols, one has the ability to clearly indicate any speech sound in any language in a way that another linguist can understand. The sounds that these symbols represent, and the relationships between them, will form the subject matter of the rest of this book, so some knowledge of sound symbols is crucial to further progress.

More important than memorizing symbols, however, is understanding the categories of place and manner. Once these are understood, you can use the chart as a reference for unfamiliar (or at least un-memorized) symbols, and be able to figure out the sounds they represent, even if it takes some practice to produce them. But it may be the blank spaces that are most interesting and important of all, since they indicate the limits of the phonetic capabilities of human speakers. The symbols answer the question "What are the occurring sounds of human language?" but the blanks answer the question "What is a possible sound of human language?" Both symbols and blanks will be discussed in turn.

As was noted above, many of these exotic-seeming sounds occur in English, given the right environment. In linguistics, the term *environment* refers to the place in a word where a sound occurs (such as initial or final position), and to the sounds that surround it (between vowels, after an [s], etc.). Languages differ not only in the sounds that they use, but in the environments where sounds may occur. We've already seen several examples of this. In English, the velar nasal [ŋ] occurs in medial and final position ("sing," "singer"), but never in word-initial position. Thai has no such restriction, and words like [ŋa:] (meaning *tusk*) are common. (The colon indicates a long vowel.) The word [ŋa:] may sound "exotic," but there is no new sound there. You already know how to pronounce [ŋ]; you just need to learn to produce it and recognize it in an unfamiliar environment. The situation is similar with the glottal stop: in English, it may occur in place of [t] after [n]. In Hawai'ian, [ʔ] can occur anywhere [p] or [k] can.

We have also already seen examples of how the environment may introduce *variation* in the way a sound is pronounced. In English, the voiceless plosives [p, t, k] are aspirated [pʰ, tʰ, kʰ] in word-initial position, but not aspirated when they occur after [s]. Thai is like English in having both aspirated and unaspirated voiceless stops, but in Thai both kinds can occur in word-initial position: [kʰâ:w] means *step*, and [kâ:w] means *rice*. (Again, the colon indicates a long vowel, and the circumflex accent indicates falling pitch.) When two sounds occur in the same environment, and create two different words (as [kʰâ:w] and [kʰâ:w] in Thai), we can be confident that the two sounds are *contrastive* (a term introduced in Chapter 2). That is, the difference between the two sounds is the only thing that is marking the difference (that is, the contrast) between the two words. Aspiration is not contrastive in English: there are no two words that differ *only* in that one has an aspirated stop and one has a non-aspirated stop. There is always some other difference, like an initial [s], that provides the environment for aspiration to occur or not. The ideas of contrast and variation are central to the study of phonetics and phonology, and are discussed throughout this book. (They are particularly important for phonology, and are given a more formal, extensive treatment in Chapter 6.) In this chapter, we will often note the fact that sounds that are positional variants in English are contrastive in some other language.

The IPA contains only enough symbols for the sounds that are used contrastively in at least some language. No language uses all of the sounds in the IPA, but for any two symbols, there is some language that uses both to create a contrast between words. There are not enough symbols to represent all the details of positional variation. Additional details of positional or dialectal variation (such as partial voicing, slight raising or lowering, or more or less rounding) can often be indicated by *diacritics*: superscripts, subscripts, or modifications to the letters to indicate the desired change.

3.1 In Focus

The largest consonant systems (which include Caucasian languages such as Kabardian and Southern African languages such as !Xóõ and Zhu|'hõasi) may contrast 80–100 or more consonants, but these include many secondary and complex articulations, combinations of the simpler symbols, along with contrasts in voice quality and airstream; see Sections 3.2.3 and 3.3. It can be difficult to get an accurate count because it is sometimes not very clear whether a particularly complex combination of constrictions should count as one consonant or a sequence of two. On the other end of the scale, consonant systems may be as small as six or eight in the languages of the Pacific Islands: for example, six in Rotokas (essentially [p, t, k, b, d, g], with nasals and fricatives occurring as positional variants) and 8 in Hawai'ian [p, k, ʔ, m, n, h, l, w]. For the record, the prize for the overall largest sound inventory probably goes to !Xóõ, which in addition to its 80+ consonants has more than 20 different vowels, and the prize for the smallest goes to Rotokas, with just five vowels in addition to its six consonants.

One final note of caution: IPA symbols are an extremely useful way to refer to sounds, but they are not themselves the "atoms" of linguistic representation. It should always be kept in mind that a phonetic alphabet is a system of labels for recurring combinations of articulatory gestures and the acoustic correlates of those gestures. The symbol [p] is a "cover term" for bilabial + plosive + voiceless, the symbol [b] is a cover term for bilabial + plosive + voiced, etc.

3.2 pulmonic consonants

3.2.1 stops, nasals, and fricatives

As is evident from the IPA chart, fricatives can be made at every place of articulation, and stops and nasals at most. There are a lot of symbols to learn, and nothing for it but to work through them systematically. I strongly recommend trying each one out as you read. While learning symbols and definitions is probably not the most interesting part of linguistics for most students, I hope that trying out some challenging new sound combinations will be rewarding. Try the sounds out by yourself in front of a mirror, or with a friend: see if you can correctly transcribe the distinctions your friend is producing, and vice versa.

At the bilabial place, the oral and nasal stops (as in [pɑ], [bɑ], [mɑ]) are familiar and straightforward. The voiceless bilabial fricative [ɸ] consists of air passing through a constriction between the lips: the same vocal tract configuration as blowing out a candle. This fricative occurs in Japanese words such as "futon" [ɸuton] and "fugo" [ɸugo]. These words are borrowed into English with an [f], but try pronouncing them without bringing the lower lip back to touch the teeth. A bilabial fricative can also be made with the lips spread and pressed together rather than pursed. Figure 3.3 shows an image of the lip position used for a bilabial fricative in Setswana (a language of Southern Africa). I think most English speakers produce this type of fricative in the exclamation usually written "phew!" [ɸju], which is not identical to "few" [fju]. (Remember that [j] stands for the palatal glide, so that [ju] is pronounced "you.") The voiced bilabial fricative [β] is made in the same way as [b], but with the lips held more loosely, allowing air to escape. In most dialects of Spanish, "b" is

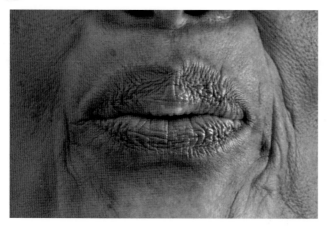

Figure 3.3   Lip position for the voiceless bilabial fricative in Setswana.

pronounced [β] when it occurs between vowels: "la bola" (the ball) is pronounced [laβola].

The labiodental fricatives are [f] and [v]. There are no labiodental plosives: a language that had them would require all its speakers to have completely perfect teeth. For real people, air is always able to escape through gaps between the teeth. It is possible, however, to articulate a labiodental nasal [ɱ]. When the velum is open, the constriction of the lower lip against the upper teeth is sufficient to divert most of the airflow through the nose. Although no language is known to use [m] and [ɱ] contrastively, labiodental nasals occur in English and other languages when a nasal precedes [f] or [v], in words like *inverse*, *infamous*, *comfort*, *symphony*, etc. Anticipating the labiodental fricative, speakers will also make the nasal at the labiodental place. You should be able to feel (and see, if you look in a mirror) that the lips never fully close in a word like "comfort." Such variation, where two sounds that are adjacent to one another become more similar, is known as *assimilation*. Assimilation is the most common kind of positional variation, and a number of examples from English will be discussed in this chapter. Assimilation is also discussed at greater length in Chapters 5 and 11.

Languages generally choose either bilabial or labiodental fricatives as part of their inventory. English chooses [f] and [v], for example, while Japanese and Setswana choose [ɸ]. Few languages contrast these types of fricatives, probably because the distinction between them is hard to hear (though not hard to see). One language that includes all four labial fricatives in its inventory is Ewe, a language of West Africa.

The dental, alveolar, post-alveolar, retroflex, and palatal consonants are all coronals, that is, made with the tongue tip or blade. The IPA gives only a single symbol [t, d, n] for the stops at the dental, alveolar, and post-alveolar places of articulation. This is because languages will generally choose only one of these places to use contrastively, and the same (simple) symbol can be used in each case. English makes these consonants at the alveolar place of articulation, while Russian and French make them dental, for example. If necessary, a dental articulation can be indicated by placing a "tooth mark" under the more general symbol [t̪ d̪], and a post-alveolar constriction can be indicated by a line under the letter [t̠ d̠].

Not many languages are known to contrast dental and alveolar place of articulation. Examples include Malayalam (Dravidian) and some of the languages of New Guinea. In each of these cases, however, the distinction in location of the passive articulator is enhanced by a further distinction in the active articulator: alveolar consonants are made with the tongue tip, and dental consonants with the tongue blade. The phonetic term for tongue-tip consonants is *apical*; tongue blade consonants are *laminal*.

While English coronal stops and nasals are alveolar in the default case, dental and post-alveolar versions occur as positional variants. Repeat the following phrases, paying attention to the position of the tongue front in the final consonant of the first word of the phrase:

(1)   Coronal assimilation in English

ten	ten times	ten things	ten roads
in	in time	in this	inroads
made	made time	made things	made rings
eight	eight times	eight things	eight rows

These examples illustrate another case of assimilation. In the first and second columns, the word-final [t, d, n] are alveolar. In the third column, however, the final consonant becomes dental [t̪, d̪, n̪] before the dental fricatives [θ, ð], and in the fourth column the final consonants become post-alveolar [t, d, n] before post-alveolar [r].

For the coronal fricatives, different symbols are used for the dental, alveolar, and post-alveolar places of articulation, because these sounds are often used contrastively, as in English. The difference between the fricatives is much more noticeable than the subtle sound difference between [t], [t̪], and [t]. One reason is that [s, z, ʃ, ʒ] are grooved fricatives, and [θ, ð] are not. The groove in the tongue creates a strong channel of airflow that produces a loud, high-pitched noise when it hits the teeth. (Again, imagine the splash when you spray water from a hose against a wall.) Try articulating these sounds a few times in succession: [s] [ʃ] [s] [ʃ] [s] [ʃ]. Can you feel that the sides of your tongue are raised for these fricatives while the center of the tongue is lowered, creating the channel? In contrast, the tongue is flat for [θ, ð], and the noise is softer and lower-pitched. Referencing this difference in pitch and volume, the alveolar and post-alveolar fricatives are termed *sibilants*, while the dentals are non-sibilants. Distinguishing among the sibilants, the post-alveolars have a somewhat lower pitch than the alveolars. Did you also notice a difference in lip rounding between [s] and [ʃ]? Rounding the lips for [ʃ], by creating a bigger space in front of the teeth, lowers the pitch of the [ʃ] even further, magnifying the difference between the alveolars and post-alveolars.

The post-alveolar fricatives [ʃ, ʒ] are laminal, made with the blade of the tongue. In order for the tongue *tip* to make a constriction in the post-alveolar region, it must be curled back. Such a configuration (apical post-alveolar) is known as *retroflex* (literally, backward-turning). As was noted in Chapter 2, the only retroflex sound in English is the rhotic, and even that may not have much if any tongue-tip raising for many speakers. Other languages, however, notably Hindi and other languages of India, have a full set of retroflex stops, fricatives, and nasals. The IPA symbols for these sounds have a little hook under the symbol, recalling the curling back of the tongue. A telltale sign of an Indian accent is substituting retroflex stops for English alveolars. Figure 3.4 shows an MRI image of a subject producing a retroflex stop. In other languages the retroflexion may not be so extreme.

Modeling your own articulation on the picture, try producing [aʈa], [aɖa], [aɳa], [aʂa], [aʐa]. The large space under the tongue that is created by the tongue tip moving up and back (the sub-lingual cavity) gives this set of sounds their distinctive quality.

Palatal articulations are usually also considered coronals, although they involve raising of both the tongue front and tongue body up to the hard palate. The symbols are [c, ɟ] for the stops, [ç, ʝ] for the fricatives, and [ɲ] for the nasal. Be careful of the differences in the direction of the hook, and where it is attached, in distinguishing palatal [ɲ], retroflex [ɳ], and velar [ŋ]. For palatal [ɲ] the hook resembles a [j], for velar [ŋ] the hook resembles a "[g]," and for retroflex [ɳ] the hook recalls the turned-up tongue.

English does not use any of palatal stops, fricatives, or nasals contrastively, although the palatal nasal may be familiar from languages such as Spanish and French: Spanish "año" (year) and French "agneau" (lamb) are both [aɲo], though with a difference in stress. The tongue positions for [ç, ʝ] are very similar to that of [j] (as in "you"). If you start with a [j] and then make it voiceless, the resulting increased airflow from the open vocal folds is likely to be sufficient to cause friction: a word such as "hue" may be transcribed [çu]. To

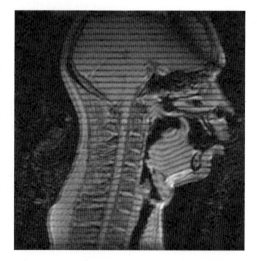

Figure 3.4 MRI image of a retroflex stop. The horizontal lines are a feature of the imaging technology, designed to track changes in muscle shape.
Source: Vocal Tract Imaging Laboratory, University of Maryland, http://speech.umaryland.edu/speech_images/mri-r.jpg. Courtesy of Maureen Stone.

create a voiced palatal fricative, again start with [j], but then raise the tongue slightly to create a narrower constriction: you will be able to hear the point at which frication begins. From [ç] and [ʝ], it is a simple matter to press the tongue up further, against the palate, to close off the airflow and create the palatal stops [c] and [ɟ]. Palatal stops, as opposed to affricates, are cross-linguistically marked, though they do occur in languages such as Akan (West Africa) and Hungarian (Eastern Europe). Because the closure involves a long portion of the tongue, it is rather difficult to release the stop closure quickly enough to avoid frication, and palatal stops often evolve over time into affricates. Many languages, like English, have alveolar and velar stops, and palatal or alveopalatal affricates. (More on the IPA symbols for affricates in Section 3.2.3.) No language contrasts palatal place and (laminal) post-alveolar place for stops or nasals, but a number of languages, including Polish and Cantonese, contrast palatal and post-alveolar fricatives.

There is actually one more possible coronal articulation. It is possible to make a stop by extending the tongue out to make a closure against the upper lip. *Linguo-labial* stops, fricatives, and nasals have been documented in languages spoken on the islands of Vanuatu, in the South Pacific. Being exceedingly rare, linguo-labial place is not accorded its own column in the IPA consonant chart, but can be indicated by placing a "seagull" diacritic (evoking the upper lip) under the corresponding alveolar symbol, as in Tangoa [n̼ata] *eye*.

The next place of articulation in the IPA chart, *velar*, is used contrastively in just about every language. Velar consonants use the tongue dorsum as the active articulator, moving up and back to make a constriction at the velum. The velar stops [k, g, ŋ] have already been discussed. Velar fricatives [x, ɣ] do not occur in English, but they are not hard to make. On the principle that a fricative is a stop with just slightly less constriction, you can make a [x] by beginning with a [k] and then lowering the tongue just enough to allow some turbulent airflow to pass through. This is the sound at the end of the German (or pretentious English) pronunciation of the name of the composer Bach. Add in voicing (and a slightly tighter constriction, to make up for the reduced airflow) to produce [ɣ].

The tongue body can also make constrictions further back, at the *uvular* place of articulation. To make the uvular stops [q] and [ɢ], begin with a [k] or [g], then move the tongue a few centimeters back. Practice contrasting [aka], [aqa], [aga], [aɢa] and then [aŋa], [aɴa]: same tongue movement each time, but with different settings for voicing and nasality. Uvular stops are common in many Native American languages. Also, the name of the Middle Eastern country Qatar is pronounced exactly the way it is spelled (as are most of the famous "q-without-u" words in the Scrabble dictionary). Once you have a feeling for the place of the stops, it is not hard to produce the fricatives [χ] and [ʁ] by loosening the constriction without changing the place. In many dialects of French, an initial "r" as in "rouge" is a voiced uvular fricative: [ʁuʒ].

Constrictions can also be made deep in the throat, with the tongue root moving back toward the pharyngeal wall. Voiced and voiceless *pharyngeal* fricatives are found in Arabic and other Semitic languages. These sounds are among the most difficult consonants for English speakers to learn to make, since they involve an active articulator, the tongue root, that is not used for English consonants at all. To make the pharyngeal fricatives [ʕ] and [ħ], I find that it's easiest to start with an [h], the laryngeal fricative, and then try to tighten the throat until a fricative sound is heard and felt. This is much easier with an open jaw and a low vowel: [aħa], [aʕa]. In fact, many of the languages that use pharyngeal fricatives do not allow high vowels to occur adjacent to them.

The tongue root itself cannot be moved far enough back to make a complete closure, but epiglottal stops and fricatives, with the epiglottis touching the pharyngeal wall, have been reported in the Caucasian language Agul. Symbols for these sounds are included in the "other symbols" section of the IPA. Only a voiceless epiglottal plosive is included, presumably because combining that much pharyngeal constriction with a laryngeal configuration consistent with voicing is not possible. Note that it is also impossible to produce a pharyngeal or laryngeal nasal stop. Knowing what you do about the anatomy of the vocal tract (look at Figure 1.8 on p. 10 if you need to) can you figure out why? (Answer at the end of this section.)

Our tour of the places of articulation finishes with the laryngeals: voiceless [h], breathy voiced [ɦ], and glottal stop [ʔ]. Note that there are only three laryngeal consonants, because there are so few degrees of freedom for laryngeal movement. Opening the vocal folds produces [h], closing them produces [ʔ], and an intermediate position, with enough airflow to cause frication but also enough tension to cause some vocal fold vibration, produces breathy voiced [ɦ]. This last sound may be produced when English [h] occurs between vowels, as in "ahead": [əɦɛd]. We already noted in Chapter 2 that the glottal stop is a positional variant of [t] in many dialects of English, frequently occurring before [n] or in word-final position: [ɪmporʔnʔ]. It should now be noted that, in other languages, the glottal stop is used as a regular consonant. For example, in Hawai'ian, the sequence [poʔo] means *head*, and [ʔoʔo] is a type of bird. In the word "Hawai'i" the apostrophe stands for a glottal stop.

We have seen in this section that fricatives can be made at every place of articulation: bilabial, labiodental, dental, alveolar, post-alveolar, retroflex, palatal, velar, uvular, pharyngeal, and laryngeal, even linguolabial. Plosives can be made at all of these but two: labiodental stops do not work because our teeth have gaps in them, and pharyngeal stops (with the one reported exception of epiglottal stops in one language) do not work because our tongues do not go back that far. For a similar reason, there is not even a column for places of articulation like "retroflex velar," if you can imagine what that would involve. (In the IPA chart, the block for labiodental stops is left blank, not shaded, because it is not physically impossible to make such a stop, just highly improbable; similarly the blocks for voiceless pharyngeal stops and for pharyngeal fricatives are left open to allow for the possibility of epiglottals.)

All the fricatives and plosives come in voiced and voiceless pairs, except for the glottal stop, which is necessarily voiceless. As was noted in Chapter 1, however, voiced and voiceless fricatives and plosives are not equal: voiced obstruents are more marked than voiceless obstruents. Voiced obstruents are difficult to produce because the vocal tract obstruction inherent in a stop or fricative necessarily interferes with the airflow necessary for vocal fold vibration. A language may have both voiced and voiceless members of a pair (like English), or just the voiceless members (like Finnish or Hawai'ian), but no language has voiced stops but not voiceless. Thus the concept of linguistic markedness may be stated in the form of an implication (an "if–then" statement): If a language has voiced obstruents, then it will also have voiceless obstruents. In more general form, "If a language has the marked option, then it will also have the unmarked option." Even in English, which contrasts words like [pɑp] and [bɑb] or [kɪk] and [gɪg], voicing tends to be slow in starting, or quick to die out, in word-initial and word-final position. A consonant that is thus at least partially "devoiced" may be indicated with an open circle under the symbol for the usually voiced sound: [b̥ɑb̥] and [g̊ɪg̊], for example.

Returning to the IPA chart, we see that nasal stops occur at all places of articulation except pharyngeal and laryngeal. The reason for this is that the pharynx and larynx are lower in the throat than the velum. If airflow is cut off at the larynx, there can be no airflow through the nasal passages, and thus no nasality.

Every language has at least one or two nasal stops, and nasalized vowels and approximants (written with a tilde, [õ] or [w̃]) are also common. But nasalized fricatives, while possible, do not work so well: venting a volume of airflow through the nose leaves a much weaker airstream with which to create a fricative. Try pronouncing [z̃] and see how fast you run out of air, if you can manage it at all.

The next sections turn to sounds whose articulatory requirements limit the places at which they can be realized.

3.2.2 laterals, trills, taps, and other approximants

A lateral sound, by definition, stops the airflow down the center line of the vocal tract, but allows air to escape along one or both sides of the tongue. The most common lateral is the alveolar lateral approximant, exemplified by English [l]. To make an [l], the tongue tip moves forward to contact the alveolar ridge, while the tongue body moves back and down, stretching out the tongue. Just as stretching a piece of gum makes it thinner, stretching the tongue also makes it thinner, so much so that the sides of the tongue pull away from the sides of the palate or the upper teeth, allowing the air to escape. This backing and lowering movement of the tongue body can be heard when an /l/ follows a high vowel: "feel" is pronounced [fiəɫ] and "pool" is pronounced [pʰuəɫ]. A lateral for which this tongue backing gesture is timed so as to be particularly evident may be termed a "dark l," or "velarized l" and symbolized [ɫ]. In English, [l]s at the end of a syllable are dark, while those at the beginning of a syllable are light: listen to difference between "leaf" and "feel."

Voiced and voiceless lateral fricatives [ɮ, ɬ] are made with the tongue in approximately the same configuration as for [l], but with a tighter constriction at the sides and/or more airflow, so that the airflow causes frication. These fricatives are common in Navajo and related languages. Note that the symbols for the "dark l" and the lateral fricative are very similar, differing only in the diacritic that runs through the center of the symbol: the "dark l" is written with a tilde [ɫ], the lateral fricative with a loop [ɬ]. Be careful not to confuse them.

Many languages also have post-alveolar laterals, symbolized [ʎ]. This is the sound written "gli" in Italian, as in "famiglia" [famiʎa] *family* and "meglio" [meʎo] *better*. Languages that have retroflex stops and nasals may also have a retroflex lateral [ɭ]. The tongue mechanics are the same for these sounds as for [l], except that the forward contact is made in the post-alveolar region (with the tongue blade for [ʎ] and the tongue tip for [ɭ]), rather than at the alveolar ridge.

It is also possible to make a velar lateral, symbolized [ʟ]. For this sound, the tongue dorsum is raised toward the velum, but with greater constriction on one side than on other. Dorsal laterals contrast with alveolar laterals in Melpa (Papua New Guinea) and in Zulu (Southern Africa). They may also occur as positional variants of [l] in some dialects of English, in words that end in "lk." Try pronouncing a word like "milk." Does your tongue tip go up to the alveolar ridge for the [l]? Even if it does, try pronouncing the word with your tongue tip held down behind your lower teeth. If you can succeed in producing a lateral sound without involving the tongue front, it will be a velar lateral.

Labial laterals, on the other hand, are impossible. Our facial muscles just do not permit an approximant articulation in which the lips are closed in the middle but open at the sides. (Try it.) Even if you could do it, such an articulation would not sound any different from [w], so it would not be worth the trouble. There are no pharyngeal or laryngeal laterals either, for obvious reasons. The IPA leaves open the possibility that a uvular lateral might exist, though none has been attested.

The next sets of sounds to be considered are the *taps* and *flaps*. These articulations are termed *ballistic*: they consist of "throwing" the active articulator against the passive articulator, so that it either strikes the passive articulator in passing (a flap) or bounces off it (a tap).

American English speakers produce a tap instead of a plosive for "t" and "d" in words like "city," "pretty," "shady," "Eddie," "felicity," "automatic," "ladder" (essentially, these consonants become taps when they occur between any two vowels, the second of which is unstressed). The IPA symbol for this tap is [ɾ]. You may also see it written as [D]. Almost all of the [d]s and [t]s are tapped in the phrase: "Dead-headed Ed edited it" (attributed to Peter Ladefoged). Try this phrase out and try to feel what your tongue is doing. In a tap, the tongue tip moves up to tap briefly against the alveolar ridge, but the two articulators do not stay in contact long enough for any pressure to build up. (The closure for typical tap is about 20 milliseconds, or $\frac{1}{50}$ th of a second, long.) Because there is no pressure build-up, a tap counts as a sonorant. Taps are so brief that the vocal folds do not have time to pull apart, so taps are also voiced. In a more careful and slow pronunciation, [t] is voiceless and [d] is voiced, but if they become taps, the distinction is lost: both are voiced. Thus you often see children spell words like "pretty" as "priddy." We once had a long discussion at my house over whether the toys Santa brings in the song "Santa Claus is Coming to Town" are cars designed for cats or for children (that is, *kitty cars* or *kiddie cars*). If all you hear is the tap, and you haven't been taught how to spell the word, the choice between "t" and "d" can be a toss up. (The medial sound in words like "Santa" and "winter" can be a nasal tap.)

> 3.2 Note that tapped alveolar stops mark a particularly American or Australian accent. Other English dialects will tend to use glottal stops or full alveolar stops where Americans and Aussies have taps. On the other hand, some dialects of British English use a tapped variant of [r]. The Scottish pronunciation of "pearl" is very like the American pronunciation of "pedal."

The words *tap* and *flap* are often used interchangeably: one often hears about "the American flapping rule," for example. However, to a phonetician, there is a difference. Technically, a tap involves an up and down motion: the tongue tip bounces off the alveolar ridge. A *flap* is a one-way motion, like a swinging door. In this text, we'll maintain the distinction, but keep in mind that it is common to call the sounds of English flaps.

Retroflex flaps [ɽ] occur in Hindi: the tongue tip curls back as for a retroflex stop, and then drops down, hitting the alveolar ridge with the underside of the tongue on the way down. The only other kind of flap that has been identified is a labiodental flap. This symbol [ⱱ] is the newest addition to the IPA (as of this writing), having been added in 2005. A labiodental flap is made by drawing the lower lip behind the upper teeth, and then pulling it forward. Labiodental flaps occur in Banda and neighboring languages of Central Africa. (See: http://www.sil.org/~olsonk/research.html).

While taps and flaps are ballistic, trills are *aerodynamic*. The active articulator is held in the correct position with the correct tension, so that the flow of air between active and passive articulator sets one or both into vibration. The best known trills are the tongue-tip "trilled rs" of Spanish and French, symbolized [r]. In a uvular trill [ʀ], it is the passive articulator, the uvula, that vibrates. You already know how to make a bilabial trill [ʙ]: as a motorboat sound or raspberry. (Just lips – no tongue involvement. Sticking the tongue out would make a linguo-labial trill – certainly doable, but not known to be used as speech sounds in any language.) Bilabial trills, however, function as regular consonants, parallel to [r] or [n] or [b], in languages such as Kele and Titan (Papua New Guinea).

The last set of consonants to be considered are those listed simply as "approximants" in the IPA chart. These sounds involve a constriction in the vocal tract, so that the active and passive articulators are brought near each other, but not so much that any frication is caused. Non-lateral approximants may be labiodental [ʋ], dental/alveolar/post-alveolar [ɹ], retroflex [ɻ] palatal [j], velar [ɰ], or labiovelar [w]. The labiodental approximant may be thought of as a severely weakened [v], and the velar as a severely weakened [g]. Bilabial approximants may also occur, though not contrastively: they may be symbolized [β̞], the diacritic standing for "a lowered version" of [β]. The glides [j] and [w] are well known to English speakers. This leaves [ɹ] for last. The sound that begins the English word "road" is an alveolar or post-alveolar approximant: a sound that is cross-linguistically much rarer than either a trill or a tap. Note also that, like [ʃ], [ɹ] is made with rounded lips.

3.3   In Focus

Transcribing the rhotics (trills, taps, flaps, and non-lateral coronal approximants) is one of the most vexing problems for beginning linguists. "Is the symbol for American English "r" [r] or [ɹ]?" The answer is: either can be correct, it depends on whether one is using broad transcription or narrow transcription. Recall that in broad transcription, only enough detail is given to distinguish all the different words of a language: the word is [rip], not [lip] or [nip], and no claim is made about the specifics of articulation. Narrow transcription provides more details. In broad transcription, [r] can be used as a cover symbol for "any rhotic," just as [t] can be used as a symbol for "any voiceless coronal stop." In broad transcription, it makes sense to use the simplest symbol available: [r] rather than [ɹ], [t] rather than [t̪]. If, however, the details of articulation are important, or if a comparison between languages is envisioned, narrow transcription is needed, and it would be incorrect to use the same symbols for the very different rhotics of English, Spanish, Czech, and Hindi. In narrow transcription, the symbol [ɹ] is used for the post-alveolar approximant of English and the symbol [r] is reserved for the much more common alveolar trill. Remember again, IPA symbols are cover terms for combinations of articulatory gestures, and they can be used in both a broad (less specific) and narrow (more specific) sense. To summarize: in broad transcription, [r] = any rhotic. In narrow transcription, [r] = alveolar trill and [ɹ] = (post-)alveolar approximant.

3.2.3 contour and complex segments

You may have noticed that the IPA chart contains no symbols for affricates. It is not that affricates are not common or contrastive – they are both – but that an affricate can always be represented by a sequence of two symbols, a stop followed by a fricative at the same place of articulation. English has only post-alveolar affricates ([t͡ʃ] and [d͡ʒ]) but affricates can be made at any place a stop and fricative can be made: bilabial as in German [p͡ɸefɐr] *pepper*, alveolar as in Japanese [t͡sunami], palatal as in Thai [c͡çɔ̂ŋwâːŋ] *blank*, velar as in Setswana [k͡xapʰa] *smear with dung*, uvular as in Oowekyala [q͡χ] *powder* or [d͡ziq͡χa] "to stop making vocal noise, e.g., stop crying." The last has both an alveolar and uvular affricate.

The real question to ask about affricates is why they "count" as just one segment, not two. You cannot necessarily tell by listening: an affricate might not be any shorter, or articulated any differently, than a sequence of two segments. The argument for their unity is not based on their physical, phonetic, characteristics, but on their phonological patterning. Edward Sapir, one of the most influential linguists of the first half of the twentieth century, answered by saying that affricates "feel" like one segment to the speakers of the language. English speakers have a sense of a "ch-sound" that is parallel to their sense of a "b-sound" or "s-sound." There's certainly something to be said for taking native speaker intuitions into account, but we might go further in finding that affricates *behave* like single segments: they appear in contexts where only single segments, not sequences, should be allowed. English generally does not allow sequences of stop + fricative at the beginning of a word: we simplify "psychology," whose root was pronounced with [ps] in Greek, to just [s], for example. But the affricates [t͡ʃ] and [d͡ʒ] are fine. Setswana goes even further, never allowing two obstruents in a row at all, but [t͡ʃ] and [d͡ʒ] are fine in Setswana too. Additionally, the two parts of an affricate always share the same place and laryngeal configuration, contributing to the sense of sameness. If [dʃ] or [pʃ] occurred, for example, they would not count as affricates. Segments like affricates are called *contour segments*: they start off as stops, but finish as fricatives.

(Arguably, there are no reverse affricates: single segments that start off as fricatives and end as stops.)

Segments can have contours in other dimensions as well. Pre-nasalized stops [ⁿd, ᵐb] start off nasal and end oral: the velum closes part-way through. There can also be stops with lateral release: [tˡ, dˡ]. The segment begins as a standard stop, but the closure is released from the side rather than from the center.

Contour segments like affricates and pre-nasalized stops have two different articulations in sequence. *Complex segments* have two different articulations at the same time. We have already discussed one complex segment: [w], the labio-velar glide, which combines an approximant constriction at both the velum and the lips. Labio-velar stops, which combine a [k] and a [p], or a [g] and a [b], at the same time, are common in many West African languages – in the name of the language Igbo, for example, or the Igbo word [k͡pa], *to weave by hand*. While double articulations at various places of articulation are not hard to make (given the independence of the active articulators), they can be hard for the ear to distinguish, so double articulations other than labio-velars are vanishingly rare. A doubly articulated fricative combining [ʃ] and [χ] is reported for Swedish, and has been recognized with the IPA symbol [ɧ]; another fricative combination, [ʃ] and [ɸ], has been reported for dialects of Setswana.

If a sound has two different articulations, but one has a greater degree of constriction than the other, the more constricted articulation is the *primary articulation*, and the more open is the *secondary articulation*. Secondarily articulations are indicated with superscripts. They include rounding (as in [kʷa], [sʷa]), palatalization ([kʲa], [sʲa]), velarization [lˠa], and pharyngealization [sˤa]. In each case the main constriction is accompanied by an approximant-like constriction at the lips, palate, velum, and pharynx, respectively.

3.3 non-pulmonic consonants

There are three kinds of non-pulmonic consonants: implosives, ejectives, and clicks. Each uses a source of airflow other than the lungs. Each creates an enclosed body of air within the oral tract, and then manipulates the pressure by enlarging or compressing the enclosed space. When the pressure is released, a distinctive sound is made. Implosives and ejectives create a space between the larynx and another place of articulation; clicks create a space between the body of the tongue and another constriction further forward (lips or tongue front). We consider each in turn.

3.3.1 implosives

Implosives may also be called *glottalic ingressive* stops. For these consonants, the main source of change in air pressure is movement of the larynx, and (to the extent that air is moving) the primary movement of air is into, rather than out of, the mouth. Implosives probably arose in languages as a way to keep voiced stops voiced. Think about what happens during a pulmonic voiced stop, such as [b]. A closure is made with the lips; by definition, no air is allowed to escape from the mouth. Meanwhile, however, air is continuing to flow out of the lungs and into the oral cavity, passing over the vocal folds and causing vibration. It does not take long, however, for the mouth to fill up with air. Within a few hundredths of a second, air pressure above the larynx is equal to the air pressure below the larynx, and at that point airflow, and voicing, will cease. Try pronouncing a syllable like [ab], and try to keep voicing going into the [b] for as long as possible, without opening the lips. Voicing will stop very quickly.

How can a speaker keep voicing going, without opening the lips? One way, of course, would be to vent the airflow through the velar port, turning the voiced oral stop into a nasal stop. If that is undesirable (since [m] and [b] are probably contrastive) another way is to somehow make the oral cavity bigger, to allow more air to fit in. The walls of the oral cavity, especially the cheeks, are somewhat pliable, and they do expand a bit in voiced stops, but the speaker can also take action by lowering the larynx. If the larynx moves down in the throat, the space in the oral cavity expands by just that much. Recall Boyle's law: if the volume of an enclosed space increases, air pressure within decreases. The decrease in air pressure, plus the action of physically pushing the vocal folds down over the air in the trachea, can keep the vibration going a bit longer.

You will probably get larynx lowering in your [ab] experiment. If you place your finger on your larynx while trying to draw out the [b], you should feel the larynx moving down in an effort to expand the oral cavity. You may also feel, for a moment, the lips being slightly drawn in by the lowered air pressure. If you open your lips at exactly the moment you feel the lips being drawn in, you will have created an implosive. Air does not exactly rush into the mouth, but the interaction of the differing pressures inside and outside the oral cavity creates a distinctive sound.

It seems to be easiest to learn to make implosives at the bilabial place of articulation, since the longer distance from larynx to lips makes for maximum oral cavity size, but languages use implosives at all places of articulation. They are especially common in languages of West Africa. As shown in Figure 3.2, the IPA symbols use a hook ascending from the symbol for the voiced plosive: [ɓ, ɗ, ɠ]. Because the aerodynamics of creating an implosive sound require both a vocal tract closure and vibrating larynx, implosives are always voiced stops. There are no voiceless implosives, and no implosive fricatives or approximants.

3.3.2 ejectives

Ejectives are the inverse of implosives. They may be called *glottalic egressive*: as with the implosives a change in air pressure is caused by movement of the larynx, but in this case direction of airflow is outward. Ejectives are written in IPA with an apostrophe following the symbol for the voiceless plosive at the same place of articulation: [p', t', k', q'].

Ejectives begin with two closures, one at the larynx (a glottal stop) the other at a different place of articulation, such as velar. The two closures enclose a body of air. In the case of the ejectives, the larynx is raised rather than lowered. Raising the larynx makes the space between the closures smaller, compressing the air and raising the pressure. Then, the forward closure is released, causing a distinctive pop. A few milliseconds later, the glottal closure is opened, and the free flow of air (and voicing) for the vowel is resumed.

In order to make an ejective, you have to first be comfortable with making a glottal stop. Practice "uh-oh" until you are familiar with the muscle configuration required. Try a glottal stop between various vowels. From there, you should be able to make a velar and glottal closure at the same time: a glottalized [kʔ]. With ejectives, it's easier to make them if the oral closure is further back, since it's easier to increase the pressure if the volume between larynx and closure is small. Once you can make a [kʔ], you need to add in larynx raising. This is the hardest part. It may help to get a feel for what's involved if you try (silently) singing a very low note and then a very high note. For the high note, the larynx rises in the throat. Try to feel the muscular sensations of larynx raising, and get it under conscious control. Finally, sequence all the parts:

1. Simultaneous closure at larynx and in the oral cavity (for example, [kʔ]).
2. Larynx raising.
3. Release of the oral closure.
4. Release of the glottal closure.

Again, it can help to place a finger on your throat so that you can feel if your larynx is moving. You'll know you are producing an ejective if you can feel the larynx rise, and if you hear a short period of silence between the release of the stop and the beginning of the vowel, when the mouth is open but the larynx is still closed. That period of silence is an important cue to distinguishing this kind of stop.

It is also possible to make ejective fricatives, affricates, and laterally-released stops. Although the fricative or lateral portion will be short, larynx raising can generate sufficient airflow for these articulations. They are found in Native American languages, and in Amharic (Ethiopia). Because the larynx must be closed, however, all ejective sounds are voiceless.

3.3.3 clicks

The third kind of non-pulmonic consonants are the *clicks*, or *velaric ingressive* consonants. You probably already know how to make clicks: the "kiss-kiss" and "tsk-tsk" sounds are clicks. The trick is to incorporate them into the speech stream as consonants.

Clicks begin with a closure of the tongue body against the velum or uvula. Then a second closure is made further forward, for example, the tongue front against the teeth. A small body of air is trapped between the two closures. The tongue body is then slid backward, without breaking the seal against the upper surface of the vocal tract, and the middle of the tongue is lowered. These actions make the pocket of air larger, and thus the air pressure in the pocket becomes lower. When the forward closure is released, a clicking sound is produced.

Clicks can be made at the labial, dental, post-alveolar, and retroflex places. The labial click [ʘ] is the "kiss-kiss" sound, though it is generally made with the lips pressed flat together rather than pursed. (The bilabial is the rarest of the clicks.) The dental click (|) is the "tsk-tsk" sound. Once you've practiced that a few times, try the alveolar (!) and palato-alveolar (ǂ) places, moving your tongue tip further back each time. You should be able to notice that as your tongue tip moves back, and the space under the tongue (the *sub-lingual cavity*) gets bigger, the pitch of the click sound gets lower. If you articulate the click slowly, you may also be able to feel the tongue body moving back and the resulting pressure change pulling back on the tongue front. The lateral click [ǁ] is made by sliding the side of the tongue down the side of the teeth. The lateral click has been described as the sound used to call horses. Once you're confident in making the different clicks in isolation, try putting them between vowels, and then into longer words.

The velaric ingressive sound is made completely in the front part of the mouth: from the tongue body forward. Therefore, clicks can be "accompanied" by other articulations going on at the back of the mouth. Clicks can be nasal, with air flowing through the open velum behind the velar closure while the click sound is being made in front of the closure. They can be voiced, voiceless, aspirated, creaky voiced or breathy voiced. They can also be affricated on release or not. For example, the !Xòõ language (spoken in Namibia and Botswana) is reported to have 83 different varieties of clicks (five places of articulation and 17 different possible accompaniments). The accompaniments can be indicated by linking the symbol for the appropriate velar stop to the click symbol: [ŋ͡|] is a nasal dental click, [g͡ǁ] is a voiced lateral click, etc.

While clicks occur as expressions, interjections, and mimetics throughout the world, they occur as regular speech sounds mostly in a cluster of languages in Central and Southern Africa: the Khoesan languages and their neighbors. Given their versatility and clear auditory distinctiveness, it is not really clear why click consonants do not occur more widely. They are "difficult" to make, certainly, requiring a high degree of articulatory coordination, but no more so than other sounds that are much more widely distributed, such as ejectives.

3.4 positional variation in English

As promised at the beginning of this chapter, we have found a number of "exotic" sounds hidden in American English pronunciations, not only the post-alveolar approximant, but species such as bilabial fricatives, glottal stops, voiceless sonorants, labiodental nasals, and even velar laterals. For those with a special interest in the pronunciation of English, for teaching, learning, or speech therapy, we pause to collate these examples into a list of some positional variants of English consonants.

In this section, because we are concerned with predictable details of pronunciation, we use narrow transcription rather than broad. In a broad transcription, transcribing the English word "pan" as [pæn] is perfectly correct, since the word does indeed consist of a voiceless bilabial plosive followed by a low front vowel followed by an alveolar nasal stop, and the symbols are sufficient to distinguish this word from all others in the language, including "ban" [bæn], "pad" [pæd], and "pin" pɪn. But many details of English positional variation are left out of the broad transcription: for example, initial voiceless stops are aspirated, vowels are nasalized before a nasal consonant, vowels are lengthened before a voiced consonant, and (at least in my dialect) the low front vowel has a high front onglide before [n]. A narrow transcription includes all these details: pʰɪæ̃:n. Of course, since sounds that are positional variants in one language may be contrastive in another, the question of how much detail to include in a broad transcription will depend on the language: aspiration will be included in a broad transcription of Thai, but not of English.

Linguists often state positional distributions in the form of rules: A is realized as B in environment Y. (For example: voiceless stops are aspirated in word-initial position.) Part of knowing how to speak English is following these rules. It is important to remember, however, that these rules are *descriptive*, not *prescriptive*. They describe how people actually *do* speak, not how people *ought* to speak. They are more like the laws of physics (if you let go of a rock, it will fall to the ground; water freezes at 0° C) than they are like the rules of "good English" you may have been taught in school (don't say "ain't"; a preposition is a bad thing to end a sentence with). It is not right or wrong to produce an intervocalic tap; it is just a fact that American English speakers do it regularly and British English speakers do not.

Chapter 10 further investigates the question of what it means to "know" a rule: even though you follow these rules (if you are a native speaker), you don't know them in the way you know your phone number, for example. Here, our goal is a description of some of the positional variants of American English consonants. You can think of them as rules for converting broad into narrow transcription.

3.4.1 laryngeal configuration

i.   Voiceless stops are aspirated in word-initial position, or beginning a stressed syllable.
ii.   Voiceless stops are unaspirated after [s]:

pit	[pʰɪt]
tall	[tʰɑɫ]
coop	[kʰup]
apart	[əpʰɑɹt]
retain	[ɹətʰeɪn]
potato	[pʰətʰeɪɾo]
accord	[əkʰɔɹd]
spit	[spɪt]

| stall | [stɑɫ] |
| scoop | [skup] |

iii.   Sonorants are devoiced when they follow an initial voiceless stop:

play	[pl̥eɪ]
pray	[pɹ̥eɪ]
tray	[tɹ̥eɪ]
clay	[kl̥eɪ]
crate	[kɹ̥eɪt]

iv.   Voiced plosives are (at least partially) devoiced, unless surrounded by voiced segments:

bad times	[b̥æd̥ˈtʰaɪmz̥]
bad guys	[b̥æd̥ˈgaɪz̥]
good news	[gʊd̥ˈnuz̥]
gag	[g̥æg̥]

v.   Sonorants are produced with creaky voice when they precede a glottal stop:

| important | [ɪmpor̰ʔn̰ʔ] |
| can't | [kʰæn̰ʔ] |

vi.   Intervocalic [h] is produced with breathy voice at the beginning of a stressed syllable, and is deleted before an unstressed syllable:

ahead	[əɦɛd]
rehabilitate	[ɹifiəbɪliteɪt]
rehearse	[ɹiɦɛɹs]
can he go?	[kʰæn i goʊ]
I like him	[aɪ laɪk ɪm]

vii.   Stops are produced without audible release when they precede another consonant:

begged	[bɛgˈd̥]
stopped	[stɑpˈt]
stop that	[stɑpˈðæt]
make noise	[meɪkˈnɔɪz̥]
met someone	[mɛtˈsʌmwən]
read books	[ridˈbʊks]

3.4.2 change in place

viii.   [n] assimilates in place of articulation to a following consonant. [m] becomes labiodental preceding [f]:

in place	[ɪmpl̥eɪs]
in case	[ɪŋkʰeɪs]
in time	[ɪntʰaɪm]
in fact	[ɪɱfækt]
in there	[ɪn̪ðeɹ]
comfort	[kʰʌɱfɪt]
symphony	[sɪɱfəni]

ix.   Alveolar [t, d] become dental before [θ, ð], and become post-alveolar before [ɹ]:

width	[wɪd̪θ]
hide this	[haɪd̪ðɪs]
hit them	[hɪt̪ðɛm]
get rich	[gɛt̠ɹɪtʃ]
not really	[nɑt̠ɹili]
bad roads	[bæd̠ɹoʊdz̥]

x.   [t] becomes a glottal stop preceding a nasal:

button	[bʌʔn]
hit me	[hɪʔmi]
litmus	[lɪʔməs]

xi.   Alveolars become postalveolars preceding [j]. (This rule is optional, but usually applies before "you" and "your," and in common phrases.)

miss you	[mɪʃju]
this year	[ðɪʃjiɹ]
bless you	[blɛʃju]
made you look	[meɪdʒəlʊk]
meet you	[mitʃju]
those years	[ðoʊʒjiɹz]

3.4.3 change in manner

xii. [t] and [d] are tapped in between two vowels, the second of which is unstressed:

city	[sɪɾi]
atom	[æɾəm]
photograph	[foɾəgɹæf]
electricity	[ilɛkˑˈtɹɪsɪɾi]
edited	[ɛɾɪɾɪd̥]
lady	[leɪɾi]
daddy	[dæɾi]
pedestal	[pʰɛɾəstəɫ]

3.4.4 other changes

xiii. [l] is velarized ("dark") at the end of a word or syllable:

feel	[fiɫ]
pool	[pʰuɫ]
call	[kʰɑɫ]
cold	[kʰoɫd]
melted	[mɛɫtəd̥]
billboard	[b̥ɪɫboɹd̥]
leaf	[lif]
loop	[lup]
lock	[lɑk]

xiv. The American English rhotic is a post-alveolar approximant [ɹ]. (Post-vocalic [ɹ] is not pronounced in some dialects: see Chapters 4 and 19 for more details).

wreck	[ɹɛk]
ripe	[ɹaɪp]
grow	[gɹoʊ]
pray	[pɹ̥eɪ]
core	[kʰoɹ]
harm	[hɒɹm]

xv. In a sequence of three consonants the second is deleted, except in very careful speech. (This rule depends to some extent on the consonants involved. It's most likely to apply if the first consonant is [s], the second is [t] or [d], and the third is a stop. The rule does not apply if one of the consonants is [ɹ]).

best man	[bɛsmæn]
desktop	[dɛstɑp]
coastline	[kʰoʊslaɪn]
hand-picked	[hæmpʰɪkt]
best friend	[bɛsfɹɛnd]
pumpkin	[pʰʌmkʰɪn]

but

| hard line | [hɑrdlaɪn] |
| straight | [stɹeɪt] |

---

chapter summary

- The symbols of the IPA chart represent all the (known) contrastive consonants in the languages of the world.
- Sounds that are contrastive in one language may be positional variants in another. The most common type of positional variation is assimilation: adjacent sounds become more similar.
- Fricatives may be produced at the bilabial, labiodental, linguolabial, dental, alveolar, post-alveolar, retroflex, palatal, velar, uvular, pharyngeal and laryngeal places of articulation. Plosives may be produced at all of these except labiodental. Nasals may be produced at all of these except pharyngeal and laryngeal.
- Lateral approximants and fricatives may be made with the tongue front or tongue body. Laterals are defined by a side-channel of airflow.
- Taps and flaps are ballistic articulations: the active articulator either bounces off the passive articulator (taps) or strikes it in passing (flaps). A trill is aerodynamic, with the movement driven by airflow.
- Contour segments combine two articulations in sequence; complex segments combine two articulations at the same time.
- The non-pulmonic consonants are ejectives (change in air pressure caused by larynx raising), implosives (change in air pressure air caused by larynx lowering) and clicks (air trapped between two tongue closures).
- Section 3.4 lists some of the positional variants of American English consonants.

further reading

No linguist describing the articulation of the sounds of the world's languages can do so without an acknowledgement of the influence of, and a debt of gratitude to, the phoneticians Peter Ladefoged and Ian Maddieson. The sounds described in this chapter and the next are covered in much more detail in the books *Sounds of the World's Languages* by Ladefoged and Maddieson, and *Vowels and Consonants* by Ladefoged. Soundfiles of example words for the languages cited can be found on the web archive compiled by Ladefoged, Maddieson, and colleagues at UCLA: http://www.phonetics.ucla.edu/.

Ladefoged, P. and I. Maddieson. 1996. *The Sounds of the World's Languages*. Oxford: Blackwell.
Ladefoged, P. 2004. *Vowels and Consonants*, 2nd Edition. Oxford: Blackwell.
Ladefoged, P. 2006. *A Course in Phonetics*, 5th Edition. Independence, KY: Thomson Wadsworth.

review exercises

1. List the active and passive articulator for each of the places of articulation listed in the Chapter Summary.
2. Define the following terms:

    environment
    variation
    contrastive
    diacritic
    assimilation
    apical/laminal
    sibilant
    tap/flap
    ballistic articulation
    aerodynamic articulation
    contour segment
    complex segment
    primary articulation
    secondary articulation
    implosive
    ejective
    click
    sub-lingual cavity
    descriptive vs. prescriptive rule

3. How is it possible for a click to be nasal?
4. The following steps are involved in making a [ɓ]. Number the steps in the correct order. (One step is not used: Cross it off.)

    _____   make a closure at the larynx.
    _____   close the lips.
    _____   release the labial closure.
    _____   lower the vibrating larynx.

5. The following steps are involved in making a [k']. Number the steps in the correct order. (One step is not used: Cross it off.)

_____	make a closure at the velum and the larynx at the same time.
_____	release the velar closure.
_____	open the larynx.
_____	raise the larynx.
_____	lower the larynx.

6. The following steps are involved in making a dental click. Number the steps in the correct order. (One step is not used: Cross it off.)

_____	make a closure of the tongue front against the teeth.
_____	release the dental closure.
_____	make a closure of the tongue body against the velum.
_____	release the velar closure.
_____	lower the larynx.
_____	lower the middle of the tongue.

7. Add three more example words or phrases to each of the sets in Section 3.4.
8. Transcribe these English sentences, first in broad transcription, then in more narrow transcription, indicating the positional variation in consonant pronunciation. (Positional variation in vowels is covered in Chapter 4.)
   a. Would you meet me at the station at five?
   b. My husband should have bought potatoes.
   c. Will he be kept back?
   d. They all wanted to be in the pictures.
   e. In fact, I hated those times.

further analysis and discussion

9. Fill in the following table to describe each consonant symbol.

	Airstream	Place	Manner	Voiced?	Nasal?	Lateral
x						
ɬ						
ɲ						
ɠ						
t						
ɸ						
j						
q'						
ǂ						
θ						

(*Continued*)

10. For each description, write the IPA symbol in the left column. One description is not articulatorily possible: draw an X through that square.

	Airstream	Place	Manner	Voiced?	Nasal?	Lateral?
	pulmonic egressive	velar	stop	yes	yes	no
	pulmonic egressive	interdental	fricative	yes	no	no
	pulmonic egressive	velar	approximant	yes	no	yes
	velaric ingressive	alveolar	stop	no	no	yes
	pulmonic egressive	post-alveolar	fricative	yes	no	no
	pulmonic egressive	uvular	trill	yes	no	no
	glottalic ingressive	bilabial	stop	yes	no	no
	pulmonic egressive	labio-velar	glide	yes	no	no
	glottalic ingressive	alveolar	stop	yes	yes	no
	glottalic egressive	alveolar	stop	no	no	no

11. Draw a mid-sagittal diagram (or series of diagrams) illustrating the crucial steps in producing each of the following sounds. Annotate the diagrams to describe the required positions and movements of the tongue, lips, velum, and/or larynx, and to indicate the order in which the steps must be carried out.
    a. [qʼ]
    b. [ŋ!]
    c. [ɗ]

12. Explain why the following articulatory combinations are impossible:
    a. labiodental plosive
    b. pharyngeal nasal
    c. retroflex uvular
    d. bilabial lateral
    e. velar tap
    f. nasal ejective

Go online Visit the book's companion website for additional resources related to this chapter at: http://www.wiley.com/go/zsiga.

references

Most of the example words in this chapter are from the author's own fieldwork. Additional examples (from Agul, Kele, Melpa, Tangoa, Titan, and Zulu) are from the database compiled at http://www.phonetics.ucla.edu/. Other sources include:

Oowekyala
Howe, D.M. 2000. Oowekyala Segmental Phonology. Ph.D. dissertation, University of British Columbia.

!Xòõ
Traill, A. 1994. A !Xòõ Dictionary. Frankfurt: University of Frankfurt.

The discussion of assimilation in English coronals is based on C. Browman and L. Goldstein (1986), Towards an Articulatory Phonology, *Phonology Yearbook* 3, 219–252.

The instructions for making non-pulmonic consonant are based on those given by Ladefoged in *A Course in Phonetics*. I don't know how I could improve on them.

4 A Map of the Vowels

Open wide, and say "ah."

The Sounds of Language: An Introduction to Phonetics and Phonology, First Edition. Elizabeth C. Zsiga.
© 2013 Elizabeth C. Zsiga. Published 2013 by Blackwell Publishing Ltd.

Vowels, by definition, are open articulations. Because the active and passive articulators never actually make contact, the dimensions of "place" and "manner" are less useful for vowels than for consonants. Instead, vowels are conceived of as occupying points in a multidimensional space, whose coordinates may be either articulatory or acoustic. In this chapter, we map out the dimensions of the vowel space. We begin in Section 4.1 with a broad view of the landscape, considering how vowels and consonants relate to each other, and how they are organized into larger constituents of syllables and stress. Section 4.2 provides our reference points: the "cardinal vowels." Sections 4.3 through 4.6 then describe the different dimensions that languages may use to define their vowel systems: height, backness, tenseness, rounding, nasality, voice quality, length, and tone. Special attention is given to central and low vowels, which are important in the English system. Section 4.7 concludes with a discussion of positional variation in English vowels.

4.1 the landscape

Vowels are the open-mouth periods separating the constrictions of the consonants. All speech is organized around this repeated closing–opening, consonant–vowel sequence, and all languages make this basic distinction. While it would be theoretically possible, no language is composed of all consonants or all vowels. Certain *words* might be all one or the other, like English [aɪ] or Oowekyala [qχ] *powder*, so one could imagine a whole language made up of such words, but no natural language works that way.

The repeated closing–opening sequence forms the basis of syllable structure. The most basic syllable type is CV: a consonantal constriction released into a vowel. Children's first words tend to be of the form [papa] or [mama], and all languages have syllables of CV shape. (Some, like English, allow syllables that are quite a bit more complicated, but all languages allow at least CV, and some allow only CV.) The vowels, in a way, form the background against which the consonantal constrictions can be heard. During the closure for a voiceless stop, after all, there is nothing but silence: we only perceive that silence as a consonant because of its contrast with the vowels around it.

A *syllable* can be defined as a grouping of segments. A more open articulation, usually a vowel, forms the syllable *nucleus*. More constricted consonantal articulations associated to the nucleus constitute the preceding *onset* and following *coda*. In the syllable [læf], [æ] is the nucleus, [l] is the onset, and [f] is the coda. Sometimes the more open articulation can be another consonant, as in Czech [vlk] *wolf*; or the "opening" can occur through the nasal passages, as in English "prism" [prɪzm̩]. In these cases, the less constricted consonant forms the syllable nucleus. These are termed *syllabic consonants*, and their status as a syllable nucleus is indicated by a vertical line beneath the symbol.

Syllables, in turn, often alternate between more prominent and less prominent, or stronger and weaker. The prominent syllables are termed *stressed*: they tend to be longer, louder, higher-pitched, and/or more clearly articulated than less prominent unstressed syllables. Not all languages make stress distinctions: in Korean, for example, all syllables are equally prominent. Those languages that do use stress vary in which phonetic parameters are used to indicate prominence. Thai speakers, for example, rely on differences in length to signal stress differences, while Russian speakers rely more on loudness. English speakers use a combination of cues, but seem to rely most on pitch. Whatever the cue, the prominent stressed syllables alternate with less prominent unstressed ones. Syllables and stress are discussed in detail in Chapters 15 and 16; they are mentioned here because they are part of the landscape within which vowels and consonants are articulated, and because syllable structure and stress patterns can often have an influence on the way segments are pronounced.

All languages make distinctions among the vowels, as they do among the consonants. Different vowel qualities are created as the tongue and lips take different positions. The vibrating vocal folds create a complex mix of frequencies. Depending on the shape of the mouth cavity, different frequencies present in the laryngeal vibration are amplified, and these differences are heard as different vowel qualities. (See Chapters 6 through 8 for details.)

As was discussed in Chapter 2, vowels can be described, rather roughly, in terms of the highest point of the tongue body: the tongue moves up for the high vowels, down for the low vowels, forward for the front vowels and back for the back vowels. (Since English has one of the larger vowel systems in the languages of the world, the discussion of the vowels of English has covered much of the ground.) The descriptors high/low and front/back have turned out to be very useful descriptions, but a number of caveats must be kept in mind when mapping from those descriptors to actual vowel articulation.

First, the shape of the vocal tract is not symmetrical. There is more room for tongue movement along the palate than there is in the pharynx. Thus there is more room for distinctions among the high vowels than among the low vowels. The vowel "space" therefore, is usually described as a quadrilateral, wider at the top than at the bottom. Second, we do not have great propriocentric feedback in the backs of our mouths: we do not have an accurate "feel" for where our tongues are, especially since, by definition, vowels do not make contact at a specific point along the surface of the vocal tract. We are much better at hearing vowel distinctions than feeling them. If this were not the case, it would be easy for people who are deaf to learn to speak; in reality, it is very hard. Third, the mapping from articulation to perception is not linear: a different amount of upward motion is required to make a front vowel sound high than to make a back vowel sound high, for example.

Therefore, when we use terms like "high" or "back," or map a vowel as a point in the vowel space, we are more accurately describing what a vowel sounds like than where our tongues really are, though as an approximation of relative tongue position, it's not that far off.

 ## 4.1   In Focus

According to Ladefoged and Maddieson in *Sounds of the World's Languages*, a very few languages (Margi in West Africa, Eastern Arrente in Australia, and Abkhaz in Central Asia) contrast only two vowel qualities, essentially high vs. low tongue position. A larger number (including Classical Arabic, North American Aleut, South American Garawa, and Australian Yidiny) have three (usually high front [i], low central [a], and high back [u]). At the other end of the spectrum, the larger vowel systems (including !Xóõ, which also has a champion-size consonant system, and West Germanic languages such as German, Norwegian, and English) contrast more than a dozen. When distinctions in length, tone and voice quality are thrown into the mix, as well as the contour vowels known as diphthongs, distinctions multiply. Hanoi Vietnamese, for example, is reported to contrast 11 different vowel qualities, six tones, and five different ways of combining vowels into diphthongs.

4.2 cardinal vowels

The idea of "mapping" vowels is due to the British phonetician Daniel Jones (1881–1967). Recall that the X-rays of tongue position shown in Figure 1.1 were done in his lab. You may want to consult that figure again, and note that what counts as "high" for [i] and [u] is not the same, nor "front" for [i] and [æ]. Realizing this problem, and knowing the impracticality of making X-rays of speakers of all the languages linguists would hope to describe, Jones developed a system, called the *cardinal vowel system*, which would allow linguists in the field to describe the vowels of any language in terms that other linguists would understand.

Just as the cardinal points of a compass (N, S, E, W) provide reference points for orientation in geography, the cardinal vowels provide reference points for orientation in the vowel space. Jones defined eighteen cardinal vowels, using a mix of articulatory and perceptual properties. The eight *primary cardinal vowels* are graphed in Figure 4.1. Cardinal vowel #1 (symbol [i]) was defined as having the tongue body as high and forward in the mouth as possible, short of creating a fricative, with the lips spread as wide as possible. Cardinal vowel #5 (symbol [ɑ]), positions the tongue as low and as far back as possible with the jaw wide open (you have to nearly swallow your tongue to make this one); while cardinal vowel #8 (symbol [u]) moves the tongue as high and back in the mouth as possible, with the lips tightly pursed. These are extremes of articulation, and don't correspond to actual vowel qualities in any particular language. They define the extreme corners of the vowel space – high front, low back, and high back – with respect to which other vowel qualities can be defined. The other cardinal vowels between 1 and 8 were described in terms of how they *sounded* relative to the three extremes. Cardinal vowel #4, for example, was described as sounding "three-quarters of the way between numbers 1 and 5." Numbers 9 through 16 (not shown in the figure) were defined as having the exact same tongue positions as numbers 1 through 8, but with opposite lip position. So cardinal vowel #9 has the tongue body as high and forward in the mouth as possible, just like #1, but with lips pursed instead of spread. Vowels 17 and 18 add in a central (neither front nor back) tongue position.

Jones trained his students to perceive and produce the cardinal vowels exactly as he had defined them, and they trained their students, and they theirs, until it was possible to write of an unknown language in the *Journal of the International Phonetic Association* that "the height of this vowel is about halfway between cardinal vowels #7 and #8," and readers would know exactly the quality of sound referred to. Vowel charts, which graphed the positions of the vowels of a language relative to the cardinal vowels, were often used.

With the advent of audio recorders and digital means of measuring sound quality, the cardinal vowel system has fallen out of use. Vowel charts made today are usually based on measurements made by a computer from a recorded sound. The cardinal vowels are still a useful system of reference when a computer isn't handy, however. You can still access a recording of Jones' pronunciations on the web (see references on the website at http://www.wiley.com/go/zsiga).

The IPA vowel chart, reproduced in Figure 4.2, is similar to Jones' cardinal vowel chart, but with some extra symbols added. (Jones was a leading member of the International Phonetic Association.) You can see the eight primary cardinal vowels around the edge of the chart. The secondary cardinal vowels are paired with them: as noted in the chart, pairs of vowels are identical in tongue position, and the vowel with

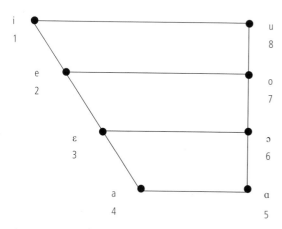

Figure 4.1   The eight primary cardinal vowels, based on Figure 10 in Jones, 1996.

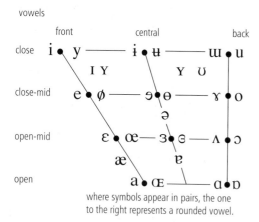

where symbols appear in pairs, the one to the right represents a rounded vowel.

Figure 4.2   IPA vowel chart.
Source: International Phonetic Association (Department of Theoretical and Applied Linguistics, School of English, Aristotle University of Thessaloniki, Thessaloniki 54124, Greece).

lip rounding is on the right. Jones' original cardinal vowels line up with the horizontal lines. Additional vowels have been placed in the spaces between. As with the consonant chart, this represents a lot of symbols to process all at once, and some are more common and useful than others.

For our discussion of the vowels, we'll begin with the most common vowel system: [i, e, a, o, u], and the basic dimensions of height and backness. From there, we'll see how more complex systems may increase their inventories.

4.3 building inventories: dimensions of vowel quality

4.3.1 height and backness

The most common number of vowels for a language to have is five. Languages as diverse as Modern Standard Arabic, Hawai'ian, Japanese, Spanish, Swahili, Tagalog, and Zulu all have five distinct vowel qualities, approximating the qualities of [i, e, a, o, u]. (Latin also had this basic inventory, giving us the five vowel letters of the Roman alphabet.) This system exploits three degrees of height (high vs. mid vs. low) and two degrees of backness (back vs. front). (Note that the IPA chart uses the term "close" for "high" and "open" for "low".) The smaller vowel systems use some subset of these. A typical five-vowel system is graphed in Figure 4.3. Example words from Spanish and Hawai'ian are shown in Table 4.1.

Note in Figure 4.3 that the vowel symbols are not graphed in the exact same location as on the cardinal vowel chart. The fact that many diverse languages have vowel systems that can be transcribed [i, e, a, o, u] does not mean that the vowels have the exact same quality as Jones' cardinal vowels. It would be unusual for a language to have an [i] or [u] as extreme as cardinal vowels #1 and #8. As is shown in Figure 4.2, the vowel transcribed as [e] is generally somewhere between cardinal vowels #2 and #3, [o] is between #6 and #7, and [a] is between #4 and #5. That is, the vowels are generally distributed fairly evenly in the vowel space, making maximal use of the space available. Nor does the transcription mean that vowel quality is exactly the same in each language. When the vowel system is small, the "area" occupied by each vowel can be rather large: there is room for quite a bit of variation before the different vowels "trespass" on one another's space and cause confusion.

Thus, the symbol [e] does not always refer to the precise same vowel quality: There are not enough symbols to cover every detail of difference in every language, let alone speaker-to-speaker variation. It is useful here to remember, however, a point that was made in Chapter 3: the IPA symbols are really just "cover terms" for combinations of articulatory gestures. So [i] refers to "high, front (unround) vowel" and [u] to "high, back (round) vowel" even if the exact degrees of height, backness, and rounding are somewhat different.

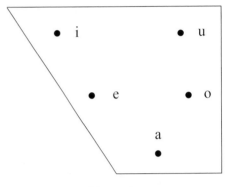

Figure 4.3 A typical five-vowel system.

Table 4.1 Five contrasting vowels in Spanish and Hawai'ian. Hawai'ian examples are taken from http://www.phonetics.ucla.edu/index/language.html

	Front	Back
Spanish		
High	[si] yes	[su] hers/his/its/yours
Mid	[se] self	[sopa] soup
Low	[sala] room	
Hawai'ian		
High	[kiki] sting	[kuku] to beat (tapa)
Mid	[keke] turnstone	[koko] blood
Low	[kaka] rinse	

4.3.2 tense/lax

Enlarging the vowel system beyond five, languages will often exploit the tense/lax distinction, contrasting lax [ɪ, ɛ, ɔ, ʊ] with tense [i, e, o, u] as shown in Figure 4.4. Examples of

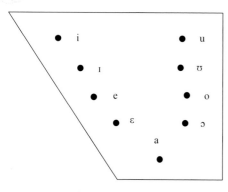

Figure 4.4 The vowel system of Akan, with both tense (advanced) and lax (retracted) vowels.

the tense/lax contrast in English and in the West African language Akan are given in Table 4.2.

Generally, when the terms "tense" and "lax" are used of vowels, the tense vowels are somewhat higher and longer than their lax counterparts, and they are said to have more "muscular tension," though that term is seldom if ever quantified. In addition, the tense vowels of English are diphthongized, with upward movement of the tongue body over the course of the vowel: [ij], [eɪ], [oʊ], [uw] (see Section 4.5 for further discussion). MRI and X-ray studies have shown that in at least some languages that make a distinction between vowels such as [i] and [ɪ], the tongue root is pulled forward for the tense member of the pair, widening the pharynx. Figure 4.5 shows a vocal tract tracing, based on MRI images, illustrating the difference in tongue root position between [i] and [ɪ] in Akan.

Table 4.2 Tense/lax vowel contrasts in Akan and English. Akan examples from Stewart (1967) and Tiede (1996). *See Section 4.3.5 for discussion of the low vowels of English.

	Front		*Back*	
	Tense/Advanced	Lax/Retracted	Tense/Advanced	Lax/Retracted
Akan				
High	[di] to eat	[dɪ] to be called	[bu] to break	[bʊ] to be drunk
Mid	[efie] home	[ɛfɪɛ] vomit	[koko] chest	[kɔkɔ] crab
Low	[kasa] language			
General American English				
High	[kijd] keyed	[kɪd] kid	[luwk] Luke	[lʊk] look
Mid	[beɪt] bait	[bɛt] bet	[boʊt] boat	[bɔt] bought
Low	*			

4.2 Native speakers of languages that do not have the tense/lax distinction (such as Spanish and Japanese) often have trouble learning to make the distinction in a language that does (such as English). I remember being shocked to hear a Spanish-speaking actor, on being asked in an American radio interview what his next project would be, reply that he was planning "to just leave this life." It took me a moment to realize he was planning to "live" and not to "leave": he just didn't distinguish [i] and [ɪ] the way a native English speaker would.

Based on such findings, some linguists have argued that the tense/lax dimension would be more accurately described as *advanced/retracted tongue root*. However, in different languages the contributions of tongue root movement, tongue body movement, length, and perhaps larynx lowering, may vary. For example, the study illustrated in Figure 4.5 found that an English-speaking subject had less of a difference in pharynx width and more of a difference in tongue dorsum height than did the Akan-speaking subject.

However, crucial involvement of the tongue root may explain why all vowel heights are not equally amenable to a tense/lax (or advanced/retracted) distinction. Pulling the tongue root forward will tend to push the tongue body up, so that tongue root advancement and tongue body raising tend to go together. It is rare for a language to make a tense/lax distinction among the low vowels, presumably because tongue root advancement is not compatible with tongue body lowering. Some languages, such as Italian and Yoruba (which is related to Akan), make a tense-lax distinction only among the mid vowels. High vowels will tend to be tense, and low vowels will tend to be lax.

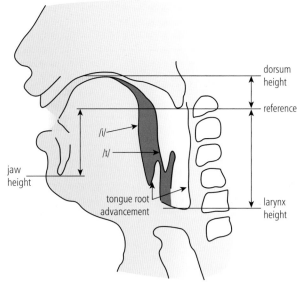

Figure 4.5   Tongue root position for [i] and [ɪ] in Akan. Source: Tiede, 1996, p. 405.) © Elsevier.

4.3.3 rounding

In the systems examined so far, rounding is predictable from backness and height: all and only the non-low back vowels are round. The incompatibility between rounding and low vowels is probably articulatory: it is harder to round the lips when the jaw is open (try it). The reason for the compatibility of rounding and backing, however, is perceptual. There is nothing difficult in articulating the front round counterpart of [i], which is symbolized [y], nor the back unround counterpart of [u], which is [ɯ]. Lips and tongue move independently: simply start with the more common vowel, and then switch lip position without moving your tongue. However, you will quickly hear that [i] and [u] sound much more distinct than do [y] and [ɯ].

The reason for this is that protruding the lips and backing the tongue have a similar effect on vowel acoustics. Rounding and backing both work to enlarge the space at the front of the mouth, while fronting the tongue and spreading the lips both work to make the front cavity smaller. Because rounding and backing reinforce each other, back round vowels sound maximally different from front unround vowels. Again, the concept of markedness may be invoked here. Back round and front unround vowels are *unmarked*: they are more common and the distinctions among them are easier to perceive. Back unround and front round vowels are marked: they are less common and harder to perceive. In general, languages will not choose a marked vowel unless the unmarked counterpart is also part of the inventory: The presence of [y] implies the presence of [i]. Thus, the most common five-vowel inventory consists of [i, e, a, o, u] while a system of just [y, ø, ɒ, ʏ, ɯ] is unattested.

Larger vowel inventories, however, may add the more marked front round vowels or back unround vowels. French and German have front round vowels in addition to front unround, Vietnamese has back unround vowels in addition to back round. Turkish has all four possibilities. The full set of symbols for front round and back unround vowels can be seen in

Table **4.3**   Vowel contrasts in French. (http://www.phonetics.ucla.edu/vowels/chapter14/french.html).

	Front		Back	
French	Unround	Round	Unround	Round
High	[li] bed	[ly] read, pst.		[lu] wolf
Mid Tense	[le] the, pl.	[lø] the, m. sg.		[lo] prize
Mid Lax	[lɛ] ugly	[lœʀ] their		[lɔʀ] during
Low	[la] there		[lɑ] tired	

Table 4.4   Vowel contrasts in Vietnamese. Unmarked vowels have mid tone; acute accent = high tone. (http://www.phonetics.ucla.edu/course/chapter11/vietnamese/vietnamese.html).

	Front		Back	
Vietnamese	Unround	Round	Unround	Round
High	[ti] bureau		[tɯ] fourth	[tu] to drink
Mid Tense	[te] numb		[tɤ] silik	[to] soup bowl
Mid Lax	[tɛ´] to fall down		[ʌŋ] favor	[tɔ] large
Low	[æŋ] to eat		[tɑ] we/our	

Table **4.5**   Vowel contrasts of Turkish, Istanbul dialect. (http://www.phonetics.ucla.edu/appendix/languages/turkish/turkish.html).

	Front		Back	
Turkish	Unround	Round	Unround	Round
High	[kis] cyst	[kys] sulky	[kɯs] turn down	[kus] vomit
Non-high	[kes] cut	[køs] dumb looking	[kɑs] muscle	[kos] island name

the IPA chart in Figure 4.2. Examples of vowel contrasts in French, Vietnamese, and Turkish are shown in Tables 4.3, 4.4, and 4.5.

Note that French and Vietnamese have a tense/lax contrast only for the mid-vowels. (One language that does contrast [ɪ] and [ʏ] is German: [bɪtən] *to ask* vs. [bʏtən] *tubs*.) While Turkish does contrast the tricky [kys]/[kɯs], it contrasts only two vowel heights. Turkish also has a system of *vowel harmony*, such that the vowels of a word will tend to agree in both backness and rounding (see Chapter 11). Such harmony not only makes articulation easier, but reinforces perception, since a separate decision on rounding and backness does not have to be made for every vowel in the word: the listener knows that if one vowel in the word is front, all the others will be as well. (Akan and Yoruba have tongue root harmony: the vowels in a word agree in whether the tongue root is advanced or retracted.)

4.3.4 central vowels

Languages tend to make their vowels as distinct as possible. If all the vowels of a language were similar, confusion could easily result. Thus, vowels tend to be *peripheral*: that is, around the edges of the vowel space, either back or front but not central. Some languages do make use of this central area, however.

The meaning of the central vowel symbols in Figure 4.2 should at this point be clear: tongue height comparable to that of the other vowels on the same horizontal line, but with a tongue body position intermediate between back and front. Lips are unrounded for symbols on the left, rounded for those on the right.

A few of the small-inventory languages are argued to be *vertical*, that is, to make no use of the front/back distinction and have all central vowels. Ladefoged and Maddieson report, for example, that the two vowels of Margi are [ɨ] and [a] and the three vowels of Kabardian are [ɨ, ə, a]. However, languages seldom, if ever, contrast back and central vowels without also making a contrast in rounding. That is, no language is definitely known to distinguish different words on the basis of [ɨ] vs. [ɯ] or [ʌ] vs. [ɤ].

There are a few possible cases for which a three-way front/central/back contrast might be needed. Ladefoged and Maddieson suggest that Nimboran, a language of Papua New Guinea, can be described as having three high unround vowels: [kip] *fire* vs. [kɨp] *lime* vs. [pakɯp] *lid*. The transcriptions are based on a written description, however, and it is notable that [ɯ] is not described as contrasting with [u]. Another candidate is Norwegian, which is described as having three high round vowels (in addition to unround [i]): [byː] *town* vs. [bʉː] *shack* vs. [buː] *live*. However, the lip position is also different for [bʉː] vs. [buː]. The lips are more compressed for the former and more protruded for the latter. Thus, it is not clear if this is a case of a three-way distinction in backness or a three-way distinction in rounding.

In practice, especially in broad transcription, the symbols for the central and back vowels that match in rounding are often used interchangeably. The non-front, non-round high vowel of Turkish is sometimes transcribed as [ɨ] and sometimes transcribed as [ɯ], for example. The distinction between a central and back symbol should be observed when a precise narrow transcription is called for.

English is one of those languages that make use of the central region of the vowel space, so a few notes on the transcription of English central vowels are called for. Some example transcriptions are given in Table 4.6.

The transcription of the English central vowels is complicated by a number of factors. The first is the influence of stress: the symbols used for stressed and unstressed vowels are different. The second is dialectal and individual variation: from place to place and person to person, pronunciation may differ. The difference is especially acute for *r-ful* vs. *r-dropping* dialects. In r-ful dialects, typified by General American, [ɹ] is pronounced at the end of a word, so that "beer," for example, is pronounced [biɹ]. In r-dropping dialects, typified by the British accent used by BBC reporters, final [ɹ] is deleted or replaced by a vowel, so that "beer" is [biə]. The dialects of Boston, New York City, and some areas of the Southeastern US are also r-dropping, as is Australian English. A different set of central vowels is used in r-ful vs. r-dropping dialects. In addition, transcriptions will differ depending on how narrowly precise the linguist chooses to be. (Finally, the exact details of the circumstances under which [ɹ] is pronounced or not are complex. For our purposes in this chapter, words are assumed to be spoken in isolation.)

To begin with the simplest case, the non-front, non-round, mid, stressed vowel of English (as in "mud") is usually transcribed as [ʌ]. (The symbol can be called "wedge.") It represents a neutral tongue position, somewhat back of central: the tongue body moves neither up, down, back (much), or forward. It is no accident that the English "filler syllable", when you open your mouth but don't quite know what to say, is "uh"; that is [ʌʌʌʌ . . .].

In the transcription of English words, the wedge symbol is only used for stressed syllables. In unstressed syllables, as in "pand_a_" or "_a_bout," the symbol [ə], schwa, is used for a vowel with neutral tongue position. Thus the word "abut" is transcribed [əˈbʌt] and "adjust" is [əˈdʒʌst]. (The teaching of phonetics must have been in vogue when I was in elementary school: I distinctly remember a page in my third-grade Language Arts workbook entitled "Schwa" with a picture of a panda bear on it. I guess I was daydreaming during the lesson that day, however, because for many years after I was convinced that a "schwa" was a black and white bear.)

There is quite a bit of variation in the way English unstressed vowels are pronounced, however. One source of variation is the surrounding consonants. Because unstressed vowels

Table 4.6 Narrow transcription of English central vowels.

symbol	example	spelling	Notes
ʌ	[mʌd] [ɹʌf]	mud rough	Used in stressed syllables
ə	[ˈpʰændə] [bəˈliv] [əˈbʌt] [ˈɹoʊzəz]	panda believe abut Rosa's	Used in unstressed syllables
ɨ	[ˈɹoʊzɨz] [ˈɹɑɾɨd]	roses rotted	Used in suffixes
ɜ	[fɜ] [ˈbɜdən]	fur burden	In "r-dropping" dialects, including Boston and BBC English
ɝ	[ˈfɝ] [ˈbɝdən]	fur burden	In "r-ful" dialects, including General American; stressed syllables
ɚ	[ˈnɛvɚ] [ˈhɛlpɚ] [ˈsʌpɚ] [fɝˈðɚ]	never helper supper further	GA pronunciation, unstressed syllables

are short, the tongue may not move very far from the positions required by the surrounding consonants. So, for example, unstressed vowels surrounded by coronal consonants such as [t, d, s, z] may tend to be fronted and raised. A reduced vowel with a higher tongue position than [ə] may be transcribed [ɨ]. The difference between [ə] and [ɨ] is contrastive for some English speakers in at least some words. Listen carefully to your own pronunciation of pairs like "Rosa's/roses", "Lisa's/leases", "Nida'd /needed" (where "Nida'd" is the contracted form of "Nida would"). For many English speakers, the vowel [ɨ] is used in unstressed plural and past-tense suffixes ("roses" and "needed" are [ɹozɨz], [nidɨd]), while the vowel [ə] is used for all other unstressed syllables ("Rosa's" and "Nida'd" are [ɹozəz], [nidəd]). Some speakers may also use [ɨ] in initial position, especially before a coronal. A word like "edition" may thus be pronounced [ədɪʃən] (homophonous with "addition") or [ɨdɪʃən] with a higher vowel. Or some speakers may give the first vowel a little bit of stress and say [ɛdɪʃən].

Things get even more complicated when transcription of the "er" sound is considered. For r-dropping dialects like BBC English, the stressed vowel in words like "bird," "fur," and "herd" is transcribed [ɜ]. As indicated by its position in the vowel chart, this vowel is intermediate between [ɛ] and [ʌ]. Unstressed "er" is simply [ə], so that "murder" is [mɜdə] and "pander" and "panda" are homophonous as [pʰændə].

For r-ful dialects like GA English, the first thing to realize is that although a word like "fur" consists of three letters, there are only two sounds. The "er" sound is not a sequence of vowel+r, but a single rhotic sound: the tongue body is in a mid-central position but the tongue front is raised (and for some speakers curled back), the same as or similar to the [ɹ] in "run." Try drawing out the word (if you are a speaker of an r-ful dialect): the sound is not [fʌʌʌʌʌʌʌɹ], but [fɹɹɹɹɹɹɹ]. So one way to write the word "fur" would be [fɹ̩], with a syllabic consonant. Most transcribers, however, consider this sound to be a separate, contrastive vowel of English – a mid, central, rhoticized (or *r-colored*) vowel – and use the symbol [ɝ]. In an unstressed syllable, as for the "-er" suffix, the symbol is [ɚ]. (Note the little hook reminiscent of a script "r.") Thus, for an r-ful dialect, "murder" is [mɜdɚ] and "further" is [fɝðɚ]. Ladefoged and Maddieson note that rhoticized vowels are known to occur in only two languages – English and Mandarin Chinese – making these sounds typologically rarer than labiodental flaps.

There is another interesting effect of vowel+r sequences in many dialects of English, including General American. In syllables where a vowel is followed by [ɹ], the 12+ vowels of English are reduced to only six: the prototypical [i, e, a, o, u], plus the syllabic rhotic itself. There is no distinction between tense and lax vowels before [ɹ] (see Figure 4.6). Thus, in most American dialects there is no distinction between "war" and "wore," and the three words "Mary", "merry", and "marry" are homophonous. (One dialect that keeps them distinct is Philadelphia.) Due to the influence of spelling, we often think we are distinguishing these words, much as we may think we are distinguishing "kitty" and "kiddie."

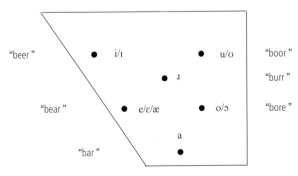

Figure 4.6   The General American English vowel system preceding [ɹ]. The tense/lax distinction is lost.

4.3.5 contrasts among the low vowels

Finishing our discussion of the dimensions of vowel quality, and the symbols of the IPA vowel chart, we turn to contrasts among the low vowels. The IPA chart gives six different low vowel symbols [æ, a, ɶ, ɑ, ɒ, ɐ], but it is unusual for any one language to contrast more than two.

Most languages, in fact, have only a single low vowel. This is true of the three-vowel systems like Classical Arabic, five-vowel systems like Spanish, seven-vowel systems like Italian, and nine-vowel systems like Akan. As has already been mentioned, there is less room for movement in the pharynx than along the palate, and it is harder to round the lips when the jaw is lower. Thus, it is common for languages, even those with larger inventories, not to exploit either a backness, roundness or tongue root contrast for low vowels, and to use only a single vowel at this height. The low vowel in these languages is usually articulated with a central tongue position, neither fronted nor backed, but there can be a lot of context-dependent variation. When there is no contrast, the one low vowel is usually transcribed as [a].

In languages with two low vowels, one usually has a more fronted tongue body position than the other. In General American English, the front low vowel in "pat" is usually transcribed [æ], while the backer vowel in "pot" is transcribed with [ɑ] (sometimes [a]). In other languages that have two low vowels, such as French, the more front vowel is not quite as far forward as the English [æ], so the distinction may be transcribed as [a] vs. [lɑ], as in Table 4.3: [la] *là* "there" vs. [ɑ] *las* "tired." The vowel quality in [la] is in between that of the vowels in "lack" and "lock."

4.3   In Focus

Two dialects of English furnish examples of a rare three-way contrast among the low vowels. British English adds a round version of the low back vowel: [ɒ]. Where General American has [pʰæk], [pʰɑk], [pʰɑɹk], for "pack," "pock," "park," British English has [pʰæk, pʰɒk, pʰɑk]. In r-dropping Boston, these three words illustrate what may be the best case for a three-way contrast between a front, central, and back vowel at the same vowel height. The vowel in "park" (as well as in "car," "Harvard," and "yard") is intermediate between [æ] and [ɑ]. There is thus a contrast between front [æ] in "pack," central [a] in "park" and back [ɑ] in "pocket," all unround. The only language known to me for which a four-way distinction among the low vowels is claimed, as well as the only language to use a front, low, round vowel, is Bavarian German, which is reported to contrast front unround [æ], back unround [ɑ], front round [Œ], and back round [ɒ].

The symbol [ɐ], which is the last vowel symbol to be discussed, indicates a raised version of [a]. It may be used as an alternative to the symbol [ə] to indicate a mid, central, *un*reduced vowel. Japanese speakers of English, for example, tend to use [ɐ] where native speakers have [ə]. This mid to low central vowel is also argued to occur in Portuguese (see Table 4.7 and Figure 4.7 on p. 66).

Table 4.7   Oral and nasal vowels of European Portuguese.

Oral vowels			Nasal vowels			
front	central	back	front	central	back
[pipu] cask	[dɨvi] (I) owed	[budɐ] Buddha	[pĩtɐ] (you) paint		[pũtu] (kind of car)
[pekɐ] (he) sins		[topu] peak	[pẽtɨ] comb		[põtɨ] bridge
[lɛvɐ] (he) takes	[kedɐ] each	[pɔtɨ] pot		[kẽtu] corner	
	[patu] duck				

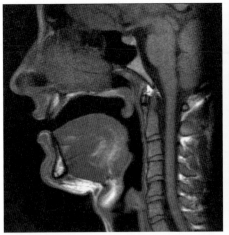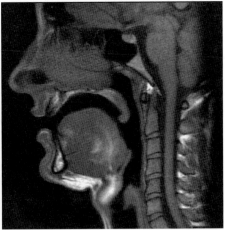

Figure 4.7   MRI images of oral [e] (left) and nasal [ẽ] (right) in European Portuguese.
Source: Martins, P., I. Carbone, A. Pinto, A. Silva, & A. Teixeira. 2008. European Portuguese MRI based speech production studies. *Speech Communication* 50: 925–952. Reprinted with permission of Elsevier.

4.4 nasality and voice quality

Thus far, we have discussed how languages make use of tongue body position (high/mid/low and front/central/back), tongue root position (advanced/retracted or tense/lax), and lip position (round/unround) to create different vowel sounds. Contrasts can also be made in nasality and in voice quality.

Commonly, vowels will become somewhat nasalized when they precede a nasal consonant. The velum, which moves rather slowly compared to the other articulators, begins opening early, in preparation for the upcoming nasal consonant, so that the vowel becomes gradually more nasal over the course of its duration. In a number of languages, however, including French, Portuguese, Polish, Chinese, Hindi, Gujarati, and others, vowels can be nasal even when no following nasal consonant is pronounced. (A nasal consonant is often written when the word is spelled, however, and may have been present historically.) Typically, the number of nasal vowels is smaller than the number of oral vowels. European Portuguese, for example, has nine oral vowels, but the inventory of nasal vowels is reduced to five (again, versions of [i, e, a, o, u]). Adding the extra resonance of the nasal cavity interferes with the acoustic cues to tongue and lip position, making nasal vowels harder to distinguish, thus leading to a smaller number of vowel contrasts. Words illustrating the oral and nasal vowel inventories of European Portuguese are shown in Table 4.7. (The vowels of Brazilian Portuguese are slightly different.) Figure 4.7 shows MRI images of an oral and nasal vowel in European Portuguese, with velum opening for the nasal vowel clearly evident. In transcription, nasality is indicated by a tilde over the vowel: [ã].

Vowels may also be distinguished by voice quality. In the unmarked case, vowels, which rely on vocal fold vibration to produce vocal tract resonance, are voiced. But in some cases vowels may have different voice qualities: they may be devoiced (or whispered), or produced with creaky voice (tense vocal folds), or breathy voice (lax vocal folds). Devoicing is transcribed with an open underdot ([ḁ]), creaky voice with a subscript tilde ([a̰]), and breathy voice with two filled underdots ([a̤]).

Sometimes voice quality differences may depend on the surrounding consonants. Unstressed vowels following aspirated stops in English, for example, may be completely voiceless: [pʰ̥ə̥tʰeɪɾo]. In Japanese, high vowels are devoiced when surrounded by voiceless consonants: [ɸu̥ton]. As with nasality, however, vowels may sometimes contrast in voice quality independent of the consonantal context. For example, Gujarati contrasts plain (or *modal*) voice vs. breathy voice on vowels, independent of a contrast in aspiration on both voiced and voiceless consonants (see Table 4.8). Mpi (a language of Thailand) contrasts modal vs. "tense" voice: [si] *to roll* vs. [si̤] *to smoke* (both with mid-rising tone, see Section 4.6 below). Jalapa Mazatec (Mexico) makes a three-way contrast: [já] *tree* vs. [ja̰] *he carries* vs. [ja̤] *he wears*.

Table 4.8 Voice quality contrasts in Gujarati. (Ladefoged & Maddieson, p. 315.)

Plain vowel	Breathy vowel	Aspirated consonat
[baɾ] twelve	[ba̤ɾ] outside	[bʱaɾ] burden
[pɔɾ] last year	[pɔ̤ɾ] early morning	[pʰɔdz] army

4.5 length and diphthongs

Vowels may also contrast simply in length. Many factors influence the amount of time it takes to articulate a given segment. A person may speak faster or slower, of course. Some differences are inherent in the articulation: low vowels, for which the mouth has to open wide, take longer than high vowels, for which little movement is necessary. As was noted above, the tense vowels of English are longer than lax vowels, and stressed vowels are longer than unstressed vowels. In some languages, however, two vowels may differ in length alone, without any other difference in stress or tongue position: the long segment and short counterpart are exactly the same, except that the former is held for a longer period of time, an extra "beat." These long segments may be written with a double symbol ([aa]), or with a colon after the usual symbol ([a:]).

Japanese and Arabic are languages that make length distinctions in both vowels and consonants. In Tokyo, you want to be careful to order [biːru] *a beer* rather than [biru] *a building* or to ask directions to a certain [toːri] *road* rather than [tori] *bird*. A linguist needs to be clear she's looking for a new [oto] *sound*, not [otːo] *husband*. In Arabic, length distinctions often have grammatical import: [kataba] is *wrote* and [kaːtaba] is *corresponded with*; [darasa] is *studied* and [darːasa] is *taught*. English has no true long consonants as found in Japanese and Arabic. English can create long consonants when two words come together – compare "stop Paul" [stɑpːɔl] to "stop all" [stɑpɔl] – but we do not distinguish long and short consonants within words. When double consonants are written, for example in "supper" vs. "super," they actually tell us about the quality of the vowel, not the length of the consonant.

Diphthongs are vowels that require a change in tongue and/or lip position, often a drastic change, over the course of their duration. (The word is from Greek: [di] *two*, [ɸθoŋgos] *sounds*.) They contrast with *monophthongs*, which hold a relatively steady state. Rarer *triphthongs* have a sequence of three vowel qualities within a single syllable. English has three true diphthongs: [aɪ] as in "hide" and "buy", [aʊ] as in "crowd" and "how," and [ɔɪ] as in "void" and "boy." The diphthongs might be thought of as contour vowels, in the way that affricates are contour consonants: they start out in one position and end in another. The English diphthongs move across the whole vowel space: from central back to high front in [aɪ], for example. Any combination of vowel sounds can be made into a diphthong, however. Dutch, for example, has [ɛɪ, œy, ɔʊ], in addition to monopthongal [i, y, ɪ, ʏ, e, ɛ, ø, u, o ɔ, ɑ]. In Vietnamese, a diphthong can begin from just about any of the 11 steady-state vowel qualities (see Table 4.4) and move up and forward to [i], up and back to [u], or from a more extreme position to the center. Vietnamese also has triphthongs, such as [iəʊ].

As was noted in Chapter 2, the crucial difference between a true diphthong and a diphthongized vowel is not the extent or direction of tongue body movement, but whether or not the movement is contrastive. In a true diphthong, deleting the offglide changes the meaning of the word: [kʰaɪt] is distinct from [kʰat] and [waʊnd] is distinct from [wand]. On the other hand, no English words are distinguished by the difference between [eɪ] and [e]. That's not to say that the difference isn't noticeable. Pronouncing the tense vowels without an offglide is a mark of a non-native speaker of English, and pronouncing [e] and [o] *with* offglides is one of the strongest marks of an English accent in French or Spanish. Changing one's typical vowel pronunciation to match a vowel in another language that is similar but not quite the same is one of the hardest tasks confronting a second-language learner (see Chapter 20). It is easier for native English speakers to learn to correctly pronounce the French word for "read" ([ly]) than it is to learn to stop asking for [kʰæfeɪ oʊ leɪ] when they want [kafe o lɛ].

4.6 tone

Last, but far from least, vowels may contrast in pitch. The use of pitch differences to create different words is called *tone*. Strictly speaking, tone is a property of a unit larger than a segment, usually a syllable or perhaps a word, but the differences in pitch are most often produced and perceived during the vowel. Tone and other linguistic uses of pitch are discussed in more depth in Chapter 17; only a few general points, particularly with regard to transcription, are covered here.

The pitch of the voice carries a lot of different kinds of information. It can tell you whether the speaker is a male or female, a large person or small, old or young. High pitch can tell you that a person is frightened; low pitch that she is angry. This sort of information isn't really linguistic, however, but physical or emotional: you could get the same messages from a dog's low-pitched growl or a puppy's high-pitched whimper.

English also makes various *linguistic* uses of pitch. It was noted above that stressed vowels tend to have higher pitch than unstressed. We also use pitch differences to convey different kinds of sentence-level or discourse-level meanings. Yes/no questions will usually have rising pitch, for example, while statements have falling pitch. We can use a more complex pitch pattern to indicate emphasis or incredulity. These discourse-level uses of pitch are called *intonation*.

Intonation distinguishes different kinds of sentences, or focuses attention on a particular word. As an example of some uses of intonation in English, try reading the following sentences out loud:

"That's a cat?"
"Yup. That's a cat."
"A *cat*? I thought it was a mountain lion!"

If you read with feeling, you should have noticed that the pitch of your voice moved in different directions on the word "cat." In the first, pitch goes up, indicating a question. In the second, pitch falls, indicating a statement or confirmation. In the third, a more complicated rise-fall pattern indicates incredulity. (Typographically, we indicate these different "readings" with a question mark, period, and italics, respectively.) In each case, the sequence [kʰæt] refers to the same object, a feline. The pitch differences indicate only the role that the reference to the feline is playing in the current conversation: asking for information about the cat, providing it, or expressing disbelief regarding the information offered.

All languages use intonation to some extent, though the patterns and meanings are not exactly the same cross-linguistically (see Chapter 17). But in addition to intonation, most languages also use pitch to distinguish different words. In English, whether you say [kʰæt] with a rising pitch or falling pitch, the word still refers to a feline; the only difference may be attitude toward the animal. In Thai, if you say [kʰa:] with rising pitch, it means *leg*; but if you say it with falling pitch, it means *value*. The two words are as different as "cat" and "cot" to an English speaker. This use of pitch, to distinguish different words, is tone.

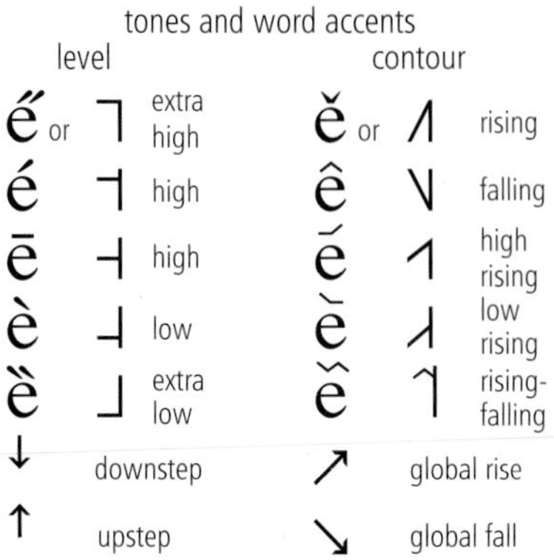

The idea of tone may seem strange to English speakers, and we may associate the term with "exotic" languages. Yet by one estimate 70% of the languages of the world are tonal, including most of the languages of Africa, and many of the languages of East Asia and of the Americas. (The major European languages and their relatives are in fact exceptional in *not* having tone. No tone languages have been reported in Australia, either.) There are certainly more native speakers of tone languages in the world than there are speakers of non-tone languages, in large part because Mandarin Chinese, native language of approximately one in six humans, is tonal.

Figure 4.8 gives the IPA symbols and diacritics for transcribing tone. As shown in the figure, tone can be transcribed using diacritics over the vowel symbols. Alternatively, if more precision is required, the linguist can use *tone letters* written after each syllable. A tone letter is a schematic diagram of the pitch pattern: the vertical line indicates the speaker's overall pitch range, while the horizontal or slanted line indicates the level and movement of the pitch pattern associated with the tone.

Implicit in these descriptions is that the pitch of tones is always relative to a speaker's overall range. The absolute pitch of a high-toned syllable spoken by a large male might be lower than the absolute pitch of a low-toned syllable spoken by a small female. But each speaker's high tones will be higher than that speaker's low tones. The pitch of tones is also sensitive to the context of surrounding syllables and to position in the sentence. Pitch tends to get lower over the course of a sentence, for example: sometimes gradually and sometimes in more dramatic *downsteps*, so that the absolute pitch of high tone at the end of a sentence might be lower than the absolute pitch of a low tone at the beginning. So the terms "high" and "low" always mean "relatively high" or "relatively low" for that speaker in that position.

In Figure 4.8, tones are divided into *level tones* and *contour tones*. Level tones do not necessarily have a perfectly level pitch, but they create contrast based on relative pitch height, not direction of pitch change. Languages that use only level tones are called *register tone* languages. More complex systems add contrasts that include crucial pitch rises and falls. These are called *contour tone* languages.

The simplest tonal system is a two-way contrast between high and non-high. Languages such as Margi (West Africa), Setswana (Southern Africa), Navajo (North America) and Mixtec (Central America) are systems with just two contrastive tones. To give just one example, in Margi, [ʃú] with high pitch, means *tail* and [ʃù], with lower pitch, means *to dry up*. An acute accent indicates a high tone and a grave accent indicates a low tone. (My mnemonic for remembering the difference is that you need to look at where the accent mark ends.) Yoruba (West Africa) is a language that contrasts three pitch levels: [wá] to come, [wā] to look, [wà] to exist. A mid tone may be indicated with a macron over the vowel, or the vowel may be left unmarked.

tones and word accents

level			contour		
e̋ or ˥		extra high	ě or ˩˥		rising
é	˦	high	ê ˥˩		falling
ē	˧	high	e᷄ ˦˥		high rising
è	˨	low	e᷅ ˩˨		low rising
ȅ	˩	extra low	e᷈ ˧˥˧		rising-falling
↓		downstep	↗		global rise
↑		upstep	↘		global fall

Figure 4.8 IPA symbols for tone.

Source: International Phonetic Association (Department of Theoretical and Applied Linguistics, School of English, Aristotle University of Thessaloniki, Thessaloniki 54124, Greece).

Table 4.9 The tones of Thai.

high	mid	low	falling	rising
ná:	nā:	nà:	nâ:	nǎ:
aunt	rice field	custard apple	face	thick
kʰá:	kʰā:	kʰà:	kʰâ:	kʰǎ:
to trade	to be stuck	galangal spice	value	leg

Table 4.9 exemplifies the tones of Thai, a contour tone language. In addition to three level tones, Thai adds rising and falling pitch patterns. The diacritic for a rising tone is (ˇ), the symbol for low (ˋ) followed by high (ˊ), while the diacritic for the falling tone is (ˆ) which corresponds to high followed by low.

The complexities of tonal systems and tonal contrasts are addressed at greater length in Chapter 17.

4.7 positional variants of the vowels of English

As we did in Chapter 3 for consonants, we end this chapter with a summary of the positional variants of the vowels of English, for those readers with a particular interest in English pronunciation. The rules exemplified here apply in most or all of the varieties of English. Keep in mind, however, that the vowels of English differ much more than the consonants based on dialect: the transcriptions here may not exactly match your pronunciation, though the general rule probably still applies. There is more variation in English vowels than can be squeezed onto the end of a general chapter, and the vowel systems of the major English dialects are discussed in Chapter 19.

i.   Vowels are nasalized before nasal consonants

ban   [bæ̃:n]
tome   [tʰoʊ̃:m]
sing   [sĩ:ŋ]

ii.   Tense vowels are diphthongized

beak   [bijk]
bake   [beɪk]
rope   [roʊp]
soup   [suwp]

iii.   Vowels are lengthened in open syllables, and before voiced consonants. Note that, with the exception of [ɔ], lax vowels do not occur in open syllables. For diphthongs and diphthongized vowels, most of the lengthening occurs on the offglide.

beak   [bijk]
bead   [bij:d]
bee   [bij:]

boost   [buwst]
booed   [buw:d]
boo   [buw:]

sought   [sɔtˀ]
sawed   [sɔ:d]
saw   [sɔ:]

bite   [baɪtˀ]
bide   [baɪ:d]
buy   [baɪ:]

iv. Stressless vowels ([ə]) may be deleted, especially preceding sonorants

| risen | [ɹɪzn̩] |
| I can go | [aɪkn̩goʊ] |

| general | [dʒɛnɹəɫ] |
| camera | [kʰæmɹə] |

v. Rhotic dialects (General American) have rhotacized mid central vowels in "bird" and "fur": [bɝd], [fɝ]. Non-rhotic dialects (RP, Australia, New Zealand, South Africa, some parts of the American South and New England) have mid central [ɜ]. In unstressed syllables with orthographic "r", rhotic dialects have [ɚ], non-rhotic have [ə].

vi. In many rhotic dialects, there is no distinction between tense and lax vowels before [ɹ], though some dialects (Irish, Philadelphia), the distinction is maintained for the mid vowels. Vowel quality preceding [ɹ] is usually in between that of the tense and lax vowel, but may be closer to one or the other depending on dialect. In non-rhotic dialects, the [ɹ] is replaced by [ə], so that "beer" [biə] rhymes with "idea."

--- **chapter summary**

- The constrictions of the consonants are superimposed on the open articulations of the vowels. Consonants and vowels are organized into syllables, which may be more or less prominent (stressed or unstressed).
- Daniel Jones created the cardinal vowel system as a map for comparing vowel qualities across languages.
- Vowels may contrast in height, backness, tense/lax, rounding, nasality, voice quality, length, and tone. Different vowel systems choose different dimensions of contrast.
- In the unmarked case back vowels are round, front vowels are unround, low vowels are lax, high vowels are tense, and vowel systems tend to be peripheral. However, languages may choose the more marked options, such as front round vowels, high lax vowels, and central vowels, in addition to the unmarked ones.
- Section 4.7 describes some of the positional variants of the dialects of English, including rhotic and non-rhotic pronunciations.

--- **further reading**

The books mentioned at the end of Chapter 3 discuss vowels as well as consonants.

For more information on linguistic tone, see Chapter 17 and Yip, M. 2002. *Tone*. Cambridge: Cambridge University Press.

review exercises

1. Define the following terms:

   syllable
   nucleus
   onset
   coda
   syllabic consonant
   stressed syllable
   vowel harmony
   peripheral vowel
   vertical vowel inventory
   r-colored vowel
   tone letters
   downstep

2. Compare and contrast each of the following pairs (or triplets) of terms:

primary cardinal vowel	secondary cardinal vowel	
advanced tongue root	retracted tongue root	
r-ful dialect	r-dropping dialect	
modal voice	breathy voice	creaky voice
monophthong	diphthong	triphthong
tone	intonation	
level tone	contour tone	

3. Why was the cardinal vowel system an important advance in cross-linguistic description? Why has it fallen out of use?

4. Why is it unusual for a language to make a tense/lax distinction among the low vowels?

5. Explain why the inventory [i, e, a, o, u] is extremely common, while [y, ø, ɒ, ɤ, ɯ] is unattested.

6. Add three more example words or phrases to each of the sets in Section 4.7.

7. Revisit your narrow transcriptions of the following sentences. Add in any positional variation in the vowels.

   a. Would you meet me at the station at five?
   b. My husband should have bought potatoes.
   c. Will he be kept back?
   d. They all wanted to be in the pictures.
   e. In fact, I hated those times.

8. Make a narrow transcription of your own pronunciation of the following sentences, indicating positional variation of both vowels and consonants. Is your dialect r-ful or r-dropping?

   a. Your brother heard the concert.
   b. Would you prefer beer or ale?
   c. I was shocked to find a shark in the shack.
   d. Her mother is searching for a cure for cancer.
   e. The senator from Ohio is never boring.

further analysis and discussion

9. Fill in the descriptions for each of the following vowels.

	Height	Backness	Rounding	Tense or lax
i				
y				
ʌ				
ɒ				n/a
ɨ				
e				
ɵ				

10. Provide the IPA symbol that matches each description.

	Height	Backness	Rounding	Tense or lax
	low	front	unround	n/a
	high	back	round	tense
	mid	front	unround	tense
	high	back	unround	tense
	mid	back	round	lax
	high	front	unround	lax
	mid	front	round	lax
	high	front	round	lax
	mid	back	unround	tense
	mid	central	unround	lax

11. The vowels in each of the following pairs differ in only one dimension: height, tenseness, backness, rounding, nasality, voice quality, length, or tone. Indicate the change. The first two have been done.

a. __i__ to__ɪ__   _____tense_____ to _____lax_____
b. __õ__ to __o__   _____nasal_____ to _____oral_____
c. __i__ to __y__   _____ to _____
d. __ɛ__ to __ʌ__   _____ to _____
e. __u__ to __o__   _____ to _____
f. __æ__ to __ɑ__   _____ to _____
g. __ɛ__ to __e__   _____ to _____
h. __ɑ__ to __ɒ__   _____ to _____
i. __é__ to __è__   _____ to _____
j. __u__ to __ɯ__   _____ to _____
k. __o__ to __o̥__   _____ to _____
l. __ɔ__ to __ɔː__   _____ to _____

(Continued)

12. Write the symbol that would result from the change. The first two have been done.

    a.   Make [ɔ] unround   __ ʌ _____

    b.   Make [e] lax   ___ ɛ ____

    c.   Make [i] rising tone   _____

    d.   Make [o] creaky   _____

    e.   Make [æ] round   _____

    f.   Make [y] back   _____

    g.   Make [ʊ] tense   _____

    h.   Make [o] front   _____

    i.   Make [a] long   _____

    j.   Make [ā] low tone   _____

    k.   Make [ɛ] high   _____

    l.   Make [ɔ] low   _____

    m.   Make [i] central   _____

further research

13. Describe the vowel system of a language that was not discussed in this chapter, either one you know or one you learn about in a reference book. Transcribe the vowels using IPA, and create a chart of the vowel space. What dimensions of contrast does the language use?

14. Make a narrow transcription of a passage of English poetry or prose.

15. Ask a non-native speaker, or someone you perceive as having a different accent from yours, to read the sentences in exercises 7 and 8 above. Make a narrow transcription of their pronunciation. What differences do you notice?

references

Ladefoged, P. and I. Maddieson. 1996. *The Sounds of the World's Languages*. Oxford: Blackwell.

Other sources, listed in alphabetical order by language:

Akan
Stewart, J.M. 1967. Tongue root position in Akan vowel harmony. *Phonetica* 16.
Tiede, M.K. 1996. An MRI-based study of pharyngeal volume contrasts in Akan and English. *Journal of Phonetics* 24: 399–421.

Bavarian German
Traunmüler 1982, cited in Ladefoged & Maddieson, 1996.

Dutch
Adank, P., R. van Hout, & H. van de Velde. 2007. An acoustic description of the vowels of Northern and Southern Standard Dutch II. *Journal of the Acoustical Society of America* 121: 1130–1141.

Portuguese

Martins, P., I. Carbone, A. Pinto, A. Silva, & A. Teixeira. 2008. European Portuguese MRI based speech production studies. *Speech Communication* 50: 925–952.

Thai

Abramson, A. 1962. The vowels and tones of Standard Thai: Acoustical measurements and experiments. *International Journal of American Linguistics*, 28, 2, part II.

5 Anatomy, Physiology, and Gestural Coordination

The centipede was happy quite
Until the toad, in fun,
said "Pray, which leg goes after which?"
Which raised her mind to such a pitch
She lay distracted in a ditch
Considering how to run.

attributed to Mrs. Edmund Craster, circa 1871

Chapter outline

The Sounds of Language: An Introduction to Phonetics and Phonology, First Edition. Elizabeth C. Zsiga.
© 2013 Elizabeth C. Zsiga. Published 2013 by Blackwell Publishing Ltd.

Of the 600–800 named muscles in the human body, a competent phonetician needs to know the names and functions of about 35. (Exactly how many muscles you count in the body depends on which source you consult, as there are differences in whether a muscle that has different sub-parts should count as one or many.) Happily, muscles tend to get named for the parts that they connect, or the function they carry out. It should not be hard to figure out the location of the *palatoglossus* (especially if you know some Latin roots) or the function of the *pharyngeal constrictors*. However, this chapter is not just a vocabulary-building exercise, or a Latin lesson.

The first goal of the chapter is for readers to gain an understanding and appreciation for speech as a biological, not just cognitive, system, down to the level of the cartilages and muscles involved. Other chapters are about the ways the mind creates language. This chapter is about how the body creates speech. Along with an understanding of the details of anatomy and physiology involved should come an appreciation for the amazing complexity of the act of speaking. Nearly every one of the 35 muscles has a carefully-orchestrated part to play in the articulation of a phrase as simple as "She ran." (I'm cheating a little by including a rhotic, which you've already learned is more complex than average, but you get the idea.)

The second goal is to further an understanding of diverse linguistics patterns and questions: how are men's and women's voices different, why do low vowels nasalize, what are the possible dimensions of contrast, how does positional variation come about? Each of these questions can be answered, at least in part, by examining the details of anatomy, physiology, and coordination of articulatory gestures.

As we did in Chapter 1, we begin with the lungs, and work our way out, considering in turn, and in detail, the anatomy and physiology of the lungs, larynx, and supra-laryngeal vocal tract. Section 5.4 then turns to the question of "orchestration": how are the movements of all these vocal tract pieces coordinated? We approach the question from the point of view of the theory of Articulatory Phonology. The chapter concludes with a description of static palatography, a fun and accessible means of investigating the details of articulation.

5.1 anatomy and physiology of respiration

This section begins like a yoga class: become aware of your breathing. (It helps if you can stand up.) Quiet, restful breathing – in and out, in and out – is known as *tidal breathing*. Notice the gentle expansion and contraction of the rib cage. Now try two further exercises. Try each one several times, paying attention to the muscles that you sense are involved. First, inhale as much air as possible, filling the lungs, then relax suddenly, releasing all the air (as in a huge sigh). Second, again inhale as much as possible, but this time exhale slowly, drawing out the exhalation as long as possible, and emptying the lungs as much as possible. Try to feel the different muscle groups that are involved at the beginning, middle, and end of the exercise. Now let's consider what is happening for breathing during speech.

Some knowledge of the anatomy of the thoracic cavity (the part of your body inside your ribs) is necessary. The human ribcage is composed of 12 pairs of ribs (Latin: *costa*). The top 10 are attached to the spinal column in the back and to the breastbone (*sternum*) in the front; the bottom two are attached only in the back. The ribcage is not completely fixed, however: if it were, breathing would not be possible. The ribs are attached to the sternum and to each other with flexible cartilage that can stretch and bend.

Muscles run along both the inside and outside of the ribcage: *the internal and external intercostals* (that is, the "inside and outside between-the-ribs muscles"). Also relevant are the abdominal muscles that run from the sternum and lower ribs to the pelvis. The largest of these is the *rectus abdominus*, which runs straight down the front of the body: this is the

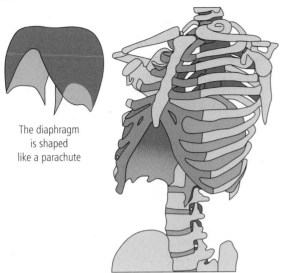

The diaphragm
is shaped
like a parachute

Figure 5.1   Shape and location of the diaphragm.

muscle whose (over-) development results in "six-pack abs." The main functions of the abdominal muscles are to position and bend the upper body, to stiffen the body for efforts like lifting weights, and to apply pressure for efforts including defecation and childbirth. But the abdominal muscles also have a role to play in respiration, as described below.

At the bottom of the ribcage, separating the lungs from the stomach and other organs of digestion, is the large, dome-shaped *diaphragm* (Figure 5.1). The diaphragm stretches over the digestive organs like a parachute, tethered at several points along the bottom edge to the pelvis, and held up at the top by attachments to the sternum, ribs, and spinal cord. Contraction of the diaphragm is the main muscular engine of respiration.

Inside the cavity created by these muscles, bones and cartilages are the lungs. The lungs are like two large sponges for air: the tiny air sacs (*alveoli*) are connected to tiny tubes (*bronchioles*) connected to larger tubes (*bronchia*), connected to the trachea, which vents to the outside world via the oral and nasal tracts. The lungs themselves have no muscles: they expand and contract only because they stick to the ribs. The lungs are covered with a membrane (the *pulmonary pleura*) and the inside of the ribs are lined with another membrane (the *costal pleura*). Because both these membranes are wet, surface tension causes them to stick together (the *pleural linkage*). Did you ever stack two wet, freshly-washed bowls or glasses on top of each other, and then discover them stuck together so firmly you couldn't pull them apart? Or do you recall, in science class, sticking the two halves of a glass slid together with a drop of water? The two halves could slide with respect to each other, but would not pull apart. The same force holds the outside of the lungs to the inside of the ribs, so that when the ribs expand, the lungs do too.

The exact amount of air the lungs can hold depends, of course, on body size. (There is a reason opera singers tend to be on the large side.) The average total lung volume for an adult male is 5 to 7 liters. (Picture to yourself seven bottles of water, each bottle being of the kind that holds 1 liter of water.) It is not possible, however, to squeeze every last bit of air out of the lungs – the ribcage cannot contract that much. The amount of air that it is possible to exchange in respiration (breathing in and blowing out as much as possible, as in the third exercise above) is called a person's *vital capacity*. Vital capacity is about 70% of total lung capacity (that is, 3.5–5 liters). We seldom use all of our vital capacity, however. Tidal breathing exchanges only about 0.5 liters per breath: only 10–15% of vital capacity, about the amount of air in a small water bottle. Speech uses anywhere from 20–80% of vital capacity, depending on loudness (about 1–3.5 liters). "Normal" speech will use about 50%.

Respiration for speech differs from that for tidal breathing not only in volume but in timing. In tidal breathing, the average person takes 12–20 breaths per minute, with about half the duration of each breath taken up with inhalation and half with exhalation. In speech there are fewer breaths per minute, and for each breath inhalation takes up only about 10%. The speaker quickly takes in a large volume of air, then exhales slowly, carefully controlling the rate of egressive airflow.

Airflow is controlled by the actions of the muscles of the thoracic and abdominal cavities working to expand and contract the ribcage. For inhalation, the external intercostals contract to pull the ribs up and out, while the diaphragm contracts to lower the floor of the thoracic cavity. The thoracic cavity and the lungs within it enlarge. When volume is increased, air pressure is lowered; therefore air rushes in from outside. (Again, inhale, feeling the contraction of the diaphragm and raising of the ribs.)

When these muscles are relaxed, the ribs and diaphragm return to their normal shape, pushing in on the lungs, increasing the pressure, and forcing air out: exhalation. If the relaxation occurred all at once, however, the air would rush out all at once, as in a sigh. For speech, exhalation is controlled. Tension on the diaphragm is released slowly. Tension in the ribcage is balanced between the external and internal intercostals: the externals continue to hold the ribs up and out while the internals pull the ribs down and in.

Once the rest position of diaphragm and intercostals is reached, additional muscle contraction is needed to further constrict the ribcage and force more air out of the lungs. The internal intercostals contract more strongly, and the abdominal muscles begin to contract to pull the bottom of the ribcage down and in. To force the very last possible milliliter of air out, the back muscles may also contract to pull the ribs down as far as possible. You should be able to feel this abdominal contraction if you attempt to hold a very long note. Maintaining better control of the abdominal muscles is one important reason why professional singers will generally stand rather than sit to perform.

One place where respiration becomes important in speech is in prosody: the way sounds are grouped together. It was once believed that the smallest prosodic unit, the syllable, might correspond to a "chest pulse": that there would be a small contraction of the diaphragm corresponding to each syllable. Measurements of muscle contraction did not bear this out, however. On the other hand, larger groupings of speech may depend on breath. The length of the average sentence is roughly the length of the average breath. A sentence-length unit is often marked by a rise in pitch at the beginning and a fall in pitch at the end (at least for statements). Such a grouping of words may be called an *intonational phrase* (see Chapter 17), or is sometimes called a *breath group*. It is tempting to attribute the gradual lowering in pitch over the course of an intonational phrase to gradually decreasing airflow. However, the thoracic muscles do an excellent job of keeping airflow constant: it appears that the decline in pitch is a linguistic choice, one that can vary in degree and timing between languages and sentence types, not an automatic consequence of lowered airflow.

5.2 anatomy and physiology of the larynx

The larynx is a structure of cartilage and muscle that sits on top of the trachea. Its non-speech function is to serve as a valve closing off the opening to the lungs, the trachea. In speech, the different parts of the larynx are minutely adjusted to produce varying speech sounds. The larynx can open or close to produce the consonants [h] and [ʔ], or it can produce different modes of vibration, or voicing, that combine with other constrictions in the supralaryngeal vocal tract to distinguish other consonants and vowels.

The larynx is composed of four cartilages: the cricoid, thyroid, and two arytenoids. One has to think in three dimensions in order to visualize this complex piece of anatomy: Figures 5.2 and 5.3 show views of the larynx from the back and top. (A side view was shown in Figure 1.7.) The *cricoid cartilage* forms the base of the larynx: it is really the topmost, enlarged, tracheal ring. It is shaped roughly like a signet ring, with the "plate" facing backwards.

On top of the cricoid plate sit the two *arytenoid cartilages*, one on each side. The arytenoids are shaped like triangular pyramids, longer than they are tall, with their long points facing inward over the opening

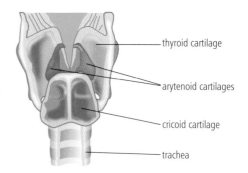

Figure 5.2   The cartilages of the larynx, viewed from the back.

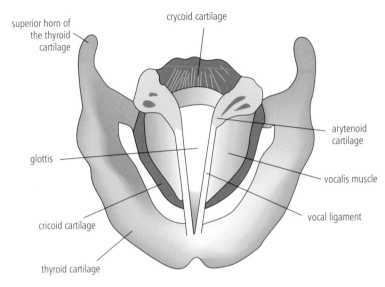

Figure 5.3   Structures of the larynx, viewed from above.

to the trachea (almost like diving boards). These forward points are called the *vocal processes*. Each arytenoid is set in a small indentation in the cricoid, and they can rock and swivel to some extent within these indentations, so that the vocal processes can be made to point down and in or up and out (maybe more like guns on a battleship than a diving board, though the range of motion is not that large).

The *thyroid cartilage* covers the front of the larynx. It is shaped like a triangular shield, folded partly back on itself, with a small notch at the top of the fold that can be felt under the skin of the throat. Two long "horns" extend from its top corners.

Once you get the names and positions of the cartilages straight, learning the muscles is straightforward, since they are named for the cartilages they connect.

The *thyro-arytenoid muscle* is also known as the *vocalis*. The vocalis is actually a set of two muscles that stretch from the vocal processes of the arytenoids in back to the center notch of the thyroid in front. Running along the inside of each muscle is the *vocal ligament*. Covered over with several layers of mucous membrane, the vocalis muscle and vocal ligament comprise the vocal folds. It is the motion of the vocal folds – pulling apart, closing together, or vibrating – that creates the speech sounds of the larynx. The space in between the vocal folds, the actual opening into the trachea, is the *glottis*.

Remember, the vocal folds are attached at the back to the long points (the vocal processes) of the arytenoid cartilages, and the arytenoid cartilages can swivel back and forth. If the vocal processes are swung apart, the vocal folds open. If the points are swung together, the vocal folds close. The folds remain attached at the front to a single point on the thyroid, so they "open" like a book whose pages remain attached to the binding. Bringing the vocal folds together is called *adduction*, moving them apart is called *abduction*. (Mnemonic: add = put together, abduct = take away.) Photos of the abducted and adducted vocal folds are shown in Figure 5.4. The pictures were taken via a rigid endoscope: a camera at the end of an aluminum rod that is held at the back of the open mouth, with the camera pointing down toward the larynx. Alternatively, a flexible endoscope can be inserted through the nasal passages and down through the velar port, so that oral tract articulation is not interfered with.

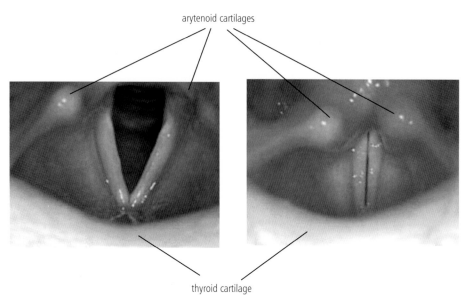

Figure 5.4   Photos of the glottis, taken via endoscope. Left: Vocal folds abducted for breathing. Right: vocal folds adducted for a sustained note. Source: http://www.voicedoctor.net/media/photo/normal/normalfemale.html.

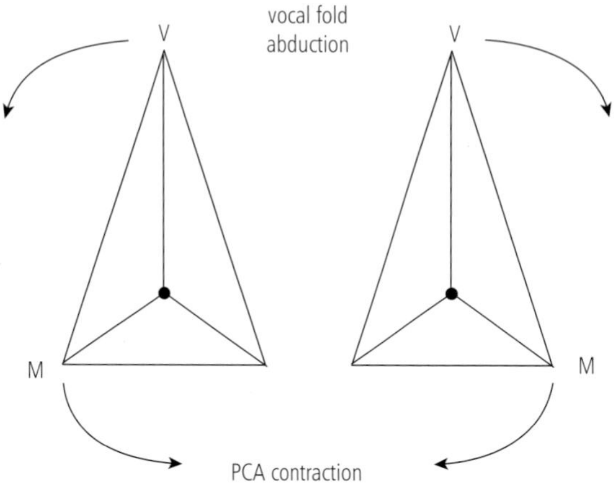

The swinging motion of the arytenoids is accomplished by muscles that attach the arytenoids to the cricoid and to each other. The *posterior crico-arytenoid muscle (PCA)*, as the name states, connects the arytenoids and cricoid at the back. (As anatomical terms, *posterior* means "towards the back" and *anterior* means "towards the front.")

The PCA fans out across the back plate of the cricoid, running from the center of the cricoid to the lower, back, outside corners of the arytenoids (the *muscular processes*). When the PCA contracts, it pulls the muscular processes in and down, causing the vocal processes to rotate up and out. Imagine rotating a pair of triangles, as in the schematic diagram in Figure 5.5. When points M (the muscular processes) are rotated toward each other by contraction of the PCA, points V (the vocal processes) are rotated away from each other, resulting in abduction of the vocal folds.

Vocal fold adduction is accomplished by two sets of muscles. The *interarytenoid muscles (IA)* run between the two arytenoid cartilages. When the IA contracts, it pulls the vocal processes together, as for voicing. Additional adduction (as for a complete glottal stop or for creaky voice) can be provided by the *lateral crico-arytenoid muscles (LCA)*. Again as the name states, these muscles connect the sides of the arytenoids to the sides of the cricoid. Contraction of the LCA brings the vocal processes together and down. The actions of the IA and LCA are schematized in Figure 5.6. Tension in the vocalis muscle itself can also be adjusted as needed.

None of these muscles causes vocal fold vibration, however: vocal fold vibration is not the result of very fast muscle contraction, like the flapping of a hummingbird's wings. Rather,

Figure 5.5   Action of the posterior crico-arytenoid muscles for vocal fold abduction. V = vocal processes, M = muscular processes.

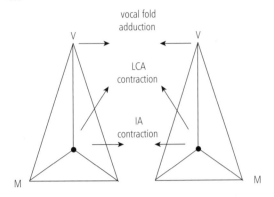

vocal fold
adduction

LCA
contraction

IA
contraction

Figure 5.6 Action of the interarytenoid and lateral crico-arytenoid muscles for vocal fold adduction.

vibration is caused by a combination of vocal fold position and tension, and airflow. If the vocal folds are adducted so that their edges are touching, and are held tautly but not clamped down so tight that no air can get through, then as air passes between them the folds will begin to vibrate. This theory of how vocal fold vibration works is the *myoelastic aerodynamic theory of phonation* (literally: muscle-tension air-power theory of voicing). In terms of the physics involved, the vibration of the larynx is no different than the vibration of the lips in a bilabial trill: hold them with the right tension, blow air between, and they vibrate.

The physical principle that causes the vibration is also the same one that keeps airplanes in the air (I have become a much more confident airline passenger since I became a phonetician). The principle is termed *the Bernoulli effect* (named after Daniel Bernoulli, a Dutch-Swiss physicist who described this effect, and other laws concerning the motion of liquids and gases, in his book *Hydrodynamica*, published in 1738). What Bernoulli discovered is that there is a drop in pressure perpendicular to the flow of a liquid or gas, and this pressure drop is proportional to the velocity of the airflow.

Consider the shape of an airplane wing: flat on the bottom and convex on the top. The convex shape means that the surface of the top of the wing is longer than the surface of the bottom, which means that air has to travel farther to pass over it, which means that the air moves faster over the top of the wing than under the bottom as the airplane moves forward. Now the Bernoulli effect kicks in: there is a pressure drop perpendicular to the flow of air, proportional to the velocity. Because air moves faster over the top of the wing than under the wing, air pressure on top of the wing is lower than under the wing. The wing, and with it the body of the plane, are literally sucked up into the sky.

How does the muscle tension in combination with the aerodynamics of the Bernoulli effect make the vocal folds vibrate? First, the IA muscles pull the vocal folds together, with contrac-

5.1 In Focus

The implications of the Bernoulli effect for flight (that is, the idea of *lift*) were understood quickly; but it took 165 years to get from *Hydrodynamica* to Kitty Hawk in part because no-one before the Wright brothers figured out how to keep an airplane *stable*: the convex shape of the wing pulled the plane both up and forward, and early attempts somersaulted into the ground. The trick turned out to be adding smaller tail flaps at the rear to keep the plane level. Someone also had to invent an engine that was light enough to get off the ground.

The convex shape of an airplane wing is also the convex shape of a modern triangular sail: square-riggers were pushed by the wind behind them; triangular-rigged sloops can be pulled nearly straight *into* the wind. Another everyday application of the Bernoulli effect is doors slamming when a breeze blows down the hall. The moving air creates lowered pressure in the hall that pulls the door shut. Finally, have you ever felt that your small car was being pulled sideways into a passing truck? Bernoulli effect again: the two vehicles traveling next to each other effectively create a moving column of air between them. Air pressure lowers perpendicular to the direction of air movement, and the car is pulled sideways.

tion of the vocalis holding the folds somewhat taut. Air flows out of the lungs through the trachea, and pressure builds up behind the closed folds. When the sub-glottal air pressure becomes sufficient to overcome the tension of the folds, they are blown open, so that air flows between them. But once airflow is established, the Bernoulli effect kicks in. There is a drop in pressure across the folds (perpendicular to the flow of air), which pulls the folds back together. The natural elasticity of the folds also aids in pulling them back. Once the folds are touching again, airflow stops, the Bernoulli effect turns off, and the cycle begins again, with pressure building up behind the closed folds. The speed with which this cycle repeats depends on a number of factors including the inherent mass of the vocal folds, the stiffness with which they are held, and the sub-glottal air pressure, but the cycle is repeated about 120 times per second for the average adult male and 220 times per second for the average adult female.

The frequency at which this cycle repeats establishes the fundamental frequency of the voice, termed *F0* ([ɛfziro]). F0 is measured in cycles per second, or *Hertz* (abbreviated Hz), in honor of Heinrich Hertz, a late nineteenth-century German physicist who made important contributions to our understanding of wave mechanics. Differences in fundamental frequency are perceived as differences in pitch: higher F0 results in higher pitch.

F0 is to a certain extent given biologically, by the mass of an individual's vocal folds. Within a given range, however, F0 is under the speaker's control. The primary way to change F0 is to tilt the thyroid cartilage forward, which stretches the vocal folds attached to it. The more the folds are stretched, the higher the frequency of vibration. (Think of tuning a guitar by adjusting the tension on the strings.) The muscle that tilts the thyroid forward is predictably named the *crico-thyroid* (CT), since it connects the front of the thyroid to the front of the cricoid. Contraction of the CT rocks the thyroid forward and down (Figure 5.7).

The function of each of these muscles of the larynx has been confirmed via testing with *electromyography (EMG)*. This technique involves inserting tiny wire probes ("hooked wire electrodes") into the muscle under examination. When the muscle contracts, the electrode picks up the electrical signal given off by the firing muscle cells, and sends the signal to a monitoring device (a computer). By coordinating the EMG signal with the speech signal, a researcher can determine which muscles are contracting for which speech sounds. It can be difficult, however, to place the electrodes correctly, and the technique is not without discomfort for the subject.

F0 adjustment, especially at the extremes of the pitch range, may also involve muscles external to the larynx, particularly the *strap muscles* of the neck (Figure 5.8). These muscles run up and down the neck from the sternum to the thyroid cartilage to the hyoid bone. The *hyoid bone* is a small horse-shoe-shaped bone that "floats" (attached to muscles but to no other bones) at the top of the throat under the chin. You should be able to feel the hyoid bone with gentle probing: press gently at the sides of the throat under the jawbone, slightly forward and above where you would feel for a pulse from the carotid artery. (Note for fans of forensic science shows: breakage of the hyoid bone or of the thyroid cartilage is considered evidence of strangulation.)

The names of the strap muscles indicate their location: the *sterno-thyroid* (from sternum to thyroid), *thyro-hyoid* (from thyroid to hyoid) and *sterno-hyoid* (all the way up from sternum to hyoid). Contraction of the thyro-hyoid pulls the larynx up in the throat. It also provides greater forward pull on the thyroid cartilage, further stretching the vocal folds, and raising F0. Contraction of the other strap muscles, the sterno-thyroid and sterno-hyoid, pulls the larynx down in the throat, with the effect of shortening and thickening the vocal folds, lowering F0. The strap muscles are also active in raising the larynx for ejectives and lowering it for implosives.

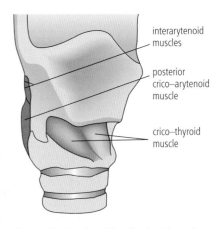

interarytenoid muscles

posterior crico–arytenoid muscle

crico–thyroid muscle

Figure 5.7   Location of the crico-thyroid muscle.

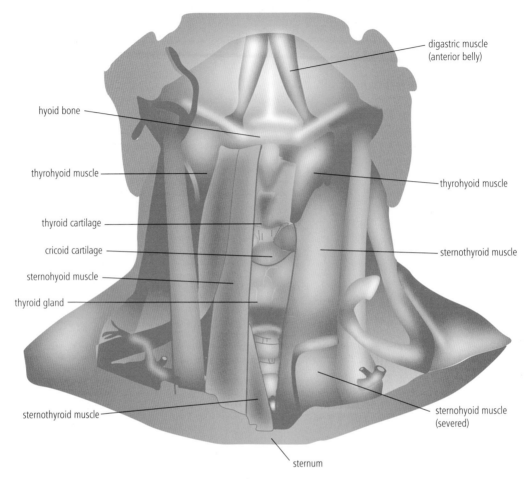

digastric muscle
(anterior belly)

hyoid bone

thyrohyoid muscle

thyrohyoid muscle

thyroid cartilage

cricoid cartilage

sternothyroid muscle

sternohyoid muscle

thyroid gland

sternothyroid muscle

sternohyoid muscle
(severed)

sternum

Figure 5.8   The strap muscles of the neck. Note that the muscles are in fact symmetrical on both sides of the neck. In the right side of the illustration, the muscles in the top layer have been cut away to reveal those that lie beneath.

Again, you can test the relationship between larynx position and pitch by placing your finger on the notch of the thryoid cartilage while humming a scale from the lowest note of your range to the highest. You should be able to feel the larynx rising as the notes get higher. (You can also ask a male friend to tilt his chin up while humming a sequence of notes: larynx raising will be more noticeable for a male than a female, because of the extra prominence of the thyroid notch in males.)

Whatever their rate of vibration, the vocal folds do not just flap open and closed like little wooden doors. They are composed of complex layers of soft tissue: the soft and massive vocalis muscle edged by the thin and stiff vocal ligament, both covered with several semi-independent membranes. The opening and closing motion is a more complex ripple: like a flag waving in the breeze, or (more viscerally), like skin waving on a flabby upper arm. Each little ripple in the vocal folds contributes to the complexity of the resulting sound (see Chapters 6–8 for details).

The larynx can create different *modes of vibration*. Vibration of the full length of the vocal folds, repeating at regular intervals, is called *modal voicing*. This is the type of voicing generally heard in the middle of vowel sounds.

Creaky voice results from clamping down on the posterior portion of the vocal folds (via contraction of the LCA) with additional vocal fold tension (contraction of the vocalis). Creaky voice is very low-pitched and irregular. (The butler, Lurch, in the TV show/movie *The Addams Family*, speaks exclusively in creaky voice: [ju̞ɹæːæ̯n]) In real speech, creaky voice often occurs in the vicinity of glottal stops [ɪmpo̞ɹʔn̩ʔ], and at the end of utterances.

Breathy voice (or *murmur*) is another mode of vocal fold vibration. Breathy voice combines vocal fold vibration with high airflow. In breathy voice the vocal folds may be held more loosely, so that they open wider and stay open longer, or the folds may never close completely at all, so that the anterior part of the folds are vibrating (held together by LCA contraction) while the posterior part of the folds are open and letting air pass through. As was mentioned in Chapter 4, some languages use creaky and/or breathy voice contrastively, as in Jalapa Mazatec: [já] *tree* vs. [ja̰] *he carries* vs. [ja̤] *he wears*.

A measure of the creaky-modal-breathy continuum is the measure of *open quotient*. The open quotient simply refers to the percentage of time in a given cycle that the vocal folds are open. In modal voicing, the open quotient is about 50%. In creaky voice, the open quotient may be 20% or less. In breathy voice, the open quotient is typically 80%, though for some women's voices the open quotient can be 100%: the vocal folds never close completely.

A number of the factors that distinguish men's and women's voices originate at the larynx. As you know, a listener can usually identify a voice as male or female without seeing the speaker. One reason is the lower pitch typical of men's voices. Due to hormone-induced growth at puberty, men's vocal folds are on average 50% longer and thicker than women's vocal folds, even when men and women are matched for overall body size. More massive vocal folds cause slower vibration and therefore lower pitch. There are other differences and cues, however. Another secondary sex characteristic of the larynx is that the arytenoid cartilages of women are set further apart and have a greater range of motion than those of men. The wider setting of the arytenoids, coupled with thinner vocal folds, results in the typically higher open quotient for women that was noted in the previous paragraph. For some women, the arytenoids are far enough apart to create a permanent *glottal chink*, such that the vocal folds never close completely. This results in a more breathy quality to the voice, but it also has another more subtle effect. For women, the sub-laryngeal and supra-laryngeal parts of the vocal tract are more closely linked, because the passage between them (the glottis) is more open. Thus it is typical for the trachea to serve as a resonating chamber for a woman's voice, but not for a man's, and this difference has an effect on voice quality. Another factor that affects voice recognition is not related to the larynx: length of the supra-laryngeal vocal tract is on average less for women than for men, because of their smaller average body size.

While these differences are biologically given as a baseline, some studies have shown that speakers may subconsciously enhance them in order to enhance gender differentiation. Women may cultivate a higher-pitched, more breathy sound, and men a lower-pitched more creaky sound than is biologically given (see Chapter 19).

5.3 anatomy of the tongue and supra-laryngeal vocal tract

5.3.1 the jaw

Moving up now into the supra-laryngeal tract, we come to the muscles of the jaw, tongue, velum, and face.

We begin with the jaw, as it is probably the simplest. The jaw, or *mandible*, is of course the large and strong bone in which the lower teeth are embedded, attached to the skull at the *temporo-mandibular joint*, from which it swings. You can feel the protuberances of this joint right in front of your ears, and feel the joint move when the jaw is opened and closed. While some limited side-to-side and front-to-back motion of the jaw is possible (as in grinding the teeth), the two motions relevant for speech are simply opening and closing, accomplished by two groups of opposing muscles. The primary muscle that accomplishes jaw opening is the *digastricus* muscle (so named because it has two sections, or "bellies"). The anterior belly (front part) of the digastricus runs under the chin from the front of the jaw to the hyoid bone (see Figure 5.8). Jaw opening is also aided by the *geniohyoid*, a smaller muscle that also runs from jaw to hyoid, on top of the digastricus. Closing of the jaw is accomplished by the *masseter* (chewing muscle), which runs along the sides of the face, under the cheeks, from the side of the jaw up to the cheekbone. If you clench your teeth you will feel the masseter bulge.

Movement of the jaw is obviously important in speech, carrying the active articulators up for consonants and down for vowels, though it is not counted as an active articulator itself, because it is never the jaw or lower teeth *per se* that effect a constriction. Jaw movement is not essential, however, and speakers can compensate for a lack of jaw movement by adjusting tongue and lip movements. Try speaking with a pencil held between the teeth, prohibiting jaw movement, and you will find that you can still produce quite intelligible speech.

5.3.2 the tongue

On top of the digastricus and geniohyoid, within the jaw, is the tongue. As was noted in Chapter 1, the tongue is a *muscular hydrostat*, similar to an elephant's trunk or octopus's tentacle. It is composed entirely of muscles, with no bones or cartilages. The tongue can change shape, but not volume, like a bag of jelly: squeeze it at one end, and the other end will protrude.

Have you ever thought about how it is possible to stick out your tongue, with no bones to stiffen it, and nothing attached to the front to pull it forward? A complex intertwining of muscles control tongue shape and position. The *intrinsic muscles* of the tongue control shape; the *extrinsic muscles* control position. In the case of sticking out the tongue, the intrinsic muscles cause it to lengthen and stiffen, while the extrinsic muscles push it forward from the back.

There are four extrinsic muscles of the tongue that are important for the articulation of speech sounds (Figure 5.9.) Each muscle connects the tongue to a different part of the vocal tract, and each is responsible for moving the tongue in a specific direction. As was the case with the muscles of the larynx, the name of the muscle indicates the parts that it connects. It each case, *glossus* means tongue.

The *hyoglossus* connects the tongue to the hyoid bone. Its function in speech is to move the tongue body down. The hyoglossus is active in low vowels, particularly [æ]. (If the tongue position is stabilized by other muscles, contraction of the hyoglossus will pull the hyoid bone up, a function that is important in swallowing.)

The *styloglossus* attaches the tongue body to the *styloid process*, a bony extension at the base of the skull, behind the jaw and below the ear. (You cannot feel the styloid process, as it is on the inside of your skull.) The function

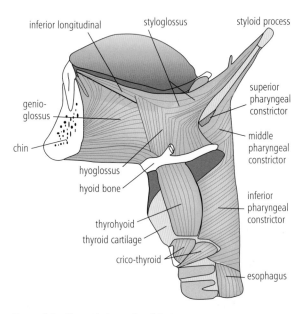

Figure 5.9   The extrinsic muscles of the tongue.

of the styloglossus is to pull the tongue up and back. It is active in velar consonants, and high, back vowels such as [u].

The *palatoglossus* connects the tongue to the soft palate. It is not shown in Figure 5.9, but it runs in front of and above the styloglossus. If you open wide and say "ah," the "arches" that you see at the back of your mouth, curving up from the floor of the mouth to the soft palate and uvula, are the membranes covering the palatoglossus muscles. The palatoglossus has several functions that are important in speech. If the velum is held steady, contraction of the palatoglossus will cause the tongue body to move up, as for a palatal consonant or the vowel [i]. By pulling up on the sides of the tongue, the palatoglossus can also help create the groove necessary for [s] and [ʃ], and can aid in the articulation of laterals. On the other hand, if the tongue body is held steady, contraction of the palatoglossus will pull the velum down, opening the velar port and allowing nasal airflow.

The palatoglossus connection between palate and tongue can have an effect on patterns of nasalization. Cross-linguistically, low vowels are more likely to be nasalized than high vowels. This connection is one reason: the hyoglossus pulls the tongue body down, the tongue body pulls down on the palatoglossus, and the palatoglossus pulls down on the velum.

The fourth extrinsic muscle of the tongue is the *genioglossus*. This large muscle originates at the front on the jaw, and fans out across the bottom of the tongue. (You can touch the membrane covering the genioglossus if you place your finger on the floor of the mouth, at the base of the tongue.) Because the genioglossus fans out to different parts of the tongue, different portions of the muscle have different functions. Or to put it another way, the tongue front and tongue body can function as separate active articulators largely because the anterior and posterior portions of the genioglossus can act independently.

Contraction of the *anterior genioglossus,* which connects the tongue front to the front of the jaw, pulls the tongue front down. This can be important in positioning the tongue for low vowels and front vowels. It will also aid the intrinsic muscles in shaping and manipulating the tongue for coronal consonants.

Contraction of the *posterior genioglossus* pulls the tongue body forward, but also squeezes the bottom of the tongue. Squeezing the bottom has the effect of pushing the top up (remember the bag of jelly), so the effect of the posterior genioglossus is to move the tongue body both forward and up.

By the way, that thin strip of tissue connecting the bottom of the tongue to the floor of the mouth is a *frenulum*. It has no linguistic purpose other than, perhaps, to prevent retroflex velar articulations. There are also frenuli connecting the upper and lower lips to the gums.

Very roughly, the muscles active in tongue positioning can be defined as follows:

down:	hyoglossus
up:	palatoglossus
back:	styloglossus
forward:	posterior genioglossus

Using just one term for each muscle is an over-simplification, since the muscle movements are not really so geometrical or linear: the styloglossus pulls both up and back, the posterior genioglossus up and forward. Creating any particular tongue position requires balancing the action of all the muscles to move the tongue body to the exact right place.

The four intrinsic muscles of the tongue control tongue shape (Figure 5.10). The fibers of these muscles are interwoven to a large extent with each other and with the extrinsic muscles, especially the genioglossus, but each has an independent function.

The *superior longitudinal* muscle runs lengthwise along the top of the tongue. This is the muscle that contracts to curl the tongue tip up and back for a retroflex articulation.

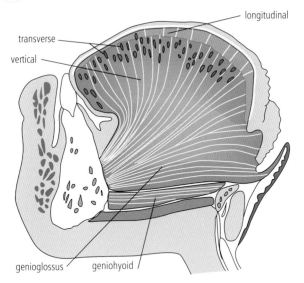

Figure 5.10   The intrinsic muscles of the tongue.

5.2   In some people, the superior longitudinal has oblique (sideways) fibers that allow the individual to "curl" the tongue from side to side. The ability to curl the tongue (like wiggling the ears or separating the digits of the hand between the third and fourth fingers) varies from person to person, and it is of no linguistic significance.

The *inferior longitudinal* runs lengthwise below the superior longitudinal (obviously). This muscle, in conjunction with the anterior genioglossus, pulls the tongue tip down. The superior and inferior longitudinal muscles work in opposition to each other for the articulation of coronal taps and flaps.

Beneath the longitudinals run the *transverse* (side to side) and *vertical* (up and down) muscles of the tongue.

The transverse and vertical muscles are intertwined with each other. Contraction of the transverse muscles narrows and lengthens the tongue: important for sticking the tongue out, but also for any articulation that requires the tongue tip to move forward, such as dentals, as well as for laterals, which require the sides of the tongue to pull in from the sides of the teeth. Contraction of the vertical muscles has the effect of flattening the tongue surface, useful for low vowels such as [æ].

5.3.3 the pharynx and velum

Our discussion of the movements of the tongue has not yet covered the tongue root, that part of the tongue that extends down into the pharynx. Movement of the tongue root is essentially one-dimensional: forward for certain vowels (tense or advanced), back for other vowels (lax or retracted), back even more for pharyngeal fricatives.

Forward movement of the tongue root is accomplished by the same muscle that pulls the tongue body forward: the posterior genioglossus. Backward movement of the tongue root is accomplished by the *pharyngeal constrictors*: rings of muscle that circle the pharynx. Their action is exactly what is stated by their name. The location of the pharyngeal constrictors is shown in Figure 5.9 on p. 86.

Movement of the velum is also one-dimensional: open or closed. As was discussed in the previous section, the palatoglossus muscle pulls the velum down (if it is not pulling the tongue up). The action of the palatoglossus is countered by the *levator palatini* (palate-raising) muscle, which attaches the velum to the base of the skull on either side. It is like a sling holding up the velum which can be either lowered or raised. Contraction of the levator muscle pulls the velum up. Closure of the velar port is aided by muscles inside the velum and uvula, the *tensor palatini* and *uvulae*, which stiffen the soft palate to create a stronger seal.

5.3.4 the lips

Finally, we consider the muscles of the lips. There are between 50 and 100 muscles in the human face (again, depending on how you count). Seven are important in labial articulation for speech. They are shown in Figure 5.11.

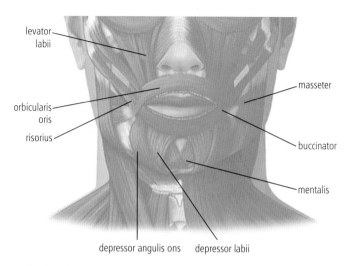

Figure 5.11   Muscles of the face.

The *orbicularis oris* circles the lips. Its contraction leads to rounding of the lips. It is no accident that we refer to rounding as pursing: constriction of the orbicularis oris acts just like pulling on purse strings.

The *mentalis* is the chin muscle. Its contraction pushes the lower lip up. You can feel the contraction of this muscle and its effect on lip position if you put your finger on your chin and make a pout. The mentalis is active in labiodental articulations and non-rounded bi-labial fricatives. Contraction of both the mentalis and orbicularis oris is needed to pull the lower lip up and in for the labiodental flap.

The aptly-named *levator labii superior* raises the upper lip and the *depressor labii inferior* lowers the lower lip.

Finally, the *risorius* (smiling) muscles pull the corners of the lips back, aided by the *buc-cinator*, or cheek muscles. These muscles are important in spreading the lips, as for the vowel [i]. The antagonist to the risorius is the *depressor angulis oris*, which, as the name states, pulls the corners of the mouth down. These would be the "frowning" muscles: contrary to popular opinion, there is no anatomical evidence that it takes more muscles to frown than to smile.

5.4 gestural coordination

Having listed all these independent parts, we have to ask, how is their movement so efficiently controlled for speech? Control does go wrong sometimes, as in a lisp, stuttering, or the occasional spoonerism, but most of the time most of us execute these extremely fast and fine-tuned movements without a thought. Think through the coordination needed to articu-late a simple phrase such as "a pan" [əpʰæn]:

The vocal tract begins in non-speech mode: tidal breathing, mouth closed, velum open. To prepare for speech, the mouth opens (geniohyoid, digastricus) and the velum closes (levator palatini). The diaphragm and external intercostals contract to draw air into the lungs. The interarytenoids adduct the vocal folds, and the vocalis tenses. Then: go! The diaphragm and external intercostals slowly relax to produce a steady airstream over the vocal folds, which begin to vibrate. The tongue stays in neutral position, and the sound [ə] emerges. The steady-state portion of this reduced vowel lasts for less than 50 ms ($\frac{1}{20}$th of a second) however, before the lips close (masseter, mentalis, orbicularis oris) for [p]. As the lips come together, the tongue body moves from its neutral position toward low front [æ] (vertical muscles and hyoglossus), and the vocal folds open (PCA) to cut off voicing. The lips open about $\frac{1}{10}$th of a second after they close, by which time the tongue body has reached its target position for [æ], and the vocal folds are wide open, producing aspiration. The folds quickly close, however, (IA), to make the majority of the vowel voiced. About the middle of the vowel, the palatoglossus begins pulling down on the velum, and shortly afterwards the tongue tip starts moving forward and up (anterior genioglossus and superior longitudinal) for the [n]. Maximum velum opening and alveolar closure are achieved simultaneously. In less than half a second, the word is over and the vocal tract is on to the next. (An average rate of speech gets in about 2.5 words per second, though double that and more are possible with practice.)

Without going into the details of neural commands and mathematical models of motor control, we can note that control and coordination of vocal tract muscles work in much the same way as control and coordination of body parts in other kinds of goal-directed motion, such as reaching, running, or dancing. The metaphor of articulation as dance was introduced in Chapter 2. A dancer will spend many hours learning and practicing routines for particular movements or steps, until they can be executed smoothly and automatically. When a dance is put together, it is the steps that are coordinated, not individual muscles: plié and sauté, not quadriceps and hamstrings. Speech works the same way. The steps in the dance of speech are articulatory gestures: goal-directed "routines" of coordinated sets of articulators. It is the gestures (labial closing, larynx opening) that are coordinated, not individual contractions of the masseter or PCA.

Coordination of muscle movements into goal-directed gestures, whether of the arms, legs, or mouth, is learned in the first months of life, as babies figure out how to coordinate their muscle movements to reach, walk, and talk. Once learned, the routines are continually reinforced, so that for the adult the gestures are effortless and without conscious thought. It is, in fact, extremely difficult to alter a learned routine, as you know if you've ever tried to change your golf swing or speak a new language (see Chapter 20).

This conception of articulatory gestures is the basis of the theory of *Articulatory Phonology*, developed by Catherine Browman and Louis Goldstein (see further reading). In this way of thinking about speech, the goal of each gesture is to use a coordinated set of articulators (e.g., jaw + lower lip + upper lip) to create a particular *constriction degree* at a particular *constriction location* (e.g., bilabial stop).

An articulatory gesture, like a dance step, has extent in both space and time. One way to diagram the temporal coordination of gestures is in a *gestural score*, as in Figure 5.12, which diagrams the utterance [pʰæn]. "Score" here is used in the sense of an orchestral score that coordinates the different instruments. Just as each instrument has its own line in an orchestral score, each articulator set has its own line in a gestural score. Articulator sets are named for the active articulator that effects the constriction: lower lip, tongue front, tongue body, velum, and larynx. Each gesture, with its specified constriction location and degree, is indicated as a box in the score. (Velum and larynx have only constriction degree, as they cannot move to different locations.)

"Pan" thus has five gestures: bilabial closing and larynx opening constitute [p], alveolar closing and velum opening constitute [n], and a single tongue body lowering gesture constitutes [æ]. Time is on the x-axis, and the length of the box indicates each gesture's *activation interval*: when active control of that articulator set begins and ends. Thus, in [pʰæn], the score shows that gestures of the lips, larynx, and tongue body begin simultaneously. In the simplest version of the theory, articulators are assumed to return to a default state when not under active control: the default is assumed to be closed for the velum and modal voicing for the larynx.

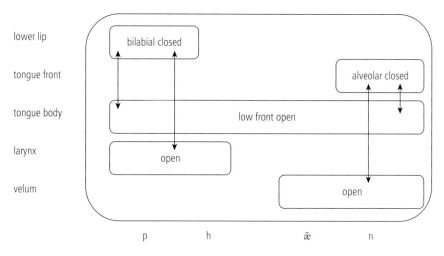

Figure 5.12   Gestural score for "pan."

Gestures are coordinated to each other, not to an external clock. Coordination between gestures is indicated in Figure 5.12 by arrows: labial closing and larynx opening are linked, as are alveolar closing and velum opening, and the constrictions of the consonants are superimposed on the opening gesture for the vowel.

An important tenet of Articulatory Phonology is that temporal coordination, particularly overlap in time, has consequences for positional variation. For example, it can be seen in Figure 5.12 that velum opening precedes alveolar closing. The result of this temporal coordination is nasalization that is heard on the vowel. Similarly, larynx opening extends beyond the duration of lip closure: the result is aspiration. There are no separate gestures for vowel nasalization or aspiration: these positional variants come about as a result of the specified temporal coordination for [p] and for [n]. If an [l] were articulated after the [p] (as in "plan"), its articulation would overlap with the open larynx, resulting in devoicing.

In some cases, gestural overlap can lead to assimilation. Consider the phrase "miss you," which, as mentioned in Chapter 2, often sounds like [mɪʃju] in American English. A gestural score for the phrase is shown in Figure 5.13. For clarity, the gestures corresponding to [ju] (palatal glide and back vowel) are shaded and some of the gestural descriptors have been simplified. Crucially, the gestural score shows that the gestures for the [s] of "miss" and [j] of "you" overlap in time. Both gestures involve the tongue front. Since a single articulator cannot be in two places at the same time, the two gestures blend, producing an intermediate articulation that begins like [s] but ends up sounding like [ʃ]. Gradual and partial change, rather than a complete switch from one type of articulation to another, is another hallmark of an Articulatory Phonology approach.

Numerous other examples of gestural coordination and positional variation can be found in the readings suggested at the end of the chapter. Or, you can go to the lists of different positional variants at the ends of Chapters 2 and 3, and see if you can work out a gestural analysis for yourself.

5.5 palatography

We conclude this chapter with directions for trying *static palatography*: a fun way to learn about place of articulation. You can make *linguograms*, which record the part of the tongue

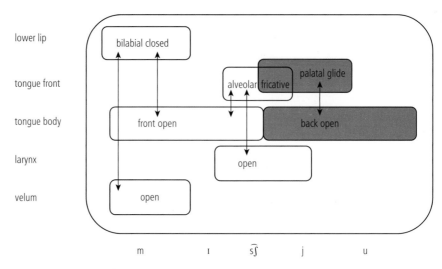

Figure 5.13   Gestural score for "miss you."

that contacts the palate, or *palatograms*, which record the part of the palate that is contacted by the tongue (Figure 5.14). The simple method described here does not allow for quantitative measurement, but it does allow you to visualize patterns of contact for different coronal articulations.

Equipment

1.   Activated charcoal. You can order a bottle of this fine black power from your local drugstore, without a prescription. Its pharmacological use is as a poison antidote. The directions on my bottle say to mix with water and drink the whole thing if you have ingested something nasty, so you can be confident that a half teaspoon is not going to hurt you. (Peter Ladefoged, in *Phonetic Data Analysis*, tells how he once made charcoal by scraping the black part off of some burnt toast, but I tried this and found it got unpleasantly soggy.)
2.   Salad oil (corn, canola, etc.)
3.   Mint extract (optional)
4.   A paper cup to mix the oil and charcoal, one for each subject
5.   A set of children's paintbrushes (fresh out of the box), one brush for each subject
6.   A small mirror, approximately two by three inches. Use one for each subject, or clean with alcohol in between uses. Cosmetic mirrors work well, or I've also found sets of small mirrors sold as favors for kids' parties. Or you can get really serious and buy a dental mirror from a supply store.
7.   A camera to record the results.

To make a linguogram

1.   Find a willing subject, who doesn't mind having his palate and tongue painted and photographed in the name of linguistic science.

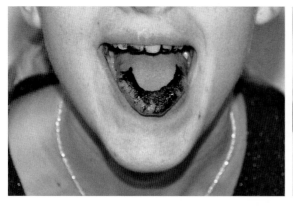 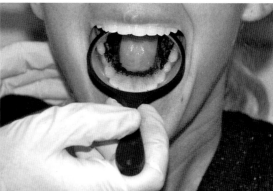

Figure 5.14   A linguogram (left) and palatogram (right) for American English [t].

2. Mix 1 teaspoon charcoal and 1 teaspoon oil in a small cup. The consistency should be that of thick paint. The mixture is tasteless, but gritty. Some people prefer to add a drop of mint extract, which makes it taste like toothpaste.

3. Have the subject tilt his head back and open wide. Using the child's paint brush, paint the subject's entire palate with the charcoal–oil mixture, from the teeth back to the beginning of the soft palate (or as far back as the subject's gag reflex will allow). Make sure to go down to the teeth on each side. You have to work quickly, as the subject will not be able to close his mouth or swallow during the procedure.

4. Have the subject articulate one syllable, such as [tɑ], [sɑ], [ʃɑ] or [lɑ], and then stick out his tongue. You can only do one consonant at a time.

5. You will see a pattern of black paint on the tongue where it made contact with the palate. Photograph the pattern on the tongue.

6. Let the subject rinse his mouth thoroughly. It doesn't hurt to swallow the mixture, but, in my experience, subjects prefer to excuse themselves to the nearest restroom or water fountain and spit.

To make a palatogram

1. Use the same procedure as for a linguogram, except that you paint the tongue. Have the subject stick his tongue out to be painted, and be sure to fully cover the tongue tip and sides.

2. Have the subject articulate the same syllable as for the linguogram.

3. In this case, the black paint will rub off the tongue onto the palate, showing the pattern of contact. In order to photograph the palate, place the mirror inside the subject's mouth, at an angle, and photograph the image of the palate in the mirror. It may take some practice or a few tries to get the angle just right. Don't let the subject close his mouth in between saying the syllable and getting the picture. Also, the subject will need to hold his breath for the few seconds the mirror is in position, or the mirror will fog up.

It is interesting to make a palatogram/linguogram pair for different utterances for the same subject, and compare the different places of articulation. If you can find subjects who speak different languages, and can compare patterns for similar sounds across languages, all the better, but never make participation coercive: not everybody is comfortable with something like this. Remember to protect your subjects' health by using a separate paint cup, a new brush, and a clean mirror for each person. You should also protect the subject's identity by editing any photos you're going to keep, to crop identifying facial features. In my experience, there are always a few adventurous souls in every class who want to try palatography for the fun of it.

chapter summary

Table 5.1 lists all of the muscles discussed in this chapter, along with their functions and representative sounds for which they are active.

Table 5.1   Muscles of the vocal tract.

Muscle	Function	Example sounds
Thorax		
Diaphragm	Expand thoracic cavity	inhalation
External intercostals		
Internal intercostals	Contract thoracic cavity	exhalation
Rectus abdominus		
Larynx: Intrinsic		
Interarytenoid	vocal fold adduction	voiced sounds
Posterior crico-arytenoid	vocal fold abduction	voiceless sounds
Crico-thyroid	vocal fold stretching	raising pitch
Lateral crico-arytenoid	strong glottal adduction	glottal stop or creak
Vocalis	vocal fold tension	voiced sonorants
Larynx: Extrinsic (strap)		
Sterno-hyoid	lower larynx, create vertical	pitch lowering
Sterno-thyroid	vocal fold tension	
Crico-hyoid	raise larynx, create vertical	pitch modulation
Thyro-hyoid	vocal fold tension	
Pharynx and Velum		
Pharyngeal constrictors	narrow phayrnx	pharyngeals
Levator Palatini	raise palate	close off nasal cavity for oral
Uvular muscles	raise uvula	sounds
Palatoglossus	lower palate	nasal sounds
Tongue: Extrinsic		
Palatoglossus	raise tongue body	velars, palatals, high vowels
Styloglossus	raise and back TB	velars, back vowels
Anterior genioglossus	lower tongue tip	/s/ and /ʃ/
Posterior genioglossus	pull tongue body forward	front vowels, alveolars
Hyoglossus	pull TB forward and down	/æ/
Tongue: Intrinsic		
Superior longitudinal	raise tongue tip	retroflex
Inferior longitudinal	lower tongue tip	/s/ and /ʃ/
Transverse	narrow and elongate tongue	alveolars and dentals, /l/
Vertical	flatten and widen tongue	low vowels

Table 5.1   (*Continued*)

Muscle	Function	Example sounds
Lips		
Orbicularis oris	round and protrude lips	round vowels, /f/
Mentalis		
Risorius	spread lips	non-round vowels, /f/
Buccinator		
Levator labii superior	raise upper lip	vowels
Depressor labii inferior	lower lower lip	
Jaw		
Masseter	jaw raising	consonants, high vowels
Anterior digastricus	jaw lowering	non-high vowels
Geniohyoid		

further reading

For further details on vocal tract anatomy and physiology:
Raphael, L.J., Borden, G., & Harris, K.S. (2007). *Speech Science Primer*, 5th Edition. Baltimore, MD: Lippincott, Williams & Wilkins.

For more information on Articulatory Phonology, the original sources are:
Browman, C. and L. Goldstein, 1986. Towards an Articulatory Phonology. *Phonology Yearbook* 3: 219–252.
Browman, C. and L. Goldstein, 1992. Articulatory Phonology: an overview. *Phonetica* 49: 155–180.

For a very accessible introduction to Articulatory Phonology:
Hall, N. 2010. Articulatory Phonology. *Language and Linguistics Compass* 9: 818–830.

review exercises

1. Define the following terms:

    a. posterior vs. anterior
    b. vital capacity
    c. pleural linkage
    d. intonational phrase (or breath group)
    e. fundamental frequency (F0)
    f. Hertz
    g. adduction vs. abduction
    h. muscular processes vs. vocal processes of the arytenoids
    i. open quotient
    j. linguogram vs. palatogram

    (*Continued*)

2. The following pairs of muscles are antagonists: they cause movement in opposite directions. Explain the functions of each pair: what do they act on, and how? Why are they important for speech?

a.	internal intercostals	external intercostals
b.	interarytenoid	posterior crico-arytenoid
c.	sterno-thyroid	thyro-hyoid
d.	levator palatini	palatoglossus
e.	styloglossus	posterior genioglossus
f.	palatoglossus	hyoglossus
g.	posterior genioglossus	pharyngeal constrictors
h.	superior longitudinal	inferior longitudinal
i.	transverse	vertical
j.	anterior belly of the digastricus	masseter
k.	risorius	orbicularis oris
l.	levator labii superior	depressor labii inferior

3. Explain the roles of these additional muscles:

a. diaphragm
b. rectus abdominus
c. lateral crico-arytenoid
d. crico-thyroid
e. uvular muscles

4. There are not too many bony parts of the vocal tract. Where are each of the following located? What are their more common names (if any)?

a. sternum
b. mandible
c. costa
d. hyoid
e. styloid process

5. Consider the English word "basketball," pronounced [bæskɪtˀbɔl]. Fill in the blanks from the word bank below to describe the muscles and articulatory configurations involved in its articulation.

In preparation for speech, the _____ muscle _____ the velum.

For the [b], the masseter muscle raises the _____.

For voicing, the _____ muscles pull on the _____ cartilages, which _____ the vocal folds.

For the vowel [æ], the _____ muscle opens the jaw. Voicing continues. The _____ muscle pulls the tongue body down. The _____ muscles help flatten the tongue.

To stop voicing for [s] and [k], the _____ muscles pull on the _____ cartilages, which _____ the vocal folds.

For [k], the _____ muscle pulls the tongue body up.

For the [t$^{?}$], the _____ help close the vocal folds tightly.

For the vowel [ɔ], the _____ muscle pulls the tongue body back. The _____ muscle rounds the lips.

For [l], the _____ muscle narrows and stiffens the tongue. The _____ muscle pulls the tongue body forward.

Word bank: some terms are used more than once, some terms are not used:

Tongue muscles	Other muscles	Bones and cartilages	Actions
genioglossus	digastricus	arytenoid	abducts
hyoglossus	interarytenoid	cricoid	adducts
palatoglossus	lateral crico-arytenoid	hyoid	lowers
styloglossus	levator palatini	mandible	raises
transverse	posterior crico-arytenoid	orbicularis oris	
vertical		thyroid	

further analysis and discussion

6. Since the lungs themselves have no muscles, how do they expand and contract? In your answer, be sure to include the muscle groups involved and the crucial role of the pleural linkage. Why would breathing be impossible if the ribcage were completely fixed?
7. Discuss the differences between:
   a. tidal breathing and breathing during speech.
   b. the typical male larynx and the typical female larynx.
8. Describe the state of the larynx, including the cartilages and muscles involved, required for modal, creaky, and breathy voice.
9. Why are low vowels more likely to be nasalized than high vowels?
10. Explain the myo-elastic aerodynamic theory of phonation. That is, how do muscle tension and airflow cause vocal fold vibration? Include a definition and discussion of the Bernoulli effect.
11. Consider the English word "point," pronounced, with a GA accent, [p^{h}ɔ̃ɪ̃nt$^{?}$]. Six different vocal tract configurations can be identified in this word, as shown in the table below. For each configuration, describe the position of the jaw, velum, lips, tongue front, tongue body, and larynx. Then, for each articulator, describe the muscle activity (name names) required to reach or maintain that position. ("Neutral/no activity" is an acceptable description.)

	p	^{h}	ɔ̃	ɪ̃	n	$t^{?}$
Jaw position						
Activity						
Velum position						
Activity						

(*Continued*)

	p	^{h}	$\tilde{\mathcirc{o}}$	$\tilde{\imath}$	n	$t^{\mathfrak{?}}$
Lip position						
Activity						
Tongue front position						
Activity						
Tongue body position						
Activity						
Larynx position						
Activity						

12. Draw a gestural score for the word "cream," and explain how gestural organization accounts for sonorant devoicing and vowel nasalization.

further research

13. Try some palatography, as described in Section 5.5.
14. The theory of Articulatory Phonology argues that final consonant deletion, as in "best buy" can also be accounted for in terms of gestural overlap: specifically, the [t] is present but "hidden" by overlap with the [b]. Draw a gestural score for this phrase, and explain how gestural hiding could lead to apparent deletion.

Go online Visit the book's companion website for additional resources relating to this chapter at: http://www.wiley.com/go/zsiga.

6

The Physics of Sound

Pendulums, Pebbles, and Waves

All science is either physics or stamp collecting.
  Ernest Rutherford, 1871–1937, winner of the 1908 Nobel Prize in Chemistry

Chapter outline

According to Rutherford, we have, up until now, been "stamp collecting": describing, ordering, and classifying the sounds of speech. We turn in this chapter to *acoustics*, the study of the physical properties of sound waves. Speech is one of the most complex sounds found in nature. It may begin in the complex undulations of the vocal folds or the turbulent eddies of a fricative, and is modified by passing through the irregularly-shaped and constantly changing chambers of the vocal tract. In order to understand speech sounds, we need to break them down into their component parts (a job which our ears and brains do effortlessly).

After defining "sound" in Section 6.1, we then describe in Section 6.2 the motion that creates the simplest sound in nature: the vibration of a tuning fork. Section 6.3 discusses how all more complex sounds can be built up from this simple motion. The next sections describe how sound travels (propagation), how sound intensity is measured (decibels), and how sound waves interact (resonance). All of this discussion builds to Section 6.7: a picture of the vocal tract as a sound-producing device.

6.1 what is sound?

In general, *sound* is a pattern of pressure variation that moves out in waves from a source. In order to count as sound, the size and rapidity of the pressure variations must be within the ranges to which the ear is sensitive: too big, and the pressure change is felt rather than heard; too small, and the changes are not perceived at all. While sound waves can travel through all kinds of materials (water, helium, apartment walls, etc.), when we think about describing the sounds of speech, we focus on sound waves as they travel through the air, from the mouth of the speaker to the ear of the listener.

Sounds can be divided into two types: *periodic*, and *aperiodic*. In a periodic sound, a pressure wave of a specific shape is repeated multiple times. Musical notes, in which a particular pitch is sustained, are periodic sounds. In an aperiodic sound, the moment-to-moment pressure variations are more random: there is no repeating pattern. Radio static, the scratching of sandpaper and the rustling of leaves are aperiodic sounds. A special category of aperiodic sound is a *transient*. A transient sound is instantaneous, like the slamming of a door, a snap of the fingers, or the crash of breaking glass. There is a momentary disturbance, not drawn out or repeated. Actual sounds that occur in nature will often combine different kinds of sound: the "hum" of an engine, the bark of a dog, and the speech of a person all have both periodic and aperiodic components.

Figure 6.1 shows *waveforms* of different types of sounds as they occur in speech. A waveform is a graphical representation of sound pressure changes over time. The x-axis shows time in seconds. Note that each waveform shows only $\frac{5}{100}$ths of a second. As we will see, variations perceived as sound happen very fast, so fast that they are commonly measured in *milliseconds* (abbreviated *ms*), that is, thousandths of a second. Each of the graphs in Figure 6.1 shows 50 ms. For the time being, the units of the pressure scale are arbitrary. (Measures of sound pressure variation are discussed below.) Positive values are moments of higher pressure (*compression*), negative values are moments of lower pressure (*rarefaction*), and the 0 value indicates equilibrium.

Figure 6.1A shows 50 ms of the vowel [ɑ], a periodic sound. The repeating pattern is evident. (Each cycle of repetition is not a perfect copy, since the sound was produced by a human and not a machine, but the pattern is there.) Figure 6.1B shows [s], an aperiodic sound. In [s], the change from positive to negative pressure is fast and random, with no pattern to be seen. Figure 6.1C shows a waveform of [z], a sound that combines periodic and aperiodic components. There is an underlying pattern that repeats, but a lot of noisy

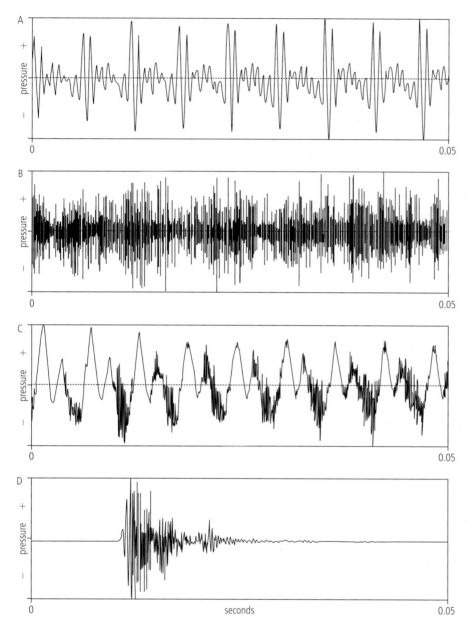

Figure 6.1   Waveforms of different sound types. A. Periodic: the vowel [ɑ]. B. Aperiodic: [s]. C. Periodic and aperiodic components combined: [z]. D. A transient: release of velar closure in an ejective [k'].

variation is laid over it. Finally, 6.1D shows a transient speech sound: the burst of noise created by the release of velar closure in the ejective consonant [k']. There is silence, then a sudden burst of sound lasting about a hundredth of a second, quickly dying down to silence again.

To understand how these patterns are created and perceived, in particular, to understand why the sound in A is heard as an [ɑ] rather than an [e], for example, we must begin with a system much simpler than the human vocal tract.

6.2 simple harmonic motion: a pendulum and a tuning fork

We begin our description of sound waves by describing the motion of a pendulum. A pendulum is too slow for its swinging to make any noise, but its movements are big enough and slow enough to be visible, and the physics underlying the motion of a pendulum is the same as that of sound waves, which cannot be seen. The motion of a pendulum bob is represented in Figure 6.2. The pendulum begins at its rest position (A), hanging straight down. To start the system in motion, the bob is pushed or pulled up to a certain displacement (B). When the bob is released, it swings back down. It passes over its rest position (A again), but does not come to a sudden stop. Instead, inertia carries it past its rest position, displacing it in the opposite direction. It will then reach a maximum displacement in the new direction (C), then swing back down again. That completes one full cycle of back and forth motion: A – B – A – C – A. Again, however, the pendulum does not stop at its rest position: the bob passes over the rest position, continues up to a maximum displacement, then swings back again. The cycle repeats over and over.

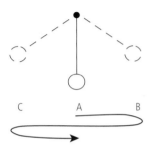

Figure 6.2 The motion of a pendulum.

As the pendulum swings back and forth, or *oscillates*, each cycle takes up exactly the same amount of time. This regularity, of course, is why pendulum clocks work. The amount of time required for each cycle is termed the *period*. If the clock is accurate, the period of its pendulum will be exactly one second (or an exact multiple of one second). The number of cycles in a given amount of time is termed the *frequency*. The frequency of a clock pendulum with a period of 1 second would thus be 60 cycles per minute. Note that the frequency is the inverse of the period: the period is $\frac{1}{60}$th of a minute per cycle, and the frequency is 60 cycles per minute. This is the most basic formula in acoustics: $F = 1/P$, where F = frequency and P = period.

Formula 6.1

$$F = 1/P$$

$$P = 1/F$$

In a pendulum, the period of a cycle is determined by the length of the string: a longer pendulum has a longer period, and thus a lower frequency. The general principle is that large, massive things oscillate more slowly, and small, less massive things oscillate more quickly.

The displacement of the pendulum (that is, how far it moves, the distance from A to B) is its *amplitude*. The amplitude depends on how much energy is put into the system: how far up the pendulum is pulled before letting go. Or consider another type of pendulum, the playground swing. The harder you push the child on the swing, the higher she will go, that is, the greater the amplitude will be. (This method of measuring amplitude, *peak displacement*, is only one possible method. Others are discussed in Section 8.2.1 on p. 161.)

In the real world, the oscillation does not last forever. You cannot give the child on the swing just one push and then go sit down for the afternoon. You have to keep pushing the swing; you have to regularly wind the clock. If you give the swing just one push, gravity and friction will exert their effects, and each cycle of the oscillation will have slightly less amplitude, until finally the swinging stops. This gradual loss of energy (and amplitude) from cycle to cycle is termed *damping*. In a *lightly-damped* system, energy loss is gradual, and the oscillations continue for a long time. In a *highly-damped* system, energy loss is quick, and the oscillations quickly die down. When it comes to speech vibrations, however, the oscillations are in many cases so fast that the loss of energy from one cycle to the next is negligible: it

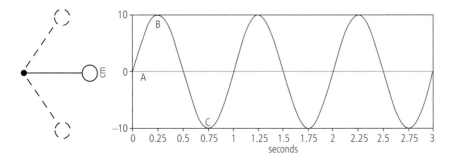

Figure 6.3   The motion of a pendulum with a period of one second and peak amplitude of 10 cm.

takes thousands of cycles for the energy to die out. The loss is so negligible that we can often get away with pretending that we are dealing with *undamped* systems, where no energy is lost at all, and amplitude stays constant from cycle to cycle. This idealization has the advantage of making the math we need to use considerably simpler.

With that basic understanding of the pendulum's motion, let's graph its change in position over time. Figure 6.3 graphs the motion of what might be a clock pendulum, with a period of one second and a peak displacement of 10 centimeters. For comparison with Figure 6.2, the picture of the pendulum has been copied, turned on its side so that the axes line up. The rest position (A, 0 cm) and points of maximum displacement (B, +10 cm, and C, −10 cm) are shown.

At time 0, the pendulum is at rest (0 displacement). When energy is applied (assume the pendulum is given a push), it moves up to B, reaching maximum displacement (10 cm) at time .25. The bob then swings back in the other direction, passing through its rest position at time .5 and eventually reaching maximum displacement in the other direction (C, −10 cm) at time .75. It then heads back to the rest position, passing through 0 displacement at time 1, having completed one cycle. Another cycle is completed between times 1 and 2, and a third cycle between times 2 and 3. Note that one full cycle includes both motion to the right (positive displacement) and to the left (negative displacement). Remember also that we are graphing a pendulum in the ideal world of mathematics, where no energy is lost and amplitude remains constant. In the real world, amplitude would slowly decrease from cycle to cycle.

The shape of the line graph in Figure 6.3 should look familiar to anyone who has taken a course in geometry: it is a *sine wave*. The name comes from the fact that a wave of this shape graphs the geometric *sin* function of an angle as it moves from 0° to 360° (one lap around a circle, that is, one cycle). A *cosine wave* (based on the *cosin* function) has the same shape as a sine wave, but begins at the maximum value (1) rather than 0. A difference in starting point is called a *phase shift*. Any wave that has the shape of a sine wave, regardless of differences in phase, is called a *sinusoid*. (Often we get lazy and call any sinusoidal wave a sine wave, but technically it is only a true sine wave if it starts at 0.) For more mathematical details on the sin function and on sinusoids, see Section 8.1.1 on p. 150.

A cosine wave graphs the *instantaneous velocity* of the pendulum bob: how fast the bob is moving (in a given direction) at a given point in time. Positive 1 is peak velocity in a rightward direction, negative 1 is peak velocity in a leftward direction, and 0 velocity is, of course, no motion at all. For a pendulum, peak velocity is reached at 0 displacement, when the bob is passing through its rest position, and 0 velocity is reached at peak displacement, the moment when the bob stops and changes direction.

These functions are important for acoustic phonetics for at least three reasons. First, any oscillating system whose period and velocity have the inverse relationship defined above and

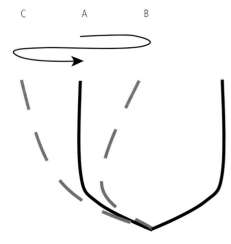

Figure 6.4   The motion of a tuning fork is simple harmonic motion.

captured by the sine and cosine waves is said to be in *simple harmonic motion*. Amplitude (displacement) moves regularly back and forth (from positive to negative, like a pendulum), velocity is 0 when displacement is greatest, and displacement is 0 when velocity is greatest. Systems that oscillate in simple harmonic motion include clock pendulums, playground swings, springs, vibrating crystals, and crucially for our purposes, the tines of a tuning fork producing a simple tone.

The jump from a pendulum to a tuning fork is a small one, since the motion of the tine of a tuning fork is exactly analogous to the motion of a pendulum. Figure 6.4 diagrams the motion of one tine of a tuning fork (exaggerated for the purpose of the diagram). The rest state of the tuning fork is of course with the tines parallel, position A. If you strike a tuning fork against a hard object, you displace the tine inward, to position B. (Both tines will actually move together because they are physically linked, but we consider only the motion of the left-hand tine.) The tine does not stay bent, because of the inherent stiffness or "springiness" of the metal: the tine springs back toward the rest position. Again, however, it does not stop instantaneously at the rest position: inertia causes it to overshoot and deform in the opposite direction, to displacement C. The end of the tine reaches a maximum displacement, slows to a stop, changes direction, moves back toward the rest position, overshoots, and continues cycling. Like the pendulum, the tuning fork is oscillating in simple harmonic motion, so its movement can be defined by a sinusoid. A tuning fork is a very lightly damped system, so it will generally take several thousand cycles before the movement dies out. You can reproduce the motion in larger, visible form by holding a long, thin stick (like a yardstick) tightly at one end. Pull the loose end back, let it go, and observe the oscillation.

The only important difference between the motion of a tuning fork and that of a pendulum or yardstick is that the oscillations of the tuning fork take place within the range of frequencies and amplitudes to which the human ear is sensitive. Generally, a young, healthy human ear responds to frequencies as low as about 20 cycles per second to as high as about 20,000 cycles per second (with the higher end dropping off rapidly with age). Frequency is proportional to pitch: the higher the frequency, the higher the "note" that is perceived. A tuning fork tuned to "orchestral A," for example, vibrates at a frequency of 440 cycles per second. Middle C is 262 cycles per second. Again, the relationship between size and frequency holds: the tuning fork for middle C is slightly larger than the one for orchestral A. Also, of course, the relationship between period and frequency holds: if the frequency is 440 cycles per second, the period is 1/440 seconds per cycle (that is, 0.022727 seconds, or 22.7 ms). For a given frequency, the amplitude of the vibration (how far the tine is displaced, which is determined by how hard the fork is struck) will be proportional to its loudness.

As was noted in Chapter 5, "cycles per second" may be abbreviated *cps*, or may be replaced by the measurement term *Hertz* (for German physicist Heinrich Hertz) abbreviated *Hz*. Because it is based on a name, the "H" in Hz is always capitalized.

6.1   Heinrich Hertz, 1857–1894, was the first person to transmit and receive radio waves. He is therefore sometimes called the father of long-distance wireless communication. Apparently he did not, however, foresee the cell phone. When he was asked what use his radio-wave receiver might be, Hertz is reported to have replied: "It's of no use whatsoever . . . This is just an experiment that proves Professor Maxwell was right . . . I do not think the wireless waves that I have discovered will have any practical application." Hertz died young (aged 36), and did not live to see Guglielmo Marconi apply his radio transmitter to the creation of a wireless telegraph.

A second reason why sinusoids are important for acoustic phonetics is that the mathematics of sinusoidal motion are well understood. Once it is known that a motion can be graphed as a sinusoid, we need only three numbers to describe it perfectly: the frequency (how fast the system is cycling); the amplitude (how big each movement is); and the phase (at what point the movement started). As it turns out, phase is not usually important for speech analysis. If you think about it, this makes sense: a sustained note does not sound any different depending on the point at which you start listening to it (though see Chapter 9 for some further discussion). With phase set aside, that means if we know the frequency and amplitude of a sinusoid (which describes anything vibrating in simple harmonic motion), we know everything important there is to know about it.

Finally, a French mathematical genius named Jean Baptiste Joseph Fourier proved in 1807 that every kind of vibration (including all the complex speech sounds graphed in Figure 6.1) can be described as the sum of a set of simple sinusoids of varying frequencies and amplitudes. With very complex sounds it takes a lot of sinusoids, but Fourier proved it can be done. Thus, an understanding of sinusoidal motion, defined by frequency and amplitude, is the key to understanding all speech sounds.

6.3 adding sinusoids: complex waves

There are many cyclic (periodic) patterns in nature, but most are not as simple as the harmonic motion of a pendulum. More complicated patterns are built up as one kind of motion is laid on another. Imagine trying to write in cursive while under the influence of too much caffeine. Your hand will still sweep through the basic motions, but there may be a tremor overlaid, so that the resulting line is bumpy rather than smooth. Or imagine our pendulum clock is now on the deck of a ship, so that the smaller motion of the pendulum is carried on the larger motion of the waves, which interferes with it. (Keeping time at sea was in fact a very real problem in navigation for hundreds of years.) There is the day-to-day variation in temperature, overlaid on the seasonal cycle. Or think of the moon, carried around the Earth, carried around the sun, carried around the spiraling galaxy. Things generally do not move to just one pattern: they are affected by many patterns at once.

To take a very simple example, imagine a child in his father's backpack, bouncing along as his father jogs along the deck of a (big) ship. The child's actual position in space will depend both on the large up and down motion of the ship and the smaller up and down motion of his father's step. Each of these motions is represented as a sinusoid in Figure 6.5: the big, slow motion of the ship in black and the small, fast motion of the jogger in orange.

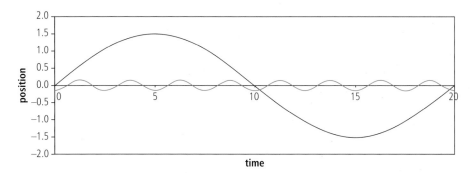

Figure 6.5   Movements of a jogger (orange) and a ship (black).

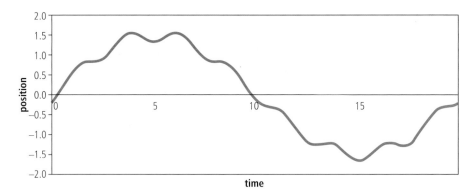

Figure 6.6   Movements of a jogger *on* a ship.

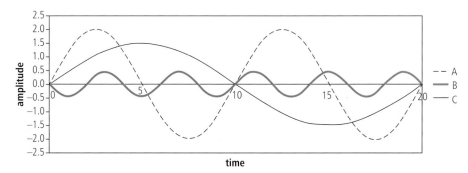

Figure 6.7   Three sinusoids: A 100 Hz, B 250 Hz, C 50 Hz.

Sometimes, the father's step will add an extra bit of height, sometimes it will subtract a bit of height. To get the child's actual position, you simply add the two waves, as in Figure 6.6.

The child is carried up and down with the ship, and on top of that, up and down with his father's stride. The wave that results from graphing the child's position is not itself a sinusoid. It is a *complex wave*, created by adding two simple sinusoids.

The algebra extends to more complicated cases. Where there are interacting forces, you simply add the amplitudes of the positive forces, and subtract the amplitudes of the negative forces. Figure 6.7 shows three sinusoids of differing frequencies and amplitudes. The amplitude scale is relative rather than absolute.

Wave A (dashed) completes one cycle in 10 ms (10/1000ths of a second). Its frequency is thus 100 Hz (1000/10). Wave B (orange) completes 5 cycles in 20 ms, for a period of 4 ms, and thus a frequency of 250 Hz (1000/4). Wave C (black) has period of 20 ms, and thus a frequency of 50 Hz (1000/20). The graph also shows that A has a peak amplitude of 2 units, B has a peak amplitude of .5 units, and C has a peak amplitude of 1.5 units. This frequency and amplitude information is displayed in bar graph form in Figure 6.8. The three waves are graphed as three bars, with frequency on the x-axis and amplitude on the y-axis. Recall that frequency and amplitude are all that we need to know to define a sinusoid (phase being unimportant for defining speech sounds). A graph of frequency and amplitude like that in Figure 6.9 is called a *spectrum*.

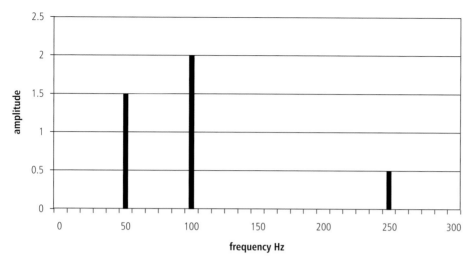

Figure 6.8   Spectrum of the three waves in Figure 6.7.

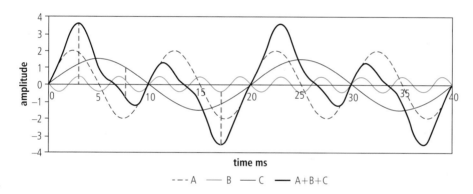

--- A   —— B   — C   —— A+B+C

Figure 6.9   Sum of the three waves in Figure 6.7.

Figure 6.9 shows the algebraic sum of the three waves. The heavy line shows the sum, the original lines are shown in lighter colors.

Every point on the heavy solid line corresponds to the algebraic sum of the values of A, B, and C at that time. A few example points, indicated by heavy dashed lines in Figure 6.9, are listed in Table 6.1.

At time 3 ms, all three waves are positive, so their sum is also positive. At time 17 ms, all three waves are negative, so their sum is also negative. At time 8 ms, the three waves are pushing in different directions: A is strongly negative, C is somewhat positive, B happens to be passing through 0. Their sum is a negative number. At time 20 ms, all three waves have completed a cycle (2 for A, 5 for B, 1 for C) and all are passing through 0. The pattern then begins again.

The result of adding the sinusoids is a *complex wave*. While not sinusoidal itself, the complex wave is periodic. Its cycle repeats every 20 ms, so its frequency is 50 Hz. Because a complex wave is made up of some number of component frequencies, this basic frequency, the rate at which the whole pattern repeats, is called the *fundamental frequency (F0)*. It is F0

Table 6.1   Sums of sinusoids.

time	A	B	C	A+B+C
3 ms	+1.9	+0.45	+1.2	+3.55
8 ms	−1.9	0	+0.88	−1.02
17 ms	−1.9	−0.45	−1.2	−3.55
20 ms	0	0	0	0

that determines the pitch (the note) of a sound wave. The loudness of the sound depends on both frequency and amplitude, but for a given F0, the greater the overall amplitude, the louder the sound. The component frequencies are called *harmonics*. The differing frequencies and amplitudes of the component harmonics give the sound its quality: what makes an A440 played on a violin different from the same note played on a piano. The syllables [la] and [lo] sung on the same note with the same loudness will have the same fundamental frequency and same overall amplitude, but different component frequencies: a different spectrum. You can think of the complex sound as a kind of chord: the effect of a whole set of tuning forks, of different frequencies and amplitudes, being struck at once. Each one adds its own contribution to the overall sound quality.

The fundamental frequency is always equal to the greatest common factor of the component frequencies. For components of 50 Hz, 150 Hz, and 250 Hz, F0 of the complex wave is 50 Hz. If you think about it, it is at the 50 Hz point (20 ms) where all the waves line up and start over again together. The more sinusoids you add together, the more complex and fast-changing a pattern you can create. (More details on the math of harmonic structure are given in Section 8.1.2 on p. 153.)

It is important to understand that Figures 6.8 and 6.9 convey *the same information*, in different ways. We know that the complex squiggle in Figure 6.10 is the sum of a set of sinusoids, and that sinusoids are defined by their frequency and amplitude. So the complex shape of Figure 6.9 is fully described by the spectrum in Figure 6.8. If we know the spectral information in Figure 6.8, we know everything we need to know about the squiggle in Figure 6.9. We know its fundamental frequency, which defines its pitch, and we know the frequencies and amplitudes of its components, which define its quality. Because the harmonic structure provides us with crucial information, the spectrum is an extremely useful way of representing speech sounds, often more useful than the more direct but unanalyzed waveform.

We have seen in this series of figures that simple waves can be added up to make complex waves. What Fourier showed in 1807 is that the process also works the other way: an arbitrary complex wave can be broken down into simple sinusoids. The math for doing a Fourier analysis is more complicated (it takes calculus rather than algebra, and is touched on in Section 8.2.3 on p. 165) but the point is that any complex wave can be broken down. This figuring out the components of a complex wave is what much of acoustic phonetics is about.

Before we can consider the complex sounds of speech, however, we need to understand the way that sound travels, beginning with the effect that the moving tuning fork has on the surrounding air. Understanding the pressure variations produced in the air by a tuning fork will also give us the tools we need to describe the range of air pressure changes to which the human ear is sensitive. Thus, we next consider how sound pressure waves move out from the source – that is, how they *propagate*.

6.4 sound propagation

Sound travels outward from the source as a *wave*. A wave is a disturbance (a change in shape or in energy level) that travels *through* a medium. The simplest example is probably a "wave" that travels around a football stadium. One person stands up and sits down, then the person next to her, then the person next to him, then the person next to him: the motion of each person is triggered by and in turn triggers the motion of an adjacent person. The stand-up-sit-down disturbance travels through the crowd, but no single person moves away from her or his seat.

A second example is the cracking of a whip. A flick of the wrist imparts energy in the form of a bulge (a wave) at the near end of the cord. The energy (bulge, wave) travels down the cord, until it is released at the far end with a snap. The wave travels down the whip, but the whip never leaves the driver's hand.

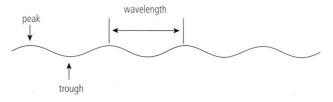

Figure 6.10   Ripples on the surface of a pond.

Third, consider dropping a pebble into the center of a calm pond. The drop of water that the pebble lands on is momentarily pushed down, then bobs up again. Just like the pendulum that overshoots its rest position after being displaced, the drop of water bobs up above its rest position, producing a small bulge, then drops down again, then bobs up. In other words, it oscillates, in simple harmonic motion, up and down. But the drop of water in the center of the pond is not alone: when it starts bobbing up and down, it pulls the adjacent droplets along with it. They too start bobbing up and down, slightly delayed from the original mover. And those droplets have an effect on the drops they are adjacent to, and those on the ones they are adjacent to, so that the bobbing motion moves out in concentric circles from the center of the pond. An observer above the pond would see ripples – waves – moving out from the center of the pond to the edges. The ripples do not carry all the water in the pond out with them: they move *through* the water, as each droplet affects the one next to it. (It is true that waves eventually crash onto the beach, carrying a volume of water with them, but the crashing occurs when increasingly shallow depth interferes with the up and down motion, holding the bottom of the wave back and causing the top to curl over. Despite all the waves crashing on the beach, the sea is never emptied.)

The movement of any one water particle, bobbing up and down in simple harmonic motion, can be described with a sinusoid. A sinusoid can also describe the shape of the surface of the pond after a few ripples have passed through. At a given moment, some areas of the pond will be at a crest (maximum positive displacement), some (a little to the right or the left) will be passing through the rest position, either on the way up or on the way down, others will be at the bottom of a trough (maximum negative displacement.). The surface will look, in fact, like Figure 6.10: another sinusoid. The amplitude of the wave in Figure 6.10 is less than that in Figure 6.3, but the shape is the same. If the x-axis in Figure 6.10 is distance, the graph describes the state of some stretch of the water at a given point in time, and the distance from one peak to the next is the *wavelength*.

Another familiar formula describes the relationship between period and wavelength:

Formula 6.2

$$\text{Distance} = \text{Rate} * \text{Time}$$

When we're talking about waves, Distance = Wavelength (the distance from one peak to the next). Rate = the speed at which the motion propagates from one particle to the next. This will depend on the properties of the medium through which the wave is moving, water vs. syrup, for example. Time = period, the amount of time it takes to generate one full cycle. That is, the distance between peaks depends on how much time elapses between the generation of each peak and how fast the disturbance propagates.

Formula 6.3

$$\text{Distance} = \text{Rate} * \text{Time}$$

$$\text{Wavelength} = \text{Speed} * \text{Period, or (since } P = 1/F)$$

$$\text{Wavelength} = \text{Speed/Frequency or}$$

$$\text{Frequency} = \text{Speed/Wavelength}$$

For sound waves, the rate at which the energy propagates through the air is approximately 340 meters per second (or 770 mph), slightly more or less depending on factors like temperature, humidity and elevation. So the wavelength of our 440 Hz orchestral A is 340 meters/sec divided by 440 cycles/sec, or 0.773 meters/cycle. The "crests" of sound pressure emanating from the first violin are spread out in space just about as far as each musician's chair is from the next.

There is an important difference, however, in the definition of the "crest" of a sound wave compared to a water wave. Each of these first three examples – the stadium wave, a whip, ripples on a pond – is what is known as a *transverse* wave. In a transverse wave, the motion of individual particles is perpendicular to the motion of the wave. Each person stands up and sits down, but the wave moves sideways through the crowd. In contrast, waves of sound are *longitudinal* waves. The motion of the individual particles is *parallel* to the motion of the wave.

Longitudinal waves are harder to visualize. One type of system through which longitudinal waves move is a spring, like a slinky® toy. Stretch out a slinky across a table (for real or in your mind's eye) and hold it at both ends. Give one end a quick push forward and back (not side to side, but parallel to the length of the spring). An area of *compression*, where the coils of the spring are pressed together, will travel down the spring and bounce back. If you stretch the spring to the right tension, the area of compression may bounce back and forth more than once. Following the area of compression will be an area of *rarefaction*, where the coils of the spring are stretched out. The compression followed by rarefaction moves down the spring just like a bulge moves down a whip or a ripple moves over a pond. This pattern of compression followed by rarefaction, moving down the line, is a particular kind of longitudinal wave, a *pressure wave*.

The step from a slinky to sound is quite simple. Imagine that the coils of the spring are molecules of air. (In order to understand sound, we need to look as small as the molecular level.) When the slinky is in its rest position, the coils/particles are evenly distributed, and the pressure is neutral. As the wave moves down the spring, the areas of compression correspond to areas of comparatively higher air pressure, and the areas of rarefaction correspond to areas of comparatively lower air pressure. The driving force is not the motion of your hand, but the push and pull of the back and forth motion of a tuning fork. The pressure wave is now a sound wave.

6.5 decibels

How big are the pressure variations in a sound wave? In one sense, not very. The loudest sound that a person can experience without pain and damage to the ear will have a peak of compression that corresponds to less than .002 pounds per sq. in. Compare that to a pressure of 30 psi in a bicycle tire.

On the other hand, the *range* of pressures to which the ear is sensitive is quite large. The loudness of a sound as we experience it is actually proportional to the amount of energy that is present in the wave, its *intensity*. Intensity is a function of both amplitude and frequency: both how big and how fast the pressure variations are. Energy is measured in watts per m^2. (The watt, of course, is another unit named after a person. James Watt improved the steam engine and helped usher in the Industrial Revolution.) The sound of a jet engine at 3 m (about the loudest sound that will be experienced as sound, the "threshold of pain") has an intensity of about 10 watts per m^2. That's just the sound wave, remember, not the actual jet propulsion. The sound of a mosquito at 3 m (about the softest sound a healthy young human can hear, the "threshold of hearing") has an intensity of 10^{-12} watts per m^2. That amount of energy moves an air particle only about a billionth of a cm. Neither of those intensities is very great in absolute terms, compared, for example, to the energy given off by a 60-watt light bulb, but the range of intensities is more than a billion to one.

Table 6.2   A logarithmic scale.

Number	Exponential notation	Logarithm
1	10^0	0
10	10^1	1
100	10^2	2
1,000	10^3	3
10,000	10^4	4
...	...	...
100,000,000,000	10^{11}	11
1,000,000,000,000	10^{12}	12

For a range that big, we need a *logarithmic* scale. A logarithmic scale compares values based on exponents, or powers of 10. A logarithmic scale for some of the numbers between 1 and 1 trillion is shown in Table 6.2. The number $100 = 10^2$, so $100 = 2$ on a logarithmic scale. The number 1 trillion $= 10^{12}$, so 1 trillion $= 12$ on a logarithmic scale. An odd point about logarithmic scales is that $1 = 0$, because $1 = 10^0$.

The logarithmic scale used for measuring sound intensity is the *decibel* scale. The unit is named after Alexander Graham Bell. (You know Bell invented the telephone, but you may not have known that both his father and grandfather were speech scientists, and that both his mother and his wife were deaf. Bell started investigating the technology that led to the telephone in order to develop a hearing aid.) The original intensity unit, the Bel, turned out to be a little too unwieldy, so it is more common to measure sound intensities in tenths of Bels, or deci-Bels, *dB*. Again, capitalize the B for Bel. The unit is defined as follows:

Formula 6.4

decibel (dB) = 10 times the log of the ratio of two sound intensities

The definition is not complicated if you break it down. First, the scale consists of comparisons (ratios) of one sound intensity to another. So it is never entirely accurate to say that some sound is a certain number of decibels loud. Rather, a sound is a certain number of decibels *louder* than another sound. (In fact, it is not accurate to say that decibels measure loudness at all. The decibel is a measure of intensity. Loudness is how we *experience* intensity – it cannot be measured with an exterior device.) Second, the scale is logarithmic: because the range of values is so big, one looks at the *log* of the ratio (the power of 10) rather than the ratio itself. Third, because we are measuring in decibels, not Bels, you have to multiply by 10. So, if sound A has an intensity 1,000 times greater than that of sound B, the ratio of A:B is 1,000 to 1. $1,000 = 10^3$, so the log of the ratio is 3. 10 times 3 = 30. Therefore, 1000 times greater intensity equals 30 dB. The sound of the jet engine has 1 trillion times the energy of the sound of the mosquito (10^{12} to 1), for a difference of 120 dB.

In measuring decibels, it is common to use the threshold of hearing (the "softest" sound detectable by human ears) as Sound B in the ratio. Some commonly cited decibel levels of various sounds, compared to the threshold of hearing, are listed in Table 6.3. Actual values, of course, will vary: obviously not all alarm clocks or trucks are the same. Distances are included because energy, and therefore intensity, drops off exponentially as distance increases.

Doubling the intensity of a sound adds 3 dB. ($2 = 10^{.3}$, so 10 times the log of the ratio 2:1 is 3) So if one mosquito is 0 dB, two mosquitoes are 3 dB. One person talking is 60 dB, two people talking are 63 dB. One motorcycle is 100 dB, two motorcycles are 103 dB. That's the nature of a logarithmic scale.

6.6 resonance

Thus far, we have seen that sound waves propagate out through a medium (air) from a vibrating source (a tuning fork). We have thus far only considered the propagation of pure

Table 6.3   Some commonly reported decibel levels.

Sound Source	Ratio of Intensities (compared to Threshold of Hearing)	dB
Mosquito at 3 m	10^0:1 (1:1)	0
Breathing	10^1:1	10
Rustling leaves, ticking watch	10^2:1	20
Whisper	10^3:1	30
Rain on the roof	10^4:1	40
Background office noise	10^5:1	50
Normal conversation	10^6:1	60
Car radio, rush hour traffic	10^7:1	70
Alarm clock	10^8:1	80
Truck traffic, from the sidewalk	10^9:1	90
Motorcycle at 1 m, chainsaw	10^{10}:1	100
Ambulance siren	10^{11}:1	110
Gunshot, fireworks, or jet engine, close range	10^{12}:1	120
Threshold of pain	10^{13}:1	130

 ## 6.2   In Focus

According to the National Institute on Deafness and other Communication Disorders (part of the American National Institutes of Health), prolonged exposure to any sound over 85 dB will cause gradual hearing loss, and exposure to any sound 130 dB or more will cause immediate damage. The decibel level at live concerts routinely reaches 120 dB and above. Crowd noise at the playoff (American) football game between the New Orleans Saints and Indianapolis Colts in January 2010 reached 102 decibels (according to Fox Broadcasting, which televised the game); crowd noise as high as 120 dB at football (soccer) matches have been reported by the BBC. The earbuds of an MP3 player at full volume, fit snugly in the ear, easily reach 100 dB, a level that can begin to cause damage after only 15 minutes of exposure. So turn your iPods down! (More info at http://www.nidcd.nih.gov/health/hearing/.)

tones, which can be defined by a sinusoid of a given amplitude and frequency. The pitch of the pure tone thus produced is proportional to the frequency of the oscillation. The loudness of the tone is proportional to its intensity, which is a function of both frequency and amplitude. We now need to consider more complex vibrations, and what happens when waves interact.

When we strike a tuning fork or push a swing, we set it into *free vibration*. The frequency of the vibration depends on the mass, shape, and stiffness of the object to which energy is applied. Every object has a basic frequency, or set of frequencies, at which it will naturally oscillate when energy is applied. This is called a *natural resonant frequency*. A pendulum has a particular frequency depending on its length. If you strike a bell, or pluck a guitar string, a certain note will be produced, and that note will depend on the physical properties of the object. A large bell will give off a lower note than a small one, because it vibrates more slowly. A thick or lax string will vibrate more slowly and give off a lower note than a thin, taut one.

Even things that do not usually make noise have natural resonant frequencies. If you thump on a table or slam a door, the sound that is made depends on the natural frequencies of the object. A big heavy door makes a deeper sound than a small, light one. The noise does not last because doors and tables are very highly damped – the vibration dies right out. A bell, like a tuning fork, is lightly damped, and continues vibrating (ringing) quite a while after the energy is applied.

Strings and bells, however, do not vibrate in simple harmonic motion. Their patterns of vibration are more complex. Since we know that complex oscillations can be broken down into the sum of a set of sinusoids (Section 6.3 above), we can think of a guitar string, for example, as vibrating at several frequencies at once. If you pluck a guitar string, there is a basic back and forth motion, which gives the fundamental frequency (F0), corresponding to the note that is played. But there are also smaller ripples moving up and down the string – like the wave moving down the whip, or like ripples in a flag. As was noted above, it is these additional frequencies (further modified by the body of the instrument) that give the note of a musical instrument a richer sound than a tuning fork. The fundamental frequency of the plucked string, as well as its component harmonic frequencies, is determined by the string length and tension. Only certain wavelengths of vibration will "fit" into the string in such a way that continued vibration can be sustained. Basically, certain waves bounce back and forth in such a way as to continually reinforce once another rather than cancel each other out. (The formulae for figuring this out are given in Section 8.1.2 on p. 153.) Patterns of vibration that are sustained by continual self-reinforcement in an oscillating system are called *standing waves*. Any frequency that can set up as a standing wave will be resonant frequency of that object.

Free vibration occurs when energy is applied once and the system is left to oscillate on its own. You strike the bell or pluck the string, and let the natural note sound. It's possible, however, to force an object to oscillate at any frequency at all, but such *forced vibration* takes the continued application of energy. Consider the playground swing again. As a pendulum, the swing has a natural frequency that depends on its length. If you want the swing to oscillate at a different rate, you could grab it and run back and forth. This would force the swing to oscillate at exactly the rate at which you're running, but a lot of energy would get used up.

To get the maximum movement from the swing with the minimum input of energy, you (as a wise caregiver, who has to last the afternoon) would want to supply energy *synchronized* with the natural frequency of the swing. If you repeatedly give the swing a push forward just when it is moving forward on its own, the swing will go higher and higher. (Happy child, rested caregiver.) On the other hand, if you try to push the swing forward when its natural frequency is causing it to swing back, the two opposite forces cancel, and movement crashes to a stop. (Tears all around.) If your frequency of pushing is synchronized with the natural frequency of the swing, the two systems (swing and caregiver) are in *resonance*. When energy is applied in resonance with a natural frequency, the amplitude of movement at that frequency is increased, because the two forces are acting together. When energy is applied that is not in resonance with a natural frequency, that energy is quickly dissipated because the forces are canceling each other out, and amplitude at that frequency dies out.

Let's return to sound waves. As the tuning fork vibrates, it forces its pattern of vibration on the surrounding air particles. Think of the tine of the tuning fork pushing and pulling on its neighboring chunk of air. Because the particles are free to move in space, the *frequency response* of open air is quite broad – the particles will resonate across any range of frequencies the tuning fork or other vibrating object imposes on them. (*Enclosed* bodies of air work differently, as discussed below.)

The sound energy, in turn, will attempt to force its pattern of vibration on objects in its path as it propagates from the source. The alternating pulses of compression will "beat" on the object they encounter, applying pushes of energy, just like the caregiver pushing the swing. Some of that energy will be transferred to the object the sound wave encounters. Certain objects, like an eardrum or the membrane of a microphone, also have a broad frequency response: they will mimic the vibration of the air particles quite accurately, within a broad range.

Other objects do not respond so freely: they are "tuned" to resonate only to a narrow frequency band (or series of bands). If the frequency of the "driving" sound energy happens to match the natural resonant frequency of the object, the object will vibrate in resonance with the sound, passing along the pattern of vibration at a high amplitude. If the frequency of the sound does not match the natural frequency of the object, the sound energy will be dissipated, and the pattern of vibration will die out. The resonating body thus acts as a *filter*, allowing only some frequencies to get through: resonant frequencies are amplified, other frequencies are lost.

6.3   Resonance is how a soprano breaks a wineglass. The glass has a natural frequency, which may be within the soprano's range. If the soprano sings loud enough on exactly the right note, the energy in her voice pulsing against the glass will cause the glass to vibrate in resonance. If the amplitude of vibration becomes big enough as more and more sound energy is applied, the glass will shatter. Not any note will break the glass, however: only one that corresponds to its own natural frequency. Other notes will not induce resonance.

At the other end of the scale, a sheetrock wall has a low natural frequency. A wall is also highly damped, so all sound vibrations that pass through it are muffled to some degree, but the low frequency sounds are transferred with the highest amplitude, while high frequency sounds are filtered out. Thus you are more likely to be able to hear the thumping bass from your neighbor's sound system than the higher tuneful notes.

6.7 the vocal tract as a sound-producing device: source-filter theory ———

What do objects like a playground swing or a wineglass have to do with speech? Though the result is different, the physics are the same. The vocal tract is a resonating system. In a vowel sound, the vibrating vocal folds provide the driving force, which induces resonance in the air trapped in the vocal tract. The energy is output as sound. This way of thinking of speech sounds is called *source-filter theory*.

Vocal tract sound *sources* may be periodic or aperiodic. The vibrating vocal folds provide a periodic source, which dominates in sonorants. An aperiodic source is most important for obstruents. The swirling turbulence created by a fricative (or by the open glottis in aspiration) is sustained aperiodic noise; the release burst of a stop is a transient. Some sounds, such as voiced stops and fricatives, combine the two sources.

We begin with the periodic source. Given the right amount of tension and the right amount of airflow, the vocal folds will flap open and closed in the column of air, providing repeated bursts of air pressure. Being thick and soft, the vocal folds undulate, with ripples moving along both their length and thickness. The complex vibration of the vocal folds provides a rich source, composed of multiple harmonic frequencies.

By itself, however, the vibration of the vocal folds does not sound like speech: it sounds like buzzing, or a duck call. Sonorant speech sounds are formed when the complex harmonics of vocal fold vibration are *filtered* by the vocal tract. Frequencies in the source that correspond to a resonant frequency of a particular vocal tract shape are amplified; those that do not match up with a resonant frequency are damped out. Which frequencies are passed through the filter and which are cancelled depends on the shape of the body of air contained in the vocal tract, which, of course, depends on the position of the articulators. Different tongue and lip positions create different resonance frequencies, and thus different vowel sounds.

Enclosed bodies of air, like the other physical systems described above, have natural resonant frequencies. The air inside the vocal tract can be considered as a column or tube. (The tube is bent around the tongue, but that matters very little, since sound propagates in all directions and easily moves around curves.) The crucial factor in determining the resonant frequencies of a column of air is the *length* of the column. We know from experience that columns of air of different lengths have different resonant frequencies, because they produce different notes. Think of a set of organ pipes: small ones have a high note, large ones a low note. The note produced by blowing over the top of a bottle depends on whether the bottle is empty (long column of air, low note) or mostly full (short column of air, high note). All of the wind instruments make music based on different resonances of columns of air of different lengths: the air inside a piccolo resonates at a high frequency, the air inside a bassoon resonates at a low frequency. The exact note is controlled by varying the effective length of the instrument, either through actually making it longer, like the slide on a trombone, or using valves to let the air out early, effectively making it shorter.

To understand why length is the crucial factor, we need to understand one more property of propagating sound waves: they bounce. When sound waves are traveling through one medium and hit another, some of the energy is transferred to the new medium through forced vibration, but some (how much depends on the relative size, shape, and materials involved) bounces back. As was noted in Chapter 1, sound travels through the air but bounces back from a cliff face or wall, creating an echo. Sound waves travel through the water but bounce off the ocean bottom or a submarine, creating a sonar image.

In the case of an echo off a mountainside, the distance is such that there is a delay between the outgoing wave and the returning wave. They do not interfere with each other, and the echo comes back clearly. In smaller enclosed spaces, however, the different waves bouncing off the walls will interact. In most cases, the interaction will be random: think of the cacophony created by sound waves bouncing around a noisy school cafeteria. In other cases, however, when specific conditions hold, the waves will interact to specific effect.

Under some conditions the outgoing wave and the echoing wave may interact to negative effect. The two waves may exactly cancel each other out, creating a "dead spot" in a room. Alternatively, the two waves may interact positively, the outgoing wave and echoing wave both pushing in the same direction at the same time. Under the right conditions (the formulas are given in Section 8.1.3 on p. 156), the right ratio of wavelength to room length or tube length, a sound wave of a given frequency, bouncing back and forth in an enclosed space, will continually reinforce itself, the interacting crests all pushing in the same direction at a given time, maintaining a high amplitude. This continual reinforcement creates a standing wave, that is, resonance. Other frequencies, of different wavelengths, interact randomly or negatively, so that their energy is quickly dissipated. The science of architectural acoustics deals exactly with this issue: managing the size and shape of a room, and the materials in it, so that bouncing sound waves do not interfere with each other in unwanted ways. Whether you want sound waves enhanced or cancelled, of course, depends on whether you are managing the acoustics of a concert hall or a school cafeteria.

In speech, different-shaped tubes of air are created by moving the tongue and lips. The complex of frequencies input by the vibrating vocal folds (or the noise of a fricative or burst) are filtered by these tubes. Resonant frequencies of particular tube lengths are amplified, other frequencies are damped out. Thus, the sound output from the lips has a different combination of component frequencies and amplitudes, a different spectrum, depending on vocal tract shape. The amplified resonance frequencies are called *formants*. The differing spectra, that is, different relationships among the formants, create different vowel qualities.

chapter summary

In this chapter, we have slowly worked our way up from the simplest of sounds to the most complex.

- Sounds can be periodic (repeating) or aperiodic (noisy).
- The simplest sound is a pure tone, such as that produced by a tuning fork. A tuning fork, like a pendulum, moves in simple harmonic motion.
- Simple harmonic motion can be graphed as a sinusoid, defined by frequency, amplitude, and phase. Frequency is correlated with pitch, and amplitude with loudness.
- Complex waves can be defined as the sum of a set of sinusoids of differing amplitudes and frequencies. The different component sinusoids are harmonics. A graph of the frequency and amplitude of harmonic components is a spectrum.
- The rate at which the overall pattern of a complex wave repeats is the fundamental frequency (F0).
- Sound waves are longitudinal pressure waves.
- Sound intensity is measured on the logarithmic decibel scale.
- All objects have natural resonant frequencies. When energy is applied at a natural resonant frequency, the source of the energy and the vibrating system are in resonance.
- In the source/filter theory of speech, the source of sound energy can be either periodic (vocal folds) or aperiodic (fricative or burst noise). The complex source is filtered by the vocal tract, whose natural resonance frequencies are determined by lip and tongue shape. Frequencies that match a vocal tract resonance are passed along with high amplitude; these frequencies are called formants. Frequencies that do not match a vocal tract resonance are filtered out.

Some basic acoustic formulas:

Period = 1/frequency

Wavelength = speed/frequency

Speed of sound (in air) = 340 m/sec

dB = 10 times the log of the ratio of two sound intensities

further reading

Fry, D.B. 1978. *The Physics of Speech*. Cambridge: Cambridge University Press.

review exercises

1. Fill in the blanks using the words in the word bank below.
   a. The three properties that define a sinusoidal wave are its
       1. _____
       2. _____
       3. _____
   b. Our perception of the _____ of a sound is determined by the amount of energy in the system (intensity), largely proportional to the amplitude of the vibration.
   c. Our perception of the _____ of a sound is determined by the frequency of the vibration.
   d. Another term for cycles per second is _____.
   e. A very brief sound (such as a bang or click) is a _____.
   f. A vibratory system, like a pendulum, that can be described by a simple sinusoid, is moving in _____.
   g. The tendency for vibrations to lose energy and die down is _____.
   h. A sound with a repeating pattern of vibration is _____.
   i. The sound produced by a simple sinusoidal wave is a _____.
   j. The component frequencies of a complex wave are called _____.
   k. A graph of the component frequencies of a complex wave is called a _____.
   l. A wave in which particle movement is parallel to the direction of wave propagation is a _____ wave.
   m. A wave in which particle movement is perpendicular to the direction of wave propagation is a _____ wave.
   n. An area of lowered air pressure is an area of _____.
   o. The frequencies at which an object or system will freely vibrate are _____ frequencies.
   p. The source of sound energy in a sonorant sound is the vibration of the _____.
   q. The resonant frequencies of a column of air depend on the _____ of the column.
   r. The resonant frequencies of a particular vocal tract shape are termed _____.

   Word bank. No term is used more than once; some terms are not used.

Amplitude	Hertz	Rarefaction
Aperiodic	Length	Resonant
Compression	Longitudinal	Simple Harmonic Motion
Damping	Loudness	Spectrum
Formants	Periodic	Transient
Fourier	Phase	Transverse
Frequency	Pitch	Vocal folds
Harmonics	Pure Tone	Watt

   (Continued)

2. Express these times in seconds:

   1,000 ms   400 ms   20 ms   3456 ms   3 ms

3. What is the frequency (in Hz) of a sine wave whose period is as follows?:

   0.02 sec   5 ms   100 ms   2 ms   .015 sec

4. What is the period (in ms) of a sine wave whose frequency is as follows?:

   300 Hz   1000 Hz   850 Hz   120 Hz

5. Calculate the wavelength (in meters), of sounds of the following frequencies. As the frequency goes up, does wavelength get longer or shorter?

   500 Hz   1200 Hz   8000 Hz

6. Convert the following ratios of sound intensities to dB.

   10,000 to 1   2:1   a million to 1

7. Convert the following dB levels to ratios of sound intensity:

   50 dB   80 dB   10 db

Go online Visit the book's companion website for additional resources related to this chapter at: http://www.wiley.com/go/zsiga.

7 Looking at Speech
Waveforms, Spectra, and Spectrograms

Acoustic phonetics is still something of a novelty for students of language, many of whom treat it either with great suspicion or with uncomprehending admiration. This state of affairs is an unhealthy one. . . . The following pages were written with the aim of doing something towards remedying this unsatisfactory situation.

Morris Halle, 1958, *The Sound Pattern of Russian*, p. 79

Chapter outline

The Sounds of Language: An Introduction to Phonetics and Phonology, First Edition. Elizabeth C. Zsiga.
© 2013 Elizabeth C. Zsiga. Published 2013 by Blackwell Publishing Ltd.

This chapter looks at the tools phoneticians use for analyzing speech sounds. In the second decade of the twenty-first century, these tools are generally computer-based, though this is of course a relatively recent development. Section 7.1 thus begins with the question: "What did phoneticians do before they had computers?" Section 7.2 examines how to get speech into a computer: the process of digitization, with practical tips for making high-quality digital recordings. The next sections discuss what to do with a speech file once you have it. The waveform is the most straightforward way of looking at speech: a representation in the time domain, it is useful for measuring duration. The spectrum is a representation in the frequency domain, useful for determining sound quality. The spectrogram combines the two, allowing the phonetician to view changes in quality over time.

The goal in this chapter is to provide enough information for you to understand these representations when you come across them in published reading. You should also be able to create these representations yourself, using simple menu commands in your chosen analysis program. Section 8.2 on p. 160 provides further in-depth information on algorithms, properties, and problems: this further information should be covered for greater competence and confidence in creating and analyzing your own acoustic representations.

7.1 pre-digital speech

At the beginning of this book, I noted that one of the difficult things about phonetic science is that you cannot see speech. Until quite recently, the phonetician's ears were the only instruments available for the analysis of sound, and they are probably still the most finely-tuned and reliable. (They are certainly still the cheapest and most convenient.) Beginning in the late nineteenth century, however, scientists began to discover ways to make sound both durable and visible.

Devices for recording sound all work by transferring the patterns of speech vibration from the air to some more durable medium. Thus Edison's phonograph (1877) used a stylus to magnify the waves resulting from sound vibrations and etch them into a revolving wax cylinder (later onto a plastic disk). When the stylus ran back over the grooves, the vibration was replicated. Magnetic recorders (invented 1898 and continually improved over the following decades) used a microphone membrane to convert sound vibrations into voltage variation in an electric current. The varying electric current was then used to create a varying magnetic field. A metal wire or tape passed through the field was magnetized in the corresponding pattern. Playback consisted of running the tape back through the magnetic "heads" of the recorder, which converted the magnetic field back to electricity back to membrane vibrations in a speaker. Thus specific sound events could be preserved and replayed.

Devices for making speech visible work on the same principle, except that the medium to which the pattern is transferred is something that can be seen. A device that worked on the same principle as the phonograph was called the *kymograph*. ("Kymo" is Greek for "wave.") Figure 7.1 shows Daniel Jones using a kymograph circa 1920. A talker spoke into a mask connected to a tube, at the other end of which was a pressure-sensitive membrane connected to a stylus. The air-pressure variations of speech caused the membrane and thus the stylus to vibrate. The stylus rested on a revolving drum covered with smoked paper, and as the drum revolved, the stylus etched out a white line that directly recorded air pressure variations.

A copy of one of Jones' kymograph recordings is shown in Figure 7.2. The periodic vibrations of the vowels are evident, as well as some very weak vibration during voiced [b]. The machine was not sensitive enough to record the complexity of the vocalic waveform, but one can clearly see the duration differences. Tense [i] is longer than lax [ɪ], and both vowels are longer preceding voiced consonants than preceding voiceless. The combination of these two tendencies results in a finding that the vowels in "beat" and "bid" are of identical length, a finding not obvious to the ear.

Oscilloscopes and *sound spectrographs*, like tape recorders, used a microphone to transfer patterns of vibration in the air into patterns of variation in electrical current. In an oscilloscope, the variations were displayed as a waveform on a screen. The sound spectrograph worked on a principle similar to Edison's revolving wax cylinder, but used an electronic filter to separate out different frequency bands. This ingenious device was invented in the 1940s at Bell Laboratories (a corporate descendant of Bell Telephone, which was founded, of course, by Alexander Graham). It could only analyze about 2 seconds of speech at a time, enough for two or three words. First, a short speech sample was recorded onto a magnetic disk, in the same way as onto a magnetic tape. Then, the sample was replayed multiple times. Each time, the output was passed through a variable electronic filter, which could be set to let pass only a specific range of electromagnetic frequencies, something like the bass/treble knob on a radio. Rather than emerging as sound, however, the output of the electronic filter was fed into a moving electric stylus, like a wood-burning tool, that would etch a dark line onto chemically-treated paper attached to a revolving drum (Figure 7.3). (It smelled awful – like burning

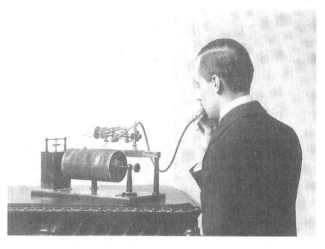

Figure 7.1 Daniel Jones using a kymograph. Source: Collins and Mees 1999, p. 256.

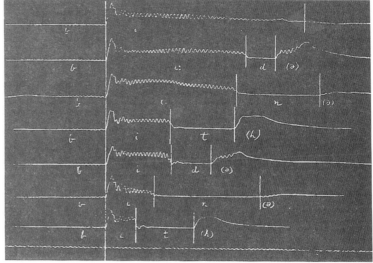

Fig. 129. Mouth-tracings of *bee, bead, bean, beat, bid, bin, bit*, showing lengths of vowels and final consonants. (⅐ original size.)

Figure 7.2 Kymograph recordings of *bee, bead, bean, beat, bid, bin, bit.*
Source: Collins and Mees 1999, p. 250. Originally published in Jones 1918, *Outline of English Phonetics*, p. 179.

rubber.) The stylus would move in increments up the drum as different frequency bands were tested. For each round, the darkness of the burned line was proportional to the amount of electricity coming through the filter, which was in turn proportional to the amount of speech energy within that particular frequency range.

7.2 digitization

At the beginning of the twenty-first century, acoustic analysis is done by computer. Computer analysis is fast, accurate, easily portable on a laptop, available in a few keystrokes, and it does not smell. But computers have an important disadvantage compared to the mechanical and electrical devices of the past: computers cannot handle analog signals.

An *analog* signal is a continuously varying wave, like a second hand sweeping smoothly around an old-fashioned clock face. No matter how closely you look, or how greatly you magnify, the motion is smooth and continuous, not jumping from state to state with pauses or blank spaces between (until you get to the molecular level, anyway). The signal looks like a ramp rather than a staircase. In the real world, speech waves are analog signals, and the electromechanical devices described above all worked on the principle of transforming one type of analog signal into another type: an air pressure wave into an etched line or a varying magnetic field. Computers cannot process these continuous signals, however. In order for a computer to process any information, that information must be represented *digitally*, that is, as a series of numbers.

recording
drum
stylus
variable filter control
magnetic
disk
tumtable
head
heterodyne
frequency
analyser
amplifier

Figure 7.3 Sound spectrograph. Source: Winckel, 1967, p. 160. Reprinted with permission of Dover Publications, Inc.

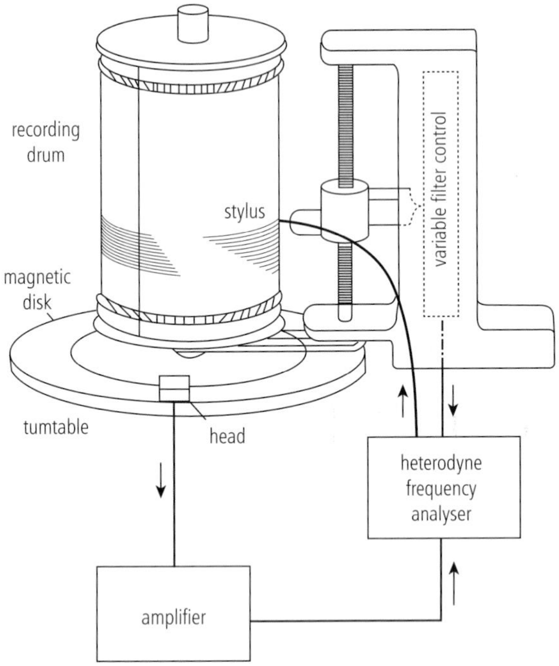

7.2.1 sampling

The analog-to-digital (A-to-D) conversion is accomplished through *sampling*. The process of sampling is nothing more than taking repeated measurements at regular intervals. That is the only way to convert any mass or extent in the

7.1 In Focus

Technically, of course, a computer can handle exactly two digits, 0 and 1, corresponding to *off* and *on*. But any arbitrarily large or arbitrarily exact number can be represented as a series of 0 s and 1 s in base-two (*binary*) notation, where place values are based on exponents of 2 rather than exponents of 10: the 1 s, 2 s, 4 s, 8 s place rather than the 1 s, 10 s, 100 s, 1000 s. The number 5, for example, is represented as 101 in base-two: 1 four, no twos, and 1 one. The conversion to binary numbers happens deep in the computer's programming, so the end user seldom has to worry about it. It is important to remember, however, that a speech signal is represented in a computer as no more and no less than a long string of numbers.

Table 7.1   Temperature sampled every hour on 7/30/2010 in Washington D.C.

temp	80	78	76	75	74	72	71	71	73	75	76	79	80	82	83	84	84	85	83	83	81	78	78	75
time	00	01	02	03	04	05	06	07	08	09	10	11	12	13	14	15	16	17	18	19	20	21	22	23

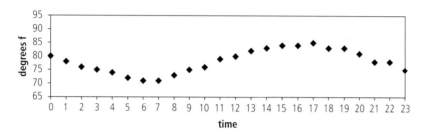

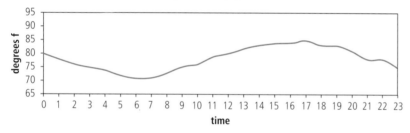

Figure 7.4   Sampled temperature in Washington, D.C. on 7/30/2010. Top, sample values; Bottom, values graphed with a smoothed line.

real world into a number: you measure it. If some value is changing (say, the temperature over the course of a day), and you want to capture the pattern of change, you make repeated measurements, at set intervals (perhaps every hour). So the digital representation of the temperature in Washington, D.C., on July 30, 2010 (according to weather.noaa.gov), might look something like the information in Table 7.1.

One could graph these numbers as a series of points, as in Figure 7.4 (top), and then connect the dots, as in Figure 7.4 (bottom). Figure 7.4 (bottom) *looks* like an analog wave, but it is really the graphical representation of a series of sampled points, the numbers in Table 7.1. Crucially, if some change happened *in between* the sampled points, it would not be captured in the digital representation.

Speech sampling works exactly the same way. A microphone converts the sound pressure wave into variation in electric current, such that the strength of the current is proportional to the air pressure. After some pre-processing (discussed below), the sound card component in the computer measures the voltage of the electric current at regular intervals, and then records the measurements. The record of measurements (a long string of numbers) is the digital representation of the speech wave, just as the record of measurements in Table 7.1 is the digital representation of the temperature.

As of this writing, even the least expensive personal computers (not to mention cell phones) come with a built-in microphone and sound card capable of analog-to-digital conversion. In order to ensure a high-quality signal, however, two questions regarding sampling must be addressed: how often to sample (*sampling rate*), and how precisely (*quantization*).

The more often samples are taken (the higher the sampling rate), the more information the resulting digital representation will contain. In our weather sampling, for example, anything that happens in between the hourly samples is lost. If a thunderstorm came through at 1:15 a.m., briefly lowering the temperature, that temporary dip would not be recorded, since it fell in between the samples taken at 1:00 a.m. and 2:00 a.m. A higher sampling rate of every 15 minutes, however, would show the dip. Relatively fast or short-lived variations can only be captured by a correspondingly high sampling rate.

In the speech domain, the time over which changes take place depends on the frequency components in the signal: high-frequency signals change very quickly (have very short periods), low-frequency signals change less quickly (have longer periods). Since speech (or any complex sound) is made up of a large number of component frequencies, the sampling rate must be fast enough to measure the highest frequencies of interest.

As speech scientists, we're not really interested in measuring frequencies that no-one can hear. Since the range of human hearing goes up to 20,000 Hz, that is pretty much the highest frequency we care about. The period of one cycle at that frequency is 0.00005 seconds. How fast do we have to sample in order to measure a change that fast? Turns out that, mathematically, in order to detect the presence of a sinusoidal component in a complex wave, you have to capture a measurement twice within its period: once in the positive phase and once in the negative phase. Therefore, you have to sample *twice* as fast as the highest frequency you want to measure. If you want to measure frequencies up to 20,000 Hz, you have to take samples 40,000 times per second (that is, every 0.000025 seconds). Computers have no problem measuring that fast. Researchers on bats and whales, animals that transmit and receive frequencies much higher than humans can perceive, routinely sample at rates of 200,000 times per second and above. High-definition video has sampling rates higher still.

The engineer who worked out the mathematical proof of required sampling rates was a Swedish-American immigrant named Harry Nyquist. In his honor, we call the highest frequency that can be captured at a given sampling rate the *Nyquist limit*. The Nyquist limit is always equal to half the sampling rate. The Nyquist limit for a sampling rate of 44,000 samples per second is 22,000 Hz; the Nyquist limit for a sampling rate of 16,000 samples per second is 8,000 Hz, etc.

7.2   Nyquist was an employee of Bell Labs, working on improving telephone communication, when he published his paper on sampling in 1928. Computers, of course, had not been invented yet, but mathematical data compression and information theory were hot topics. Since Nyquist was Swedish, it really should be called the [nykvist] limit, with a front round vowel, but the term has been anglicized to [naɪkwɪst].

An odd effect occurs if frequencies above the Nyquist limit are present in the signal being sampled. This effect, called *aliasing*, is illustrated in Figure 7.5. The original analog signal, in black, has a frequency of 160 Hz (the period is 6.25 ms, and 1/.00625 = 160). The black dots indicate the measured samples, taken every 4 ms. That is a sampling rate of 250 samples/ second, for a Nyquist limit of 125 Hz. That is, 125 Hz is the highest frequency that could be accurately represented at that sampling rate. What happens if a 160 Hz signal is sampled at this rate? Once the signal is sampled, the information between the sampled points is lost. When the computer then connects the dots between the sampled points (the orange line), the wrong shape appears: the connected dots take the shape of a wave of much longer period (therefore much lower frequency). This is aliasing: a high frequency masquerades as a low frequency. Obviously, aliasing would result in distortion of the digital signal.

Aliasing is avoided by removing all frequencies above the Nyquist limit from the sound signal *before* the analog-to-digital conversion takes place. This is generally done automatically by the A-to-D conversion program when the signal is at the electrical stage, by passing the current through a low-pass filter: All frequencies above the Nyquist limit are blocked. The speech scientist therefore does not need to worry about aliasing, but needs to remember that the frequencies in the digital signal are limited: no frequencies above the Nyquist limit are present. If the researcher is interested in measuring high frequencies, she needs to ensure that the sampling rate is high enough: at least twice the highest frequency of interest.

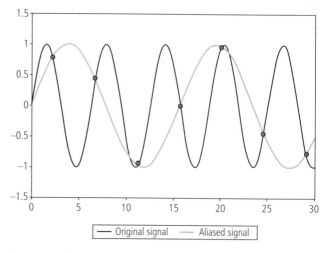

Figure 7.5   Aliasing.
Source: http://commons.wikimedia.org/wiki/File:Aliasing.jpg.

Exactly how to set the sampling rate for a given computer set-up will be highly system-specific, but options should be found among the sound input or recording menus. For engineering reasons (compatibility between the physical properties of different storage and transmission media), the industry standard for digital audio is commonly set to 44,100 samples per second, more than enough to capture the full range of human hearing, and many computer systems default to this rate. Older files, for space-saving reasons (see below), may have been sampled at lower rates, so always check before deciding to use archived material.

7.2.2 quantization

Why not just measure at extremely high sampling rates (high enough for bats, for example) just to be on the safe side? One reason is that sound files very quickly become very big objects. Forty thousand numbers per second take up a lot of computer space (in both storage and in processing), especially if you want to record more than a short sentence or so: why double or triple that number to represent information you are not going to use? Exactly how much space a speech file takes up depends on the precision with which each sample is measured, that is, on *quantization*.

Whenever we take a measurement, we need to decide how precise our measurement needs to be. How much rounding error can we accept? Do we need to be accurate to the nearest kilometer, meter, centimeter, or micron?

In a digital representation, more precise measurements mean allocating more decimal places, and therefore more computer space. A measurement of 1.00001 is more precise than a measurement of 1.0, for example, but those extra zeroes take up more space. In binary notation, every decimal place takes up one bit of storage space (one opportunity to enter 0 or 1). As more bits are assigned, precision increases exponentially, as shown in Table 7.2. If we allocate two bits, we can record four levels (2^2): 00 (very low), 01 (medium low), 10 (medium high), 11 (very high). Going up to 6 bits means we can record up to 64 (2^6) distinct sound pressure levels, and allocating 16 bits per sample is more than 1000 times more precise than

Table 7.2   Relationship between bits per sample and precision of measurement.

Number of bits per sample	Number of levels available
1	$2^1 = 2$
2	$2^2 = 4$
3	$2^3 = 8$
4	$2^4 = 16$
5	$2^5 = 32$
6	$2^6 = 64$
7	$2^7 = 128$
8	$2^8 = 256$
12	$2^{12} = 4,096$
16	$2^{16} = 65,536$

that. Sixty-five thousand levels is slightly more precise than marking off a kilometer in 2 cm intervals.

Generally, as of this writing, computer audio systems will default to 16 bits per sample, although speech sampled at 8 bits does not sound bad. At a sampling rate of 44,100, 16-bit sampling means that each second of speech takes up approximately 705,600 bits, or 88,200 bytes. (The number is approximate because a few bits in each file are needed for other purposes.)

File size was a big problem when computer processing speeds were slower and storage was expensive. If you have occasion to use older digital recordings, it is likely that lower sampling rates and bit rates (16 K or 20 K and 8 bit) were used to save space. (Though some quality is lost, most of the useful information in speech is below 5000 Hz, as we will see.) When processors are fast and terabytes of storage are cheap, file size is much less of a problem, so high sampling rates are commonly used, even if the increase in quality is marginal.

7.2.3 digital recording

Actually recording speech onto a computer or digital recorder is no more difficult than opening an audio program and pushing the record button. Many computers come with audio software installed, and many acoustic analysis programs are available for purchase or download. A very popular program among phoneticians is *Praat* (Dutch for *speech*), developed by Paul Boersma and David Weenink, and (as of this writing) available as a free download at www.praat.org. The waveform and spectrogram figures in this book were created using Praat. Specific keystrokes and menu choices will differ from program to program, but the underlying processes and algorithms are generally consistent.

Done properly, digital recordings will be of better quality than analog tape recordings. In analog recordings, the plastic or metal tape would inevitably stretch and distort, and the noise from the turning cogs and the hiss of the tape traveling through the heads could never be completely eliminated. But digital recordings will not automatically be good just because they are digital, and care needs to be taken in choosing, setting up and using the recording equipment.

Overall, the goal is to maximize the *signal-to-noise ratio (SNR)*. The recording should be as clean and clear as possible: more signal, less noise. In order to get the most signal, the phonetician doing the recording needs to take full advantage of the system's *dynamic range*. The system is set up to respond to a certain range of amplitudes: the incoming signal should use the full range, taking advantage of all the + or − 32,768 levels that a 16-bit system makes available. Turning up the input volume is like using a zoom lens on a camera. You want to adjust the lens so that your image fills the field of vision, and detail in the object is evident. You don't want a frame filled with blank sky, with your subject an indistinct dot in the middle. In the same way, you want your input to use the full available dynamic range.

There will always be a certain amount of background noise. Some of this noise is *quantization error* (or rounding error) in representing the continuous analog signal as a series of discrete levels. The amount of quantization noise is constant, depending on the bit rate. The higher the bit rate, the more levels available, and the lower the quantization error.

Of course, other sources of background noise should be eliminated as well, to the extent possible. You can easily carry your laptop or digital recorder to where your speakers are, but be aware of what else is going on during the recording. It's easy to "tune out" traffic, a TV in the next room, a fan or air conditioner, or people in the hallway, not noticing the level of noise until it's too late. If speakers are reading from a script, they have a tendency to shuffle or turn the pages while they are speaking. Phoneticians who make their recordings in the "field" (that is, anywhere outside a sound-treated laboratory) will always have humorous stories (at least humorous in retrospect) of recordings ruined by a passing rainstorm or herd of goats. (Both true.) For better or worse, however, "the field" is generally where the people are, so do the best you can.

Figure 7.6 shows three digital waveforms from three different recordings of the utterance [ɑb]. The higher-amplitude, more complex portion of the wave is the vowel [ɑ], the lower amplitude portion corresponds to [b]. (These syllables were cut out of longer utterances, another advantage of digital representations: cutting and pasting is no harder in a speech file than in a text file.) The top waveform has a good SNR: it was sampled at 40 K, 16-bits, with very little background noise, and the details in the shape of the wave are clearly evident. The second waveform was digitized in the same way, but recorded in an environment with

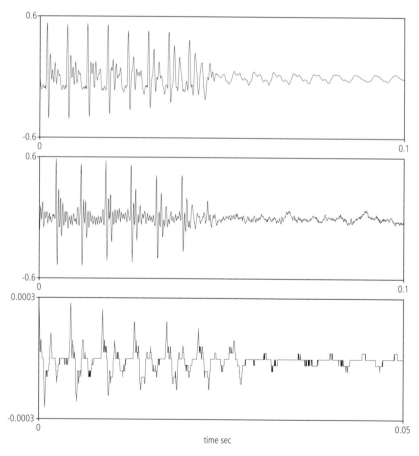

Figure 7.6   Top: 100 ms extracted from the utterance [ɑb], including the end of the vowel and the beginning of the consonant, recorded with a high signal-to-noise ratio. Middle: 100 ms extracted from the utterance [ab], recorded with high background noise, and thus a low signal-to-noise ratio. Bottom: 50 ms from the utterance [a], with an extremely low signal level, and thus low signal-to-noise ratio. Low input volume results in significant quantization noise.

background noise. Note how the noise obscures the details in the [ɑ], and makes it impossible to see the low-amplitude periodicity during the [b]. The third waveform was also sampled at 40 K and 16-bits, but the signal was input with such low amplitude that only about the first +/− 16 levels around 0 were utilized. (If the amplitude scale were not enlarged by a factor of 20,000 compared to the first two signals, the signal would not be visible at all.) Because so few levels are utilized, quantization error is a big factor. The effect is the same as attempting to enlarge a small image in a digital photo: if the object in the image is too small, the enlarged image becomes a blurred collection of pixels, and all detail is lost. The example is extreme, but makes the point that dynamic range matters.

It is important to maximize the dynamic range and minimize background noise, but on the other hand, do not turn the volume up too far. If the amplitude of the incoming signal is greater than the maximum amplitude the system can measure, the result is *clipping*: the high amplitude peaks are cut off, resulting in distortion. (Again, like a camera: don't zoom in so far that part of your image is out of the frame.) Two digital waveforms of the vowel [ɑ] are shown in Figure 7.7. The top waveform fully utilizes the dynamic range: from +1 to −1 (where 1 = 100%). In the bottom waveform, the initial high peaks of each period are cut off, distorting the signal: information about the actual relative amplitude of the different peaks has been destroyed.

In practice, fully utilizing the dynamic range without clipping can be tricky. Speakers tend to raise and lower their voices, turn their heads, shift their bodies around. A head-mounted microphone, set to the side of the speaker's lips, can reduce some of this variation. Always keep an eye on the level meter that should be available on your recorder or in your program, and adjust the input volume, or the position of the microphone, to keep the signal within acceptable levels. If there is not a level meter, use a different system.

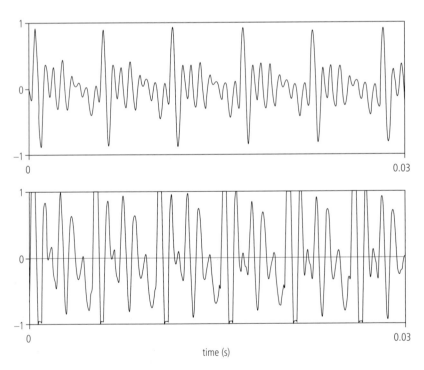

time (s)

Figure 7.7   Top. 30 ms from the vowel [ɑ], using the full dynamic range. Bottom. 30 ms from the vowel [ɑ], with clipping.

Be careful to pick a good microphone. Read the specifications. The best microphones will have a frequency response that is close to the full range of human hearing and a dynamic range of more than 100 dB. You could have the highest sampling rate and bit rate possible, but if the data being fed into the system from a cheap microphone is deficient, so will the digital recording be, and you'll be wasting all those bits. Uni-directional microphones are designed to be used with a single talker: they pick up sound primarily from one direction, so are good at reducing background noise. Omni-directional microphones pick up sound from all directions, so are best for recording more than one speaker on a single channel. The built-in microphone on a laptop is almost never good enough.

Finally, *never* record someone without his or her knowledge. Participants in your research should always know the purpose for which the recording is being made, how the data will be used, and how their privacy will be protected. You may need to get approval for your study from an Institutional Review Board for the protection of human subjects. It might seem unlikely that recording someone's voice could harm them, but research participants have a right to know what's going on, and researchers have a responsibility to protect the participants' interests.

7.3 looking at waveforms

Now that you've got a high-quality speech file into your computer, what can you do with it? Understanding the file as a string of numbers opens up a huge range of possibilities. It is simple to select, cut and paste, amplify portions (multiplication), or play the speech backwards (just reverse the column of numbers). In the remainder of this chapter, we will concentrate on just a few basic skills: looking at and understanding waveforms, spectra, and spectrograms.

The most basic presentation of a speech file is as a waveform. A waveform is a graph of changes in amplitude (air pressure) over time. While it usually is not possible to read the identity of specific segments from a waveform, different classes of sounds have different defining characteristics. These different patterns are illustrated in Figure 7.8, which shows 200 ms waveforms extracted from the utterances [mɑ], [dɑ], [spɑ], [pʰɑ], and [zɑ], spoken by an American English speaker in the frame "Say _____ now."

- In each of the waveforms, it can be seen that vowels will have the highest relative amplitude (remember the mouth is most open), and a complex repeating (periodic) pattern. Differences between the absolute amplitude of the vowels in the different waveforms are just due to variation in how loudly each utterance was spoken.
- Sonorant consonants such as nasals ([mɑ]) and laterals will look a lot like vowels, but with lower amplitude and usually less complexity.
- Voiced stops ([dɑ]) are also periodic, but have a much lower amplitude (the sound of vocal fold opening and closing is "beating" through a closed vocal tract). They will usually have a transient burst at the moment when the closure is released into the vowel. In American English, the periodic energy in [b, d, g] will often die down during the closure, unless the stop is between other voiced sounds.
- Voiceless fricatives have no repeating pattern, but appear as random noise. Strident fricatives ([s], [ʃ]) will have high amplitude, as in [spɑ]. Non-strident fricatives (such as [θ]) may have very low amplitude, and may be hard to distinguish from voiceless stops, especially if the SNR is not excellent. One cue is that fricatives are not followed by a burst.
- Voiceless stops are easy to spot: they are silent during the closure phase (no amplitude) and so appear in a waveform as a flat line (modulo any background noise). They will

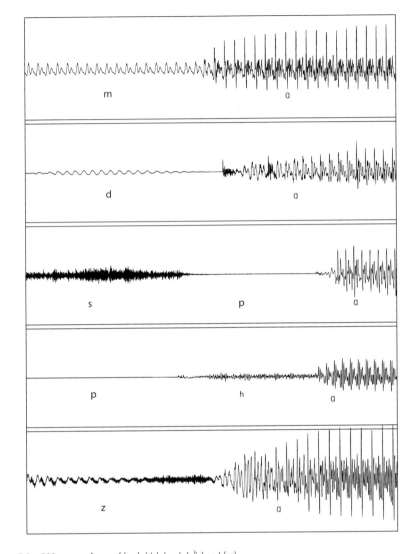

Figure 7.8   200 ms waveforms of [mɑ], [dɑ], [spɑ], [pʰɑ] and [zɑ].

usually be followed by a burst. Aspirated stops will be followed by aspiration noise. Note that the /p/ in [pʰɑ] is aspirated and the /p/ in [spɑ] is not.

- Voiced fricatives combine periodicity and noise. As with voiced stops, the periodicity may die out toward the end of the consonant.

Note that extensive magnification of the waveform is necessary to pick out the details: the waveforms in Figure 7.8 each show only ⅕ of a second. In viewing longer portions of the waveform, different types of segments can usually be picked out by differences in amplitude, as in Figure 7.9, where the distinct segments have been marked in a file two seconds long. Speech analysis programs should allow for easy zooming in and out to different magnifications. The task of marking off the segments is called, reasonably enough, *segmentation*. This particular utterance was chosen as one where landmarks between segments, such as points of closure and release, would be easy to pick out, but this is not always the case. One cannot

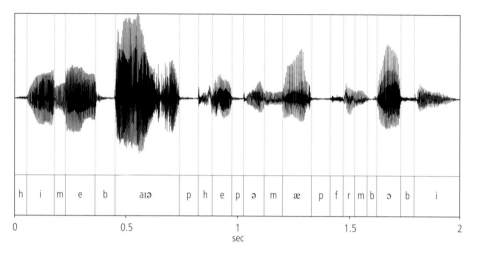

Figure 7.9   A segmented waveform, 2 seconds long: "He may buy a paper map from Bobby."

mark a point in time, for example, where the diphthong changes from [a] to [ɪ]. There is gradual change in the position of the tongue, and thus gradual change in the waveform.

One of the most useful types of information that can be gleaned from a waveform representation is duration of different speech events: how long is a vowel, a consonant closure, a burst? The difference between aspirated and unaspirated consonants is found in differences in *voice onset time (VOT)*: the amount of time that elapses between the release of the consonant and the onset of periodicity for the vowel. In Figure 7.7, the VOT for the in [pʰɑ] is 76 ms and the VOT for the in [spɑ] is 11 ms. While these measures are important, it is very difficult to determine exact segment quality from a waveform. While stops look different from nasals, which look different from vowels, one cannot necessarily tell a [b] from a [d], an [n] from an [l], or an [e] from an [o]. To analyze segment quality, spectral analysis is needed.

7.4 spectra

As was discussed in Chapter 6, complex waves, such as vowel sounds, can be understood as the sum of some number of simple sinusoids. The *quality* of the sound ([e] vs. [o], for example) depends on the frequencies and relative amplitudes of the different sinusoidal components. Spectral analysis allows us to quantify, visualize, and analyze these component frequencies, and thus to quantify, visualize, and analyze the details of sound quality.

Some algorithms for doing spectral analysis are covered in more detail in Sections 8.2.3 and 8.2.4 on p. 167. Essentially, they all involve mathematically analyzing the signal in order to accomplish what the electronic filters in the sound spectrograph did: to test the strength of different frequencies that might be present. In this chapter, we take the math for granted, and examine the results, with the aim of understanding how different frequency components determine different sound qualities.

7.4.1 spectrum of the glottal source

The vibration of the vocal folds is a complex motion. There is the underlying cycle of opening and closing: the fundamental frequency. But overlaid on this fundamental cyclic motion are smaller ripples, which add up a more complex motion.

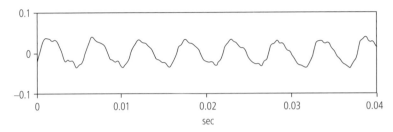

Figure 7.10   Waveform of voicing, an approximation of the glottal waveform.

The actual waveform of glottal vibration, the pressure changes that a microphone would measure if held directly above the vocal folds, before the wave passes through the vocal tract, looks something like Figure 7.10. (This waveform was actually taken from the sound of voicing during [b].)

The shape approximates a "sawtooth" wave: a steep upslope, corresponding to the pressure increase when the vocal folds are blown open, followed by a more gradual decrease, corresponding to their being pulled together by the Bernoulli effect. The pattern is obviously periodic. By looking at the figure, you ought to be able to estimate the period of one cycle of opening and closing, and thus the speaker's fundamental frequency, using the formula F = 1/P. (You also ought to be able to use that information to determine whether the speaker was likely male or female.)

A sawtooth wave, like any other complex wave, can be analyzed as the sum of a set of sinusoidal components (harmonics). As discussed in Chapter 6, a graph of the frequency and amplitude of these sinusoidal components, with frequency on the x-axis and amplitude on the y, is called a spectrum.

In a sustained vibrating system, the harmonic structure is not random. More background and formulas are given in Section 8.1.2 on p. 153. Here, it is important to know that, because of the physics of the vibrating system, the harmonic frequencies of vocal fold vibration will always occur at *integer multiples* of the fundamental frequency. (Basically, the period of each sub-vibration has to fit exactly into the period of the fundamental: see Section 8.1.2 on p. 153.) Thus, if a voice has a fundamental frequency of 100 Hz, harmonics will occur at 200 Hz, 300 Hz, 400 Hz, etc. A voice with an F0 of 210 Hz has harmonics at 420 Hz, 630 Hz, 840 Hz, etc. Further, in vocal fold vibration, as the harmonics increase in frequency they gradually fall off in amplitude: every time the frequency is doubled, about 6 dB of energy is lost.

The graph of these component frequencies is the spectrum of the glottal wave. An idealized glottal spectrum for a wave like that in Figure 7.10 (assuming that the cycle continues for an indefinitely long time without any change from period to period, a condition that is not met in the real world) is shown in Figure 7.11. Each line indicates a harmonic at the particular frequency, and the height of the line indicates its amplitude. Because the physics of vocal fold vibration are essentially the same from person to person, any glottal spectrum will have approximately this shape: frequency components at integer multiples with gradually decreasing amplitude.

As you should have been able to infer from Figure 7.10, the speaker's F0 is approximately 200 Hz (period of approximately .005 sec.), typical of a woman's voice. Thus, in Figure 7.11, we find harmonics at integer multiples of F0: 200, 400, 600, etc.

Figure 7.12 shows an idealized spectrum for a voice with an F0 of 100 Hz. The overall shape of the spectrum is the same, but harmonics are found at multiples of 100 Hz rather than 200 Hz.

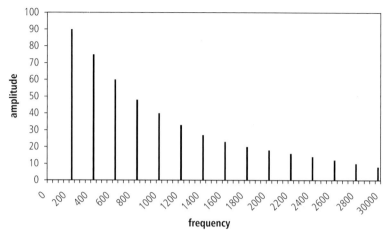

Figure 7.11 Approximation of the spectrum of the glottal waveform in Figure 7.10.

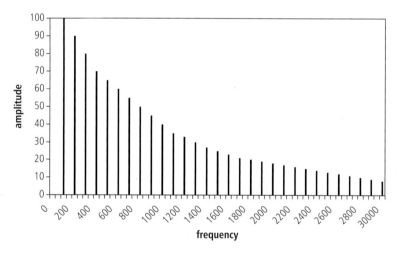

Figure 7.12 Approximation of the spectrum of a different glottal waveform, with lower F0.

When looking at spectra, it is important to remember that the spacing of the harmonics depends on F0. The *lower* the voice, the *more dense* the harmonics. There are twice as many harmonics below 3000 Hz for a voice with an F0 of 100 Hz than for a voice with an F0 of 200 Hz.

When comparing spectra, the rate at which the harmonics decrease in amplitude (degree of *spectral tilt*) reflects differences in voice quality. Creaky voice quality (with smaller, more abrupt glottal changes) has more energy in the higher harmonics (less spectral tilt.) Breathy voice quality causes greater high-energy loss, and thus greater spectral tilt.

It is worth noting that women's voices are thus in a sense doubly disadvantaged when it comes to spectral analysis. With typically higher F0, there are fewer harmonics present, and with typically more breathiness, those harmonics that are present may have lower amplitude, particularly at higher frequencies. We discuss these factors as they interact with vocal tract resonances in section 7.4.3. First, Section 7.4.2 turns to aperiodic sound sources.

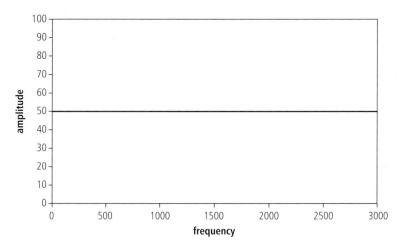

Figure 7.13   Spectrum of white noise.

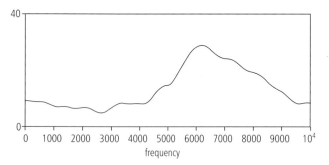

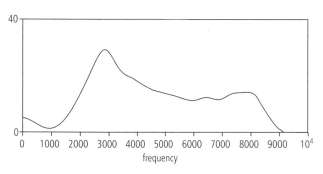

Figure 7.14   Spectra of [s] (top) and [ʃ] (bottom).

7.4.2 spectrum of a noise source

White noise is an aperiodic sound where the pressure variations are completely random. Radio static is one real-world example. The spectrum of a white noise source is flat: all frequencies are equally present, as graphed in Figure 7.13. Since there are no particular repeating patterns that can be singled out as harmonic components, the graph is not drawn with bars, but with a connected line across all frequencies. The amplitude in the graph was chosen at random. Actual source amplitude would depend on the intensity of the signal: turning the volume on the radio up or down.

Not all noise is "white", however. The spectrum may have a concentration of higher amplitude noise in certain regions of the frequency space. Figure 7.14 shows spectra of [s] and [ʃ]. As with the white noise, there is no harmonic structure, so the spectra are shown as line graphs rather than bar graphs. The spectra are not flat, however: [s] has a concentration of higher amplitude energy in the region of 6000 Hz, while [ʃ] has higher amplitude energy in the region of 3000 Hz. Thus [s] sounds higher-pitched than [ʃ] (though the term "pitch" is used loosely where aperiodic sounds are concerned). Such spectral differences characterize the different fricative sounds.

Transient sounds – clicks and bursts caused by sudden changes in air pressure – are also an important part of the speech signal. Like fricatives, transients are aperiodic, and may have energy concentrated in different frequency regions.

Either the vibrating vocal folds or the aperiodic noise of fricatives or bursts can be a source of energy for speech sounds. These sounds, however, do not make it out of the mouth unaltered. They are filtered by the resonances of the vocal tract.

7.4.3 spectra of vowels

The air in the vocal tract filters the vibrations of the sound source. As was noted in Chapter 6, every object has certain resonance frequencies: frequencies at which it will vibrate if energy is applied. The resonant frequencies of an object depend on its physical characteristics. For a swing or other pendulum, the frequency is determined by the length of the string; for a gong, by the mass and thickness of the vibrating metal. For a column of air the crucial characteristic is the length of the column.

The vibrating vocal folds apply energy to the air in the vocal tract at multiple harmonic frequencies. Some of these frequencies will happen to match or come close to a resonant frequency of the particular vocal tract shape assumed at the moment. Those resonant frequencies (*formants*) will be amplified as the repeating waves reinforce each other. Frequencies produced by the vocal folds that do not come close to a resonant frequency of the vocal tract will be damped out – their energy will be randomly dispersed. Thus the vocal tract is a filter.

Importantly, it is a moving filter. As the shapes of the tongue and lips move, the formant frequencies change. In a spectrum, formant frequencies are visible as broad peaks: areas of higher amplitude overlaid on the underlying harmonic structure. Remember: harmonics are a product of the vocal fold source, occurring at integer multiples of the fundamental. Formants are a product of the vocal tract filter, amplifying certain harmonics at the expense of others. The overall spectral shape is the product of the interaction of harmonics and formants.

There are different models of exactly how formant frequencies are derived: see Sections 8.1.3 and 8.1.4 on pp. 156 and 159 for further discussion and formulas. *Tube models* picture the vocal tract as a series of linked tubes of different lengths, each of which has different resonant properties. *Perturbation models* picture one long tube, then describe the effect of constricting that tube at different locations. In this chapter, we'll assume a simple tube model. For example, one might consider the oral cavity as one tube and the pharynx as another: any sound that raises the tongue body and thus effectively lengthens the pharynx will cause the resonances of the pharyngeal tube to drop (because longer = lower). In the vowel [i], the high front tongue position creates a small tube in the front of the mouth (over the top of the tongue), and a long tube in the back of the mouth (behind the tongue), creating one high and one low resonant frequency. The vowel /u/, on the other hand, moves the tongue body back, creating two long tubes roughly equal in length, and thus two similar and fairly low resonant frequencies.

Noise sources can be filtered in the same way, though the output sound will be aperiodic rather than periodic. This is what is occurring in whispering: the vocal tract is passing along noise near certain frequencies, rather than periodic vibration. Burst noise can also be filtered. Try pronouncing [kʰə] and [tʰə]. Can you hear that the burst noise of the [k] is lower pitched than that of the [t]? Part of the reason for that is that the tube of air in front of the [k] is longer than that in front of the [t], creating a lower-frequency filter.

Here, we concentrate on observed spectral patterns for different vowel sounds. There are known relationships between spectral patterns and vocal tract shapes.

Figure 7.15 shows spectra from three different vowels: [æ], [ɔ], and [i], derived from the words "map," "Bob(by)," and "he" in the utterance pictured as a waveform in Figure 7.9. These are actual spectra, not idealized, so the first thing to note is that the harmonics appear as narrow peaks, not single lines. Because the signal being analyzed is not perfectly invariant

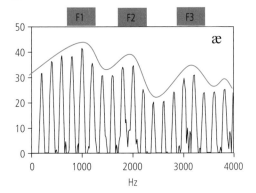

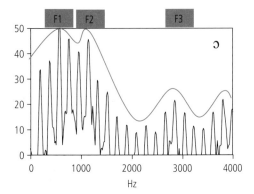

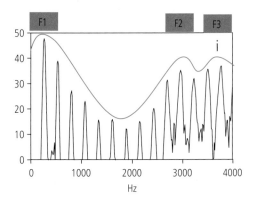

Figure 7.15   Spectra for [æ], [ɔ], and [i].

nor perfectly free of noise, and is limited in both time (about 200 ms for each vowel) and frequency (at the Nyquist limit of 22.5 K), the spectral analysis algorithm (*Fast Fourier Transform* in this case) can narrow down each frequency value only to a narrow range, not a single point. As in the spectra shown above, frequency (in Hz) is on the x-axis, and amplitude (dB) on the y. The analysis will find harmonics up to the Nyquist limit, but only the first 4000 Hz are shown in the graph, as this is the range in which vowels are distinguished. Note that time (ms) is *not* represented in a spectrum. The frequencies and amplitudes represented are averaged over the period of time being analyzed: in these cases a portion of a vowel that is relatively steady-state.

First, note the regular spacing of the harmonics. If you count the individual peaks in the first spectrum, you'll see that the 10th harmonic is equal to about 2000 Hz, giving an F0 of 200 Hz. (This is an efficient way to read F0 from a spectrum.) The F0 in the second spectrum is about the same. What about the third? In the third spectrum, harmonics are spaced further apart, and the 10th harmonic lands at about 2800 Hz, for an F0 of 280 Hz. Since we know that these vowels are all from the same speaker in the same utterance, we can deduce that her voice was higher at the beginning of the utterance than at the end, and/or that there was some emphasis placed on the word "he."

Now consider the differences in spectral shape for each vowel. In each case, the smooth spectral roll-off of the glottal spectrum has been altered, with broad peaks pushed up in different areas. The location of these peaks has been emphasized by the drawing of a solid line across the tops of the individual harmonics. These broad peaks are the formants. In each spectrum, the first three peaks have been labeled: F1, F2, F3 (for formant 1, 2, 3). It is the relationship between the locations of the first three formants that most strongly determine perceived sound quality.

Note that, as we move from [æ] to [ɔ] to [i], the frequency of the first formant decreases: F1 is about 900 Hz for [æ], 600 Hz for [ɔ] and 300 Hz for [i]. This general relationship holds consistently: *F1 is inversely proportional to vowel height*. F1 is high for low vowels, and low for high vowels. Exact values will differ from speaker to speaker, since no two vocal tracts are identical, but these values are typical for a female voice; and for any speaker, F1 for [i] will be lower than F1 for [æ]. In a tube model, F1 for many vowels corresponds to the column of air in the pharynx: as the tongue body moves up, the pharyngeal tube is effectively lengthened, and the resonant frequency goes down.

Now consider the spacing between F1 and F2. The two formants are very far apart for [i], very close together (almost indistinguishable) for [ɔ], and intermediate for [æ]. This relationship is also consistent: *the distance between F1 and F2 is inversely proportional to vowel backness*. The more back the vowel, the closer F1 and F2 are; the more front the vowel, the further apart F1 and F2 are. Moving the tongue body back tends to equalize the space in front of the tongue (F2 resonance) and the space behind the tongue (F1 resonance).

Finally, lip rounding tends to lower all the formants (effectively lengthening the entire vocal tract), especially F2 and F3 (front cavity resonances). Thus backing and rounding have reinforcing acoustic effects: both lower F2. This explains the cross-linguistic tendency for back vowels to be round and front vowels to be unround. Rounding a front vowel will lower F2, bringing F2 and F1 closer together, making the vowel sound more back; and unrounding a back vowel will raise F2, making the vowel sound more front. The vowels [y] and [ɯ] have similar acoustic spectra, while [i] and [u] have F2 values at opposite ends of the range.

Graphing F1 and F2–F1 shows how vowels are distributed in the space defined by the dimensions of backness and height. A graph of F2–F1 on the x-axis and F1 on the y (with the origin at upper right) creates a graph of the vowel space comparable to the charts that were made based on auditory quality alone, relative to the cardinal vowels (see Chapter 4). Such charts, whether auditory or acoustic, roughly approximate tongue body position. Figure 7.16 shows such a graph for the vowels of Japanese, as produced by a female speaker. Note that this graph confirms the auditory impression that Japanese /u/ can accurately be more narrowly transcribed as [ɯ].

Thus spectra are very useful representations, allowing the phonetician to distinguish different vowel qualities, as well as F0 information. Their drawback, however, has already been mentioned: there is no time in the representation. Because the sounds of speech change so rapidly, the phonetician is often interested in seeing how spectral quality changes over time. One could, of course, examine a series of spectra. To be able to see changes in the amplitude of a set of frequencies over time in a single graph, however, we need a graph with three dimensions: one for time, one for frequency, and one for amplitude. This type of graph is called a *spectrogram*.

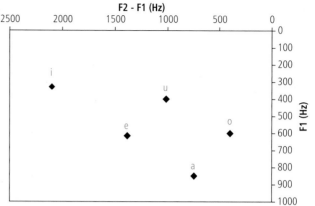

Figure 7.16   Graph of the Japanese vowel space.

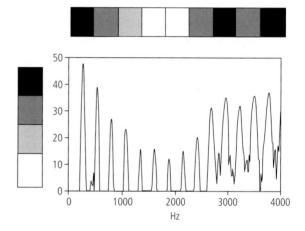

Figure 7.17   Spectrum of [i] with frequency on the y-axis, and amplitude represented with shading. Formant frequencies show up as dark boxes.

7.5 spectrograms

In a spectrogram, time is shown on the x-axis and frequency on the y-axis. The amplitude of a given frequency at a given time is represented by color, or in a black and white print, darkness. Figure 7.17 shows the spectrum of [i] from Figure 7.15 turned on its side, so that frequency is on the y-axis, with higher frequencies at the top. In addition, a darkness scale has been added, to represent different amplitudes. Amplitude of over 35 dB is represented as black, between 25 and 35 dB as dark gray, 15 to 25 as light gray, and any amplitude under 15 dB as white. The column of squares on the left then represents, in bands of color, the information in the spectrum. F1 (about 300 Hz), F2 (2800 Hz) and F3 (3800 Hz) show up as dark squares.

In order to add time to the representation, all that is needed is to take spectral information at repeated intervals, and graph additional columns for each interval, as shown in Figure 7.18. This might represent the diphthong [ɔi]. At time t1, F1 is high and F2 is low, indicative of a lower back vowel. Over time, as the tongue body moves up and forward, F1 lowers and

F2 rises, until by time t6, the typical pattern for [i] has been reached. The changing resonance patterns, that is, the formant movement, can be traced as a dark line. Figure 7.18 is a schematic spectrogram.

A real spectrogram, created in the Praat signal analysis program, from the sequence [baɪəp] ("buy a p[aper]," Figure 7.9) is shown in Figure 7.19. The procedure for making the spectrogram is essentially the same as that diagrammed in Figures 7.17 and 7.18. Spectra are taken at repeated intervals (in the case of Figure 7.18 about every 5 ms), and the amplitude of energy in different frequency bands is computed. When the information from sequential spectra is graphed over time, with amplitude coded as darkness, the formants (regions of high-amplitude energy) show up as dark stripes that move over time, reflecting changes in resonance frequencies as vocal tract articulators change position. The F2 stripe moves gradually from about 1500 Hz at time 50 ms, indicative of central [a], to 2400 at 200 ms, indicative of front [ɪ], then down again to about 1700 Hz, indicative of [ə]. The white areas at beginning and end correspond to the stop closures, when there is no high-amplitude energy in the signal.

This type of spectrogram is called a *wide-band* or *broad-band spectrogram*, because the formant frequencies show up as broad bands. In a wide-band spectrogram, spectra are taken from very short "windows" of the speech signal at frequent intervals, so that changes that take place over very short time periods are evident. The burst at the release of the [b] shows up as a line of energy at about 30 ms, for example. Each vertical striation corresponds to a period of vocal fold vibration (one beat of sound energy). The irregular vertical lines between 200 and 250 ms indicate glottalization, irregular vocal fold vibration, between "buy" and "a."

If larger "windows" at less frequent intervals are used, the result is a *narrow-band spectrogram*, as shown in Figure 7.20. This spectrogram is of the exact same speech sample as in Figure 7.19. You should be able to pick out the same formant patterns. By taking a larger sample for each spectrum, more accurate frequency information can be computed: in a narrow-band spectrogram, individual harmonics can be distinguished. (At time 150 ms, for example, the 10th harmonic is at 2500 Hz.) The time dimension is less precise,

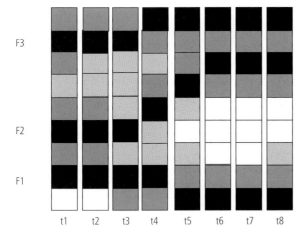

Figure 7.18   A schematic spectrogram of [ɔɪ].

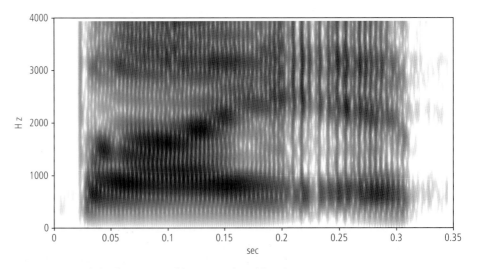

Figure 7.19   A wide-band spectrogram of the sequence [baɪəp] from the utterance in Figure 7.9.

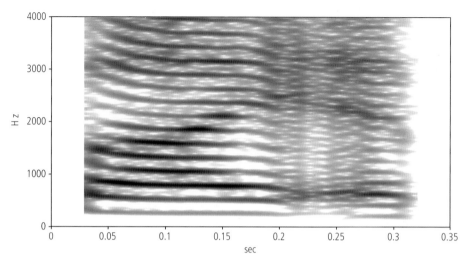

Figure 7.20   Narrow-band spectrogram of the same utterance as in Figure 7.18.

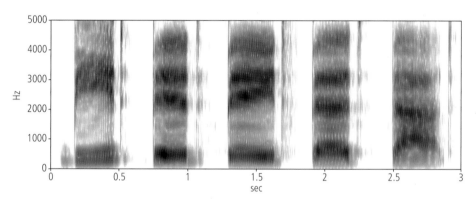

Figure 7.21   Spectrogram of the American English words *bead, bid, bayed, bed, bad.*

however: bursts, glottalization, and the transitions between vowel and stop are no longer evident. Because the point of using a spectrogram rather than a spectrum is to investigate changes over time, broad-band spectrograms are more commonly used.

The following figures illustrate spectrographic patterns typical of different (English) sounds.

Broad-band spectrograms of the English words "bead, bid, bayed, bed, bad" are shown in Figure 7.21. Note how F1 gets higher as the vowels get progressively lower, and F2 gets lower as the tongue moves further back. (Each of these vowels counts as a "front" vowel, because each has a counterpart further back, but the spectrogram shows that they do not all have the same degree of tongue fronting.) Movement of F2 during "bayed" confirms the diphthongized nature of this English vowel.

Figure 7.22 shows the back vowels in the words "booed, book, boat, bought, body, bud." The first two formants are much closer together than in any of the words in Figure 7.21. (Compare the first and second syllables of "body", between times 2 and 2.5 seconds. The white space in between them is the closure for the [d], during which there is only faint low-frequency

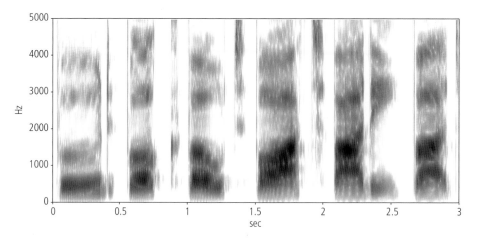

Figure 7.22   Spectrogram of the American English words *booed, book, boat, bought, body, bud.*

Table 7.3   Formant cues to consonant place of articulation.

Articulation	Formant transition cue	Plausible connection
Voiced stops	Lower F1	Lowering the larynx preparatory to voicing lengthens the pharynx
Labials	Lower all formants, especially F2 and F3 (similar to rounding)	Lengthened vocal tract, especially the front cavity
Alveolars	Relatively high F2 (1600–2000 Hz)	Raising the tongue front makes the front cavity smaller
Velars	F2 and F3 approach each other: "velar pinch"	Front and back cavities equalize
Palatals	Raise F2, F3, and F4 (similar to [i])	Constriction in the whole front of the oral cavity
Retroflexes	Lower F3	Large sub-lingual cavity (area under the tongue)
Pharyngeals	Raise F1 (similar to low vowels)	Constriction in the back of the mouth shortens the pharynx

energy, indicative of voicing.) You can also note some typical characteristics of English vowels: [u] is not really very back (F1 and F2 are comparatively far apart), and [oʊ], like [eɪ], is diphthongized. (For this speaker, the vowel in "bought" is also diphthongized.)

You may also notice formant movement near the beginnings and ends of the vowels. In "bud," for example, F1 is arced, not flat, and F2 takes a steep upturn at the end. These changes are due to the influence of surrounding consonants, as the articulators move toward different closures. Since there is generally very little energy during the actual constriction of a consonant, these *formant transitions* into and out of consonant closures provide crucial cues, both in acoustic analysis and in real listening, to consonant identity, particularly place of articulation.

Some crucial cues to place of articulation are summarized in Table 7.3. For each cue, a plausible connection between articulator movement and vocal tract (tube) resonance is provided. It is not possible to make a one-to-one correspondence between vocal tract cavity and formant number: each "tube" has more than one resonance, and exactly which resonance of which cavity turns out to be lowest or highest depends on numerous factors and interactions. See the references at the end of the chapter for further information and more exact calculations.

Some of these cues are illustrated in Figure 7.23, spectrograms of the words "bab, dad, gag." The arced shape of F1 is due to the voicing of the consonants. Differences in F2 and F3 encode consonant place: sloping down for [b], flat for [d] (F2 pointing to 2000 Hz), pinching together for [g]. In back vowels, for which F2 is low, there will be a sharp upturn in F2 into a velar or alveolar consonant, as in Figure 7.22. For this reason, if you are measuring vowel formants, you want to be as far away from velars and alveolars as possible.

Sonorant consonants have vowel-like resonances, but lower amplitude. The glides [j] and [w] look like low-amplitude [i] and [u], as shown in Figure 7.24. Note how all the higher

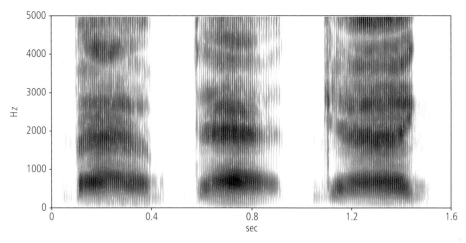

Figure 7.23   "Bab, dad, gag."

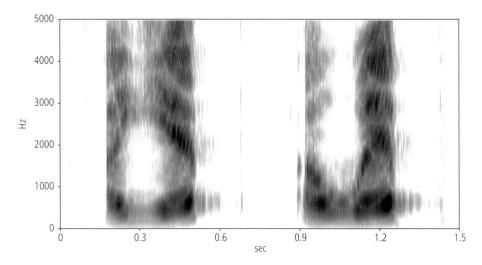

Figure 7.24   "A yip, a whip."

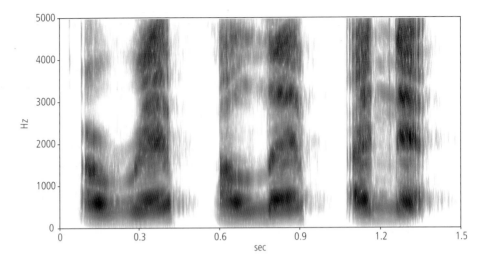

Figure 7.25   "A rip, a lip, a nip."

formants sweep upward for [j], while F2 nosedives for [w]. Because glides do not involve a closure or change in voicing, there is no sharp discontinuity between vowel and glide.

The English rhotic approximant also has no sharp discontinuities. Its spectral signature is a very low F3, as illustrated in Figure 7.25. Laterals and nasals may be easier to pick out as separate consonants, but they can be harder to distinguish from each other. Especially for nasals, resonance patterns distinct from the surrounding vowels often appear. Nasals will introduce extra resonances from the nasal cavity, often in the area of 200 Hz and 2500 Hz. Interaction with nasal resonance can also "cancel" oral formant structure, muddying the vocalic formants. Laterals often have a resonance around 1200 Hz, an effect of the side channel.

Finally, fricatives show up as noise in a spectrogram. Consistent with the spectra discussed in Section 7.4, they have no formant structure, but show up as bands of noise with concentrations in different parts of the frequency spectrum. One often has to look at higher frequencies to distinguish fricatives than to distinguish vowels and other consonants. Consequently, the frequency range in Figure 7.26 has been adjusted, showing frequencies up to 10,000 Hz rather than the 5000 Hz in previous figures.

Figure 7.26 shows the utterances "sash" and "thief". The strident fricatives [s] and [ʃ] have higher overall energy, and thus appear darker. Again, consistent with the spectra in Figure 7.14, [s] has the highest frequency, almost all above 5000 Hz. [ʃ] has energy concentrated around 3000 Hz. The energy in [θ] and [f] is much more diffuse. In practice, [θ] and [f] are very difficult to distinguish, both in reading spectrograms and in real speech perception. This may be one reason why [θ] is rare cross-linguistically, and why these fricatives bear a very light "functional load" in English: very few utterances depend on the difference between [θ] and [f] to convey their distinct meanings.

chapter summary

- Before computers, sound recording and analysis consisted of transferring analog patterns of speech vibration from the air to some more durable medium, such as a wax cylinder, magnetic tape, or etching on a chemically-treated paper.

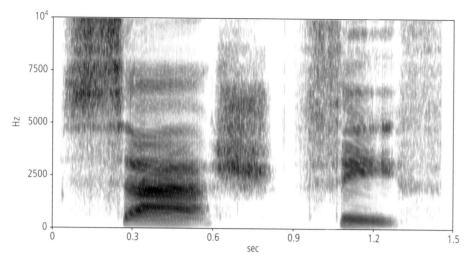

Figure 7.26   "Sash, thief."

- Digital recording takes place via the process of sampling, taking measurements at repeated intervals. Sampling rate refers to how often samples are taken, quantization to how precise each measurement is. Current default sampling and quantization rates are 44,100 samples per second at 16 bits per sample.
- The highest frequency that can be faithfully digitally recorded, without aliasing, is called the Nyquist limit, and is equal to one-half the sampling rate.
- Waveforms graph sound pressure changes over time. They are most useful for measuring durations of segments and voice onset time (VOT).
- Spectra graph the frequency and amplitudes of harmonic components, but do not represent time. They are useful for measuring sound quality during relatively steady-state intervals.
- Harmonics, which occur at integer multiples of the fundamental frequency, are a product of the glottal source.
- Formants are peaks in the spectrum, where the harmonics that correspond to vocal tract resonances have been amplified. The height of F1 is inversely proportional to vowel height; the distance between F1 and F2 is inversely proportion to vowel backness. (See Figures 7.15, 7.21, and 7.22.)
- Spectrograms graph spectral changes over time.
- Formant transitions provide information about consonant constrictions. See Table 7.3, and Figures 7.23–7.26.

further reading

Johnson, K. 1997. *Acoustic and Auditory Phonetics*. Oxford: Blackwell.
Stevens, K. 2000. *Acoustic Phonetics*. Cambridge, MA: MIT Press.

review exercises

1.   What does a kymograph do? A sound spectrograph?
2.   Twenty years ago, speech was routinely sampled at 8000 samples per second and 8 bits. Today, defaults are 44,100 samples/sec and 16 bits. What is gained at the higher sampling and bit rates? What is the downside?
3.   What is the relationship between F1 and vowel height? What spectral information correlates with vowel backness? With rounding?
4.   Fill in the blanks
     a.   In a spectrum, the _____ change depending on F0. (harmonics/formants)
     b.   In a spectrum, the _____ change depending on tongue position. (harmonics/formants)
     c.   In a spectrogram, amplitude is represented by _____. (distance on x-axis/distance on y-axis/darkness)
     d.   Another term for analog-to-digital conversion is _____. (Fourier transform/sampling/output)
     e.   If frequencies above the Nyquist limit are present in a digitized signal, this may cause _____. (aliasing/clipping/ quantization)
     f.   In the source/filter theory of speech production, the filter is the _____. (vibrating larynx/air in the vocal tract/speed of sound propagation)
     g.   If you want to digitally analyze frequencies up to 10,000 Hz, you need to use a sampling rate of at least _____. (5000 Hz/10,000 Hz/20,000 Hz/44,000 Hz)

further analysis and discussion

5.   Match the waveforms to the following utterances:

     Say chat now.   _____   Say mad now.   _____
     Say mash now.   _____   Say dish now.   _____

     a.   In each waveform, draw vertical lines to indicate the boundaries between each segment. Assume burst and aspiration are part of the consonant. Label each interval with the correct phonetic symbol.
          i.   Indicate burst and aspiration as part of the consonant.
          ii.   Indicate the two parts of the affricate separately.
          iii.   Diphthongs count as one segment.
     b.   From the waveforms, estimate (to the nearest 20 ms)
          i.   the length of the vowel in *mad*.
          ii.   the length of the fricative in *mash*.
          iii.   the length of the final [t] closure in *chat*.
          iv.   the length of the burst for [d] in *dish*.

A

0   0.1   0.2   0.3   0.4   0.5   0.6   0.7   0.8   0.9   1   1.1   1.2   1.3   1.4   1.5

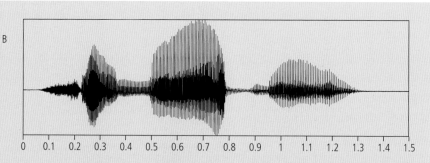

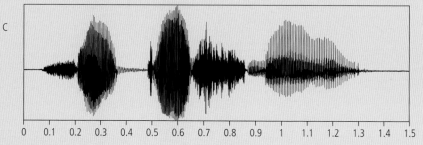

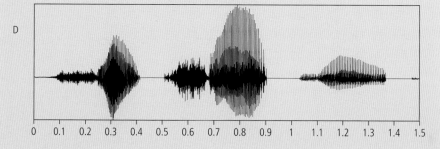

6. Examine the spectra below. The spectra represent the vowels [e] and [o] pronounced
    with relatively high or low pitch.
    a. In spectrum A, estimate:
        i.   the frequency of the 5th harmonic _____
        ii.   F0 _____
        iii. the frequency of the first formant _____
        iv.   the frequency of the second formant _____
        v.   the frequency of the third formant _____
    b. In spectrum B, estimate:
        i.   the frequency of the 10th harmonic _____
        ii.   F0 _____
        iii. the frequency of the first formant _____
        iv.   the frequency of the second formant _____
    c. The vowels [e] and [o] are approximately the same height. Thus all four spectra
        have approximately the same _____.
    d. Match the spectra to the utterances:
        i.   [le] with high tone _____
        ii.   [le] with low tone _____

(*Continued*)

iii.   [lo] with high tone _____
iv.   [lo] with low tone _____

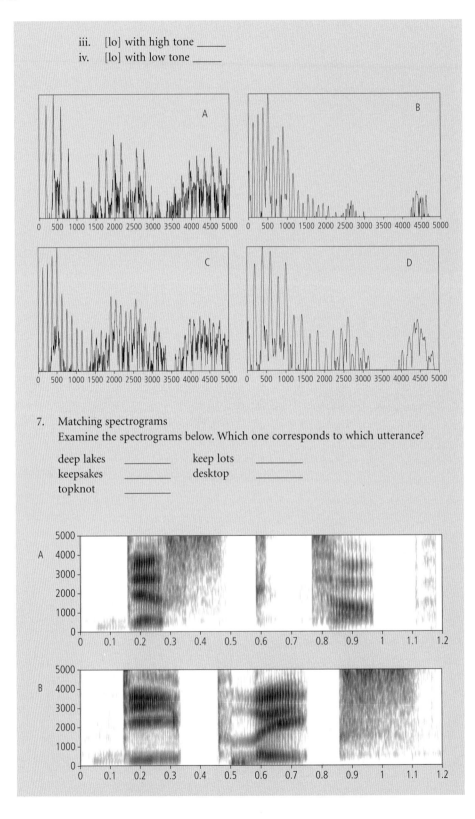

7.   Matching spectrograms
     Examine the spectrograms below. Which one corresponds to which utterance?

deep lakes   _____   keep lots   _____
keepsakes   _____   desktop   _____
topknot   _____

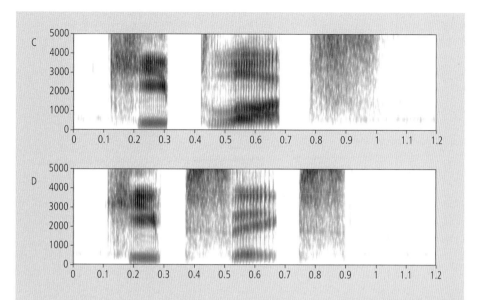

8. Try decoding the spectrogram below. The utterance is a significant date in American history, in the form of month, day, year, so the choice among possible words is limited. (If you don't recognize the significance, look it up!) Look for obvious landmarks, then fill in ambiguous sections using both phonetic and lexical knowledge.

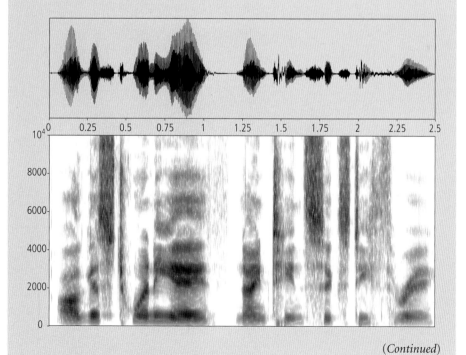

(Continued)

further research

9. Make a spectrogram of your own "mystery utterance", and share it with others in your class. Can they decipher it?

Note: Some further ideas for practicing spectrographic analysis are found at the end of Chapter 8.

Go online Visit the book's companion website for additional resources related to this chapter at: http://www.wiley.com/go/zsiga.

references

Collins, B. and I.M. Mees. 1999. *The Real Professor Higgins: The Life and Career of Daniel Jones*. Berlin: Mouton de Gruyter.

Winckel, F. 1967. *Music, Sound and Sensation*. New York: Dover Publications, Inc.

Text description of the spectrograph is based on:

Lieberman, P. and S. Blumstein. 1988. *Speech Physiology, Speech Perception, and Acoustic Phonetics*. Cambridge: Cambridge University Press.

8 Speech Analysis
Under the Hood

To the acoustician . . . a speech event is completely characterized by the pressure changes in the air at some point in front of the speaker, for a record of such pressure changes suffices to reconstitute the observed acoustical event with any desired degree of fidelity. To the student of language, on the contrary . . . unless he can discover in the acoustical signal reflexes of the complicated hierarchical organization of language, acoustic studies have little practical importance.

Morris Halle, 1958, The Sound Pattern of Russian, p. 79

The essence of mathematics is not to make simple things complicated, but to make complicated things simple.

Stanley Guddar, Professor of Mathematics,
University of Boulder, author of A Mathematical Journey

Chapter outline

The Sounds of Language: An Introduction to Phonetics and Phonology, First Edition. Elizabeth C. Zsiga.
© 2013 Elizabeth C. Zsiga. Published 2013 by Blackwell Publishing Ltd.

In this chapter, we revisit a number of the topics discussed in Chapters 6 and 7, and here we do the math. A student does not need to know and be able to work with these mathematical formulas in order to have a qualitative understanding of acoustic phonetics. One can understand the information in a spectrogram, for instance, without understanding how the analysis was done. If one wants to have creative control, however – to have the ability to synthesize a tone or a vowel, create one's own spectrograms, or fix them when something in the algorithm goes wrong – then a deeper mathematical knowledge is needed. It's the difference between being able to drive a car – knowing which levers or knobs on the dashboard to push or pull to get a certain result – and being able to look under the hood, knowing what each hose and wire is for, and being able to fix the faulty connection that keeps the car from starting.

Section 8.1 discusses some of the formulas necessary to build sounds up: understanding sinusoids as circular motion, calculating harmonic structure, and understanding formants as the resonances of a column or air. Section 8.2 turns to breaking sounds down: the algorithms used for computer speech analysis, including RMS amplitude, autocorrelation pitch tracking, Fourier analysis, and linear predictive coding. While this chapter represents a level of depth beyond Chapters 6 and 7, it still is very elementary. The physics of speech sounds and the algorithms of speech analysis go well beyond what can be covered in an introductory text. Further reading is suggested at the end of the chapter.

8.1 building sounds up

8.1.1 sinusoids as circular motion

In Section 6.2 on p. 102, we learned that the sound wave that produces a pure tone can be graphed as a sinusoid, and that a sinusoid is defined by its frequency, amplitude, and phase. We saw in Section 6.3 that all complex waves can be broken down into sinusoidal components. We learned that the pitch of a sound, either simple or complex, is correlated with the fundamental frequency of the wave (the frequency with which the overall pattern repeats). Its loudness is correlated with intensity, the amount of energy in the system, which depends on both frequency and amplitude. The quality of a complex sound is determined by the frequencies and relative amplitudes of its sinusoidal components. Therefore, an understanding of the *sin* function is crucial to all speech analysis. In this section, we look more closely at the math underlying the sinusoid, and ask the question, "What does simple harmonic motion have to do with the trigonometric *sin* function, the ratio of opposite side to hypotenuse in a right triangle?"

The formula for a sinusoid is given in Formula 8.1:

Formula 8.1: defining a sinusoid wave

$$y = a \sin \omega t$$
a = amplitude
ω = frequency
t = time (phase)

The three components that define the wave are represented. The variable *y* stands for the value on the y-axis, the value that is to be computed. The variable *a* stands for the amplitude. Since the result of *sin* ω *t* is multiplied by *a*, the larger the value of *a*, the greater the value of *y*: the bigger the sine wave is. The variable *t* stands for how much time has elapsed since the start of the oscillation, and thus represents phase. Finally, ω stands for frequency, expressed as *circular motion*. The cycles of simple harmonic motion can be understood as motion around the circumference of a circle. Once around the circle equals one cycle.

Imagine a dot painted on the side of a bicycle tire. As the tire spins, the dot moves around the circumference. How far and how fast does it move? One way to measure circular motion references the fact that a circle consists of 360°. Thus, we can ask how many degrees the dot moves through in one second. If the cycle takes one second to complete, the dot is moving at 360° per second. If the cycle takes 4 seconds to complete, the dot is moving at 90° per second. When circular motion is measured in degrees it is called *angular motion*.

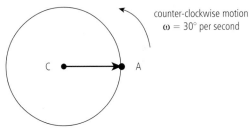

Figure 8.1   Circular motion.

This is where the *sin function* comes in, because the *sin* is measured from angles. Instead of a bicycle tire, imagine a clock with a second hand. On a real clock, of course, the second hand sweeps through one cycle (360°) in one minute. Our imaginary clock has a few differences: we will imagine that we can change the rate of circular motion to anything we want and that we can start the second hand at any position we want. We'll also make it run counter-clockwise (this makes the math easier). We'll start our clock as in Figure 8.1. The length of the "second hand" (line CA), is equal to the radius of the circle, which we'll set to be equal to 1. We'll start the second hand lying flat and pointing straight to the right (position A). And we'll imagine that the hand sweeps through 30° per second (so it will take 12 seconds to finish the whole 360° cycle): that is, ω = 30°/second.

Figure 8.2 shows the position of the second hand at subsequent points in time. At time 1 (1 second, shown in orange), the hand has swept through 30° ($\frac{1}{12}$ of the circle). At each point in time, the angle between the second hand and

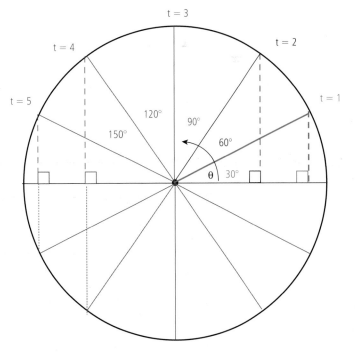

Figure 8.2   The sin function on a circle.

the horizontal radius is referred to as θ: at t = 1, θ = 30°. After two seconds have elapsed (t = 2, shown in black), the hand has swept through 60° (θ = 60°).

To relate Figure 8.2 to our sine wave formula (8.1), θ is the result of multiplying ω (degrees per second) by t (number of seconds elapsed). If ω is 30° per second and t = 2 seconds, then θ = 60°. So we can reformulate Formula 8.1 as Formula 8.2:

Formula 8.2: defining a sinusoid (version 2)

$$\theta = \omega\, t$$
$$y = a \sin \theta$$

The variable *a*, representing amplitude, corresponds to the size of the circle as determined by the radius. The bigger the radius, the bigger the circumference, and thus the greater the distance our dot has to travel. In Figure 8.2, however, we have defined the radius as equal to 1, so we can ignore *a* for the moment.

Now all we need to add is the *sin* function. To do that, imagine that we drop a straight line down from the end of our second hand, forming a right angle with the diameter of the circle. At t = 1, this will be the light dashed line in Figure 8.2. Dropping this perpendicular line makes a right triangle to which we can apply our trigonometric functions.

If you recall your high school trig, you'll remember that the *sin* function is a ratio relating the sides of a right triangle. The *sin* of an angle is the ratio of the length of the side opposite the angle to the length of the hypotenuse (sin = opposite/hypotenuse). This is shown in Figure 8.3. The *sin* of angle θ is the ratio of BC (opposite) to BA (hypotenuse).

In Figure 8.2, length of the orange dashed line is the sin of 30°. This line is opposite the 30° angle, and the hypotenuse, the radius of the circle, is defined as 1. The sin of 30° is .5. (That is, if θ is 30°, BC is half as long as BA. Check it on your calculator.)

One second later, the hand has swept through 60°. If we drop a new line down to the diameter (the black dashed line) its length will equal sin 60°, or .867. At t = 3, the hand has swept through 90°, and the sin of 90° = 1: the perpendicular line is equal to the length of the radius. Continuing around, we find the sins of 120°, 150°, 180°, etc. (These subsequent points are shown in gray in Figure 8.2). The sin functions of angles in 30° increments, from 0° to 360° are listed in Table 8.1.

Note the patterns and symmetry. As the second hand sweeps through the angles from 0° to 90°, the *sin* function increases from 0 to 1. From 90° to 180°, the *sin* decreases in exactly proportional pattern, from 1 to 0. The *sin* of 120° is the same as that of 60°, the *sin* of 150° is the same as 30°. The *sin* of 180° is 0. Between 180° and 270°, the lower left quadrant of the circle, the second hand is below the diameter, so the length of the line is a negative number: the *sin* of 210° is −.5. (Only two negative lines have been drawn in Figure 8.2 to keep the diagram from becoming too cluttered. You ought to be able to imagine the rest.) The *sin* function gets more and more negative, until at 270° it reaches a maximum negative value of −1. Finally, between 270° and 360°, the *sin* function moves from −1 to 0.

This all should sound and look familiar. If we graph the *sin* values from t = 1 to t = 12, we get the graph in Figure 8.4: the sine wave. (Intermediate values have been interpolated, and connected with a smooth line.)

To get a sine wave of higher frequency, we increase the number of degrees per second. If ω = 60° per second instead of 30°, you get through two cycles (720°) in 12 seconds instead of one: double the frequency. To increase the amplitude,

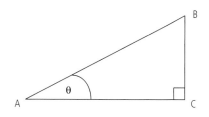

Figure 8.3 Sin θ = BC/BA. If BA = 1, then sin θ = BC.

Table 8.1 The sines of some angles.

t	θ	sin θ
0	0°	0
1	30°	.5
2	60°	.867
3	90°	1
4	120°	.867
5	150°	.5
6	180°	0
7	210°	−.5
8	240°	−.867
9	270°	−1
10	300°	−.867
11	330°	−.5
12	360°	0

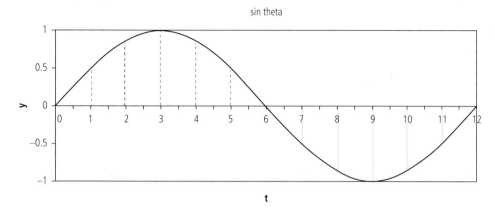

Figure 8.4 The sine wave based on the circular motion in Figure 8.2. Dashed lines correspond to the measures in Table 8.1.

increase the radius of the circle (a), which multiplies each value by some amount. Thus, we can use Formula 8.1 to define any sinusoid wave, and then use algebra to sum sinusoids to create complex waves, building up a complex sound. Section 8.2 discusses algorithms for reversing the process. Section 8.1.2 now turns to the question of how complex sounds are created in the real world.

8.1.2 harmonics: standing waves in a string

The source of periodic energy in the vocal tract is the vibrating vocal folds. While the vocal folds are not strings, the physics of their vibration have some things in common with the physics of string vibration. Recall that the vocal folds are complex flaps of tissue with many layers – an innermost muscular layer, several layers of mucosa, and a stiff cartilaginous edge. Given the right amount of tension and the right amount of airflow, the folds will flap open and closed in the column of air, providing repeated bursts of air pressure, at a basic rate between about 120 Hz for men and 220 Hz for women. The folds do not open and close like trapdoors, however. Being thick and soft, the vocal folds undulate, with ripples moving along both their length and thickness, like a flag rippling in the wind.

These waves (ripples) move through the vocal folds in much the same way that waves of vibration move along the string of an instrument such as a guitar or piano. Properly tuned, the A string will vibrate back and forth at a basic rate (fundamental frequency) of 440 Hz. The vibration of the string is not simple harmonic motion, however. The string has other ripples of motion, other components (harmonics), which give it a richer, more complex sound.

The fundamental frequency of the plucked string, as well as its component harmonic frequencies, are determined by the string length, composition, and tension. Certain wavelengths travel up and down the string in such a way as to continually reinforce one another, allowing that pattern of vibration to be sustained where others die out. As was noted in Chapter 6, patterns of vibration that are sustained by continual self-reinforcement in an oscillating system are called *standing waves*. The frequencies that can set up as a standing wave determine the set of harmonics in the vibration of a string. There are formulae to determine which frequencies will set up standing waves. We'll work through the formulae using the example of a guitar string, because it is easier to visualize, but keep in mind that the formulae apply equally to the ripples that move through the vocal folds.

For a string, the crucial factor is the relationship between the length of the string and the wavelength of the vibration. Only certain wavelengths "fit" into the string length in the proper way. Recall from Formula 6.2, repeated here as Formula 8.3, that wavelength is determined by the speed of propagation and the frequency of oscillation (distance = rate * time). Since the speed of sound through catgut (or its modern synthetic counterpart) remains a constant, there will be a regular relationship between frequency and wavelength: in a given medium, the shorter the wavelength, the higher the frequency.

Formula 8.3: relationship between frequency and wavelength

Wavelength = Speed/Frequency or
Frequency = Speed/Wavelength

In order to set up a standing wave, certain *boundary conditions* must hold. That is, what happens at the edges of the system is crucial. For the string of a musical instrument like a piano, violin, or guitar, the critical boundary condition is that the string is fixed at both ends: the ends of the string cannot move. Any pattern of vibration that would require these fixed points to move (and that will include most frequencies) will obviously be "resisted" by the physical characteristics of the string, and cannot be sustained. Only those few frequencies that allow the ends of the string to remain still (that is, that respect the boundary conditions) will set up as standing waves.

A point in a standing wave that does not move is called a *node*; a point of maximum motion is an *antinode*. Consider the basic back-and-forth motion of the string, as diagrammed in Figure 8.5. As the string vibrates back and forth, its ends (nodes) do not move. The middle of the string, with maximum displacement, is an antinode.

This pattern "fits" into the string in that the pattern of vibration does not require the ends of the string to move. What is the relationship of wavelength to string length? From Figure 8.5, you should be able to see that the upward movement of the string corresponds to the positive half of a sinusoid, and the downward movement corresponds to the negative half of a sinusoid. This is made explicit in Figure 8.6. The length of the string is equal to ½ of the wavelength of the sinusoid. This is the first (lowest frequency) standing wave in a string: string length (L) = ½ wavelength (WL).

Another pattern that "fits" in the string length, with nodes at each end, is one where the two halves (that is, one whole wave) fits into the string length. In fact, any wave for which the string length is any multiple of the half-wavelength will fit as a standing wave: ½, ²⁄₂, ³⁄₂, ⁴⁄₂, ⁵⁄₂, etc. The progression is shown in Figure 8.7.

Each of these patterns of vibration will set itself up as a standing wave in the string, creating a harmonic frequency. The general

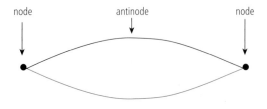

Figure 8.5   Boundary conditions for a vibrating string: each end is a node.

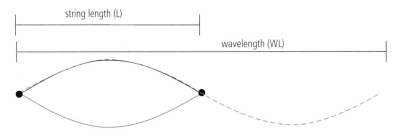

Figure 8.6   The first standing wave in a string: string length = ½ wavelength.

equation for computing standing waves in a string is given as Formula 8.4. Substitute any integer for *n* to get the *n*th wave. The 4th standing wave, for example, is one where the WL is equal to ²⁄₄ (or ½) the string length, illustrated in Figure 8.7C. For the 5th standing wave (8.7D), the wavelength is ²⁄₅ string length, etc.

Formula 8.4: standing waves in a string

$$WL_n = 2L / n$$
WL = wavelength
L = string length
n = any integer

The actual frequencies that correspond to these wavelengths will depend on the speed of propagation in that particular medium, by Formula 8.3.

Other frequencies of vibration, which do not meet the boundary conditions, will die out (Figure 8.8). Wavelengths that do not have a node at the ends of the string would require those fixed points to move, a physical impossibility, so frequencies that do not fit the formula do not set up standing waves. They expend all their energy, as it were, trying to move a fixed point.

The actual shape of the string at any given moment will be the algebraic sum of all the standing waves (that is, of all the harmonic frequencies). It is the presence of the harmonic frequencies (modified by the body of the instrument, as discussed below) that gives a stringed instrument a richer, more natural sound than the simple tone of the tuning fork.

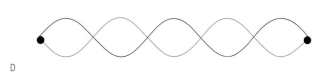

Figure 8.7   Other standing waves in a string. String length is any multiple of the half wavelength.

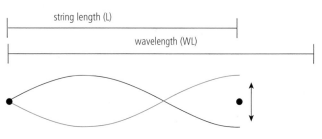

Importantly, the harmonic frequencies will form a progression. By Formula 8.3, Frequency = speed/WL. Because speed is constant, frequency will increase as the *inverse* of the WL: frequency gets higher as wavelength gets shorter. The wavelength of each standing wave decreases as a fraction of the first: the wavelength in 8.7A is ½ the wavelength of 8.6, B is ⅓ the wavelength of 8.6, C is ¼, D is ⅕. Therefore, the frequency of each standing wave *increases* as an integer multiple

Figure 8.8   A wavelength that does not meet the boundary conditions for a string: WL = 4/3 L.

of the first: A is twice the frequency, B is 3 times, C is 4 times, D is 5 times. This brings us to another crucial formula: for a resonating system (like a string) with a node at each end, *harmonics occur at integer multiples of the fundamental frequency*. If the string is the A piano string, its fundamental will by 440 Hz, and it will have additional harmonic frequencies at 880 Hz, 1320 Hz, 1760 Hz, etc. If you change the string length by introducing a node at a new location, for example by placing a finger on the fret of a guitar, you change the note, and with it the whole harmonic structure.

Getting back to speech, the waveform of glottal vibration is not exactly the same as the waveform of string vibration, but crucially, the same boundary conditions hold: the only standing waves are those for which there is a node at each end. Therefore, Formula 8.4 also holds for the vibrating vocal folds, as does its corollary: for voiced speech sounds, where the

8.1 In Focus

Harmonic structure is what makes musical chords sound "consonant" rather than dissonant: in a major chord, the harmonics overlap. Consider the major triad C-E-G. The fundamental frequency of C3 (the C below middle C) is 131 Hz. Its harmonics (multiples of the fundamental) are given in Table 8.2. Every doubling of the frequency (the 2nd, 4th, and 8th harmonics) corresponds to an octave increase. The third, fifth, and sixth harmonics of C3 correspond to multiples of other notes of the major chord: because these notes share harmonics, they will resonate with each other, producing a pleasant sound. Note that the 7th harmonic of C is listed as "not quite B$^\flat$" (it is about 25 Hz off). The way the math works out, the 7th harmonic does not match any other note of the scale. It is thus considered dissonant, and is often suppressed. Violins are bowed and piano hammers hit at just about $\frac{1}{7}$ of the way along the string, suppressing movement at exactly that point where the 7th harmonic would require an antinode, suppressing that pattern of vibration.

Table 8.2   The harmonics of C3.

	Harmonics of C3	Corresponding note
H1	131	Fundamental
H2	262	Middle C (C4)
H3	393	G above middle C
H4	524	High C (C5)
H5	655	E above high C
H6	786	G above high C
H7	917	Not quite B$^\flat$
H8	1048	C6

source of periodic energy is the vibrating vocal folds, harmonics occur at integer multiples of the fundamental frequency. (Look back at Figures 7.10 and 7.11 on pp. 132 and 133.)

8.1.3 formants: resonances of a tube of air

As was noted in Chapter 6, the vocal tract may be considered as a tube of air in between the larynx and the lips. Thinking of the vocal tract as a tube is to some extent an oversimplification, since the sides of the vocal tract are not really smooth and straight. In fact, the soft sides and deviations from perfect symmetry, along with the irregular shape and imperfect vibrations of the vocal folds, are factors that make our voices sound human rather than robotic. For the basic determination of speech sounds, however, the crucial factor is the length of the tube.

As we make constrictions with the tongue and lips, we can create a series of tubes of different lengths. We begin, however, with considering an open vocal tract from larynx to lips, with no particular constriction in any particular place, essentially characteristic of a mid, central, unround vowel [ʌ]. The tube of air that is created for this sound is (more or less) a single tube open at one end (the lips) and closed at the other (the larynx). The fact that it bends in the middle does not matter, because sound propagates equally in all directions. The vibrating larynx does not make a complete closure, of course, but the partial closure and difference in air pressures above and below the glottis are generally sufficient to provide separation between the sub-glottal and supra-glottal systems. (Again, the simplification is more apt for men than for women, because of the greater open quotient typical of women's voices.) At the lips, the difference in volume and air pressure between the inside and outside of the vocal tract is sufficient to make the air in the vocal tract behave as an independent system, but the opening is great enough that air particles at the lips have a great deal of freedom of motion.

What patterns of vibration will set themselves up as standing waves in a column or tube of air? As sound energy echoes back and forth inside the column of air, most wavelengths will interact randomly, such that energy is quickly dissipated. Certain wavelengths, however, will interact to positive effect, such that the interacting forces reinforce each other, pushing or pulling simultaneously. As with strings, the crucial determinant is the necessary boundary conditions.

For a tube of air open at one end and closed at the other, the boundary conditions that must hold for resonance is that the closed end of the tube must be a *velocity node*, and the open end must be a *velocity antinode*. Like the fixed ends of the musical string, the particles of air at the closed end of the tube have nowhere to move. At the open end of the tube, there is maximum freedom of movement.

Picture the oscillating yardstick we used as a picture of simple harmonic motion: one end is fixed and does not move at all (velocity node), while the other end experiences maximum movement (velocity antinode). Or picture a spring (like a slinky) fixed at one end and hanging free at the other. The spring is a more apt illustration, since the waves in a spring are longitudinal. If left to oscillate, the free end will bounce around (velocity antinode), while the fixed end stays put (velocity node).

The fixed end of the spring is both a velocity node and a pressure antinode. Because the point does not move at all in space, it experiences extremes of compression and rarefaction as the spring coils up and stretches out. It cannot move back to avoid being compressed, or move forward when it is pulled. The free end is the opposite. It is both a velocity antinode, moving back and forth freely, and a pressure node. Because the free end moves in response to the forces of the spring, it never experiences a change in pressure. But whether pressure or velocity is considered, the boundary conditions are met: a node at one end of the spring and an antinode at the other.

Only wavelengths with a node at one end and an antinode at the other will set up as standing waves in a spring fixed at one end. The fixed end cannot be forced to move; the free end cannot be kept from moving. The same is true of the air in the vocal tract: there is maximum particle movement (minimum pressure change) at the lips, and minimum particle movement (maximum pressure change) at the vocal folds. In the figures that follow, velocity nodes and antinodes will be graphed, as they are easier to visualize.

The distance from a node to an antinode is ¼ of the wavelength, as shown in Figure 8.9. So the first standing wave for a tube open at one end and closed at the other is one where tube length (L) = ¼ WL. At ⅔ of the wavelength, however, is a second node. This does not meet the boundary conditions, so will not resonate as a standing wave. When L = ¾ WL, the distance is node to antinode again, but not at ½ of the wavelength.

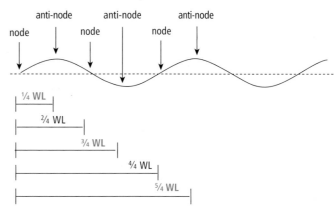

Figure 8.9 The distance from node to antinode is odd multiples of the ¼ wavelength.

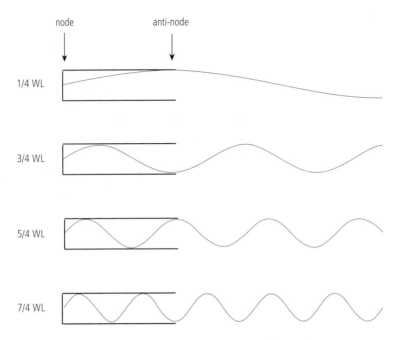

Figure 8.10 First four standing waves in a tube open at one end and closed at the other.

The general principle is that a standing wave is set up *when the tube length is equal to odd multiples of the quarter wavelength*. The progression is shown in Figure 8.10, and the general formula is given as Formula 8.5a.

Formula 8.5a: For a tube open at one end and closed at the other, a standing wave will occur when:

$$L = \frac{(2n-1)WL}{4}$$

L = tube length
WL = wavelength
n = any integer (thus 2n − 1 = any odd integer)

Because our perception of sound is relative to frequency, it is important for phoneticians to determine the frequencies that correspond to these standing waves. Since we know (by Formula 8.3), that WL = speed/frequency, we can rewrite Formula 8.5a as Formula 8.5b.

Formula 8.5b: For a tube open at one end and closed at the other, a standing wave will occur when:

$$L = \frac{(2n-1)*\text{speed}}{4*\text{frequency}}$$

Finally, solve for frequency, and we get Formula 8.5c:

Formula 8.5c: For a tube open at one end and closed at the other, a standing wave will occur when:

$$F_n = \frac{(2n-1)*\text{speed}}{4\,L}$$

All that remains is to calculate actual frequencies that correspond to actual tube lengths. For our purposes, we want to know about very specific waves: what are the frequencies of sound waves that resonate in the human vocal tract? The speed of sound in air is a constant 340 meters/second. (Slight variations due to temperature, humidity, and atmospheric pressure can be disregarded.) The average male vocal tract has a length of 17 cm (.17 m) from larynx to lips. (We begin with the male vocal tract for the pedagogical reason that the math comes out rather neatly.) Substituting these numbers into our formula gives us Formula 8.5d:

Formula 8.5d: The first three resonances of a 17-cm vocal tract:

$$F_1 = \frac{(1)*340}{4*.17} \quad \frac{340}{.68} \quad = \quad 500$$

$$F_2 = \frac{(3)*340}{4*.17} \quad \frac{1020}{.68} \quad = \quad 1500$$

$$F_3 = \frac{(5)*340}{4*.17} \quad \frac{1700}{.68} \quad = \quad 2500$$

Thus, the first three resonant frequencies of the average male vocal tract with no constrictions are 500 Hz, 1500 Hz, and 2500 Hz. These are the first three formants of the mid central vowel [ʌ]. Calculating the average formant frequencies for the female vocal tract is left for the student as an exercise.

8.1.4 calculating resonances for other vocal tract configurations

Movements of the lips and tongue modify the basic vocal tract tube in various ways. In this short chapter, we are able to consider only a few representative examples of how these variations could be modeled. As was noted in Chapter 7, *perturbation models* consider the effect of constricting (squeezing) the tube at different locations, while *tube models* picture the vocal tract as a series of tubes of different sizes with different boundary conditions.

Figure 8.11 repeats from Figure 8.10 the first four standing waves (that is, the first four formant frequencies) in a tube open at one end and closed at the other. In Figure 8.11, only the part of the wave inside the vocal tract tube is considered. In addition, labels indicating vocal tract landmarks have been added: the pharynx is at the closed end, the lips at the open end, the velum approximately half way along. Perturbation theory focuses on the location of nodes and antinodes in these standing waves, and on the inverse relationship between pressure and frequency (a pressure node = a velocity antinode, and vice versa). In the figure, the waves show velocity nodes and antinodes: antinodes (maximum velocity variation) occur at places where the line touches the top or bottom of the tube, and nodes (minimum velocity variation) occur at places where the line is in the middle of the tube. The crucial insight of perturbation theory is that increasing the pressure (that is, making a constriction) near a velocity antinode will *decrease* particle velocity, and thus frequency.

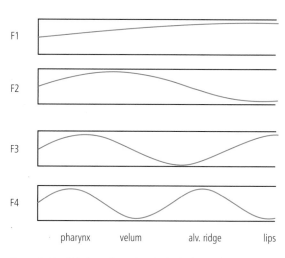

Figure 8.11 Velocity nodes and antinodes in the vocal tract.

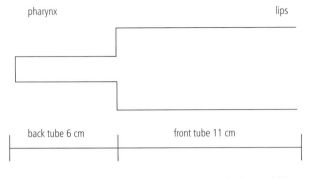

pharynx   lips

back tube 6 cm   front tube 11 cm

Figure 8.12   Tube schematic for vocal tract constriction for the vowel [ɑ].

Conversely, increasing the pressure near a velocity node will *raise* the frequency.

For example, by definition, the lips constitute a velocity antinode for all standing waves in the vocal tract. Therefore, constricting the lips lowers all formants. The pharyngeal region is closest to a velocity node for F1. Therefore, a constriction in the pharynx raises F1. F2 has a velocity node near the alveolar ridge: alveolar constrictions raise F2. F2, F3, and F4 all have velocity nodes in between the velum and alveolar ridge, that is, the palatal region: palatal constrictions raise all these formants. Perhaps most compelling, the third formant has three velocity antinodes: one in uvular region, one in the post-alveolar region, and one at the lips. English [ɹ] makes constrictions at all three locations: the tongue body backs and raises to the uvular region, the tongue tip raises toward the post-alveolar region, and the lips are rounded. The articulation seems to be designed for the exact purpose of lowering F3 as much as possible.

Another way to think about the acoustic consequences of vocal tract constrictions is to consider the vocal tract as a series of linked tubes. The vowel [ɑ], for example, can be modeled as two tubes. The "back tube" is narrow, corresponding to the narrow pharynx created by the low back constriction. The "front tube" is wider, corresponding to the open space in the front of the mouth created by the lowered tongue and open jaw. The front tube is longer than the back tube (say, for a 17 cm vocal tract, 6 cm for the back tube and 11 cm for the front tube). This is diagrammed in Figure 8.12.

The differences in diameter between the tubes are great enough that both can be considered effectively closed at one end and open at the other, so we can use Formula 8.5c to calculate the first three resonance frequencies of each tube, using 11 cm and 6 cm instead of 17 cm for tube length. Calculations are given as Formula 8.5e.

Formula 8.5e: The first two resonances of two tubes, 11 cm and 6 cm:

$$F_n = \frac{(2n-1)*\text{speed}}{4\,L}$$

		front tube (11 cm)		back tube (6 cm)	
First	=	$\dfrac{(1)*340}{4*.11}$	= **773**	$\dfrac{(1)*340}{4*.06}$	= **1417**
Second	=	$\dfrac{(3)*340}{4*.11}$	= **2318**	$\dfrac{(3)*340}{4*.06}$	= **4250**

The three lowest of these resonance frequencies constitute the first three formants: F1 = 773, F2 = 1417, F3 = 2318. If you compare these numbers to the spectrogram in Figure 7.22, you'll find them not a bad approximation for [ɑ]. (The match is not exact because the speaker in Figure 7.22 does not have a vocal tract of exactly 17 cm.)

Other configurations become progressively more complicated, but these formulae should be enough to give the beginning student an idea of how vocal tract resonance works. Resources for further reading are provided at the end of the chapter.

8.2 breaking sounds down

In Section 8.1, we gradually built sounds up, from simple-tone sinusoids to vowels with complex resonance patterns. In this section, we proceed to break sounds down. Starting from the complex waveforms that we digitize, how do we extract the acoustic information we need to analyze the sounds? Amplitude, pitch, and spectral analysis are considered in turn. Again, different signal analysis programs will have slightly different menus, displays, and steps. We concentrate here on the underlying algorithms that the different programs should have in common.

8.2.1 RMS amplitude

The amplitude of a signal could be important for a number of reasons. The amplitude of the signal as it is digitized is an important determinant of signal-to-noise ratio. Varying or controlling for amplitude could be important for tests of hearing and speech perception. The phonetician is also often concerned with *relative amplitude* – differences in amplitude between comparable speech segments. One might want to explore the role amplitude plays in conveying stress differences between syllables, for example, or to look at amplitude differences as a measure of reduction.

In one sense, every digitized sample is a measure of amplitude. However, measuring signal amplitude at a given point in time is not very useful as an overall characteristic of the speech wave, as amplitude varies constantly, from positive to negative and back again. Another possible measure is peak amplitude: find the highest point in the waveform portion of interest, and read off its amplitude value. The problem with measuring peak amplitude, however, is that it does not really correspond to how humans perceive loudness. The perception of loudness, as you may recall from Section 6.5 on p. 110, is correlated with sound intensity – the amount of energy in a sound wave – which varies depending on both amplitude and frequency.

The amplitude measure that corresponds most closely to the perception of loudness is the *Root Mean Square (RMS)* method. To compute the RMS amplitude over a window of time, you take a set of samples, square each value, find the mean, then take the square root. Working with squared values makes positive and negative values comparable. Otherwise, taking the mean of positive and negative numbers would result in 0.

Two example waves are shown in Figure 8.13. Measured sample values are shown. Simple waves are used for clarity, but the point would hold of any signal. Both waves have the same peak amplitude, 5 units, but wave B has a higher frequency. The method of taking RMS amplitude for each wave is shown in Table 8.3.

The result is that Wave B, which has the same peak amplitude as A, but higher frequency, is found to have the higher RMS amplitude, corresponding to the way the loudness of the two signals would be perceived.

In measuring RMS amplitude, the analyst can make the *window* of samples, the part of the waveform analyzed, as large or small as required. It is always the case that a smaller window will give more precision in the temporal domain, but sometimes the average over a longer period, even the whole utterance, might be what is needed.

8.2.2 autocorrelation pitch analysis

In the strict sense, it is impossible to measure pitch from an acoustic signal. Pitch refers to the way a sound is perceived. What can be measured from a signal is fundamental frequency (F0), which is correlated with, but not identical to, perceived pitch. Over the full range of human hearing, the correlation between F0 (acoustic measure) and pitch (perceptual measure) is not linear, but logarithmic – the higher the frequency, the greater change that is required in F0 in order to create the perception of equal change in pitch (see Section 9.3.1, p. 186). However, below 500 Hz, the correlation is close to linear. Therefore, in the range of F0 values common in human speech, the terms F0 and pitch are loosely used interchangeably.

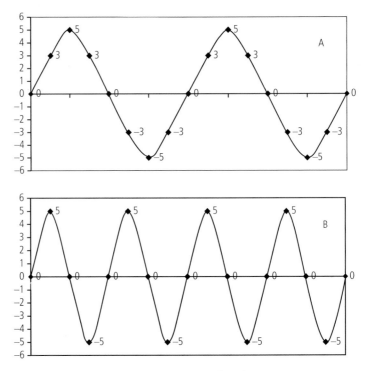

Figure 8.13   Two waves with the same peak amplitude but different frequency.

Table 8.3   Measuring RMS amplitude.

	Wave A	Wave B
Measured samples	0 3 5 3 0 −3 −5 −3 0 3 5 3 0 −3 −5 −3 0	0 5 0 −5 0 5 0 −5 0 5 0 −5 0 5 0 −5 0
Square each sample	0 9 25 9 0 9 25 9 0 9 25 9 0 9 25 9 0	0 25 0 25 0 25 0 25 0 25 0 25 0 25 0 25 0
Find the mean	10.12	11.76
Take the square root	3.18	3.42

Measuring F0 at one point in time is simple. Find the period (duration) of one cycle, and then take the inverse (F = 1/P). If the period is 5 ms, the F0 is 200 Hz (1/.005 = 200). Since there will always be slight variation from cycle to cycle in any human voice (more so for some voices and voice qualities than others), it can be useful to measure the duration of 10 periods, take the inverse of the whole, and then multiply by 10, to average out these small differences.

However, linguists are often more interested in how F0 changes over the course of an utterance, studying whether pitch is rising or falling, and how high and low points line up with the string of segments. A graph of F0 values over time is known as a *pitch track*. Taking numerous repeated measurements is tedious for a human, but exactly what computers were made for.

One common computational method of creating pitch tracks is *autocorrelation*. As the name indicates, the analysis consists of correlating a signal with a delayed version of itself. It relies on the definition of periodicity: a pattern of a certain duration repeats itself. Autocorrelation finds the duration of that chunk of the waveform that most clearly repeats.

Figures 8.14 A–D illustrate the process. First, the window of speech to be analyzed for each measurement is chosen. Window size determines the range of values that can be

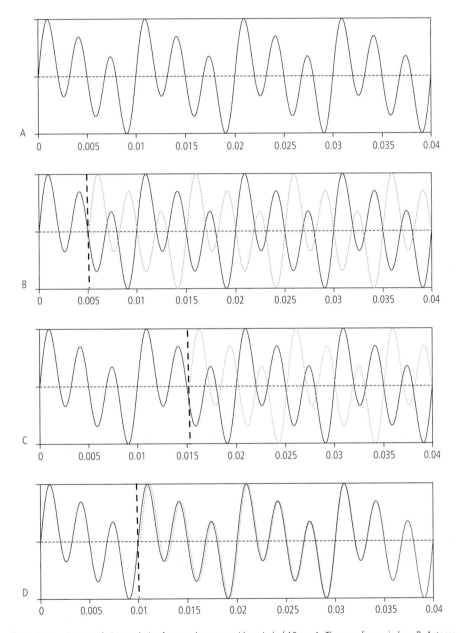

Figure 8.14   Autocorrelation analysis of a complex wave with period of 10 ms. A. The waveform window. B. Autocorrelation with a period that is too short. C. Autocorrelation with a period that is too long. D. Autocorrelation with the correct period.

detected: the window has to be long enough to contain more than one period, but short enough to remain fairly stable from cycle to cycle. Figure 8.14A shows a periodic waveform of 40 ms, a typical window size. It is not difficult for a human to "eyeball" the wave, discern the repeating pattern, and conclude that the period of one cycle is 10 ms, for an F0 of 100 Hz. Computers, however, are not nearly as good as humans at pattern matching. The computer must come to this conclusion by trial and error.

The autocorrelation algorithm tries out a range of periods, and calculates which one best matches the actual repeating pattern. The computer chooses a certain period, offsets (delays) the windowed waveform by exactly that much, and then compares the offset waveform to the original. If the selected lag time in fact corresponds to the actual period, the delayed waveform and the original should still line up: that is, their values will correlate. If the lag time does not correspond to the actual period, the two waves will be out of sync.

The computer might begin by trying out a period that is too small, as shown in Figure 8.14B. As shown in the figure, the actual and delayed waveforms do not line up. Another failed attempt is shown in Figure 8.14C. For this attempt, the period is too long. Autocorrelation of the actual period is shown in 8.14D. The computer will try a whole range of possible periods, pick the one for which the difference between offset wave and actual wave is the least, and return that value as the F0 for that window of the waveform. The window is then moved down an increment to the next part of the waveform, and the process repeats.

An actual pitch track, along with an approximately-segmented corresponding waveform, is shown in Figure 8.15. You can see that the voice is a rather deep man's voice, that the emphasis in the utterance fell on the words *you* and *year*, and that not all English questions end with a pitch rise. Note also the break in the "track" corresponding to the [g]: periodicity was not strong enough during the stop for the algorithm to compute any correlation. If there is no voicing, there is no period to measure, and thus no F0. In order to maintain the strongest periodic signal, studies designed to test F0 patterns will use as many sonorants as possible.

Two caveats in doing F0 analysis must be kept in mind. First, autocorrelation analysis is error-prone, especially when the SNR is low, or voicing is irregular. It is particularly common for the algorithm to return the best correlation over two periods (resulting in *pitch halving*) or over half a period (resulting in *pitch doubling*). Sudden and implausible jumps in F0, especially to half or double the previous value, should be corrected by adjusting the window size to rule out the implausible values. Suspect values should be hand-checked by directly measuring periods from the waveform.

Figure 8.16 shows an example of pitch doubling. The utterance is [volimo neven], *We love marigolds* in Serbian. (It was chosen for its many sonorants, not its meaning.) The pattern of rise–fall on each word is typical of the accent pattern expected in this language. At the end of the utterance, however, the autocorrelation pitch track jumps suddenly from 140 Hz to 280 Hz, even though no jump in pitch was heard. The problem was that the voicing became somewhat irregular at the end of the utterance, and the algorithm found a better

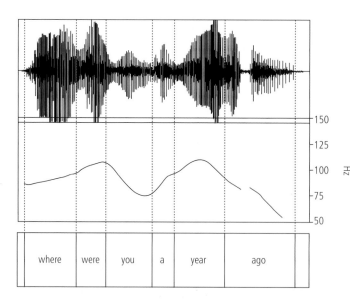

Figure 8.15   Pitch track for "Where were you a year ago?"

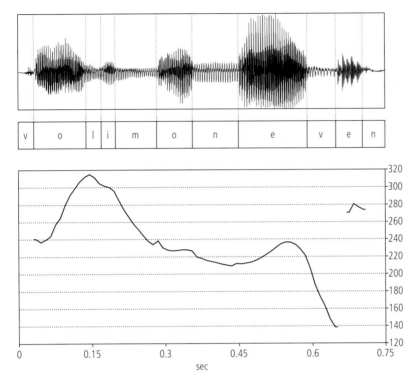

Figure 8.16   An example of pitch doubling in autocorrelation analysis.

match over half a period than over a single period, and it returned the wrong value. To get an accurate value, this portion of the waveform had to be measured by hand, using P = 1/F, and the ability of a human to see a pattern the computer couldn't.

8.2.3 Fourier analysis

A *Fourier analysis* is a mathematical analysis of a complex wave into its component frequencies. Computers perform a version called a *Fast Fourier Transform (FFT)* –*Transform* because the algorithm transforms the signal from the time domain into the frequency domain, *Fourier* because the original math goes back to Jean Baptiste Fourier, and *Fast* because the algorithm uses some mathematical shortcuts to make waveforms with a large number of samples more easily computable.

The exact formulae are beyond the scope of this text, though they can be found in any introduction to signal processing. Essentially, however, Fourier analysis is also a type of correlation. In this case, the signal is not correlated with itself, but with a series of sine waves. If the complex signal has a high amplitude component at a given frequency, there will be a strong correlation between the complex signal and a sinusoid of that frequency. The higher the amplitude, the greater the correlation.

Figure 8.17A shows a complex wave that was created by adding together two sinusoids, one with a frequency of 100 Hz and the other with a frequency of 500 Hz. The 100 Hz wave had twice the amplitude of the 500 Hz wave. You can see that the fundamental frequency of the complex wave is the greatest common factor of the component waves: 100 Hz.

Figure 8.17B overlays a sinusoid of 100 Hz on the complex wave. The correlation would compute the average sample-by-sample difference between the two waves, resulting in a

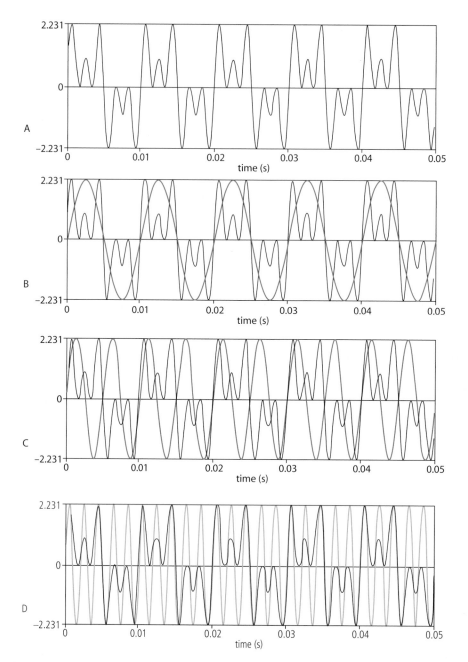

Figure 8.17 Comparison of a complex wave with three different sinusoids. A. A complex wave with components at 100 Hz and 500 Hz. B. Compared to a 100 Hz sinusoid. C. Compared to a 200 Hz sinusoid. B. Compared to a 500 Hz sinusoid.

number indicative of how similar the two waves are. Without going through the math, you can see from Figure 8.17 that the correlation would be fairly good: when the sinusoid is positive, the complex wave is also positive, when one is negative the other is negative. They tend to both be moving up or moving down at the same time. A high correlation indicates that presence of a high-amplitude component at that frequency.

Figure 8.17C compares the complex wave to a sinusoid with a frequency of 200 Hz. Here, the correlation is not so good. The complex wave is often highly positive when the sinusoid is highly negative, and they are often moving in opposite directions. This would return a low or negative correlation, indicating that this frequency is not present in the signal.

Finally, 8.17D shows the correlation with a 500 Hz sinusoid. The correlation is lower than that of B but higher than that of C, indicating a lower-amplitude frequency component.

In a real FFT of a speech sample, of course, the wave is more complex and the frequencies tested more numerous. The number of frequencies that can be tested, and therefore the frequency resolution, depends on the number of samples available for analysis, and thus on the window size. As was noted in Chapter 7, a longer window gives more samples, and thus greater frequency resolution, but resolution in the time domain is sacrificed. A long window gives a narrow-band spectrum or spectrogram (see Figure 7.21 on p. 139), while a smaller window gives a wide-band spectrum or spectrogram (see Figure 7.20 on p. 139). One window of FFT analysis produces a spectrum; numerous spectra taken at sequential points in time produce a spectrogram.

8.2.4 linear predictive coding

A different algorithm for spectral analysis of a digital signal is *Linear Predictive Coding (LPC)*. LPC also relies on the definition of a periodic signal: certain patterns repeat at regular intervals, and the intervals correspond to the periods of the component frequencies. This is, in one sense, a type of autocorrelation: samples that are separated by one period will be highly correlated with each other. If we know, for example, that the period of a wave is 5 ms, then the value of sample X will be a good predictor of the value of X + 5 ms. This holds true whether the period in question is the fundamental frequency, or a component frequency.

LPC works, then, by computing the intervals at which sample values are most highly correlated. The basic formula for LPC is given in a simplified form in Formula 8.7.

Formula 8.7: Linear Predictive Formula:

$x_n = a_1x_1 + a_2x_2 + a_3x_3 \ldots$
x_n equals some sample value
$x_1, x_2, x_3,$ etc. = previous sample values
$a_1, a_2, a_3,$ etc. = weights assigned to those previous sample values

Informally, the formula states that in a periodic signal, the value of any given point in time can be determined by the values of previous points in time (that is the linear predictive part), when those previous points are each assigned a weight. Higher weights correspond to samples that are separated by the period of a component frequency.

In order to compute what the weights should be, the algorithm works through a process of autocorrelation. The signal is offset by a certain number of samples, the original and offset waves are multiplied, and the mean product computed. If the result is positive (which will occur when both numbers tend to be positive or both numbers tend to be negative), the correlation is positive. If the result is negative (which will occur when one signal is positive and the other is negative), the correlation is negative. The highest correlations will occur when the offset is equal to the period of a component frequency.

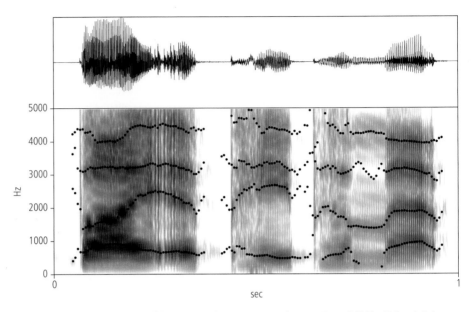

Figure 8.18   FFT and LPC analysis of the utterance "buy a paper map" (same as Figure 7.9). The LPC analysis is set to find four formants.

The intervals examined are smaller than those used in autocorrelation pitch analysis, because the goal of the analysis is to determine the higher frequency components. Instead of returning just one value as the fundamental period, the algorithm returns a set of the strongest correlations, which by hypothesis correspond to the formant frequencies. As with an FFT analysis, an LPC analysis can be computed over just one window, which will return a single set of numbers for formant frequencies, or it can be repeated sequentially, showing how the formant frequencies change over time.

The result of an LPC analysis is shown in Figure 8.18, overlaid on a spectrogram created by FFT analysis. The utterance is "buy a paper map," the same utterance as in Figures 7.18, 7.19, and 7.20. The dots in Figure 8.18 indicate the results of the LPC analysis at successive windows. Note that the LPC and FFT confirm one another: the line of dots lie over the bars of the spectrogram. It is important to remember, however, that they were computed independently.

LPC is more precise than FFT analysis. It will return an exact number in Hz for each formant, where FFT will show a band of frequencies within which the formant frequency falls. For example, in the utterance above, FFT analysis will tell us that F2 in the vowel of "map" is about 1800 Hz. LPC analysis returns an exact value of 1884.4 Hz (more precision, in fact, than is necessary). Because of this precision, LPC can often separate out formants that are close in frequency and that may seem on a spectrogram to have merged. LPC is not necessarily more accurate, however. Note the number of spurious values (random dots) found for voiceless portions of the signal. These should just be ignored.

An important feature/drawback of LPC analysis is that it will return exactly as many formant frequencies as requested. For Figure 8.18, the analysis was set to return four formants below 5500 Hz, which corresponds in fact to the number of formants in this range for this speaker. For Figure 8.19, six formants were requested, so six formants are returned. The analysis finds spurious values in between F1 and F2 and in between F2 and F3. (These likely correspond to harmonics rather than formants.) The user needs to be aware of the power

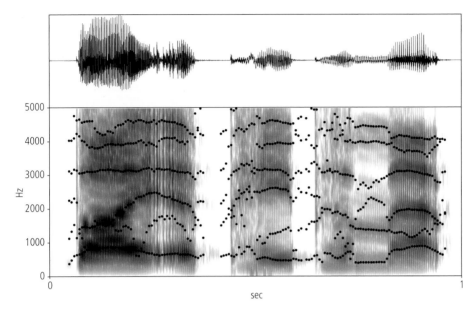

Figure 8.19 Same utterance as in Figure 8.18, with LPC analysis set to find 6 formants.

of this setting, and tune it correctly for the particular voice being analyzed. Because formant frequencies depend on the length of the vocal tract, women's voices will tend to have formants more spread out in the frequency range than men's, and thus have fewer formants below 5000 Hz. Four formants would be typical of a smaller female adult, 6 formants for a larger male adult.

LPC and FFT are best used together, as in Figure 8.18, where the FFT spectrogram can be used to confirm the accuracy of the LPC analysis. Finally, there is no substitute for an informed analyst, who knows what spectral patterns are to be expected for different speech sounds, and who can make intelligent and appropriate adjustments.

chapter summary

building sounds up

- A sinusoid is defined as circular motion:

  $y = a \sin \omega t$, where a = amplitude, ω = frequency, and t = time

  or

  $y = a \sin \theta$, where $\theta = \omega t$

- The vocal folds produce a source of sound energy that is rich in harmonics. The harmonic frequencies correspond to standing waves, which occur for all wavelengths that meet the required boundary condition: there must be a node (a fixed point) at each end. This condition is found for all waves where string length is a multiple of the half wavelength.

  $WL_n = 2L / n$, where WL = wavelength, L = string length, and n = any integer

- Because wavelength and frequency are in an inverse relationship (wavelength = speed/frequency), in such systems, harmonics occur at integer multiples of the fundamental.
- The air in the vocal tract filters the complex source, amplifying harmonics that correspond to a resonant frequency of that particular vocal tract shape (a formant), and damping out others. The boundary condition for resonance in a tube open at one end and closed at the other, like the air in the vocal tract, is that there must be a node at one end and an antinode (point of maximum change) at the other. This condition holds for all waves where tube length is an odd multiple of the quarter wavelength. The formula for the resonant frequencies of a tube of air is:

$$F_n = \frac{(2n-1) * \text{speed}}{4 L}$$

- This formula is used to compute formant patterns for particular vocal tract shapes, and thus particular vowels. Perturbation models consider the effect of constricting the tube at different locations, while tube models picture the vocal tract as a series of tubes of different sizes.

techniques of speech analysis

- RMS amplitude computes signal amplitude in a way that corresponds to our perception of loudness.
- Autocorrelation pitch analysis correlates a signal with an offset version of itself. The offset that returns the best match corresponds to the period, from which F0 is computed.
- A Fast Fourier Transform correlates the signal with a range of sinusoidal components. The strength of the correlation corresponds to the amplitude of that component in the signal, and from those amplitudes a spectrum or spectrogram can be created.
- Linear Predictive Coding computes the intervals at which sample values are most highly correlated. These intervals correspond to the periods of component formant frequencies.

further reading

Johnson, K. 1997. *Acoustic and Auditory Phonetics*. Oxford: Blackwell.
Lyons, R. 2011. *Understanding Digital Signal Processing*, 3rd Edition. Harlow: Pearson Education.
Stevens, K. 2000. *Acoustic Phonetics*. Cambridge, MA: MIT Press.

review exercises

1. What is circular motion, and how is it related to angular motion?
2. How does θ change as a point moves around a circle? How does $sin\,\theta$ change?
3. Define node and antinode.
4. What is a standing wave?
5. What boundary conditions are required to set up a standing wave in a string fixed at both ends?
6. What boundary conditions are required to set up a standing wave in a tube open at one end and closed at the other?

7. The tube model of vocal tract resonance models the vowel [ɑ] as two tubes (Figure 8.12). How do these tubes relate to a real vocal tract configuration? Which tube corresponds to F1? F2?

8. According to the perturbation model of vocal tract resonance, making a constriction near a velocity antinode will _____ (increase/decrease) frequency; and making a constriction near a velocity node will _____ (increase/decrease) frequency.

9. How does the perturbation model explain why rounding lowers all formants? How does it explain the very low F3 of English [ɹ]? (Refer to Figure 8.11.)

10. What is the difference between F0 and pitch?

11. Which utterance would work better for making a pitch track? Why?
    a. MaryAnne will nominate the mayor.
    b. Pete took six pieces of chalk.

further analysis and discussion

12. The average female vocal tract is about 15 cm. long. Calculate the first three resonance frequencies:
    a. for a uniform tube with no constriction (vowel [ʌ]).
    b. for a back tube length of 5 cm and a front tube length of 10 cm (vowel [ɑ]).
    c. Compare these to the results for the average male vocal tract found in the text. In general, how does a smaller vocal tract affect formant frequencies?

13. A larger male might have a vocal tract 18 cm in length. Calculate the first 3 resonance frequencies
    a. for a uniform tube with no constriction (vowel [ʌ]).
    b. for a back tube length of 6.5 cm and a front tube length of 11.5 cm (vowel [ɑ]).
    c. Compare these to the results for the average male vocal tract. In general, how does a larger vocal tract affect formant frequencies?

further research

14. To practice speech analysis, you need to work with actual digital files. Here are some ideas:
    a. Record two utterances that differ only in that one is said as a statement and one is said as a question, such as those below. Make pitch tracks for both. How does pitch signal the difference between statements and questions in English?

       (Who will run in the rain?) <u>Molly</u> will run in the rain.
       <u>Molly</u> will run in the rain? (I don't think so.)

    b. Record two utterances that differ only in which word or syllable is stressed, such as those below. Compare pitch, amplitude, and duration in the stressed and unstressed versions. How do these factors signal stress in English?

       Mary will win the <u>medal</u>.
       <u>Mary</u> will win the medal.
       Mary will win the <u>medallion</u>.

Go online Visit the book's companion website for additional resources relating to this chapter at: http://www.wiley.com/go/zsiga.

references

Chiba, T. and M. Kajiyama. 1941. Perturbation theory. In *The Vowel: Its Nature and Structure*. Tokyo: Kaiseikan.

Fant, G. 1960. Tube models. In *Acoustic Theory of Speech Production*. The Hague: Mouton.

9 Hearing and Speech Perception

The chief function of the body is to carry the brain around.

Thomas Edison

The Sounds of Language: An Introduction to Phonetics and Phonology, First Edition. Elizabeth C. Zsiga.
© 2013 Elizabeth C. Zsiga. Published 2013 by Blackwell Publishing Ltd.

The preceding chapters have covered the topic of how speech sounds are created by the vocal tract – articulatory phonetics. They have also covered the topic of how the speech waves thus created propagate through the air, and how they can be mathematically analyzed – acoustic phonetics. This chapter is about how speech sounds are analyzed by the human ear, and the human brain. What happens in the ear is *hearing*; what happens in the brain in *speech perception*. Hearing refers to the physiological process of transferring energy from sound waves to nerve impulses. Speech perception refers to the mapping of sounds into linguistic representations.

We begin with the anatomy and physiology of the ear, then cover a little bit of neuro-anatomy, and finally discuss some current issues in speech perception, including the nonlinear relationship between acoustic and perceptual measures, problems of variability and invariance (including normalization and categorical perception), cue integration, top-down processing, and the question of the units of perception and thus of linguistic representation.

9.1 anatomy and physiology of the ear

The ear has three parts: outer, middle, and inner. The parts of the ear are shown in Figure 9.1. The outer ear, or *auricle*, consists of the visible shell of the ear (the *pinna*) and the ear canal leading down to the eardrum (*tympanic membrane*). The shell of the human ear, though smaller and less mobile than that of many other mammals, helps to capture sound waves, and aids in sound localization. The ear canal serves, first, to keep our eardrums safely inside our heads, shielded from changes in temperature and humidity, as well as from sharp objects. The ear canal is also a resonator, amplifying sounds especially in the 3000 Hz range, a crucial frequency area for speech sounds. (If you do the math for the resonances of a tube closed at one end and open at the other, you'll find that that means that the average ear canal is 2.8 cm long.)

The fact that we have two ears allows us to locate sounds in space, and to keep track of a particular sound source in a noisy environment. Because the ears are separated by a head's width, there is a slight delay in time between when a sound reaches one ear and when it reaches the other, and a slight decrease in intensity, due to the "shadow" of the head. In addition, sounds actually echo within the folds of the pinna in characteristic ways, depending on the direction of propagation. The brain interprets these small differences in phase, intensity, and frequency to determine the location of the sound source.

The middle ear consists of the eardrum and the *ossicles*: three tiny bones called the *malleus*, *incus*, and *stapes* (or hammer, anvil, and stirrup). They are, as you learned in Biology class, the smallest bones in the body; the stapes is the smallest of the three, at about 2.5 mm long. The ossicles connect the eardrum to a second membrane, the *oval window* of the fluid-filled inner ear, and their job is to efficiently transfer sound patterns from one membrane to the other. Having this additional stage of transfer minimizes the reflection of energy, amplifies soft sounds, and protects the inner ear from very loud sounds.

Soundwaves travel down the ear canal and impact the eardrum, causing it to vibrate, mimicking the complex patterns of vibration in the soundwave. The middle ear is an air-filled chamber, and vibration of the eardrum is maximized when air pressure on both sides of the membrane is equal. Under normal circumstances, pressure equalization is achieved via the *Eustachian tube*, which creates a passageway between the middle ear and the mouth,

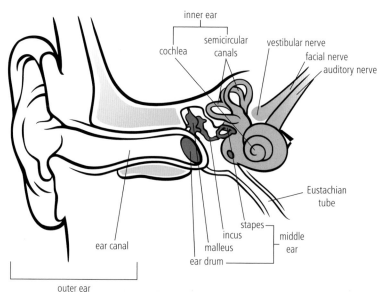

Figure 9.1 Anatomy of the ear.

and thus the outside world. Abnormal circumstances, such as a tube blocked by infection, or a sudden change in altitude as at takeoff, result in pressure build-up in the middle ear, and an earache. Swallowing or chewing gum activates the muscles around the Eustachian tube, which can induce the exchange of air and release of pressure that makes the ears "pop." Extreme pressure differences, as can be experienced in scuba diving, can cause the tympanic membrane to rupture.

> 9.1   The Eustachian tubes were discovered by Bartolomeo Eustachius, an Italian Renaissance anatomist (d. 1574), who worked primarily via autopsy. Due to the views of contemporary officials on the legality of cutting up dead bodies, Eustachius' anatomical drawings were not published until 140 years after his death.

If soundwaves in the air directly impacted the oval window, without the mechanical transfer of energy through the ossicles, the difference in viscosity between the air and the inner-ear fluid would cause almost all of the sound energy to be reflected. (Fish, whose ears have fluid both inside and outside, have no middle ear.) In humans, as the energy is transferred from eardrum to malleus to incus to stapes to oval window, the force (the amount of "push" at a given point) is increased at each step. As can be seen in Figure 9.1, the eardrum is not flat, but conical, and the first bone in the middle-ear chain, the malleus, is attached to the apex of the eardrum, where force is concentrated. (Remember playing with a parachute in grade-school gym class? The children hold the edge of the parachute, and the teacher places a ball in the middle. When the children shake the edges, the waves travel to the center and shoot the ball high into the air: all the energy it takes to move the whole large parachute travels inward and is concentrated at the apex.) Then, the malleus is longer than the incus, and acts like a lever: the force transferred to the smaller arm is greater, because its displacement is less. The incus transfers energy to the stapes, and the "footplate" of the stapes is attached to the oval window. The oval window is much smaller than the eardrum: a force that creates only a small displacement of the eardrum causes a much greater displacement of the oval window. Thus, through a series of transfers through the middle ear, sound energy is amplified.

A different process, called the *middle ear reflex*, can impede the transfer of energy in very loud sounds. The reflex is an involuntary contraction of the muscles attached to the ossicles (the *stapedius* and *tensor tympani*), in response to any very high-intensity stimulus (above 80 dB). Like the bone to which it is attached, the stapedius muscle is the smallest in the body. The muscle contraction pulls the bones away from the membranes, and damps the vibration, protecting the oval window from being displaced too much. The protection, however, is only partial (10 to 20 dB reduction in amplitude) and not quite instantaneous, so very loud sounds can still cause significant damage.

The inner ear is encased in the thickest part of the skull, the temporal bone. The inner ear consists of two connected parts: the *vestibular system* for balance and the *cochlea* for hearing. Within the vestibular system are the three *semicircular canals*, loops oriented in different planes at right angles to each other, which sense motion in three dimensions, and the smaller, ovoid *utricle* and *sacchule*, which sense horizontal and vertical acceleration. Each of these vestibular organs is filled with fluid and lined with tiny hair cells (*cilia*), each of which is attached to a nerve fiber. When the head moves, the motion of the fluid causes the hair cells to bend, which triggers the nerves to fire. The brain interprets the patterns of activation as movement and orientation of the body in space, providing feedback to maintain balance, fix the gaze, and coordinate body motion.

9.2   Interestingly, there are small crystals of calcium carbonate floating in the fluid in the utricle and sacchule, which further stimulate the cilia. These crystals are called *otoliths*, literally ear-stones. You really do have rocks in your head.

Our interest as phoneticians, however, lies in the cochlea. The cochlea is a coiled tube like a snail shell, no bigger than a marble (see Figure 9.1). It takes 2½ turns on itself; unrolled (Figure 9.2), it would be about 3.5 cm long. The cochlear tube is divided lengthwise into three parts, or *scalae*: the *scala vestibuli* on the top, the *scala tympani* on the bottom, and the *scala media* (also known as the *cochlear duct*) in the middle.

The end of the cochlea adjacent to the middle ear is the *basal* end, the far end is the *apex*. The *helicotrema*, at the apex of the cochlea, connects the scala vestibuli and scala tympani. Like the vestibular organs, the cochlea is filled with lymphatic fluid.

As shown in Figure 9.2, the stapes connects to the oval window at the basal end of the scala vestibuli. Sound vibrations pass through the eardrum, through the ossicles, to the oval window. The vibration of the oval window causes complex pressure waves to move through

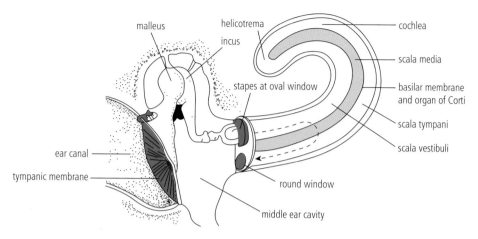

Figure 9.2 Middle and inner ear, showing the cochlea "unrolled."

the lymphatic fluid in the cochlea. The waves move up the scala vestibuli, around the helicotrema, and down the scala tympani. At the basal end of the scala tympani is another membrane, the *round window*, which expands and contracts as the waves impact it, acting as a pressure release valve. As these pressure waves, corresponding to sound pressure variations, move through the cochlea, they cause deformation of the cochlear duct. It is this deformation that results in hearing.

In order to understand how hearing takes place, we need to magnify even further, to examine the structures *inside* the cochlear duct. These are shown in Figure 9.3, which, for comparison, shows three stages of magnification: (a) the entire cochlea; (b) a cross-section of the three scalae; and (c) a close-up of the inside of the cochlear duct.

As shown in Figure 9.3, the cochlear duct is separated from the scala vestibuli on the top by the *vestibular membrane*, and from the scala tympani on the bottom by the *basilar membrane*. The basilar membrane is connected to a protrusion of the temporal bone, a "bony shelf" that supports the inner ear. On top of the basilar membrane runs a tunnel-shaped set of structures collectively known as the *organ of Corti*.

> 9.3   Marquis Alfonso Corti was an Italian medical doctor and anatomist who lived 1822–1876. He worked first in Vienna, until his lab was taken over and his papers destroyed in the revolution of 1848. He then moved to Germany, where he published a paper (in French) describing the organs of hearing inside the cochlear duct. That same year (1851), Corti's father died, and he inherited a title and an estate. He moved back to Italy, took up residence on the estate, and gave up science.

The organ of Corti consists of a set of hair cells spread out along the cochlear duct. Each hair cell is connected to a nerve cell, and from each hair cell a bundle of fine filament hairs (*stereocilia*) protrudes (about 1.5 million in each ear). Covering the stereocilia is the *tectorial membrane*, which is described by numerous sources as a "gelatinous flap." The whole organ

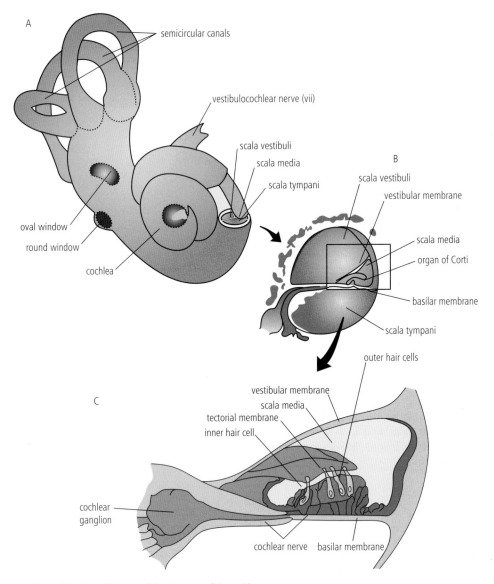

Figure 9.3 Magnified view of the structures of the cochlea.

is bathed in the lymphatic fluid that fills the cochlear duct. As pressure waves reverberate through the scalae, corresponding movement of the basilar and tectorial membranes cause the stereocilia to deform, and their connected nerves to fire. The nerve signals, carried through the auditory nerve to the brain, are interpreted as sound.

Spookily, the stereocilia also send out their own very-low-amplitude signals, moving in a delayed response to, or sometimes in the absence of, external stimulation. These *oto-acoustic emissions* can be picked up by a sensitive microphone placed in the ear, and are a sign of a healthy auditory system. While no-one is completely sure what causes them, it may be an effect of the cochlea fine-tuning itself to receive and process signals at the appropriate frequencies and amplitudes.

The ability to distinguish *different* sounds depends on the structure of the basilar membrane. Crucially, the basilar membrane is not uniform along its length. At the basal end, it is thin (less than .1 mm) and stiff, supported almost all the way across by the bony shelf. At the apex of the cochlea, the bony shelf tapers off and the basilar membrane is thicker (.5 mm) and much less stiff. Because of its tapered shape, the basilar membrane creates a fine-tuned analog spectral analysis of the incoming pressure wave.

As the oval window vibrates and sends pressure waves through the scalae, the basilar membrane deforms in response to these waves. The place at which the greatest deformation occurs depends on the frequency. The thin end of the basilar membrane responds strongly to high frequencies, the thick end of the basilar membrane responds strongly to low frequencies, and the middle responds differentially to every frequency in between. The exact places along the membrane that respond to different frequencies are diagrammed in Figure 9.4. (Hungarian scientist Georg von Békésy won the 1961 Nobel Prize in Medicine and Physiology for figuring this out.)

For a complex sound, the different parts of the basilar membrane will respond to the different component frequencies. The amplitude of vibration of the basilar membrane at a certain point will depend on the relative amplitude of that frequency in the signal: greater amplitude causes greater displacement, which causes a stronger firing of the nerves. Thus the organ of Corti creates a complete spectral analysis: both frequency and amplitude information are encoded in the message sent to the brain.

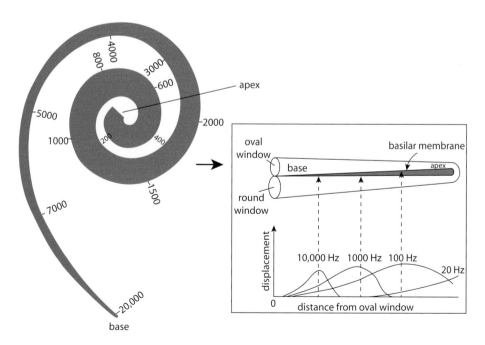

Figure 9.4 The place theory of hearing: response of the basilar membrane to different frequencies. Reproduced with permission from Dr Kathleen E. Cullen and the McGill Molson Medical Informatics Project.

Note that in Figure 9.4, areas of frequency response are not evenly distributed along the basilar membrane, resulting in a non-linear relationship between acoustic frequency and perceived pitch. Over half of the length of the basilar membrane is devoted to frequencies between 200 and 3000 Hz, those frequencies most important for distinguishing speech sounds. Because most of the cochlea is devoted to this range, humans can discriminate sounds in this range much more precisely than sounds either lower or higher. As frequencies get progressively higher, the cochlea is less able to distinguish them. No part of the cochlea responds to frequencies above 20,000 Hz; therefore such frequencies are not perceived by humans as sound. The cochlea of other animals are configured differently, and they therefore perceive a different range of sound frequencies. Dogs can hear up to 40,000 Hz, bats and dolphins over 100,000 Hz.

We have described the healthy hearing system as a complex chain of energy transfer. If any point in the chain is damaged, hearing loss results. If sound is not being properly transferred from outer to middle to inner ear the hearing loss is termed *conductive*. If the inner ear is not properly responding to the sounds it receives the hearing loss is termed *neurosensory*. Congenital deafness (from birth) occurs when some part of the ear does not develop normally. Later in life, the delicate structures of the middle and inner ear can be damaged by disease, especially infections and tumors. Certain medications can cause neural or hair-cell damage as a side-effect. Prolonged exposure to high amplitude noise, or even instantaneous exposure to very high amplitude noise, can damage the ear in numerous ways. Most commonly, stereocilia of the inner ear can be permanently damaged by over-stimulation: they are quite fragile and break off easily. The most common cause of hearing loss is aging. As with everything else in the body, the structures of the ear stiffen up over time, and stereocilia are gradually damaged and lost. Hearing loss is greatest in the higher frequencies, as shown in Figure 9.5.

Hearing aids function to undo partial hearing loss, boosting the amplitude of frequencies to which the ear has lost sensitivity. Cochlear implants bypass the ear completely. These devices directly stimulate the auditory nerve cells in the way that the cochlea would if it were working. Like the cochlea, implants detect the level of sound energy at different frequencies, and stimulate the appropriate nerves accordingly. The frequency bands are not as finely tuned as in natural hearing, but speech is intelligible.

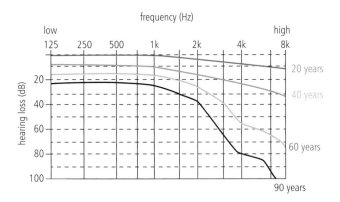

Figure 9.5   Average hearing loss as a function of age.
Source: Reproduced by permission from 'Journey into the World of Hearing' http://www.cochlea.org, by R. Pujol et al., NeurOreille, Montpellier.

9.2 neuro-anatomy

9.2.1 studying the brain

We do not understand exactly how the brain creates the perception of language. It is a complex, multi-leveled process. We know that one end of the process – the speech signal – consists of pressure modulations at different frequencies and amplitudes, and that the other end of the signal – the linguistic message – consists of a meaningful sequence of words. We do not fully understand, however, how the brain turns one into the other, although we are gaining more information about it all the time. Since perception takes place inside the brain, there are two general ways to study it. The first set of methodologies look directly at brain activity.

One traditional way of doing neuroscience involves experimenting on animals, tracing the biological and behavioral effects of stimulating or destroying parts of the nervous system or the brain. The subjects in these experiments are often rats or cats, whose auditory systems turn out to be reasonably similar to those of humans. In humans, we can study brains that have been affected by disease or injury, hopefully helping the sufferers as well as advancing science. Two pioneers in the study of brain anatomy were Pierre Paul Broca, a French physician who lived 1824–1880, and Carl Wernicke, a German physician who lived 1848–1905. Both men worked with patients whose speech had been affected by brain damage. Broca discovered that patients who had suffered damage to a small area toward the front of the left cerebral hemisphere were unable to put words together into sentences, while Wernicke found that patients who had damage to an area somewhat further back had trouble associating sound and meaning. They were among the first scientists to claim that different parts of the brain have specific functions. This claim turned out to be somewhat too simplistic, and speech scientists today accept that language processing and other brain functions are more widely distributed, but *Broca's area* and *Wernicke's area* remain well-known brain landmarks.

Today, neurosurgeons often operate on patients who are conscious. Because the brain itself has no pain receptors, only local anesthesia to the scalp is necessary during brain surgery. Prior to excising a tumor, the surgeon may electrically stimulate different parts of the exposed brain while talking to the patient, testing the effect on the patient's movement, perception, or speech. The immediate goal is to preserve as much brain function as possible when a part of the brain must be removed, but much information about functions of different parts of the brain – as well as person-to-person variation and the ability of other parts to compensate – has been gained in this way.

Non-invasive techniques for measuring brain activity include *EEG (electro-encephalography)* and *ERP (event-related potentials)*, which measure electrical activity in different parts of the brain using external electrodes. *PET (positron emission tomography)* and *f-MRI (functional magnetic resonance imaging)* both measure increased blood flow, PET scans based on the metabolization of (very-low-dose) radioactive sugars ingested by the patient for the purpose of the test, and f-MRI based on the magnetic response of iron in hemoglobin. These all rely on the insight that parts of the brain that are "working" will have both increased electrical activity and increased blood flow relative to the parts that are not immediately involved in a specific task.

All these means of directly measuring brain activity, both animal and human, invasive and non-invasive, require sophisticated labs and expensive instrumentation. The second family of methods is simpler, if less direct. The investigator plays sounds (either natural or altered), and asks people what they hear. The physical family of methods gives us information about physical pathways, while perception experiments give us information about the results.

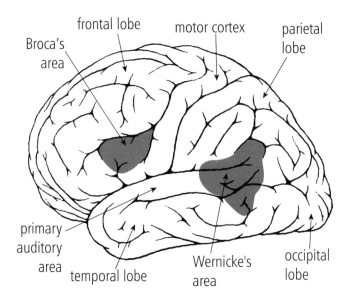

Figure 9.6   The left hemisphere of the brain.

In order to be understood as language, speech stimuli must reach the *auditory cortex* in the temporal lobe of the brain (Figure 9.6). Note that the auditory cortex is centrally located, in between Broca's and Wernicke's areas, and not far from the *motor cortex*, which controls all muscular movement, including speech articulation. Figure 9.6 shows the left side (*hemisphere*) of the brain: if this brain were in a person, she would be facing to the left.

Our brains are *lateralized*: the two hemispheres of our brains often specialize in different functions, and for most people language processing takes place predominantly in the left side of the brain. (For a minority of left-handed people, the specializations are reversed, or are more equal. Most of our neural wiring crosses at the top of the spinal column, so right-handed people tend to be left-brain dominant, and vice versa, though the degree of functional lateralization differs from person to person.) Because of lateralization, speech scientists most often look at brains from the left. Lateralization is not complete, however, and there is an auditory cortex on both sides of the brain. Rhythm and prosody, like music, seem to be processed more on the right.

No single nerve connects the cochlea straight to the auditory cortex, however. Along the way are several relays, like station stops, where temporal, spectral, and amplitude information is extracted and integrated. The chains of nerves that carry signals from the ears to the brain are called the auditory pathways. The *primary auditory pathways* carry signals from the cochlea to the auditory processing centers of the brain. The *non-primary pathways* connect the signals from the cochlea to nerves that handle all incoming stimulation, and thence to the parts of the brain that control awareness and attention. These centers determine, for example, whether you'll consciously follow the conversation at the next table or tune it out and focus on your book, what noises wake you up and what you'll sleep through, and how you'll divide your attention between driving and a phone call. Here, we concentrate on the primary auditory pathways.

9.2.2 primary auditory pathways

In order for speech perception to take place, information about spectrum, amplitude, and timing must be extracted from the signal, and the different types of information must be integrated with each other. This processing take place as the signal is sent through the relays of the auditory pathways.

Frequency information is encoded in the fact that, at every stage of the pathway, neurons are *tonotopically organized*, as they are in the cochlea. That is, neurons that respond to different frequencies remain on separate tracks, and eventually feed into separate parts of the auditory cortex. Thus the brain can interpret the firing of specific bundles of neurons as the presence of specific frequencies in the signal, based on the location along the basilar membrane where the chain began. The tonotopic organization of the auditory nerve is illustrated in Figure 9.7.

The bottom portion of Figure 9.7 shows a spectrogram of the utterance "Joe took father's green shoebench out." (This particular utterance, which contains a variety of speech sounds, originated at Bell Labs in the 1950s, where it was used for testing telephone equipment.) The top portion of Figure 9.7 shows a *neurogram*, indicating the firing of bundles of nerve fibers in the auditory nerve of a cat, in response to hearing the utterance. (Figure 9.7 does not show that the cat understood the utterance, of course, only that it heard the sounds in a way similar to that of a human.) Each line of the neurogram represents activity in a bundle of nerve fibers tuned to a specific frequency band, low frequency on the bottom, high frequency on the top. The neurogram and spectrogram are time-aligned. Across the top of Figure 9.7, white arrows point to bursts of activity in nerve bundles attuned to high frequencies, around 3000 and 4000 Hz. These bursts of activity correspond to fricative and burst noise for alveolars and palatoalveolars: [ʤ], [t], [z], [ʃ], [tʃ]. Across the bottom of Figure 9.7, black arrows point to bursts of electrical energy in nerve bundles attuned to low frequencies. These firings correspond to the onset of voicing and F1 for every vowel. Finally, the circled portions of the neurogram and spectrogram show that as F3 rises from about 1000 to 3000 Hz in the sequence [gri], bundles of nerves attuned to successively higher frequencies fire in sequence.

Amplitude information is encoded in the strength of the firing: the greater the amplitude of a given pressure wave in the cochlea, the greater the displacement of specific hair cells, which results in stronger electrical charges being sent through the neurons associated with those frequencies. Stronger electrical charge is interpreted as higher amplitude.

Information about timing is more complex, and it involves the coordination of different streams of information as the signal is sent through the relays of the auditory pathway. These relays are illustrated in Figure 9.8 and summarized below.

Step 1: auditory nerve: initial transmission. The hair cells of the cochlea are connected to fibers of the *cochlear nerve*, which join with nerve fibers from the vestibular system to form the *auditory nerve* (cranial nerve VII). When a hair cell is sufficiently stimulated, an electrical charge is sent into the pathway. Each nerve fiber is associated with a particular frequency, determined by its place along the basilar membrane.

Step 2: cochlear nuclei: first-level processing. The auditory nerve transmits signals to the *cochlear nuclei* in the brain stem, which extract basic frequency, amplitude, and temporal information from the incoming signals. One way that timing is extracted from the signal is through the firing of *onset neurons*. These neurons are cued to fire whenever another neuron sets off a sudden burst of energy. They thus keep track of when certain auditory events begin. Different onset neurons will *phase-lock* (fire in coordination with) other neurons that are activated at specific periodic intervals. Some will tend to

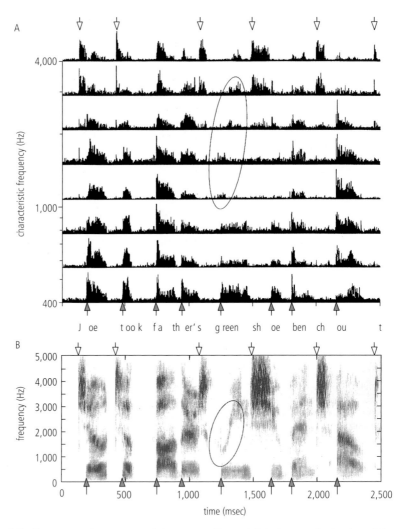

Figure 9.7 Neurogram and spectrogram of the sentence "Joe took father's green shoebench out." See text for explanation.

Source: From Delgutte, Bertrand. 1997. *Auditory Neural Processing of Speech.* (Figure 16.1 in W. Hardcastle and J. Laver, *The Handbook of Phonetic Sciences,* 1st Edition).

phase-lock to the large-scale amplitude bursts that occur at rates of 3 to 5 times per second, corresponding to the onsets of segments or syllables. Others will phase-lock to lower amplitude changes at rates of 100 to 300 Hz, corresponding to the smaller bursts of energy that characterize each glottal pulse, and will thus fire in a pattern corresponding to F0. Coordination of these different temporal signals is interpreted further up the chain.

Steps 3 and 4: superior olivary cortex and inferior colliculus: binaural and audio-visual integration. The next relay is the *superior olivary cortex* (named for its olive shape) where information from both ears is integrated, and sent on to the *inferior colliculus* in the

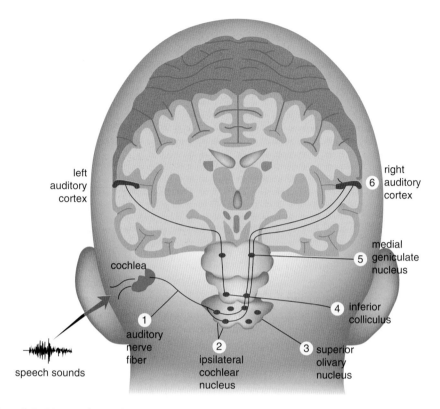

Figure 9.8 Primary auditory pathway.

midbrain. The superior olivary cortex and inferior colliculus, by integrating information from the two ears, are responsible for sound localization. The inferior colliculus also serves as a switchboard for other incoming sensations, and integrates incoming auditory and visual information. The middle ear reflex (tamping down the ossicles in response to high-amplitude input) is triggered in the olivary cortex.

Step 5: medial geniculate nucleus: relative timing and auditory/motor integration. The next relay is the *medial geniculate nucleus*, in the thalamus, which is part of the cerebrum. Timing and intensity differences from different frequency streams, sent up from previous relays, are further processed here: for example, the time delay between consonant burst and onset of voicing that corresponds to VOT may be extracted. It is also at this stage that incoming auditory signals are matched up with motor neurons, particularly motor neurons associated with speech articulation. The perception of a sound will cause activation in areas of the brain associated with speech production, without any actual accompanying movement of the articulatory apparatus. A number of linguists propose that this neural link between acoustics and articulation is a crucial part of the speech perception process (see Section 9.3.4).

Step 6: auditory cortex: speech perception. Finally, the pre-processed auditory signal is sent to the *auditory cortex.* Prior to this point, different auditory cues have been extracted, as described above: frequency and timing of energy bursts, fundamental frequency,

frequency changes that correspond to formant transitions, amplitude variations corresponding to syllables, etc. It is in the auditory cortex and associated areas, however, where actual speech recognition takes place. The incoming stimulus is matched to a stored linguistic unit, and the units are assembled into linguistic meaning.

Our brain-scanning devices can show us what areas of the brain are active during different tasks, but they cannot tell us exactly what are brains are *doing*, that is, exactly how the incoming stimulus is matched up with linguistic meaning. Questions such as "What units are stored?" "How are they activated by the incoming signal?" and "How are different streams of information integrated and processed?" are subjects of much research and debate.

9.3 speech perception

9.3.1 non-linearity

Sections 9.1 and 9.2 have detailed the multiple transfers that occur from sound stimulus to auditory cortex, with opportunities at every stage for aspects of the signal to be enhanced or lost. It should therefore not be surprising that auditory information as it is processed by the brain is not exactly the same as acoustic information that is recorded by a microphone. The mapping from acoustics to perception is non-linear: equal changes in frequency and amplitude do not necessarily result in equal responses in the perceptual system.

9.4   In Focus

The smallest difference that can be detected is called the *just-noticeable difference (jnd)*. A scientist tests the jnd by playing slightly different sounds to a listener, and asking him "Are those two sounds the same or different?" or "Which sound in this set is different?" For tones under 1000 Hz, heard under ideal conditions (listening to pure tones over headphones in a lab), a young healthy ear can distinguish notes that differ by only 2 or 3 Hz or less than 1 dB. However, because of the unequal frequency distribution along the basilar membrane (Figure 9.4), the jnd gets exponentially larger as frequency increases. A listener may be able to distinguish a tone at 500 Hz from one at 503 Hz, but 5000 Hz and 5100 Hz will sound the same. At 10,000 Hz, a listener needs a 1000 Hz change before he will identify two signals as different.

Because of this non-linear mapping, phoneticians concerned with speech perception generally do not work with and report raw frequency values, but will mathematically transform the numbers to a logarithmic scale that better matches perceptual sensitivities. A number of different mathematical transformations are available: these include the semitone scale, the Bark Scale, the Mel scale, and the ERB scale. The most straightforward may be the Bark scale (another eponym: German physicist Heinrich Barkhausen, 1881–1956). The Bark scale divides the frequency range of human hearing into 24 bands, such that each step from one

Table 9.1   The Bark scale.

Hz	Bark	Hz	Bark	Hz	Bark
20	1	920	9	3150	17
100	2	1080	10	5300	18
200	3	1270	11	6400	19
300	4	1480	12	7700	20
400	5	1720	13	9500	21
510	6	2000	14	12000	22
630	7	2320	15	15500	23
770	8	2700	16	200000	24

band to the next sounds about equal. The upper edge (in Hz) of each band of the Bark scale is given in Table 9.1.

The logarithmic nature of the scale is seen in that, in the lower frequency ranges, it takes only 100 Hz to increase by 1 Bark (e.g., between Bark 2 and 3), but in the higher ranges (e.g., between Bark 22 and 23), it takes over 3000 Hz. Note, however, that below 500 Hz, the mapping from Hz to Bark is nearly linear.

9.3.2 variability and invariance

The case of the difference between F0 and perceived pitch is just one instance of a much larger issue. At many levels, and all the time, we perceive sounds that are measurably different as though they were the same, and sometimes sounds that are the same as though they were different. One example is the same utterance said by two different people, for example, a large male and small child. Because of differences in vocal tract anatomy, the formant values in a simple utterance like "Mom" will be completely different for these two speakers. For the man, F1 might be 700 Hz and F2 might be 1100 Hz in the middle of the vowel, while the child's F1 might be as high as her father's F2: 1100 Hz for F1 and 2000 Hz for F2. How can a listener perceive such different signals as the same word? This is the problem of *normalization*.

We perceive all speech frequency (and timing) values as relative. Our brains use information in other parts of the signal to *normalize* a particular stimulus, that is, to interpret values relative to other values, not to an external standard. High F0 and wide spacing of harmonics within the given vowel, and high formant values in other vowels, will all cue the listener to the smallness of the child (or the opposite to the largeness of the man), and values will be interpreted accordingly in decoding the linguistic message. At the same time, the personal and social information will be extracted and stored as well: listeners recognize both the message and the person saying it.

Thus acoustically different items (such as vowels with formants at 700 and 1100 Hz vs. 1100 and 2000 Hz) can be heard as the same linguistic item. Another effect of normalization is that the *same* item can be perceived differently when embedded in different contexts. The same syllable can be heard as high tone or low tone, as /ɪ/ or /ɛ/, depending on the characteristics of the other syllables around it.

Another example of a case where measurably different acoustic patterns are perceived as the same stimulus is the case of formant transitions. As was discussed in Chapter 7, stop consonants are acoustically distinguished from one another primarily by formant changes in adjacent vowels. During the stop closure, there is little or no sound energy, and the silence (or low-level voicing) produced by a [b] closure is no different from the silence (or low-level voicing) produced by a [d] or [g] closure. Instead, the different places of articulation are cued by the effect they have on neighboring vowels, as the articulators move away from the closure position to the position required for the vowel. This was shown in Figure 7.25, which illustrated formant transitions for different consonants before the same vowel.

The opposite situation, the same consonant before different vowels, is illustrated in Figure 9.9, which shows a spectrogram of the utterances "dee, day, doe." If you ask listeners whether they "hear a *d*" in each of these utterances, they will say "yes." But in what does the perception of [d] inhere? Because this is English, there is no voicing during the stop phase, so the [d] cannot be identified there. It must be the formant trajectories. The problem is that the trajectories are different in each case: F2 is rising out of the closure for [di], staying flat for [de], and falling for [do].

A different type of normalization is at work here. The listener interprets the formant transition relative to the following vowel. A rising F2 transition is associated with [d] in the context of [i], and a falling [F2] transition is associated with [d] in the context of [o].

9.5   In Focus

The first scientists to experiment with formant transitions were Pierre Delattre, Alvin Liberman, Franklin Cooper, and colleagues working at Haskins Laboratories in the 1940s and 1950s. They were working on developing a speech synthesizer that could serve as a "reading machine" for blind people, and were thus studying the correspondences between speech sounds and acoustic patterns as revealed by the newly-invented sound spectrograph. Their analog speech synthesizer, called the "pattern playback" used a bright light reflecting off of white-painted formant patterns to power a photocell connected to an amplifier. The Haskins scientists were hoping to find a single pattern that would represent [d] in all contexts, and they found themselves frustrated that they had to paint different patterns depending on the surrounding vowels. Their frustration, however, led to major advances in the study of acoustic cues and contextual variation.

Probably the most-discussed example of a case where measurably different acoustic patterns are perceived as the same linguistic item is the case of *categorical perception*. Listeners are good at distinguishing sounds that fall into different categories in their language, and poor at distinguishing sounds that fall into the same category, even if the degree of acoustic difference is the same. Categorical perception was first demonstrated with F2 transitions differentiating ba-da-ga, but it can be demonstrated with any continuum of values that differentiates linguistic categories.

In one categorical perception experiment in the early 1970s, phoneticians Arthur Abramson and Leigh Lisker synthesized a series of syllables with voice onset time (VOT) ranging from −150 ms (a long period of voicing preceding the release burst) to +150 ms (a long lag before voicing began following the release burst). They then played the tokens to listeners, in two tasks. In the identification task, listeners were asked to name the syllable, for example,

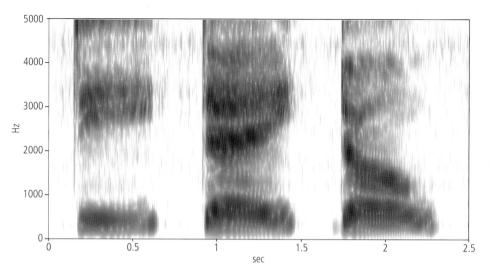

Figure 9.9   Spectrograms of [di], [deɪ], and [doʊ].

either "ba" or "pa." In the discrimination task, listeners were played two tokens, and asked whether they were the same or different.

Abramson and Lisker found that, for English speakers, the *category boundary* between /ba/ and /pa/ occurred around 30 ms VOT. All tokens with a VOT of less than 30 ms (including tokens with pre-voicing) were identified as "ba," and all tokens with a voice onset time of more than 30 ms were identified as "pa." In the discrimination task, when listeners heard two tokens within a category, they did not discriminate between them: all the tokens within a category were judged as "same," even when they were measurably different. Tokens were tagged as different only when they were from different sides of the category boundary.

In addition, the location of the category boundary was found to differ by language experience. For Spanish speakers, who produce /b/ with prevoicing (negative VOT) and /p/ as voiceless unaspirated (short-lag VOT), the /b/ vs. /p/ boundary fell at 15 ms positive VOT. For Thai speakers, who produce a three-way contrast between pre-voiced /b/, voiceless unaspirated /p/, and aspirated /pʰ/, the continuum was divided into three categories: /b/ was identified for any VOT less than −20 ms, /p/ for VOT between −20 and +40 ms, and /pʰ/ for VOT above +40 ms. Like the English speakers, the Thai and Spanish speakers showed poor discrimination of tokens within a category, and heightened discrimination of tokens across a category boundary. That is, Spanish speakers heard tokens of −30 and +20 as different, but +20 and +50 as the same, where English speakers heard −30 and +20 as the same and +20 and +50 as different, because their category boundaries were in different places. Thai speakers discriminated all three. These results are summarized in Figure 9.10.

Abramson, Lisker and their colleagues concluded from their research that human speech perception is special, processed by cognitive systems different from any other kind of perception, including that of music and other non-linguistic sounds. (They argued, in fact, that perception of speech involves direct perception of articulatory gestures; see discussion in Section 9.3.4.) These claims were weakened by findings that categorization happens in other domains, such as visual perception, and that animals (notably chinchillas) also demonstrate categorical perception of speech sounds. Further, the claim that humans cannot hear any

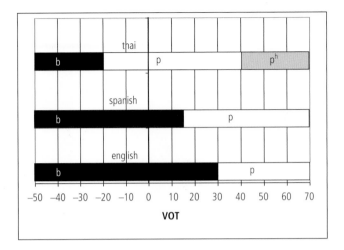

Figure 9.10 Category boundaries depend on language experience.
Source: Results from Abramson, A. and L. Lisker (1970: Discriminability across the voicing continuum: Cross-language tests, *Proceedings of the 6th International Conference of Phonetic Sciences*; and 1973: Voice-timing perception in Spanish word-initial stops. *Journal of Phonetics* 1).

difference at all between tokens in a category turned out to be too strong, and was to some extent an artifact of the primitive quality of synthesized speech in the 1970s. As was argued above, it cannot be the case that listeners "discard" the phonetic details after a sound has been placed into a category.

Nonetheless, it remains clear that human speech perception is affected by (if not completely determined by) our differing linguistic categorizations. The interaction of acoustic cues and speech categories continues to be an important area of research, especially in second language acquisition. Speakers of Thai, English, and Spanish have a great deal of trouble learning one another's consonant systems as adults, and part of the problem is certainly the fact that speakers of different languages do not perceive differences between speech sounds in exactly the same way. (See Chapter 20 for further discussion.)

9.3.3 cue integration

Cue integration means that the brain creates a single object, the percept, from multiple pieces of information that it receives. A [p], for example, consists of a sequence of acoustic events: silence, followed by a burst of a certain frequency and amplitude, followed by aspiration, with rising F2 and F3 formant transitions. Take away or change any one of these cues, and a different consonant will be perceived: removing aspiration changes [p] to [b]; changing F2 from rising to flat changes [p] to [t]. A naive listener, however, is not aware that [p] contains this sequence: it generally takes extremely slow and exaggerated movements, or a waveform demonstration, to teach someone what a [p] consists of. Yet listeners easily identify various words as containing [p]: the different cues – silent interval, burst, aspiration, formants – are integrated into a single perceived object. As was noted in Section 9.2, these pieces of information are not only separated in time, but are extracted at different points in the auditory pathway. In the auditory cortex, however, they are put back together again.

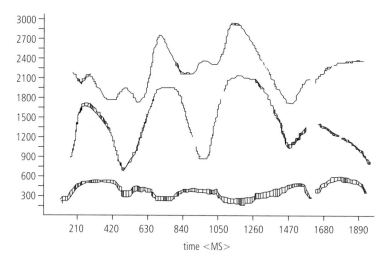

Figure 9.11 Sine wave speech pseudo-spectrogram of the utterance "Where were you a year ago?"
Source: http://www.haskins.yale.edu/featured/sws/swssentences/sentences.html. Remez, R.E.; Rubin, P.E.; Pisoni, D.B.; Carrell, T.D. (1981). "Speech perception without traditional speech cues". *Science* 212 (4497): 947–950.

Another example comes from the integration of formant information to create perceived vowel quality. The difference between [i] and [u] lies in the height of F2. But a listener does not hear high and low F2: she hears vowel sounds. The effect can be demonstrated in *sine wave speech*, another perceptual effect first created at Haskins Laboratories. Sine wave speech is made up of three sinusoidal tones, with frequencies that vary continuously to match changing formant frequencies in human speech. An example of a sine wave utterance is shown in Figure 9.11. If each tone is played separately, it sounds like a varying whistle. When the three tones are combined, however, the percept becomes speech (even if not quite human). The sentence is "Where were you a year ago?" The integration effect also works if one of the tones is played into one ear and the other two are played into the other ear.

9.6   In Focus

Sine-wave speech is how parrots "talk." The vocal tracts of birds are not shaped at all like ours, so they cannot make speech sounds the way we do. Most bird species have an organ called a syrinx, which they use for vocalizations. The syrinx is an air-filled sac at the base of the trachea. Inside the syrinx is a membrane that vibrates when air passes over it. Birds sing different "notes" by using muscles to adjust the size of the syrinx. Parrots and other talking birds have two syringes, one for each lung, which they can control independently. Parrots who can talk use the syringes to mimic the changing formant patterns in human speech. For at least some parrots it has been claimed that they not only can mimic speech sounds, but can associate words to meanings.

Cue integration takes place not only within the speech stream, but also across perceptual modalities. The most striking example of multi-modal perception is probably the McGurk effect (discovered by Harry McGurk and John McDonald in 1976), which illustrates the integration of auditory and visual input. The effect falls somewhat flat in print, but several audio-visual demonstrations can be accessed online (search for McGurk effect).

The effect is created by a mismatch between visual and auditory information. A video of a talker saying "ga ga" is dubbed with audio saying "ba ba." If you listen to the audio with your eyes closed, "ba ba" is clear; if you watch the video without sound you can probably guess from the movements of the mouth that the utterance is "ga ga." When both are perceived together, however, the percept is neither one nor the other, but "da da." (Surprisingly, the effect works even if you know the trick.) The brain seems to be doing its best to interpret the two conflicting stimuli consistently. It knows that the picture cannot be "ba", because there is no lip closure. It also knows that the audio cannot be "ga": F2 is rising, not falling. So the percept is mapped to "da."

9.3.4 top-down processing

A different kind of information that can also affect perception is *top-down processing*. Acoustic cues come into the brain from the bottom up. But they are met in speech processing with top-down predictions that are made from experience. In running speech, we have very strong expectations of what we are about to hear, and we tend to perceive what we expect.

For example, compare the utterances: (a) "The baker burned the bread;" and (b) "The plane closed the fish." In sentence (a) the word "bread" is highly predictable from the context: what else is a baker likely to burn? Further, the initial stops of "baker" and "burned" make the brain especially ready (*primed*) to hear another word starting with /b/. In tests with human listeners, such an utterance is identified as a grammatical string faster, and is repeated much more accurately, than the equally grammatical but much less predictable utterance (b). (For this reason, tests of the quality of speech synthesis systems tend to use nonsense sentences like (b). Listeners would be likely to identify the word "bread" in sentence (a) no matter how bad the synthetic speech was.)

Top-down processing is also responsible for the phenomenon of *phoneme restoration*. (See Chapter 10 for a definition of the term "phoneme"; here it is used just to mean "speech segment.") In this kind of experiment, a speech sound is digitally replaced with a non-speech sound. It works best if the two sounds are somewhat similar: for example, an [s] replaced with a cough. Listeners will hear the cough, but they won't notice that the speech sound is missing. The perceptual system restores the sound to its rightful place when the word is recognized. For example, in the sentence "The governor convened the legislature in the capital city," listeners do not notice if the first [s] is replaced. It seems that the brain matches the acoustic signal of the word to "legislature," which is obvious from the context, and then moves on. Since "legislature" contains an [s], an [s] is perceived, even if it is not there.

Top-down processing is obviously an important aid to real-world communication in a noisy environment. Most of the time, people do say what is expected, so having the brain fill in pieces that are not perfectly evident in the auditory signal is helpful. Speech recognition is fastest and most accurate when all the cues – auditory, visual, and top-down – are working together.

9.3.5 units of perception

As the above discussion should have made clear, the perception of speech does not really take place until all the available information is used to match the signal to a stored linguistic representation. The final, and perhaps most interesting question, is "What are the units of perception?" To what linguistic representation is the speech signal mapped?

Traditional answers to this question are based on *prototype models*. These models assume that an abstract, idealized version of a linguistic unit is stored in memory, and the incoming stimulus is matched to the prototype it most closely resembles. This accounts straightforwardly for categorical perception: all [pɑ] stimuli sound the same because they are mapped to the same prototype. Differences in detail are not noticed unless they cause a mapping to different stored representation. Models differ, however, in claims about the linguistic level to which the prototype corresponds.

One idea is that *feature detectors* pick up distinct acoustic events, such as aspiration noise, a nasal formant, or low-frequency periodicity and match them to segment characteristics (which may differ from language to language). After segments are identified, they are assembled into words. Listeners can definitely recognize individual segments, despite the fact that segment boundaries are not evident in connected speech. However, experiments have found very few invariant cues to specific features or specific segments that the detectors could pick up on. Findings such as the different formant patterns that can cue [d] before different vowels (Figure 9.9), have led some researchers to propose that the units of perception are demi-syllables (CV or VC combinations) or syllables as a whole. If syllables are the objects of perception, however, then the problem becomes one of how listeners break them down into segments. (Being taught the alphabet may be an important influence. Studies have shown that children who have difficulty learning to read may get stuck on just this point – they find it hard to hear a word like "cat" as being made up of three distinct segments.) Finally, effects of top-down processing and phoneme restoration can be interpreted as evidence that word-level prototypes are stored.

Lisker and colleagues argued that the units of perception are articulatory gestures themselves. This view is called the *Motor Theory of Speech Perception*. Proponents make an analogy to visual perception. In vision, they argue, varying wavelengths of light are the medium *by which* we see, but the things *seen* are the objects that caused the pattern. By analogy, sound patterns are the medium by which we hear, but the objects heard are the articulatory movements that caused the sounds. Proponents of the Motor Theory argue that speakers learn the acoustic patterns that correspond to particular speech gestures by listening to their own utterances as babies, and they point to the neural link between the auditory and motor cortex in the brain as further support. On the contrary side, the facts that we can perceive as speech noises that no real vocal tract could create (such as sine wave speech), and that brain injury often affects production and perception independently, makes a strong version of the motor theory difficult to maintain.

Prototype models assume that after the match to the linguistic unit is made, detailed information in the signal is discarded, and speech processing proceeds on the abstract level. In contrast to prototype models, *exemplar models* assume that extremely detailed memory traces are retained and referenced. These *episodic traces* are linked together at multiple levels into multi-dimensional clouds. For example, a memory of a specific pronunciation of the word "cat" by your brother Mike would be associated in one cloud with "car," "kitchen," "course" and all other words starting with [k]; with "tap," "patch," "asteroid" and all other words containing [æ] in another; with bunnies and other cute furry things (or rats, ghosts and scary things, depending on your opinion); and with everything else that Mike says to you. It is not claimed that everything is remembered perfectly – old memory traces fade, and the cloud is continuously updated with new examples – but it is claimed that the stored exemplars are detailed and specific, unlike abstract prototypes, and that the details matter. Categorization does take place, when the mind labels a particularly dense cluster of exemplars that have formed over time, but the label is in addition to, not a replacement of, the specific instances. Importantly, incoming stimuli are not compared to an abstract prototype, but find a place in different clouds: the more similar the new stimulus is to exemplars in the center of the cloud, the faster and more accurate the categorization. If new stimuli continue to be similar to old stimuli, the category label is reinforced and the boundaries between categories sharpen; if new stimuli are not very similar, the category may shift, causing language change.

Exemplar models are supported by psycholinguistic research that shows the details do matter, and that connections exist at multiple levels. The word "cat", for example, is recognized faster if the listener is shown a picture of a car (priming [k]), an apple (priming [æ]), a witch (priming a semantic area in which cats are prominent), or just by hearing the same voice that said "cat" the last time. Exemplar models are also consistent with *frequency effects*, which show that how often you hear a sound makes a difference. Frequency effects make sense if categories are clouds of examples which are subject to change and are being constantly updated; but such effects are not predicted if categories consist of unchanging abstract prototypes. Work remains to be done, however, in reconciling these findings with others that show the important effects of categorization, particularly in the question of how categories are formed and labeled in the first place.

Overall, the question of the units of speech perception is far from solved, and remains an area of research and debate. It is clear, however, that linguistic interpretation of the speech signal involves the integration of stored and incoming information at multiple levels of analysis.

chapter summary

- The processes of hearing and speech perception involve a chain of events in the ear and brain that transform sound pressure waves to nerve impulses, and then match patterns of nerve impulses to linguistic representations.
- The outer ear protects the tympanic membrane (eardrum), aids in sound capture and echolocation, and amplifies frequencies important for speech.
- The job of the middle ear is to efficiently transfer sound patterns from the tympanic membrane to the inner ear.
- The inner ear consists of the vestibular system and the cochlea. The vestibular system helps maintain balance and coordination.
- In the cochlea, different regions of the tapered basilar membrane respond more or less strongly to different incoming frequencies, performing an analog spectral analysis. Nerve fibers attached to stereocilia in the organ of Corti transform the movements of the basilar membrane into electrical signals.
- The primary auditory pathways carry the nerve signals from the cochlea to the auditory cortex. Different relays along the pathway extract different kinds of information.
- The mapping from acoustics to perception is non-linear: equal changes in frequency and amplitude do not necessarily result in equal responses in the perceptual system. A logarithmic scale, such as the Bark scale, better represents perceptual differences.
- The process of normalization, by which our brains interpret values relative to other values rather than to an external standard, allows us to interpret acoustically different patterns as the same linguistic item.
- The phenomenon of categorical perception shows that speech perception is affected by language-specific linguistic categorization. Listeners have difficulty distinguishing sounds that fall into the same category in their language.

- Listeners integrate distinct frequency, temporal, and even visual cues into a single linguistic percept, such as [p] or [i].
- Top-down processing means that listeners often perceive what they expect to perceive, even when it doesn't match what the signal actually contains.
- Different theories propose different units of speech perception. Prototype models assume the incoming stimulus is compared to a stored idealized representation, which might correspond to a segment, demi-syllable, syllable, or word. The Motor Theory of Speech Perception argues that the objects of perception are articulatory gestures. Exemplar models assume the stimulus is placed in a cloud of detailed episodic traces, which may be associated with category labels.

further reading

Goldstein, E.B. 2007. *Sensation and Perception*. Independence, KY: Thomson Wadsworth.

review exercises

1. What is the difference between?
    a.   hearing and speech perception
    b.   conductive and neurosensory hearing loss
    c.   left and right hemispheres of the brain
    d.   auditory cortex and motor cortex
    e.   primary and secondary auditory pathways
    f.   prototype models and exemplar models of speech perception
2. Fill in the blanks, using the words from the word bank. Note two words are not used.

    The _____, the smallest bone in the body, transfers patterns of vibration to the _____, which in turn transfers the vibration to the fluid that fills the cochlea. Inside the cochlea, pressure waves travel down the _____, around the _____, and then down the _____. The _____ bulges out as a pressure valve. Inside the central cochlear duct, otherwise known as the _____, lies the tapered _____, on which sits the organ of _____. Inside this organ, vibrations of the gelatinous _____ and delicate _____ cause the firing of nerve cells, whose patterns the brain interprets as sound.

basilar membrane	round window	stereocilia
Corti	scala media	tectorial membrane
Eustachius	scala tympani	utricle
helicotrema	scala vestibuli	
oval window	stapes	

    (Continued)

3. Match each aspect of speech perception to the place in the auditory pathway where it occurs:
   1. tonotopic organization of the auditory nerve
   2. cochlear nuclei
   3. superior olivary cortex
   4. inferior colliculus
   5. medial geniculate nucleus
   6. auditory cortex
       a. match perceived sound to linguistic unit
       b. integrate relative timing of acoustic events
       c. combine sound from both ears
       d. combine information from eyes and ears
       e. extract frequency information
       f. track timing of onsets of syllables and segments

4. Define each term, and explain its importance in hearing or perception.

   auricle
   Eustachian tube
   middle ear reflex
   utricle and sacchule
   oto-acoustic emissions
   just-noticeable difference
   tonotopic organization
   onset neuron
   neurogram

5. True or false?
   a. The vestibular system responds only to high-amplitude noise.
   b. Most people process speech segments on the right side of the brain.
   c. The McGurk effect demonstrates the integration of audio and visual information.
   d. Discrimination improves when two sounds are within the same linguistic category.
   e. Categorical perception demonstrates that people who speak different languages perceive speech sounds in the same way.
   f. Sine wave speech demonstrates cue integration.
   g. Phoneme restoration demonstrates top-down processing.
   h. Exemplar models are not consistent with frequency effects.
   i. Prototype models consist of episodic traces.
   j. Normalization allows us to understand different voices saying the same thing.

further analysis and discussion

6. Why do we have two ears?
7. How do the ossicles accomplish the function of the middle ear?
8. What is the place theory of hearing? Why would we not be able to hear speech sounds if the basilar membrane were not tapered?
9. What did Drs Broca and Wernicke do?

10. What do each of the following stand for, and what do they measure?

    EEG
    ERP
    PET
    f-MRI

11. According to the Motor Theory of Speech Perception, what do we actually perceive when we listen to speech? How is this analogous to vision?
12. Why is the tonotopic organization of the auditory nerve important?

Go online Visit the book's companion website for additional resources relating to this chapter at: http://www.wiley.com/go/zsiga.

references

Corti: http://www.ncbi.nlm.nih.gov/pubmed/18652163.

Talking birds:
Larsen, O. and F. Goller. 2002. Direct observation of syringeal muscle function in songbirds and a parrot. *Journal of Experimental Biology* 205: 25–35.

Chinchillas:
Kuhl, P. and J.D. Miller, 1975. Speech perception by the chinchilla. *Science* 190, 69–72.

Phoneme restoration:
Warren, R.M. 1970. Perceptual restoration of missing speech sounds. *Science*, 167, 392–393.

The Motor Theory of Speech Perception:
Galantucci, B., C.A. Fowler and M.T. Turvey. 2006. The motor theory of speech perception reviewed. *Psychonomic Bulletin and Review* 13, 361–377.
Liberman A.M., F.S. Cooper, D.P. Shankweiler and M. Studdert-Kennedy. 1963. Perception of the speech code. *Psychological Review* 74: 476.

Exemplar theory:
Johnson, K. (1997). Speech perception without speaker normalization: An exemplar model. In K. Johnson and J. Mullenix, eds. *Talker Variability in Speech Processing*, San Diego: Academic Press, 145–166.
Pierrehumbert, J. (2001). Exemplar dynamics: Word frequency, lenition and contrast. In J. Bybee and P. Hopper, eds. *Frequency Effects and Emergent Grammar*, Amsterdam: John Benjamins, 137–157.

10 Phonology 1
Abstraction, Contrast, Predictability

[N]o entity in human experience can be adequately defined as the mechanical sum or product of its physical properties.

Edward Sapir, "The Psychological Reality of the Phoneme," 1933, (reprinted in *The Collected Works of Edward Sapir*, 2008)

Chapter outline

In Chapters 1–9, we have been studying phonetics: how the sounds of language are produced, transmitted, perceived, and measured. In Chapters 10–17, we turn to the study of *phonology*. Phonologists ask questions such as:

- What sound patterns are found among the languages of the world? Which are common and why? What patterns are not found?
- What is the relationship between more abstract cognitive patterns and more concrete production and perception? How abstract should phonology be?
- What sorts of formal tools and symbols provide the best way to understand and talk about these patterns?

Chapters 10–14 concentrate on segmental phonology: how sounds relate to one another in linear strings. Chapters 15–17 cover suprasegmental phonology: how sounds are grouped into larger, hierarchical constituents such as syllables, feet, words, and phrases. The current chapter introduces the arguments for abstract phonological knowledge (Section 10.1), and the central concepts of contrast and predictability, as instantiated in phonemic analysis (Section 10.2). Some complicating factors are covered in Section 10.3. Chapter 11 discusses phonological alternations, including more practice in solving phonology problems, and a survey of the types of alternations that are common in the languages of the world. Chapters 12–14 then turn to the question of phonological formalism: representations that are designed to express not only the actual phonologies of the world, but the set of *possible* human phonologies.

10.1 the necessity of abstraction

An understanding of the physical aspects of sound production and perception is certainly crucial to linguistic study: it is no accident that most courses of linguistic study, including this one, begin with phonetics. But the next step is to move beyond the physical character-istics to study the more abstract systematic relationships between sounds: the behavior of sounds within a patterned cognitive system. This study is termed *phonology*. Even though you cannot print out phonological patterns like a spectrogram, or measure them in milli-seconds, they are as much a part of a speaker's knowledge of the sounds of language as is the ability to accurately make and perceive an [i] or a [t]. In fact, particular perceptions and productions are inextricably linked to the patterns in which they participate.

But what does it mean to talk about "an abstract cognitive pattern"? How do you know one when you see one? One such pattern has already been mentioned in Chapter 3: the relationship of *contrast* vs. *positional variation*. We noted in Chapter 3 that two sounds that distinguish different words in one language might be just "two ways of saying the same sound" in another language. The question of which sounds are contrastive, and which are positional variants (discussed at length in Section 10.2) is central to any phonological analysis.

There is also the pattern of *phonotactics*: which sounds are allowed to "touch" each other, that is, licit and illicit sequences of sounds. A sequence that is possible in one language may not be allowed in another. The sequence [pne] is a perfectly good way to begin a word in Greek (as in "pneu" *breath*), but if we want to talk about "pneumonia" in English, the [p] has to go. Phonotactic constraints give rise to *alternations*: a word or morpheme may be pronounced in different ways depending on the context. (A *morpheme* is any entry in your mental dictionary; it can be a word or a part of a word, like a prefix, suffix, or root.) Thus while the [p] is not pronounced in "pneumonia," it is retained in "apnea," where the preced-ing [æ] provides a licit context for the [p] to be pronounced.

Is there, however, really any evidence that the generalization "[pn] is an illicit way to begin a word" is part of your knowledge of English? In all likelihood, you have never considered the relationship between "pneumonia" and "apnea" until I (or some other teacher) brought it to your attention. Isn't it possible that you (and all English speakers) just learned the words of English in their various forms, and that any relationships between them (like between "pneumonia" and "apnea") are just historical accidents – patterns that an analyst might uncover, but that play no role in everyday speech and communication?

There is evidence that patterns of contrast, phonotactics, and alternation, abstract though they may be, play a crucial role in speaking and hearing. One of the most influential papers written on the subject is an article entitled "The psychological reality of the phoneme," published by the linguist Edward Sapir in 1933. (Actually, it was entitled "La réalité psychologique des phonèmes," as the article was published in the French *Journal de Psychologie Normale et Pathologique*, presumably in the *Normale* section). The term "phoneme" is defined below, but Sapir's article addressed various kinds of abstract phonological knowledge. Sapir begins with the point quoted in part at the head of the chapter: "no entity in human experience can be adequately defined as the mechanical sum or product of its physical properties" but must be understood as "a functionally significant point in a complex system of relatednesses." That is, phonological patterns are necessarily abstract: summing up the physical properties of sounds is not sufficient to understand human language.

The idea that all human activity can only be understood as part of a "complex system of relatednesses" is a central tenet of the *Structuralist* approach to social science, within which phonology developed in the first half of the twentieth century (see Section 10.4). Sapir goes beyond this, however, in arguing that these abstractions are not just out there in the world for an analyst to discover as she pores over dictionaries or texts or compares different dialects. Rather, these patterns are part of every individual speaker's *knowledge* of his language. In his article, Sapir describes several experiences in learning, teaching, and studying language that led him to make this controversial claim.

In one of his most-often-cited examples, Sapir describes an interaction between himself and a man named John Whitney, who was a native speaker of Sarcee, a language spoken in Western Canada. (Sapir spent many years working on linguistic descriptions of Native American languages.) Sapir reports that he was questioning Whitney about possible homophones (words that sound alike) in Sarcee. Among the potential homophones, Sapir had listed [dìní] "it makes a sound" and [dìní] "this one." (Recall that the grave accent represents a low tone and the acute accent a high tone.) To Sapir's trained ear, the two words sounded identical, but Whitney insisted there was a difference. Sapir pressed Whitney to come up with a phonetic distinction – perhaps a slight difference in tone, in stress, or in voice quality – but Whitney rejected each suggestion. "The one tangible suggestion that [Whitney] himself made," Sapir reports, "was obviously incorrect, namely, that the *-ní* of 'it makes a sound' ended in a 't'" (2008, p. 545). Whitney insisted so strongly on this "phantom 't'" that Sapir gave up trying to talk him out of it.

Why did Whitney "hear" a [t] that wasn't there? What Whitney knew, and Sapir did not (until he learned more Sarcee grammar), is that both "this one" and "it makes a sound" can take a relative suffix [-i] (among other suffixes, of course). When this suffix is added to [dìní] meaning "this one", the result is a long final vowel. When the suffix is added to [dìní] meaning "it makes a sound" the result is [dìnítí]. The "phantom" [t] appears. Where did it come from? Sapir argues that Whitney's knowledge of the word "it makes a sound" included a "latent" consonant, which appeared in some forms but not others. Whitney knew the /t/ was part of the word, even if it was not always pronounced. Essentially, in Whitney's mental dictionary, "this one" was stored as /dìní/, but "it makes a sound" was stored as /dìnít/. It was this more abstract form, not any actual pronunciation, that Whitney was referencing when he insisted "it makes a sound" ended in a consonant. Linguists later in the century would refer to this more abstract form as the *underlying representation*.

Note that there was a switch in formalism in the middle of the preceding paragraph. When the reference is to sounds as actually pronounced, square brackets are used: [t]. When the reference is to a more abstract level (the underlying representation), slashes are used: /t/.

Speakers of Athabaskan languages are not the only ones to hear phantom segments. When Sapir was not working on language descriptions, he was teaching linguistics and anthropology at the University of Chicago and at Yale. In the same article in which he reports on his experience with John Whitney, Sapir reports a similar phenomenon among his English-speaking Ivy League undergraduates. The students in Sapir's phonetics classes, having been taught about the existence of glottal stops, started hearing them in many words where they had not been pronounced. As part of their training in phonetics, Sapir would give his students exercises in transcribing nonsense words. The students, Sapir reports, would often transcribe words that ended with a stressed lax vowel, like ['smɛ] or [pi'læ], as [smɛʔ] or [pi'læʔ]. Sapir considers the hypothesis that "students who have learned a new sound like to play with it" (2008, p. 551), but concludes that that does not explain why his students consistently heard glottal stops in some words but not others. Something else must account for their collective "phonetic illusion."

In this case, the culprit is their knowledge of English phonotactics. As English speakers, they know that words are "not allowed" to end with a lax stressed vowel. So, for example, "see," "say," "so," "sue," and "sigh" are fine, but [sɪ], [sɛ], [sʊ], and [sæ] are not possible English words. When confronted with an actual pronunciation that their knowledge of English tells them is not possible, they unconsciously supply the missing final consonant, choosing a glottal stop as the least obtrusive consonant possible.

Further examples of the effects of phonological knowledge abound in the mistakes made by language learners, both children and adults. Sometimes the problems of a language learner are "just" in production. I, for example, simply cannot get my tongue to make a Spanish-like alveolar trill, and thus my accent in Spanish is terrible. Many learners of English have trouble with the tongue shape for our post-alveolar approximant [ɹ], and substitute a different sound. But there is often more to the problems of language learners than errors in producing segments. Often, the mistake is the misapplication or overapplication of a phonological pattern.

In one of my favorite instances, I overheard a conversation between my four-year-old neighbor Johnny, and his older playmate. Johnny was bored with playing school. When he was told by his older playmate that "two plus two equals four," Johnny asserted his independence by declaring (perhaps truthfully): "I knowed that before you teached me it!"

We can smile at the fact that Johnny doesn't know the irregular forms "knew" and "taught," but his eight-word utterance in fact reveals a lot of sophisticated linguistic knowledge. Note that he manages the correct linguistic forms for subordinate clauses, case marking on pronouns ("I" vs. "me"), the double-object construction (deriving "teach me it" from "teach it to me"), and reference to internal mental states, abstract entities such as mathematical formulae, and complex temporal relations (all of which, by the way, he "knowed" without being "teached"). For our purposes, we want to examine his knowledge of sound structure. Though the spelling does not convey it, he pronounced "knowed" as [nod] and "teached" as [tʰitʃt] Why the [d] ending in the first case and the [t] in the second?

Since the English speakers around him say "knew" and "taught," Johnny couldn't have been repeating memorized forms he had heard others use before. Nor were his mistakes random. Rather, he was applying his knowledge of a phonological alternation: a "rule" he had learned, based on other forms he had heard. You may have been taught a rule in school that says that to make a past tense, you should "add *ed*," but Johnny's rule could not have taken this form. Four-year-old Johnny cannot read or spell, so he does not know what letters he's adding. Rather, he has generalized from other words he has heard, like "mowed" and "reached," that the past tense meaning is related to a certain set of *sounds* – that the past tense for words that end in sounds like [o] take [d], and words that end in sounds like [ʧ] take [t]. (We'll return to the more complete statement of this rule in Chapter 11.) For the present we note that this knowledge – a "rule" for pronouncing the past tense forms depending on the environment – is phonology. And because he applied this rule in a novel way, we can conclude that his knowledge of this rule is more general than a list of memorized forms.

10.1   This ability of children (and others) to apply linguistic generalizations to novel forms was formally tested in a famous experiment conducted by linguist Jean Berko Gleason in 1958. Gleason drew imaginary creatures, one of which she called a "wug," and she asked pre-school children what they would call two of them (Figure 10.1). Reliably, four-year-old children reported seeing two [wʌgz], not [wʌgs] or [wʌgəz], demonstrating that they could correctly apply the rule for English plurals to new words. Since then, an experiment that tests for the ability of a speaker to generalize a rule to words that have not been heard before has been called a "wug-test."

Figure 10.1   This is a wug.
Source: Figure 5.9 from the article: Berko, Jean (1958). The child's learning of English morphology. *WORD* 4: 150–177, 'This is a wug' Reprinted with permission of International Linguistic Association.

Other examples of the over-application of a rule come from non-native speakers of English. Sue is a college student who was born and raised in Seoul, Korea, and who has taken English classes since elementary school. She reads and writes English fluently, and excels in her classes at an American university, so much so that she has been selected as a teaching assistant, with responsibility for leading several classes. Her American students, however, have trouble understanding her speech. One particular problem is that she pronounces phrases such as "Pick me up," as "Ping me up", "got me" as "gon me" or "keep Matt" as "keem Matt."

Sue in general has no trouble pronouncing a final [p] or [k] in words like "keep" and "pick." It's just phrases like "keep me" or "pick me" that she has trouble with. Why? Like Johnny, who has never heard the adults around him use "knowed," Sue has never heard an English speaker say "ping me" for "pick me." But she has heard and produced many Korean phrases where a word-final stop precedes a word-initial nasal. In Korean, such sequences are nasalized. In Korean, for example, the word for "soup" is [kuk], and one form of the verb "eat" is [mekta]. Put together, "ate soup" is not [kuk mekta] but [kuŋ] mekta]. (The word order is "soup ate", because in Korean the verb comes last.) The point is that /k/ is pronounced as [ŋ] before [m]. (Note again the uses of slashes to mark a more abstract form that is not actually pronounced.) Similarly, "rice" is [pap], and "ate rice" is [pa**m** mekta]. See the pattern? Sue, as a Korean speaker, learned the phonotactic pattern that stops must be nasalized before nasal consonants. Her mistake is applying the pattern learned for Korean to words belonging to English.

We end this section with a final example illustrating the importance of phonological contrast. Mazi was born in Tokyo, but has lived in the United States for decades. His speech has almost no trace of a foreign accent: listening to him on the phone, you wouldn't guess he was not a native speaker of English. He even correctly produces the distinction between [ɹ] and [l], a distinction notoriously difficult for native speakers of Japanese. But he does report one continuing problem: he often cannot remember whether a new word, like an unfamiliar street name, begins with "r" or "l." He reports that he hears the word and thinks he remembers it, but when he tries to recall it later, he cannot recall whether the new restaurant is on "Wright St." or "Light St."

Mazi has mastered the phonetic production of English [ɹ] and [l]. But he has not completely shaken off the effects of the Japanese phonological system. In Japanese, there is only one non-nasal coronal approximant: the lateral tap [ɺ]. In English, of course, there is contrast: "row" and "low" are different words. It seems that in organizing his mental dictionary, Mazi sometimes stores new words under the single Japanese category: non-nasal coronal approximant. Once words have been sorted into this more general "bin," the memory of exactly which non-nasal coronal approximant it is gets lost.

These extended examples, I hope, have made the point that phonological knowledge, including concepts such as contrast, alternation, and phonotactics, is part of our knowledge of language. It influences what we produce and what we perceive. Specifically, phonological knowledge governs the way words are stored in our mental dictionaries and controls the realization of different words in different contexts. We now turn to more detailed discussion of what our phonological knowledge consists of.

10.2 contrast and predictability: phonemes and allophones

10.2.1 defining the phoneme

The idea of the phoneme is central to phonological reasoning, but the concept is notoriously difficult to define. The term "phoneme" is obviously based on the Greek word for "sound," and has been used by different linguists to refer to various "units of sound" for centuries. The term *fonema* was probably first used in something close to its current sense in the late nineteenth century by the Polish linguist Jan Badouin de Courtenay and his student and colleague Nikolaj Kreszewski. Badouin de Courtenay and Kreszewski were among the first European linguists to place an emphasis on the analysis of currently-spoken languages (as opposed to historical change), and to argue for a more important role for abstraction and mental representation in the study of sound systems. They probably borrowed the term "phoneme" from the more well-known contemporary Swiss linguist Ferdinand de Saussure, though they used it in a different way. Their work, in turn, influenced the linguists of the Prague Circle, including Nikolaj Trubetskoy and Roman Jakobson, who were leaders in developing phonological theory throughout most of the twentieth century. "Phonemic analysis" per se has gone in and out of style in phonological theory, but the underlying concepts of contrast and predictability remain central.

Here's a preliminary attempt at a definition: A *phoneme* is a label for a set of sounds that all count as basically the same. This definition obviously needs fleshing out: what does "count as basically the same" mean? Before we turn to that problem, however, notice that a phoneme is an abstraction. It is a label for a *set* of sounds, not a particular sound in itself. As such, a phoneme cannot actually be pronounced. The individual sounds within the set, which *can* be pronounced, are the *allophones* of that phoneme. Crucially, the allophones are positional (or contextual) variants: which allophone appears (that is, which version of the sound gets used) depends on the context.

One commonly-used analogy is that a phoneme is a *family* of sounds. The Simpson family may consist of five individuals: Homer, Marge, Bart, Lisa, and Maggie. As a part of the larger society, they function in some ways a single unit: they may have the same last name, live in the same home, fill out a single tax return. In some cases, the whole family may be called by the name of one of its prominent members (in American society, this tends to be the Dad): the Homer Simpson family. But this does not mean that Homer *is* the family, or even the family member most frequently seen or heard. His name is just used as a label for the group.

The family analogy emphasizes the concept of the phoneme as a group of sounds that function as a unit, but it breaks down in that it is possible to see a family group all together at one time, say, for a portrait. With phonemes and allophones, the different family members (the allophones) never appear in the same place at the same time. In that respect, a phoneme is more like Miley Stewart/Hannah Montana: high school student by day, pop star by night. Miley/Hannah (or Clark Kent/Superman or Bruce Wayne/Batman; pick your favorite cultural icon) is just one person, but she appears as one personality or the other, depending on the context. In the school context, Miley appears; in the stage context, Hannah appears. Again, the analogy is not perfect, but you might say that the complex character encompassing both Hannah and Miley is the phoneme. Hannah is one allophone of that character; Miley is another.

Let's return to linguistics. Analogies aside, how do you know if two sounds are "members of the same family" or "two sides of the same character"? How do you know if two sounds "count as the same" and are thus allophones of one phoneme, or not? We could appeal to psychology here, as Sapir did, and state that two sounds form a phoneme when a language user "feels" that the two sounds count as the same. There is undoubted truth to this: the English speaker has a strong conviction that the [pʰ] in [pʰɪl] and the [p] in [spɪl] are identical. It generally takes some demonstration of the aerodynamics of aspiration to convince her that they are not. We conclude that, in English, [pʰ] and [p] are allophones of the same phoneme: they form a set of sounds that speakers count as the same.

But this sort of introspection is not always easy or possible. Instead, phonemic analysis can be based on the distribution of sounds in a set of data. (Presumably, it is the knowledge of this distribution that leads the speaker to her conviction.) If two sounds are *contrastive*, they must be members of different phonemes. If two sounds are in *complementary distribution*, they are more likely allophones of the same phoneme.

Consider the case of [d] and [ð] in (General American) English and (Castilian) Spanish. In General American English, [d] and [ð] are contrastive: the difference between them can create a difference in meaning. There are several pairs of words that differ only in that one has [d] where the other has [ð]: "den" [dɛn] and "then" [ðɛn], "eider" [aɪdɚ] and "either" [aɪðɚ], "bade" [bed] and "bathe" [beð]. Pairs of words that differ in only a single sound in the same position within the word are called *minimal pairs*. (If you pronounce "either" as [iðɚ], then you have a *near-minimal pair*, two words that are almost exactly alike.) The existence of minimal pairs is proof that two sounds are contrastive, and thus belong to different phonemes. Think about it: if the two sounds "counted as the same," then the two words wouldn't be distinguished. (If Clark Kent and Superman ever appeared in the same room at the same time, you would know they were two different people.)

We can also note that, if two sounds are contrastive, their distribution is unpredictable. If I tell you I'm thinking of an English word that rhymes with "when," and starts with either [d] or [ð], you cannot predict which sound I have in mind.

Now compare this to the situation in Spanish. Some Spanish words with [d] and [ð] are given below:

[dama]	lady
[demonios]	demons
[dulse]	sweet
[disfras]	disguise
[laðo]	side
[universiðað]	university
[inbaliðo]	invalid
[granaða]	Granada

In Spanish, there are no minimal pairs for [d] and [ð]. There is no [ðama] to contrast with [dama], no [lado] to contrast with [laðo]. The [d] versus [ð] difference in sound is never used in Spanish to signal a difference in meaning. Instead, the two sounds have different, non-overlapping (that is, *complementary*) distributions. Like Hannah and Miley, they're never seen in the same place. In initial position, there is only [d], never [ð]. After a vowel, there is only [ð], never [d]. If you know the *context* (the position in the word, or the surrounding sounds), you can predict whether [d] or [ð] will be used. (For example, even if you don't know Spanish, you should be able to predict how the word "nada" *nothing* is pronounced.) The situation is somewhat more complicated when contexts other than phrase-initial and post-vocalic are considered, but the principle of complementary distribution holds. There is only [d] after [n], for instance, and only [ð] after [r].

Thus, we can use distributions to diagnose phoneme membership. When two sounds in a language form minimal pairs (that is, if their distribution is unpredictable and contrastive), those two sounds represent different phonemes. When two sounds in a language are in complementary distribution (that is, their distribution is predictable and non-contrastive), the two sounds are likely to be allophones of the same phoneme. Remember the sets of terms that go together:

Minimal pairs—unpredictable—contrastive—separate phonemes
Complementary distribution—predictable—non-contrastive—allophones of one phoneme

We may diagram the English and Spanish situation as in (1):

(1) Family trees of /d/ and /ð/ in English and Spanish

Note that I have written the phonemes between slashes, and the allophones between brackets. Note also that I have "named" the Spanish phoneme with the symbol "d", though in principle it would have been just as valid to choose the other family member to represent the group. Section 10.3.1 below returns to the problem of choosing one form or another as "basic."

10.2   In Focus

In English, there are two separate, contrastive sounds (phonemes). In Spanish, there is only one contrastive sound (one phoneme), with two variant pronunciations (two allophones). To the Spanish speaker, if she pays any conscious attention at all, [ð] is just "a way of saying 'd'." She knows, as a speaker of the language, when the [d] variant is called for and when the [ð] variant is appropriate. If you're learning Spanish as a second language, you may have been taught this distribution as a rule, something like "the sound [d] is pronounced as [ð] after a vowel." There is no such rule relating [d] and [ð] in English. They belong to separate phonemes.

This extended example has shown a case where a distinction that is contrastive in English is not contrastive in another language. The reverse occurs too, of course. Consider the case of voiceless stops in Thai and English.

Speakers of both Thai and English produce a full set of aspirated [pʰ, tʰ, kʰ] and unaspirated [p, t, k]. Though the inventory of voiceless stops is the same, the languages use the inventory in different ways. Some Thai and English words using these sounds are shown below.

Thai:

Aspirated:		Unaspirated:	
pʰàt	to stir fry	pàt	to wipe
tʰun	a fund	tun	to hoard
kʰâ:w	step	kâ:w	rice

English

Aspirated:		Unaspirated:	
pʰɪl	pill	spɪl	spill
tʰɪl	till	stɪl	still
kʰɪl	kill	skɪl	skill

In Thai, aspiration is contrastive. The difference between [p] and [pʰ] makes a difference in meaning, and thus minimal pairs with aspirated and unaspirated stops (such as [pʰàt] and [pàt]) are easy to find. [p] and [pʰ] represent two different phonemes. To the speaker of Thai, [p] and [pʰ] are as different as [t] and [k].

There are, however, no minimal pairs for aspiration in English. Aspiration is never the *only* difference between two words. There is always some other difference on which the aspiration depends. At the beginning of a word, a voiceless stop will be aspirated; after /s/, it will be unaspirated. In English, the single phoneme /p/ has (at least) two allophones: [p] and [pʰ].

Differences in phonemic and allophonic distribution pose significant problems for speakers of one language learning to speak another. A native speaker of English learning Thai will have problems perceiving and producing the set [kʰâ:w] versus [kâ:w]. According to the principles of English, unaspirated [k] cannot occur in initial position, so she will tend to hear and say either [kʰâ:w] or [gâ:w], sequences that are licit for her. (She might or might not get the tones right.) A native speaker of Spanish learning English will have trouble with the distinction between "den" and "then." To her, [d] and [ð] count as the same sound, so she will tend to hear them that way, and to pronounce them according to the principles of her own language. She may tend to say [dɛn] for "then" (using the word-initial allophone), and [aðɪʃn] for "addition" (using the intervocalic allophone). These are not random errors, but a result of imposing the phonological organization of the first language onto the sounds and words of the second.

10.2.2 phonemic analysis

To illustrate how to determine "families of sounds" based on distributions in the data, let's work through some examples from languages that readers probably won't know. More practice examples can be found in the exercises at the end of the chapter.

An analysis must begin, always, with some data. To start from scratch, of course, a linguist would have to find a speaker or group of speakers of the language under investigation, start asking for words and word meanings, and get transcribing. After collecting a few thousand words and phrases, the linguist would begin to have a pretty good idea of the sound inventory: the set of vowels and consonants that occur in the language. Then she could begin the next step of figuring out how the sounds go together into families: which sounds belong to different phonemes, which are allophones of the same phoneme, and what the rules are that determine which allophones appear where.

In the interests of time, we'll skip step one and assume that data has already been accurately collected. (The assumption of accuracy is sometimes a dangerous one. One should always consider the reliability of secondary sources, and double-check with native speakers whenever possible. However, relying on secondary sources is sometimes inevitable: life is short and the list of languages to be investigated is long.) Further, in textbook exercises like the ones here, where available time and space is even more limited, the reader has to trust that the author has chosen the example words to be representative. In a real analysis, larger data sets would be required.

After the data has been amassed, the second step in a phonemic analysis is to identify a set of sounds that are suspected to belong to the same family. They might be chosen because they are very similar (that is, there is a family resemblance), or because they have turned out to be related to each other in a number of other languages. (Chapter 11 provides a survey of likely candidates.) In our first example, we examine the distribution of [ɔ] and [o] in Swahili. (References for all languages cited can be found at the end of the chapter.)

(2)   Some lexical items of Swahili

ŋgoma	drum	watoto	children
bɔma	fort	ndoto	dream
ŋɔmbe	cattle	mboga	vegetable
ɔmba	pray	dʒogo	rooster
ɔna	see	ʃoka	axe
pɔɲa	cure	okota	pick up
ɲɔɲa	nurse	modʒa	one

ɔɲdʒa	taste	mtego	trap
ɔŋgeza	increase	kʰɔndo	sheep
ɲɔŋga	strangle	karɔŋgo	wash-out

Having collected and organized our data set, we proceed to search for patterns. First, look for minimal pairs. If any can be found, the analysis is finished: the two sounds are contrastive and therefore must belong to different phonemes. Here, we find no minimal pairs: there is no [boma] to match the existing word [bɔma]; no [ʃoka] to match the word [ʃoka]. So we suspect that the distribution of [o] and [ɔ] may be predictable by context. The next step, then, is to look closely at the environments in which each sound occurs. It can be helpful to list the immediately preceding and following sounds in each case: this helps to focus on the part of the word most likely to be relevant. Looking at immediately adjacent sounds does not always work – sometimes sounds can affect each other from some distance away (see Chapter 11) – but it is a good place to start. This is done in (3), where a blank indicates the occurrence of each sound. The symbol # indicates the edge of a word, so that #__ indicates a word-initial sound, and __# indicates a word-final sound.

(3)   Environments for [o] and [ɔ]

[ɔ]	[o]
g__m	t__t
b__m	d__t
ŋ__m	b__g
#__m	dʒ__g
#__n	ʃ__k
p__ɲ	k__t
ɲ __ ɲ	m__d
#__ɲ	g__#
#__ŋ	d__#
r__ŋ	#__k
kʰ__n	t__#

Look at the lists in (3). Try to determine whether there's anything that all the environments in one list have in common, but that does not occur in the other list. Sometimes the pattern jumps out at you; sometimes a little more thought and work is needed. (Here, it is pretty obvious, but bear with me for the sake of learning the process: it won't always be this easy.)

There does not seem to be anything systematic about the preceding sound that could condition the choice of a different vowel in this data set. Both lists contain a variety of preceding nasals and voiced and voiceless consonants. Particularly, both [o] and [ɔ] can follow [g], and both can occur at the beginning of a word. So we cannot predict which vowel will occur based on preceding sound.

On the other hand, there *is* a pattern to the sounds that follow the vowel. The vowel [ɔ] only occurs before [m, n, ɲ, or ŋ], and the vowel [o] never occurs before any of these consonants. This establishes that the two sounds are in complementary distribution. Because the two sounds are in complementary distribution, we conclude that they belong to the same phoneme.

To complete the analysis, we need to state the rule for which allophones occur where. It would be correct to say that [ɔ] occurs before [m, n, ɲ, ŋ], and [o] occurs before [t, d, k, g] and in word-final position, but to just give a list of sounds is missing something. Phonological distributions seldom, if ever, depend on random lists of sounds with nothing in common. Phonological distributions depend on *natural classes*: sets of sounds that have something in common. (Natural classes will be defined more formally in Chapter 12.) Here, we note that the sounds [m, n, ɲ, ŋ] have something in common: they are all nasal consonants. The complement set [t, d, k, g, #] does not have any property in common: we can call this the *elsewhere case*. Thus, we can state our analysis as follows: [o] and [ɔ] are in complementary distribution and allophones of one phoneme in Swahili: [ɔ] occurs before nasal consonants, [o] occurs elsewhere. This is diagrammed in example (4):

(4)

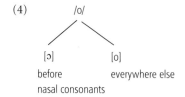

/o/

[ɔ]   [o]
before   everywhere else
nasal consonants

The pattern can be restated as a generalization: The phoneme /o/ is pronounced [ɔ] before nasals.

It is simpler to state a generalization when the elsewhere case is chosen as the basic form, and the more restricted variant as the derived form. Statement *a* is simpler than statement *b*:

a.   /o/ becomes [ɔ] before nasals.
b.   /ɔ/ becomes [o] before non-nasal consonants or at the end of a word.

It is not always possible to definitively choose one environment as the elsewhere case (see Section 10.3.1), but all things being equal, the simpler analysis is always to be preferred. One should always try to make the analysis as simple and general as possible, consistent with the data.

Let's look at another example. The words in (5) show the distribution of [k] (voiceless velar stop) and [x] (voiceless velar fricative) in Florentine Italian. Do [k] and [x] belong to different phonemes, or are they allophones of the same phoneme?

(5)   [k] and [x] in Florentine Italian

laxasa	the house	kwando	when
poxo	little	kapella	chapel
bixa	stack	blaŋko	white
amixo	friend	makkina	machine
fixi	figs	kabina	booth
kwuoxo	cook		

Step 1 is to look for minimal pairs. None occur in this data, so we move to step 2. Step 2 is to list the environments where each sound occurs. This has been done in (6).

(6)   Environments for [k] and [x]

[x]	[k]
a__a	#__w
o__o	#__a

```
[x]              [k]
i__a             ŋ__o
i__o             a__k
i__i             k__i
```

Step 3 is to look for a pattern. Is there anything that all the environments in one list or the other have in common? There is a pattern here, though it is a little different from the one seen in Swahili. Here, both sides of the consonant are relevant: the sound [x] occurs only between vowels. The sound [k] occurs if another consonant precedes or follows, or if the consonant is in word-initial position. (Note that word-final position is missing from both lists: no obstruents appear in word-final position in this dialect.) Thus, we conclude our analysis: The sounds [x] and [k] are in complementary distribution and allophones of one phoneme in Florentine Italian: [x] occurs between vowels and [k] occurs elsewhere. Because [k] is the elsewhere case, we choose /k/ as the label for the underlying phoneme: /k/ is pronounced as [x] between vowels.

One more example. The data in (7) is from Venda, a language of Southern Africa. Recall that [n] is an alveolar nasal and [n̪] is a dental nasal. These two sounds are very similar, so we might suspect that they are allophones of one phoneme.

(7)   [n] and [n̪] in Venda

han̪u	at your place	ene	he
lin̪o	tooth	hana	childhood
mun̪a	master	kʰouno	there
n̪ari	buffalo	vatanu	five
pfen̪e	baboon	vonami	see!
van̪a	four	zino	now

A scan of the data reveals no exact minimal pairs, so we move on to step 2, and consider the environments in which each sound appears.

(8)   [n] and [n̪] in Venda

```
[n̪]              [n]
a__u             e__e
i__o             a__a
u__a             u__o
#__a             a__u
e__e             a__i
a__a             i__o
```

When we examine the environments in which [n̪] and [n] occur, however, no pattern emerges. They can occur between identical sets of vowels: [a__a], [e__e], and [i__o] occur in both lists, for example.

The possibility that some more distant sound could be conditioning the difference has to be considered. The initial consonant, for example, might explain the difference. But words like [han̪u] and [hana] or [van̪a] and [vonami] show that we cannot make a prediction on that basis. It is not the case that "words that begin with [h] must have a dental nasal," for example. (That sort of random association would be pretty unlikely anyway.) We conclude that the distribution of [n] and [n̪] in Venda is not predictable, and that they therefore belong to different phonemes, even though no exact minimal pairs are available.

As was noted above, two words that are almost minimal pairs, but not quite, are called *near-minimal pairs*. Near-minimal pairs are not as perfect in proving phonemic status as are true minimal pairs, but sometimes they're the best one can do. In the Venda dataset, [haṉu] and [hana] are a near-minimal pair, as are [liṉo] and [zino] or [pfeṉe] and [ene]. The words with the same vowels show that vowel quality cannot predict the alveolar/dental distinction, and the words that begin the same show that the initial consonant is not predictive either. If you can collect a number of near-minimal pairs, each of which differ in a different way, you can still be on firm ground in arguing that a distribution is unpredictable and contrastive, and thus that two sounds represent different phonemes.

10.3   In Focus

The need to use near-minimal pairs may arise if one of the sounds in question occurs in the language, but not very often. In English, this situation arises with /ʒ/. English speakers have the intuition that /ʃ/ and /ʒ/ are different sounds, but since /ʒ/ is rather rare, and doesn't occur in all positions, true minimal pairs are hard to come by. One true minimal pair is "Confucian" vs. "confusion." Some near-minimal pairs are "mission" vs. "vision," and "Aleutian" vs. "illusion." As a rule, it is best not to use personal or place names, since names may be of foreign origin and may keep some of their native phonology, but sometimes it cannot be helped.

10.3 some complicating factors

10.3.1 is one allophone always "basic"?

We saw in the previous section that the absence of true minimal pairs can make a phonemic analysis more difficult. Another difficulty that can arise is that it is not always straightforward to choose one allophone as basic. This can occur when the distribution of allophones is such that neither can be described as the "elsewhere" case. One example is the distribution of "light l" [l] and "dark l" [ɫ] in English. As shown in (9), [l] occurs in at the beginning of a word or syllable (essentially, before a vowel) and [ɫ] occurs in syllable codas.

(9)   [l] and [ɫ] in English

leaf	[lif]	feel	[fiɫ]
loop	[lup]	pool	[pʰuɫ]
led	[[lɛd]	dell	[dɛɫ]
lame	[lem]	male	[meɫ]
blame	[blem]	help	[hɛɫp]

Clearly, the two sounds are in complementary distribution, and belong to a single phoneme. If they notice the difference at all, English speakers consider [l] and [ɫ] to be two versions of the same sound. But which is basic? It is equally simple to say /l/ becomes [ɫ] in the syllable coda, or /[ɫ]/ becomes [l] in the syllable onset. We might have a tendency to choose [l] with the idea that it's a simpler sound, but our intuition is really more that [l] is a more familiar symbol. In terms of articulation, the two sounds are equally complex. And this sort of equal distribution – one allophone in the syllable onset and another in the syllable coda – is not uncommon cross-linguistically. In Korean, [ɾ] occurs only in the syllable onset, and [l] only in the syllable coda. Which is more "basic": [ɾ] or [l]?

Since it works either way, one could pick one at random, but linguists do not like randomness: presumably speakers do not vary randomly in how they mentally represent their sound inventory. Another alternative is to avoid identifying the phoneme with *any* one of its allophones. One could just call the "family" of [l] and [ɫ] the "lateral" family. One member of the family does not have to be singled out as most important.

(10)   /lateral/

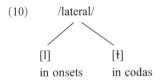

[l]   [ɫ]
in onsets   in codas

To state the distribution informally: In English, the lateral is light in the syllable onset and dark in the syllable coda.

10.3.2 phonetic similarity and complementary distribution

One reason the more abstract alternative is attractive is that it captures the sense that there is an "invariant core" of phonetic characteristics shared by all the allophones of a phoneme. It is true that allophones tend to have a "family resemblance." Some features of the sound may vary by position, but the "core" often remains unchanged. Thus [l] and [ɫ] are member of the "lateral" family, [p] and [pʰ] are allophones of the "voiceless labial stop" family, [m] and [m̥] are members of the "labial nasal" family, etc.

We will return to the idea of using phonetic features to define contrastive sounds in Chapter 12. But here we should note that, just as family resemblances do not always hold of every member in human family, so an "invariant core" of features is not always shared by every allophone. Consider, for example, all the allophones of /t/ in American English that we have run across so far:

(11)   Allophones of English /t/

aspirated	[tʰɑp]	top
unaspirated	[stɑp]	stop
glottalized	[kʰæt̚ʔ]	cat
glottal stop	[kʰæ̃ʔ]	can't
tap	[kʰɪɾi]	kitty
affricate	[mɛtʃju]	met you
zero (Ø)	[mospipəl]	most people

To an (American) English speaker, each of these sounds counts as "a way of saying /t/," and it would make sense to say that they belong to the "voiceless alveolar stop" family. But there is no one phonetic feature that every allophone shares (even if we ignore the "zero" case, where /t/ has no phonetic realization at all.) The sound [ʔ] is not alveolar, for example, and [ɾ] is not voiceless. On the other hand, each allophone (again leaving aside Ø) does have at least one of the "family characteristics": [ʔ] is a stop, [ɾ] is alveolar, [tʃ] is voiceless. As in human families, this is usually, though not necessarily, the case.

Taken together, however, the case of [n] and [n̪] in Venda and the case of /t/ in English show that the sharing of phonetic characteristics is a good clue, but not a reliable determinant of phonemic or allophonic status. We see cases, like Venda, where sounds that seem very similar (at least to our ears) count as separate phonemes, and other cases, where sounds that seem very different (such as [ʧ] and [ʔ] are allophones of one phoneme.

On the other hand, complementary distribution alone is not necessarily sufficient for determining allophonic status either. Consider the case of [h] and [ŋ] in English. The two sounds are in complementary distribution: like [l], [h] occurs only in the syllable onset, and like [ɫ], [ŋ] occurs only in the syllable coda. So there have been linguists who have argued that they must be allophones of a single phoneme. Yet, despite the complementary distribution, English speakers have no sense that [h] and [ŋ] are two ways of saying the same sound.

It is true that [h] and [ŋ] are not phonetically similar. But more importantly, there are no sets of related words where one form of the word has [h] and another form has [ŋ]. That is, an allophonic relationship is not supported by alternations. Compare this to [ʧ], [ʔ], and [ɾ]. Each can occur in a possible pronunciation of the word "at," as shown in (12).

(12)   Alternations in the pronunciation of "at."

at you	[æʧju]
at noon	[æʔnun]
at another time	[æɾənʌðəˑtʰaɪm]

Depending on the environment in which the word is placed, a different variant of /t/ appears. The fact that [æʧ], [æʔ], and [æɾ] are all variant pronunciations of the same word contributes to the English speaker's certainty that [ʧ], [ʔ], and [ɾ] are alternate ways of saying the "same" sound. We pick up the topic of alternation again in Chapter 11, but first we must consider two other factors that complicate the phoneme/allophone relationship: free variation and positional neutralization.

10.3.3 free variation

So far, we have discussed two possible distributional relationships that sounds may enter into. The first is contrast: two sounds may occur in the same environment, and so create a difference in meaning, as in [saɪ] vs. [ʃaɪ]. The second is complementary distribution: two sounds do not occur in the same environment, and so never contrast, as in [pʰɪt] vs. [spɪt]. A third possible type of distribution is *free variation*. Sounds that are in free variation occur in the same context, and thus are not predictable, but the difference between the two sounds does not change one word into another. Truly free variation is rather hard to find. Humans are very good at picking up distinctions in ways of speaking, and assigning meaning to them, so finding distinctions that are truly unpredictable and that truly have no shade of difference in meaning is rare.

One case of possibly free variation in English is the pronunciation of a /t–j/ sequence when /t/ is the end of one word and /j/ the beginning of another. You may have spotted this problem when only one pronunciation of "at you" was given in (12). Actually, there are two. Consider the sentence "You forgot your book." Before reading the next paragraph, say this over to yourself, and transcribe your pronunciation of "forgot your."

For some English speakers, the pronunciation will be [fɚgɑtʔjɚ], with glottalization. For others, it's [fɚgɑʧjɚ], with affrication. Which did you say? Is the other pronunciation possible?

In general, an English speaker may use either [tʔ] or [ʧ] in this environment. The meaning of the utterance is not changed, so this is neither complementary distribution nor contrast, but free variation. Because the difference does not change meaning, we would say that [tʔ] and [tʃ] are both allophones of /t/ in this position: they count as two different ways of saying the same thing.

I continue to call this, however, a *possible* case of free variation. It may well be that the choice between the two variants is not entirely unpredictable. It may be conditioned by social factors such as dialect, gender, or conversational situation. Is one pronunciation perhaps more forceful, more casual, more typical of a certain region? To my knowledge, however, a study showing exactly which of these factors might be relevant in this particular case has not yet been done.

10.3.4 positional neutralization

The most complicated and confusing distribution may be *positional neutralization*. In this case, two sounds are contrastive in one position, and not contrastive in another. The two sounds still belong to two different phonemes: if minimal pairs exist, the sounds are capable of bearing contrast. But that contrast may be neutralized in certain positions.

One example from English is tapping of intervocalic /t/ and /d/. Numerous minimal pairs demonstrate that /t/ and /d/ are contrastive: "time" vs. "dime," "mate" vs. "made," "write" vs. "ride." As was already noted in Chapter 3, however, in American English /t/ and /d/ both becomes taps ([ɾ]) in between two vowels, the second of which is unstressed. Thus "city" is pronounced [sɪɾi] and "lady" is pronounced as [leɪɾi]. This change can lead to a situation where two words that differ only in medial /t/ vs. /d/ are pronounced alike. Thus both "kitty" and "kiddy" are pronounced [kʰɪɾi], and it may not be clear whether a child who wants to be a [raɪɾɚ] is more interested in words or horses. If you do not already know the spelling, or cannot tell from the context which word was meant, you cannot tell whether /t/ or /d/ was intended. The phonemic difference between /t/ and /d/ is neutralized in this intervocalic position.

But just as a linguist must be careful in claiming that free variation is truly free and unpredictable, a linguist must be careful in claiming that a distinction is truly neutralized. There may remain a slight difference between the allophones that can clue a listener in to which phoneme was intended.

In English, a difference in the preceding vowel may provide clues as to whether a tap corresponds to /t/ or to /d/. English speakers pronounce vowels with a longer duration, and sometimes with a slightly different quality, depending on whether the following stop is voiced or voiceless. The difference is very slight in a lax vowel like [ɛ] or [ɪ], but it may be quite noticeable in a diphthong like [aɪ]. The vowel in "ride" is longer and probably lower than the vowel in "write." For at least some dialects and some speakers, the vowel difference persists even when the following /t/ or /d/ is tapped. Listen to yourself saying "ride" and "right," and then "rider" and "writer." Can you hear a difference?

10.4 Structuralism, Behaviorism, and the decline of phonemic analysis

As was noted in Section 10.1, phonemic analysis was an important part of the Structuralist approach to linguistic theory. Recall that a Structuralist analysis emphasizes working out the "complex system of relatednesses" between items in human experience. For phonology, this meant fully specifying the phonemic and allophonic relationships among the sounds of a language.

The dominant psychological paradigm in the first half of the twentieth century, when Structuralism was at its height, was *Behaviorism*, exemplified by the psychologist B.F. Skinner in his 1957 book, *Verbal Behavior*. Another important proponent of the Behaviorist model of linguistics was Leonard Bloomfield, a colleague of Edward Sapir at the University of Chicago, and one of the founding members of the Linguistic Society of America. In Behaviorism, as the name implies, language is understood to be something that a person *does*, not something that a person *knows*. Language is learned through imitation and reinforcement, and requires nothing more psychologically complex than hearing a word or phrase, remembering it, and repeating it under appropriate circumstances. Thus, anything systematic about language is to be found by studying verbal production, not by trying to figure out the mind of an individual speaker. Bloomfield wrote, for example, that "the meaning of a linguistic form [is] the situation in which a speaker utters it, and the response which it calls forth in the hearer" (1935, p. 139). As a Behaviorist, Bloomfield was often at odds with Sapir, who was more concerned with internal "psychological reality" than external "verbal behavior."

10.4   Although both Sapir and Bloomfield both went on to have a lasting influence on linguistic theory, they apparently were not friends. They wrote competing books, each entitled "Language," Sapir in 1921, and Bloomfield in 1933. A contemporary linguist who knew them both, Charles Hockett (1970, cited by Anderson, 1985, p. 220), writes that Bloomfield called Sapir a non-scientific "medicine man" and Sapir referred to Bloomfield's "sophomoric psychology." Anderson notes that Bloomfield could not have been happy "when most of the best students at Chicago left to follow Sapir to Yale in 1931."

By the middle of the twentieth century, linguists were beginning to question the value of Structuralist phonemic analysis. Complications such as free variation and positional neutralization, which contradict a simple and fully specified mapping between phonemes and allophones, as well as the failure of complementary distribution to fully predict allophonic status (as in English [h] and [ŋ]), led them to question whether it was always possible or necessary to completely determine the "family" relationships between sets of sounds.

Instead, linguists such as Noam Chomsky, building from Sapir's emphasis on "psychological reality," and in tune with the rise of cognitive science as a serious discipline, turned their attention to language as cognitive construct. They asked: What does it mean for a speaker to *know* a language? (In asking this question, Chomsky placed himself in direct opposition to the Behaviorists. His 1959 review of Skinner's book is often politely described as "scathing.") The focus of investigation turned from *performance* (what does a speaker do?) to *competence* (what does a speaker know?).

With respect to the sound systems of language, three areas of knowledge became increasingly important. A speaker certainly must know a memorized set of lexical items. But in addition to the real words of his language, a speaker also knows whether or not a particular string of sounds is a *possible* word in his language. And, third, the speaker knows a set of rules that convert stored lexical items (*underlying representations*) into actual pronunciations (*surface representations*), with the correct positional variants. While the principles of contrast and positional variation remain crucial to phonological theory, in the second half of the twentieth century, the focus of phonological investigation began to shift from completely determining systematic family relationships among the sounds of a language, to underlying representations and rules that derive surface representations from them.

chapter summary

- Phonology is the study of systematic relationships between sounds, including contrast, positional variation, phonotactic restrictions, and alternations.
- Phonetic illusions and the mistakes of language learners clue us in to the necessity of a level of phonological knowledge more abstract than actual pronunciation.
- Contrast and positional variation can be studied through phonemic analysis, which was a particular hallmark of the Structuralist approach. A phoneme is a unit of contrast (that is, a "family" of sounds that all "count as the same"). The allophones of a phoneme are the positional variants that make up the phoneme.
- Minimal pairs diagnose different phonemes; complementary distribution diagnoses allophonic status.
- The basic or underlying form of a phoneme typically corresponds to the "elsewhere case," but a more abstract underlying form is sometimes necessary or preferable.
- Free variation and positional neutralization complicate phonemic analysis, because they create an unpredictable mapping between allophone and phoneme.
- In the first half of the twentieth century, Structuralism and Behaviorism were the dominant theories in phonology, both of which emphasized relationships among surface forms. In the second half of the twentieth century, phonologists began to focus more on the question of linguistic knowledge, and on the mapping from underlying to surface representations.

further reading

For more information on the history of phonology, see:

Anderson, S. 1985. *Phonology in the Twentieth Century*. Chicago: University of Chicago Press.

Historical references in the present chapter are based on Anderson's analysis.

review exercises

1. Which terms go together? Write A if the term is indicative of an allophonic distribution, P if it is indicative of a phonemic distribution.

   ____ unpredictable
   ____ complementary distribution
   ____ contrastive
   ____ predictable
   ____ minimal pairs
   ____ non-contrastive
   ____ positional variation

2. Define the following terms:

   morpheme
   alternation
   phonotactic constraint
   natural class
   elsewhere case
   free variation
   positional neutralization

3. Explain how free variation and positional neutralization contradict a perfectly pre-dictable mapping between phoneme and allophone.

4. Explain the difference between:

   minimal pair and near-minimal pair
   underlying representation and surface representation

5. Match the name with the accomplishment or idea.

   ___ Jan Badouin de Courtenay
   ___ Leonard Bloomfield
   ___ Noam Chomsky
   ___ Edward Sapir
   ___ B.F Skinner

   a. Wrote "The psychological reality of the phoneme."
   b. First used the term "phoneme" to mean "unit of contrast."
   c. Wrote "Verbal Behavior."
   d. Wrote a scathing critique of "Verbal Behavior."
   e. Wrote a book called *Language*, from a Behaviorist perspective.

further analysis and discussion

6. Section 10.1 tells several stories meant to illustrate the point that there's more to learning the sounds of a language than knowing how to pronounce the sounds. Which story (if any) did you find most convincing, and why?
   a. Sapir, Whitney, and the [t] that wasn't there
   b. Sapir, the Yalies, and the [ʔ] that wasn't there
   c. "I knowed that before you teached me it"
   d. "keem Matt"
   e. "Light Street or Wright Street?"

7. Give examples of minimal pairs for each of the following contrastive sounds in English. Illustrate the contrast in initial, medial, and final position. (Do not reuse the same lexical item.) The first has been done.

	initial	medial	final
/s/ vs. /ʃ/	sip/ship	fist/fished	mass/mash
/m/ vs. /n/			
/z/ vs. /d/			
/ʃ/ vs. /tʃ/			

(Continued)

	initial	medial	final
/p/ vs. /b/			
/l/ vs. /ɹ/			

8. List three pairs of words that demonstrate that the tense/lax distinction is contrastive for English vowels. What problem do pairs of words such as these present to a native speaker of Spanish learning English?

9. Consider the distribution of [l] and [lʲ] in Russian. Do they represent two different phonemes, or are they allophones of a single phoneme? Argue for your answer, either by citing (near-)minimal pairs from the data, or by describing the distributions of the two sounds. (Data courtesy of Maria Gouskova.)

words with [l]

lat	agreement
gala	gala
polka	shelf
mel	chalk
pol	floor

words with [lʲ]

milʲ	of miles
nebilʲ	imaginary tale
lʲat	demon
lʲot	ice
molʲ	moth
polʲka	polka

10. In Farsi, spoken in and around Iran, the trill [r], voiceless trill [r̥], tap [ɾ], and retroflex approximant [ɻ] are all in complementary distribution and form one phoneme. Describe the distribution of each allophone. (Data courtesy of Narges Mahpeykar.)

[r]

ræd̥	trace
ræhbær̥	leader
rumizi	tablecloth
ræis	boss
rubah	fox
riz	tiny
ruzname	newspaper
rahzden	robber

[r̥]

pær̥	feather
dir̥	late
pænir̥	cheese
aχær̥	final
aʒir̥	alarm
mædʒbur̥	forced
æŋur̥	grapes
mar̥	snake
mæsir̥	path
didar̥	meet

[ɾ]

piɾuz	victorious
aɾam	quiet
biɾun	outside
sæɾiʔ	fast
kæɾim	generous
hæɾas	fear
kæɾe	butter
tiɾe	dark
toɾab	dust
suɾaχ	hole

[ɻ]

ɢæɻtʃ	mushroom
soɻb	iron
sæɻv	cedar
zæɻf	dish
mæɻd	man
geɻd	round
keɻm	warm
tʃæɻm	leather
æɻz	width
laɻv	insect eggs

11. Tiwi, a language spoken on Bathhurst and Melville Islands on the north coast of Australia, has both dental [t̪] and alveolar [t]. Do they belong to different phonemes, or are they allophones of the same phoneme? Argue for your answer.

tijoni	yam	t̪apaliŋa	star
tampajani	stone axe	t̪apit̪api	paddle
mant̪aŋa	woman friend	mant̪aŋa	stick
taka	tree	t̪alikaɹat̪i	fishing spear
taŋku	flat fighting stick	taŋkənaŋki	white-breasted sea eagle
təmani	land	t̪əmpala	sail
tiliwini	neck	t̪ilamaɹa	paint
tua	finished!	t̪əraka	wallaby
tuniwa	black	t̪uma	paper bark
tuwaɹa	tail	t̪uwaɹti	spit
tiŋati	sand	maɹakat̪i	spear grass
kuta	show it to me	kut̪aluwi	Fire clan
maɹatiŋa	dinghy	marit̪i	rainbow
maɹakata	fine rain	maɹakat̪a	knee cap
t̪ipita	crab claw	t̪ipət̪ini	soft

Source: C.R. Osborne. *The Tiwi Language*. Australian Aboriginal Studies #55. Australian Institute of Aboriginal Studies. 1974.

further research

12. Create your own phoneme/allophone problem, based on a language you know, or data you find in a published grammar or language description.
13. Find minimal pairs in another language for the sounds in #7. If the sounds occur but are not contrastive, illustrate and describe the distributions.
14. Can you think of another example of possibly free variation in English?
15. Try your own mini perceptual experiment. Record yourself (or better yet, a friend) saying "She wants to be a writer" and "She wants to be a rider" five times each. Then play the recordings, in random order, back to 10 other people. Can they tell which word is which? Is the difference between /t/ and /d/ truly neutralized?

Go online Visit the book's companion website for additional resources relating to this chapter at: http://www.wiley.com/go/zsiga.

references

Bloomfield, L., 1935, Linguistic aspects of science. *Philosophy of Science* 2: 499–517, reprinted in Hockett, C.F. (ed.), 1970, *A Leonard Bloomfield Anthology*. Bloomington, IN: Indiana University Press.

Sapir, E. 2008. *The Collected Works of Edward Sapir*, edited by Pierre Swiggers, Mouton de Gruyter.

Florentine
Villafana, C. 2006. *Consonant Lenition in Florentine Italian*. Doctoral dissertation, Georgetown University.

Swahili and Venda
Gleason, H. 1955, *Workbook in Descriptive Linguistics*.

Other language data is from the author's own fieldwork.

11 Phonotactics and Alternations

Phonology studies the social and mating habits of speech sounds.
Paul Smolensky and Geraldine Legendre, *The Harmonic Mind*, 2006, p. 26

The Sounds of Language: An Introduction to Phonetics and Phonology, First Edition. Elizabeth C. Zsiga.
© 2013 Elizabeth C. Zsiga. Published 2013 by Blackwell Publishing Ltd.

In this chapter, we begin to investigate the question, "What does it mean to know a language?" focusing on the evidence from *phonotactics* (possible sound sequences) and *alternations* (positionally-conditioned changes). As Smolensky and Legendre put it in the epigraph, phonotactics might be considered the *social habits* of speech sounds: what sounds go together, and where can they be found? Alternations might be considered *mating habits*: when sounds get together they interact, things happen, and new sequences come into being. We begin in Section 11.1 with a discussion of phonotactic constraints: how does a speaker know whether a word is possible in her language or not? What form does the knowledge take? How are phonotactic constraints evidenced in borrowings? The bulk of the chapter, however, is devoted to alternations: what happens to sequences of sounds when phonotactic constraints are violated? Section 11.2 discusses general procedures for diagnosing and describing alternations in a phonological analysis. Section 11.3 then provides a survey of the most common types of alternations found in the languages of the world, with the goal of giving students a sense of what to expect in their own phonological explorations.

11.1 phonotactic constraints

11.1.1 actual words and possible words

One thing that a proficient speaker knows about his language is the set of vocabulary items. (An adult may know 100,000 or more words, depending on background and education.) Lexical items must simply be memorized, as there is in general no natural relationship between the meaning of a word and the sequence of sounds used to encode it. There is nothing particularly canine about the sequence [dɔg]. It might just as well have been [kanis], as it was in Latin, or [aso] as it is in Tagalog (Filipino). Even onomatopoeia is conventional-ized: dogs say "bow-wow" in America but "wan-wan" in Japan. Ferdinand de Saussure, in his lecture series *Cours de Linguistique Générale* (delivered in Paris in 1906), called this arbi-trary pairing of sound and meaning "*the arbitrariness of the sign.*"

But a speaker knows more than the actual words of his language. He also knows whether a string of sounds could be a *possible* word. For example, the word for dog in Swahili is [mbwa]. This sequence could never be a word in English. Not because it isn't "doggy" enough, but because English does not allow the sequence [mbw] at the beginning of a word. Constraints on sequences that are allowed or disallowed are termed *phonotactic constraints* (phono = sound, tacti = touching).

There is one sense in which speech sounds are like numbers. We have discussed how language is combinatorial: just as we can take the digits 3, 2, 1 and make 123, 321, and 213, we can take the sounds [m], [e], [d] and make [med] *made*, [dem] *dame*, and [emd] *aimed*. But while any combination of digits is a possible number, not every combination of sounds is a possible word: 312 is perfectly valid, but [dme] is not (at least in English). Like the previously-mentioned [pneu], [dme] violates a phonotactic constraint of English: you cannot begin a word with a stop followed by a nasal (or with a nasal followed by a stop).

Morris Halle (in a 1962 article *Phonology in Generative Grammar*) illustrated the difference between actual word, possible word, and impossible word with the triplet [bɹɪk], [blɪk], [bnɪk]. The sequence [bɹɪk] is an actual word: English speakers happen to have associated the meaning "building block" to it. The sequence [blɪk] is a possible word: it does not happen to mean anything, but it does not violate the phonotactic constraints of English. Possible words could become actual words, if someone decided to start using them and they caught on. Impossible words, on the other hand, are sequences that could not become words because they do violate a phonotactic constraint, like [bnɪk] or [mbwa]. Even though you have heard neither [blɪk] nor [bnɪk], you can reference your implicit knowledge of the constraints of English to determine that one is possible and the other is not. We use an asterisk to indicate a sequence that is impossible (that is, ungrammatical): *[bnɪk].

The sequences ruled out by phonotactic constraints vary from language to language. English allows neither stop-nasal nor nasal-stop sequences in initial position. Swahili allows nasal-stop ([mba]) but not stop-nasal (*[bma]). Greek is the opposite: [pneu] is fine, but *[mba] is not. Senufo (West Africa) allows no consonant clusters at all. Discovering phonotactic constraints in different languages, and accounting for how they may differ or be similar cross-linguistically, is one of the important jobs of phonological theory.

Though phonotactic constraints may vary, they are not random. No language, for example, allows complex sequences like Greek [pneu] without allowing the simple [pe] and [ne]. The constraints rule out more difficult, marked, sequences, while permitting those that are unmarked. Many phonotactic constraints are based on syllable structure, and we will cover these in more detail in Chapters 14 and 15. Here, by way of illustration, we mention two constraints on sequences of sounds that contribute to positional variation. These constraints hold for English and many other languages.

One of the most common phonotactic constraints across languages is "Nasals must agree in place of articulation with a following stop." Think of English words that have a sequence of nasal + oral stop: "camp," "hamper," "bombard," "paint," "intelligent," "wind," "window." Though there are some exceptions, the general pattern is that the bilabial stops [p] and [b] are preceded by the bilabial nasal [m], and the alveolar stops [t] and [d] are preceded by the alveolar nasal [n]. With [k] and [g] we write the nasal as "n," but the pronunciation is usually velar [ŋ]: as in *think* [θɪŋk] and *linguistics* [lɪŋgwɪstɪks]. (Many words whose spelling ends in "ng", like "sing" and "rang", actually end in just the nasal [ŋ], with no [g] stop at all.) Exceptions occur when prefixes and suffixes are added, but there are no simple English words (that is, *monomorphemic* words; words with only one part) like "blimk" to contrast with "blink", or "ranp" to contrast with "ramp." This is a case of positional neutralization: nasals do not contrast in place of articulation when they occur before a stop. In these monomorphemic English words, however, the constraint is a *static generalization*: we don't see different forms of the word "blink," we just look across the language and notice the absence of words like "blimk." Static generalizations are often called *morpheme structure constraints*.

A similar constraint is that sequences of obstruents must match in voicing. This time, think of monomorphemic words that have a sequence of obstruents: "fist," "raft," "ask," "axe," "captive," "act," "adze," "rugby." There is no "rugpy", no "azk." Because we do not see different forms of "fist," this is again a static generalization, but it is true across the English lexicon.

11.1.2 absolute and statistical generalizations

That is, it is almost always true. There are a few exceptions: the word "obstruent," in fact, has a [bst] voiced-voiceless sequence. What to do about exceptions, and generalizations that are almost always, but not quite always, true, continues to be a challenge for phonology. One strategy is to ignore the exceptions, assume they are unimportant because they are not numerous, and concentrate on what is generally true. Another strategy pursues the idea that exceptions may teach us something important about phonological knowledge: that it is never absolute.

Recent work in psycholinguistics has revisited the question of what it means to *know* a phonotactic constraint. Halle divided sequences into possible and impossible, grammatical and ungrammatical. But recent studies have shown that phonotactic constraints are not absolute. Speakers do not necessarily judge sequences as possible or impossible, but better or worse (or perhaps likely vs. unlikely). Some sequences are very much better and some are very much worse, but there are gray areas. Studies by Janet Pierrehumbert and colleagues have shown that when speakers are asked to rate how "English-like" different nonsense words are, their responses are gradient: that is, they are willing to rate words as 8, 5, or 2 on a scale of 0 to 10, not just 0 for impossible and 10 for possible. Further, ratings are strongly correlated with how frequently the different parts of the words are heard. For example, the nonsense word [mrupation], which Halle would mark as totally ungrammatical, gets a surprisingly high rating. The sequence [mru] never occurs within a word, but [ation] is very, very frequent, so on average the word isn't too bad.

It is not clear, however, that asking people to think about and rate words gets at the same kind of knowledge that speakers access when they actually use language. (The way you rate how much you like various foods, for example, might or might not match what you actually eat.) Linguists continue to debate the best way to incorporate statistical generalizations into phonological theory. Whether absolute or gradient, however, phonotactic constraints do embody an important kind of phonological knowledge.

11.1.3 borrowings

A fun place to look at the effect of phonotactic constraints is in lists of new words that are entering a language: possible words that become actual. Japan, for example, has borrowed the game of baseball from America, and many of the terms that go with it. But Japanese allows many fewer consonant clusters than English does, and English baseball terms are adapted to the constraints of the Japanese language. A common strategy is to insert extra vowels to break up the consonant clusters. So "bat" becomes [batto], "strike" becomes [sutoraiku] and "baseball" becomes [besubaru]. (For simplicity, the symbol [r] is used for the Japanese alveolar lateral tap, which corresponds to both English [ɹ] and English [l]. Note also that the preferred vowel to insert is [u], except after [t]. The vowel [o] is inserted after [t], because Japanese has another constraint that rules out sequences of [tu]! See Chapter 14 for further analysis and discussion.)

New words enter the English language all the time. Merriam-Webster maintains an "open dictionary" online where people can submit new English words they've come across (http://www3.merriam-webster.com/opendictionary/). Thousands of entries are submitted every year, though only a few of these make it into the official dictionary. Many candidates are combinations of already-existing words, like "frenemy," which already obey the constraints of English. Others are borrowings from other languages, however, and have to be adjusted to meet the English rules.

For example, in 2009 Merriam-Webster officially added "goji" [godʒi], a kind of fruit or fruit juice, to the dictionary. In Mandarin Chinese, the source language, the pronunciation is [kotɕi]. English phonotactic constraints do not allow unaspirated [k] in initial position, so we pronounce the word with a [g] instead. The medial palatal affricate, a sound that does not exist in English, becomes [dʒ].

Another word that Merriam-Webster added in 2009 is "vlog" ([vlɑg]): an abbreviation of video-log on the model of "blog." The addition of this word actually addresses a real question in English phonology. Do we have a constraint against consonant clusters that begin with [v]? We have plenty of words that begin with [fr] ("friend, free, frame, frog," etc.) and plenty that begin with [fl] ("flag, flee, flow, flounder"), but almost none with [vl] or [vr]. There is onomatopoetic "vroom," "Vlasic" pickles, and the name "Vladimir," but sounds and names don't quite have the status of real meaningful words. While "Vladimir" is perfectly pronounceable, it still feels foreign. So it is a real question: do English speakers have a constraint *vC, to which "vroom" and "Vladimir" are exceptions, or is the fact that so few English words begin with [vl] just an accident of history? The addition of [vlɑg] as a vocabulary word suggests the latter. How would you rate "vlog" on a scale of 1 to 10? Does the fact that it is similar to the frequent (and trendy) word "blog" make it better?

11.2 analyzing alternations

The previous section addressed how phonotactic constraints give rise to systematic gaps: sequences that simply fail to occur, and which native speakers judge to be ill-formed (whether absolutely or relatively). Phonotactic constraints also give rise to *alternations*. Alternations occur when morphemes are put together in different combinations. If an illicit sequence is created, a change may occur in the way the morpheme is pronounced.

We saw above that within morphemes in English, nasals agree with the place of articulation of a following stop, as in "camp", "wind", and "think." Because these nasals are within a single morpheme, we never see alternations in how they are pronounced. But some English prefixes that end with a nasal are pronounced differently when the prefix is added to words beginning with different sounds. Consider the negative prefix "in-". Before a vowel or an alveolar, "in-" is pronounced [ɪn]: "inedible," "inaudible," "indelible," "intolerable," "insufferable." But before the bilabials [m], [b], or [p], it becomes [ɪm]: "immobile," "imbalance," "impossible." And before [k] or [g], it's usually pronounced [ɪŋ]. We don't change the spelling, because English does not have a separate letter for the velar nasal, but listen to your pronunciation of a word like "incorrect" and you'll realize the nasal is velar rather than alveolar. The phonotactic constraint "Nasals must agree in place of articulation with a following stop" applies not just within morphemes (like "camp" and "wind"), leading to a static generalization, but also when morphemes are combined, giving rise to positional variation (and sometimes positional neutralization).

One way to think about alternations is to assume that each morpheme has only a single entry in the mental lexicon: this is its *underlying form* or *basic form*. Just as an underlying phoneme has different positional variants termed allophones, a morpheme has different positional variants termed *allomorphs*. The different allomorphs (the words that are actually pronounced) may also be termed *surface forms*. As with phonemes, we can usually identify the underlying form of the morpheme with the elsewhere case, and assume that the more restricted surface forms are derived. Noam Chomksy and Morris Halle, in their 1968 book, *The Sound Pattern of English*, argued that an important part of a speaker's knowledge of a language is the rules that derive surface forms from underlying forms. The rules *generate* (create) the surface forms from underlying forms; thus linguistic descriptions that follow this basic model are termed *generative grammars*. The approach can be illustrated by one extended example: the alternation between [d] and [t] that led four-year-old Johnny to say "knowed" and "teached."

The first step in doing an analysis of phonological alternation is to identify the different forms of the morpheme that need to be accounted for. The past tense suffix in English has three forms: [t] as in "reached" [ritʃt], [d] as in "mowed" [mod], and [ɨd] as in "rotted" [raɾɨd]. Example (1) gives a list of various words that take each suffix. The transcriptions show the pronunciation of the unsuffixed verb: transcription is broad, and non-contrastive details not relevant to the alternation are not included.

(1)　Allomorphs of the English past tense suffix:

[t]		[d]		[ɨd]	
reached	[ritʃ]	mowed	[mo]	rotted	[rɑt]
ripped	[rɪp]	fibbed	[fɪb]	prodded	[prɑd]
laughed	[læf]	loved	[lʌv]	lifted	[lɪft]
camped	[kæmp]	rammed	[ræm]	boosted	[bust]
missed	[mɪs]	blazed	[blez]	carded	[kɑrd]
reversed	[rivɝs]	blared	[bler]	handed	[hænd]
refreshed	[rifɹɛʃ]	edged	[ɛdʒ]	created	[kriet]
picked	[pɪk]	begged	[bɛg]	crafted	[kræft]
inked	[ɪŋk]	banged	[bæŋ]	ranted	[rænt]
helped	[hɛlp]	canned	[kæn]	belted	[bɛlt]
milked	[mɪlk]	failed	[fel]	hated	[het]
hoped	[hop]	sued	[su]	asserted	[əsɝt]

As analysts, we want to discover if the alternation is conditioned by phonological environment. Therefore, the next step (as with an allophone problem) is to list the environments where each allomorph occurs. The steps in solving a phoneme/allophone problem and a morpheme alternation problem are in fact pretty much the same. The difference is one of focus. In a phoneme/allophone problem the linguist is looking at the distribution of sounds across the entire lexicon (though of course in a given problem one can only look at a subset of representative words). In a morpheme alternation problem, the linguist is looking at the variant forms of a specific word or affix. In both cases, however, the overall goal is the same: to discover which aspects of sound structure are contrastive and which are predictable according to the environment.

　　The environments for the variants of the English past tense suffix are shown in (2). Since the alternating morpheme is a suffix, we can begin with the hypothesis that it is the final sound of the stem that conditions the change.

(2)　Environments for the English past tense suffix:

[t]	[d]	[ɨd]
tʃ __	o __	t __
p __	b __	d __
f __	v __	
s __	m __	
ʃ __	z __	
k __	ɹ __	
p __	dʒ __	
	g __	
	ŋ __	
	n __	
	l __	
	u __	

We can immediately note that the allomorphs are in complementary distribution: no sound occurs in more than one list. We can also note that each list forms a class that can be defined in phonetic terms: [ɨd] occurs following alveolar stops (if intervocalic, these will actually be pronounced as taps), [t] occurs following all other voiceless sounds, and [d] occurs following all other voiced sounds.

Further, we can see the activity of phonotactic constraints in driving the alternation. The [ɨ] is inserted to break up a cluster of consonants ([td] or [dd]) that would otherwise not be licit at the end of a word. The change from [d] to [t] after voiceless consonants brings the sequence into line with the constraint that requires obstruent clusters to agree in voicing. As was noted above, the phonotactic constraints rule out marked structures: the clusters that are "fixed up" are either hard to hear (like a second [d] in [hændd]), or hard to produce (like switching voicing twice in the middle of a consonant cluster like [lpd]).

To finish the analysis, we need to decide on the underlying form of the morpheme, and state the generalizations that derive each of the surface forms. Here, we can be secure in choosing [d] as the elsewhere case, as the set of sounds that take [d] is the most diverse: vowels, sonorants, and voiced obstruents. We ensure that words that end with alveolars get the correct suffix form by applying the rule for the most specific case first. (This idea of taking the most specific case first, thus getting it out of the way so that succeeding statements could be made more generally, is originally due to the ancient Indian grammarian Pāṇini, and is still known as *Pāṇini's Theorem*.)

The overall generalization for forming English plurals is given in (3):

(3)　Deriving the English past tense suffix:

    a.　The underlying form of the past tense suffix is /d/.
    b.　If the suffix is added to a word that ends with an alveolar stop, a vowel is inserted to derive the surface form [ɨd], *otherwise*
    c.　If the suffix is added to a word that ends with a voiceless consonant, the surface form is [t], *otherwise*
    d.　The surface form is [d].

This is the "rule" that four-year-old Johnny knew and applied in his spontaneous utterance "I knowed that before you teached me it."

Another, somewhat more complex, example comes from Zoque ([zoke]), a language spoken in Southern Mexico. The phonology of this language was described in detail by William Wonderly in a series of articles published in 1951, and has been much discussed in the phonological literature since. (The word set presented here is somewhat simplified.) Example (4) illustrates the different forms of the Zoque prefix meaning "my." (You may also notice the mixture of native words and borrowings from Spanish, though the history of the word does not seem to affect how it takes a possessive prefix.)

(4)　Zoque possessives:

pama	clothing	m-bama	my clothing
plato	plate	m-blato	my plate
burru	burro	m-burru	my burro
tatah	father	n-datah	my father
trampa	trap	n-drampa	my trap
disko	phon. record	n-disko	my phonograph record
kaju	horse	ŋ-gaju	my horse
kwarto	room	ŋ-gwarto	my room
gaju	rooster	ŋ-gaju	my rooster

waka	basket	n-waka	my basket
jomo	wife	n-jomo	my wife
ʔane	tortilla	n-ʔane	my tortilla
faha	belt	faha	my belt
ʃapun	soap	ʃapun	my soap
sʌk	beans	sʌk	my beans
rantʃo	ranch	rantʃo	my ranch
lawus	nail	lawus	my nail

As with English, we begin by listing the different forms of the prefix, and the environments in which they occur. For the cases in which no prefix appears (*belt, soap, beans, ranch,* and *nail*), a "zero" allomorph (Ø) is listed.

(5)   Distribution of Zoque first-person possessive allomorphs:

[m]	[n]	[ŋ]	[Ø]
pama	tatah	kaju	faha
burru	disko	gaju	ʃapun
plato	trampa	gwarto	sʌk
	waka		rantʃo
	jomo		lawus
	ʔane		

The second step is to look for patterns. Is there overlap between the lists, or is the distribution of the prefix forms predictable? If predictable, what aspect of the context determines the form? Do the lists of words that take the different prefix forms have anything in common?

(6)   Predictable distribution of Zoque first-person possessive allomorphs:

[m]: labial stops
[n]: alveolar stops, glides, and glottal stop
[ŋ]: velar stops
[Ø]: consonants that are not stops

The set of sounds that follow [n] constitute the elsewhere case: [d], [t], [j], [w] and [ʔ] have nothing particular in common. We therefore choose /n/ as the basic form of the first person possessive prefix. (Words in Zoque do not begin with vowels, so we cannot tell for sure what form the prefix would take before a vowel, but we can guess that it would be [n], the basic form.) The other forms are derived by rule. Part of the pattern clearly involves the requirement that nasals agree in place of articulation with a following stop: labial [m] before labial stops, velar [ŋ] before velar [k] and [g]. What about the case where the prefix does not occur at all? The set of fricatives, [r], and [l] constitute the set of consonants that have a significant constriction in the oral cavity, but that don't make a complete closure like a stop. (Linguists label these the *continuant* consonants.)

The overall generalization is given in (7):

(7)   Deriving the Zoque first person possessive prefix:

a.   The underlying form of the prefix is /n/.
b.   If the prefix is added to a word that begins with an stop consonant, the nasal agrees in place of articulation with the following stop, *otherwise*

    c.   If the prefix is added to a word that begins with a continuant consonant (frica-tive or liquid), the nasal prefix is deleted, *otherwise*

    d.   The surface form is [n].

Another set of alternations in seen in the data in (8): some of the nouns show an alternation in their first segment when the nasal prefix is added.

(8)   Voicing alternations in Zoque:

word-initial	post-nasal
[pama]	[bama]
[plato]	[blato]
[tatah]	[datah]
[trampa]	[drampa]
[kaju]	[gaju]
[kwarto]	[gwarto]

no alternation:

word-initial	post-nasal
[burru]	[burru]
[disko]	[disko]
[gaju]	[gaju]

The nouns that alternate have a voiceless stop in word-initial position, and a voiced stop following a nasal. There are in principle two possibilities here: either the voiceless stop is underlying, and it becomes voiced in post-nasal position, or the voiced stop is underlying and it becomes voiceless in word-initial position, as listed in (9):

(9)   Voicing alternations:

    a.   Voiceless stops become voiced in post-nasal position?

    b.   Voiced stops become voiceless in word-initial position?

Either example (9a) or (9b) is plausible phonetically: getting voicing going in a stop is dif-ficult at the beginning of a word and easy after a nasal. But the full set of data in example (8) is compatible only with (9a). If there were a process of word-initial devoicing in Zoque, we would expect it to apply to words like [burru], [disko], and [gaju] as well as [pama], [tatah], and [kaju]. Why would devoicing apply to "horse" but not to "rooster"? We could list, for every word, which devoices and which does not, but every time we resort to a list, we give up the idea that there is any generalization to be made. Instead, we explain the dif-ference between "horse" and "rooster" as a difference in underlying representation. The alternating forms begin with a voiceless stop in underlying representation, and the rule makes them voiced in post-nasal position. The non-alternating forms begin with a voiced stop in underlying representation, and they remain unchanged.

    An example involving vowel alternations can be found in Igbo, spoken in Nigeria, as described by William Welmers (1973). In Igbo, the third-person singular subject prefix (*he, she* or *it*) alternates between [ó] and [ɔ́], as shown in (10).

    There is a lot of phonology going on in these Igbo words. Recall that acute accents indicate high tones and grave accents indicate low tones. Tonal alternations are also ubiquitous in Igbo and related languages, but are not a focus here (see Chapter 17). We can also note that the past tense affix in Igbo is *reduplicative*: it copies the vowel of the verb. In English, we sometimes copy parts of words to convey a pejorative, diminutive sense: "teeny-tiny," "itsy-bitsy," or the more dismissive "syntax-schmintax." But in other languages, copying can be a regular part of the sound system, as in the Igbo past tense.

(10)   Igbo 3s subject prefix:

   a. [ó]
   ó rìrì   he ate
   ó sìrì   he cooked
   ó mèrè   he did
   ó gbùrù   he killed
   ó zòrò   he hid

   b. [ɔ́]
   ɔ́ pìrì   he carved
   ɔ́ sìrì   he told
   ɔ́ sàrà   he washed
   ɔ́ zùrù   he bought
   ɔ́ dòrò   he pulled

In Igbo, it cannot be the case that the immediately adjacent sound conditions the alternation in the prefix. The consonants [s] and [z] appear as initial consonants of verbs in both lists. Rather, it is the vowel of the verb that determines the form of the prefix:

(11)   Predictable distribution of the Igbo 3s subject prefix:

   [ó]: when the verb contains [i, e, o, u]
   [ɔ́]: when the verb contains [ɪ, a, ɔ, ʊ]

No vowel occurs in both lists, and each list constitutes a natural class: a set of sounds with some phonetic description in common. As was described in Chapter 4, [i, e, o, u] are all made with the tongue root advanced, and [ɪ, a, ɔ, ʊ] are all made with the tongue root retracted. (These sets are described as tense and lax in English, though Welmers is careful to explain that in Igbo it is the retracted set that involves more muscular tension.) Alternations where a vowel in one syllable conditions the quality of the vowel in another syllable, regardless of intervening consonants, is known as *vowel harmony*. (Another example, from Turkish, is given in Section 11.3.2 below.)

The distribution of the Igbo prefix is another of those cases where neither alternant can be described as the elsewhere case (see Section 10.3.1), so we cannot decide, based on the data, whether [ó] or [ɔ́] is more basic. We will fall back on the strategy of defining the prefix simply as a mid, back, high-toned vowel, with tongue root position unspecified, and write our generalization as in (12)

(12)   Deriving the Igbo 3s subject prefix:

   a.   The prefix is a mid, back, high-toned vowel.
   b.   If the prefix is added to a verb that contains a vowel with advanced tongue root, the prefix is realized as advanced [ó], *otherwise*
   c.   If the prefix is added to a verb that contains a vowel with retracted tongue root, the prefix is realized as retracted [ɔ́].

It is worth emphasizing that the step from (11) to (12) is an important one. (11) lists a set of sounds, with no indication of what, if anything, they have in common. (12) states a generalization, defining the natural classes over which the rule operates. Distributions should always be stated in a form that is as general as possible (consistent with the data, of course). Making a list of environments is an important step in solving an alternation problem, but it is only an intermediate step.

In fact, we can take a further step with Igbo vowel alternations. It is not only the subject prefix that undergoes vowel harmony. A sampling of Igbo words shows that vowel harmony holds as a morpheme structure constraint. As shown in (13), monomorphemic words generally will contain vowels from only the advanced or retracted set:

(13) Vowel harmony in Igbo monomorphemic words:

Only advanced-tongue-root vowels		Only retracted-tongue-root vowels	
íhé	thing	ńkítá	dog
úbì	farm	òdí	sort, kind
ésú	millipede	ḿmádó	people
òsè	stream	ótá	shield

In addition, vowel harmony applies to other prefixes and suffixes, illustrated in (14) with the verb roots [si] "cook" and [sɪ] "tell."

(14) Vowel harmony in Igbo affixes:

si-e	cook!	sɪ-a	tell!
o-si-ghi	he did not cook	ɔ-sɪ-ghɪ	he did not tell
i-si	to cook	ɪ-sɪ	to tell
o-si	the cook	ɔ-sɪ	the teller
e-si	cooking	a-sɪ	telling

The imperative suffix alternates between [e] and [a], the negative between [i] and [ɪ]. The infinitive, agentive, and continuous prefixes show the alternations [i ~ ɪ], [o ~ ɔ], and [e ~ a] respectively. (The symbol ~ can be read "alternates with.") In each case, the affix harmonizes to the stem. In summary, we can make a general statement as in (15).

(15) General statement of Igbo vowel harmony:

Vowels in Igbo words must agree in advanced or retracted tongue root. Affix vowels agree with the root vowel in tongue root position: affix vowels are advanced if the root vowel is advanced, and retracted if the root vowel is retracted.

 11.1 In Focus

Remember, phonology is about contrast and predictability. If you are a phonologist working to describe a previously unknown language, probably the first thing you want to figure out is what the inventory of sounds is – what sounds does the language use? But the second thing you want to figure out is which dimensions of sound are *contrastive* – which sound differences does the language use to encode differences between words? What are the phonemes? Then, we want to be able to predict the contexts in which the different allophones of a phoneme, or allomorphs of a morpheme, appear. Sometimes we do this by studying lists of words in order to discover different kinds of sound distributions. Sometimes we look at what happens to borrowed words. Another way is by studying alternations. In each case, we seek to discover the relationship between underlying and surface forms, and the different phonotactic constraints that determine what sounds appear where.

Section 11.3 now turns to a survey of the different kinds of alternations common in the languages of the world, giving us a broader understanding of the range of facts for which any theory of phonology needs to account (as well as a better ability to discern the types of patterns we're likely to find in new datasets.)

11.3 alternations: what to expect

The goal of this section is to illustrate different kinds of phonological alternations, so that you may come to know what to expect. The material is summarized in Table 11.1, which lists common alternations, their definition, and the examples that are listed here. For reasons of space, only a few examples from a few languages are given, but the examples have been chosen to be representative of what can be found across a wide variety of languages. Some cases are well known and much-discussed in the literature (and therefore worth becoming familiar with); others are less well known. References for each set of data are found at the end of the chapter. The terms are, to the extent possible, descriptive rather than formal. Chapters 12 through 14 return to a discussion of more formal ways of representing these alternations.

11.3.1 local assimilation

The most common type of alternation is *assimilation*: two sounds that are different become more alike. Each of the examples in Section 11.2 is one of assimilation: obstruent voicing assimilation in English affixes, nasal place assimilation and post-nasal voicing assimilation in Zoque, and vowel harmony in Igbo. The first three are *local assimilations*: the sound undergoing the change is immediately adjacent to the trigger of the change. Harmony is a *long-distance assimilation*: vowels affect each other even though consonants intervene.

More examples of local assimilation are shown in (16) through (24). These examples are the most numerous, as local assimilation is the most common type of alternation. Example (16) shows obstruent assimilation in Russian. The facts are similar to English obstruent assimilation in suffixes, except that in Russian the alternating morphemes are prepositions, illustrated here by /ot/ *from* and /s/ *with*. Voicing assimilation is not triggered by sonorants, so that the underlying voiceless forms are heard in [ot mamɨ] and [s mamoj]. Russian, like many other Slavic languages, allows long consonant clusters, such as [fspl] and [vzb], and within these clusters as well, all obstruents must be either all voiced or all voiceless.

(16)   Russian: an obstruent agrees in voicing with a following obstruent:

ot papɨ	from papa
ot fspléska	from a splash
od babuʃki	from grandma
od vzbútʃki	from a scolding
od vzlóma	from breaking in
ot mamɨ	from mama
s papoj	with papa
z babuʃkoj	with grandma
s mamoj	with mama

Table 11.1 Summary of the most common types of phonological alternation.

Name	Definition	Examples cited here
Local assimilation	Two adjacent segments become more similar	Russian voicing assimilation Catalan nasal place assimilation Malayalam nasal place assimilation Korean nasal assimilation Oowekyala rounding English palatalization Japanese palatalization Syrian vowel lowering Arabic lateral assimilation
Long-distance assimilation (Harmony)	Two segments that are not immediately adjacent become more similar	Turkish vowel harmony Chumash consonant harmony Shona tone spreading
Coalescence	Two segments merge into one. The resulting segment shares some properties of both	Indonesian nasal fusion Xhosa vowel coalescence
Dissimilation	A segment becomes less similar to another segment	Chontal voicing dissimilation Ancient Greek fricative dissimilation Llogoori glide formation Latin lateral dissimilation
Lenition	Weakening	Spanish voiced stop lenition Florentine voiceless stop lenition English vowel reduction American English tapping
Debuccalization	A consonant changes to [ʔ] or [h]	Slave debuccalization Spanish debuccalization English glottalization
Fortition	Strengthening	Setswana post-nasal hardening English aspiration
Epenthesis	A segment is inserted	Yowlumne vowel epenthesis Basque glide epenthesis English consonant epenthesis
Deletion	A segment is deleted	Tagalog medial vowel deletion Lardil final deletion
Lengthening	A short segment becomes long	Komi compensatory lengthening
Shortening	A long segment becomes short	Yawelmani vowel shortening
Metathesis	Segments switch order	Hanunoo glottal stop metathesis

Nasal place assimilation, as was illustrated in Zoque (4) and in English ("indecent" vs. "impossible") is nearly ubiquitous cross-linguistically. Two more examples are shown from Catalan (Southwest Europe) (17) and Malayalam (Southern India) (18). Comparison of the different examples cited shows that languages may differ in whether or not post-nasal voicing also applies (yes in Zoque, no in Catalan and Malayalam), whether or not nasals assimilate to fricatives and liquids (yes in Catalan, no in Zoque), and whether or not all nasals are affected (just /n/ in Catalan, /n/ and /m/ in Malayalam).

(17)   Nasal place assimilation in Catalan. /n/ assimilates in place of articulation to a following consonant:

só[n] amics	they are friends
só[m] pocs	they are few
só[ɱ] feliços	they are happy
só[n̪] [d̪]os	they are two
só[n̺] rics	they are rich
só[ɲ] [lʲ]iures	they are free
só[ŋ] grans	they are big

(18)   Nasal place assimilation in Malayalam. /n/ and /m/ assimilate in place of articulation to a following stop:

awan	he
awam-paraɲɲu	he said
awan̪-t̪aṭiccu	he became fat
awaɲ-ca:ṭi	he jumped
awaŋ-karaɲɲu	he cried
kamalam	proper name
kamalam-paraɲɲu	Kamalam said
kamalan̪-t̪aṭiccu	Kamalam became fat
kamalaɲ-ca:ṭi	Kamalam jumped
kamalaŋ-karaɲɲu	Kamalam cried

In addition to voicing assimilation and place assimilation, the quality of nasality often assimilates from one segment to another. This is often seen in allophonic vowel nasalization: vowels are nasalized preceding a nasal consonant, as in English *cat* [kʰæt] vs. *can* [kʰæ̃n]. As was noted in Chapter 10.1, an example of consonant nasalization is seen in Korean (19).

(19)   Assimilation of nasality in Korean: a consonant becomes nasal when a nasal consonant follows:

pap	rice	pam mekta	eat rice
ot	clothes	on man	only clothes
jak	medicine	jaŋ mekta	take medicine

While local assimilations often affect consonant clusters, vowels and consonants may also assimilate to each other. Consonants often assimilate the rounding or fronting properties of adjacent vocalic articulations. For example, in Oowekyala (Northwest North America), velar and uvular consonants become round when a round vowel precedes. Thus each of the suffixes in (20) has two allomorphs: a plain version following consonants and most vowels, and a rounded version following [u]. (The suffix [χs], meaning something like *aboard*, is a personal favorite.)

(20)   Rounding assimilation in Oowekyala: velar and uvular consonants become round when they follow [u]:

pusq'a-xʔit	to become very hungry
tl'u'xwalasu-xʷʔit	to become sick
məja-gila	make (draw or carve) a fish
ʔamastu-gʷila	make kindling

waka-k'ala	sound of barking
tu-k'ʷala	sound of footsteps
k'wa's-χs	to sit in a boat
q'atu-χʷs	to assemble on the boat

Consonants may become fronted (*palatalized*) adjacent to a front vowel or glide. In English (21), word-final alveolar consonants become alveopalatals when a suffix beginning with /j/ is added. Obligatory within words, English palatalization applies optionally across word boundaries, especially in very common phrases. Japanese (in example 22) illustrates two kinds of palatalization: alveolars become alveopalatals preceding /i/, while velar and labial consonants take on a secondary palatal articulation without changing their primary place.

(21)   English palatalization before /j/:

d ~ dʒ	grade	gradual	could you	[kʰʊdʒjə]
t ~ tʃ	habit	habitual	bet you	[bɛtʃjə]
s ~ ʃ	press	pressure	this year	[ðɪʃjir]
z ~ ʒ	please	pleasure	could use your help	[kʰʊdʒjuʒjərhɛlp]

(22)   Japanese palatalization before /i/:

kas-anai	lend-NEG	kaʃ-ita	lend-PAST
kat-anai	win-NEG	katʃ-itai	win-VOLITIONAL
wak-anai	boil-NEG	wakʲ-itai	boil-VOLITIONAL
job-anai	call-NEG	jobʲ-itai	call-VOLITIONAL

Sometimes, vowels assimilate to adjacent consonants. For example, in some Arabic dialects, the feminine suffix [e] lowers and backs to [a] adjacent to a uvular, pharyngeal, or laryngeal consonant: those made in the back of the throat.

(23)   Vowel lowering in Syrian Arabic:

daraʒ-e	step
ʃerk-e	society
madras-e	school
wa:ʒh-a	display
mni:ħ-a	good
dagga:ʀ-a	tanning

As the examples above have illustrated, local assimilation can target just about any phonetic parameter, including but not limited to voicing, place, and nasality. In each preceding case, however, the assimilations have been *partial*: adjacent sounds became similar but not identical. Nasals take on the place of the following consonant, but remain nasal; or obstruents take on the voicing or nasality of the following consonant, but retain their underlying place.

Complete assimilation occurs when two adjacent sounds become identical. One well-known example involving complete assimilation of /l/ comes from Modern Standard Arabic, shown in (24). The definite prefix [ʔal] is realized with a final alveolar lateral before the set of words beginning with the "moon letters", so called because of the canonical example [ʔal-qamr]. Before the "sun letters," however, typified by [ʔaʃ-ʃams], the lateral becomes identical to the following consonant. Can you determine the phonetic parameter that defines the class of sun letters?

(24)   Complete assimilation of [l] in Arabic:

Sun letters:

ʔaʃ-ʃams	the sun
ʔat-tidʒa:ra	the commerce
ʔaθ-θaqa:fa	the culture
ʔad-di:n	the religion
ʔað-ðahab	the gold
ʔar-rab:	the lord
ʔaz-zuhu:r	the flowers
ʔaʒ-ʒil:	the shadow
ʔan-nu:r	the light

Moon letters:

ʔal-qamr	the moon
ʔal-badw	the Bedouin
ʔal-filfil	the pepper
ʔal-ħaʒ	the luck
ʔal-xardal	the mustard
ʔal-ɣarb	the west
ʔal-kanz	the treasure
ʔal-markaz	the center
ʔal-handasa	the engineering
ʔal-wiza:ra	the ministry

Local assimilation is ubiquitous because strong articulatory, perceptual, and processing requirements all favor it. In articulation, it can be difficult to switch positions quickly, and it is impossible to do so instantaneously. It is easier to maintain a single state across adjacent articulations than it is to switch back and forth from voiced to voiceless, from nasal to oral, or from front to back in the middle of a cluster. Then, coarticulation between segments can lead to the perception that a category change has taken place: if an [s] is coarticulated with the high tongue body position of a following [i] or [j], for example, it may sound like [ʃ] (see the discussion in Chapter 5). Certain positions and certain segments may be better or worse carriers of perceptual contrast. Nasal stops, with their complex resonance patterns, are particularly poor at conveying contrastive place information, especially if they are followed by a stop whose strong release conveys place information very clearly. The sequences [np] and [mp] just do not sound very different. Finally, in terms of speech processing, word recognition can be speeded if there are fewer decisions that need to be made to identify a word. When a single articulatory state is maintained (all consonants voiced or all voiceless) there are fewer decisions.

11.3.2 long-distance assimilation

Long-distance assimilation is known as *harmony*. Two segments become more similar, even though they are not immediately adjacent. An example of vowel harmony was already seen in the Igbo data in examples (13) and (14) above: all vowels in a word must agree in having either advanced or retracted tongue root, and suffix vowels alternate to match the root vowel, regardless of intervening consonants.

Another well-known case of vowel harmony is found in Turkish (example 25). Turkish has an eight-vowel system, including front round and back unround vowels: [i, y, u, ɯ, o, ø, e, ɑ]. All suffix vowels alternate to match the root vowel in backness. In addition, high vowels also match the preceding vowel in rounding. Thus, the accusative suffix, which is underlyingly high, has four different allomorphs: [i, y, ɯ, u]. The plural suffix, which is underlyingly non-high, alternates between [ler] following front vowels and [lɑr] following back vowels.

(25)   Vowel harmony in Turkish:

Nominative	Accusative	Genitive	Nom. plural	Gen. plural	Gloss
jel	jel-i	jel-in	jel-ler	jel-ler-in	wind
diʃ	diʃ-i	diʃ-in	diʃ-ler	diʃ-ler-in	tooth
gyl	gyl-y	gyl-yn	gyl-ler	gyl-ler-in	rose
gøl	gøl-y	gøl-yn	gøl-ler	gøl-ler-in	sea
kɯz	kɯz-ɯ	kɯz-ɯn	kɯz-lɑr	kɯz-lɑr-ɯn	girl
dɑl	dɑl-ɯ	dɑl-ɯn	dɑl-lɑr	dɑl-lɑr-ɯn	branch
kol	kol-u	kol-un	kol-lɑr	kol-lɑr-ɯn	arm
kul	kul-u	kul-un	kul-lɑr	kul-lɑr-ɯn	slave

Consonant harmony, where non-adjacent consonants assimilate to each other, is rarer than vowel harmony, but is sometimes attested. Chumash (Northwest North America) is one well-known example. In Chumash, the sibilant consonants in a word ([s], [ʃ], [tʃ]) must be either all alveolar or all post-alveolar, agreeing with the final sibilant in the word, as shown in example (26). The basic form of the third singular prefix is [s], as in [s-ixut], but it becomes [ʃ] before [ʃ]-final [ilakʃ]. Conversely, the basic form of the dual prefix is [iʃ], but it becomes [is] when [s] is final. Similar long-distance assimilations between alveolars and post-alveolars are found in related languages. Long-distance assimilation of nasality and laryngeal features are also attested, but long-distance assimilation of primary place is rare or non-existent.

(26)   Consonant harmony in Chumash:

s-ixut	it burns
s-aqunimak	he hides
ʃ-ilakʃ	it is soft
ʃ-kuti-waʃ	he saw
saxtun	to pay
ʃaxtun-itʃ	to be paid
p-iʃ-anan'	don't you two go
s-is-tisi-jep-us	they two show him

A very common long-distance assimilation involves tone. High or low tone often "spreads" from one syllable to the next. The example in (27) is from Shona (East Africa). The high tone from a verb root spreads rightward, causing all the suffixes to become high-toned.

(27)   Tone assimilation in Shona:

téng	buy	ereng	read
ku-téng-á	to buy	ku-ereng-a	to read
ku-téng-és-á	to sell	ku-ereng-es-a	to make read
ku-téng-és-ér-á	to sell to	ku-ereng-es-er-a	to make read to
ku-téng-és-ér-án-á	to sell to each other	ku-ereng-es-er-an-a	to make read to each other

11.3.3 coalescence

Coalescence is a phonological alternation closely related to, but not identical to, assimilation. In assimilation, two adjacent sounds become more similar, but remain a sequence of two distinct segments. In coalescence, which applies in many of the same environments as local assimilation, two segments merge into one, with the merged segment displaying some properties of each of the input segments.

A process known as *nasal fusion* applies to sequences of nasal plus voiceless stop in Indonesian and related languages. As shown in example (28), the nasal and stop merge into a single nasal segment that has the place of the stop. (The capital N is used to indicate a nasal stop whose underlying place is undetermined.) An example of vowel coalescence is found in Xhosa (Southern Africa) (example 29), in which a sequence of /a/ followed by a high vowel results in a mid vowel with the backness and rounding features of the second vowel.

(28)   Indonesian nasal coalescence:

məN + pilih	->	məmilih	to choose
məN + tulis	->	menulis	to write
məN + kasih	->	məŋasih	to give

(29)   Vowel coalescence in Xhosa: high vowel + low vowel = mid vowel:

wa + inkosi	->	wenkosi	of the chiefs
wa + umfazi	->	womfazi	of the woman
na + um + ntu	->	nomntu	with the person
na + impendulo	->	nempendulo	with the answer

11.3.4 dissimilation

The opposite of assimilation is *dissimilation*: a segment changes to become *less* similar to another segment. Though much rarer than assimilation, dissimilation can take place both locally (adjacent segments) and long-distance (non-adjacent segments). It is thought that the grounding of dissimilation is mostly perceptual: two similar segments may be confusable, and change to become less so.

An example of systematic voicing dissimilation comes from Chontal, a language of Mexico (30). The imperative suffix alternates between [ɬaʔ], which begins with a voiceless lateral, and [laʔ], which begins with a voiced lateral. The voiceless form is the basic, elsewhere case. The voiceless form becomes voiced when a voiceless fricative, such as [x] or [ʃ], precedes.

(30)   Voicing dissimilation in Chontal: [ɬ] becomes [l] when preceded by a voiceless fricative:

ko-ɬaʔ	say it!
mi:-ɬaʔ	tell him!
pu-ɬaʔ	dig it!
kan-ɬaʔ	leave it!
panx-laʔ	sit down!
fuʃ-laʔ	blow it!

Ancient Greek (example 31) also exhibited a process of dissimilation between fricatives. The past perfect suffix alternates between [-θik] and [tik]. The fricative becomes a stop when adjacent to another fricative.

(31)   Fricative dissimilation in Ancient Greek:

agap-i-θik-e	he was loved
fer-θik-e	he was carried
stal-θik-e	he was sent
akus-tik-e	he was heard
ðex-tik-e	it was received
ɣraf-tik-e	it was written

Vowel sequences sometimes undergo dissimilation. It is common for a high vowel to become a glide when it precedes another vowel. For example, in Llogoori (spoken in Kenya), all nouns take a prefix, which depends on their class. (The class system, which is typical of Bantu languages, functions like the "masculine" and "feminine" noun classes in Romance languages, except that Llogoori has 20 classes instead of two.) The class 11 prefix is [rʊ] before a consonant-initial noun, but [rw] before a vowel-initial noun: [rʊ-ba:ho] *board*, but [rw-i:ga] *horn*. The class 1 prefix alternates between [mu], as in [mu-ðạ:ð̣i] *boy*, and [mw], as in [mw-a:na] *child*.

Latin provides an example of long-distance dissimilation (32). The adjectival suffix [-alis] became [-aris] if another [l] preceded anywhere in the word. Thus, the forms are [navalis] and [totalis], but [lunaris] and [solaris]. The exception is that if an [r] intervenes between the two laterals, as in [later-alis], the dissimilation is blocked. Many of these lexical items have come down into English, explaining why some adjectives end in [-al] (*naval*) and others in [-ar] (*solar*).

(32)   Lateral dissimilation in Latin:

nav-alis	lun-aris
tot-alis	sol-aris
coron-alis	vel-aris
espiscop-alis	pol-aris
reg-alis	angul-aris
autumn-alis	milit-aris
voc-alis	stell-aris
anim-alis	popul-aris
capit-alis	
flor-alis	
littor-alis	
sepulchr-alis	
later-alis	

11.2   It is not surprising that dissimilations often involve fricatives, laterals, and rhotics, sounds that require precise articulator placement, and this hints at a further articulatory impetus for dissimilation. It can be very tricky to quickly articulate a sequence of sounds that are very similar, but not exactly the same. This is, in fact, the basis of most tongue twisters like "She sells seashells" and "The sixth sheik's sixth sheep's sick."

11.3.5   lenition and fortition

Another type of alternation is *lenition*: sounds become weaker or more open. Among consonants, stops change to fricatives, and fricatives change to approximants. The Spanish alternation discussed in Chapter 10, where [b, d, g] alternate with [β, ð, ɣ] is an example of lenition. Florentine Italian (33), also mentioned in Chapter 10, has a similar process, except it is the voiceless stops that are lenited.

(33)   Consonant lenition in Florentine Italian: voiceless stops become fricatives in between vowels:

indefinite	definite	gloss
[kaza]	[la xaza]	house
[torta]	[la θorta]	cake
[palla]	[la ɸalla]	ball

In casual speech, intervocalic [x] can further lenite to [h], making this a process of debuccalization (see below).

The opposite of lenition is *fortition*: weaker, more open sounds become more constricted (stronger). One common variety of fortition is *post-nasal hardening*: fricatives become stops or affricates following nasals. The example in (34) is from Setswana (Southern Africa).

(34)   Post-nasal hardening in Setswana:

supa	point at	xo-supa	to point at	n-t͡sʰupa	point at me
ʃapa	hit	xo-ʃapa	to hit	ɲ-t͡ʃʰapa	hit me
xapa	capture	xo-xapa	to capture	ŋ-k͡xʰapa	capture me

Lenition of vowels is often simply called *reduction*, and is often related to stress. In English unstressed syllables, vowels are not pronounced with full contrastive quality, but reduce to schwa, as in the words in example (35). Note also the alternation between the full stops [d] or [tʰ] and shorter, weaker [ɾ]. Stressed syllables realize full stops and full vowels, while unstressed syllables realize lenited taps and reduced vowels.

(35)   Fortition, lenition, and stress in English:

atom	[ˈærəm]	atomic	[əˈtʰɑmɪk]
adding	[ˈærɪŋ]	addition	[əˈdɪʃən]
metal	[ˈmɛɾəl]	metallic	[məˈtʰælɪk]

An extreme case of lenition is *debuccalization*, literally "cutting off the mouth." In debuccalization, a consonant loses its oral articulation and becomes either [h] or [ʔ]. In Slave ([slevi],

Northwest Canada), all word-final consonants are pronounced as [h] (example 36). The basic form of "hat", for example, is /ts'ad/ and this form surfaces when a suffix, such as the possessed, is added. When the consonant is final, however, it surfaces as [h].

(36) Debuccalization in Slave: word-final consonants become [h]:

possessed	non-possessed	
ts'ad-é	ts'ah	hat
mil-é	mih	net
dzéeg-é	dzéeh	gum
tédh-é	téh	cane

ts'é-ʔáh	one eats
ts'e-ʔal-íle	one does not eat
ts'e-ʔal-ole	one is going to eat

11.3   In Focus

Slave is an excellent illustration of the principle that the unsuffixed form is not necessarily the one that realizes the basic form. How do we know that the form of the noun that occurs in the possessed form is basic? If the non-possessed, [h]-final, form was the one stored in the mental lexicon, there would be no way of predicting which consonant would appear when a suffix is added. Why [d] in "hat" and [l] in "net"? Instead, we assume that the final consonant is stored in memory as part of the word, so that "hat" = /ts'ad/ and "net" = /mil/, and then a general rule reduces each one to [h] in final position. The principle is that unpredictable information is stored in the lexicon, so that rules can be formulated as generally as possible.

Debuccalization is not uncommon. In many dialects of Caribbean Spanish, syllable-final [s] is pronounced as [h], so that "las gatas" *the (female) cats* would be [lah gatah]. In English, [t] can be pronounced as [ʔ]. Depending on the dialect, debuccalization of [t] might occur in word-final position ([kʰæʔ], [donʔ]), before nasals ([bʌʔn], [kʰaʔn], [ʌʔmost]), or inter-vocalically ([prɪʔɪ], [baʔəl]).

11.3.6 epenthesis

Epenthesis means insertion. Usually, epenthesis applies to break up a sequence of segments that violates the phonotactic restrictions of the language. Epenthesis in loanwords (as in Japanese [sutoraiku] from English *strike*) was discussed in Section 11.3. The realization of the English plural /z/ as [ɪz] and past tense /d/ as [ɪd] are also examples of epenthesis. In the plural, the epenthetic vowel breaks up a sequence of two strident fricatives: /wɪʃ-z/ becomes [wɪʃɪz]. In the past tense, the vowel breaks up a sequence of two alveolar stops: /bæt-d becomes /bætɪd/ (and then bærɪd] by tapping).

Example (37) shows epenthesis in Yowlumne, a nearly-extinct language of California. The verbs in example (37a) show that a verb root with the shape CVC (such as /xat/) is unchanged when a suffix is added. (Suffix vowels that match in height will undergo rounding harmony.) In example (37b), however, the verb roots end with two consonants: CVCC. These remain unchanged when a vowel-initial suffix is added, as in [paʔtal]. When a consonant-initial suffix is added, however, that creates a sequence of three consonants, which the phonotactics of Yowlumne never allow. A high vowel is inserted to break up the sequence: /paʔtmi/ becomes [paʔitmi], *fighting*. If it happens that the root vowel is both high and round, as in /ʔugn/, the epenthetic vowel will also undergo rounding harmony: [ʔugunmu], drinking.

(37)   Epenthesis in Yowlumne: CCC –> CVCC

dubitative	gerundive	imperative	gloss
a.			
xat-al	xat-mi	xat-ka	eat
xil-al	xil-mi	xil-ka	tangle
bok-ol	bok-mi	bok-ko	find
dub-al	dub-mu	dub-ka	lead by the hand
b.			
paʔt-al	paʔit-mi	paʔit-ka	fight
lihm-al	lihim-mi	lihim-ka	run
logw-ol	logiw-mi	logiw-ka	pulverize
ʔugn-al	ʔugun-mu	ʔugun-ka	drink

> **11.4** Yowlumne, also known as Yawelmani, was described by the linguist Stanley Newman in 1944. Newman worked with a small group of speakers living in the foothills of the Sierra Nevada mountains of northern California. Many sources list the Yowlumne dialect as now extinct, but the Survey of California and Other Indian Languages, conducted by linguists at the University of California, Berkeley, identified up to two dozen speakers still living in 2011. Yowlumne has an elegant, complex phonology that has often been cited in phonological theorizing. (Only a few of the more straightforward aspects are mentioned here.) And we nearly missed it!

While vowel epenthesis is most common, consonants and glides can also be epenthetic. In Basque (Western Europe), the glide [j] is inserted to break up a sequence of two vowels: [mutil-e] *the boy*, but [ari-j-e], *the thread*.

(38)   Glide epenthesis in Basque:

agin	tooth	agim bet	a tooth	agin e	the tooth
mutil	boy	mutil bet	a boy	mutil e	the boy
erri	village	erri bet	a village	erri je	the village
ari	thread	ari bet	a thread	ari je	the thread

In English, as shown in example (39), an epenthetic consonant can break up a sequence of nasal followed by fricative, so that "prince" and "prints" are homophones.

(39)   Consonant epenthesis in English:

[sʌmpθɪn]	something
[warmpθ]	warmth
[tʰɛnts]	tense
[prɪnts]	prince

11.3.7 deletion

The opposite of insertion is *deletion*: a segment that is part of the underlying form of the word is not pronounced. Sometimes deletion rather than epenthesis can apply to repair a difficult or illicit sequence of consonants. In English, for example, the medial consonant of three will often delete: "desktop" is pronounced [dɛstɑp] and "grandmother" is pronounced [græmmʌðɚ] in all but the most careful speech.

Tagalog (Philippines) has an alternation that is in some ways the opposite of the Yowlumne epenthesis illustrated above. Yowlumne inserts vowels when a consonant-initial suffix is added; Tagalog deletes vowels when a vowel-initial suffix is added. In Tagalog, verb roots have a basic shape of CVCVC. As shown in example (40), when a vowel-initial suffix is added, the second vowel of the root deletes. (The source does not give a gloss for the suffixes /–in/ and /–an/, except to say they are "derivational.")

(40) Vowel deletion in Tagalog:

bukas	buks-in	buks-an	open
kapit	kapt-in	kapt-an	embrace
tubos	tubs-in	tubs-an	redeem
damit	damt-in	damt-an	fulfill
putol	putl-in	putl-an	cut
banig	baŋg-in	baŋg-an	mat
ganap	gamp-in	gamp-an	fulfill

In the last two forms there is a two-step process. Deletion brings an /n/ adjacent to a stop, and the /n/ then assimilates in place: /ganapin/ –> /ganpin/ –> [gampin].

When there are alternations in a root, such that a vowel appears in one form but not in another (that is V ~ Ø), it can be difficult to decide if the process is epenthesis or deletion. In Yawelmani, [paʔt] alternates with [paʔit], and in Tagalog [kapt] alternates with [kapit]. How is one to know that in the former the underlying form is [paʔt] and the second vowel in [paʔit] is epenthetic, while in the latter the basic form is [kapit] and in [kapt] the vowel is deleted? Essentially, the quality of epenthetic vowels is predictable, and the quality of deleted vowels is not. In Yawelmani, the alternating vowel is always [i], except when the conditions for vowel harmony are right and it surfaces as [u]. In Tagalog, the only way to know that there is an /i/ in the word for "embrace," an /o/ in the word for "redeem" and an /a/ in the word for "fulfill" is if those vowels are part of the underlying form. Of course, things get more complicated if the rule of deletion targets only a single vowel quality, such as u-deletion in Hanunoo (see example 44). In that case, the analyst just has to try it both ways and see which results in a better account of the system.

One of the most extreme cases of deletion is found in Lardil, an Austronesian language. In Lardil, the only consonants allowed in word-final position are apical (tongue tip) consonants such as [l, n, r]. Lardil has a rule of word-final vowel deletion, however, which can leave non-apical consonants in word-final position. Should this occur, the "exposed" consonants are deleted as well, as shown in example (41). (Lardil nouns are inflected to agree with the verb, in either future or non-future tense. Marking the difference between the (non-future) fish I'm eating now and the (future) fish I hope to eat tomorrow seems like it would be a very useful distinction.)

(41)   Deletion in Lardil:

uninflected	future	UR	gloss
puta	putaka-r	/putaka/	short
ŋawuŋa	ŋawuŋawu-r	/ŋawuŋawu/	termite
murkuni	murkinima-r	/murkinima/	nullah
muŋkumu	muŋkumuŋku-r	/muŋkumuŋku/	axe
tʃumputʃu	tʃumputʃumpu-r	/tʃumputʃumpu/	dragonfly

Again, Lardil serves as a dramatic warning against assuming that the uninflected form is always going to be equivalent to the underlying form.

11.3.8 lengthening and shortening

Sometimes, long segments can become short, and short segments can become long. An example of lengthening is found in Komi (related to Finnish, spoken in Northwest Russia). In Komi, /l/ deletes in either pre-consonantal or word-final position (42). After the deletion, the vowel then lengthens, as though to make up for the loss of the lateral. Such lengthening after deletion is known as *compensatory lengthening*.

(42)   Compensatory lengthening in Komi:

kɨl-i	I heard	kɨ:-nɨ	to hear
sulal-i	I stood	sulo:-nɨ	to stand
vøl-ys	from a horse	vø:	horse
nyl-ys	from a daughter	ny:	daughter

The opposite of compensatory lengthening is closed-syllable shortening. Example (43) shows some additional verbs from Yowlumne.

(43)   Vowel shortening in Yowlumne:

	future	dubitative	gerundive	imperative	gloss
a.	xat-en	xat-al	xat-mi	xat-ka	eat
	xil-en	xil-al	xil-mi	xil-ka	tangle
	bok-en	bok-ol	bok-mi	bok-ko	find
b.	la:n-en	la:n-al	lan-mi	lan-ka	hear
	me:k-en	me:k-al	mek-mi	mek-ka	swallow
	wo:n-en	wo:n-ol	won-mi	won-ko	hide

In example (43a) the verb roots have short vowels throughout the paradigm: we assume that they are short underlyingly. The alternating roots in example (43b), have underlyingly long vowels that surface unchanged before vowel-initial suffixes ([la:n-al]) but shorten before a cluster of two consonants ([lan-mi]).

11.3.9 metathesis

Metathesis means "changing places": two segments switch in order. In the history of English, metathesis occurred in r + vowel sequences. The word "horse" used to be [hros], for example, and "bird" used to be [bridde]. A contemporary example is found in Hanunoo (the Philippines). First, Hanunoo has a process of medial vowel deletion. The environment for deletion is similar to that of its neighbor Tagalog (example 40), but the Hanunoo deletion targets only /u/. Examples of words with no alternation are shown in example (44a), and words with /u/ deletion in example (44b). Once the /u/ is deleted, a sequence of two consonants is created. If the first of those two consonants happens to be a glottal stop, as in example (44c), the glottal stop and the second consonant switch places. Thus /ka-ʔusa/ *once* becomes /kaʔsa/. Then metathesis switches /ʔs/ to /sʔ/ resulting in [kasʔa].

(44)   Metathesis in Hanunoo:

    a. no alternation
lima	five	ka-lima	five times
pitu	seven	ka-pitu	seven times

    b. /u/ deletion
duwa	two	ka-dwa	twice
tulu	three	ka-tlu	three times

    c. /u/ deletion and metathesis
ʔusa	one	ka-sʔa	once
ʔupat	four	ka-pʔat	four times
ʔunum	six	ka-nʔum	six times

11.3.10 morphological interactions

Sometimes, phonological alternations apply generally, whenever the appropriate conditions are met. Most of the examples that have been cited in this chapter are like this. The English tapping rule, for example, applies whenever a /t/ or /d/ is between two vowels, the second of which is unstressed. It does not matter if the sequence is within a morpheme ("atom"), across a morpheme boundary ("added"), or even across a word boundary ("up and 'em"). These very general rules also tend to have very clear phonetic conditioning: it is easy to see what phonotactic constraint is being violated, and what the difficulty in the prohibited configuration would be. A weaker constriction in an unstressed (short, non-prominent) syllable, for example, makes perfect phonetic sense.

Sometimes, however, phonological alternations apply only in specific morphological contexts. One common pattern is for alternations to apply to affixes, but not within roots. Nasal assimilation in Zoque, for example, applies to prefixes, but not within words, as illustrated by [ɲ-dʒoʔngoja] *my rabbit*. (This more complicated case was left out of the general description in Section 11.2). Nasal place assimilation applies to the prefix (/n + dʒ/ → [ɲdʒ]), but not to the [ng] sequence within the noun. In other cases, an alternation may apply only to a limited class of affixes. In English, for example, nasal place assimilation is obligatory for the prefix "in-" ("imbalance") but optional for the prefix "un-" ("unbalanced"). We don't change the spelling of "un-", but the pronunciation may vary between [n] and [m]. Or, there may be certain words that are just marked as exceptions. In Turkish, for example, there are some words where front and back vowels co-occur, such as [mɑvi] "blue," and in Igbo there are some words where retracted and non-retracted vowels co-occur, such as [akpi], "scorpion." Alternations that make reference to lexical information, such as the difference between affix and root or to specific lexical classes or items, are called *lexical rules*, for obvious reasons. The more general, exceptionless rules are often called *post-lexical*, following Pāṇini's theorem that the more general occurs after the more specific. Many phonologists, and diverse phonological theories, have investigated the differences between lexical and post-lexical rules, and thus the interaction of phonology and morphology. Some additional reading is suggested below; see also Chapter 16.5.4.

We should note in conclusion, however, that lexical rules sometimes seem to lack phonetic grounding: they do not seem to make the word either easier to say or easier to hear. They thus might not fit into any of the categories discussed above. Often, if one looks back into the history of the language, a phonetic motivation can be found, but sometimes the trigger of the alternation undergoes sound change itself, and is lost (see Chapter 17).

chapter summary

- Phonotactic constraints determine licit and illicit sequences of sounds.
- Recent research has indicated that grammaticality judgments may be gradient (better vs. worse) rather than absolute (grammatical vs. ungrammatical), and are related to frequency of occurrence, where more frequent = better.
- Alternations in the pronunciation of a morpheme (different allomorphs) often occur when illicit sequences are created.
- The theory of generative grammar proposes that every morpheme has a single underlying representation, and that different surface representations (allomorphs) are generated by the application of a sequence of rules.
- Common alternations found in the languages of the world are listed in Table 11.1.

further reading

A good place to start for more information on the phonology/morphology interface would be some introductory textbooks on morphology, such as:

Aronoff, Mark and Kirsten Fudeman. (2005). *What is Morphology?* Oxford: Blackwell.
Haspelmath, Martin and Andrea Sims. (2010). *Understanding Morphology*. Oxford: Oxford University Press.

For some more advanced reading:
Kaisse, Ellen. (2005). "The interface between morphology and phonology." In *Handbook of English Word Formation* edited by P. Štekaur and R. Lieber. Dordrecht: Foris.

Though it's not easy reading, you might also try Paul Kiparsky's 1985 article, "Some consequences of Lexical Phonology" in *Phonology Yearbook 3*. Cambridge: Cambridge University Press, 1986.

review exercises

1. Define each of the following terms:

   arbitrariness of the sign
   generative grammar
   phonotactic constraint
   alternation
   allomorph
   underlying form
   surface form

Pāṇini's Theorem
continuant consonant
compensatory lengthening
epenthesis
dissimilation
debuccalization
metathesis

2. Why are "morpheme structure constraints" called "static generalizations"?
3. List three differences that characterize lexical vs. post-lexical rules.
4. Identify the author(s), year of publication, and at least one main idea for each:

    a. *Cours de Linguistique Générale*
    b. *Phonology in Generative Grammar*
    c. *The Sound Pattern of English*

5. Characterize each of the following alternations as assimilation, coalescence, dissimilation, lenition, debuccalization, fortition, epenthesis, or deletion. If assimilation or dissimilation, indicate whether it is local or long-distance.

    a. In some dialects of English, [ð] and [θ] are pronounced as [d] and [t].
    b. In the Boston dialect of English, "linking-r" occurs between two vowels: "Cuba[r] is an island."
    c. In Aklanon, spoken in the Philippines, the prefix meaning "one" alternates depending on the initial consonant of the noun. (Source: Zorc, D. and de la Cruz, B. 1968. *A Study of the Aklanon Dialect*. Kalibo: Aklan Printing Center.)

saŋkurot	little bit
saŋgantaŋ	one ganta
saŋgatos	one hundred
sambilog	one (referring to inanimate entity)
sambato	one (referring to animate entity)
sambuean	one month

    d. In Serbo-Croatian (Eastern Europe), adjectives of the form CVCC surface as CVCaC unless followed by a vowel-initial suffix.
    e. In Moro (Sudan) the locative prefix is pronounced [ék-] if the first consonant of the noun stem is voiced, but as [ég-] if the first consonant of the noun stem is voiceless. (Source: Sharon Rose, talk presented at 2011 Annual Conference on African Linguistics.)

ék-ómón	in the tiger	ék-ógovél	in the monkey
ég-atʃóŋgʷár	in the bird of prey	ég-ətám	in the neck

    f. In English, "support" is often pronounced the same as "sport."
    g. In Hungarian, the dative suffix is pronounced [-nek] after words that contain all front vowels, and as [-nɑk] after words that contain back vowels.
    h. In Yucatec Maya, /k/ is pronounced as [h] when it precedes another [k]. (Source: Straight, S., *The Acquisition of Maya Phonology*. New York: Garland, 1976.)

[k-]	1 pl. prefix
[kool]	clearing (noun)
[h- kool]	our clearing

(Continued)

[kolik]   clearing (verb)
    [k'a:s]   brush
    [kolih k'aas]   clearing brush

i. In Japanese, high vowels are devoiced between two voiceless consonants

    ki̥ppari   clearly
    ki̥to: prayer
    ɸu̥kaɸu̥ka   soft
    koku̥sai   international
    su̥ʃimai   sushi rice

j. In Kinyarwanda (East Africa), [u] becomes [w] preceding [i]. (Source: Scott Myers: http://www.laits.utexas.edu/phonology/kinyarwanda/)

k. Also in Kinyarwanda, [β] becomes [b] following [m].

l. Vowels are nasalized before a nasal consonant.

m. In many dialects of English, sonorants are produced with creaky voice when they precede a glottal stop.

n. In Norwegian, a sequence of [ɾ] followed by another consonant is realized as a single retroflex consonant (Source: Kristofferson, G. 2007. *The Phonology of Norwegian*, Oxford: Oxford University Press, 2000).

    ʋoɾ + tejn   –>   ʋo:ʈæjn   spring sign
    ʋoɾ + dag   –>   ʋo:ɖa:g   spring day
    ʋoɾ + sul   –>   ʋo:ʂul   spring sun
    ʋoɾ + nat   –>   ʋo:ɳat   spring night
    ʋoɾ + luft   –>   ʋo:ɭuft   spring air

further analysis and discussion

6. What is the phonetic parameter that defines the class of "sun letters" in Arabic (example 24)?

7. Noah's ark (adapted from an exercise in M. Halle and N. Clements, *Problem Book in Phonology*, Cambridge, MA: MIT Press, 1983).

    a. Consider the following animal names. What if you had two of them? Divide the list of animals into three groups, depending on whether the plural is formed with [s], [z], or [ɨz]. Add a few more animal names (or general nouns, if you cannot think of animals) to each list.

lion	tiger	bear	slug	horse	cat
dog	giraffe	snake	chimp	mosquito	bird
nuthatch	dove	cow	finch	walrus	moth
lark	wallaby	tadpole	midge	bee	duck
pig	thrush	kite	platypus	cow	cub
snail	beetle	cheetah	sloth	rat	zebra

    b. Now consider the hypotheses below. Which hypothesis best fits the data? It shouldn't be hard to guess which one the teacher wants you to choose, but be prepared to argue for your answer.

    H1: We memorize the plural for every animal name we learn.
    H2: We choose a plural based on the *letters* at the end of the word.

H3: We choose a plural based on the *sounds* at the end of the word. We memorize a list of which sounds take which endings.

H4: We choose a plural ending based on *sound categories*: sounds that share particular characteristics take a particular ending.

  c. What about words like *sheep, fish, ox, goose, mouse,* and *octopus*? Does this change how you evaluate hypotheses 1–4?

  d. A four-year-old child of my acquaintance (not the same one who "knowed" 2+2) generally got his plurals correct, but mistakenly talked about [dʒə'ræfɪz] and ['mɔθɨz]. Does this change how you evaluate hypotheses 1–4?

8. Based on your answer question #1, and following the model for the analysis of the English past tense in Section 11.2, describe the plural alternation in English. Your answer should take the form found in example (3) in Section 11.2.

9. Diminutives in Dutch. (Source: Booij, G., *The Phonology of Dutch*. Oxford: Clarendon Press, 1995.) The Dutch diminutive suffix has several different allomorphs, as listed below. Determine the underlying representation of this affix, and describe the environments where each allomorph occurs. Your answer should take the form found in example (3) in Section 11.2. (There is in fact one more allomorph, [ətjə], the occurrence of which is influenced by stress and syllable structure. We ignore this complication for the purposes of this exercise.)

[-jə]		[-pjə]	
lɑx-jə	little laugh	rim-pjə	little belt
hɑnt-jə	little hand	bɔm-pjə	little tree
gɛk-jə	crazy kid	bodɛm-pjə	little bottom
lif-jə	sweetheart	albʏm-pjə	little album
klɑs-jə	little class	hɛlm-pjə	little helmet

[-kjə]		[-tjə]	
konɪŋ-kjə	little king	re-tjə	little deer
palɪŋ-kjə	little eel	tran-tjə	tear drop
		wil-tjə	little wheel
		har-tjə	little heart
		dɔktɔr-tjə	little doctor
		profesɔr-tjə	little professor
		ze-tjə	little sea

10. In Maga Rukai, an Austronesian language spoken in Taiwan, certain prefixes show an alternation between a mid vowel and a high vowel. What determines whether the prefix vowel is mid or high? (Only one rule is needed to cover all the examples.) What kind of rule is this? (Source: Hsin, Tien-Hsin, Aspects of Maga Rukai phonology. Doctoral dissertation, The University of Connecticut, 2000.)

o ~ u	dynamic verb marker		
o-kamɨ	back	u-cŋulu	connect
o-dranɨ	make a road	u-ḍmiɲi	make a road
o-lapɨ	hunt without dogs	u-lupu	hunt with dogs

(Continued)

e ~ i	negative marker		
e-kaplii	not hold with hands	i-tukruu	not hit with stones
e-lalpɨɨ	not hunt (without dogs)	i-ulpuu	not hunt (with dogs)
se ~ si	to wear		
se-kceŋe	wear pants	si-slivi	wear beads
se-kcabu	wear leggings	si-krɨkrɨ	wear a necklace
te ~ ti	to make		
te-kceŋe	make pants	ti-slivi	make beads
te-tovnaa	build a hut	ti-kunu	make a skirt
te-sdamraa	cook a side dish	ti-krɨkrɨ	make a necklace
ke ~ ki	harvest		
ke-teθo	harvest turnip	ki-sito	harvest peanut
ke-bləblə	harvest bamboo shoot	ki-lpɨlpɨ	harvest peas
ke ~ ki	passive		
ke-ɖoɖoo	be awaited	ki-klukluɖu	be frightened
ke-kθabɨ	peeled	ki-tɨtɨ	be bitten

11. Another process in Maga Rukai is shown below. Characterize the alternation:

/aɖa – i – kanɨɨ/	→	aɖe kanɨɨ	don't eat!
/aɖa – i – mumuu aθoo/	→	aɖe mumuu aθoo	don't kiss dogs!
/aɖa – i – ptemuduu troka/	→	aɖe ptemuduu troka	don't kill chickens!
/maka – uŋulu/	→	makoŋlu	finish drinking
/maka – inunuu/	→	makenunu (ŋaa)	already sat
/ma – ibubu/	→	me bubu	mix
/pa – ibubu/	→	pe bubu	cause to mix
/pa- innuu/	→	pe nnuu	cause to sit

Go online Visit the book's companion website for additional resources relating to this chapter at: http://www.wiley.com/go/zsiga.

references

Data for which no source is listed are from the author's own fieldwork.

Arabic (Modern Standard)
Ryding, K. 2005. *A Reference Grammar of Modern Standard Arabic*. Cambridge: Cambridge University Press.

Arabic (Syrian)
Cowell, M. 1964. *A Reference Grammar of Syrian Arabic*. Washington, DC: Georgetown University Press.

Basque
Kenstowicz, M. 1994. *Phonology in Generative Grammar*. Oxford: Blackwell.

Catalan
Mascaró, J. 1976. *Catalan phonology and the phonological cycle*. Doctoral dissertation, Massachusetts Institute of Technology.

Chontal
Waterhouse, V. 1949. Oaxaca Chontal: Sentence types and text analysis. *Mexico Antigua* 7: 229–314, cited in M. Kenstowicz and C. Kisseberth, 1979, *Generative Phonology*. San Diego: Academic Press.

Chumash
Applegate, R.B. 1972. *Ineseño Chumash grammar*. Doctoral dissertation, University of California, Berkeley.

Dakota
Shaw, P. 1980. *Theoretical Issues in Dakota Phonology and Morphology*. New York: Garland.

English phonotactics
Pierrehumbert, J. 1994. Syllable structure and word structure: A study of triconsonantal clusters in English. In P. Keating (ed.), *Papers in Laboratory Phonology III*. Cambridge: Cambridge University Press, 168–188.

Greek (Ancient)
Smyth, H. 1920. *Greek Grammar*. Cambridge, MA: Harvard University Press.

Hanunoo
Gleason, H. 1955. *Workbook in Descriptive Linguistics*. New York: Henry Holt and Company.

Igbo
Welmers, W. 1973. *African Language Structures*. Berkeley, CA: University of California Press.

Indonesian
Halle, M. and G.N. Clements. 1983. *Problem Book in Phonology*. Cambridge, MA: MIT Press.

Japanese
Vance, T. 1987. *An Introduction to Japanese Phonology*. Albany, NY: State University of New York Press.

Komi
Kavitskaya, D. 2002. *Compensatory Lengthening: Phonetics, Phonology, Diachrony*. New York: Routledge.

Korean
Davis, S. and S.-H. Shin. 1999. The syllable contact constraint in Korean: An Optimality-Theoretic analysis. *Journal of East Asian Linguistics* 8: 285–312.

Lardil
Hale, K. 1973. *Deep-Surface Canonical Disparities in Relation to Analysis and Change*, cited in M. Kenstowicz and C. Kisseberth, *Generative Phonology*. San Diego: Academic Press, 1979.

Llogoori
Leung, E. 1971. The tonal phonology of Llogoori: A study of Llogoori verbs. *Working Papers of the Cornell Phonetics Laboratory*, Volume 6, New York.

Malayalam
Mohanan, K.P. 1993. Fields of attraction in phonology. In J. Goldsmith (ed.), *The Last Phonological Rule: Reflections on Constraints and Derivations*. Chicago: University of Chicago Press, 1993, 61–116.

Oowekyala

Howe, D. 2000. *Oowekyala segmental phonology*. Doctoral dissertation, University of British Columbia.

Russian

Jakobson, R. 1978. Mutual assimilation of Russian voiced and voiceless consonants. *Studia Linguistica* 32: 107–110.

Setswana

Tlale, O. 2006. *The phonetics and phonology of Sengwato, a dialect of Setswana*. Doctoral dissertation, Georgetown University.

Shona

Myers, S. 1987. *Tone and the structure of words in Shona*. Doctoral dissertation, University of Massachusetts, Amherst.

Slave

Rice, K. 1989. *Grammar of Slave*. The Hague: Mouton.

Tagalog

Kenstowicz, M. and C. Kisseberth. 1979. *Generative Phonology*. San Diego: Academic Press.

Turkish

Clements, G.N. and E. Sezer. 1982. Vowel and consonant disharmony in Turkish. In H. van der Hulst and N. Smith (eds), *The Structure of Phonological Representations*, Part II. Dordrecht: Foris Publications, 1982, 213–255.

Xhosa

Casali, R. 1996. *Resolving hiatus*. Doctoral dissertation, University of California, Los Angeles.

Yawelmani

Kenstowicz and Kisseberth 1979 and Kenstowicz 1994 give a full explication of data originally reported by Newman in 1947.

Zoque

Wonderly, W. 1946. Phonemic acculturation in Zoque. *International Journal of American Linguistics* 12: 92–95.

12 What Is A Possible Language?
Distinctive Features

Languages differ from one another without limit.

Edward Sapir, *Language*, 1921

In examining the phonetic frameworks tested on a large number of languages . . . one cannot fail to be impressed by the small number of features involved.

Morris Halle, *The Sound Pattern of Russian*, 1971, p. 20

The Sounds of Language: An Introduction to Phonetics and Phonology, First Edition. Elizabeth C. Zsiga.
© 2013 Elizabeth C. Zsiga. Published 2013 by Blackwell Publishing Ltd.

The preceding chapter provided a survey of common phonological alternations in the languages of the world. As phonologists, however, we want to know more. We want to understand not only the set of things that *do* happen, but the set of things that *can* happen. We want to answer the questions: "What is a *possible* phonological contrast?" and "What is a *possible* phonological alternation?"

The chapter begins with an excursus on why this is an important question, and how formal representations help us to answer it. Section 12.2 then surveys one formal theory of how the possible contrasts and alternations in human language can be encoded: distinctive feature theory. There is not complete agreement among phonologists concerning the exact content and enumeration of features – we will consider several hypotheses, and conclude the chapter with an evaluation of how our hypotheses have fared.

12.1 introduction

12.1.1 phonological universals

Imagine that you are the one to discover a language previously unknown to the world of the Linguistics Society. Traveling up a tributary of the Amazon in Brazil, or descending into a hidden valley in Papua New Guinea, you come into contact with an isolated people, and have the opportunity to learn their language. (Stephen Pinker, in his book *The Language Instinct*, provides a humorous but telling account of just such an encounter.) Do you have any idea what this new language will be like? Can you make any predictions about how the contrasts and alternations of this language will be similar to languages already known, or about the parameters along which they might vary?

We want to know whether there are any *phonological universals*, properties that are true of all languages. If there are universals, we want to know what they are, and why they occur. Edward Sapir hypothesized that languages could differ "without limit." Later phonologists hypothesized that differences between languages were in fact very limited, and that all languages were built on the same basic pattern, from the same building blocks provided by a *Universal Grammar*.

If there is such a thing as Universal Grammar, where does it come from? Some linguists (prominently, Noam Chomsky and his students, including Pinker) argue that the universal properties of language are programmed into our DNA. On this view, the structure of human language and our ability to use it are part of our genetic endowment, in the same way that the structure of our eyes and our ability to produce liver enzymes are a product of our genetic endowment. Just as we are genetically programmed to perceive light of a certain wavelength, and to digest food of a certain kind, we are genetically programmed to be sensitive to the difference between a sonorant and an obstruent (or a noun and a verb).

Other linguists argue that where language is concerned our genetics give us only powerful brains that are good at classifying things and mouths of a certain shape and mobility, and that all the other purported universals of language come about because of a universal desire to communicate with each other, shared pathways for learning, and a common experience of the world. On this view, nouns and verbs are not pre-programmed mental constructs, but concepts that are learned through repeated interaction with actual objects and actions. The difference between sonorant and obstruent is not given, but is learned, as infants try out the effects of different vocal tract configurations in babbling. Since we all share the same basic anatomy and physiology, and experience more or less the same world, the same categories emerge every time.

Both these views emphasize the importance of the process of learning, but differ on what is innate and what is learned from the environment. A third view places the emphasis on language change rather than on human cognition. This view argues that humans could learn any language that the environment presented them with. Languages turn out to have a lot in common simply because certain changes are more likely than others, which over time tend to produce languages with similar properties.

The debate over the existence and nature of a genetically-given Universal Grammar rages on, and won't be resolved here. We can, however, examine the nature and description of language universals: properties that do seem to hold across all 7,000-plus human languages that have been investigated, and are predicted to hold of the next human language to be discovered as well. In order to examine these properties, we will examine five hypotheses that have been argued to be true across all languages. In formulating and testing these hypotheses, we will begin to use some more formal descriptions: terms and symbols that may have more in common with algebra and geometry than with English prose.

12.1.2 why bother with formalism?

Why bother with formal language? The question is a valid one. Why not just make our generalizations in English prose and be done with it? Why introduce possibly confusing technical terms and symbols? One reason is that we want our predictions to be as precise as possible.

In order for a hypothesis to be interesting, it must be *falsifiable*. A hypothesis is falsifiable if we can decide whether it is true or false based on observable data. And in order to decide if a statement is true or false, we must understand precisely what each of its terms mean. Consider, for example, a hypothesis that has been previously discussed:

Hypothesis 1:
Phonological alternations target natural classes.

Is this true or false? In order to test the hypothesis, we must examine alternations in the languages of the world, discover the classes of sounds that are targeted, and determine whether those classes are "natural" or not. If we find a class of sounds that is not natural, we conclude that our hypothesis is not supported. Our decision, however, depends on the definition of "natural class." The English word "natural" has many different meanings. Sometimes the term means "found in nature," as opposed to "invented or man-made," and thus linguists will speak of "natural languages" as opposed to computer languages. If "natural class" means a class of sounds found in any natural language, then our hypothesis is (uninterestingly) always true: any set of sounds we might find in a natural language would be by definition a natural class. It would not matter what the data actually was, so it would be a waste of time to compile it. Or maybe we could define "natural" as "whatever feels easy and uncontrived." Again, this is not a useful definition. What counts as easy, and to whom? We are all competent users of our native languages, so all alternations are easy to the native speaker. Without a precise and useful definition of "natural," our hypothesis is unfalsifiable and thus completely uninteresting. In Section 12.2, we consider how to precisely define natural classes in terms of a proposed universal set of *distinctive features*. The formal use and definition of these parameters lead us to clear hypotheses that can truly be tested against the data.

In addition to wanting our hypotheses to be precise, we want them to be *constrained*. The more specific a hypothesis is, the more things it rules out, the more interesting the hypothesis and the theory behind it is. Imagine that I have a theory of weather patterns that leads me to make the prediction: "The high temperature in Washington D.C. on July 4 will be between 20° and 110°F." The prediction is falsifiable: it could in principle reach 111° or drop down to 19°, but even in the event the prediction is proven true, it doesn't mean I have a very good theory of weather. My theory is too unconstrained; it allows too many possibilities; it says little if anything about what July in Washington is really like. If, on the other hand, I make the highly constrained prediction that on July 4 it will reach a high of 94° at 2 p.m., and *that* prediction is confirmed, you might conclude that my theory of weather patterns is a pretty good one.

Every linguistic hypothesis is part of a theory of what human language is like. The more constrained our hypotheses are, the more possibilities we can rule out, the more we understand what real human languages are actually like. For example, I might hypothesize that our newly-discovered language will use sounds generated by the vocal tract. This is falsifiable – it is logically possible that this group of people communicates using complicated foot stomping – but once the hypothesis turns out to be true (yes, they do use spoken language), we don't have much more to say. A more constrained hypothesis might predict, for example, that "this language will syllabify VCV sequences as V-CV not VC-V." If that hypothesis turns out to be true, we can ask interesting follow-up questions about why syllabic organization is universal, and why syllables of CV form are preferred. Following up on our more constrained hypotheses, we may learn something really interesting about possible human languages.

For the purposes of hypothesis testing, English prose descriptions are both too vague and too powerful: Too vague in that English words are not necessarily precisely defined, and too powerful in that our prose can describe anything and everything. Instead of describing alternations in English prose, we will propose a constrained set of descriptors, and consider the hypothesis that these, and only these, parameters are available for human language phonology. Every proposed feature or feature set is a hypothesis about what phonological grammars can manipulate. We will see that not all of the phonetic parameters and relationships that the mouth can produce, the ear can perceive, or the analyst can describe turn out to be part of phonology.

12.1.3 some hypotheses

Here are the hypotheses we will consider. They formed the starting point of the book *The Sound Pattern of English* (Chomsky and Halle, 1968), which laid out the program of generative phonology.

Hypothesis 2:
Phonological contrasts, classes, and alternations can be defined in terms of a closed set of phonetic parameters that is the same across all languages: the set of *distinctive features*.

Hypothesis 3:
Features are defined in terms of *binary* (+/−) oppositions that are specified for every segment (e.g., every segment is either [+voice] or [−voice]).

Hypothesis 4:
Every lexical item has a unique *underlying representation (UR)*, which is defined in terms of combinations of distinctive features.

Hypothesis 5:
Underlying representations are converted into contextually-varied *surface representations (SR)* by the operation of a set of feature-changing rules.

Hypotheses 1, 2, and 3 concern the nature of distinctive features in codifying contrasts and alternations. Hypotheses 4 and 5 concern the role of features in mediating underlying and surface representations. We begin in Chapter 12 with hypotheses 1–3 and the discussion of the definition of distinctive features. Chapter 13 continues with URs, SRs, and hypotheses 4 and 5.

12.2 distinctive features

12.2.1 background

The idea of a set of distinctive phonological features rests on the tenet that language is discrete and combinatorial. Sentences are made up of words, words are made up of segments, and segments are made up of features that define the categories to which the segments belong, and determine the alternations in which they participate.

The idea of *binary* distinctive features began with the Structuralist idea that all objects must be understood as part of a system: the nature of any sound in a given language can only be understood in terms of its *opposition* to other sounds in the system: [p] holds a certain place in the linguistic system because it contrasts with [b]. Nikolay Trubetskoy, in his work *Grundzüge der Phonologie* (*Foundations of Phonology*, 1939), suggested a large set of possible dimensions of contrast. Trubetskoy's student Roman Jakobson further defined and developed the idea in important ways: it was Jakobson who proposed that featural oppositions should be binary, that the set of features is universal, and that every feature should be unambiguously defined in both articulatory and acoustic terms.

Jakobson's work on phonology spanned most of the twentieth century. Jakobson wrote extensively on markedness, language acquisition, and language typology (that is, types of contrasts and alternations that are common or uncommon cross-linguistically). The clearest exposition of Jakobson's distinctive feature system is found in his co-authored work with Gunnar Fant, a phonetician, and Morris Halle, Jakobson's colleague and former student. Jakobson, Fant, and Halle published *Preliminaries to Speech Analysis: The Distinctive Features and Their Correlates* in 1952. While the set of accepted distinctive features has undergone significant revisions in the decades since, the features currently in common use grew out of those proposed by Jakobson, Fant, and Halle.

12.1   Jakobson lived from 1896 to 1982, and was active in research, writing, and teaching up until his death. He began his career as a student of Trubetskoy in Moscow in 1915 and became a prominent member of the influential Prague Linguistics Circle in the 1920s. He fled across Europe and eventually came to New York City during World War II, and ended his career as colleague to Morris Halle and Noam Chomsky at MIT.

In order to test hypotheses about distinctive features, phonologists consider the different systems of contrast and alternation in the languages of the world, with the goal of determining whether a particular set of features correctly characterizes the required classes. It is to this consideration that the following sections now turn.

12.2.2 major class and manner features

We have seen that phonological alternations often reference large classes of sounds: consonants vs. vowels, sonorants vs. obstruents, stops vs. fricatives, nasal consonants, approximant consonants, lateral consonants. Any set of distinctive features must include parameters that distinguish these classes of sounds. A widely-accepted set of such features is defined below. As originally proposed by Jakobson, we define each dimension in terms of a binary (+/−) contrast, and define each parameter in both acoustic and articulatory terms.

[+/− syllabic]

Articulatory definition: [+syllabic] sounds form the nucleus of a syllable.

Acoustic definition: [+syllabic] sounds have higher amplitudes than neighboring sounds.

Typical natural classes and alternations: vowels are [+syllabic], as opposed to consonants which are, in the default case, [−syllabic]. Glides are also [−syllabic]. Consonants may become [+syllabic] if they form the nucleus of a syllable on their own, as in [bʌʔn̩], for example. We will find this feature to be useful in defining these natural classes at this point, but will revisit the need for a [+/− syllabic] feature in Chapter 15, on syllable structure.

[+/− consonantal]

Articulatory definition: [−cons] = having no significant vocal tract constriction

Acoustic definition: [−cons] = high amplitude resonance

Typical natural classes and alternations: Vowels and consonants are often targeted separately: alternations often apply to just one or the other, or are conditioned by just one or the other. For example, vowel harmony skips consonants, place assimilation applies to just consonants. Vowels and glides are [−consonantal], consonants are [+consonantal].

[+/− sonorant]

Articulatory definition: [−sonorant] = build-up of pressure behind an oral constriction.

Acoustic definition: [−sonorant] = lower amplitude.

Typical natural classes and alternations: The feature [+/− sonorant] classifies the sonorant vs. obstruent consonants. Oral stops, affricates, and fricatives are [−sonorant] while nasals, approximants, and laterals are [+sonorant]. Vowels and glides are also by definition [+sonorant]. Alternations in voicing and assimilation often target obstruents and sonorants separately.

[+/− continuant]

Articulatory definition: [−continuant] = complete closure in the oral cavity.

Acoustic definition: [−continuant] = period of silence or low amplitude followed by abrupt release.

Typical natural classes and alternations: Oral stops and affricates are [−continuant], fricatives and approximants are [+continuant]. Vowels and glides are [+continuant]. Nasal stops, by virtue of their complete closure in the oral cavity, as well as their

Table 12.1   Major classes of sounds.

	Plosives	Fricatives	Nasals	Approximants	Laterals	Glides	Vowels
Syllabic	−	−	−	−	−	−	+
Consonantal	+	+	+	+	+	−	−
Sonorant	−	−	+	+	+	+	+
Continuant	−	+	−	+	(+)	+	+
Nasal	−	−	+	−	−	−	− (or +)
Lateral	−	− (or +)	−	−	+	−	−

common patterning with oral stops, are [−continuant]. [Continuant] is the active feature in many alternations of lenition and fortition.

[+/− nasal]

Articulatory definition: [+nasal] sounds are articulated with an open velum.

Acoustic definition: [+nasal] sounds have nasal resonance.

Typical natural classes and alternations: Assimilation of nasality is common; nasal stops are often targeted as a class. For example, nasal stops assimilate in place of articulation, most commonly to another stop.

[+/− lateral]

Articulatory definition: vocal tract closed at the center line, open at the side.

Acoustic definition: a particular resonance pattern.

Typical natural classes and alternations: l-sounds often form a class unto themselves in assimilations (as in Catalan, Arabic, and Komi).

Table 12.1 summarizes how these features distinguish these major sound classes.

Note that every column in Table 12.1 is unique: each class of sounds is defined by a unique combination of features. Plosives and fricatives share most of their features, but are distinct in that plosives are [−continuant] and fricatives are [+continuant]. Glides are distinct from approximant consonants in that they are [−consonantal] and distinct from vowels in that they are [−syllabic].

Note also that every cell in the table is filled. Every column has either a plus or minus value for every feature. The cells with "− or +" do not indicate uncertainty, but the possibility of two different classes: vowels may be either nasal or non-nasal, and fricatives may be either central or lateral.

There are a few cases where values are in question. There is genuine debate over the continuant value of [l]. This is on the one hand a question of definition: should we define [−continuant] as having a *complete* closure in the oral tract (which would make laterals, with their open side channel, [+continuant]), or only a closure at the *center* of the oral tract (which would make laterals [−continuant])? Either position is phonetically coherent, so we need to look at the phonological behavior of [l] to answer the question: does [l] usually form a natural class with the [−continuant] stops or with the [+continuant] fricatives? The jury is still out on this one: some language data points one way, some the other. It has been suggested that laterals may be defined as [+continuant] in some languages and [−continuant] in others, contradicting the hypothesis that features and feature definitions are truly universal. Acknowledging that this point is controversial at present, we tentatively define [l] as [+continuant], but see Section 12.3 below.

Another question is how to handle the continuant value of affricates. Because of the difficulty of the question, I have left affricates out of Table 12.1 entirely. In terms of articulation, affricates are both [−continuant] and [+continuant]: [−continuant] during their closure phase and [+continuant] during their release phase. However, it would go against Jakobson's conception of distinctive features to say that they are both plus *and* minus continuant. He considered the plus/minus distinction to indicate mutually exclusive categories to which a segment must be assigned. To say that a segment is both +F and −F at the same time would be, for him, like saying a number is both positive and negative, a switch is both on and off, or a direction is both East and West: it's a logical contradiction. Crucial, however, is the observation that affricates are not minus and plus continuant *at the same time*, but in sequence. Jakobson's system, however, had no way of accounting for changes in the middle of a segment.

Here, provisionally, we will assign the affricates to the [−continuant] class, on the basis of our definition (they do have a complete closure) and on our preliminary observation that they seem to pattern with the stops, making the [−continuant] segments a natural class. (In English palatalization, for example, [t] alternates with [tʃ] while [s] alternates with [ʃ], and in Zoque we saw that nasals assimilate to both stops and affricates but delete before fricatives.) How then are stops and affricates to be distinguished? In English, and in many other languages, affricates and stops are distinct in place of articulation: [t] is alveolar and [tʃ] is post-alveolar. There are many languages, however, where there are stops and fricatives at the same place of articulation, so another feature is needed. We will adopt the solution of stating that affricates have all the same features as stops, except that affricates are marked as [+delayed release].

[+/− delayed release]
Articulatory definition: [+delayed release] = opening from a stop into a fricative, rather than being fully released into an open vowel articulation.
Acoustic definition: [+delayed release] = period of frication upon release.
Typical natural classes and alternations: affricates are [+delayed release]; stops and all other segments are [−delayed release].

This works for distinguishing stops and affricates, but it introduces an interesting asymmetry: we may often find reason to refer to the class of sounds that are affricates, but we never seem to have occasion to refer to the class of all the sounds that are *not* affricates. The same holds true for the features [nasal] and [lateral]: the class of [+nasal] and [+lateral] are very useful. For example, nasals assimilate in place of articulation to a following stop, or laterals assimilate in place of articulation to a following coronal. But the class of "sounds that are not nasal" or "sounds that are not lateral" don't seem to be a classes at all, but more like an elsewhere case.

This is in contrast to other features, where both + and − values are equally useful. We refer equally often to the class of [−sonorant] obstruents as to the class of sonorants, and equally often to the class of [−consonantal] vowels and glides as to the class of consonants. That is, some contrasts, like [+/− sonorant], [+/− consonantal] and [+/− continuant] seem to be truly binary, while others like [nasal], [lateral] and [delayed release] seem more one-sided. Recognizing this asymmetry, most linguists have departed from the requirement of binary symmetry (and from our Hypothesis 3) and have argued that features like [nasal] and [lateral] do not have plus and minus values. They are *unary* rather than binary. If a sound has an open velum, it is designated [nasal], sometimes abbreviated [N], otherwise, no specification for this feature is given.

Note the differing predictions that are made by the use of binary vs. unary features. If [−nasal] is among the set of features universally available, then we would expect that lan-

Table 12.2   Revised feature values for the major classes of sounds, including affricates and some unary features.

	Plosives	Fricatives	Affricates	Nasals	Approx.	Laterals	Glides	Vowels
Syllabic	–	–	–	–	–	–	–	+
Consonantal	+	+	+	+	+	+	–	–
Sonorant	–	–	–	+	+	+	+	+
Continuant	–	+	–	–	+	(+)	+	+
Nasal				N				
Lateral						L		
Delayed rel			DR					

guages would make use of it. If in fact they do not (as seems to be the case), we should remove it from the set, making our prediction about possible human languages more constrained. Given our current state of knowledge, most phonologists work within a system that has some binary feature values and some unary feature values. Here, we will mark some features as binary and some as unary, recognizing, however, that these are hypotheses subject to further testing and refinement (Table 12.2).

Finally, consider how these features work to define specific natural classes. The set of sonorant consonants is defined as the set of sounds that are [+sonorant, +consonantal]: all and only the sonorant consonants share these two features. The set of fricatives is [+continuant, –sonorant]: all and only the fricatives share these two features. Using the table above, which features would you use to define the natural class of glides? Try to create your specifications using as few features as possible.

One might ask, at this point, how is it that [+continuant, –sonorant] is better than "fricative"? Isn't saying "fricative" simpler? It is, but it is also less predictive. By using distinctive features, we are making a specific, testable hypothesis that all natural classes can be defined in terms of these parameters (for the moment, those in Table 12.1.)

For example, imagine a phonologist is working on language similar to Zoque (call it *A*), and she discovers that the segments [m, n, ŋ] delete before the sounds [f, s, ʃ, v, z, ʒ] in this language. She will immediately note that these lists of sounds are not random, but constitute a class of sounds that have certain phonetic parameters in common. Further, these parameters are among those given by the list of distinctive features: the sounds [m, n, ŋ] constitute the class of sounds in this language that are [nasal, +consonantal], and the sounds [f, s, ʃ, v, z, ʒ] constitute the class of sounds in this language that are [+continuant, –sonorant]. All is well: her hypotheses about the way phonology works are supported. This phonological alternation targets natural classes defined in terms of the proposed distinctive features. (Of course, if the language's phonetic inventory were slightly different, the set of sounds specified by these features would be different as well: if the language happened to have [x] and [ɣ], they also would be included in the set. However, there is no need to worry about excluding sounds that do not occur in the language under study. For language *A*, the features [+continuant, –sonorant] designate the set of all the fricatives that occur in *A*.)

Now imagine that, in the next city, the linguist finds a different dialect (*B*) which has a somewhat different alternation: nasal consonants delete before [f, s, ʃ, v, z, ʒ, p, b], but not [t, k, d, g, m, n, ŋ]. That is, nasals delete before fricatives and labial oral stops. I can certainly describe this class in English prose, but I cannot describe it in terms of a single set of distinctive features. (Try it.) There is no set of features that define all and only the fricatives and labial stops. Thus, by hypotheses 1 and 2, Dialect *A* is a possible human language, and Dialect

Table 12.3   Laryngeal features.

	Voiceless	Voiced	Voiceless aspirated	Voiced aspirated	Ejectives and ʔ	Creaky voice
Voice	−	+	−	+	−	+
Spread glottis			SG	SG		
Constricted glottis					CG	CG

B, which targets the set [f, s, ʃ, v, z, ʒ, b, p] within a single rule, is not. The set is not a natural class. Should such a rule actually turn out to exist, we will have to revise our hypotheses.

12.2.3 laryngeal features

Languages often make use of contrasts and alternations involving laryngeal distinctions. Languages such as French may contrast [p] and [b], languages like Thai may contrast [p] and [pʰ], languages like Quechua may contrast plain [p] and glottalized or ejective [p'], and languages like Hindi may make a four-way contrast between plain voiceless [p], voiceless aspirated [pʰ], plain voiced [b], and breathy voiced [bʱ]. Finally, some languages, such Hausa, may contrast plain voice vs. creaky, or glottalized, voice, usually on sonorants. Features sufficient for describing these contrasts are defined below, and shown in Table 12.3. It is generally accepted that the features [spread glottis] and [constricted glottis] are unary. Some linguists argue for a unary analysis of [voice] as well, arguing that "plain" voiceless stops are just that: they have no laryngeal specification at all. Unary-feature analyses of voicing assimilation would take us beyond the scope of this book, however, so the feature [voice] is here assumed to be binary.

[+/− voice]
> Articulatory definition: sounds that are [+voice] have vibrating vocal folds.
> Acoustic definition: [+voice] sounds are periodic (have a regularly-repeating pattern).
> Typical natural classes and alternations: Many languages have alternations involving voicing, especially among obstruents.

[spread glottis]
> Articulatory definition: large glottal opening gesture
> Acoustic definition: extended period of voicelessness upon release
> Typical natural classes and alternations: aspirated stops have the feature [spread glottis].

[constricted glottis]
> Articulatory definition: constricted vocal folds
> Acoustic definition: irregular glottal pulses
> Typical natural classes and alternations: ejectives, glottal stop, and creaky-voiced sonorants have the feature [constricted glottis].

12.2.4 major place distinctions

Our list of distinctive features must also account for contrasts and alternations in place of articulation (abbreviated POA). All languages make place of articulation contrasts among consonants, and many alternations either target a class of sounds based on place (such as vowel lowering adjacent to uvulars) or manipulate place (as in place assimilations). However, developing a set of features for place of articulation has not proved straightforward.

Trubetskoy conceived of POA as a multi-valued feature. The distinctive feature was PLACE, and its values were bilabial, labiodental, dental, alveolar, etc. This corresponds to an accepted understanding of the set of phonetic distinctions, but does not allow for any natural classes that group places together. For example, given the places of articulation bilabial, labiodental, and dental, we might assign bilabial to 1PLACE, labiodental to 2PLACE, and dental to 3PLACE. Under this system, labiodental is equidistant from both bilabial and dental; and involving as it does both the lips and the teeth we would expect labiodental to form a natural class with labial sounds and with dental sounds equally often. This is not the case, however. Rather, labiodentals consistently form a class with the bilabials, but not with the dentals.

In English, for example, [w] cannot follow a labial consonant, where "labial" includes both bilabials and labiodentals: we have "twill," "swill," and "quill," but not *pwill or *fwill. ([θw] is uncommon, but acceptable, as in "thwart." Clusters with voiced consonants are marginal at all places, but "Gwen" and "dwell" are better than *bwell.) In Korean and other languages that do not have [f], the labiodental fricative is consistently borrowed as [p], not [t]: "fish" is borrowed into Korean as [piʃi], not [tiʃi]. In Setswana, which does not have [v], "university" is [unibesiti], not [unidesiti]. To cite just one more example, Turkish exhibits a class of words that violate the principle of rounding harmony discussed in Chapter 11 (example 25). In general, [u] cannot occur in a non-initial syllable in Turkish unless the initial vowel is also round: [dɑlɯ], *branch*, and [kolu] *arm*, are fine, but not *[dɑlu]. The only exceptions are words where a labial consonant, either bilabial or labiodental, intervenes: [karpuz] *watermelon*, and [havlu] *towel* are both acceptable.

This is the common pattern cross-linguistically: labiodentals and bilabials form a natural class, and labiodentals and dentals do not. Dentals, however, form a class with other consonants made with the tongue front: the *coronals*. Evidence for the natural class of coronals comes from alternations such as Arabic [l] assimilation (Chapter 11, example 24). Some examples are repeated here:

(1)   Arabic /l/ assimilation:

ʔaʃ-ʃams	the sun
ʔat-tidʒaːra	the commerce
ʔaθ-θaqaːfa	the culture
ʔað-ðahab	the gold
ʔaz-zuhuːr	the flowers
ʔaʒ-ʒilː	the shadow

Compare:

ʔal-qamr	the moon
ʔal-badw	the Bedouin
ʔal-filfil	the pepper
ʔal-xardal	the mustard

In Arabic, [l] assimilates completely to a following dental, alveolar, or post-alveolar, all coronal consonants (the "sun letters.") All other consonants (the "moon letters," including [f]) induce no change. A similar example is found in Catalan (example 2): [l] assimilates in place of articulation to a following dental, post-alveolar, or retroflex, but not to a labial or labio-dental.

(2)   Catalan /l/ assimilation:

e[l p]a   the bread
e[l f]oc   the fire
e[l̪ d̪]ia   the day
e[ɭ ʈ]ic   the rich
e[ʎ ʒ]ermà   the brother

Finally, consider the alternations between stop and fricative in Sudanese Arabic shown in example (3).

(3)   Assimilation in Sudanese Arabic:

book	*daughter*	*fish*	
kitaːb	bit	samak	*X*
kitaːf fatʰi	bit fatʰi	samak fatʰi	*Fathi's X*
kitaːp samiːr	bis samiːr	samak samiːr	*Sameer's X*
kitaːp ʃariːf	biʃ ʃariːf	samak ʃariːf	*Sharif's X*
kitaːp xaːlid	bit xaːlid	samax xaːlid	*Halid's X*
kitaːp ħasan	bit ħasan	samak ħasan	*Hasan's X*

The pattern is that the word-final stop assimilates to a following fricative just in case the two share an active articulator. Bilabial [b] assimilates to labiodental [f] (shared labial articulator), alveolar [d] assimilates to both alveolar [s] and postalveolar [ʃ] (shared tongue front articulator), and [k] assimilates to [x] (shared tongue body articulator). No stop assimilates to pharyngeal [ħ], because no stop shares the tongue root articulator with [ħ].

Alternations such as those listed above have led phonologists to propose a set of unary place features based on active articulator, as listed below. These features depart from the Jakobsonian pattern in two ways: they are unary, and they are defined in purely articulatory, not acoustic, terms. They do however, seem to work. That is, they make accurate predictions about the possible natural classes found in the languages of the world.

[labial]
> Definition: constriction at the lips
> Natural class: bilabials and labiodentals

[coronal]
> Definition: constriction made with the tongue front
> Natural class: dentals, alveolars, alveopalatals, retroflexes, palatals

[dorsal]
> Definition: constriction made with the tongue body
> Natural class: palatals, velars and uvulars. Palatals have been found to involve an extended constriction of both tongue blade and tongue body against the upper surface of the vocal tract, so they may be considered both coronal and dorsal.

[pharyngeal]
> Definition: constriction made with the tongue root
> Natural class: pharyngeal fricatives

Table 12.4   Features based on active articulator. The fricative symbol stands for all sounds made at the corresponding place of articulation.

	ɸ	f	θ	s	ʃ	ʂ	ɕ	x	χ	ħ	h
Labial	L	L									
Coronal			C	C	C	C	C				
Dorsal							(D)	D	D		
Pharyngeal										Ph	
Laryngeal											Lar

[laryngeal]
> Definition: constriction at the glottis
> Natural class: [h] and [ʔ].

Additional features are necessary to make distinctions with each of the classes defined by the features in Table 12.4. These subsidiary place features are listed in Table 12.5 and discussed below.

12.2.5 subsidiary place distinctions

No language has all of the fricatives shown in Table 12.5, or uses all these places of articulation, but for any pair, there is some language that creates a contrast between those two sounds. Therefore, we need a set of features sufficient to uniquely identify each column.

We begin with the coronal consonants, since there are five different possible places of articulation that can be contrasted within the coronal articulator. For a first distinction, the feature [anterior] divides sounds made at or in front of the alveolar ridge ([+anterior]) from those made behind the alveolar ridge ([−anterior]). Many languages have alternations similar to the palatalization rule of English: [t, d, s, z] become [tʃ, ʤ, ʃ, ʒ] before the glide [j]. This alternation can be analyzed as assimilation of the feature [−anterior]: [+anterior] /s/ changes to [−anterior] [ʃ] before [−anterior] [j].

The feature [anterior] was first used by Jakobson to make a binary division of the whole vocal tract, at the alveolar ridge, dividing [f] and [s] from [ʃ] and [x]. We have just seen, however, that this makes the wrong predictions: [f] and [s] don't go together. To fix the problem, and properly constrain the domain of the feature, we will define [anterior] as pertaining to coronals only: it distinguishes [s] from [ʃ], but does not apply to non-coronal sounds such as [f] and [x].

[+/− anterior]
> Definition: [+anterior] sounds are made with the tongue front at or in front of the alveolar ridge; [−anterior] sounds are made with the tongue front behind the alveolar ridge.
> Natural classes: dentals and alveolars are [+anterior]; postalveolars, retroflexes, and palatals are [−anterior]. Non-coronal sounds are not specified for [anterior].

Within the [+anterior] class, we need to distinguish [θ] vs. [s], and within the [−anterior] class we need to distinguish [ʃ] vs. [ʂ] vs. [ɕ]. One way to do this is to reference the distinction between tongue tip (apical) and tongue blade (laminal) consonants. While we could have named a feature for this distinction [+/− apical] or [+/− laminal], the term commonly in use is [distributed], going back to a Jakobsonian feature that was proposed to apply across all places of articulation.

[+/− distributed]

Definition: [+distributed] sounds have a relatively long constriction. In practice, this means that laminal consonants are [+distributed] and apical consonants are [−distributed].

Natural classes: [s] and [ʂ] are [−distributed]; [θ], [ʃ] and [ç] are [+distributed].

Thus among the coronal fricatives, [θ] is [+anterior, +distributed], [s] is [+anterior, −distributed], [ʃ] is [−anterior, +distributed] and [ʂ] is [−anterior, −distributed]. Stops and nasals at the same places of articulation would be distinguished in the same ways.

Among the coronals, that leaves the distinction between post-alveolar [ʃ] and palatal [ç]. One observation to make about this contrast is that no language is known to contrast post-alveolar and palatal stops or nasals: this distinction seems to apply only to fricatives and affricates. Thus we can appeal to the fact that these fricatives sound very different: [ʃ] and [s] (known as "sibilants") have a noise component that is both high-amplitude and high-frequency, while the other coronal fricatives are softer. A feature that references this difference is [+/− strident]. This is one of the few features that has a primarily acoustic definition. The feature [strident] has the added advantage of being able to distinguish higher-pitched labiodental [f] from softer bilabial [ɸ], another place distinction that applies only to fricatives. It can also distinguish [θ] from [s] for those who make [θ] with the tongue tip.

[+/− strident]

Definition: [+strident] sounds have high-amplitude, high-pitched frication.

Natural classes: sibilants (alveolar and post-alveolar fricatives and affricates), as well as labiodental and uvular fricatives and affricates are [+strident]. All other fricatives and affricates are [−strident]. This feature is only defined for fricatives and affricates.

The features [anterior] and [strident] sometimes seem to duplicate effort: the distinction between [s] and [θ], for example, can be defined in terms of either [+/− strident] or [−/+ distributed]. But the features define different natural classes, both of which seem to be useful. [+strident] is crucial in defining the class of sibilant consonants. For example, the English plural allomorph [ɨz] occurs only after the coronal sibilants: [coronal, +strident]. On the other hand, the feature [strident] is not available for stops and nasals, and there are languages (such as Tiwi, see Chapter 10 exercises) that distinguish laminal dental vs. apical alveolar, or laminal postalveolar vs. apical retroflex, stops and nasals.

As was noted in the definition, the feature [strident] can be used to distinguish [−strident] velar fricatives from harsher [+strident] uvular fricatives. But another feature is needed to distinguish velar and uvular stops and nasals. The feature [distributed] will not do it, as both velars and uvulars are made with the same articulator, the tongue body. The most salient distinction between these two is position of the tongue body: the feature [high] can be recruited to distinguish these sounds. This feature, which is defined only for sounds that use the tongue body as an active articulator, is mostly active for vowels, and is defined (straightforwardly) in Section 12.2.6.

The aforementioned set of features is hypothesized to be sufficient for accurately and succinctly describing all the consonantal contrasts and natural classes that are found in the languages of the world.

There is one consonantal natural class that has not yet been covered, however. Languages that utilize the uvular, pharyngeal, and laryngeal places of articulation (including the Semitic languages, and a number of Caucasian and Native American languages) often group these consonants into a natural class (which does not include the velars). For example, we saw in Chapter 11 that, in Syrian Arabic, [e] lowers to [a] when it follows a uvular, pharyngeal, or laryngeal consonant. The data are repeated in example (4):

(4) Syrian Arabic:

daraʒ -e   step
ʃerk-e   society
madras-e   school

wa:ʒh-a   display
mni:ħ-a   good
dagga:ʀ-a   tanning

This class is often referred to as the class of *guttural consonants*, and [guttural] is sometimes proposed as a unary articulator feature, parallel to [labial], [coronal] and [dorsal]. Unlike those three features, however, [guttural] does not refer to a single active articulator: uvulars use the tongue body, pharyngeals the tongue root, and laryngeals the larynx. (One intriguing possibility, still speculative however, is that the guttural consonants may comprise the class of consonants that do not involve raising of the jaw.) In part, the issue is difficult to resolve because pharyngeal consonants, which are crucial to determining the correct generalizations, are not among the most common. Here, while we recognize that the issue is far from resolved, we will note the affinity of guttural consonants and low vowels, and specify uvulars, pharyngeals and laryngeals as [+low]. Like [+/− high], [+/− low] is most often a feature of vowels, and it is to features of vowels that we now turn.

Table 12.5 Expanded table of place distinctions.

	φ	f	θ	s	ʃ	ʂ	ɕ	x	χ	ħ	h
Labial	L	L									
Coronal			C	C	C	C	C				
Dorsal							(D)	D	D		
Pharyngeal										Ph	
Laryngeal											Lar
Anterior			+	+	−	−	−				
Distributed			+	−	+	−	+				
Strident	−	+	−	+	+	−	−	−	+	−	−
High							+	+	−		
Low									+	+	+

12.2.6 features for vowels

Vowels always involve movement of the tongue body, as thus are always considered to be [dorsal]. In addition, since rounding is implemented with the lips, round vowels are [labial]. The distinctive features needed to distinguish vowels are straightforward: [+/− high], [+/− low], [+/− back], [+/−advanced tongue root] (ATR) and [+/− round]. A subset of these features can also be used to indicate secondary articulations on consonants (vowel-like constrictions articulated simultaneously with the consonant): [+low] for pharyngealization,

[+back] for velarization, [−back] for palatalization, and [+round] for rounding. The feature [+/− round] must be distinct from [labial], as languages may distinguish [p] ([labial]) from [pʷ] ([labial, +round]); and [t], for example, can become [+round] [tʷ] without becoming labial [p].

Vowel features can be defined in both articulatory and acoustic terms. Each lip and tongue body position results in a typical resonance pattern. (If you haven't studied acoustic phonetics (Chapters 6 to 8), and these descriptions of resonance patterns mean nothing to you, ignore them and concentrate on the articulatory definitions.)

[+/− round]
Articulatory definition: [+ round] segments have pursing of the lips.
Acoustic definition: rounding lowers all resonances.
Typical natural classes and alternations: round vowels, including [u, ʊ, o, ɔ, y, œ] are [+round], as are rounded consonants such as [tʷ, sʷ, gʷ].

[+/− high]
Articulatory definition: for [+high] segments, the tongue body is raised from the neutral position.
Acoustic definition: [+high] segments have low F1.
Typical natural classes and alternations: high vowels, including [i, u, ʊ, ɨ y,] are [+high], all other vowels are [−high]. May also be used to distinguish [+high] palatals and velars from [−high] uvulars.

[+/− low]
Articulatory definition: for [+low] segments the tongue body is lowered from the neutral position.
Acoustic definition: [+low] segments have high F1.
Typical natural classes and alternations: [ɑ], [a] and [æ] are [+low]. Guttural consonants may also be described as [+low].

[+/− back]
Articulatory definition: for [+back] segments, the tongue body is moved back from the neutral position.
Acoustic definition: for [+back] vowels, the first two resonances (F1 and F2) are close together, for [−back] vowels, F1 and F2 are farther apart.
Typical natural classes and alternations: Front vowels (including [i, ɪ, e, ɛ, æ] are [−back]. Back *and central* vowels (including [u, ɨ, o, ʌ, a] are [+back]. See discussion below.

[+/− advanced tongue root] ([+/− ATR])
Articulatory definition: [+ATR] vowels have the tongue root pulled forward.
Acoustic definition: [+ATR] vowels have lowered F1 compared to their [−ATR] counterparts.
Typical natural classes and alternations: [i, e, u, o] are [+ATR], [ɪ, ʊ, ɛ, ɔ] are [−ATR]. The [ATR] feature is active in vowel harmony in a number of West African languages, such as Igbo (Chapter 11, example 14). In other languages, [+ATR] vowels may be termed [+tense]. See discussion below. Low vowels are sometimes considered to be [−ATR], or may be undefined for [ATR].

Vowel features are in general quite straightforward, but there are a few points worth noting. First, a note on vowel height. The usually-accepted features for vowel height are [+/− low] and [+/− high]. There is no distinctive feature [mid]. The mid vowels [e, ɛ, o, ɔ, ʌ] are [−high, −low]. Other apparent or subsidiary differences in tongue body height may be subsumed with the feature [+/−ATR]. There may be a difference in tongue body height between [i] and [ɪ], but the primary distinction is that [i] is [+ATR] and [ɪ] is [−ATR].

Concerning the feature [ATR], we will use [+ATR] for the English vowels that are usually described as tense, and [−ATR] for the English vowels that are usually described as lax. Introducing a separate feature [+/− tense] would, first, create redundancy, since [+/− ATR] and [+/− tense] target what are essentially the same vowel contrasts. Second, it would make wrong predictions. Generally, we expect features to cross-classify: if we have features [+/− high] and [+/− back], we expect that all four combinations [+ back, +high], [+back, −high], [−back, +high] and [−back, −high] should occur. With [ATR] and [tense], the combinations [−ATR, +tense] and [+ATR, −tense] would never occur. One possible approach would be to assume that some languages use [ATR] and some languages use [tense], contra the claim that features are universal. Less radically, one could propose that [ATR] and [tense] refer to a single universally-available dimension of contrast (essentially [i] vs. [ɪ]) and should therefore be represented by a single distinctive feature (whichever term is chosen), but that languages may differ somewhat in the exact phonetic implementation. This is the solution chosen here. This weakens the requirement that features have a universal, shared, phonetic definition, and thus opens the possibility that some distinctive features might not be phonetically-based at all. The subject of the precise phonetic definition of features continues to be one of debate.

The central vowels, such as [ɨ] and [ʌ], can be defined in featural terms as [+back, −round]; and they contrast with [u] and [o] that are [+back, +round]. That is to say, although there are three degrees of backness phonetically (front, central, back), there are only two dimensions of contrast phonologically: [−back] front vowels and [+back] back and central vowels. In retrospect, it would have been better to have named the feature [+/− front], but Chomsky and Halle happened to choose [back], and it seems to be too late to change it now.

12.2   In Focus

There are few, if any, cases of languages contrasting a back vs. central vowel without also making a contrast in rounding. There are no completely convincing cases of languages that contrast central [ɨ] and back [ɯ], or central [ʌ] and back [ɤ]. A few possible back vs. central contrasts, in Nimboran, Norwegian, and Bostonian are discussed in Section 4.3 on p. 59, but each is subject to re-analysis. Bostonian, for example, contrasts "shack" [ʃæk] vs. "shock" [ʃɑk] vs. "shark" [ʃak], but in that case [a] may be argued to be underlying (ar), so that back /ɑ/ and central /a/ are not really contrastive.

Table 12.6 gives the feature values of a representative set of vowels. The [ATR] values shown in parentheses are tentative, as these vowels do not commonly participate in [ATR] contrasts or alternations, so definitive data as to their value is lacking.

Finally, note that, secondary articulations aside, the set of "place" features for vowels and consonants are largely mutually exclusive. Only consonants can be [coronal], for example, and only vowels are specified for [ATR]. For the most part, consonants are not specified as [high], [back], or [low]. This is by design, allowing for simpler and more general statements of the alternations that affect only consonants or only vowels, which constitute the majority.

Table 12.6　Place features for a representative set of vowels.

	i	*ɪ*	*e*	*ɛ*	*æ*	*u*	*ʊ*	*o*	*ɔ*	*a*	*y*	*ø*	*ɨ*	*ʌ*
Back	–	–	–	–	–	+	+	+	+	+	–	–	+	+
High	+	+	–	–	–	+	+	–	–	–	+	–	+	–
Low	–	–	–	–	+	–	–	–	–	+	–	–	–	–
ATR	+	–	+	–	(–)	+	–	+	–	(–)	+	+	(–)	(–)
Round	–	–	–	–	–	+	+	+	+	–	+	+	–	–

This decision, however, complicates cases where vowels and consonants interact. Palatalization is a case in point. The alternation "[s] is realized as [ʃ] before [i]" is quite common, and its phonetic grounding is clear: the fronted and raised tongue body position of [i] is more compatible with [ʃ] than with [s], making palatalization a kind of assimilation. This compatibility is not captured in features, however. The change from [s] to [ʃ] is one of [+anterior] to [–anterior], a feature that is not even defined for [i]. Reacting to this problem, some phonologists have proposed a unified set of features for vowels and consonants, suggesting that front vowels should be [coronal] instead of [–back]. This fails to account, however, for the many times that coronal consonants and [i] fail to interact. Finding a single representation that elegantly captures both interactions and lack of interactions between vowels and consonants continues to be a matter of research and debate.

There are two more vowel features that we will find useful at this point to define natural classes and alternations. We need a feature [+/– long] to distinguish vowels that differ in length but not quality, such as are found in the Japanese words [biru] *building* vs. [biːru] *beer*, and to capture alternations like compensatory lengthening and closed syllable shortening. We will also find it useful to refer to a feature [+/– stress] in order to account for alternations that are conditioned by stress, such as English tapping and vowel reduction. We will see, however, that a more carefully-elaborated theory of timing, syllable structure, and stress, to be developed in Chapters 15 and 16, will obviate the need for these two features. Chapter 17 will discuss the features necessary to account for alternations and contrast in tone.

12.3　how have our hypotheses fared?

We began this chapter with a set of hypotheses about natural classes in human languages. Hypotheses 2 and 3 are repeated here:

Hypothesis 2:
Phonological contrasts and natural classes can be defined in terms of a closed set of phonetic parameters that is the same across all languages: the set of *distinctive features*.

Hypothesis 3:
Features are defined in terms of binary (+/–) oppositions (e.g., every segment is either [+voice] or [–voice]).

The bulk of this chapter has been spent specifying the set of distinctive features. Is this set able to account for all phonological contrasts and natural classes? As far as contrasts go, the hypothesis is pretty well supported. The features are defined clearly enough that we know what kind of data would render them inadequate: a language that required six degrees of vowel height could not be accounted for with the features [+/− high] and [+/− low], or a language that contrasted four degrees of rounding could not be accounted for with the feature [+/− round]. Thus far, languages such as these hypothetical cases have not been described.

As far as natural classes go, the story is more complicated, and we have seen that the set of distinctive features has undergone significant revisions since the original work of Jakobson, and new revisions continue to be proposed. We have seen that there are numerous cases for which hypothesis 3 has not been supported. The lack of evidence for targeted classes such as [−nasal] and [−lateral] have led to the suggestion that at least some features are unary rather than binary. In particular, unary features for place of articulation based on active articulator have proven to be useful.

Once unary features are introduced, it becomes clear that not all segments are specified for every feature. A lack of complete featural specification of a given segment is termed *underspecification*. Absence of a unary feature (as when non-nasal consonants simply have no [nasal] specification) is one type of underspecification. Another type is when a binary feature is not defined or not available for a certain class of sounds: [+/− anterior] is defined only for coronal consonants, for example, and [+/− strident] is defined only for fricatives and affricates. Other types of underspecification are possible. For example, if we know that all nasals are [+voice], do we need to specify nasal consonants as both [+nasal] and [+voice] in underlying representations? There is reason to think we should not. This and similar cases are discussed in Chapter 13.

Cases that continue to be the subject of research and debate include the definition of the feature [continuant], the possibility of unary [voice], features of guttural consonants, the relation between "tenseness" and ATR, the best representation for vowel height, and the interaction or non-interaction of vowels and consonants. These specific cases feed into larger questions of whether the set of distinctive features is truly universal, how clearly-defined in articulatory or acoustic terms each feature must be, and whether features are learned or innate. Different hypotheses have been put forward, each one in service of a slightly different theory of what human languages can be like. All the problems have not been solved – if they were, phonologists would be out of a job. In that case, we could declare that we had learned all there is to know about human language contrasts and alternations, and retire to our respective beach houses. We're not there yet, but the set of features described in this chapter does hold up very well against the data. We will use this set of features in subsequent chapters as we investigate the next set of hypotheses regarding the relationship between underlying and surface representations.

chapter summary

- The set of distinctive features constitutes a hypothesis about the dimensions of contrast and alternations available in human languages. As such, they define the space of possible languages.
- The distinctive features proposed by Jakobson, Fant, and Halle were binary, defined in both articulatory and acoustic terms, and fully specified for all segments.
- Subsequent analyses, based on a range of cross-linguistic contrasts and alternations, have suggested that some features are unary, some are based on the active articulator used, and not all features are specified for all segments.
- A suggested set of features and feature values are found in Table 12.2 (major class features), Table 12.3 (laryngeal features), Table 12.5 (place features), and Table 12.6 (vowel

features). Definitions of each feature accompany the tables. These are the features that will be used in for the description of phonological contrasts and alternations in the following chapters.

further reading

Take a crack at R. Jakobson, G.M. Fant, and M. Halle 1952. *Preliminaries to Speech Analysis: The Distinctive Features and Their Correlates.* Cambridge, MA: MIT Press.

For an entertaining and accessible extended argument in favor of Universal Grammar as a genetic endowment, see Stephen Pinker's *The Language Instinct* (London: Perennial, 1994/2007). Geoffrey Sampson offers counter-arguments in *The Language Instinct Debate* (London: Continuum, 1997).

review exercises

1. What makes a hypothesis falsifiable?
2. Why is it better for a hypothesis to be more constrained?
3. What is the difference between binary and unary features?
4. Review the definitions of:

   a. Major class and manner features
   b. Laryngeal features
   c. Place features
   d. Features for vowels

further analysis and discussion

The best way to learn the features is to practice using them.
5. List the feature corresponding to the major active articulator (labial, coronal, dorsal, pharyngeal, laryngeal) for each of the following sounds:

   a. k
   b. ɗ
   c. h
   d. ħ
   e. e
   f. s
   g. ɸ
   h. m
   i. v
   j. χ

6. In each pair listed below, the segments differ in the value of one or more binary features. Fill in the difference.

   a. p __−voice____   b ___+voice_____
   b. s _____   ʃ _____

c.	ʃ _____	ʂ _____
d.	i _____	ɪ _____
e.	j _____	i _____
f.	k _____	x _____
g.	q _____	k _____
h.	æ _____	ɑ _____
i.	u _____	o _____
j.	ɸ _____	f _____
k.	t _____	θ _____

7. In each pair listed below, the segments differ in the presence or absence of a unary feature. Fill in the feature on the sound for which it is specified.

a.	p _____	pʰ _____SG_____
b.	m __Nasal_____	b _____
c.	ʤ _____	d _____
d.	õ _____	o _____
e.	k' _____	k _____
f.	l _____	d _____

8. Imagine a language that has the inventory shown below. Nine of the circled sets of sounds are natural classes. Describe each class in terms of distinctive features, using only the features defined in this chapter, and being mindful of which features are unary and which binary. Use as few features as possible to uniquely identify each set relative to the whole inventory. Indicate the set that is not a natural class. [ɭ] is a retroflex approximant.

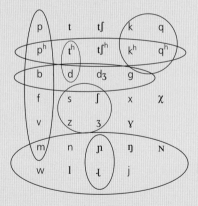 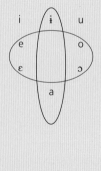

9. Assuming the same inventory, list the features that define the following natural classes:

   a. fricatives
   b. high vowels
   c. velar stops
   d. voiced affricate
   e. glides

(Continued)

10. Assuming the same inventory, list the sounds that comprise the following natural classes:

   a. [−voice, +continuant]
   b. [dorsal, +consonantal]
   c. [+anterior]
   d. [round]
   e. [+delayed release, +voice]

further research

11. Find a grammar book or dictionary that lists the segment inventory of a language, and repeat exercises 8 to 10 with that inventory. Circle groups of sounds that you suspect should be natural classes, and see if you can define them using the features presented here.
12. Repeat exercise 11 with a made-up inventory. Repeat with different sets of sounds until you feel confident in your ability to define natural classes with distinctive features.

Go online Visit the book's companion website for additional resources relating to this chapter at: http://www.wiley.com/go/zsiga.

references

The historical exposition in this chapter follows that of S. Anderson, *Phonology in the Twentieth Century*. Chicago: University of Chicago Press, 1985,

Catalan
Mascaró, J. 1976. Catalan phonology and the phonological cycle. Doctoral dissertation, Massachusetts Institute of Technology.

Sudanese Arabic
Hamid, A.H. 1984. The phonology of Sudanese Arabic. Ph.D. dissertation: University of Illinois, cited in M. Kenstowicz, *Phonology in Generative Grammar*. Oxford: Blackwell, 1994.

Turkish "labial attraction"
Kornfilt, Jaklin. 1997. *Turkish*. London: Routledge.

13 Rules and Derivations in Generative Grammar

I have assumed that an adequate description of a language can take the form of a set of rules – analogous perhaps to a program of an electronic computing machine – which when provided with further special instructions, could produce all and only well-formed (grammatical) utterances in the language in question. This set of rules . . . we shall call the grammar of the language.

Morris Halle, *The Sound Pattern of Russian*, 1971, p. 12.

The Sounds of Language: An Introduction to Phonetics and Phonology, First Edition. Elizabeth C. Zsiga.
© 2013 Elizabeth C. Zsiga. Published 2013 by Blackwell Publishing Ltd.

In this chapter, we consider in more detail the approach to phonology (and to linguistics in general), known as Generative Grammar, particularly rule-based Generative Grammar. The basic idea of this approach, as has been noted in previous chapters and as Halle states in the epigraph, is that a "grammar" consists of a set of rules that produce, or "generate" all the well-formed utterances of a language. This chapter examines phonological rules and their operation in more detail, especially the question of what formal devices should be used in writing rules. Section 13.1 reviews the basic tenets of the theory in its historical context. Section 13.2 discusses the representation of underlying representations, and Section 13.3 covers the specifics of writing and evaluating phonological rules. Section 13.4 considers an alternative rule formalism, that of autosegmental representations.

13.1 generative grammars

As was noted in previous chapters, Generative Grammar was first developed by the linguist Noam Chomsky, who applied this approach to both phonology and syntax, beginning in the 1950s. The generative approach to phonology was popularized in the 1968 publication *The Sound Pattern of English*, co-authored by Noam Chomsky and Morris Halle. *The Sound Pattern of English* was so influential that it became familiarly known as *SPE*, and "SPE-style" grammars for other languages proliferated.

In contrast to the Structuralist emphasis on relationships between surface forms, Generative Grammar focused on deriving surface pronunciations from abstract underlying forms (entries in the lexicon). In contrast to the Behaviorist conception of language as stimulus and response, Generative Grammar focused on language as knowledge: a speaker's competence (what she knows how to do) rather than her performance (what she actually does in any given instance). The central premise of Generative Grammar as set out in SPE is that what it means to know a language is to know a set of underlying representations and a set of rules. The approach is called *Generative* Grammar because the rules apply to generate the surface forms from the underlying representations. The process of generating surface representations (SRs) from underlying representations (URs) is called a *derivation*. The following two hypotheses are crucial to an SPE-style generative grammar:

Hypothesis 4:
Every morpheme has a unique underlying representation, which is defined in terms of combinations of distinctive features.

Hypothesis 5:
Underlying representations are converted into contextually-varied surface representations by the operation of a set of feature-changing or feature-filling rules.

One can make an analogy to a manufacturing process. The lexicon is like a warehouse, where all the morphemes one needs to make words and sentences are stored. The grammar is like the factory where the morphemes are assembled into the finished product. To launch a derivation, the morphemes are taken from the lexicon and put together in order to make words and sentences. After the syntactic part of the grammar has gotten the word order straightened out, the ordered set of morphemes is sent down a phonological assembly line. Each "station" on the assembly line consists of a particular rule. The rule looks for a certain configuration – maybe a word-final voiced stop, maybe a fricative preceding a nasal – and when it finds this configuration, the rule makes an adjustment according to the instructions that it has been given – perhaps devoicing the stop, or deleting the fricative. If a particular string of morphemes does not happen to contain the specified configuration, that lexical item passes by the rule's station unchanged. After the lexical item has passed by each station on the assembly line, the finished SR is sent off to be pronounced. Languages will differ in having different items in their warehouses, and in having different assembly lines, that is, different rules applying in different orders.

In the decades since the publication of SPE, this model of grammar as assembly line has undergone significant revision. The nature of underlying representations, and the mechanisms by which SRs are generated, have been re-evaluated. In some versions of generative phonology, the layout of the factory is made much more elaborate. In one of the more recent versions (Optimality Theory), there are no rules whatsoever. (Chapter 14 considers how Optimality Theory gets from UR to SR without the operation of rules.) What makes each of these a generative grammar, however, is the basic conception of language as a process or algorithm that generates all possible SRs from a set of URs that can be concatenated in various ways. The goal is always to make the algorithm as simple and general as can be, such that all of the possible forms of a language are possible outputs of the grammar, and none of the impossible forms are generated (as it were) by mistake.

We begin with a closer look at underlying representations.

13.2 underlying representations

Standard models of Generative Grammar assume that each lexical item has a unique UR. This is the entry in the mental dictionary, where arbitrary sound-meaning relationships are stored. The URs are encoded in terms of "bundles" of distinctive features. Two examples of feature bundles, for the words "pen" and "sad" are shown in example (1).

(1) Underlying representations as feature bundles:

PEN	=	labial	dorsal	coronal
		+consonantal	−consonantal	+consonantal
		−syllabic	+syllabic	−syllabic
		−sonorant	+sonorant	+sonorant
		−continuant	+continuant	−continuant
		−voice	+voice	+voice
			−back	+anterior
			−high	−distributed
			−low	nasal
			−ATR	

SAD	=	coronal	dorsal	coronal
		+consonantal	−consonantal	+consonantal
		−syllabic	+syllabic	−syllabic
		−sonorant	+sonorant	−sonorant
		+continuant	+continuant	−continuant
		−voice	+voice	+voice
		+strident	−back	+anterior
		+anterior	−high	−distributed
		−distributed	+low	

Note that not every feature is specified for every segment. In the feature system we are developing here, unary features are absent from most segments. Thus [n] is [nasal], but none of the other segments have a specification for this feature. Further, not all binary features are defined for all segments: non-fricatives are not specified for [+/− strident], for example, and stops are not specified for vowel features. As was noted in Chapter 12, leaving certain feature values out is known as *underspecification*.

One view of underlying representations is that they should contain as few features as possible: only information that is truly unpredictable should be stored in the lexicon. Predictable features should be absent from underlying representations, and then filled in by rule. Feature values might be predictable for different reasons. In some cases, feature specifications are *redundant*: all nasals are sonorants, for example, so [+sonorant] is redundant if [nasal] is specified. Or features might be completely positionally-determined (non-contrastive). Aspiration is not contrastive for any segments in English, so [SG] can be left unspecified in English URs, and filled in later by rules such as "voiceless stops are aspirated in word-initial position." Leaving out redundant and positionally-determined features is known as *Contrastive Underspecification*. Representative feature bundles are shown in example (2).

(2)   URs based on Contrastive Underspecification:

PEN	=	labial	dorsal	coronal
		−voice	−consonantal	nasal
		−continuant	−back	
			−high	
			−low	
			−ATR	

SAD	=	coronal	dorsal	coronal
		+continuant	−consonantal	−continuant
		−voice	−back	−sonorant
		+strident	+low	+voice
		+anterior		+anterior

Vowels, once they are specified as [−consonantal], need no further underlying specification for [sonorant], [continuant], or [voice], because [−consonantal] sounds do not contrast for these features. Once [n] is specified as [coronal] and [nasal] no further features are necessary: there is only one coronal nasal in the English inventory. Specifying [p] as [−voice] makes [−sonorant] redundant (no voiceless sounds are underlyingly [+sonorant]) in English), but voiced sounds may be sonorant or not, so [d] is marked as [−sonorant]. In general, enough features are specified to uniquely identify each sound in the language, but no more.

13.1   In Focus

One idea behind underspecification is that it makes the lexicon more efficient. Instead of specifying every nasal segment in the language as both [nasal] and [+sonorant] one could save "shelf space," by specifying just the feature [nasal], along with the general rule that "Nasals are sonorants." Storing and implementing one rule, the argument goes, is more efficient than specifying tens of thousands of separate lexical entries with the same information.

The problem with that argument is that it is not clear that our brains are wired to store information with maximum efficiency. We are discovering that the brain has plenty of storage space, so that storing one piece of information multiple times is no great cost: we have plenty of neurons available. Further, it may be that storing redundant information is a plus rather than a minus, speeding recall and processing time.

The argument for underspecification must rest on phonological grounds. For example, recall the observation that sonorants often do not participate in rules of voicing assimilation. In Russian, for example, we saw that the final consonant in the prefix meaning "from" assimilates in voicing to a following obstruent: [ot papɨ] *from papa*, [od babuʃki] *from grandma*. Sonorants, however, have no effect: [ot mamɨ] *from mama*. The theory of underspecification argues that the reason that sonorants do not participate in voicing assimilations is that at the time the rule of assimilation applies, nasals have no [voice] specification for the obstruents to assimilate to.

That is, the rule that says "sonorants are voiced" is a few stations down the assembly line from the rule that says "consonant clusters must agree in voicing." The agreement rule is looking for clusters where one consonant is voiced and the other voiceless, such as /ot babuʃki /. In the early stages of the derivation, however, the morpheme [mamɨ] is not specified as [+voice] on its nasal segments. Therefore, when the agreement rule examines the /t+m/ cluster, it sees only one [−voice] specification, not a minus-plus mismatch, so it lets the form pass unchanged. (It must be understood that rules are not very bright: they follow their instructions exactly, never looking ahead nor back.) Later down the assembly line, the "sonorants are voiced" station fills in the [+voice] value, so that the nasal is in fact pronounced with vibrating vocal folds, but it's too late for the voicing assimilation rule to have any effect.

Because arguments for underspecification depend on issues of what information must be accessed at what point in the derivation, different views of how the derivation proceeds result in different theories of underspecification. See the suggested readings on p. 299 for further discussion.

13.3 writing rules

13.3.1 SPE notation

We now take a closer look at the form and operation of phonological rules. How should they be written? Chomsky and Halle argued that the general form of rules should be:

A –> B / C __ D

where *A*, *B*, *C* and *D* may be matrices of features or one of a small set of special symbols, including # for word boundary, + for morpheme boundary, Ø for null. Because the set of parameters that can be referenced is limited, the set of rules that can be written (and thus processes that are predicted to occur) is made more constrained. *A* specifies the natural class of sounds targeted by the rule, and *B* specifies the featural change. Insertions and deletions are represented using the Ø symbol. The arrow can be read as "become" or "are." Some featural changes are shown in (3):

(3)   Rule formalism: A –> B:

      a. [−sonorant] –> [−voice]
         "obstruents become voiceless"
      b. [−voice, −continuant] –> [SG]
         "voiceless stops are aspirated"
      c. [−consonantal, +syllabic] –> Ø
         "a vowel is deleted" (that is, a vowel becomes null)
      d. Ø –> [−consonantal, −back, +high, +ATR]
         "insert [i]" ("null" becomes a vowel with these features)

The / separates the part of the rule that specifies the change from the part of the rule that specifies the environment in which the change occurs. It is sometimes called the "environment slash" and can be read "in the environment of." The underline indicates where the targeted class occurs, C indicates the required preceding environment (if any) and D indicates the required following environment (if any). In some cases, both C and D are absent: this would indicate a rule that applies in all environments. The following are some typical rules with their translations.

(4)   SPE rule formalism:

      a. [−sonorant, +continuant] –> [−continuant] / [nasal] _____
         "a fricative becomes a stop in the environment of a preceding nasal"
      b. [+voice, −continuant, −sonorant] –> [+continuant] / [+continuant] ___
         "a voiced stop becomes a fricative in the environment of a preceding segment that is also [+continuant]"
      c. [−sonorant] –> [−voice] / ___ #
         "an obstruent becomes voiceless in word-final position"
      d. Ø –> [laryngeal, CG] / # ___ [−consonantal, +syllabic]
         "insert a glottal stop preceding a word−initial vowel"
      e. [+syllabic, −consonantal, +high] –> [−voice] / [−voice] __ [−voice]
         "a high vowel becomes voiceless when it occurs between two voiceless segments"
      f. [nasal] –> [+voice]
         nasals are voiced (in all contexts)

13.3.2 derivations

Derivations show sequential rules operating to change URs into SRs. Recall from Chapter 11 the generalizations for forming the English regular past tense, repeated here as (5). Translation into SPE formalism is shown in (6). Check that you can read the rules in (6) as corresponding to the prose generalizations in (5).

(5)   Deriving the English past tense suffix:

      a. The underlying form of the past tense suffix is /d/.
      b. If the suffix is added to a word that ends with an alveolar stop, a vowel is inserted to derive the surface form [ɨd], *otherwise*

   c. If the suffix is added to a word that ends with a voiceless consonant, the surface
      form is [t], *otherwise*
   d. The surface form is [d].

(6)   English past tense rules in SPE:

   i-epenthesis

   Ø –> [+syllabic, +high, +back, −round] /
         [coronal, −continuant, +ant] _____ + [coronal, −continuant, +ant]

   voicing assimilation
   [−son] –> [−voice] / [−voice] + _____

These rules then apply in a step-by-step derivation, as shown in example (7). As is common,
the forms are written out in IPA, with each IPA symbol therefore standing as a cover term
of the appropriate set of features.

(7)   Derivations for "snowed", "missed" and "lifted":

UR	sno + d	mɪs + d	lɪft + d
R1) i-epenthesis	—-	——	lɪft i d
R2) voicing assimilation	—-	mɪs t	——
SR	snod	mist	lɪftɪd

Note that the underlying representation for the affix is /d/ in every case. The different allomorphs are derived by rule application. Instances where a rule does not apply because its
required environment is not met are indicated with a dash.

   Note also that the order in which the rules apply matters, as shown in example (8). If
voicing assimilation applied before epenthesis broke up the cluster, assimilation would apply
to /lɪft/ as well as /mɪs/, resulting in the wrong surface form.

(8)   Incorrect derivation:

UR	sno + d	mɪs + d	lɪft + d
R2) voicing assimilation	—-	mɪs t	lɪft t
R1) i-epenthesis	—-	——	lɪft i t
SR	snod	mist	*lɪftɪt

Thus, knowledge of the phonological grammar must include not only the rules, but the order
in which they apply.

13.3.3 rule complexity

Certain *abbreviatory conventions* are accepted as ways to make rules simpler, or to combine
two similar rules. Because they occur so often, the natural class of consonants ([+consonan-
tal]) is often abbreviated C, and the natural class of vowels ([−consonantal, +syllabic]) is
often abbreviated V, but it should be kept in mind that these are just abbreviations and don't
have any status beyond the feature values they stand for. Parentheses can be used for optional
elements, as in example (9a). A subscript "$_0$", as in example (9b), means "zero or more." Braces
indicate "either/or," as in example (9c).

(9)   Abbreviatory conventions:

   a. V –> [+round] / V (C) ____
                 [+round]
      A vowel becomes round if the preceding vowel is round, whether or not a con-
      sonant intervenes

b. V –> [+round] /   V   C₀ ___

    $\qquad\qquad$ [+round]

A vowel becomes round if the preceding vowel is round, regardless of the number of intervening consonants.

c. C –> Ø / C ___ $\left\{ \begin{matrix} C \\ \# \end{matrix} \right\}$

Delete a consonant if it follows another consonant and precedes either another consonant or the end of a word. (This rule, for example, would delete the [k] in both "desk" and "desktop.")

SPE used other conventions as well, to express more complex logical relations, but these should do to get on with.

When specifying the class of sounds that undergoes the change, as well as natural classes of sounds that are required in the environment, one should use the minimum number of features required to specify all and only the sounds in the class. When indicating the featural change, specify only the features that change. Thus "[−sonorant] –> [−voice]" is sufficient for indicating "obstruents become voiceless." One does not need to add [−sonorant, +consonantal], because all obstruents are consonantal: the added feature adds no new information. Don't use two features to specify a class when one will do. Nor is it necessary to say [−sonorant, +voice] –> [−sonorant, −voice]." There is no need to specify features on both sides of the arrow if they don't change ([−sonorant] –> [−sonorant]). Specify the targeted class on the left and the change on the right. It is also not necessary to specify that only voiced sonorants become voiceless. Adding the extra [voice] feature on the left ([−sonorant, +voice] instead of just [−sonorant]) makes the rule more complicated and has no effect on the output, which is that all obstruents, regardless of their initial specification, end up voiceless after the rule has applied.

In the SPE approach, it was argued that simpler rules were more likely to occur cross-linguistically. Rule complexity was computed by feature counting: the more features necessary to write the rule, the more complex the rule, and therefore the less likely the rule was predicted to be. Consider the two rules in examples (10a) and (10b).

(10)   Rule complexity:

    a. [−sonorant, −continuant] –> [−voice] / ___ #
    b. [−sonorant, −continuant, coronal] –> [−voice] / ___ #

Rule (10a) states that "stops become voiceless in word-final position." Rule (10b) states that coronal stops (but not labial or velar stops) become voiceless in word final position. The more specific rule takes one extra feature to write, and is thus judged more complex. It is therefore predicted to be less likely, which is in fact the case. Feature-counting turns out, however, to be an imperfect rubric for predicting whether or not a rule is likely to occur.

One problem with SPE formalism is that it turned out to be very easy to write rules that were highly unlikely to occur. The two rules in example (11) are equally simple by the feature-counting metric. However, (11a) is very common, and (11b) is unattested.

(11)   Rule complexity:

    a. [−sonorant] –> [−voice] / ___ [−voice]
    b. [−sonorant] –> [+voice] / ___ [+continuant]

Where (11a) is a common rule of assimilation, (11b) is a random collection of features. Yet there is nothing in the formalism that disallows or disfavours rules such as (11b).

SPE does have a special convention for representing rules of assimilation: *alpha notation*. In this notation, Greek letters (α, β, γ) stand for variables whose possible values are + and −.

As with algebraic variables, every instance of the variable must be filled in with the same value.

The rule of Russian voicing assimilation serves as a good example: voiced obstruents become voiceless before a voiceless obstruent, and voiceless obstruents become voiced before a voiced obstruent. Without alpha-notation, this assimilation takes two rules to write, as in example (12).

(12) Russian voicing assimilation, without alpha-notation:

    a. [−voice] −> [+voice] / ___ [−sonorant, +voice]
    b. [+voice, −sonorant] −> [−voice] / _____ [−voice]

But writing two rules is surely missing a generalization. There is one process here, not two: obstruents must *agree* in voicing. Alpha notation allows the concept of agreement to be expressed directly, by the use of the same variable on both sides of the environment slash, as in example (13).

(13) Russian voicing assimilation, with alpha-notation:

    [−sonorant] −> [α voice] / ___ [−sonorant, α voice]

If the variable α is filled in with "−", then the rule states that an obstruent becomes voiceless before a voiceless obstruent. If the variable α is filled in with "+", then the rule states that an obstruent becomes voiced before a voiced obstruent. Thus the single rule in (13) more succinctly makes the same statement as the two rules in (12): obstruents must match in voicing.

While alpha-notation does provide a simpler way to represent some rules of assimilation, it does not solve the problem of being able to write impossible rules, such as the rule in example (14).

(14) Obstruent voicing must match the value for [+/− back]:

    [−sonorant] −> [α voice] / _____ [−sonorant, α back]

Again, rule (14) is equal in simplicity to rule (13), but rule (13) is common and rule (14) is unattested. On this account, SPE formalism, while more precise and constrained than English prose, is still too powerful. As a theory of phonology, it still predicts too many processes that do not occur.

On the other hand, for other cases SPE formalism is not powerful enough. The formalism does not deal well with any assimilation that involves more than one feature, particularly the common and straightforward process of place assimilation. Recall the process of nasal place assimilation in Catalan, repeated here in (15).

(15) Nasal place assimilation in Catalan:

só[n] amics	they are friends
só[m] pocs	they are few
só[ɱ] feliços	they are happy
só[n̪] [d̪]os	they are two
só[n] rics	they are rich
só[ɲ] [lʲ]iures	they are free
só[ŋ] grans	they are big

The nasal comes to share all of the place features of the following consonant: [labial], [coronal], [dorsal], [anterior], and [distributed]. How can this rule be written in SPE? We would certainly want to use alpha-notation to indicate agreement, yet if place features are unary, they do not have + and − values for alpha variables to represent. Thus we would be forced to write three different rules, as in example (16), or revert to binary place features, as in example (17).

(16)   Catalan nasal assimilation using alpha notation and unary place features:

a.   [+nasal] –> $\begin{pmatrix} \text{labial} \\ \alpha \text{ distributed} \end{pmatrix}$ /____ $\begin{pmatrix} \text{labial} \\ \alpha \text{ distributed} \end{pmatrix}$

b.   [+nasal] –>   [dorsal]   /____   [dorsal]

c.   [+nasal] –> $\begin{pmatrix} \text{coronal} \\ \beta \text{ anterior} \\ \delta \text{ distributed} \end{pmatrix}$ /____ $\begin{pmatrix} \text{coronal} \\ \beta \text{ anterior} \\ \delta \text{ distributed} \end{pmatrix}$

(17)   Catalan nasal assimilation using alpha notation and binary features:

[+nasal] → $\begin{pmatrix} \alpha \text{ coronal} \\ \beta \text{ anterior} \\ \gamma \text{ back} \\ \delta \text{ distributed} \\ \varepsilon \text{ high} \end{pmatrix}$ /____ $\begin{pmatrix} \alpha \text{ coronal} \\ \beta \text{ anterior} \\ \gamma \text{ back} \\ \delta \text{ distributed} \\ \varepsilon \text{ high} \end{pmatrix}$

Neither solution is very attractive. Phonological formalism should be able to represent in straightforward fashion a rule that is so ubiquitous and that has such a clear phonetic motivation. We should not have to resort to three separate rules or half the Greek alphabet to say "nasals assimilate in place of articulation to a following stop." The situation with complete assimilations, which are also fairly common, would be even worse: every feature would have to be listed in the rule.

There are a number of positive aspects to SPE formalism. It is very precise: rules can be stated in an unambiguous fashion. It is also very general: this approach has been successfully used to describe a wide variety of languages. Finally, because it uses carefully-defined distinctive features, this formalism is more constrained than English prose. Thus SPE formalism was, and continues to be, a very useful descriptive tool. Between 1968 and (about) 1985, many phonological descriptions were written using this formalism, and phonologists today continue to use SPE formalism as a means of succinctly stating generalizations about the alternations that occur in their data. Proficiency with this formalism is an important tool for any phonologist.

However, it soon became clear that as a theory of possible phonological alternations, SPE formalism is inadequate. It is too powerful because it predicts that many alternations that are in fact unattested ought to be common. And some alternations that do commonly occur are so complicated in this formalism that they are predicted to be impossible. Thus, beginning in the 1980s, new ways of writing rules began to be developed. We turn to these formalisms in the next section.

13.4 autosegmental representations and Feature Geometry

13.4.1 autosegmental representations for tone

Possibilities for rethinking the SPE "feature bundle" approach to rule writing came from the study of tone languages. Three linguists who pioneered the new approach were Nancy Woo (MIT Ph.D. 1969), William Leben (MIT Ph.D. 1973), and John Goldsmith (MIT Ph.D. 1976), all students of Chomsky and Halle. Woo can be credited with arguing for the basic elements of the new approach in her analysis of Mandarin tone; the approach was further developed, generalized, and popularized by Leben and by Goldsmith.

The basic insight of the new approach was that although tone is realized as a pitch contrast on vowels (high pitch vs. low, or falling vs. rising), tone features are independent of the segments that realize them: tones can easily jump from one vowel or syllable to the next, they can stay behind when a vowel is deleted, they can crowd onto one vowel or spread out over many. That is, tones are autonomous from segments: they behave like "auto-segments," and this approach is termed *autosegmental phonology*. Some examples from African languages illustrate the point.

Leben cites the following data from Etsako, a language of Nigeria. Recall that an acute accent indicates a high tone [á], a grave accent indicates a low tone [à], and a hacek indicates a rising tone [ǎ].

(18) Tone stability in Etsako:

/ówà # ówà/ –> [ówǒwà]   every house (*lit.* house – house)
/ídù # ídù/ –> [ídwǐdù]   every lion (*lit.* lion – lion)

The strategy for dealing with two vowels in a row should be familiar: in a sequence of two vowels, the first deletes (if it is a non-high vowel) or becomes a glide (if it is a high vowel). The interesting part is what happens to the tone after the vowel is gone. If the original tone sequence was [low-high], the remaining vowel is realized with a rising tone. Consider how we would have to derive [ówǒwà] in an SPE feature-bundle approach, in which the features of tone are [+/− hightone], [+/− lowtone], and [+/− risingtone], and are specified in the feature bundle like any other vowel feature, such as [+/− high], [+/− low] or [+/− back]. The vowel deletion rule is straightforward, as in rule (19):

(19) Vowel deletion:

V –> Ø / ___ V

How then are we to deal with the tonal alternation? Deletion rules target whole segments: if the vowel is deleted, it takes all of its features with it. In a feature-bundle notation we do not have a way of saying "delete all the features of a segment except one." So we have to do the tonal change first, as in rule (20):

(20) Tone assimilation:

[+hightone] –> [−hightone, +risingtone] / [+lowtone] ___

First, the second vowel is changed from High to Rising by rule (20). Then the triggering vowel is deleted by rule (19), deriving the correct output. The derivation is given in example (21):

(21) Derivation of "every house"

UR   ówà – ówà
tone assimilation   ówà – ǒwà
vowel deletion   ów – ǒwà
SR   ówǒwà

This gets the right output, but there are at least two problems here. First, it seems evident that the tone change occurs *because* the vowel is deleted. Making the tone change first loses this connection: we get the effect before the cause.

Second, and more important, if [hightone], [lowtone] and [risingtone] are separate features, it is unclear why High would change to Rising after Low. It would be similar to saying that a vowel that is [−high] becomes [+back] before another vowel that is [−ATR]: just a list of three unrelated features. But Woo's insight was that Low, High, and Rising are not unrelated: A Rising tone is nothing more than a sequence of Low followed by High. If "rising tone" is simply a sequence of Low-High crowded onto one vowel, then the change makes perfect sense. Further, Woo and Leben went on to argue that [hightone] and [lowtone] should be pulled out of the feature bundle and represented as *autosegments*: separate features that are linked to the vowel, but not really part of the vowel. The features are represented by capital H for [hightone] and capital L for [lowtone]: note that the autosegments are considered to be unary. The linking is shown by the convention of an *association line*, as in example (22).

(22)   Sequence of [à ó] represented with tonal autosegments:

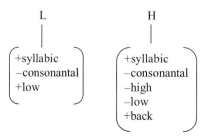

For convenience, the bundle of non-tone vocalic features can be represented by V. Because the tone is autonomous from the segment, when the vowel is deleted, the tone stays behind. The untethered *floating* tone then reassociates to the vowel to its right. The autosegmental derivation is shown in example (23). Reassociation is indicated with a dotted line.

(23)   /à ó/ becomes [ǒ]:

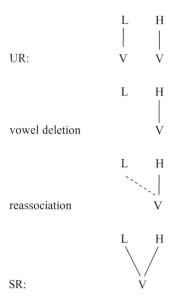

The graphical representation takes up a little more room on the page, but the introduction of tones as autosegments solves the two problems with rule (20). First, reassociation is shown to result from deletion: the vowel deletes, the tone is left floating, and it needs to "dock" onto another vowel to be realized. Second, the Rising tone is shown to result from the combination of Low followed by High on the original vowel sequence. The same tones are present, but they are realized on one vowel instead of two.

Example (23) thus illustrates a many-to-one association: two tones, one vowel. One-to-many associations also occur, in which a single tone can spread out over more than one vowel. Such *tone spreading* neatly accounts for long-distance tone assimilations, such as are found in Shona (data repeated from Chapter 11, example 27):

(24)   Tone spreading in Shona:

téng	buy	ereng	read
ku-téng-á	to buy	ku-ereng-a	to read
ku-téng-és-á	to sell	ku-ereng-es-a	to make read
ku-téng-és-ér-á	to sell to	ku-ereng-es-er-a	to make read to
ku-téng-és-ér-án-á	to sell to each other	ku-ereng-es-er-an-a	to make read to each other

Shona has only a two-way contrast is tone. Here we will assume that high tones are specified as H, and that non-high tones are unmarked (both orthographically and featurally). As the data in example (24) show, verbs in Shona can be either High-toned or not, and suffixes alternate based on the tone of the verb. All the suffixes in a long string come to agree with the underlying tone of the verb.

One could represent this long-distance assimilation with an SPE rule that changed one vowel at a time, and was repeated over and over until the end of the word was reached (*iterative* application). However, autosegmental formalism allows a more straightforward representation, by using tone spreading. The high tone begins by being associated only to the verb, but then spreads rightward, ending up associated to every vowel in the word, as shown in example (25).

(25)   Derivation of "to sell to each other" in autosegmental formalism:

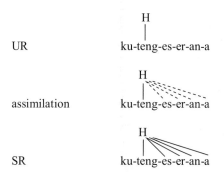

There is good independent reason to believe that sequences of high-toned syllables should be represented with one-to-many linking, as in (25). One piece of evidence comes from a tonal alternation that occurs in many Bantu languages, including Shona. It is known as Meeussen's Rule, after Achilles Meeussen, the Belgian linguist who first described the alternation to European linguists.

(26)   Meeussen's Rule in Shona:

a. mbwá   dog   né-mbwa   with a dog
    hóvé   fish   né-hove   with a fish
    mbúndúdzí   army worms   sé-mbundudzi   like army worms
    hákáta   diviner's bones sé-hakata   like diviner's bones

b. bénzíbvunzá   inquisitive fool   sé-benzibvunzá   like an inquisitive fool
    badzá   hoe   né-badzá   with a hoe

As shown in example (26a), a high-toned noun loses its tone when it is preceded by certain high-toned affixes, including "with" and "like." Crucially, if the noun has a sequence of high-toned syllables, as in the word for "army worms," *all* the high tones in the sequence are deleted. This applies, however, only when the sequence of high tones is not interrupted by a low-toned syllable. Only the first two tones are deleted in the word for "inquisitive fool," and there is no tone change in the word for "hoe." These patterns can be simply explained if a sequence of high-toned syllables within a morpheme is represented with a single autosegment linked to multiple vowels, as shown in rule (27) and example (28).

(27)   Meeussen's Rule: a high tone is deleted when preceded by a high-toned affix:

H –> Ø / H + ___

(28)   Meeussen's Rule: autosegmental derivations:

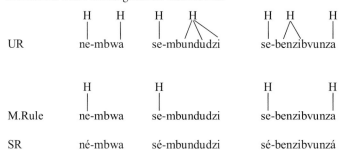

As example (28) shows, exactly the correct high tones are deleted when multiple linking across a sequence of syllables within a morpheme is assumed. Multiple linking is always assumed when the sequence of tone-bearing syllables is uninterrupted. Thus words like the Shona word for "fish" are always represented as in example (29a) rather than example (29b).

(29)   Adjacent identical elements are prohibited:

Multiple linking can be enforced by a principle that has come to be known as the *Obligatory Contour Principle (OCP)*: "Adjacent identical elements are prohibited." The representation in (29b) violates the OCP by having identical H tones linked to adjacent syllables. The representation in (29a) does not violate the OCP because there is only a single H. Meeusen's Rule itself can be seen as a response to an OCP violation: an illicit sequence is created when the high-toned affix is added, and the violation is repaired by the deletion of one of the tones.

A final piece of evidence for the autonomy of tone features comes from *tonal morphemes*: cases where meaning is altered by a tone change without any accompanying segmental change. In these cases, the morpheme is argued to consist of just a tonal autosegment without any associated vowel. In the West African language Igbo, for example, "jaw" is [àgbà] and "monkey" is [ènʷè] (all low tones), but "jaw of a monkey" is [àgbá ènwè], with raising of the second syllable from low tone to high. In autosegmental formalism, the morpheme meaning "of" is represented by an H tone with no underlying segmental content. In the course of the derivation, the tone is associated to the final vowel of the first noun, as shown in example (30).

(30)   A tonal morpheme in Igbo:

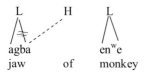

agba   en ʷe
jaw   of   monkey

The original tonal specification is "delinked" from the [a], shown by a cross-hatch through the association line.

13.4.2 autosegmental representations for other features

Once autosegmental representations for tone features were accepted, the question quickly arose: "Do any other features exhibit similar autonomous behavior?" The answer is yes. In fact, *most* other features exhibit many-to-one association, one-to-many long-distance spreading, stability, and OCP effects. (Single-feature morphemes are rarer outside of the tone domain.)

In example (23), we saw that two tones could be associated to a single vowel, creating a Rising contour from a sequence of L H specifications. Autosegmental contours can be created with other features as well, accounting for other types of segments where feature values change part-way through, such as pre-nasalized stops, diphthongs, and affricates. Just as a Rising tone can be represented as a sequence of H and L associated to a single vowel, an affricate can be represented as a sequence of [−continuant] and [+continuant] associated to a single consonant (example 31).

(31)   Contour segments:

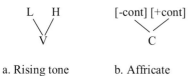

a. Rising tone   b. Affricate

Using autosegmental notation allows us to represent an affricate as having a sequence of continuant values, in keeping with its actual phonetic realization. It also allows us to do away with the feature [delayed release], making phonological theory that much simpler. (One issue that remains, however, is that while there are both Rising and Falling tones (LH and HL), there are no "backwards affricates" that consist of a fricative followed by a stop. No completely satisfactory explanation for this gap has been found, and other theories of the features of affricates have been proposed as well.)

While many-to-one association provides a useful way of formalizing contour segments, one-to-many association proves useful for formalizing assimilation, especially harmony. The first application of autosegmental representation to non-tonal phonology was Goldsmith's analysis of vowel and consonant harmony. In harmony systems, a feature that starts out associated with one segment (usually in a root) comes to be associated with other syllables in the word. In Turkish, for example, all suffix vowels agree in backness with the root vowel.

This harmony can be represented in terms of autosegmental spreading of the feature [+/−back], as shown in (32) and derivation (33). (As was seen in Chapter 11, high vowels also agree with the root vowel in rounding, but for simplicity only backness harmony is shown in the derivation.)

(32)   Turkish vowel harmony:

Nom. sg.	Nom. pl.	Genitive pl.	Gloss
dɑl	dɑl-lɑr	dɑl-lɑr-ɯn	branch
kɯz	kɯz-lɑr	kɯz-lɑr-ɯn	girl
jel	jel-ler	jel-ler-in	wind
diʃ	diʃ-ler	diʃ-ler-in	tooth

(33)   Turkish vowel harmony: autosegmental representation:

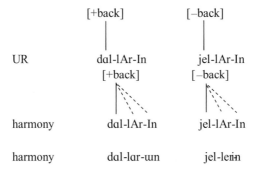

The capital letters A and I in (33) stand for suffix vowels that are not specified for backness or roundness in underlying representation: A = [−high] and I = [+high]. Their values for back and round are determined by the root. Spreading of the feature [back] in example (33) is parallel to the spreading of the H tone in example (25).

Other features exhibit long-distance spreading as well. There is, for example, spreading of the feature [nasal] to all sonorants in Sundanese (examples 34, 35), and spreading of the feature [-anterior] to all coronal sibilants in Chumash (examples 36, 37).

(34)   Nasal spreading in Sundanese:

mĩãk	to stand aside
ɲãĩãn	to wet
mãhãl	to be expensive
ɲãhõ	to know

(35)   Autosegmental spreading of [nasal]:

(36)   Anterior harmony in Chumash:

    s-ixut   it burns
    s-aqunimak   he hides
    ʃ-ilakʃ   it is soft
    ʃ-kuti-waʃ   he saw

Recall from Chapter 11 that in Chumash, all coronal sibilants agree with the rightmost sibilant in the feature [+/− anterior]. This is formalized in (37) by spreading of the feature [anterior], with delinking of the underlying specification.

(37)   Autosegmental spreading of [+/− anterior]:

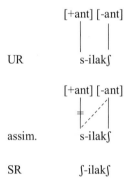

        UR   s-ilakʃ

        assim.   s-ilakʃ

        SR   ʃ-ilakʃ

A system such as Chumash, where two coronal sibilants can "see" each other despite multiple vowels and other consonants intervening, is especially difficult to formalize in linear SPE notation.

   A good case for feature stability (that is, a feature being left behind when the rest of the segment deletes) is found for the feature [nasal]. In French, word-final nasal consonants are deleted, but the nasalization remains behind, and is realized on the preceding vowel (example 38). Other cases of coalescence, where a segment is deleted but leaves one or more of its features to be realized on a neighboring segment, can be analyzed the same way.

(38)   Nasal stability in French:

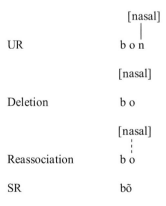

        UR   b o n

        Deletion   b o

        Reassociation   b o

        SR   bõ

A variety of features exhibit OCP effects as well. In general, processes of dissimilation can be seen as taking place to repair an OCP violation: if there are two adjacent identical elements, one must change. Recall the Latin -al/-ar dissimilation. The suffix [-al] occurs in most words, but [-ar] is used when the root contains another [l]. Thus the language has [nav-al-is] and [tot-al-is], but [sol-ar-is] and [lun-ar-is]. This can be analyzed as delinking of the feature [lateral] from the suffix when there is another [lateral] specification in the root. The derivation is shown in example (39).

(39)   Latin dissimilation as an OCP effect:

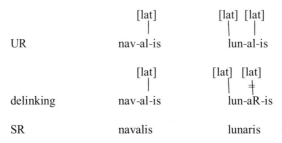

	[lat]	[lat] [lat]
UR	nav-al-is	lun-al-is
	[lat]	[lat] [lat]
delinking	nav-al-is	lun-aR-is
SR	navalis	lunaris

In autosegmental representations, it is assumed that if a feature is delinked, it will be deleted unless another rule explicitly re-links it to another segment. After the feature [lateral] is delinked, feature-filling default rules will cause the [coronal, +consonantal, +sonorant, +continuant] segment (indicated as R) to be realized as [r].

Once we allow autosegmental spreading for long-distance assimilation, there is no reason not to use it for local assimilation as well. Korean local nasal assimilation (40, 41) is represented in the same way as Sundanese long-distance nasal assimilation.

(40)   Local nasal assimilation in Korean:

[pap]	*rice*	[pam mekta]	*eat rice*
[ot]	*clothes*	[on man]	*only clothes*
[jak]	*medicine*	[jaŋ mekta]	*take medicine*

(41)   Nasal assimilation in Korean as autosegmental spreading:

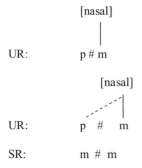

	[nasal]
UR:	p # m
	[nasal]
UR:	p # m
SR:	m # m

Autosegmental formalism has an advantage over SPE formalism in that the most common types of phonological alternation – assimilation and dissimilation – are represented very simply, as the addition or deletion of an association line. (If lenition and fortition are considered as assimilation of [+/− continuant], a reasonable analysis, then these processes are covered as well.) Conceptualizing assimilation as feature sharing or spreading rather than feature copying is also in line with the phonetic facts: a single vocal tract state is extended over more than one segment. It is possible to represent random feature switches, such as [+high] –> [+back] / __ [+ATR], by delinking one feature and then inserting another. However, such a multi-step process is more complicated to formalize, thereby correctly predicting it should be rarer. We can also get rid of the alpha-notation device. It is no longer needed if agreement is expressed in terms of multiply-linked features.

If assimilation, dissimilation, lenition, and fortition are all formalized in terms of spreading and/or delinking, then we must assume that any feature that is subject to any of these processes is autosegmental. That is, there is almost nothing left of the feature bundle: almost all features are autosegmental. That leaves us with a representation something like that in (42): a "wagon wheel" or "bottle-brush" representation. An X represents the segment, and all of the features are independently linked to it. A string of X's, each with its associated halo of features, makes up a morpheme. The Xs make up the *timing tier*: they keep track of how many segments are in the word. Features may then be associated with one or more segments, as they are spread or realigned by the autosegmental rules.

(42)   A wagon-wheel model of [s]:

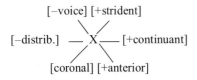

[−voice] [+strident]

[−distrib.] — X — [+continuant]

[coronal] [+anterior]

Thus we have seen arguments for the superiority of autosegmental representation over SPE notation. The new notation more simply describes alternations that are common, like assimilation, while making more random changes harder to represent. It solves a number of other problems such as the representation of affricates, feature stability, and aspects of harmony systems. A further development is necessary, however, to account for feature dependencies and for groups of features that assimilate together.

13.4.3 Feature Geometry

Feature Geometry imposes more organization on the autosegmental representation of features than does the "wagon-wheel" model. Instead of each feature necessarily connecting directly to the timing tier, features are grouped together based on their phonological behavior. While consensus has not been reached on the exact structure, one commonly-used model is shown in (43). No individual sound would have all of these features, but the model shows where any given feature would be placed.

(43)   One model of Feature Geometry:

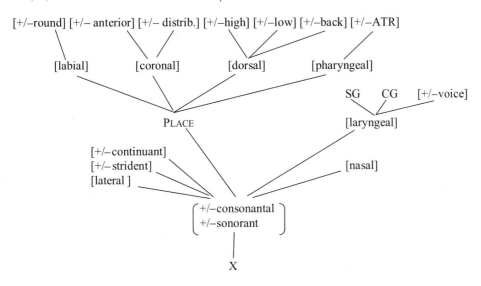

[+/−round] [+/− anterior] [+/− distrib.] [+/−high] [+/−low] [+/−back] [+/−ATR]

[labial]   [coronal]   [dorsal]   [pharyngeal]

SG   CG   [+/−voice]

PLACE   [laryngeal]

[+/−continuant]
[+/−strident]
[lateral]   [nasal]

⎛ +/−consonantal ⎞
⎝ +/−sonorant ⎠

X

Most of the features represented in (43) are the same as those that were defined in Chapter 12. Binary features are still binary; unary features are still unary; all features keep the same definitions. What has changed is: (1) certain features are shown to be in a dependency relationship; (2) the class node PLACE has been added; and (3) certain features are no longer needed.

Feature dependencies were noted earlier: here they are indicated graphically. The feature [round] is defined as "having pursed lips." Therefore, [round] is dependent on [labial]: by definition, it can be present only in sounds that use the labial articulator. The features [anterior] and [distributed] refer to the position of the tongue tip and blade, so they depend on the presence of [coronal]; [high], [low], and [back] refer to the tongue body and thus depend on [dorsal]; and [ATR] depends on [pharyngeal]. The features [SG], [CG], and [voice] are realized with the laryngeal articulator.

The features [continuant], [strident], [lateral], and [nasal] cross-classify across different places of articulation, and thus are not shown as being dependent on any particular articulator: stops and fricatives contrast, and nasals are found, at all different places of articulation. There is a fairly good case for [lateral] and [strident] to be bound to the coronal articulator instead, as these features are most often contrastive only for the coronal sounds. A few languages have been found to have dorsal laterals, however, and [strident] is occasionally needed to distinguish certain non-coronal fricatives, such as [f] and [ɸ].

In addition to each of these features, a new *class node*, PLACE, has been added. The PLACE node groups together the labial, coronal, dorsal, and pharyngeal articulators. As will be shown below, addition of PLACE allows the set of place features – all the daughters of this node – to be targeted as a group.

Finally, only two features, [consonantal] and [sonorant] are left inside the bracketed "feature bundle." These two features constitute the *ROOT* node. All other features depend on them. These two features are represented as the root of all the others for two reasons. First, all languages contrast sonorants vs. obstruents and consonants vs. non-consonants: there is no sound for which these features are not defined. Second, these are the two features that have *not* been shown to exhibit autosegmental behavior – they do not assimilate or dissimilate independently, and never exhibit long-distance behavior or stability when other features of the segment are deleted.

Two features that were listed in Chapter 12 are not listed at all in (43). The feature [delayed release] is absent because it is no longer needed: in autosegmental phonology, affricates can be represented by multiple linking of the feature [continuant]. The other missing feature is [syllabic]. The absence of [syllabic] means that vowels and glides are not represented with contrasting feature sets: [j] has the same features as [i], while [w] has the same features as [u]. Vowels and glides are distinguished, instead, by how they fit into the larger geometry of syllable structure. Syllable structure will be discussed in Chapter 15. For the time being, a feature [+/− syllabic] could be inserted into the root node if necessary. Also absent are the tonal features H and L. Their place in the geometry is discussed in Chapter 17.

13.2   Note that (43) should be used as a guide for where features are to be attached when they are needed. It is not the case that all features will be present for all sounds. In general, the features that are needed to define a segment or a natural class in autosegmental notation are the same ones that were needed in SPE notation. The only difference is that "daughter" features must be chaperoned: they are only allowed into the representation if their mothers are present as well. (The analogy could just as easily have been to sons and fathers, but reference to "mother" and "daughter" relationships to describe hierarchical dependencies is traditional in Generative Grammar.)

Autosegmental representations of "pen" and "sad" are shown in diagrams (44) and (45). With the exception of ROOT node features, which are assumed to be always present, only contrastive features (and their mothers, when needed) are indicated. So, for example, in "pen", only the [p] has a Laryngeal node with a specified [−voice] feature, since voicing is only contrastive for obstruents.

(44)   Autosegmental representation of the UR for "pen":

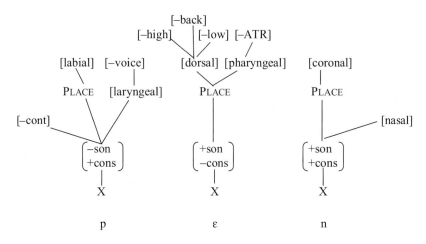

(45)   Autosegmental representation of the UR for "sad":

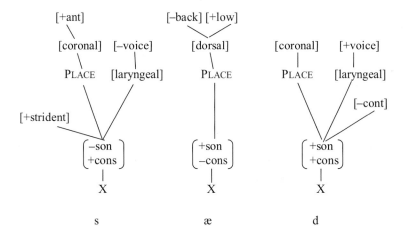

The extra structure provided by Feature Geometry gives us the ability to refer in a simple fashion to a group of features. Any node in the geometry can be targeted by autosegmental rules of spreading and delinking. The change is that when a mother is targeted, all her daughters come along for the ride. Thus, single-feature spreading, such as for nasal assimilation, works exactly the same way as was previously described (examples 33, 35, 37). In addition, however, a rule can target the set of daughter features by spreading or delinking the mother node instead. Four examples illustrate the point: Lateral assimilation in Catalan, nasal assimilation in Catalan, complete assimilation in Arabic, and debuccalization in Slave. In each case the data is given, followed by (b) the crucial generalization in English prose; (c) SPE notation; and (d) the feature-geometrical representation.

(46)   Lateral assimilation in Catalan:
a.   Data

e[l p]a	the bread
e[l f]oc	the fire
e[l̪ d̪]ia	the day
e[ɭ r]ic	the rich
e[ɭ r]ic	the brother

b.   English prose
The lateral consonant becomes dental before a dental, retroflex before a retroflex, and palatal before a palatal.
c.   SPE notation

[+lateral] –> [α distributed, β anterior] / ___ [coronal, α distributed, β anterior]

d.   Feature Geometry

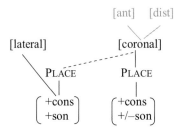

In feature-geometrical notation, the assimilation is shown as spreading of the [coronal] node. The two daughters of [coronal], [anterior] and [distributed], are shown as grayed out because they do not need to be specified as part of the rule. The rule spreads [coronal], and any daughters of [coronal] will automatically be included.

(47)   Nasal assimilation in Catalan:
a.   Data: see example (15) above.
b.   English prose
A nasal assimilates in place of articulation to a following consonant.
c.   SPE notation (repeated from example (17) above).

$$[+\text{nasal}] \longrightarrow \begin{pmatrix} \alpha \text{ coronal} \\ \beta \text{ anterior} \\ \gamma \text{ back} \\ \delta \text{ distributed} \\ \varepsilon \text{ high} \end{pmatrix} \;/\; \underline{\qquad} \begin{pmatrix} \alpha \text{ coronal} \\ \beta \text{ anterior} \\ \gamma \text{ back} \\ \delta \text{ distributed} \\ \varepsilon \text{ high} \end{pmatrix}$$

d.   Feature Geometry

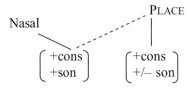

The rule in example (47d) states simply that the nasal comes to share any and all of the place features of a following consonant. There is no need to state each feature separately, as in (47c): the theory of Feature Geometry tells us what the place features are.

Spreading of the place node results in assimilation; delinking of the place node results in debuccalization, as shown in example (48).

(48)   Debuccalization in Slave:
    a. Data

possessed	non-possessed	
ts'ad-é	ts'ah	hat
mil-é	mih	net
dzéeg-é	dzéeh	gum
tédh-é	téh	cane

    b. English prose
       Word-final consonants become [h].

    c. SPE notation

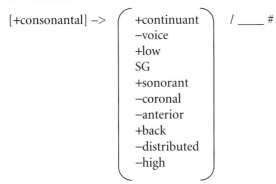

$$[+\text{consonantal}] \rightarrow \left(\begin{array}{l} +\text{continuant} \\ -\text{voice} \\ +\text{low} \\ \text{SG} \\ +\text{sonorant} \\ -\text{coronal} \\ -\text{anterior} \\ +\text{back} \\ -\text{distributed} \\ -\text{high} \end{array}\right) \quad / \underline{\quad} \#$$

    d. Feature Geometry

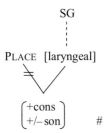

Rules of debuccalization are particularly hard to write in SPE. Every single feature of any possible consonant must be changed into features appropriate for [h]. In Feature Geometry, turning a consonant into [h] or glottal stop is recognized simply as a loss of all the place features: delinking of the PLACE node. All that is left is the laryngeal node, which receives a [SG] specification.

(49)   Complete assimilation in Arabic:
    a. Data

ʔaʃ-ʃams	the sun
ʔat-tidʒaːra	the commerce
ʔaθ-θaqaːfa	the culture
ʔad-diːn	the religion

ʔal-qamr	the moon
ʔal-badw	the Bedouin
ʔal-filfil	the pepper
ʔal-ħaʒ	the luck
ʔal-xardal	the mustard

b. English prose
   The lateral consonant assimilates completely to a following coronal consonant.
c. SPE notation

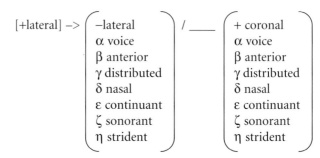

d. Feature Geometry

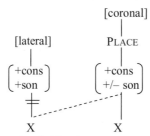

A similar situation holds of complete assimilation: in SPE, every feature must be listed separately. In Feature Geometry, every feature is encompassed by spreading of the ROOT node. A single root node shared between two X-slots (that is, two timing slots) is used to represent any long or doubled consonant or vowel, allowing us to get rid of the ad-hoc feature [+/− long] as well.

13.5 how have our hypotheses fared?

Parallel to Chapter 12, we began this chapter with hypotheses concerning the representation of possible alternations in the languages of the world. They are repeated below:

Hypothesis 4:
Every morpheme has a unique underlying representation, which is defined in terms of combinations of distinctive features.

Hypothesis 5:
Underlying representations are converted into contextually-varied surface representations by the operation of a set of feature-changing or feature-filling rules.

In general, this chapter has shown that rule-based derivational accounts based on hypotheses 4 and 5 have proven useful in describing alternations in the languages of the world. Formal rules and derivations provide a precise and concise language for stating phonological generalizations. Theories of how rules should be written have changed in the decades since SPE, however. Rule formalisms using autosegmental representation and Feature Geometry allow for a simpler, more constrained, more predictive theory of the types of alternations that can take place.

The introduction of Feature Geometry does not solve all of our phonological problems, however. To begin with, phonologists have not reached a consensus on what model of feature geometry is best. It is not always clear exactly where a feature should be attached ([lateral], for instance), nor is it clear that daughters will always behave as a group. A particular problem is spreading of [round] and [back] together, as in Turkish vowel harmony (example (25) in Section 11.3.2). These two features are not sisters, they do not share an active articulator, yet it is clear that they pattern together in phonology. Other unsolved issues include vowel and consonant interactions: sometimes vowels and consonants interact with each other (as in palatalization and vowel lowering), and in other cases they ignore each other (harmony systems). There is also the class of guttural consonants to be accounted for (see Section 12.2.5).

Other issues do not seem to be amenable to a feature-geometry analysis at all. No formalism we have examined so far seems to have a good way to deal with metathesis, for instance. But the biggest problem facing any rule-based analysis is the interaction of rules and constraints: what has been termed the "conspiracy" problem. It is to rule and constraint conspiracies, and the possible abandonment of hypothesis 5, that we turn in Chapter 14.

chapter summary

- In the theory of Generative Phonology as laid out in SPE (Chomsky and Halle, 1968), each morpheme has a unique underlying representation composed of bundles of distinctive features (hypothesis #4). Rules apply in a sequential derivation, adding and changing features as necessary to generate surface representations (hypothesis #5).
- According to theories of underspecification, predictable features are absent from underlying representations and are filled in by rule.
- In SPE notation, rules take the form A –> B / C __ D, where A, B, C, D are composed of features and a small set of special symbols. SPE notation is more precise and constrained than English prose, but it is both too powerful and not powerful enough: unattested rules can be simply written, while common rules like place assimilation are difficult and complicated to represent.
- Autosegmental notation, which began as a representation for tonal phenomena, represents features as autonomous units that are associated to segments, not as parts of a feature bundle that constitute the segment. Autosegmental notation has an advantage over SPE notation in that common processes of assimilation and dissimilation are represented as simple linking and delinking.
- Feature Geometry imposes a hierarchical organization on autosegmental features, such that groups of features that pattern together are represented as grouped under a single class node.

further reading

Have a crack at N. Chomsky and M. Halle, *The Sound Pattern of English* (New York: Harper and Row, 1968), to get a feel for its style and argumentation. See how many of the rules you can read.

For more information on underspecification in derivational phonology, try
D. Steriade, Underspecification and markedness, in *The Handbook of Phonological Theory* (John Goldsmith, ed., Oxford: Blackwell, 1996).

There is also a second edition of the book, composed of nearly entirely new chapters:

Goldsmith, J., Riggle, J. and Yu, A.C.L. (eds), 2011. *The Handbook of Phonological Theory*, Second Edition, Oxford: Wiley-Blackwell.

You might find other articles in the Handbooks interesting as well.

One of the first and clearest arguments for autosegmental representation of tone features is W. Leben, The representation of tone, in *Tone: A Linguistic Survey* (V. Fromkin, ed., New York: Academic Press, 1978).

Another classic text that provides a clear explication of the SPE model is *Generative Phonology* by Michael Kenstowicz and Charles Kisseberth (San Diego: Academic Press, 1979).

An overview of further arguments for Feature Geometry can be found in J. McCarthy, Feature geometry and dependency: A review. *Phonetica* 43 (1988): 84–108.

review exercises

1. What does a Generative Grammar "generate"?
2. What is the difference between competence and performance? Which one does Generative Grammar emphasize?
3. Define the following terms:

    derivation
    underspecification
    alpha notation
    iterative rule application
    tonal morpheme

4. Write out the meaning of each of these symbols:

    ->
    /
    #
    +
    Ø
    ( )
    { }

5. Write out these common phonological abbreviations:

    SPE
    UR
    SR
    OCP

further analysis and discussion

6. Write out the URs for the English words "node" and "cliff" assuming:
    a. Full specification using feature bundles (see example 1).
    b. Contrastive underspecification using feature bundles (see example 2).

c. Contrastive underspecification using Feature Geometry (see example 44).

For exercises 7–9, assume a language that has the inventory shown below.

p	t		k	i		u
b	d		g	e		o
m	n		ŋ	ɛ		ɔ
f	s	ʃ	x		a	
v	z	ʒ	ɣ			
	l	ɭ				
w		j				

7. Translate the following rules from SPE to English.
    a. [+syl, +high] –> [−voice] / [−voice, +cont] ____ [−voice, +cont]
    b. [dorsal, −cont, −son, +voice] –> [+cont] / [+syl, +back] ____ [+syl, +back]
    c. [−son, +cont] –> [−cont] / ____ #
    d. [+voice, −cont, −son] –> Ø / [Nasal] ____ #
    e. [+syl, +low] –> [−low, +round] / ____ C₀ [+syl, +high, −back]

8. Translate the following rules from English to SPE.
    f. Nasals delete preceding fricatives, l, and r.
    g. In a sequence of two (non-nasal) stops, the first becomes a fricative.
    h. Voiceless stops and fricatives become voiced between sonorants.
    i. [ɭ] becomes [l] preceding [l].
    j. Mid vowels agree with the vowel of the preceding syllable in ATR value.

9. Rewrite rules 7b, 8g, 8i, and 8j in autosegmental formalism.

10. Revisit some of the alternations discussed in previous chapters, and try representing them in both SPE and autosegmental formalisms. Recommended data sets include but are not limited to:
    a. Lenition in Florentine (Ch. 10, #5)
    b. Allophones of English /t/ (Ch. 10, #11)
    c. Igbo vowel harmony (Ch. 11, #s 10–15)
    d. Oowekyala rounding (Ch. 11, #20)
    e. Vowel lowering in Syrian (Ch. 11, #23)
    f. Voicing dissimilation in Chontal (Ch. 11, #30)
    g. Vowel deletion and nasal place assimilation in Tagalog (Ch. 11, #40). Two rules: show the necessary rule ordering.
    h. Deletion in Lardil (Ch. 11, #41). Three rules: show the necessary rule ordering.
    i. Yucatec Maya debuccalization (Ch. 11, Exercise 5h)
    j. Kinyarwanda nasal hardening (Ch. 11, Exercise 5k)
    k. English glottalization (Ch. 11, Exercise 5m)

11. In Twi, a language of Ghana, the prefix meaning "not" alternates depending on the initial consonant of the verb. This initial consonant also sometimes undergoes an alternation, as shown. (Data from J. Redden and N. Owusu. 1963. *Twi Basic Course*. U.S. Foreign Service Institute; supplemented with data courtesy of Alfred Opoku.)
    a. List the allomorphs of the negative prefix. Write the rule for the alternation in both SPE and autosegmental format.

(Continued)

b. List the verbs for which the initial consonant alternates and those for which it does not. Write the rule for the alternation in both SPE and autosegmental format.

me-pɛ	I like	me-m-pɛ	I do not like
me-ba	I come	me-m-ma	I do not come
me-fa	I take	me-m-fa	I do not take
me-te	I speak	me-n-te	I do not speak (a lg.)
me-dɔ	I love	me-n-nɔ	I do not love
me-nom	I drink	me-n-nom	I do not drink
mi-si	I wash	mi-n-si	I do not wash
me-ɲa	I receive	me-ɲ-ɲa	I do not receive
me-ҫɛ	I wear	me-ɲ-ҫɛ	I do not wear
me-ɟa	I leave	me-ɲ-ɲa	I do not leave
me-cɛ	I am late	me-ɲ-cɛ	I am not late
me-jɛ	I do	me-ɲ-jɛ	I do not do
me-ka	I say	me-ŋ-ka	I do not say
me-gu	I pour	me-ŋ-ŋu	I do not pour
mi-hu	I see	mi-ŋ-hu	I do not see

12. Another alternation in Twi affects prefix vowels. The vowel inventory of Twi consists of {i, u, e, o, ɛ, ɔ, a}.

a. Fill in + and − values in the feature chart below. Circle the values that would be represented in the UR according to contrastive underspecification (features that are not predictable). Write the rules that would be needed to fill in the predictable values.

	i	u	e	o	ɛ	ɔ	a
high							
back							
low							
round							
ATR							

b. Note the vowel alternations in the pronominal prefixes below, and, assuming these verbs and prefixes are representative, write the rules necessary to account for the alternations (two rules are needed). Write each rule in a) English prose, b) SPE formalism and c) autosegmental formalism.

	jɛ *do*	dɔ *love*	te *speak*	nom *drink*	hu *see*	si *wash*	ka *say*
I	me-jɛ	me-dɔ	me-te	me-nom	mi-hu	mi-si	me-ka
you (sg.)	wo-jɛ	wo-dɔ	wo-te	wo-nom	wu-hu	wu-si	wo-ka
he/she/it	ɔ-jɛ	ɔ-dɔ	ɔ-te	ɔ-nom	o-hu	o-si	ɔ-ka

	jɛ / do	dɔ / love	te / speak	nom / drink	hu / see	si / wash	ka / say
we	jɛ-jɛ	jɛ-dɔ	jɛ-te	jɛ-nom	je-hu j	e-si	jɛ-ka
you (pl.)	mo-jɛ	mo-dɔ	mo-te	mo-nom	mu-hu	mu-si	mo-ka
they	wɔ-jɛ	wɔ-dɔ	wɔ-te	wɔ-nom	wo-hu	wo-si	wɔ-ka

further research

14. Try writing some of the other rules in Exercises (7) and (8) in autosegmental formalism. What problems do you encounter?
15. Go to the library and browse through some descriptive grammars written in the first half of the twentieth century.
    a. Identify some of the phonological alternations described, and practice rewriting them in SPE and autosegmental formalism.
    b. Can you discover any examples of necessary rule ordering?
    c. What difficulties do you encounter in formalizing your rules? Do these difficulties suggest that revisions are needed to our formal representations, either of distinctive features or of rule application?

Go online Visit the book's companion website for additional resources relating to this chapter at: http://www.wiley.com/go/zsiga.

references

Etsako
Leben, W. 1978. The representation of tone, in *Tone: A Linguistic Survey* (V. Fromkin, ed.), New York: Academic Press.

Igbo
Williamson, K. 1986. The Igbo associative and specific constructions. In *The Phonological Representation of Suprasegmentals*. (J.M. Stewart *et al.*, eds.)

Meeussen's Rule in Shona
Odden, D. 1980. Associative tone in Shona. *Journal of Linguistic Research* 1/2: 37–51.

Sundanese
The Sundanese data is much cited in the literature, but originates with R.H. Robins, *Vowel Nasalization in Sundanese*, 1957.

14 Constraint-based Phonology

The standard phonological rule aims to encode grammatical generalizations in this format:

A –> B / C __ D

The rule scans potential inputs for structures CAD and performs the change on them that is explicitly spelled out in the rule: the unit denoted by A takes on property B. For this format to be worth pursuing, there must be an interesting theory which defines the class of possible predicates CAD (Structural Descriptions) and another theory with defines the class of possible operations A–> B (Structural Changes). If these theories are loose and uninformative, as indeed they have proved to be in reality, we must entertain one of two conclusions:

(i)   phonology itself simply doesn't have much content, is mostly 'periphery' rather than 'core', is just a technique for data-compression, with aspirations to depth subverted by the inevitable idiosyncrasies of history and the lexicon; or
(ii) the locus of explanatory action is elsewhere.

We suspect the latter.

Alan Prince and Paul Smolensky, Optimality Theory:
Constraint Interaction in Generative Grammar (1993/2004), p. 4

The Sounds of Language: An Introduction to Phonetics and Phonology, First Edition. Elizabeth C. Zsiga.
© 2013 Elizabeth C. Zsiga. Published 2013 by Blackwell Publishing Ltd.

Chapter outline

Prince and Smolensky level a serious charge against rule-based analyses such as those we have been developing in the previous chapters. Phonological rules, these authors claim, are just "a technique for data compression." Formal rules provide way to write things down in a kind of short-hand, but offer no interesting theory of what kinds of alternations are possible and what kinds aren't. Rule-based phonology, they claim, does not get us anywhere in answering the central linguistic question, "What is a possible language?" Our choices, they suggest, are to stop pretending that phonology has any interesting linguistic content (option 1), or to abandon rule-based formalisms and look for explanations elsewhere (option 2). In this chapter, we consider the basics of the theory that Prince and Smolensky propose in pursuing option 2. We begin, in Section 14.1, with a description of some of the problems that led phonologists to question rule-based formalism: duplication, blocking, and conspiracy. Section 14.2 lays out the basic tenets of Prince and Smolensky's alternative approach, Optimality Theory, a phonology based on constraint interaction rather than rule application. Section 14.3 provides some examples of how a generative phonology can operate without rules, and Section 14.4 concludes with some challenges and directions for future research.

14.1 constraints and rules in linguistic theory

It has long been recognized that constraints on possible representations are an important part of phonological knowledge. It was in 1962 that Morris Halle pointed out that speakers know that "blick" is a possible word of English while "bnick" is not, even though neither one is an actual vocabulary item, because English speakers know that "bnick" violates a phonotactic constraint specifying that words cannot begin with a sequence of stop+nasal. Phonotactic constraints are similar across languages, in that they always rule out more marked structures, such as complex syllable structures or difficult featural combinations (including front round vowels or voiced obstruents), while allowing simpler structures such as CV syllables, front unround vowels, and voiceless obstruents. On the other hand, constraints are not universally true of all surface structures in all languages: Greek allows words to begin in [pn], German allows front round vowels, and English allows voiced fricatives.

Thus, in rule-based Generative Grammar, constraints are considered to be language-specific statements, even though they often reflect universal tendencies. Language-specific *Morpheme Structure Constraints* (*MSCs*), such as *#bn in English, limit possible underlying representations, requiring lexical entries to conform to the phonotactic restrictions of the language.

In addition to describing possible and impossible underlying lexical entries, however, constraints often seem to play a role in ongoing derivations, bringing derived items into conformity with what the MSCs require. We have noted, for example, that in English and many other languages, nasal+stop sequences in monomorphemic words always agree in place of articulation: we have words such as "camp," "wind," and "thank," but not "canp" or "thamk." Speakers know that words like "thamk" are not good English, so we may posit the existence of an MSC that states: "nasals must agree in place of articulation with a following stop." We do not have any evidence from alternations that [kʰæmp] is derived from underlying /kænp/, so there is no reason to believe that a rule has applied. However, we *do* need a rule for other cases, such as alternation in the form of the prefix "in-": "inability" vs. "impossibility". It looks like the rule "nasals assimilate in place of articulation to a following stop" is taking place to bring the prefix-root sequence into conformity with a constraint that already holds at underlying representation for other words.

To take another example, we saw in Chapter 11 that Lardil has a morpheme structure constraint that allows only tongue-tip (apical) consonants in word-final position: Lardil has words like [kentapal] *dugong* and [kethar] *river*, but never *[kentapam] or *[kethak]. If a non-apical consonant becomes word-final due to vowel deletion, the violating consonant is deleted: /muŋkumuŋku/ –> [muŋkumuŋk] –> [muŋkumu]. The rule is applying to bring the word into conformity with the MSC.

Thus, in a rule-based grammar, it was often found that a generalization had to be stated twice: once to cover static generalizations that hold over URs, and again as part of a rule. The Lardil MSC states: only apical consonants can occur in word-final position. The Lardil rule states: non-apical consonants in word-final position are deleted. The problem of constraints and rules both saying the same thing in different form is known as the *Duplication Problem*. Because it seemed that the constraint was *causing* the rule to apply, phonologists began to suspect that the constraints were the more important aspect of phonological knowledge.

However, while we can analyze a rule as applying to "repair" a violation, we cannot necessarily predict what form the repair will take. Repairs might include changing a feature (English "impossible"), deleting an offending segment (Lardil [muŋkumu]), or inserting segments to change the environment, as in Japanese [besubaru]. Another option is that a rule that would create a violation might be blocked from applying in the first place. A famous example of blocking is Japanese compound voicing, known as "Lyman's Law" (after a European linguist) or "rendaku" in Japanese.

In native Japanese vocabulary there are words like [Φuta] *lid*, [Φuda] *sign*, and [buta] *pig*, but no words like [buda]. To account for this gap, we posit an MSC: a word may not contain two voiced obstruents. (This type of restriction is an OCP effect; see Chapter 13.)

Rendaku, however, creates voiced consonants: The rule states that when two words are put together into a compound, the first consonant of the second word becomes [+voice], as illustrated in example (1).

(1)   Japanese rendaku:

kami	paper	ori-gami	folded paper
ke	hair	eda-ge	split hair
ʃita	tongue	neko-dʒita	cat's tongue (aversion to hot food)
seme	torture	mizu-zeme	water torture

The interesting cases, however, are those where the voicing alternation does *not* happen: if the second word happens to have a voiced obstruent in it already, the first consonant stays voiceless, as shown in (2): /kita-kaze/ "north wind" does not become *[kita-gaze]. (Note that, as with many other voicing alternations, sonorants do not count, so words like [ori-gami] are fine.)

(2)   Rendaku does not apply:

kaze	wind	kita-kaze	*kita-gaze	north wind
ʃinogi	avoiding	taikutsu-ʃinogi	*taikutsu-dʒinogi	avoiding boredom (time-killer)

The analysis is that if the voicing rule applied to compounds like those in (2), it would create two voiced obstruents in the same word, and so violate the MSC. To prevent the violation, rule application is blocked. But how can a constraint that holds over underlying representations have the power to reach down and stop a rule in its tracks? As was noted in Chapter 13, rules in general are blind to the eventual results of their output: they simply scan for a certain environment, and apply when the conditions are met. For blocking to take place, a rule has to look ahead and know that the results of its application would be unfortunate, and therefore refrain from applying. Analysts uncomfortable with such "smart" derivations suggested that the rendaku rule went ahead and applied, but then another repair rule stepped in immediately to undo what the rendaku rule had done.

> **14.1**   This kind of sequence of rule application, where a rule applies and is then undone, is known as a Duke of York gambit, after the nursery rhyme: *The grand old Duke of York/ He had 10,000 men/ He marched them up to the top of the hill/ And he marched them down again.* Allowing Duke of York moves into a phonological derivation adds a level of abstraction that made many phonologists uncomfortable: how do we know that rules aren't being done and undone all over the place?

Blocking or repair are not the only options. Sometimes, as in Lardil, the rule creating the violation applies, and then rather than that rule being undone, another rule applies to repair the damage. Or sometimes, the violation is tolerated. Hindi, for example, has the usual MSC requiring place agreement between nasals and following stops. A rule of medial vowel deletion, however, can bring mismatched consonants together: /tsəməka/ –> [tsəmka], "to shine." The rule is not blocked, and the violation is not repaired. The [mk] sequence remains.

Looking across languages, it becomes clear that constraints and rules are interacting in interesting ways, but it does not seem possible to predict what the interaction would be in any particular language. Would there be blocking or not? Would there be repair? If so, what would the repair be? The duplication problem was acknowledged, but rules still were deemed to be necessary to specify what exactly would happen in a particular language.

One final problem for rule and constraint interactions is the problem of *conspiracies*. In a conspiracy, different rules seem to be working together to make sure that MSCs are obeyed. One example is found in another part of Japanese phonology.

Japanese has an MSC prohibiting an alveolar stop followed by a high back vowel: *[tu]. (While this vowel is phonetically [ɯ], for simplicity, we will follow the convention that allows for using the simplest symbol in the neighborhood when there is no contrast, and transcribe it broadly as [u]. Similarly, [ɹ] is transcribed as [r].) Because of the MSC *[tu], there are words like [tsunami] and [tsukidʒi] (the name of Tokyo's famous fish market), but no words like *[tunami] and *tsukidʒi. ([ts] is an alveolar affricate.)

If a [t-u] sequence arises by morpheme concatenation, a rule applies to repair the sequence. Thus /kat-u/ "wins" becomes [kats-u]. Compare [kat-anai], "did not win." The present-tense suffix also alternates, between [u] and [ru]: so the derivation actually consists of three steps:

/kat-ru/ –> /kat-u/ –> [kats-u].

(3)   Repair #1 for Japanese /tu/:

t –> ts / ___ u

A different rule applies in borrowings. As has been noted previously, Japanese allows very few consonant clusters or final consonants. This is enforced over underlying representations via MSC, and in borrowing, via epenthesis (another example of the duplication problem). The usual epenthetic vowel in Japanese is [u]: "baseball" becomes [besubaru]. But, just in case a [tu] sequence would be created, [o] is inserted instead. Thus, "strike" is pronounced [sutoraiku] not [suturaiku] and not [sutsuraiku]. Thus, we need a special rule of epenthesis after [t], which must apply before the more general rule of epenthesis before all other consonants.

(4)   Repair #2 for Japanese /tu/:
       a.   Ø –> o / t ___ {C, #}
       b.   Ø –> u / C ___ {C, #}

(5)   Derivation of [sutoraiku]:

UR	straik
o-epenthesis	storaik
u-epenthesis	sutoraiku
SR	sutoraiku

Thus, epenthesis in Japanese applies in a very intelligent fashion: the rule seems to recognize that inserting [u] after [t] would create a problem, so it inserts an alternative vowel instead. We have to state the "no cluster" prohibition three times: once as an MSC holding over URs, once as part of the rule for o-epenthesis, and once as part of the rule for u-epenthesis. And we have to state the *tu constraint three times: once as an MSC, then in two different rules that enforce it in different ways. Overall, the rules are found to be conspiring: working in different ways, but toward the same goal of producing an output that contains only acceptable syllable structures.

14.2 the basics of Optimality Theory

Throughout the 1980s and early 1990s, a number of phonologists noted and tackled these issues in different ways, but no approach was widely adopted. In 1993, an unpublished manuscript began to circulate on the then-new internet, co-authored by a professor of linguistics at Rutgers University (Alan Prince, a former student of Chomsky and Halle) and a professor of computer science at the University of Colorado (Paul Smolensky, a specialist in creating algorithms that model inputs and outputs in complex systems). Prince and Smolensky brought their ideas together to create an approach that completely removed rules from the grammar, and relied entirely on constraints to map URs into SRs. They called their new approach *Optimality Theory (OT)*. As of this writing, OT has become the dominant paradigm in phonological theory (and it is a contender in syntax as well). The manuscript *Optimality Theory: Constraint Interaction in Generative Grammar* was finally published in book form in 2004. In this section, we discuss the main points of OT.

One important point to keep in mind is that OT is still a generative grammar. The role of the grammar is to generate SRs from URs. One begins with an underlying representation (in most versions, still in terms of features, and still using feature geometry). The grammar operates, and the output is a surface pronunciation. The question is, how do you get from URs to SRs without rules? Several different components and assumptions have to come together. An OT grammar has four parts: the Lexicon; the constraint set (Con); the generator (Gen); and the evaluator (Eval). As in other versions of generative grammar, the Lexicon records the arbitrary pairings of sound and meaning. The other parts of the grammar are very different. We will discuss each in turn.

14.2.1 Con

Con is the set of constraints. Some constraints in Con are *markedness constraints*, of the type that should be familiar: no front round vowels, no consonant clusters, nasals agree in place of articulation with a following consonant, obstruent clusters agree in voice, nasal consonants are preceded by nasal vowels, etc. It is a convention in OT to give constraints names, which are written in caps or small caps. The constraint "nasals agree in poa with a following stop" might be named Agree-Nas-Place, and the constraint against consonant clusters might be named *CC, etc.

In addition to familiar markedness constraints, OT posits a new kind of constraint, called *faithfulness constraints*. Faithfulness constraints mediate relations between UR and SR, requiring that SRs should match URs along particular dimensions. (Since OT was created in part by a computer scientist, URs are often referred to as *inputs*, and SRs as *outputs*.)

One set of faithfulness constraints are *Identity* constraints. The constraint Ident-Place, for example, requires that corresponding segments in SR and UR have the same place of articulation. A formal theory of correspondence is beyond the scope of this introduction, but it's generally not hard to determine which segments correspond to which. If the UR is /ɪn-pʊt/ and the SR is [ɪmpʊt], then /n/ corresponds to [m], and Ident-place has been violated. Ident-voice requires that corresponding segments have the same value for voice. If the UR is /kæt-z/, and the SR is [kæt-s], then Ident-voice has been violated, because the SR of the plural morpheme does not match the UR in voicing. There is an identity constraint for every feature.

Another set of faithfulness constraints require correspondence between UR and SR in the number of segments (regardless of feature change): in effect, they prevent deletion or epenthesis. The constraint that prevents deletion is called Max, the constraint that prevents epenthesis is called Dep. They are defined in (6).

(6) Faithfulness constraints MAX and DEP:
  a. MAX: every segment in the input must have a correspondent in the output (that is, outputs should be *Maximal*).
  b. DEP: every segment in the output must have a correspondent in the input (that is, output segments should *Depend* on inputs).

In effect, MAX prevents deletion, because a deleted segment has no representation in the output. And DEP prevents epenthesis, because an epenthetic segment is new and does not correspond to any segment in the input. However, note that the constraints are carefully worded not to mention any process. Rather, they describe a state of affairs between UR and SR. If the UR is /muŋkumuŋku/ and the SR is [muŋkumu], then MAX is violated three times: the three segments /ŋku/ don't make it into the SR. If the UR is /straik/ and the SR is [sutoraiku], then DEP is violated three times, because there are two [u]s and an [o] in the SR that are not present in the UR. Sometimes, MAX and DEP violations are diagrammed as in (7), with segments in correspondence indicated by connecting lines.

(7) Violations of MAX and DEP:

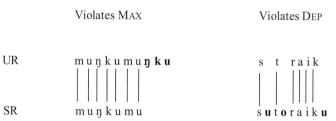

Both markedness and faithfulness constraints must be *grounded*: all constraints exist for a reason, and that reason is to be found in articulation (e.g., it is hard to switch vocal fold vibration on and off in the middle of a consonant cluster), acoustics (e.g., front round and back unround vowels are not perceptually distinct) or processing (e.g., we can more easily detect word boundaries if all initial voiceless stops are aspirated, or all final syllables are stressed). Faithfulness constraints are grounded in processing: if URs and SRs were randomly different, and allomorphs of the same UR were randomly different from each other, it would be awfully hard to keep track of the sound-meaning correspondence.

Constraints are argued to be universal: all languages have the same constraints. One could say that the universal constraint set arises because of grounding: the same articulatory, acoustic, and processing limitations are operative in every language. Alternatively, one could appeal to a genetically-given Universal Grammar. This claim of universality is a significant departure from pre-OT approaches, in which MSCs were considered to be

 ## 14.2 In Focus

Grounding is an important constraint on constraints, or a limit to the power of OT analyses. The analyst can't just make up constraints for anything and everything. Recall that one of the problems with SPE was that random feature-changing rules were allowed. Grounding of constraints works against this kind of random alternation being stated in OT formalism.

language-particular: Japanese had its own set of MSCs, English had its set, etc. The claim that constraints are universal leads to (at least) two big questions:

1. *If all languages have the same constraints, why aren't all languages the same?*

OT answers that constraints are *ranked*, on a language-specific basis. Languages have the same set of constraints, but prioritize them differently. In Japanese, having a simple syllable structure is very important, so the language is willing to tolerate a few extra vowels here and there in order to keep the syllable structure in the desired form. English is much more tolerant of a complex syllable structure, but much less tolerant of epenthetic vowels.

2. *If constraints are universal, why aren't they always obeyed? For example, if there's a universal constraint against epenthetic vowels (DEP), then why does Japanese allow them?*

OT answers that constraints are *violable*. Just because a constraint is present in a language doesn't mean that it will always be obeyed. Violability of constraints leads to one more big question:

3. *What's the good of saying constraints are universal if a language can just choose to violate them any time?*

Crucially, languages cannot violate them *any* time. OT answers that *violation must be forced*. Languages do not violate constraints randomly: English does not allow random combinations of consonants to become syllables, and Japanese does not randomly stick in vowels everywhere. Constraints can be violated, but only under one condition: a lower ranked constraint can be violated if the violation helps to meet a higher-ranked constraint. Japanese tolerates extra vowels if and only if those extra vowels improve syllable structure. English tolerates changes in place if and only if it results in a cluster that obeys place agreement. The UR *ɪn-* can be matched with the SR *[im]-perfect* (violating IDENT-PLACE) because *imperfect* has place agreement where *in-perfect* didn't. English ranks the markedness constraint AGREE-NASAL-PLACE higher than the faithfulness constraint IDENT-PLACE. The rankings are reversed in Russian: Russian ranks IDENT-PLACE over AGREE-PLACE, so Russian does not have nasal-place agreement. In general, the ranking of Markedness over Faithfulness will result in alternation, and the ranking Faithfulness over Markedness results in lack of alternation.

Note, however, that no ranking of IDENT-PLACE and AGREE-NASAL-PLACE will ever produce the mapping of *in-perfect* to *iŋ-perfect*. The form *iŋ-perfect* violates IDENT-PLACE, but for no good reason. Changing the place of articulation hasn't made the cluster any better. Thus we see that a constraint like IDENT-PLACE in English may still be active, preventing random changes, even if it is out-ranked, and thus often violated. Further, if no constraint ranking produces the mapping *in-perfect* to *iŋ-perfect*, the OT correctly predicts that no language will contain this alternation.

In summary, then, CON = a set of grounded, universal, violable constraints. Language universals arise because all languages have the same features and the same constraints. Language differences arise because languages rank the constraints differently. Alternations arise (or not) due to conflicts between markedness and faithfulness constraints. If a markedness constraint is ranked higher than faithfulness to the marked feature or configuration, changes occur to repair the more marked structure. If faithfulness to the marked structure is ranked higher than the markedness constraint against it, the marked structure remains.

14.2.2 Gen

Gen , the *Generator*, creates UR:SR (or input:output) pairings. A factory analogy may again be useful. Gen is like a factory. Unlike the well-organized and ordered assembly line of SPE however, the Gen factory is a mess. Gen takes URs and makes random changes to them, in random order, inserting segments here, deleting segments there, changing features everywhere, or maybe just leaving everything unchanged. (In the original conception of "Classic" OT, changes made by Gen are totally random. Later versions have modified this, allowing only changes that result in some improvement somewhere, but that still randomly apply or not, and in random order.) The result is that for any UR, Gen generates not just one SR, but an indefinitely large set of SRs, called the *candidate set*. The candidate set will always include one member that has avoided any change at all and matches the UR perfectly (called the *faithful parse*), but it will also include various other candidates that differ from each other and from the UR in multiple different ways.

So, if the input is /kæt-z/, the SR candidate set will include faithful [kætz], but also [kæts], [kædz], [kædɨz], and [kæz], each of which offers some improvement over in the difficult /tz/ cluster. In addition, (in Classic OT) the candidate set will contain [kætʒ] and [ketz] and [gæts], where feature changes have been made for no good reason, not to mention hopeless candidates like [dagz], where multiple feature changes have made the original input unrecognizable.

Gen is made to operate randomly because OT is a constraint-based grammar. The constraints are "the locus of explanatory action" as Prince and Smolensky put it. All the interesting generalizations arise from the constraints and constraint interactions. Gen, the part of the grammar that makes the actual changes, is as unstructured and "unintelligent" as possible.

14.3 In Focus

Students often ask how OT can operate with an indefinitely large candidate set. If the grammar has to consider an infinite number of candidates, how does it ever find the right one? This question assumes, incorrectly, that the grammar must sift through the set one candidate at a time. If it did that, it would indeed never finish. However, algorithms exist that allow the grammar to dispense with whole classes of impossible candidates with one fell swoop, narrowing down the alternatives to a manageable plausible set without too much difficulty. Exact computational implementations of OT are beyond the scope of what we can cover here, but I offer one comforting analogy (suggested by John McCarthy and others): we solve computational problems that involve infinite sets all the time. It's called arithmetic. The fact that the set of integers is infinite does not prevent us from developing strategies that allow us to find the one correct answer, and those strategies do not involve trying out every integer in turn to determine if it happens to be the right one.

14.2.3 Eval

Eval is the part of the grammar that brings together Gen and Con. It is the job of Eval, the *Evaluator*, to choose the input-output pairing (of all those created by Gen) that best matches the language's constraint hierarchy (Con). That is, Eval selects the *optimal* input-output pair. Note that it does not select the *perfect* input-output pair: every UR:SR pair violates some constraint, either faithfulness or markedness. If the UR is left unchanged, then some markedness constraint is violated. If the SR differs from the UR, then some faithfulness constraint is violated. It is the job of EVAL to pick the form that obeys the high-ranked constraints of the language, at the expense of the low-ranked ones.

Note, also, that EVAL does not choose the optimal *SR*, it chooses the optimal *UR:SR pair*. There is no such thing as a single optimal pronunciation. An SR must be the optimal pronunciation for some particular UR. The form [pʰa] may be the optimal pronunciation for the input /pa/, but it is not the optimal pronunciation for the input /no/.

The following extended analogy may help in understanding how EVAL, and thus all of OT, works. OT-like constraint evaluation can be applied to all sorts of issues in everyday life that involve possibly-conflicting priorities. Let's imagine you decide to buy a car, and make up a list of five things that you desire:

1. It must pass state inspection.
2. It must go 0–60 in less than 6 seconds.
3. It must get more than 35 miles per gallon.
4. It must be red.
5. It must cost no more than $20,000.

So you go to the car lot. This lot has all the cars you can imagine, and some you couldn't. Some are fast, some are fuel-efficient, some are very expensive, some are cheap, they come in all colors. Some could have been on the cover of *Car and Driver*, others hardly look like cars at all: they may be missing the front seat, or have only three wheels. Nonetheless, you discover that none of the cars in the lot meets all five of your criteria: in large part because some of your criteria are mutually exclusive.

So, do you give up and go home carless? No – you rank your criteria. You can't have everything you want, so you decide what is most important.

Suppose you only *have* $20,000. That constraint has to be top-ranked. There might be a beautiful red car on the lot with an experimental new battery system that gets both great mileage and great acceleration, already complete with state tags, but if it costs $75,000, you can't have it. In OT, this concept is known as *strict domination*: if a candidate violates just one high-ranked constraint, and there are other candidates that don't, then the violator of the high-ranked constraint is out of contention, even if it obeys all the rest of the lower-ranked constraints. Not all versions of OT assume strict domination, but most do. So all of the expensive cars are ruled out.

Similarly, a car you cannot register won't be any use to you, so ability to pass state inspection is also high-ranked. All the clunkers with missing pieces or misplaced parts are also ruled out.

This will still leave a pretty big set of cars. Some are big, older cars with big engines that have great acceleration. Some are small, newer cars with great gas mileage. Both come in all colors, but sadly, in your price range, there are none that have both great acceleration and great mileage. Again, you have to rank which is more important to you. Based on your personality, you choose either the small carbon footprint or the fun ride. Within the small set of cars that's left, you choose the red one, and bring it home.

The analogy to phonological theory should be clear. GEN is the factory that created all the cars, some wonderful, some plausible, some crazy. CON is the list of desires. And EVAL is you, choosing the car that best satisfies your ranked list. There is no perfect car, one that fulfills all your desires. You have to settle for the one that *best* satisfies the constraints on your list, giving priority to the ones ranked highest. And the car that is best for you is not necessarily the one that's best for your friend. If she inherited a big sum of money, price might be the lowest consideration on her list, and she might go home with the car that has the powerful experimental battery, great acceleration and great gas mileage. If you're lucky, she might give you a ride.

14.3 example problem solving in OT

14.3.1 vowel sequences in three languages

Let's apply these ideas to a real linguistic example. We have seen that, in many cases, languages will not tolerate two different vowels in a row. We can formalize this tendency with a markedness constraint, as in example (8). (We will revisit this constraint in Chapter 16, on syllable structure.) Our analysis will also need the two faithfulness constraints MAX and DEP, defined above.

(8)   A markedness constraint:

*VV: do not have two vowels in sequence

The activity of this markedness constraint is seen in Yoruba, as the data in example (9) show.

(9)   Vowel deletion in Yoruba:

[ri]   see
[r-igba]   see a calabash
[r-aʃɔ]   see cloth
[r-ɔbɛ]   see soup

In Yoruba, if two vowels occur in sequence, the first is deleted: /ri-aʃɔ/ "see cloth" is realized as [r-aʃɔ]. In OT terms, this must mean that the markedness constraint *VV is ranked above MAX, the constraint that prohibits deletion.

The analysis is shown via a *tableau*: a table that indicates the input/UR, the ranked constraints, possible candidates and their constraint violations, and the winning candidate/ actual SR.

(10)   Partial tableau for vowel deletion in Yoruba:

ri-aʃɔ	*VV	MAX
ri-aʃɔ		
r-aʃɔ		

The top-left cell of the tableau shows the UR: in this case the Yoruba phrase for "see cloth." The leftmost column shows the candidate set: different possible outputs for this input. In principle, the candidate set is indefinitely long, and consists of every possible change that could be made to /ri-aʃɔ/. In practice, phonologists tend to list only plausible candidates. Here, for starters, we list just two (which should always be included): the faithful parse identical to the UR and the actual SR, the winning candidate. The top row of the tableau shows the constraints, in ranked order from left to right.

Thus far, the tableau has shown the operation of GEN and CON. CON supplies the constraints, and GEN gives the possible pairings: ri-aʃɔ : ri-aʃɔ and ri-aʃɔ : r-aʃɔ. It is now up to

EVAL to choose the optimal pair. EVAL does this by assigning and evaluating constraint violations. These are indicated with asterisks in tableau (11). If a candidate violates a constraint, an asterisk is placed in the corresponding cell. An (!) indicates a fatal violation: a constraint violation that renders a candidate out of contention.

(11)   Tableau for vowel deletion in Yoruba: operation of EVAL:

ri-aʃɔ	*VV	MAX
ri-aʃɔ	*!	
→ r-aʃɔ		*

The faithful parse [ri-aʃɔ] violates the markedness constraint *VV, and [r-aʃɔ] does not. Because *VV is highest ranked, violation of this constraint is fatal, and [ri-aʃɔ] is ruled out of contention. The remaining candidate, [r-aʃɔ], is declared the winner. Its status as the winning candidate is indicated by an arrow pointing to it. (Prince and Smolenksy used the icon ☞ to indicate the winning candidate in their tableaux, but the orthographic device used to indicate the winner doesn't matter.) The output [r-aʃɔ] is not perfect – it violates lower-ranked MAX, but it is the optimal candidate given this input and this constraint ranking. (We leave aside for the moment the question of which vowel will be deleted.)

Now let's consider a slightly larger candidate set. The violation of *VV could have been repaired in other ways, for example by epenthesis. A candidate with an epenthetic glide is shown in tableau (12).

(12)   Tableau for vowel deletion, not epenthesis:

ri-aʃɔ	*VV	DEP	MAX
ri-aʃɔ	*!		
→ r-aʃɔ			*
ri-jaʃɔ		*!	

We know that the epenthetic candidate, [ri-jaʃɔ], does not win. Therefore, it must be ruled out because it violates some constraint. Clearly, that constraint is DEP. Further, DEP must be higher ranked than MAX: this formalizes the idea that Yoruba would rather delete than epenthesize to repair violations. The tableau shows that the violation of DEP incurred by [ri-jaʃɔ] is fatal. In principle, the candidate that violates only the lowest ranked constraint is the candidate that wins. Any candidate that violates a high-ranked constraint is eliminated (assuming another competitor is still left standing).

Note that while we know that both *VV and DEP must outrank MAX, we cannot determine the relative ranking of the two. Since the winning candidate violates neither, we would get the right result whichever way *VV and DEP were ranked. Because we do not know the ranking between the two constraints, the line between them is dotted. (Phonologists differ on whether all constraints must be *fully* ranked, such that all constraints occur in strict order from highest to lowest, or whether ties are ever allowed. Different kinds of constraint rankings are allowed in different versions of OT. For now, we'll stick with the simplest.)

If the rankings of DEP and MAX were switched, then the epenthetic candidate would be the winner. This is exactly the case in Basque, as the data in example (13) show:

(13)   Glide epenthesis in Basque:

    [agin]   tooth   [agin e]   the tooth
    [erri]   village   [erri je]   the village

(14)   Tableau for glide epenthesis, not deletion:

erri e	*VV	MAX	DEP
erri e	*!		
→ erri je			*
err e		*!	

In tableau (14), the deletion candidate is ruled out and the epenthetic candidate wins, because MAX outranks DEP. (Again, we leave aside for the moment the problem of determining *which* segment will be epenthesized, but return to the problem below.)

The third possibility would be to have the markedness constraint, *VV, lowest ranked. In that case, the vowel sequence would be tolerated. This situation is illustrated by English, as shown by tableau (15). The sequence /i#e/, as in "see eight," is not altered.

(15)   Tableau for no alternation:

i # e	DEP	MAX	*VV
→ i # e			*
i # je	*!		
e		*!	

Thus we see that the three languages, Yoruba, Basque, and English, have the same three constraints: DEP, MAX, and *VV. They differ in their rankings of the constraints. Because Yoruba ranks MAX lowest, it repairs its vowel sequences via deletion. Because Basque ranks DEP lowest, it repairs its vowel sequences via epenthesis. And because English ranks *VV lowest, it leaves its vowel sequences alone. The task of trying out different constraint rankings to determine if the rankings correspond to actual languages is called *factorial typology*. OT predicts that every different ranking of constraints should produce a possible, if not an actual, language.

14.3.2 nasal place assimilation

Let's consider how OT handles nasal place assimilation, which posed problems for SPE notation. To deal with this alternation, we need a markedness constraint that requires nasal place agreement, and a faithfulness constraint that requires that place of articulation not change from UR to SR. These are shown in (16).

(16)   Markedness and Faithfulness in nasal place agreement:

1.   AGREE-NASAL-PLACE: If a nasal stop occurs before another stop, the two stops must share all PLACE features.
2.   IDENT-PLACE: PLACE features must be identical between a segment in the UR and its correspondent in the SR.

We'll use Setswana as our example. The morpheme meaning "me" is a nasal consonant that agrees in place of articulation with a following consonant. (For simplicity, we'll look only at place assimilation to voiceless stops and affricates. Aspiration is contrastive in this language.)

(17)   Nasal place agreement in Setswana:

m-pitsa   call me
m-pʰaɲa   slap me
n-tamola   squeeze me
n-tʰaɲa   wake me up
ɲ-tʃʰalɛla   make fun of me
ŋ-kopa   ask me
ŋ-kʰʷaɲa   tap me

Tableau (18) shows the analysis of [ŋ-kopa]. The UR /n-kopa/ is shown in the upper left, and possible output forms are shown in the left column. (We represent the UR as /n/, though this choice is not in fact crucial.) Assimilation does take place in this language, so the markedness constraint requiring agreement outranks faithfulness to place in the underlying form.

(18)   Tableau for nasal place agreement in Setswana:

n-kopa	AGREE-NASAL-PLACE	IDENT-PLACE
nkopa	*!	
→ ŋkopa		*
mkopa	*!	*

Here, [nkopa] and [mkopa] both violate the high-ranked constraint AGREE-NASAL-PLACE, and [ŋkopa] does not. Therefore, [nkopa] and [mkopa] are out of contention (their violations are fatal), and the remaining candidate, [ŋkopa] is declared the winner.

If the constraint rankings were different, the result would be different. Tableau (19) shows the result of switching the ranking of AGREE and IDENT. This would be the ranking for a language with no place assimilation.

(19)   Tableau for no agreement:

n-kopa	IDENT-PLACE	AGREE-NASAL-PLACE
→ nkopa		*
ŋkopa	*!	
mkopa	*!	*

Under this ranking, [nkopa]is the winner, since it obeys high-ranked IDENT-PLACE. Note that [mkopa] never wins: because it violates both constraints, it is not optimal under any constraint ranking. OT therefore predicts that the mapping /n-kopa/ –> [mkopa] will not be found in any language. This prediction seems to be borne out.

Again, let's consider a larger candidate set. There could be other ways of resolving the violation of AGREE-NASAL-PLACE. Why, for example, not change the obstruent instead of the nasal?

(20)   A tie on IDENT-PLACE:

n-kopa	AGREE-NASAL-PLACE	IDENT-PLACE
nkopa	*!	
? ŋkopa		*
? ntopa		*

The SR [nkopa] is definitely out (for Setswana), since it violates high-ranked AGREE. But [ŋkopa] and [ntopa] tie: neither violates AGREE-NASAL-PLACE, and both violate IDENT-PLACE. How is the winner chosen? There must be some other constraint to distinguish the two candidates.

In fact, cross-linguistically, it is always the nasal that changes in nasal-stop clusters, so there must be some reason. One posited explanation that accounts for a general tendency in all kinds of clusters is that the onsets of syllables are privileged: faithfulness to onsets is more important than faithfulness in other positions. (This may be because onsets are more perceptually salient and clearly produced than segments in other positions. Changes to onsets are therefore more noticeable, and are therefore not preferred.) The idea that faithfulness can be relative, with faithfulness to more prominent positions being more important than faithfulness to less prominent positions, is known as *positional faithfulness*.

We can indicate privileged faithfulness to the onset with a positional faithfulness constraint, as defined in example (21).

(21)   Positional faithfulness:
ID-PLACE(ONSET): PLACE features must be identical between a segment in the UR and its correspondent in the SR, *if the segment is in onset position in the SR.*

If the positional faithfulness constraint outranks the general faithfulness constraint, as shown in tableau (22), then [ŋkopa] is again correctly declared the winner.

(22)   Positional faithfulness resolves the tie:

n-kopa	AGREE-NASAL-PLACE	ID-PLACE(ONSET)	ID-PLACE
nkopa	*!		
→ ŋkopa			*
ntopa		*!	*

A version of positional faithfulness could also be used to solve the problem of which vowel deletes in Yoruba. Cross-linguistically, word-initial syllables have also been found to be prominent and to resist alternation. Therefore, we can posit a positional faithfulness constraint for MAX. MAX-INITIAL requires faithfulness to word-initial vowels. Added to our tableau for Yoruba, (example 23), violation of MAX-INITIAL rules out an analysis where the second vowel is deleted instead of the first.

(23)   Positional faithfulness in Yoruba:

ri-aʃɔ	*VV	DEP	MAX-INITIAL	MAX
ri-aʃɔ	*!			
→ r-aʃɔ				*
ri-ʃɔ			*!	*
ri-jaʃɔ		*!		

Returning to Setswana, other possible repairs to the mis-matched place cluster must be considered. One could insert a vowel to break up the cluster, violating DEP. Or delete the offending nasal, violating MAX. Since candidates that violate these constraints are not optimal, it must be that these constraints are ranked higher, as shown in tableau (24). The winning candidate is the one that violates only the lowest ranked constraint.

(24)   No epenthesis or deletion in Setswana:

n-kopa	AGREE-NASAL-PLACE	DEP	MAX	IDENT-PLACE
nkopa	*!			
→ ŋkopa				*
kopa			*!	
nakopa		*!		
mkopa	*!			*

Again, we do not know the ranking between AGREE, DEP, and MAX. Since the winning candidate does not violate any of them, we would get the same result regardless of their ranking. We just know that IDENT-PLACE is the lowest.

14.3.3 Japanese /tu/

Finally, let's take a look at how OT solves the problem of the conspiracy against [tu] in Japanese.

First, we account for the change /tu/ –> [tsu] by positing a markedness constraint *TU, which is grounded in the articulatory incompatibility between anterior tongue-tip consonants and a high, backed tongue body. This markedness constraint outranks the faithfulness constraint for the feature [continuant], as shown in (25). Constraints such as IDENT-VOWEL PLACE must also be high-ranked, to rule out other repairs, such as changing /u/ to [o].

(25)   Affrication of /tu/ in Japanese:

kat-u	*TU	IDENT-VOWEL PLACE	IDENT-CONTINUANT
katu	*!		
kato		*!	
→ katsu			*

In addition to accounting for alternations, *TU also works to keep undesirable words out of the lexicon. In OT, there are no constraints that apply specifically to underlying representations, the way MSCs did. If a form does not surface in a language, it must be because of constraint interaction in CON as mediated by EVAL, not because of a separate MSC. Because there are no separate MSCs, *any sequence* is a possible input. (This idea is called *Richness of the Base*.) For example, if there were an input such as /tunami/ in example (26), it would (correctly) surface as [tsunami]. It is up to CON and EVAL to make sure that even unattested inputs are matched with an output that is a possible word of the language.

(26)   /tu/ –> [tsu] in Japanese monomorphemes:

tunami	*TU	IDENT-VOWEL PLACE	IDENT-CONTINUANT
tunami	*!		
tonami		*!	
→ tsunami			*

In order to account for epenthesis, we posit another markedness constraint that states that all syllables must be of the form CV. (This is an oversimplification, but it works well enough for the present example.) The constraint interaction is illustrated in tableau (27), showing the Japanese output for the English borrowing "baseball." (For simplicity, we leave aside the treatment of /l/, and transcribe the Japanese lateral flap as [r]. This l/r correspondence would be handled with a separate set of constraints not considered here.)

(27)   Epenthesis in Japanese:

besbal	CV	MAX	DEP
besbar	*!*		
beba		*!*	
→ besubaru			**

In tableau (27), DEP is lower ranked than both the CV constraint and MAX, resulting in the candidate with epenthetic vowels being chosen as optimal. Note that [besbar] violates the syllable constraint twice, once for [bes] and once for [bar], so it gets two asterisks, one for each violation. Similarly, [beba] violates MAX twice, because two consonants have been deleted. In both cases, however, even one violation would have been fatal, so the "!" goes after the first asterisk.

Why is the vowel [u] epenthesized, and not some other quality? Analyses usually run along the lines that a language will insert the vowel that it finds least objectionable. The choice of epenthetic vowel is not the same cross-linguistically, so OT handles the difference with differences in constraint ranking. Here, we will assume that Japanese finds that extra [u]s are less objectionable than extra [o]s. We will formalize this by ranking a constraint against [o] higher than a constraint against [u], as shown in tableau (28).

(28) Epenthesis in Japanese: [u] rather than [o]:

besbal	CV	Dep	*o	*u
besbar	*!*			
besobaro		**	*!*	
→ besubaru		**		**

Note that because [besobaro] and [besubaru] tie on their violations of Dep (two each), we move to the next constraint down, *o, to choose the winner. Because *o outranks *u, [u] will be the default epenthetic vowel.

To account for why we get [o] after [t], we simply incorporate the *TU constraint we already have. Thus, [u] will be the default epenthetic vowel, except when it would create a violation of *TU.

(29) Epenthesis in Japanese: [o] rather than [u] after [t]:

straik	*TU	CV	Dep	*o	*u
straik		*!*			
suturaiku	*!		***		
sotoraiko			***	**!*	
→ sutoraiku			***	*	**

Finally, we need to check that the analysis of epenthesis is consistent with the rest of the phonology. Tableau (30) shows that underlying vowels, as in [kats-u], will remain unchanged as long as IDENT-VOWEL PLACE continues to outrank both *u and ID-CONTINUANT (compare tableau (26)).

(30) Epenthesis in Japanese: [o] rather than [u] after [t]:

straik	*TU	CV	Id-V-Pl	Dep	*o	*u	Id-cont
straik		*!					
suturaiku	*!			***			
sotoraiko				***	**!*		
→ sutoraiku				***	*	**	
tat-u							
tatu	*!						
→ tatsu					*	*	
tato		*!			*		

14.4 challenges and directions for further research

It is hoped that these few simplified examples have given a sense of how an OT analysis works. There are many issues that are being addressed in ongoing research, however, and not all phonologists accept that good solutions can be found. Among current research questions are:

1   What is the nature of CON? How many constraints are there? What are they? Are all constraints really universal? Are all constraints really grounded?
2   What is the nature of GEN? Is it really random?
3   Can we necessarily find one constraint ranking that works for all the lexical items in a language? What if we can't?
4   Are constraints fully ranked or can there be ties? Are constraints ranked in strict domination, or can lower-ranked constraints sometimes "gang up" on higher-ranked ones?
5   What computational algorithms work best?
6   How is an OT grammar learned?
7   How does OT deal with variation?

The biggest challenge for OT, however, may be the problem of *opacity*. An opaque interaction occurs when one process obscures the operation of another. In contrast to the multi-stage derivations of rule-based phonology, OT is in general a "surface-oriented" theory: both markedness and faithfulness constraints directly reference SRs. This orientation makes it difficult to deal with alternations whose operation or motivation are not transparently visible in the surface form. The problem of opacity has caused some phonologists to reject OT entirely and return to (or remain with) rule-based formalisms, and has led others to propose various emendations to the theory.

Turkish provides a simple example of an opaque generalization, one that is very easy to account for in a rule-based derivation, but very difficult to account for in OT. The opacity comes from an interaction of processes of vowel epenthesis and velar deletion. The relevant data is shown in example (31).

(31)   Epenthesis and deletion in Turkish:

a. Epenthesis

/baʃ-m/ –>   baʃɯm   my head
/jel-m/ –>   jelim   my wind

b. Velar deletion

/ajak-I/ –>   aja-ɯ   his foot
/inek-I/ –>   ine-i   his cow

c. Interaction

/ajak-m/ –>   a.ja.ɯm   my foot
/inek-m/ –>   i.ne.im   my cow

As shown in example (31a), when a suffix that consists only of a consonant is added to a consonant-final stem, a high vowel is inserted to break up the cluster. (The backness and roundness of the vowel are determined via harmony with the stem.) As shown in example (31b), a velar stop is deleted when it occurs between two vowels. Then, as shown in example (31c), in some forms both epenthesis and deletion apply: the inserted vowel creates the intervocalic environment that leads to velar deletion. The two processes are formalized as SPE rules in (32).

(32)   Rules for epenthesis and deletion in Turkish:

   a. Ø –> [-cons, +high] / C __ C #
   b. [dorsal, -cont, -son] –> Ø / V __ V

SPE has no problem deriving the forms "my foot" and "my cow," in which both epenthesis and deletion have applied. The epenthesis rule just needs to be ordered first, as shown in (33).

(33)   Derivations:

UR	jel-m	inek-I	inek-m
epenthesis	jellm	—	ineklm
vowel harmony	jelim	ineki	inekim
velar deletion	—	inei	ineim
SR	jelim	inei	ineim

SPE thus gets the right results. How does OT fare?

OT has no problem dealing with the two alternations independently. We will need two markedness constraints: one to rule out word-final clusters, and the other to rule out intervocalic [k]. The first is a familiar markedness constraint against complex syllables. The second constraint may be grounded in the fact that vowels and velar consonants both call on the same articulator, and require incompatible positions: open vs. closed. Intervocalic velars are often the target of lenition cross-linguistically; Turkish takes the lenition to an extreme and deletes the velars completely. These markedness constraints interact with the faithfulness constraints DEP and MAX. None of these four constraints is controversial.

(34)   Constraints for epenthesis and deletion in Turkish:

   a. *CVCC: no consonant clusters at the end of a word
   b. *VkV: no intervocalic velar stops

In order to get vowel epenthesis, the constraints must be ranked with *CVCC and MAX above DEP, as shown by tableau (35). As shown in tableau (36), the ranking necessary for velar deletion is *VkV over MAX. So far, so good.

(35)   Tableau for epenthesis in Turkish:

jel-m	*VkV	*CVCC	MAX	DEP
jelm		*!		
jem			*!	
→ jelim				*

(36)   Tableau for velar deletion in Turkish:

inek-I	*VkV	*CVCC	MAX	DEP
ineki	*!			
→ inei			*	

The problem comes in trying to get both epenthesis and deletion to apply to the same word.

(37)   Tableau for epenthesis and deletion in Turkish:

inek-m	*VkV	*CVCC	Max	Dep
inekm		*!		
inekim	*!			*
→ inem			*	
ineim			*	*!

As shown in tableau (37), the winner *should be* [inem]. If the velar consonant is not present on the surface, there is no need for the epenthetic vowel. The word that actually surfaces in Turkish, [ineim], has an extra (unforced) Dep violation, which will always make it lose to [inem]. No ranking of these constraints will ever make [ineim] the winner. The consonant cluster that triggered the epenthesis is no longer present on the surface, so surface-oriented markedness constraints will not be able to capture this interaction.

The problem is difficult, but not impossible to solve: see the list of suggested readings. One approach to dealing with problems like this is to make markedness constraints more complicated, allowing them to reference underlying as well as surface representations, for example. Or one could make faithfulness constraints more complex, requiring output forms that would not normally undergo an alternation to match other forms where the alternation has taken place. Or one might allow some intermediate stages or ordering restrictions back into the grammar. Whatever solution is chosen, problems of opacity make OT more complex and thus less attractive.

Thus, we end our discussion of segmental phonological theory at the same place we began it in Chapter 10: with the fact that our knowledge of grammar includes abstractions that are not "surface true." Debates over the role of abstraction in phonology, over different versions of OT, and over rule-based vs. constraint-based approaches in general, continue. Stay tuned.

chapter summary

- Interactions of constraints and rules raise problematic issues for phonological theory, such as the duplication problem, where rules and constraints repeat the same generalization, conspiracies, where different rules apply to create the same result, and blocking, where a constraint stops a rule from applying.
- Optimality Theory proposes to eliminate these problems by eliminating rules and relying on constraints and constraint rankings to map URs into SRs.
- The parts of an OT grammar are the Lexicon, Con (the constraint set), Gen (which generates UR:SR pairings) and Eval (which chooses the optimal pairing based on violations of ranked constraints).
- In an OT grammar, cross-linguistic universals come about because constraints are universal, and cross-linguistic differences come about because constraints can be differently ranked.
- Markedness constraints rule out difficult or complex surface structures, faithfulness constraints require URs and SRs to match. Contrast is preserved when faithfulness outranks markedness; alternations occur when markedness outranks faithfulness.
- Section 14.3 provides examples of how this works in practice.

- One of the biggest challenges for OT is the problem of opacity: accounting for generalizations that are not "surface true."

further reading

McCarthy, J. 2001. *A Thematic Guide to Optimality Theory*. Cambridge: Cambridge University Press.
McCarthy, J. 2008. *Doing Optimality Theory*. Oxford: Wiley-Blackwell.
Prince, A., and P. Smolensky. 1993/2004. *Optimality Theory: Constraint Interaction in Generative Grammar*. Cambridge, MA: MIT Press.

review exercises

1. What is an MSC?
2. Why is the "duplication problem" a problem?
3. What do CON, GEN, and EVAL stand for? What part does each play in an OT grammar?
4. What does MAX rule out? What does DEP rule out? What do IDENT constraints rule out? Are these markedness or faithfulness constraints?
5. Define the following terms:

   candidate set
   faithful parse
   factorial typology
   strict domination
   richness of the base

6. How is positional faithfulness different from general faithfulness?
7. Explain in your own words how OT answers the following questions:

   a. If all languages have the same constraints, why aren't all languages the same?
   b. If constraints are universal, why aren't they always obeyed?

8. What does it mean to say "constraint violation must be forced"? Use this idea to explain why *in-perfect* will never map to *iŋ-perfect*.

further analysis and discussion

Describe the following alternations (all from Chapter 11), using OT formalism. In each case (except the last) the constraints you need to answer the questions are provided, and in all cases you don't need to consider candidates other than those given.

9. Post-nasal hardening in Setswana. In this tableau, we deal only with the fricative-affricate alternation, not the nasal place alternation.

(Continued)

[supa]	point at	[xo-supa]	to point at	[n-tsʰupa]	point at me
[ʃapa]	hit	[xo-ʃapa]	to hit	[ɲ-tʃʰapa]	hit me
[xapa]	capure	[xo-xapa]	to capure	[ŋ-kxʰapa]	capture me
[ruta]	teach	[xo-rutʼa]	to teach	[n-tʰuta]	teach me

Constraints:

*NS: nasal-fricative sequences are prohibited.
IDENT-CONTINUANT
DEP

a. Indicate which of the above constraints are Markedness constraints and which Faithfulness constraints.
b. What is the ranking of *NS and IDENT-CONTINUANT? How do you know?
c. What is the ranking of IDENT-CONTINUANT and DEP? How do you know?
d. Fill in the tableau below. Write the constraint names across the top in their rank order, and indicate the constraint violations and the winning candidate.

n – supa			
nsupa			
ntsʰupa			
nisupa			

10. Igbo vowel harmony

si-e	cook!	sɪ-a	tell!
o-si-ghi	he did not cook	ɔ-sɪ-ghɪ	he did not tell
i-si	to cook	ɪ-sɪ	to tell
o-si	the cook	ɔ-sɪ	the teller
e-si	cooking	a-sɪ	telling

Constraints:

AGREE-ATR: all vowels in the word must have the same ATR value.
IDENT-ATR: vowels have the same ATR value in SR as in UR.
IDENT-ATR-ROOT: vowels in the verb root must have the same ATR value in SR as in UR.

a. Indicate which of the above constraints are Markedness constraints and which Faithfulness constraints. Which is a Positional Faithfulness constraint?
b. What is the ranking of AGREE-ATR AND IDENT-ATR? How do you know?
c. What is the ranking of IDENT-ATR and IDENT-ATR-ROOT? How do you know?
d. Fill in the tableau below.

si-a *cook-imperative*			
sia			
sie			
sɪa			

11. Vowel lowering in Syrian Arabic

     daraʒ-e   step   waːʒh-a   display
     ʃerk-e   society   mniːh-a   good
     madras-e   school   daggaːʁ-a   tanning

Constraints:

AGREE-LOW: A consonant specified as [+low] must be followed by a low vowel.
IDENT-LOW(V): vowels have the same value for [+/- low] in SR as in UR.
IDENT-PLACE: a consonant has the same place features in both SR and UR.

a.   Indicate which of the above constraints are Markedness constraints and which
     are Faithfulness constraints.
b.   What is the ranking of AGREE-LOW and IDENT-LowV? How do you know?
c.   What is the ranking of IDENT-LowV and IDENT-PLACE? How do you know?
d.   Fill in the tableau below.

daggaːʁ-e			
daggaːʁe			
daggaːʁa			
daggaːɣe			

12. Tagalog

     bukas   buks-in   buks-an   open
     kapit   kapt-in   kapt-an   embrace
     tubos   tubs-in   tubs-an   redeem
     damit   damt-in   damt-an   fulfill
     putol   putl-in   putl-an   cut

     banig   baŋ-in   baŋ-an   mat
     ganap   gamp-in   gamp-an   fulfill

Constraints:

*MEDIAL-CV: open syllables with short vowels (CV) are prohibited in the middle of
the word. (This may seem counter-intuitive, but think about English words like
chocolate, camera, and veteran, which show effects of the same constraint.)
MAX.
IDENT-NASAL-PLACE: Nasal consonants must have the same place in SR as in UR.
IDENT-OBSTRUENT-PLACE: Obstruent consonants must have the same place in SR as
in UR.
AGREE-NASAL-PLACE: Nasals must agree in place of articulation to a following stop.

a.   Indicate which of the above constraints are Markedness constraints and which
     Faithfulness constraints.
b.   What is the ranking of *MEDIAL-CV and MAX? How do you know?
c.   What is the ranking of IDENT-NASAL-PLACE and AGREE-NASAL-PLACE? How do
     you know?

(Continued)

d. What is the ranking of IDENT-NASAL-PLACE and IDENT-OBSTRUENT-PLACE? How do you know?

e. Fill in the tableau below.

ganap-in				
ganapin				
ganpin				
gampin				
gantin				

13. Review the allomorphs of the English past tense suffix (Chapter 11, example 1). A few examples are repeated here.

[t]		[d]		[ɨd]	
picked	[pɪk]	mowed	[mo]	rotted	[ɹɑt]
ripped	[ɹɪp]	fibbed	[fɪb]	prodded	[pɹɑd]
laughed	[læf]	loved	[lʌv]	lifted	[lɪft]
missed	[mɪs]	roar	[ɹoɹ]	carded	[kɑɹd]

There are two alternations here. Assume that the UR of the past tense suffix is /d/.

a. Consider the voicing alternation, exemplified in [læft] vs. [lʌvd]. What faithfulness constraint is violated? What markedness constraint seems to be driving the alternation? What is the ranking of these markedness and faithfulness constraints?

b. Consider the vowel/Ø alternation, exemplified in [ɹoɹd] vs. [kɑɹdɨd]. What faithfulness constraint is violated? What markedness constraint seems to be driving the alternation? How might such a markedness constraint be grounded? What is the ranking of these markedness and faithfulness constraints?

c. Note that [pɪkt], the actual pronunciation of "picked" is more optimal than [pɪgd] (for the input /pɪk-d/). How can Positional Faithfulness account for this pattern? Propose a constraint.

d. Another way to resolve the markedness violation in *b* would be to just drop the final consonant. What does the fact that [kɑɹdɨd] wins over [kɑɹd] as the optimal pronunciation of /kɑɹd-d/ tell us about the ranking of MAX and DEP?

e. The past tense of "craft" is [kɹæftɨd] not [kɹæftɨt]. In SPE, we accounted for this by rule ordering: epenthesis precedes voicing assimilation. In OT, we use the idea that "violation must be forced". Explain.

f. That should give you six constraints: two proposed in *a*, two in *b*, and one additional constraint in each of *c* and *d*. Add the constraints to the tableau below, and indicate in the proper cells the constraint violations needed to ensure the winning candidates for both "laughed" and "carded." Constraint ranking must be consistent for both lexical items. I've started you off by indicating solid and dotted lines: two constraints are crucially violated in the winning candidates, the other four are not. The ranking of the bottom two constraints also makes a difference: make sure that [læfɪd] does not win.

læf – d					
læfd					
læft					
lævd					
læfɪd					
læf					
kaɹd – d					
kaɹdɪd					
kaɹdd					
kaɹdɪt					
kaɹd					

further research

14.   Return to any other data set you've seen in previous chapters, or that you found for yourself, and craft an OT analysis.
15.   Did your search in Exercise 14 turn up any examples of opacity? What problems do you encounter when you attempt an OT analysis?

Go online Visit the book's companion website for additional resources relating to this chapter at: http://www.wiley.com/go/zsiga.

references

The term "Duke of York" was first used in the linguistic sense of doing and undoing a rule by Geoffrey Pullum in 1976.
Pullum, G. 1976. The Duke of York gambit, *Journal of Linguistics* 12.

Early discussion of the Duplication Problem can be found in:
Kenstowicz, M. and C. Kisseberth. 1979. *Generative Phonology*. San Diego: Academic Press.

Japanese Rendaku
Itô, J. and A. Mester. 1986. The phonology of voicing in Japanese. *Linguistic Inquiry* 17: 49–73.

Turkish
Kager, R. 1999. *Optimality Theory*. Cambridge: Cambridge University Press.

15 Syllables and Prosodic Domains

The ear perceives syllabic division in every spoken chain; it also perceives a sonant in every syllable. One can accept both facts and still wonder why they should hold true.

Ferdinand de Saussure, *Course in General Linguistics*, 1915(ed. C. Bally and A. Sechehaye; trans. Wade Baskin, 1966, p. 58)

The Sounds of Language: An Introduction to Phonetics and Phonology, First Edition. Elizabeth C. Zsiga.
© 2013 Elizabeth C. Zsiga. Published 2013 by Blackwell Publishing Ltd.

Thus far, we have focused our phonological analysis on segments: contrasts between segments, the features of which segments are comprised, and strings of segments and their influences on each other. But speaking does not involve just running off segments in a linear string. Segments group into units at different levels, and some phonological patterns are better described in terms of these higher-level organizational units. When we talk about aspects of speech that are defined over groups of sounds rather than strings of single segments, we label them *suprasegmentals*. Suprasegmental aspects of speech include syllable structure, phrasing, stress, tone, and intonation.

In the next three chapters we examine the phonological evidence for suprasegmental groupings, and consider their phonological representation. The first half of Chapter 15 considers syllables: the need for reference to syllables in Section 15.1.1, the definition of the syllable in Section 15.1.2, and two ways of representing syllable structure in Sections 15.1.3 and 15.1.4. Section 15.2 discusses higher-level prosodic groupings: the phonological word and phonological phrase, providing evidence that these units are distinct from morphological words and syntactic phrases. Chapter 16 then moves on to examine stress systems in more detail, and Chapter 17 turns to tone and intonation.

15.1 syllables

15.1.1 does phonology need syllables?

How many syllables are in the word "suprasegmental"?, "syllabification"?, "antidisestablishmentarianism"? It should have been easy for you to come up with the answers 5, 6, and 12, though you probably had to say the words out loud and count on your fingers to do it. English speakers seem to have no trouble counting the number of syllables in a word, so to the extent that we want our phonological theory to account for speakers' knowledge of their language, phonological theory needs to account for this ability.

Further, the syllable often seems to be the appropriate unit for making phonological generalizations. Consider, for example, the allophonic distribution of the consonants /t/ and /l/ in English, which we have thus far codified as word-initial and word-final variants. We have seen that /t/ is aspirated in word-initial position ([tʰæk]) and glottalized in word-final position ([kʰætʔ]). Likewise, we've seen that English [l] is "light" in word-initial position [lif], and "dark" or velarized in word-final position [fiəɫ]. What happens to these consonants in word-medial position? It depends. In words like "atlas" [ætʔlɪs], /t/ appears with its word-final glottalized allophone and /l/ appears with its light word-initial allophone. In "attack", however, /t/ takes its aspirated word-initial version. Similarly, the /l/ in "almost" is dark, and the /l/ "allow" is light. What determines the pattern? The correct generalization emerges when English speakers are asked to break the words down into syllables, as shown in (1). A dot indicates the syllable boundary.

(1) Syllable-based allophony of /t/ and /l/:

.tʰæk.   .lif.
.kʰætʔ.   .fiəɫ.
.ætʔ.lɪs.   .aɫ.most.
.ə.tʰæk.   .ə.lau.
.ætʔ.læn.tʰɪk.

The phoneme /t/ is glottalized in syllable-final, not just word-final position, and /l/ is velarized in syllable-final, not just word-final, position. (For words in isolation at least, word-final is necessarily syllable-final, and word-initial is necessarily syllable-initial.)

Syllable structure also often seems to be driving alternations. As noted in the previous chapter, insertions and deletions often take place in order to bring lexical items into conformity with constraints on permissible syllable structure. Consider, for example. a process of glide deletion in Icelandic, shown in (2). Recall that the palatal glide is transcribed [j] while [y] is a high, front, round vowel.

(2)   Glide deletion in Icelandic:

	storm	bed	valley
	storm	bed	valley
accusative sg.	byl	beð	dal
genitive sg.	byl-s	beð-s	dal-s
dative pl.	bylj-um	beðj-um	dœl-um
genitive pl.	bylj-a	beðj-a	dal-a

The glide [j] appears in the dative and genitve forms of "storm" and "bed," but not in the accusative and genitive forms. We know that the glides must be part of the underlying representation of these morphemes ("storm" = /bylj/ and "bed" = /beðj/) and that this is therefore a rule of deletion rather than insertion, because glides are not generally inserted before vowel-initial suffixes in Icelandic, as shown in the paradigm for "valley." (The change from /a/ to [œ] in "to the valleys" is the result of a general "umlauting" process that applies to [aCu] sequences in Icelandic, and is not an issue here.) What, then, is the proper generalization expressing the environment for glide deletion? The rule can be formalized using SPE notation, as in example (3).

(3)   Glide deletion in Icelandic: SPE formalism:
       [j] –> Ø / C ____ {#, C}

That is, [j] is deleted following a consonant that is *either* at the end of a word *or* followed by another consonant.

This environment, {#, C} comes up a lot, in many languages, and especially for processes of insertion and deletion. What, for example, is the environment for vowel epenthesis in Japanese borrowings from English, such that "baseball" becomes [besubaru] and "strike" becomes [sutoraiku]? Insert a vowel following a consonant that is either at the end of a word or followed by another consonant. Lateral deletion in Komi? Delete /l/ either at the end of a word or before another consonant. A fourth example comes from a process of obstruent de-voicing in German. In each of the words in example (4), the underlying form of the alternating obstruent is voiced. In German, obstruents become voiceless when they occur either at the end of a word ([lob-es] ~ [lop]) or when they are followed by another consonant ([reg-en] ~ [rek-nen]), as formalized in (5).

(4)   Obstruent devoicing in German:

lop	*praise*	loben	*to praise*
leit	*sorry*	leiden	*to suffer*
sark	*coffin*	sɛrge	*coffins*
reknen	*rain*	regen	*to rain*
jakden	*hunting*	jagen	*to hunt*

(5)   Obstruent devoicing in German: SPE formalism:
       [-sonorant] –> [-voice] / ____ {#, C}

Many other examples of reference to the environment { __C, __#} could be listed. There is a problem here, however. We have learned that phonological rules should refer to natural classes. What is natural about the class of {C, #}? Whenever we need to state a disjunction (*a or b*), we have to consider that we are missing a larger generalization, something that *a* and *b* have in common. The fact that the environment {C, #} comes up so often in the description of phonological alternations in various languages suggests that the generalization we're missing is in fact very large.

One analysis is that the missing generalization is syllable structure. Strings of segments are organized into syllables, and languages impose constraints on what kinds of syllables are possible. When sequences arise that do not meet the constraints, alternations ensue. In Icelandic (and most other languages, for that matter), a consonant followed by a glide is not allowed at the end of a syllable. Neither [.bylj.] nor [.byljs.] is a possible syllable of Icelandic. Glides are fine at the beginning of a syllable, however, so [byl.ja] and [byl.jum] are acceptable. The correct generalization is that glides in Icelandic are deleted when they cannot be syllabified according to the syllable-structure constraints of the language. In Japanese, vowels are inserted following consonants that cannot otherwise be syllabified. And in German, obstruents are devoiced in syllable-final position.

It is often noted that Chomksy and Halle's SPE did not even use the word "syllable." However, it soon became clear that phonological theory needed to reference this unit. Dissertations by Daniel Kahn (MIT 1976: *Syllable-based Generalizations in English Phonology*) and Junko Ito (University of Massachusetts, Amherst 1986: *Syllable Theory in Prosodic Phonology*) made strong cases based on a range of data for the importance of syllable structure. However, in spite of the clear evidence for the phonological necessity of the syllable, and the fact that native speakers can in most cases count syllables without difficulty, linguists have a hard time defining what a syllable is.

15.1.2 syllables and sonority

What is a syllable? Phoneticians have at times suggested that a syllable corresponds to one opening-closing cycle of the jaw, or to a single contraction of the muscles of respiration (a "chest pulse"), but these hypotheses were not supported. One preliminary answer might be that a syllable equals "a vowel and its surrounding consonants." Most of the syllables we encounter, in words like "pin," "print," or even "sprints," fit this definition. However, it is perfectly possible to have a syllable without a vowel. We would all agree that "hidden" has two syllables, even if I pronounce it, as I usually do, as [hɪdn̩], with my tongue stuck to the alveolar ridge between the [d] and the [n], so that there is no opening, and thus no possibility of a vowel, between the two consonants. The slash under the [n̩] is the IPA symbol for just this possibility: a syllabic nasal. Syllabic consonants are not uncommon, in English (the second [l] in "ladle", the [m] in "prism") or in other languages ([m̩pata] "look for me" in Setswana, [vl̩k] "wolf" in Czech, even [tfk] "to shine" and [tχ.zn̩t] "you stored" in Berber.)

Further, defining a syllable as a vowel and the consonants around it does not help us understand that some sequences of consonants are allowed, and others are not. The sequence [prɪnt] is acceptable as a syllable in English, but the sequence [rpɪtn] is not. What principle determines which sequences are acceptable as syllables and which aren't?

The best, though not perfect, answer lies in the concept of sonority. (Sonority is obviously related to, but not identical to, the feature [+/− sonorant]: sonority is a relative scale, [+/-sonorant] is a binary contrast.) Sonority can be defined as relative openness of the vocal tract, which corresponds directly to the relative loudness of a sound. The most sonorous sounds are the low vowels: the mouth is wide open, and the sound flows freely out. The least sonorous sounds are the voiceless stops: the mouth is completely shut, and no sound is made at all. Other sounds range between these two extremes, as shown in the list in (6).

(6)   Sonority scale, from most sonorous to least:
1.   low vowels
2.   mid vowels
3.   high vowels and glides
4.   rhotics
5.   laterals
6.   nasals
7.   fricatives
8.   plosives

Thus the doctor tells you "open wide and say 'ah'" when she wants to see your throat, not "open wide and say 'ee' or 'lll' or 'mm'"; and if you have to yell for assistance, you're likely to call out "heeeeelp!", prolonging the loudest part of the word, not "hhhhhhelp", or worse yet "helpppppp!" (unless you're panicked into speechlessness, of course).

The speech stream is organized into peaks and valleys of sonority. In the unmarked case, languages alternate low sonority consonants with high sonority vowels: each stands out better against the background of the other. A syllable, then, may be defined as a way of organizing sounds around a peak of sonority.

Take the simple syllable "pin." The vowel [ɪ] is the most sonorous sound in the sequence, flanked by less sonorous consonants. Thus there is a single sonority peak, and a single syllable. The syllable "print" also follows the principle of sonority. Sonority rises from [p] (voiceless stop) to [r] (rhotic) to [ɪ] (vowel), then falls from vowel to [n] (nasal) to [t] (stop). A single peak, a single syllable. Even the seemingly unlikely syllables [vl̩k] and [tʃk] follow the principle of a single sonority peak. (Maybe more like a small sonority hill than much of a peak, but a rise in sonority nonetheless.) Meanwhile, the sequence [rpɪtn] has three peaks: the [r], [ɪ], and [n] are interrupted by lowest sonority [p] and [t]. Thus, if it is a possible word at all, it has three syllables, not one. Sonority peaks are illustrated in Figure 15.1.

Sonority can also explain why two vowels can sometimes form a single syllable: a diphthong. Diphthongs usually consist of a mid or low nucleus followed by a high offglide or preceded by a high onglide. Just as consonants can constitute a syllable peak if they happen to be the most sonorous sound available, a high vowel will *not* constitute a peak if it is adjacent to a vowel more sonorous than itself. As shown in Figure 15.2, words like "crowd" or "crime" are monosyllabic.

> 15.1   Disagreements between native speakers about the number of syllables in a word generally arise only when there are two or more adjacent sounds of very similar sonority, forming a "sonority plateau" rather than a clear peak or valley. How many syllables are there, for instance, in "file," "film," or "Carl"? Do "our" and "bower" rhyme?

Figure 15.1   The syllable as sonority peak.

non-high vowel –
high vowel –
rhotic –
lateral –
nasal –
fricative –
plosive –

k r a ʊ d

k r aɪ m

Figure 15.2 Diphthongs.

Sonority seems to capture most of our intuitions about syllable structure, and explains a lot about possible syllables in the languages of the world. But sonority does not account for everything. There are some words that clearly violate the principle of sonority (Figure 15.3). The word "sprints," mentioned above, is one example. Following the sonority sequencing principle, this should be three syllables, not one, since [s] is more sonorous than [p] or [t]. English also allows monstrous syllables like "sixths" [sɪksθs], with coronal fricatives hanging off the end of the syllable like a tail.

non-high vowel –
high vowel –
rhotic –
liquid –
nasal –
fricative –
plosive –

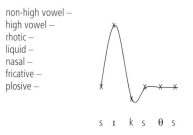

s ɪ k s θ s

s p r ɪ n t s

Figure 15.3 Sonority-violating syllables.

Linguists are not sure exactly how to deal with syllables like this. English seems to have a rule that says you can add coronal fricatives (s, z, θ, ð) to the end of a word, and [s] to the beginning of a word, without penalty. This seems to be related to the fact that many of our important suffixes (plural, possessive, past tense, ordinal) are coronals; but do we allow these sounds so we can say the suffixes, or do we choose these sounds as suffixes because we're allowed to say them? As linguists, we could just say that there is a special rule allowing coronals into the syllable, even though they violate sonority, or we could say that they are not really part of the syllable at all; rather they are tacked on in an "appendix" to the end of the word, just as an appendix is tacked on to the end of a book, but isn't really part of the story. Motivation for the latter solution comes from the fact that these anti-sonority sequences are allowed only at the ends of words. If they were "regular" syllables, they ought to be able to occur anywhere, yet words like [sɪksθ.pa] are impossible.

A further problem comes from the fact that syllable structure is not completely predictable from sonority, even within a given language. There are a few cases where sequences of the same sounds can be syllabified in two different ways. For example, the phrase "hid names" [hɪd.nemz] is bisyllabic, but the phrase "hidden aims" [hɪd.n̩.emz], with the exact same sequence of segments, is tri-syllabic. This variable syllabification is most likely to occur with high-sonority consonants, and demonstrates that the problem of defining the syllable is still not completely solved.

15.1.3 syllable structure constraints 1: onsets and codas

Phonologists often find that they need to refer to the constituent parts of a syllable, and so propose models of *syllable structure*. One model divides syllables into onset+rhyme, and rhymes into nucleus+coda. The most sonorous element of a syllable, the peak itself, is the *nucleus*. Lower sonority sounds preceding the nucleus are grouped into the *onset*, and those following the nucleus are grouped into the *coda*. The nucleus and coda together form the *rhyme*. A syllable, by definition, will always have a nucleus, but syllables that lack codas (like

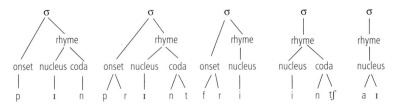

Figure 15.4   Syllable-structure trees for some English words.

"free"), onsets ("inch"), or both ("eye") are possible. Syllables that have a coda are termed *closed*, and syllables without a coda are termed *open*.

Some syllable structure tree-diagrams, showing how the parts of the syllable are grouped together, are shown in Figure 15.4. The Greek letter sigma (σ) is often used to symbolize the syllable constituent.

The sub-constituents shown in Figure 15.4 are important for the statement of a number of syllable structure generalizations. The rhyme, of course, is important in poetry. Languages differ in the segments or sequences of segments that are allowed in the onset, the nucleus, or the coda.

One of the most basic constraints on syllable structure is the *sonority sequencing constraint*, which codifies the requirement that sonority must rise through the onset to the nucleus, and then fall from the nucleus through the coda, as in "print." Languages may differ in the level of sonority required for a nucleus: While some languages require a vowel (Hawai'ian), many languages allow syllabic sonorants (Setswana [m̩pata], Czech [vl̩k]). Berber is unusual in allowing syllabic obstruents ([tʃ̩k], [tχ̩.zn̩t]). In careful speech, English requires every syllable to have a vocalic nucleus ([prɪ.zəm], [pʰə.tʰe.ro]), but syllabic sonorants are common in less careful speech ([prɪ.zm̩],), and in some cases "reduced" syllables seem to consist only of an obstruent. If there is a vowel in the first syllable of a fast-speech production of [pʰ.tʰe.ro], it is very short and completely devoiced. Note, however, that if a language allows less sonorant sounds as syllable nuclei, it will also allow more sonorant sounds as nuclei: the more sonorant the nucleus, the less marked the syllable.

Universally, languages prefer syllables of the CV type (with an onset, without a coda). This is the least marked type of syllable. All languages allow syllables of this type, and children usually start out with syllables of this form ([ma.ma], [dɑ.dɑ]). Some languages, like the West African language Senufo, allow only CV syllables, so that utterances are always of the alternating form CV.CV.CV.CV . . . Even in languages that allow more complex syllables, a CVCV string will generally be syllabified as CV.CV, rather than CVC.V. (Consider English "cu.pi.di.ty" or "ca.ma.ra.de.rie".) This tendency to place a consonant into an onset whenever possible is known as *priority of onsets*.

Avoidance of onsetless syllables can also be seen in the cross-linguistic tendency to avoid sequences of vowels without an intervening consonant. In some cases the missing onset is supplied via epenthesis, as in Basque /a.ri.e/ –> [a.ri.je] *the thread*. (Though note that word-initial position is protected: see Section 14.3.2.) In other cases, the CV.V sequence is changed to CV, either through deletion (Yoruba /ri.a.ʃɔ/ –> [ra.ʃɔ] *see cloth*), dissimilation (Llogoori /mu.a.na/ –> [mwa:.na] *child*) or coalescence (Xhosa /wa.um.fa.zi/ –> [wom.fa.zi] *of the woman*).

We can break down the preference for CV syllables into two constraints: "syllables must have onsets," and "syllables must not have codas." In OT (see Chapter 14), these constraints are transparently named ONSET and NOCODA. (ONSET can replace the previously-proposed *VV). In general, principles of syllable structure are easily amenable to an OT-type analysis: see the exercises at the end of this chapter.

Languages may prioritize (rank) these constraints differently, however. Hawai'ian, for example, has a strict ban on any codas, but is fine with syllables that do not have onsets. It allows syllables of the type V and CV, but never CVC. Other languages allow CV and CVC but not VC: every syllable must have an onset, and codas are optional. Arabic and German are languages of this type. Words that are spelled with initial vowels in these languages are actually pronounced with a glottal stop: [ʔapfel] "apple" in German, and [ʔal] "the" in Arabic. Note that while some languages ban codas and other languages tolerate them, no language requires codas. Conversely, no language forbids onsets.

15.2 Hawai'ian is also famous for having one of the smallest segmental inventories around: only five vowels [i, e, a, o, u] and 8 consonants [p, k, ʔ, l, w, n, m, h]. That gives a grand total of 45 possible syllables (5 V and 40 CV) to encode the thousands of words in the language. How do you use 45 syllables to make thousands of words? Hawai'ian words get very, very long, with lots of repetition, as in the state fish, the [hu.mu.hu.mu.nu.ku.nu.ku.a.pu.a.ʔa]. Note that every syllable is either CV or V, and that [ʔ] functions as a regular consonant.

The Onset/Coda typology can be diagrammed as in Figure 15.5. In OT terms, this typology follows from language-specific constraint ranking: languages that prohibit codas rank NoCODA high in the hierarchy, languages that require onsets rank ONSET high.

Many languages that allow codas put restrictions on the sounds that can occur there. These restrictions are called *coda constraints*. In Thai, for example, [p], [pʰ],

	Codas prohibited (NoCODA ranked high)	Codas allowed (NoCODA ranked low)
Onsets required (ONSET ranked high)	CV Senufo	CV, CVC German, Arabic
Onsets not required (ONSET ranked low)	CV, V Hawai'ian	CV, CVC, V, VC English

Figure 15.5 Onset-Coda typology.

and [b] may occur in onsets, but only [p] in the coda. Similarly, in German as was seen above, [b] and [p] occur in onsets, only [p] in codas. In Japanese, the only coda consonants allowed are nasals, or the first half of geminates: [nip.pon] *Japan*, [ʃim.bun] *newspaper*, [gak. ko] *school*. In Korean, coda fricatives are banned. Constraints on onsets exist (such as the prohibition on [ŋ] in onsets in English and Japanese), but are much rarer.

Many languages allow at most one consonant in the coda and one in the onset. Onsets and codas with multiple consonants, such as English [.**print**.] or [.**flæsk**.] are termed *complex*, and are quite marked cross-linguistically. Even when complex onsets and codas are allowed, the sequences are usually highly constrained. In all but the most exceptional cases (including words like "sixths", mentioned above, and sequences like [**fspl**eska] *a splash*, in Russian) they must follow sonority sequencing: the closer a consonant is to the nucleus, the more sonorous it must be. (Again, sonority-violating sequences may be better represented as appendix rather than part of the syllable proper.)

In addition to sonority sequencing, languages may impose *sonority distance* requirements. Such constraints specify that consonants in a cluster must be a certain distance apart on the sonority scale. In English onsets, for example, segments that come from adjacent sonority classes are disallowed: stops cannot be followed by fricatives *[psa], fricatives (other than [s]) by nasals *[fna], or nasals by laterals *[mla]. Other languages are more lenient: French [psi.ko.lo.ʒi] *psychology*, Serbian [mlada] *bride*. English codas also do not impose sonority distance constraints: sequences ruled out in onsets are fine in codas, even in monomorphemes, as in [bæ**nd**], [klæ**sp**], [fi**lm**].

15.3   In Focus

Other more specific constraints may also come into play. English, for example, generally disallows onset clusters that begin with a voiced fricative: *free* is fine, but *vree* is not. (Though see the discussion of words like "vlog" in Section 11.1). English also disallows the onset cluster [tl], while allowing the onset cluster [tr]. (Thus there is a glottalized [tˀ] in *Atlantic*, but an aspirated [tʰ] in *atrocious*.) It's not clear if these are idiosyncratic facts about English, or instantiations of more general tendencies. Voiced fricatives are more marked than voiceless fricatives, so perhaps the combination of a marked sound type in a marked syllable type is too much. The ban on [*tl] might have to do with the fact that [t] and [l] are both alveolar, and languages tend to avoid sequences of sounds that are very similar but not identical. (On this account, [tr] is ok because [r] is post-alveolar.) Harder to explain is the American English ban on sequences of coronal consonant followed by [ju], which is fine in British English. The words *tune*, *dune*, *enthuse* are [tʰjun], [djun], [ɛnθjuz] in Oxford, England and [tʰun], [dun], [ɛnθuz] in Oxford, Connecticut.

As has been noted previously, syllable-structure constraints often give rise to alternations, either when unsyllabifiable strings are created by morpheme concatenation, or when a more constrained language borrows a word from a less constrained language. A common strategy is to insert extra vowels to break up consonant clusters. Epenthesis arising from morpheme concatenation has already been illustrated with the English past tense (/ɹɑt + d/ –> [ɹɑɾɪd]), Turkish possessives (/baʃ + m/ –> [baʃɯm] *my head*) and Yowlumne verbal suffixes. A subset of the Yowlumne data from Chapter 11 is repeated here as example (7). This language bans complex onsets or codas, so strings of more than two consonants cannot surface. If the verb root /paʔt/ *fight*, for example, is followed by a vowel-initial suffix, such as dubitative /-al/, syllablification can divide the word into two CVC syllables without futher modification: [paʔ.tal]. If a consonant initial suffix such as gerundive /-mi/ is added, however, the resulting string, /paʔtmi/, cannot be syllabified unless a vowel is inserted to provide an extra nucleus: [pa.ʔit.mi]. Note that the intervocalic consonant syllabifies as an onset rather than a coda (*[paʔ.it.mi]), respecting priority of onsets.

(7)   Epenthesis in Yowlumne:

verb root	Dubitative /-al/	gerundive /-mi/	imperative /-ka/	gloss
/xat/	xa.tal	xat.mi	xat.ka	eat
/paʔt/	paʔ.tal	pa.ʔit.mi	pa.ʔit.ka	fight
/lihm/	lih.mal	li.him.mi	li.him.ka	run

Regarding borrowings, we have already discussed how Japanese uses epenthesis to turn "strike" into [sutoraɪku], and English uses deletion to turn [pn] into [n] in "pneumonia." Hawai'ian has the double challenge of a restricted inventory and restricted syllable structure. The phrase "Merry Christmas" becomes [meli kalikimaka] in Hawai'ian. It sounds unrecognizable, but you can easily work it out: change [r] into [l], [s] into [k], and add vowels as needed. Note that even English speakers do not pronounce the [t].

15.1.4 syllable structure constraints 2: moras and syllable weight

While onset, nucleus, and coda do turn out to be useful constructs, there are other generalizations that do not seem to be easily captured in terms of the these structures. For a number of important cross-linguistic patterns, the crucial question seems to be *how many* elements are in the rhyme, regardless of whether those elements are in the nucleus or coda.

One example is a common alternation termed *closed-syllable shortening*. The data in (8), repeated from Chapter 11, also come from Yowlumne.

(8)   Closed syllable shortening in Yowlumne:

verb root	dubitative /-al/	non-future /-hin/	gloss
/xat/	[xa.tal]	[xat.hin]	eat
/xil/	[xi.lal]	[xil.hin]	tangle
/la:n/	[la:.nal]	[lan.hin]	hear
/me:k/	[me:.kal]	[mek.hin]	swallow

As the data in example (8) show, there is a contrast between long and short vowels when the verb root is followed by a vowel-initial suffix such as dubitative /-al/; but when the verb is followed by a consonant-initial suffix such as non-future /-hin/, all vowels are short. Syllable structure provides the generalization: Yowlumne allows syllables with a long vowel, or syllables with a coda consonant, but not syllables with both. When a verb root is followed by a vowel-initial suffix, the root-final consonant syllabifies as the onset of the second syllable, so the long vowel is allowed to remain: /la:n + al/ is syllabified as [la:.nal]. If the second syllable already has an onset consonant, the root-final consonant must become the coda of the first syllable, and the vowel shortens to make room for it: [dos.hin] but not *[do:.shin] or *[do:s.hin]. It is as though the Yowlumne rhyme has only two "slots," and those two slots can be taken up by one long vowel, or by a short vowel and one consonant, but no more.

A situation that is very nearly the converse is found in Thai, which is governed by a *minimal word constraint*. In Thai, most words are monosyllabic, and these single syllables may have a long vowel (as in [na:], *rice field*), or a short vowel with a coda consonant (as in [làk], *stake*), or both (as in [là:k] *various*) but a short vowel with no coda is not allowed to stand as a single word. There are no words *[na] or *[la]. Here, the constraint is that at least two slots in the rhyme *must* be filled, but again it does not matter whether they are filled with a long vowel or with a short vowel plus consonant. (Open syllables with short vowels are allowed in longer words in Thai, which are mostly borrowings, as in [sàri:] *sari*, but they cannot be stressed.) The same minimal word constraint holds of English, if our tense, diphthongized, vowels are considered long. We have words like [beɪ] and [boʊ] with long vowels, and [bɛt] and [bʌt] with short vowels plus coda, but no words like *[bɛ] and *[bʌ]. Some languages use compensatory lengthening to ensure that two rhyme slots remain filled: if a coda consonant is deleted, the vowel lengthens to take up the slot (Komi /nyl/ *daughter* –> [ny:], Ch. 11, example 42).

This same class of syllables (CV: or CVC) is also often important in assigning stress (to be discussed in more detail in Chapter 16). In Hixkaryana (an Amazonian language), for example, all syllables that have either a long vowel or a coda consonant are stressed, and open syllables with short vowels are not: ['nak.'ɲoh.'jatʃ.ke.'na:.no] *they were burning it*, ['ak.ma.'ta:.rɨ] *branch*. In English monomorphemic nouns (though there are exceptions), stress will usually fall on the second-to-last syllable, *if* that syllable is closed ([ə.'dʒɛn.də]) or has a long vowel ([hə.'raɪ.zən]). If the second-to-last syllable is open with a short vowel, stress falls one syllable back (['mɛ.lə.di], [ə.'lu.mɪ.nəm]). See Chapter 16.5 for further discussion of English stress.

Again, then, we find ourselves with a disjunction: long vowel *or* coda consonant. What do these two syllable types have in common? They have more substance, or *weight*, or take longer to say, than a short vowel with no coda. Phonologists refer to syllable weight directly with the unit called a *mora* (symbolized μ). Short vowels have a single mora, long vowels have two, as shown in example (9).

(9)   Moraic representation of vowel length:

In some languages, those that group CV: and CVC syllables together like Yowlumne, Thai, English, and Hixkaryana, coda consonants are also assigned a mora. Syllables with two moras (*bimoraic*) are *heavy*, and syllables with one mora (*monomoraic*) are *light*.

(10)   Moraic representation light and heavy syllables:

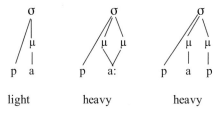

light   heavy   heavy

Note that onset consonants do not get a mora: addition of onset consonants does not make a syllable heavy. The sequence [sprɛ] is no more acceptable as an English word than the sequence [sɛ]. (In some languages, coda consonants do not get a mora either: in these languages closed syllables and long vowels do not form a natural class.) In general, the addition of more coda consonants does not make a syllable *extra-heavy*, so it doesn't seem that every consonant in a complex coda has its own mora. Additional consonants in a complex coda can be gathered under a single mora, or attached directly to the syllable node, as onsets are.

15.4   The mora is an important unit in Japanese. Each mora has a separate symbol in the writing system, and mora counting is the basis of many poetic forms. Despite what your elementary school teacher told you, a haiku has the pattern 5–7–5 moras, not 5–7–5 syllables, as shown in this example by Basho. The word [nan.de] *why* counts for three out of seven beats in the second line.

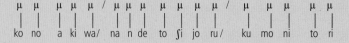

This autumn   Why am I aging so?   Toward the clouds, a bird

Sensitivity to moraic structure can explain minimal word constraints, closed-syllable short-ening, and certain stress effects. We can state the generalizations that, in English and Thai, words must be *at least* two moras long, and that bimoraic syllables attract stress. In Yowlumne, we can say that every vowel and coda consonant must have a mora, and syllables can be *no more* than two moras long.

(11) Closed syllable shortening in Yowlumne: moraic representation:

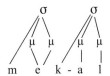

swallow, dubitative
me:kal

swallow, non-future
mekhin

Finally, the affinity between heavy syllables and stressed syllables can be used to shed light on one more facet of English syllabification: *ambisyllabicity*. An ambisyllabic consonant is one that belongs to two syllables at once. This seems to occur in English when a single con-sonant is in between a stressed and unstressed syllable, as in "happy." If English speakers are asked to syllabify this word, they're likely to suggest "hap.py", but of course if one considers sounds rather than spelling, there is only a single intervocalic consonant. Which syllable does it belong to? Priority of onsets ("Be in the onset if you can") prefers [hæ.pi], but the principle of stress-to-weight ("Stressed syllables should be heavy") prefers [hæp.i]. One possible com-promise is that the consonant is both coda and onset at the same time.

Since both the onset-nucleus-coda representation and the moraic representation capture important generalizations, it seems that both are necessary. As we have begun to see, moraic structure is certainly important for defining stress systems, and we will see more of this structure in Chapter 16.

15.2 the prosodic hierarchy

The mora is a *sub*-syllabic constituent. Segments are grouped into moras, and moras are grouped into syllables. Larger domains, above the syllable, have also been proposed, creating a multi-layered *prosodic hierarchy*. Just as phonological alternations may be sensitive to syl-lable structure, alternations may be sensitive to larger domains as well, applying only within a certain domain, or in some cases at a specific domain boundary. Crucially, these domains are defined in phonological terms, and do not always align with morphological or syntactic constituents. One commonly-accepted version of the prosodic hierarchy, with commonly-used symbols, is shown in (12), and the possible organization of an English sentence is diagrammed in (13).

(12) The prosodic hierarchy:

Utterance (U)
Intonational Phrase (I)
Phonological Phrase (φ)
Phonological Word (ω)
Foot (F)
Syllable (σ)

(13)   Prosodic structure of an English sentence:

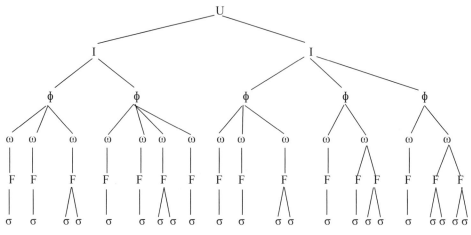

my friend Alice made blueberry pie, but Pat's cousin, who's   Italian, made tiramisu

Syllables (σ) are grouped into feet (F), feet into phonological words (ω), words into phono-logical phrases (φ), phonological phrases into intonational phrases (I), and intonational phrases into utterances (U). The grouping of syllables into metrical feet is most important for the systematic description of linguistic stress, and thus foot structure is treated extensively in Chapter 16, specifically Section 16.4. Similarly, the intonational phrase is discussed in the chapter on tone and intonation (Section 17.3). In this chapter, then, we concentrate on evidence for the phonological word and phrase.

15.2.1 the phonological word

The word as a linguistic unit is hardly in dispute. Words – nouns, verbs, adjectives, etc. – are associated with specific meanings and constitute the pieces from which sentences are built. But words may also constitute *phonological* domains: that is, phonological alternations may apply only within words, or in some cases only at or across word boundaries.

Vowel harmony and consonant harmony typically apply from one syllable to the next across a whole word, but not across word boundaries. In Turkish, all vowels within a word must agree in backness, and high vowels also agree in rounding. (See Chapter 11, example 25.) Across word boundaries, however, no harmony applies. As shown in example (14), the first-person singular suffix harmonizes with the vowel of the root, but nouns and verbs with front and back vowels combine freely without alternation.

(14)   Vowel harmony in Turkish applies within but not between words:

kuʃ gør-dym   kuʃ bul-dum
birds saw-1sg   *birds found-1sg*
I saw birds   I found birds

diʃ gør-dym   diʃ bul-dum
tooth saw-1sg   *tooth found-1sg*
I saw a tooth   I found a tooth

In Chumash (example 15), all sibilants within a word must agree with the rightmost sibilant in anteriority: that is, all sibilants in a word must be either alveolar ([s] and [ts]) or post-alveolar ([ʃ] and [ʧ]). (See Chapter 11, example (26)). Sibilants do not harmonize across a word boundary, however, even though in some cases the two non-interacting sounds may be adjacent in the string of segments.

(15)   Chumash sibilant harmony

    s-ʔip-us   ʃ-iʃtiʔ-ʧij
    3s-say-to 3s-meet-indef.obj
    she said she is meeting someone

    ʃ-ijaqujep-ʃ   sʰeseʔ
    3p-scavenge-pl.obj bones
    they scavenge bones

These examples from Turkish and Chumash illustrate that it is not nearness in the string of segments that matters in defining whether or not harmony will apply, but the grouping of segments together within a word.

An example of reference to the *edge* of a word comes from word-final devoicing. Example (16) comes from Russian. Voiced obstruents devoice in word-final position, as shown in example (16a), even when the next word begins with a voiced sound, as shown in example (16b). The existence of words like [po.jez.**d**a], *of the train*, demonstrate that devoicing in Russian is a word-final, not syllable-final, phenomenon. (Compare German, [ja.**g**en] *to hunt*, [jak.**d**en] *hunting*, from example (4) above).

(16)   Russian word-final devoicing:

    a.   Words with and without affixes

genitive	nominative sg.	gloss
gub-a	gup	lip
sled-a	slet	track
knig-a	knik	book
raz-a	ras	occasion
plaʒ-a	plaʃ	beach

    b.   Word-final devoicing in phrases

/otkaz lenɨ/ –>	[otkas lenɨ]	Lena's refusal
/sad mixaila/ –>	[sat mixaila]	Mikhail's garden
/grob rozɨ/ –>	[grop rozɨ]	Rosa's grave

Sometimes, what counts as a word for the phonology can be either smaller or larger than what counts as a word for syntactic purposes. A clear case of this kind of mismatch comes from compound words – these often count as two words in the phonology, but one in the syntax. One specific example comes from compound verbs in Igbo. As was noted in Chapter 11, vowels in Igbo words must agree in ATR value: [i, e, o, u] are advanced [+ATR] and [ɪ, a, ɔ, ʊ] are retracted [-ATR]. All the vowels in a word must be taken from either the advanced or retracted set (17a), and when affixes are added, they alternate, appearing with [+ATR] vowels in [+ATR] words and [-ATR] vowels in [-ATR] words (17b). (In these examples, low tones are marked, unmarked vowels have high tone.)

(17)   Igbo vowel harmony (from Chapter 11, examples 13 and 14):

    a.   monomorphemic words

ùwe	clothing	ùwà	world
ego	money	àtɔ	three
obì	heart	ɔ́ʊ̀	grub

b.   harmony to affixes

i-si	to cook	ɪ-sɪ	to tell
o-si	the cook	ɔ-sɪ	the teller
e-si	cooking	a-sɪ	telling

In addition, Igbo has a very productive process of verbal compounding. While individual verb roots are all monosyllabic, complex verbal meanings can be built up by combining verbs with other verbs, nouns, and adverbials into compounds, as shown in example (18).

(18)   Igbo compound verbs:

go	+	pù	=	gopù
buy		*go out*		*completely buy up*
gba	+	ɣà + lù	=	gbaɣàlù
run		*pass make*		*leave alone, forgive*
bi	+	kɔ	=	bikɔ
live		*together*		*live together*
kù	+	fu	=	kùfu
strike		*hit*		*kick away*
ɣa	+	gbu	=	ɣagbu
turn		*hurt*		*cheat*

As can be seen in the examples, [+ATR] and [-ATR] morphemes combine freely, without regard to ATR value, indicating that the phonology treats the parts of a compound as two separate words. When these compound verbs are put into sentences however, the syntax treats them as a single verb, taking a single suffix and a single set of inflectional affixes. Most interesting, prefixes harmonize to the leftmost verbal morpheme of a compound, suffixes harmonize to the rightmost, as shown in example (19).

(19)   Affixes harmonize with the adjacent verbal morpheme in compounds:

àɲɪ   a - kùfu - ole   ja
1pl.   infl. - kick away - perf. 3s.obj
we have kicked it away

Ibè   à - ɣagbu - go   m
I.   infl. - cheat - past   1s.obj.
Ibe cheated me

fàa   bikɔ̀ - rɔ̀   e - bikɔ   n - ebe ahù
3pl.   live together - indic.   part. - live together   in - place that
They really live together there
(Repeating the verb in participial form indicates emphasis: compare English *She likes him likes him.*)

Thus, in [a - kùfu - ole], *kicked away*, the prefix has [-ATR] [a], harmonizing with [-ATR] [ʊ]; and the suffix has [+ATR] [o, e], harmonizing with [+ATR] [u], but the two halves of the verb don't harmonize with each other. The split is the same for [bikɔ], *live together*, which takes the [+ATR] prefix [e] and [-ATR] suffix [rɔ].

The conclusion is that the phonology treats compounds as two separate phonological words, and thus two separate harmony domains, even though the verb is a single word with respect to the syntax. The mismatch is shown in (20).

(20) Mismatch between the phonological and syntactic word:

```
[ -ATR ]  [ +ATR ]
[phol wd] [phol wd]
  a - kù    fu - ole
[    syntactic word    ]
```

The mismatch can also go the other way: the phonology may treat as a single word strings that the syntax breaks into two. A clear example comes from copula reduction in (General American) English: the verb *is* will often be shortened to just a fricative, as in *Pat's tall* or *Doug's a good friend*.

Normally, voicing assimilation in English takes place only within the word domain. As has been seen previously, past tense and plural suffixes assimilate in voicing to the final consonant of the stem: *cats and dogs* [kʰæts n̩ dagz], *hits and runs* [hɪts n̩ rʌnz]. There is no voicing assimilation across word boundaries: /s/ and /z/ don't assimilate in phrases like *big sale* [bɪg sel] or *work zone* [wɝk zon].

The subject and verb are obviously two separate constituents in the syntax. However, when the copula verb is reduced, it attaches itself to the right edge of the noun, and the phonology treats the noun+verb complex as a single word domain. Assimilation applies. The mismatch is shown in example (21): example (21a) shows a sentence with a non-reduced verb, where phonological and syntactic boundaries do not conflict; example (21b) shows a sentence with a reduced verb, where the main syntactic division in the sentence (subject noun phrase vs. verb phrase) occurs in the middle of what the phonology considers a single word.

(21) Reduced copulas in English: one word in the phonology, two in the syntax:

   a. non-reduced form: Pat is tall

```
[phol wd]      [phol wd]      [phol wd]
  pʰæt           iz             tʰɑl
[noun]         [verb]         [adjective]
```

   b. reduced form: Pat's tall

```
[    phol wd    ]              [phol wd]
  pʰæt      s                    tʰɑl
[noun] [ verb ]                [adjective]
```

Similar reductions and assimilations are common cross-linguistically, particularly with *function words*: words that are small in number of segments, but that have important syntactic functions.

These small syntactic constituents that attach to and form a unit with an adjacent phonological word are sometimes termed *clitics*. In a number of languages, pronominal elements will form a phonological unit with the verb. Examples in (22) are from Cypriot Greek. In this language, voiced fricatives delete in between vowels, as long as the sequence occurs within a word (22a). Across word boundaries, there is no deletion (22b). In a sequence of preverbal pronoun + verb (22c, d), however, the fricative *will* delete, indicating that the phonology does not treat pronoun + verb as two separate words, even though the syntax does.

(22) Voiced fricative deletion in Cypriot Greek:

   a. iðok - en   -> [ioken]
       give - pst.3s   he gave

   b. eval - a   ðeka   -> [evala] [ðeka] (no change)
       put - pst.1s ten   I put on ten

    c.   na   mu   ðokis   ->   [na] [mu okis]
         subj.   me   give   to give me

(*na* marks the clause as *subjunctive*, roughly translated with the English infinitive)

    d.   na   to   ðis   ->   [na] [to is]
         subj.   it   see   to see it

The exact conditions under which cliticization takes place are complex, and beyond the scope of this introductory chapter. Some phonologists consider a clitic plus phonological word as just a larger phonological word; others argue that the *clitic group* forms a unique constituent in the prosodic hierarchy, with its own definition and properties. Crucially, however, these small constituents clearly form an independent functional unit for the syntax, but not for the phonology. Overall, these examples show that while the "word" is an important unit in both syntax and phonology, syntactic words and phonological words are not always coextensive.

15.2.2 the phonological phrase

At the next level up, phonological words may be grouped into phonological phrases. Just as some rules apply only within a word, but not across word boundaries, other rules apply within a phrase, but not across phrase boundaries. Igbo again serves as a good example. It was shown above that vowel harmony applies within Igbo words. Across word boundaries, a rule of vowel assimilation may apply, as shown in example (23): when two vowels become adjacent at a word boundary, the first assimilates to the second.

(23)   Igbo vowel assimilation:

    a.   ì - tʃɔ̀ - rɔ̀   ego   ->   [ìtʃɔ̀rèego]
         2sg - want - past   money   you want money

    b.   o - gò - rò   àlà   ->   [ogòrààlà]
         3sg - buy - past   land   s/he bought some land

    c.   ihe   ɔzɔ   ->   [ihɔɔzɔ]
         thing   other   another thing

    d.   ŋkìtà ɔtʃa ɔma ʊnù   ->   [ŋkìtɔ̀otʃɔɔmʊʊnù]
         dog white beautiful your   your beautiful white dog

    e.   nà ime   ʊlɔ̀   ->   [nìimʊʊlɔ̀]
         in inside   house   inside the house

We know that these sequences are not just becoming one big word, because [+ATR] and [-ATR] vowels can co-occur, as in [ìtʃɔ̀rèego] *you want money*. Rather, the separate words are grouped into a larger phonological phrase, and the rule of vowel assimilation references the phrase as its domain. The phonological phrase is typically about the size of a syntactic phrase, as is the case in example (23): a verb phrase in examples (23a, b), noun phrase in examples (23c, d), and prepositional phrase in example (23e). Subject and verb generally do not phrase together: there is no assimilation, for example, between subject and verb in the phrases in example (19) above: [ibè] [àɣagbugo] *Ibe cheated*, not *[ibàày̆agbugo].

    Depending on vowel quality, speech rate, familiarity of the phrase and other factors, the assimilations in (23) may be partial rather than complete. The first vowel in the sequence may retain some of its underlying quality. Some phonologists would argue, in fact, that phrasal assimilations are always partial: see, for example, the discussion of Articulatory Phonology in Chapter 5.

A phrase-domain rule involving voicing is found in Korean. In Korean, as shown in example (24), voiceless unaspirated stops become voiced between two sonorants. The rule can apply within a word (example 24a) or across word boundaries, as long as all the segments are within a single phonological phrase. As in Igbo, the phonological phrase is roughly, but not exactly, equivalent to the syntactic phrase. A noun will form a single phrase with a preceding determiner or adjective (example 24b), as will a verb with its object (example 24c). A subject, however, always forms a separate phrase from object and verb (examples 24d, e). Korean word order is subject – object – verb.

(24)   Korean voicing assimilation:

    a.   apeci   –>   [abeʤi]
        father   father

    b.   motun kulim   –>   [mo**d**ungulim]
        every picture   every picture

    c.   kulimul pota   –>   [kulimul**bo**da]
        picture look at   look at a picture

    d.   kajka canta   –>   [kaj**g**a] [can**d**a]
        dog sleeps   the dog sleeps

    e.   kajka papul meknunta   –>   [kaj**g**a] [pa**b**ulmeŋnunda]
        dog rice eats   the dog eats rice

One can, in fact, construct a phrasal minimal pair, where the exact same segmental string can be phrased in different ways, and the application of voicing depends on the phrasing. Example (25) depends on the Korean words /paŋ/ *room* and /kapaŋ/ *bag*, and the fact that the nominative suffix /-ka/ is optional.

(25)   A minimal phrasal pair for Korean voicing assimilation:

    a. / apeci-ka   paŋ-e   tɨleka - si - nta/   –> [abeʤi**g**a] [paŋedɨrəgaʃinda]
        father - nom. room - loc. enter - hon. - plain   Father entered the room

    b. /apeci   kapaŋ-e   tɨleka - si - nta/   –> [abeʤi] [kabaŋedɨrəgaʃinda]
        father   bag - loc.   enter - hon. - plain   Father entered the bag

The phrase break comes at the end of the subject noun phrase. If /ka/ is a suffix on the word for *father*, then /k/ is intervocalic within its phonological phrase, and becomes voiced. If, on the other hand, /ka/ is the first syllable of the word for *bag*, then /k/ is *initial* in its phonological phrase, and remains voiceless. The application or non-application of voicing is surely an aid to the listener in figuring out which phrasing is intended.

The exact nature and definition of the prosodic hierarchy remain an area of active research. Questions that are currently being debated include:

1.   What are the right categories? For example, is there a clitic group in addition to the phonological word? Do phonological phrases come in different types?
2.   How are the categories defined? What syntactic relations must be accessed?

3. Are the categories exhaustively parsed and strictly layered? That is, is it the case that every element at level n is incorporated into a constituent at level n+1, and every constituent at level n+1 is composed of only elements of level n? Strict layering would be violated, for example, if a syllable could attach directly to the word level, without being part of a foot, or if one larger phonological word contained two smaller phonological words.

Whatever the answers to these questions turn out to be, the data presented in this chapter has hopefully been convincing that segments are grouped into larger, hierarchical, prosodic constituents, and that these constituents make a difference in the operation of phonological alternations.

chapter summary

- Phonology needs an account of syllable structure both because syllable counting is part of a native speaker's knowledge, and because alternations and allophonic distributions make reference to syllabic constituency.
- Syllables organize segments around a peak of sonority: the most sonorous segment is the nucleus. Following the principle of sonority sequencing, preceding consonants are grouped into the onset, following consonants into the coda.
- The least-marked syllable type is CV: with an onset, and without a coda. Many languages enforce a constraint that all syllables must have onsets, or a constraint that no syllables may have codas. Other constraints may impose coda conditions, prohibit complex onsets or codas, or restrict sonority distance.
- Reference to moraic structure formalizes the natural class of heavy syllables, which can be important for stress patterns, minimal word constraints, and alternations involving lengthening and shortening.
- The prosodic hierarchy (see example 12) groups segments into a multi-leveled constituent structure. Phonological rules may apply within these constituent domains, or at domain boundaries.
- Phonological words and phonological phrases may or may not be co-extensive with the syntactic word and phrase.

further reading

On syllables:

Blevins, J. 1995. The syllable in phonological theory. In J. Goldsmith (ed.), *The Handbook of Phonological Theory*. Oxford: Blackwell.

Cairns, C. and E. Remy. 2010. *Handbook of the Syllable*. Leiden: Brill.

For an alternative theory that accounts for the natural class {__C, __#} by referencing cue perception rather than syllable structure per se, see:

Steriade, D. 2001. Directional asymmetries in place assimilation: a perceptual account. In E. Huma and K. Johnson (eds), *The Role of Speech Perception in Phonology*. New York: Academic Press.

On the prosodic hierarchy:

Inkelas, S. and D. Zec 1990. *The Phonology/Syntax Connection*. New York: Academic Press.

Kaisse, E. 1985. *Connected Speech*. New York: Academic Press.

Nespor , M. and I. Vogel, 1986. *Prosodic Phonology*. Dordrecht: Foris.

1. Order each list of sounds from most to least sonorous, according the scale in (6) above.

   [s   r   e   t   j]
   [d   m   ɑ   u   l]
   [i   n   p   z   o]

2. Transcribe the following English words into IPA, indicating syllable boundaries with a period. <u>Underline</u> each closed syllable.

   freedom   octopus   create   myself   angry

3. Refer to the discussion of Icelandic glide deletion in the text (example 2), and draw a sonority profile (following Figure 15.1) for the Icelandic word [beðj-um] *to bed*, and for the potential but ungrammatical form *[beðj] *bed*. Explain how sonority sequencing prevents [beðj] from being organized into a single syllable.

4. Transcribe the following English words into IPA, and draw a syllable structure tree for each, indicating the onset, nucleus, coda, and rhyme constituents. (Assume priority of onsets.) <u>Underline</u> the syllable that violates sonority sequencing.

   English   sequencing   structure   nucleus   friendship
   concreteness   fractals   Georgetown   Atlantic   representative

5. Transcribe the following English words into IPA, indicating syllable boundaries with a period. Assuming that coda consonants are moraic, underline each heavy syllable.

   veranda   Believe   reply   ransom   papaya

6. Draw a syllable structure tree for each of the words in Exercise 5, showing moraic constituency.

7. Which of the following English words may be analyzed as having an ambisyllabic consonant? Explain your choice, making reference to "priority of onsets" and "stress-to-weight."

   contains   follow   onset   cryptic

8. Fill in the appropriate levels of the prosodic hierarchy for the sentence "MaryAnne aced Economics, didn't she?"

_____	[me	ri	æn	est	ɛ	kə	na	mɪks	dɪd	n? ʃi]
_____	[me	ri	æn	est	ɛ	kə	na	mɪks]	[dɪd	n? ʃi]
_____	[me	ri	æn]	[est	ɛ	kə	na	mɪks]	[dɪd	n? ʃi]
_____	[me	ri	æn]	[est]	[ɛ	kə	na	mɪks]	[dɪd	n?] [ʃi]
_____	[me	ri]	[æn]	[est]	[ɛ	kə]	[na	mɪks]	[dɪd	n?] [ʃi]
_____	[me]	[ri]	[æn]	[est]	[ɛ]	[kə]	[na]	[mɪks]	[dɪd]	[n?] [ʃi]

9. If voicing assimilation in English applies only within words (ca[ts], but not wor[k z]one), why does it apply to the fricative in "Rick's late again"?

   (Continued)

10. Prosodic phrasing can disambiguate different meanings of identical sequences of words. What are the two different meanings that correspond to the phrasing below?

The ads target [young]$_\phi$ [men and women]$_\phi$
The ads target [young men]$_\phi$ [and women]$_\phi$

further analysis and discussion

Exercises 9–11 use OT formalism to analyze a set of data that references syllable structure. If you have not covered this phonological formalism (introduced in Chapter 14), you may simply discuss in English prose the relevance of syllable structure to describing the patterns in each language.

9. Refer to Exercise 3 above and example (2) in the text. Fill in the table below, indicating the relative rankings of MAX, DEP, and SONORITY SEQUENCING in Icelandic, and the constraint violations for each candidate.

beðj			
beðj			
→ beð			
beðja			

10. Refer to the discussion of Yowlumne epenthesis in the text (example 7). Fill in the constraints MAX, DEP, *COMPLEX, ONSET and NOCODA in the table below: remember that constraints violated by the winner must be lowest ranked. Although the ranking for the other constraints is undetermined, indicate which candidates violate which constraints.

paʔt-mi					
paʔt.mi					
→ pa.ʔit.mi					
pat.mi					
paʔ.it.mi					

11. In Setswana, all nasals that do not precede a vowel are syllabic:

m̩ .ma.la	color
m̩ .pʰa.ɲa	slap me
e.m̩ .pa	evil
pa.ŋ̩ .ka	walk bow-legged
mʊ.na.ŋ̩	mosquito

Assume a constraint, PEAK-V, that is violated whenever anything other than a vowel is the syllable nucleus. What must be the relative ranking of MAX, DEP, NOCODA, and

PEAK-V in this language? (For the sake of the exercise, complications involving stress and morphological conditioning are ignored: see A. Coetzee, Nasal-only Syllables in Tswana. *RuLing Papers 2: Working Papers of Rutgers University*, 2001.) Fill in the table below. Explain why [m.ʊ.n.a.ŋ], where every nasal is syllabic, does not win.

mʊnaŋ			
→ mʊ.na.ŋ			
mʊ.naŋ			
m.ʊ.n.a.ŋ			
mʊ.na			
mʊ.na.ŋa			

12. In Northern Italian dialects, intervocalic [s] is voiced in certain cases, as shown. What is the domain of s-voicing in Italian (Nespor and Vogel, 1986)?

i[z]ola	island
a[z]ola	button hole
a[z]ilo	nursery school
ca[z]e	houses
re[z]istenza	resistance
divi[z]ione	division
la [s]irena	the siren
hanno [s]eminato	they have seeded
lo [s]apevo	I knew it

Voicing does not apply when the [s] occurs at the boundary between the two parts of a compound. What does this tell you about the prosodic status of compound words in Italian?

tocca-[s]ana	cure-all
ri-[s]ud-divi[z]ione	re-sub-division

13. What is the domain of palatalization in English? (A ligature indicates that palatalization may apply, a slash indicates that it will not.)

habit‿ual	press‿ure
last‿year	this‿year
that dog might bite‿you	I miss‿you
that dog might bite, / you know	the batter will miss, / you said
Matt, / you can go.	Miss, / you can go

Does your idiolect (your way of speaking) match the examples? If not, what is the domain of palatalization in your phonological system?

references

Chumash sentences
http://www.chumashlanguage.com/texts/Crane-woman.pdf.
http://www.chumashlanguage.com/texts/Dog-Girl.pdf.
Samala Chumash texts narrated by Maria Solares in 1919 and transcribed by John P. Harrington.

Cypriot

Revithiadou, A. 2008. A cross-dialectal study of cliticisation in Greek. *Lingua* 118: 1393–1415.

German

Lombardi, L. 1999. Positional faithfulness and voicing assimilation in Optimality Theory. *Natural Language and Linguistic Theory* 17: 267–302.

Icelandic

The analysis of glide deletion is based on that of M. Kenstowicz, *Generative Phonology* (San Diego: Academic Press, 1994, p. 79), which in turn is based on data from J. Oresnik, On the epenthesis rule in modern Icelandic, *Arkiv för Nordisk Filologi* 87 (1972): 1–32.

Igbo

Zsiga, E. 1992. A mismatch between morphological and phonological domains: Evidence from two Igbo rules. *Phonology* 9: 101–135.

Korean

Silva, D. 1992. *The phonetics and phonology of stop lenition in Korean. Doctoral dissertation*, Cornell University, New York.

Russian

Padgett, J. 2002. *Russian voicing assimilation, final devoicing, and the problem of [v]. ms*, University of California, Santa Cruz.

Turkish

Feizollahi, Z. 2010. *Two case studies in the phonology-phonetics interface: Evidence from Turkish voicing and Norwegian coalescence*. Doctoral dissertation, Georgetown University.

16 Stress

Everything has rhythm, everything dances.

Maya Angelou

You put the wrong em**pha**sis on the wrong syl**lab**le.

Mike Myers (as John Whitney in *View from the Top*)

The Sounds of Language: An Introduction to Phonetics and Phonology, First Edition. Elizabeth C. Zsiga.
© 2013 Elizabeth C. Zsiga. Published 2013 by Blackwell Publishing Ltd.

We may think that "meter" applies only to poetry, but the rhythm and beat of language is important in every utterance. *Metrical Phonology*, the study of meter as it applies to all spoken language, is an important part of linguistics. As we saw with Japanese haiku in Chapter 15, the units of poetry – the mora, the syllable, the metrical foot – are also the units of everyday language. Every utterance "dances." The choreography followed by a speaker in unscripted conversation may be different, and less self-conscious, than that used by a poet, but as we will see, it is no less rule-governed. Less poetically, as Mike Myers reminds us, if you put the wrong em**pha**sis on the wrong syl**la**ble, you won't be understood.

The linguistic principles that determine varying levels of emphasis on the different syllables in a word are termed *stress systems*. The definition and uses of linguistic stress are discussed in Section 16.1. Section 16.2 surveys the different kinds of stress systems found in the languages of the world, and 16.3 lays out the reasons why a feature [+/− stress] is inadequate to cover the data. Section 16.4 then introduces the hierarchical grid and tree structures that have been proposed to account for stress patterns, and introduces different types of metrical feet. Section 16.5 concludes with a discussion of the complex stress patterns of English, including the interaction of phonological and morphological information.

16.1 what is linguistic stress?

Linguistic stress can be defined as a prominence relation between syllables. Just as we can usually count the number of syllables in a word, native speakers of English can also pick out the one syllable that is most prominent: phoNOlogy, phoNEtics, SYNtax. So, as with syllable structure, stress is a native-speaker competence that a theory of phonology must account for.

Stress can sometimes be contrastive: In Russian, for example, if the string of segments /muka/ is stressed on the first syllable the words means "torment" and if it's stressed on the second it means "flour." In English, sometimes the only difference between a verb and a noun is the pattern of stress: we re**ject** the **re**ject, re**cord** the **re**cord, con**vert** the **con**vert, in**sult** someone with an **in**sult, etc.

Linguistic stress is always a matter of *relative* prominence, and speakers can distinguish multiple relative levels. Consider the word "Alabama." We should all agree that [bæ] is the most prominent, and bears the main stress of the word. But the other three syllables are not equal. The first has a full vowel quality [æ], though it is not quite as long or loud as the third, while the second and fourth syllables are short and weak, with the tongue not moving far from its central position. We say that the first syllable has secondary stress, where the second and third are completely unstressed. In IPA transcription, main stress is indicated by a superscripted line preceding the syllable, secondary stress by a subscripted line. (More familiarly, dictionaries tend to use an acute accent for primary stress (é) and a grave accent for secondary stress (è), but IPA needs these symbols for high and low tone, respectively.) Recall that schwa [ə] is used in transcribing English as a special symbol for the "reduced" vowel in an unstressed syllable. Thus in IPA "Alabama" is [ˌæləˈbæmə].

One way to keep track of different levels of stress is to number them. Four distinct levels of stress are illustrated in example (1). In this example, "1" indicates the greatest degree of stress and "4" the lowest. If you say these phrases out loud, do you hear all the distinctions?

(1)   Up to four levels of stress:
    a.   one who keeps a lighthouse

1	3	2	4
light	house	kee	per

b.   one who does light cleaning

2	1	3	4
light	house	kee	per

1 = primary stress
2 = secondary stress
3 = not stressed but not reduced (tertiary stress)
4 = reduced

It should be clear from example (1) that the stress pattern has to do with the morphological structure, and with creating compounds. In English, when a compound gets created, the element on the left gets more prominence than the one on the right. In a phrase, it is the other way around. Thus we have stress-based minimal pairs like "**hot**dog" (which you eat) and "hot **dog**" (Fido in August). Other pairs include compound "**White** House" (1600 Pennsylvania Avenue) vs. phrasal "white **house**" (your neighbors), and "**green**house" (which is made of glass) and "green **house**" which isn't. In example (1a), the "light" in "lighthouse" gets the main stress because it is the leftmost member of a compound (twice over, first for "lighthouse" then for "lighthouse keeper"). In example (1b) "light" is an adjective in a phrase describing "housekeeper," which gets the main stress. Following Chomsky and Halle (1968), the rule for compounds ("stress on the left") is called the *Compound Stress Rule* and the rule for phrases ("stress on the right") is called the *Nuclear Stress Rule*.

> 16.1   Some phonologists (Chomsky and Halle among them) have proposed more levels than four, particularly in multiple compounds and complex phrases, where the stress rules are argued to apply multiple times, adding a new level of stress with each application. (How many levels of stress in "lighthouse keeper's daughter's wedding invitation scandal"?) In actual conversational speech, however, psycholinguists have found that speakers are able to distinguish only three or four levels, no matter what the phrasal complexity.

Stress is often an important determinant for other allophonic generalizations: certain allophones occur in stressed syllables, others in unstressed syllables. The American English data in example (2) show two allophonic patterns that are determined by stress: tapping and vowel reduction.

(2)   Tapping and vowel reduction in American English

atom	[ˈærəm]	atomic	[əˈtʰɑmɪk]
adding	[ˈærɪŋ]	addition	[əˈdɪʃən]
metal	[ˈmɛrəl]	metallic	[məˈtʰælɪk]
dramatize	[ˈdrɑməˌtʰɑɪz]	dramatic	[drəˈmærɪk]
photograph	[ˈforəˌgræf]	photography	[fəˈtʰɑgrəfi]
addict (noun)	[ˈærɪkt]	addiction	[əˈdɪkʃən]
melody	[ˈmɛləri]	melodic	[məˈlɑrɪk]
fatal	[ˈferəl]	fatality	[fəˈtʰælɪri]
phonetician	[ˌfonəˈtʰɪʃən]	phonetic	[fəˈnɛrɪk]

When suffixes such as "-ic," "-tion," and "-ity" are added to a root, the stress shifts to the syllable directly preceding the suffix (see Section 16.5). Here we want to note the segmental changes that follow from the stress change. Intervocalic /t/ is realized as [tʰ] when it is in the onset of a stressed syllable, but as [ɾ] when it is in the onset of an unstressed syllable. (The tap is often analyzed as ambisyllabic.) There is also an alternation between a full vowel quality in stressed syllables ([æ] in "atom," [o] in "photograph," [e] in "fatal," vs. a reduced schwa in the corresponding unstressed syllables in "atomic," "photography," and "fatality." (For some people the first syllable in "fatality" is completely reduced, for others it retains some level of stress and an unreduced vowel quality.) For both tapping and vowel reduction we see fortition in stressed syllables and lenition in unstressed syllables.

Lenited, "weaker" allophones are one phonetic correlate of the stress distinction, but there are others. Stress is unlike other phonological features in that it does not have just one, invariant phonetic realization. A syllable may be made prominent, made to stand out from other syllables, in a number of different ways. A stressed vowel may be longer or louder than other syllables; it may have higher pitch, and its consonants and vowels may be more clearly articulated. Different languages may choose to emphasize different dimensions of stress. In English, each of these factors is present to some extent, but pitch differences seem to be most important to English-speaking listeners. In Thai, on the other hand, stressed syllables are longer than unstressed, but do not have higher pitch. For Russian, loudness seems to be the most important correlate.

16.2 cross-linguistic typology

Some languages do not use stress at all. In Japanese, for example, it is perfectly possible for all the syllables in a word to be pronounced with equal prominence. This gives quite a bit of trouble to English speakers. In 1996, for example, when the Winter Olympics were held in Japan, English commentators had a great deal of trouble deciding how to say the name of the host city. What it **Na**gano? Na**ga**no? Perhaps Naga**no**? The answer is "None of the above." The word is pronounced with all syllables equally stressed (or equally unstressed), a difficult task for an English speaker. Conversely, Japanese speakers have trouble with the English concept of "reduced vowel," and tend to pronounce [ə] as [a], sounding overly careful to English ears.

For languages that do use stress (most of the languages of the world), patterns of stress can be classified as *lexical*, *paradigmatic*, or *positional*. In a lexical stress system (sometimes also known as *free stress*), the placement of stress is largely unpredictable. A speaker simply has to learn which syllable in a word is prominent, in the same way she has to learn whether the word begins with a [b] or a [p]. There is no real pattern to it. Russian is often cited as a lexical stress system, though it is not completely unpredictable.

In a paradigmatic stress system, the stress pattern depends on morphological information: for example, whether the word is a noun or a verb, or on whether a particular affix has been added. The English system is largely paradigmatic, though it is really a mixed system, with some predictable and some unpredictable aspects. English stress in some cases must just be memorized: there is no phonological rule to explain the fact that "ba**na**na" is stressed on the second syllable while "**a**nimal" is stressed on the first, for example. Historical origin is often at play, but the fact that "animal" is a descendant of Latin while "banana" is a later borrowing from Spanish is not accessible to the language-learner.

There are some patterns, however. Generally, English verbs and adjectives follow one set of rules, nouns another. Verbs tend to have stress on the final syllable (re**ject**, in**sult**), while nouns have stress on the second-to-last or third-to-last (**re**ject, **in**sult, **a**nimal, ba**na**na). Word structure, particularly suffixes, is also important. The suffix "y," for example, tends to leave stress alone, thus "**pre**sident/**pre**sidency," but "-ial" pulls stress back to the syllable immediately preceding, as in "presi**den**tial." Volumes have been written on predicting English stress, and the topic could easily be a course in itself. Section 16.5 discusses some of the basic patterns in more detail.

Systems like Russian (mostly lexical with some paradigmatic aspects) and English (mostly paradigmatic with some lexical aspects) are the most complicated types of phonological stress patterns. Much more straightforward are the completely predictable positional stress (or *fixed stress*) systems. In a positional stress system, whether or not a syllable is stressed depends on its position in the word (though other factors, like vowel length, sometimes come into play as well, and these factors can sometimes interact in complex ways).

In some cases, a language may pick out a single syllable to bear stress. In Czech, Finnish, and Georgian for example, stress is always on the initial syllable. In French, stress is always on the last syllable; and in Polish always on the second-to-last. Because of the importance of word-position in stress systems, linguists have special terms for final and near-final syllables: *ult* is final, *penult* is second to last, *antepenult* is third to last. (First, second, and third suffice for the beginnings of words.) Cross-linguistically, main stress seldom falls on a syllable other than one of the first two or last three, even in words of more than six syllables, though *pre-antepenultimate* stress is possible in English, if you use the right suffixes ("**pre**sidency," for instance). No language consistently stresses the *middle* syllable of all its words, for example.

Because stressed syllables occur near the edges of words, stress patterns provide excellent information on how to break down the continuous stream of speech into discrete words: that is, stress is *demarcative*, it marks edges. Studies with infants have shown that they are sensitive to the stress patterns of their language, and seem to use the information to group syllables together. For example, if you play a French infant (about eight months old) a string of three syllables in which the middle one is stressed (e.g., [ba.**da**.ga]), the child will remember [ba.**da**] but not [**da**.ga], arguably because French is a final-stress language, and the child is able to make a pretty good guess that [ba.**da**] is likely to be a word and [**da**.ga] is not. (See Chapter 20 for more discussion of infant speech perception.)

While main stress always occurs near word edges, some positional stress systems have alternating secondary stress across the entire word. The examples in (3) (from Bruce Hayes' 1981 monograph, *A Metrical Theory of Stress Rules*), are typical. (Segmental transcription from the source, including [y] for the palatal glide, is followed.) Preference for an alternating pattern is called the *rhythmic property* of stress.

(3)   Four basic types of alternating stress
   a.   Maranungku (Australia)
        primary stress on the initial syllable, and secondary stress on every other syllable thereafter:

'ti ralk	saliva	'lang ka ˌra te ˌti	prawn
'me re ˌpet	beard	'we le ˌpe ne ˌman ta	kind of duck
'yan gar ˌma ta	the Pleiades		

   b.   Weri (Papua New Guinea)
        primary stress on the final syllable, with secondary stress on each preceding alternate syllable

ŋin 'tip	bee	u ˌlu a 'mit	mist
ˌku li 'pu	hair of arm	ˌa ku ˌne te 'pal	times

   c.   Warao (Venezuela)
        primary stress on the penult, with secondary stress on each preceding alternate syllable

yi ˌwa a 'na e	he finished it
ˌya pu ˌru ki ˌta ne 'ha se	verily to climb
e ˌna ho ˌro a ˌha ku 'ta i	the one who caused him to eat

d.   Araucanian (Chile)
primary stress on the second syllable, and secondary stress on alternating syllables thereafter

wu 'le	tomorrow
ti 'pan to	year
e 'lu mu ˌyu	give us
e 'lu a ˌe new	he will give me
ki 'mu ba ˌlu wu ˌlay	he pretended not to know

English, of course, also often has alternating stress across the word, even though the position of the main stress is not as completely predictable as for the languages cited by Hayes. The pattern of stressed and unstressed syllables alternating is seen most clearly in long place names, such as "Apalachicola" [ˌæ pə ˌlæ tʃɪ 'ko lə], "Massachusetts" [ˌmæ sə 'tʃu sɪts] or "Canandaigua" [ˌkæ nɛn 'de gwə], but any polysyllabic word is likely to show an alternating pattern: ['al tɚ ˌne ɾɪŋ].

Two adjacent stressed syllables create a *stress clash*, a violation of the rhythmic property of stress. When two syllables with primary stress become adjacent across a word boundary in English, the resulting clash may force a *stress shift*. For example, stress on the word "sixteen" is usually on the final syllable, but it will (optionally) shift back to the first if the next word begins with primary stress. Try reading the dialog in example (4a) aloud. Does stress shift sound natural? Other examples are given in example (4b).

(4)   Stress clash and stress shift in English:

a.
How old are you?
Six**teen**.
Who came to your party?
Sixteen **friends**.

b.

kanga**roo**	**kan**garoo **court**	
Tennes**see**	**Ten**nessee **Titans**	**Ten**nessee **Waltz**
Pali**sades**	**Pali**sades **Park**way	

The rhythmic property is based in the definition of stress as a prominence relation: in order for a syllable to be prominent, it must have a less prominent background to stand out from.

Prominence is also related to a final factor in stress typology: *quantity sensitivity*. As was discussed in Chapter 15, syllable weight often makes a difference in stress patterns. Some syllables are already more prominent by virtue of having more segmental material in the rhyme, specifically a long vowel or a coda. In some languages, these heavy syllables attract stress. If a language has a stress system that pays attention to syllable weight, the system is termed *quantity-sensitive*. If weight does not matter, the system is *quantity insensitive*. All of the languages in example (3) are quantity-insensitive. Two examples of quantity-sensitive positional stress patterns are shown in example (5).

(5)   Interaction of syllable weight and position in quantity-sensitive systems:

a.   Meadow-Mari (Siberia)
Stress the rightmost long vowel, otherwise the first vowel.

ʃiːn 'tʃaːm	I sit
ʃlaː 'paː ʒəm	his hat
'pyː gəl mə	cone

'ki: də ʃtə ʒə	in his hand
'tə lə zən	moon's

b. Ojibwa (North America)

In words lacking a long vowel, stress falls on even-numbered syllables counting from the beginning of the word. In addition, the final syllable of every word is stressed.

ni 'bi mo ˌse	I walk
ni 'ni ˌba	I sleep
na 'ga ˌmo	he sings
ni 'na ga ˌmo ˌmin	we sing

In addition, stress all long vowels

bi 'mo ˌse:	he walks
ni 'bi mo ˌse: ˌmin	we walk
ni 'ni ˌba: ˌmin	we sleep

In both Meadow-Mari and Ojibwa, the introduction of quantity-sensitivity makes the system more complicated, but the different factors can be separated out. Meadow-Mari is essentially an initial-stress language, like Czech, but initial stress is over-ridden when an inherently-prominent long vowel pulls the stress away. Ojibwa is basically an alternating-stress language like Araucanian (3d), but additional stresses are overlaid on inherently-prominent syllables (long vowels and final syllables.)

The tendency for heavy syllables to attract stress is called the *Weight-to-Stress principle* ("If heavy, then stressed"). The opposite also holds: underlying light syllables that are in a position to be stressed may become heavy, by the *Stress-to-Weight principle* ("If stressed, then heavy"). The Stress-to-Weight principle was illustrated by the phenomenon of ambisyllabicity in English (Section 15.1.4), and is further illustrated by "rhythmic lengthening" in Hixkaryana, an Amazonian language. In Hixkaryana, as shown in example (6a), all closed syllables are stressed. In addition, every other syllable counting from the beginning of the word (or from the rightmost closed syllable) is stressed (with the exception that the final syllable is never stressed). There is no underlying distinction in vowel length, but all vowels in open stressed syllables are lengthened. (The source does not distinguish between primary and secondary stress.)

(6) Rhythmic lengthening in Hixkaryana:

closed syllables are stressed

'nak 'ɲoh 'jatʃ ke 'na: no	they were burning it
'ak ma 'ta: rɨ	branch

a. vowels in stressed syllables are lengthened

to 'ro: no	small bird
ne 'mo: ko 'to: no	it fell
'toh ku 'rʲe: ho na	to Tohkurye
'toh ku 'rʲe: ho 'na: ha 'ʃa: ha	finally to Tohkurye

When described in English prose, the pattern sounds complicated, but the complication arises from interacting factors, which are themselves not difficult: the rhythmic property ("every other syllable"), Weight-to-Stress ("all closed syllables are stressed"), and Stress-to-Weight ("all stressed syllables are heavy"). The last property, "no final stress," is also not uncommon: it crops up in other languages such as Latin and in English nouns. It is sometimes the case that a syllable or segment at the end of the word is excluded from consideration: this is known as *final extrametricality*. We will return to extrametricality in our account of English stress in Section 16.5.

16.3 a feature for stress?

The examples in the preceding sections have demonstrated that stress can be contrastive in some languages (like Russian), that in other languages (like French and Maranungku) its distribution can be predicted by rule, and that it can condition other phonological alternations (like tapping in English and lengthening in Hixkaryana). These properties indicate that stress must have a phonological representation. However, the examples in the preceding sections have also highlighted several different qualities of stress that set it apart from other phonological features. These properties are summarized here:

- *Stress has no single phonetic correlate.* Other features have a clear phonetic definition: [nasal] means an open velum, [coronal] means a tongue tip constriction, [+round] means pursing of the lips. But stress can be realized by a variety of different phonetic correlates, including length, pitch, loudness, and clarity of articulation.
- *Stress is multi-leveled.* We need to refer to three or four levels of stress. This is in contrast to other features, which are either binary or unary.
- *Stress is alternating.* Many languages require (or at least prefer) that every other syllable be stressed. We haven't seen cases where a language requires, for example, that every other vowel be round, or every other consonant be voiced.
- *Stress is culminative.* Culminativity means that stress marks a single prominence on every word. In languages that use stress at all, every content word has at least one stressed syllable, and only one stressed syllable is marked as primary. Other features are not culminative. No language has a requirement that there should be one and only one fricative per word, or one and only one nasal consonant.
- *Stress is positional.* The placement of stress is usually determined by the overall shape of the word: penultimate, initial, every other syllable counting from the left edge. No other feature has this sort of distribution.
- *Stress is demarcative.* Main stress is usually found near word edges, not in the middle of words. More so than other features, stress marks the boundaries between words.

All of these special qualities suggest that a feature [+/− stress] marked on an individual vowel is not the best representation. Rather, we can account for the fact that stress is inherently a multi-leveled relational property by incorporating syllables in a multi-leveled, relational *metrical structure*. We can account for the alternating nature of stress by basing the structure on groups of two. And we can account for the positional, demarcative, and culminative properties of stress by building the structure across a whole word.

16.4 metrical structure

We capture the alternating nature of stress by introducing the notion of a *metrical foot*. A foot is a grouping of one or more syllables, one of which (the *head*) is stressed. In the simplest case, a foot consists of two syllables. If the syllable on the left is stressed (left-headed) the foot is a *trochee*. If the syllable on the right is stressed (right-headed) the foot is an *iamb*. (It is unfortunate that the word "iamb" happens to be a trochee. One way to keep the two terms straight is to remember which side the consonant cluster is on: **tr**ochees are left-headed, ia**mb**s are right-headed.) The terms are borrowed from poetic analysis. Iambic pentameter, in which a line consists of five iambic feet, is one of the most common forms of English poetry, as illustrated by the lines in example (7). Trochaic rhythm is much less common, except in nursery rhymes, see example (8).

(7)   Iambic pentameter

(Know then) (thy**self**,) (pre**sume**) (not **God**) (to **scan**);
(The **prop**) (er **stud**) (y of) (man**kind**) (is **man**).

Alexander Pope, An Essay on Man

(Something) (there **is**) (that **does**) (not **love**) (a **wall**)
(That **sends**) (the **froz**) (en **ground**) (swell **un**) (der **it**)

Robert Frost, Mending Wall

(8)   Trochaic rhythms

(**Ring** a) (**round** the) (**ro**sy)
(**Po**cket) (**full** of) (**po**sies)

(**Twin**kle), (**twin**kle), (**litt**le) (star)
(**How** I) (**won**der) (**what** you) (are)

Good poets, of course, will mix things up a bit by occasionally switching the rhythm (as both Pope and Frost do in the first words of these selections), and by not always aligning feet with word boundaries. The principle that linguistic feet should be binary is simply stated as *foot binarity*.

16.2   In Focus

In versification, other kinds of foot structure may be used. Anapests (weak-weak-**strong**) and dactyls (**strong**-weak-weak) are ternary feet. Clement Moore's *A Visit from St. Nicholas* is written in anapests: ('Twas the **night**) (before **Christ**) (mas and **all**) (through the **house**). Tennyson's *Charge of the Light Brigade* uses dactyls: (**Can**non to) (**left** of them), (**Can**non to) (**right** of them), (**can**non in) (**front** of them), (**vol**leyed and) (**thun**dered). Ternary feet never seem to be necessary for linguistic word stress, however.

Parsing (that is, dividing up) words into trochaic or iambic feet accounts nicely for the four patterns of (quantity-insensitive) alternating feet described by Hayes. The languages also differ in whether they build feet to align at the end of the word (right edge) or at the beginning of the word (left edge). Two kinds of feet times two kinds of alignment equals four alternating stress patterns. Alignment is important in words with odd numbers of syllables: after the word has been broken down into bi-syllabic feet, there will be one syllable left over, either at the beginning of the word or at the end. In some languages (here, Maranungku and Weri), the leftover syllable will form a monosyllabic foot of its own. In other languages, (here, Warao and Araucanian), the leftover syllable is left *unfooted* (or, *unparsed*).

(9)   Alternating stress as foot structure:

    a.   Maranungku: trochaic feet aligned at the left edge

        ('yan gar) (ˌma ta)   the Pleiades
        ('lang ka) (ˌra te) (ˌti)   prawn
        ('we le) (ˌpe ne) (ˌman ta)   kind of duck

    b.   Weri: iambic feet aligned at the right edge

        (u ˌlu) (a 'mit)   mist
        (ˌa) (ku ˌne) (te 'pal)   times

    c.   Warao: trochaic feet aligned at the right edge

        (ˌya pu) (ˌru ki) (ˌta ne) ('ha se)   verily to climb
        e (ˌna ho) (ˌro a) (ˌha ku) ('ta i)   the one who caused him to eat

    d.   Araucanian: iambic feet aligned at the left edge

        (e 'lu) (mu ˌyu)   give us
        (e ' 'lu) (a ˌe) new   he will give me
        (ki 'mu) (ba ˌlu) (wu ˌlay)   he pretended not to know

Whether or not all syllables in an odd-numbered word are incorporated into feet can be seen as a conflict between two principles. On the one hand is the imperative to make feet binary (Foot Binarity). On the other hand is the imperative to incorporate all syllables of the word into feet (Parse). In some languages Parse wins out, and a foot of a single syllable is created. In others, Foot Binarity wins out, and the odd syllable is left unfooted. Whether or not a stress clash would be created can also be important: in examples (9c) and (9d), creating a foot and thereby stressing the leftover syllable would have created two stressed syllables in a row, while in examples (9a) and (9b) the alternating stress pattern is preserved.

As with syllable structure, these conflicting principles translate in straightforward fashion to an OT analysis (see Chapter 14). Parse, FootBinarity, Align-Left, Align-Right, and *Clash can be formulated as constraints which languages rank differently. Some exercises in accounting for stress patterns using ranked constraints are provided at the end of this chapter.

Main stress can be distinguished from secondary stress by choosing one foot in the word, either the rightmost or leftmost, to be the *head foot* of the word. These layers of prominence – one syllable is prominent in the foot, one foot is prominent in the word – can be graphically represented in either a *metrical tree* or a *bracketed metrical grid*. In a tree structure, each branch is labeled either strong or weak. In a grid structure, each mark in the grid (that is, each *x*) indicates a level of prominence. Grids and trees for words in Warao and Araucanian are shown in examples (10) and (11).

(10)   Stress in Warao: "verily to climb":

a. metrical grid

```
                        x
( x     x     x     x   )
( x  x )( x  x) ( x  x) ( x  x)
(ˌya pu) (ˌru ki) (ˌta ne) ('ha se)
```

b. metrical tree

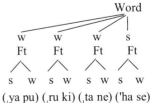

```
(ˌya pu) (ˌru ki) (ˌta ne) ('ha se)
```

(11) Stress in Araucanian: "he pretended not to know":

a. metrical grid   **b. metrical tree**

In general, trees and grids convey the same information, just in different graphical formats. Grids, however, may be more convenient for showing stress shift, as in English "Tennessee Titans." In the grid in example (12), primary stress is indicated by a column with three marks, secondary stress by a column with two marks, and unstressed syllables get only a single mark. Stress clash is indicated by two 3-mark columns adjacent to each other. Rhythmic regularity is restored by shifting the primary stress mark from the third syllable to the first.

(12) Stress shift in English: metrical grids

```
          x    x                    x                   x
x         x    x                    x           x       x
x    x    x    x    x                x     x    x    x   x
Ten  ne   see  Ti   tans   →   Ten  ne   see   Ti   tans
```

For languages that do not have alternating stress, but just a single stressed syllable at either the left or right edge, the alignment constraint takes precedence over other considerations: only a single foot, perfectly aligned to one edge or the other, is allowed. Final stress requires an iamb at the right edge; initial stress requires a trochee at the left edge. Penultimate stress requires a trochee at the right edge. The advantage to a single stressed syllable is that the edge of the word is more clearly demarcated.

There are two strategies for dealing with the rest of the word in such single-stress languages. One strategy is to build a single binary foot at the edge, and leave the other syllables unparsed. The other strategy is to create a single *unbounded* foot that encompasses the whole word. The former strategy obviously violates the PARSE constraint, the latter the FOOTBINARITY constraint. The two strategies are illustrated in example (13). Unfortunately, it is difficult to find empirical evidence that would distinguish between the two.

(13) Final stress in French: a single foot aligned at the right edge:

binary foot: psi ko (lo **ʒi**)   unbounded foot: (psi ko lo **ʒi**)

To account for quantity-sensitive systems, we need to recognize that foot structure can be sensitive to the distinction between light and heavy syllables. In Chapter 15, we discussed syllable weight in terms of moras. Heavy syllables have two moras, light syllables have one, as shown in example (14).

(14) Moraic representation of light and heavy syllables:

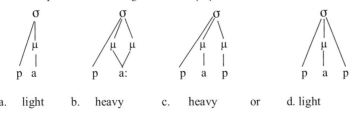

a. light   b. heavy   c. heavy   or   d. light

In all languages, short vowels will have one mora and long vowels will have two (that's what makes them long). Languages will differ in whether coda consonants are moraic or not: that is, some languages choose representation (14c) for closed syllables and some choose (14d). In languages where syllables with long vowels attract stress, but closed syllables do not (such as Meadow-Mari), we can infer that coda consonants are not moraic. In languages where closed syllables attract stress (Hixkaryana), we can infer that coda consonants are moraic.

We can account for quantity sensitive languages by revising the principle of Foot Binarity: "Feet must be binary at the syllable *or moraic* level." Allowing bimoraic as well as bisyllabic feet allows a single heavy syllable to be a foot on its own. The possible types of feet in quantity-senstive languages are shown in (15). The letter L stands for "light," the letter H for "heavy." The stressed syllable is bold.

(15)   Foot inventory in quantity-sensitive languages:

Trochee: (**L** L) or (**H**)
Iamb: (L **L**) or (**H**) or (L **H**)

A trochee can consist either of two light syllables (with the left one as the head), or of a single heavy syllable. Both are bimoraic. Conversely, an iamb can consist of two light syllables (right-headed). A heavy syllable can also be an iamb, if that is what the system demands. (You can only tell if a system is trochaic or iambic by looking at words with light syllables.) The preferred option for quantity-sensitive iambic systems, however, is **the uneven iamb** (L **H**), a bisyllabic foot that consists of a light syllable followed by a heavy syllable. Several different tendencies converge in creating uneven iambs: Stress-to-Weight and final lengthening both prefer (L **H**) to (L **L**), and an alternating stress pattern prefers (L **H**) to (**H**). Uneven trochees, which would be (**H** L), seem to be rare or non-existent.

Meadow-Mari is a quantity-sensitive trochaic system. A foot can consist of a heavy syllable, or two light syllables (example 16). Codas are not moraic in this language: the coda in the final syllable of the word for "moon's" does not make the syllable heavy. There is only one foot per word.

(16)   Foot structure in Meadow-Mari:

('ki:) də ʃtə ʒə   in his hand
(**H**)

('tə lə) zən   moon's
(**L** L)

Ojibwa is a quantity-sensitive iambic system. As in Meadow-Mari, feet can consist of two light syllables or one heavy syllable. Unlike Meadow-Mari, this language requires all syllables to be gathered into feet, even if a non-binary foot is created, and even if it causes a stress clash (as in the word for *I sleep*).

(17)   Foot structure in Ojibwa:

(ni 'bi) (mo ˌse)   I walk
(L **L**) (L   **L**)

(bi 'mo) (ˌse:)   he walks
(L **L**)   (**H**)

(ni 'ni) (ˌba)   I sleep
(L **L**) (**L**)

Hixkaryana is a slightly different quantity-sensitive iambic system. Feet may be (**H**) or (L **H**), and are aligned at the left edge. In a sequence of open syllables, the head syllable of the foot undergoes vowel lengthening to create an uneven iamb (L **H**). Some example words are shown in example (18).

(18)   Rhythmic lengthening in Hixkaryana:

('nak) ('ɲoh) ('jatʃ) (ke 'na:) no   they were burning it
(**H**)   (**H**)   (**H**)   (L **H**)

(to 'ro:) no   small bird
(L **H**)

('toh) (ku 'rʲe:) (ho 'na:) (ha 'ʃa:) ha   finally to Tohkurye
(**H**) (L **H**)   (L **H**)   (L **H**)

('toh) (ku 'rʲe:) ho na   to Tohkurye
(**H**) (L **H**)

Note that in the word "to Tohkurye," the last two syllables of the word remain unfooted. This is because of Hixkaryna's strict foot structure requirements (iambs only!) and its ban on final stress. If the last two syllables were made into an iamb, then stress would be final; if stress were non-final, then the foot wouldn't be an iamb. Caught in this bind, the language gives up and leaves the syllables unfooted.

16.5 stress in English

16.5.1 overview

This section turns to a brief overview of stress in English. English stress is more complicated than any of the purely positional systems discussed in section 16.4. First, as noted above, stress in English is not predictable in all cases. Is it ['kʰɑmɪri] "comedy" or ['kʰə'mɪri] "committee"? Why are "canal" and "giraffe" stressed on the final syllable but "camel" and "tariff" on the first? For some English words, you simply need to memorize the stress pattern as you do the meaning. That is, English is at least partly a lexical stress system.

The parts of the English stress system that are predictable are still quite complex – as witnessed by the number of book-length treatments of the subject. In large part, the complexity comes from the fact that the English system is paradigmatic – when there are rules, they're different depending on the part of speech. Thus "**ob**ject" (a thing) and "ob**ject**" (to protest) seem to be an unpredictable minimal pair, but "**ob**ject" perfectly follows the rule for nouns, and "ob**ject**" the rule for verbs. There are, in addition, numerous sub-rules that cover classes of apparent exceptions. We have space here to cover only the most general rules: See the list of readings at the end of the chapter for more detailed discussion.

In our discussion of English stress, we begin with the rule for nouns, then for verbs and adjectives, then discuss the role of affixation, keeping in mind that any of the rules described here can be over-ridden by a lexical specification, so that there will always be counter-examples. The original generalizations (and word lists) can be traced back to Chomsky and Halle (1968); the analysis in terms of metrical structure follows that of Hayes (1981). Additional examples, particularly for affixes, are taken from Kreidler (1989).

16.5.2 nouns

A set of words illustrating the English stress pattern for monomorphemic nouns is given in (19).

(19)   English noun stress

Group A:	Group B:	Group C:
Ari**zo**na	Ne**bras**ka	A**me**rica
di**plo**ma	a**gen**da	**ca**mera
pa**pay**a	ap**pen**dix	**al**gebra
ma**ri**na	a**mal**gam	**la**byrinth
cerebrum	co**nun**drum	as**pa**ragus
fac**to**tum	ve**ran**da	a**lu**minum
af**fi**davit	e**nig**ma	**sy**llable

In groups A and B, stress falls on the penult, and in group C, it falls on the antepenult. The distinguishing factor is the weight of the penult: English stress is quantity-sensitive. If the penultimate syllable is heavy (that is, contains a long vowel as in group A or a coda consonant as in group B), then the penult is stressed. This is the Weight-to-Stress principle at work. (Note that, for stress purposes, the tense vowels of English count as long.) If the penult is light, as in group C, then stress skips the penult and lands on the antepenult.

How does this translate into foot structure and alignment? English stress counts from the right edge (penult, antepenult), but in nouns that follow the regular pattern, the final syllable itself never receives main stress. As with Hixkaryana, we can call on the principle of final extrametricality to account for this. In English nouns, the final syllable is extrametrical: it is not incorporated into metrical structure. Once the last syllable is excluded, then we can account for the pattern by constructing a trochaic foot at the right edge of the word (not counting the final syllable), as shown in example (20). The trochee can consist of one heavy syllable, resulting in penultimate stress (groups A and B); or of two syllables, the second of which is light, resulting in antepenultimate stress (group C).

(20)   English noun stress: right-aligned trochaic feet with final syllable extrametricality:

L L H	L L H	L L
(æ.rɪ) (zoʊ) < nə >	(æ.nə) (kɑn) < də >	ə (mɛ. rɪ) < kə >
ˌAriˈzona	ˌanaˈconda	Aˈmerica

Additional feet are created across the word, resulting in alternating secondary stress, as long as there are enough syllables to create binary trochees. If there are multiple feet, the head foot (main stress) is rightmost.

It follows from final-syllable extrametricality that bisyllabic nouns will generally be stressed on the initial syllable, regardless of the weight of the second: "**al**cove, **ter**mite, **tex**tile." The counter-examples, including "ca**nal**" and "gi**raffe**," are mostly relatively recent (within the past few hundred years) borrowings from French, which idiosyncratically preserve their source stress pattern. For these words, stress must be marked in the lexical entry and memorized. In longer words, like "cigarette" and "magazine," pronunciation may vary between final stress (French pattern) and antepenultimate stress (English pattern).

If the noun is monosyllabic, then the principle of culminativity (all content words must be stressed) takes precedence over extrametricality, and the only available syllable is stressed: **girl, boy**. The syllable must be heavy, however: there is no way to make a binary foot out of a single light syllable, so words such as *[bɛ] are not allowed.

16.5.3 verbs and adjectives

English verbs also fall into groups, based on syllable structure. Representative examples are shown in (21). Most non-derived adjectives follow the same pattern as verbs, as shown in (22).

(21)   English verb stress:

Group D:	Group E:	Group F:
main**tain**	col**lapse**	as**to**nish
e**rase**	**tor**ment	**ed**it
ca**rouse**	e**lect**	i**ma**gine
sur**mise**	u**surp**	**can**cel
de**cide**	ob**serve**	in**ter**pret
de**vote**	a**dapt**	em**bar**rass
de**lay**	ex**empt**	re**mem**ber
re**ply**	in**volve**	so**li**cit

(22)   English adjective stress:

Group D:	Group E:	Group F:
su**preme**	ab**surd**	**so**lid
sin**cere**	cor**rupt**	**fran**tic
se**cure**	im**mense**	**hand**some
re**mote**	oc**cult**	clan**des**tine

For verbs and adjectives, the crucial syllable is the ult. If the ult has a long vowel, it is stressed (group D). If the ult has a short vowel followed by a consonant cluster, then it also receives stress (group E). However, if the ult has a short vowel followed by only one consonant, stress moves back to the penult (group F).

The analysis here is that while nouns have final *syllable* extrametricality, verbs and adjectives have final *consonant* extrametricality. As shown in (23), for verbs and adjectives the final consonant is marked as extrametrical, and then footing proceeds as for nouns: build a trochaic foot aligned to the right.

(23)   English verb and adjective stress:
right-aligned trochaic feet with final consonant extrametricality

H	H	L L
dɪ (saɪ) < d >	kə (læp) < s >	ɪ (mæ. gɪ) < n >
de'cide	col'lapse	i'magine

H	H	L L
rə (moʊ) < t >	kə (rʌp) < t >	(sɑ. lɪ) < d >
re'mote	cor'rupt	'solid

For verbs with a long final vowel (group D), the ult is heavy with or without a final consonant, so a bimoraic trochee can be built on the final syllable, and thus stress is final. In group E, where the verb ends in a consonant cluster, the final segment can be marked extrametrical and still leave another coda consonant to make the final syllable heavy. Again, a bimoraic trochee can be built on the single syllable, and stress is final. If there is only one consonant at the end of the word, however (group F), marking that consonant as extrametrical leaves the final syllable light. In that case, the penult must be incorporated as the head of the trochaic foot, resulting in penultimate stress.

16.3   In Focus

As noted above, in general, English tense vowels count as long, and thus attract stress, as in "re**mote**," and "ce**re**brum." An interesting sub-generalization, however, is that verbs that end in [-i] (usually spelled "y" as in "carry") and [-o], (usually spelled "ow" as in "follow"), act as though they have a lax, short vowel, not a tense, long vowel, in the final syllable. These verbs thus fall into group F, with penultimate stress, not group D. These final vowels are variously analyzed as (exceptionally) extrametrical, as underlying non-syllabic glides, or as underlying lax vowels. In the latter two cases, a special rule must apply to change the vowel quality, *after* stress has been determined.

If a verb has three or more syllables, and the final syllable is heavy, another variation on the stress pattern occurs: call it group G, illustrated in examples (24) and (25). In this case, where more than one trochaic foot can be built across the word, the *non-final* foot is chosen as the head. Main stress falls on the antepenult, with secondary stress falling on the ult.

(24)   Longer English verbs with antepenultimate stress (group G):

      in'timi‚date
      'illu‚strate
      'ridi‚cule
      'galli‚vant

(25)   Footing of group G verbs:

    L L **H**   L L   **H**
   (rɪ. dɪ) (kju) <l>   (gæ lɪ) (væn) <t>
   'ridi‚cule   'galli‚vant

This pattern only emerges in cases where the word is long enough to preserve the alternating character of stress, so that an unstressed syllable intervenes between main and secondary stress. The demarcative property of stress is also implicated: main stress never moves more than three syllables from the right edge (in non-derived words), so this pattern can occur only if the final syllable is heavy, taking up one foot by itself.

16.5.4 words with affixes, and lexical phonology

All the words in Sections 16.5.2 and 16.5.3 are monomorphemic. In this section, we briefly discuss some stress patterns for derived words, exemplifying three different types of suffix: *neutral* suffixes, *tonic* suffixes, and *post-tonic* suffixes. "Tonic syllable" is another term for "stressed syllable."

The neutral suffixes are the simplest. They have no effect on the stress pattern of the word to which they attach. Neutral suffixes include "-hood, -like, -ing, -ness, -less, -ship, -able, -y." A few examples are given in (26).

(26)   Words with neutral suffixes:

      'neighbor‚hood
      de'ciding
      'galli‚vanting

'purpose‚less
com'pleteness
'presidency
con'federacy
in'habitable
'partisanship

The tonic suffixes attract stress to themselves. These are mostly French borrowings (as you would expect), and include "-aire, -ee, -eer, -ese, -ette, and -ique," as in the words in (27) illustrate.

(27)   Words with tonic suffixes:

‚millio'naire
‚detai'nee
‚Japa'nese
‚kitche'nette
‚tech'nique
‚racke'teer

Notice that if the root word to which a tonic suffix attaches is one that would otherwise have final stress, the root stress shifts back one syllable in order to avoid clash and preserve an alternating pattern over the word: [ʤə'pæn] but [‚ʤæpə'nis].

The third type, the post-tonic suffixes, cause stress to shift to the syllable immediately preceding the suffix. These include "-ic, -al, -ity, -ify and -(t)ion," as shown in (28). Other examples were given in (2).

(28)   Words with post-tonic suffixes:

'atom	a'tomic
'acid	a'cidic
'parent	pa'rental
de'partment	de‚part'mental
'mortal	‚mor'tality
'humid	‚hu'midity
'person	per'sonify
'product	pro'duction

Accounting for the paradigmatic stress system of English forces the phonologist to confront the interaction of phonological and morphological information, the domain of *lexical phonology*. Stress patterns show us that phonological alternations are not always determined by phonological information alone, but that morphological information must sometimes be accessed as well.

One way to think about the interaction of morphology and phonology is to divide the lexicon into separate modules, or *levels*, and associate different phonological rules with each level. Words are then built in a step-wise derivation, with morphemes added one by one, and the relevant batch of phonological rules applies each time a new morpheme is added. In English, for example, post-tonic suffixes might be assigned to one level, compounds to another, with different stress rules applying for each. The neutral suffixes are added at a level where no stress rules apply, so they have no affect on word stress. Finally, phrasal rules apply. Example (29) shows a level-ordered derivation of different phrases built on the word "parent."

(29)   Interleaving of phonology and morphology:

root level	parent	parent	parent
root stress	'parent	'parent	'parent
level 1 affixes	—-	'parent + al	—-
level 1 stress	—-	pa'rental	—-
level 2 affixes	—-	—-	step + 'parent
compound stress	—-	—-	'step‚parent
level 3 affixes	'parent + ing	—-	—-
(no stress rules apply)			
phrasal level	'parenting 'skills	pa'rental 'rights	'new 'step‚parent
nuclear stress rule	‚parenting 'skills	pa‚rental 'rights	‚new 'step‚parent

The number of levels, and the assignment of morphemes and rules for each, is decided on a language-specific basis.

In a non-derivational approach, where multiple levels are not available, morphology/phonology interactions must be handled by different means. One way is to "index" constraints to specific morphemes, so that different lexical items are subject to different phonological patterns, but without an assumed derivational relationship. Another approach is to require that related words in a paradigm should have similar stress patterns. In both cases, morphological information is incorporated directly into the content of the constraints. The question of how to handle interactions between phonology and morphology remains an active area of study, with stress patterns often at the center of the debate.

chapter summary

- Linguistic stress is a prominence relation between syllables.
- Stress systems may be lexical (free), paradigmatic (making reference to morphological information), or positional (determined by position in the word). The English stress system is largely paradigmatic.
- Unlike other features, stress is multi-leveled, alternating, culminative (one main stress per word), positional, and demarcative (marking word edges). A binary or unary feature for stress cannot capture these properties.
- Alternating stress patterns are created by a series of binary feet. Trochaic feet are left-headed (strong-weak) and iambic feet are right-headed (weak-strong). Foot structure can be represented in bracketed grids or hierarchical trees.
- In a quantity sensitive stress system, heavy syllables attract stress. In a quantity-insensitive system, syllable weight has no effect on the stress pattern.
- Principles for constructing regular stress patterns include the following. These principles/constraints may be conflicting, and languages may rank them as more or less important.

PARSE: all syllables must be grouped into feet.
FOOTBINARITY: feet must be binary at the syllabic or moraic level.
ALIGN-FT-LEFT/ALIGN-FT-RIGHT: align feet at the left/right edge of the word.
ALIGN-HEAD-LEFT/ALIGN-HEAD-RIGHT: the leftmost/rightmost foot bears main stress.
*CLASH: stressed syllables must not be adjacent.
WEIGHT-TO-STRESS: heavy syllables must be stressed.
STRESS-TO-WEIGHT: stressed syllables must be heavy.

- To the extent that English stress is predictable, the system is paradigmatic and quantity-sensitive. English nouns are (generally) stressed on the penult if it is heavy, otherwise the antepenult (quantity-sensitive trochaic foot at the right edge of the word, with final syllable extrametricality). English verbs are generally stressed on the ult if it has a long vowel or ends in a consonant cluster, otherwise on the penult (quantity-sensitive trochaic foot at the right edge of the word, with final consonant extrametricality).
- English suffixes may be tonic, post-tonic, or neutral with respect to stress.
- Incorporating morphological information into phonological alternations, as is required for paradigmatic stress systems, is the purview of lexical phonology. Morphological information may be accessed by the phonology though a multi-leveled derivation, or via direct incorporation of morphological information into the statement of constraints.

further reading

Hayes, B. 1981. *A Metrical Theory of Stress Rules*. New York: Garland.
Hayes, B. 1995. *Metrical Stress Theory*. Chicago: University of Chicago Press.
Kiparsky, P. 1985. Some consequences of Lexical Phonology. *Phonology* 2: 85–138.
Lehiste, I. 1970. *Suprasegmentals*. Cambridge, MA: MIT Press.

review exercises

1. Define:

   linguistic stress
   final extrametricality
   ult, penult, antepenult
   iamb
   trochee

2. Explain what is meant by each of the following properties of stress systems:

   multi-leveled
   alternating
   culminative
   positional
   demarcative

3. What makes a stress system quantity-sensitive or quantity-insensitive?

4. Transcribe each of the following English words into IPA and indicate the stress patterns for each, using ' for primary stress and ˌ for secondary stress. Syllables with secondary stress will have full vowel quality, and completely unstressed syllables will have reduced vowel quality.

   secondary
   elementary
   stupendous
   appendicitis
   canine
   equivocation

(Continued)

5. Draw a metrical grid and metrical tree for each word in (4).

6. Give three more examples of the Compound Stress Rule and of the Nuclear Stress Rule. Can you think of any more minimal pairs, where compound and phrase are distinguished only by stress?

7. Put each of the following nouns into group A, B, or C (as in example 19), and explain for each word why the stress falls where it does.

   anaconda
   arithmetic
   elephant
   horizon
   synopsis
   tornado

8. Put each of the following verbs and adjectives into group D, E, or F (as in example 21) and explain for each word why the stress falls where it does.

   achieve
   exhaust
   careen
   convince
   consider
   promise
   certain
   distinct
   inane

9. Indicate whether each of the following words has a tonic, post-tonic, or neutral suffix

   auctioneer
   curiosity
   photographic
   dinette
   solidify
   personhood
   idiocy
   idiotic
   adulthood

further analysis and discussion

10. Consider the stress systems of the five languages below. For each, answer the following questions:
    a. Are feet aligned on the left or on the right?
    b. Are feet iambs or trochees?
    c. Does the main stress fall on the rightmost or leftmost foot?
    d. In words with an odd number of syllables, are leftover syllables made into a non-binary foot, or are they left out of the foot structure?
    e. Is the system quantity-sensitive? (If there is insufficient evidence to decide, you may assume the system is *not* QS.)

Two words in each language are shown in bold. Show the foot structure of each word (following the format in examples 16, 17, and 18 in the chapter).

11. Yimas. (Data from Foley, W. 1991. *The Yimas Language of New Guinea*. Stanford, CA: Stanford University Press.)

'waŋ.kaŋ	'bird'
'a.wak	'star'
'ki.aŋ	'cough'
'awt.maj.ŋi	'sugarcane'
'war.kap.wi	'wallaby'
'na.ma.rawt	'person'
'ma.ra.ˌŋa.pa	'type of basket'
'wan.ka.ˌna.wi	'insect'
'ta.pu.ˌka.niŋ	'bamboo'

12. Setswana place names. (Data courtesy of One Tlale.) Glosses are given only for names that are transparently meaningful. (Recall that nasals that do not precede a vowel are syllabic.)

'na.ta	
'ka.ɲe	
'o.tse	
mo.'re.mi	person who chops
lo.'ba.tse	
se.'ro.we	small hills
ma.'u.n	
ˌxa.bʊ.'ro.ne	it is befitting
ˌma.ha.'la.pʲe	
ˌle.tlʰa.'ka.ne	little reeds
ˌbo.bo.'no.ŋ	
m.ˌma.di.'na.re	mother of buffaloes
ma.ˌkxa.di.'kxa.di	
mo.ˌle.po.'lo.le	
ˌle.n.ˌtsʷe.le.'ta.u	a rock and a lion
ˌxa.le.ˌkxa.tʃʷʰa.'wa.ne	
m.ˌma.tʰu.ˌbu.du.'kʷa.ne	

Give the correct stress pattern for

se.le.bi.pʰi.kʷe

13. Fijian. (Data originally from A. Schütz 1985. *The Fijian Language*. Honolulu: University of Hawai'i Press, cited in McGarrity, L. 2003.)

'la.ko	go
bi.'na.ko	good
se.'ŋai	no
ki.'la:	know
ˌnre:.'nre:	difficult
pa.ˌrai.ma.'ri:	primary
ˌndai.ˌre:.ki.'ta:	director
te.ˌre.ni.ˌsi.si.'ta:	transistor
pe.ˌre.si.'te.ndi	president

(*Continued*)

further research

14. Translate your analyses of the languages above into OT terms.
    a. What is the ranking of ALIGN-FEET-LEFT and ALIGN-FEET-RIGHT?
    b. What is the ranking of FT-FORM=IAMB and FTFORM=TROCHEE?
    c. What is the ranking of ALIGN-HEAD-LEFT and ALIGN-HEAD-RIGHT?
    d. What is the ranking of PARSE and FOOT-BINARITY?
    e. What is the ranking of WEIGHT-TO-STRESS and the constraints on foot form and alignment?
15. Describe the stress system of another language, either known to you or that you've found in a descriptive grammar.

Go online Visit the book's companion website for additional resources relating to this chapter at: http://www.wiley.com/go/zsiga.

references

Stress typology
Hayes, B. 1981. *A Metrical Theory of Stress Rules*. New York: Garland.
Hayes, B. 1995. *Metrical Stress Theory*. Chicago: University of Chicago Press.
Kager, R. 1999. *Optimality Theory (Ch. 4)*. Cambridge: Cambridge University Press.
McGarrity, L. 2003. Constraints on patterns of primary and secondary stress. Doctoral dissertation, Indiana University.

English stress rules
Chomsky, N. and M. Halle. 1968. *The Sound Pattern of English*. Cambridge, MA: MIT Press/
Kreidler, C. 1989/2004. *The Pronunciation of English*. Oxford: Blackwell.

17 Tone and Intonation

A shocking number of people concerned with African languages still seem to think of tone as a species of esoteric, inscrutable, and utterly unfortunate accretion characteristic of underprivileged languages – a sort of cancerous malignancy afflicting an otherwise normal linguistic organism. Since there is thought to be no cure – or even reliable diagnosis – for the regrettable malady, the usual treatment is to ignore it, in hope that it will go away of itself.

William Welmers, *African Language Structures*, 1973, p. 73

Chapter outline

Linguistic tone is not, in fact, going to go away. As was noted in Chapter 4, it is the major Indo-European languages that are exceptional in *not* having tone, rather than the other way around, and the student of phonology cannot afford to ignore the role of tonal contrast and alternation in thousands of languages around the world. However, as Welmers goes on to say,

> The presence of tone need not cause us to tremble in our scientific boots. . . . [T]he varieties and functions of tonal contrasts in language are of the same order as the varieties and functions of any other contrasts; the problems of tonal analysis are simply typical problems of linguistic analysis.

This chapter follows up on Welmers' assertion by discussing tone as a phonological system. Section 17.1 discusses contrasts, alternations, and representations in tone languages. Section 17.2 discusses intonation, the use of pitch to convey discourse meaning, which both tonal and non-tonal languages exhibit.

Various aspects of tonal phonetics and phonology have been touched on in earlier chapters:

Chapter 4.6: definition of tone and intonation; transcription of contrastive tone
Chapter 5.3: laryngeal anatomy and control of F0
Chapter 8.2.2: making pitch tracks
Chapter 9.3.1: pitch perception
Chapter 13.4: basics of the autosegmental representation of tone

In this chapter, we build on these introductory notes to create a fuller picture of tonal and intonational phonology.

17.1 tone

17.1.1 tone contrasts

Tone is the use of pitch to create lexical contrast. In a tone language, two or more words can have identical segments, but differ in meaning because they are produced with a different pitch pattern. In the simplest tone system, each syllable is produced with either relatively high or relatively low pitch. Such a system is exemplified by many Bantu and Athabaskan languages, including Setswana (1) and Navajo (2). High tones are marked with an acute accent on the vowel; low tones with a grave accent.

(1) Setswana tone contrasts:
    a. Two patterns on monosyllables:

High		Low	
xá	his	xà	not
ú-	s/he	ù-	you (sg)

    b. Four patterns on disyllables:

High – High		Low – Low		High – Low		Low – High	
ńná	many men			ńnà	stay	ǹná	me
		hùlà	graze	húlà	shoot		
		bùwà	skin (v.)	búwà	speak		
		tàlà	hunger	tálà	fill up	tàlá	green

(2) Navajo tone contrasts:

High		Low	
jí	he	jìs	I

High – High	Low – Low	High – Low	Low – High
jí-dzí:s	jìʃ-tʃà	jí-tʃà	jìs-dzí:s
he dragged it	I cry	he cried	I drag it

Note that, in Setswana, syllabic nasals may bear tone, indicating that tone is not just a property of vowels (see Section 17.1.2 below).

Yoruba (Nigeria) and Punjabi (Pakistan) are typical of the many languages that contrast high vs. mid. vs. low tones.

(3) Yoruba tone contrasts: three levels:

High		Mid		Low	
wá	to come	wa	to look	wà	to exist
kɔ́	to teach	pa	to kill	kɔ̀	to divorce

(4) Punjabi tone contrasts: three levels:

High		Mid		Low	
kár	boil	kar	bottom	kàr	chisel
kóra:	leper	kora:	whip	kòra:	horse

Figure 17.1 graphs the F0 patterns of the three Yoruba tones. It is not the case that pitch is absolutely flat over the course of the syllable, but the contrast is between relative pitch heights.

Languages contrasting four and five tone levels have also been described, as illustrated by Mazatec, spoken in Mexico (5), Grebo, spoken in Liberia (6), and Black Miao, spoken in Southern China (7). In these complex and more densely-specified systems, numbers are typically used to indicate relative pitch height, rather than a large set of diacritical marks. In an unfortunate but long-standing terminological inconsistency, Meso-American and African linguistic descriptions usually use the numeral 1 for the highest tone and 4 or 5 for the lowest, while Asian linguistic descriptions use 1 for lowest and 5 for highest.

(5) Chiquihuitlan Mazatec tone contrasts: four levels:

high	mid-high	mid-low	low
tʃa¹	tʃa²	tʃa³	tʃa⁴
I talk	difficult	his hand	he talks

(6) Grebo tone contrasts: four levels:

high	mid-high	mid-low	low
to¹	na²	mɔ³	fã⁴
store	fire	you-sg	herring

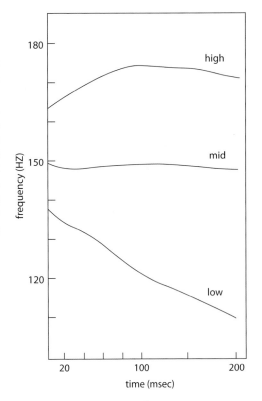

Figure 17.1 Three tones in Yoruba.

Source: Gandour, J. 1978. The perception of tone. In V. Fromkin (ed.), *Tone: A Linguistic Survey*. New York: Academic Press.

(7)   Black Miao tone contrasts: 5 levels and 3 contours:

extra high (5)	high (4)	mid (3)	low (2)	extra low (1)	high-rising (35)	low-rising (13)	high-falling (51)
[la] short	[la] a classifier	[la] cave	[la] to move away	[la] candle	[la] to squeeze	[ɬju] to rescue	[laqa] to mow
[ta] to take	[xan] to walk	[tjo] broom	[tɔ] far	[tju] waist	[ta] to break	[tɔ] not	[tano] to fall

Languages that contrast only relative pitch levels may be termed *register tone languages*. Other languages, termed *contour tone languages*, add an additional dimension, making use of patterns in which the pitch necessarily moves up or down (or both) over the course of the syllable. In contour tone languages the course and timing of these pitch rises and falls, not just different pitch levels, are crucial in distinguishing lexical items. As illustrated in example (7), Black Miao is argued to contrast three different contours, two different rises and a fall, in addition to its five level tones. Other contour tone languages include Thai (example (8), and Figure 17.2), Mandarin (example (9) and Figure 17.3), and Cantonese (example 10). (The different "dialects" of Chinese (more accurately described as different languages spoken in China) have very different tone systems. As shown in the figures, in these languages the actual tone contour shapes can be quite complex, and don't necessarily match up perfectly with their linguistic labels: the "high" tone in Thai, for example, is only high at the very end, and the "rising" tone is low for most of its duration.)

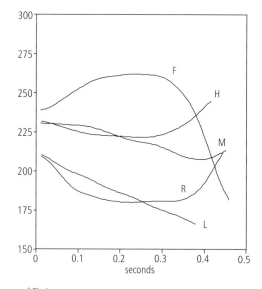

Figure 17.2 The five tones of Thai.
Source: Morén, Bruce and Elizabeth C. Zsiga (2006). The lexical and post-lexical phonology of Thai tones. *Natural Language and Linguistic Theory* 24(1): 113–178. Reprinted with permission of Springer.

(8)   Thai tone contrasts:

High	Mid	Low	Falling	Rising
ná	na	nà	nâ	nǎ
aunt	custard apple	rice field	face	thick
kʰá	kʰa	kʰà	kʰâ	kʰǎ
trade	galangal	be stuck	value	leg
lám	laŋ	làŋ	lâm	lǎŋ
go beyond	crate	flow	sturdy	back

(9)   Mandarin tone contrasts:

High (tone 1)	High-rising (tone 2)	Fall-Rise ("dipping", tone 3)	Falling (tone 4)
má	mǎ	mǎ	mâ
mother	hemp	horse	scold

(10)   The seven tones of Cantonese:

high (5) [siː] poem	mid-high (4) [siː] to try, taste	mid-low (3) [siː] affair, undertaking	low (21) [siː] time	high-rising (35) [siː] to cause, make	low-rising (24) [siː] market, city	high-falling (53) [siː] silk

In many tone languages, pitch and voice quality vary together. In Mandarin, for example, the "dipping" tone has noticeable laryngealized quality at the point of lowest pitch. Low tones are also glottalized in Burmese and in Munduruku (Brazil), but glottalization can be associated with either extreme of the pitch range. High tones are glottalized in Navajo. It makes sense that there should be interactions between pitch and voice, as both distinctions are produced by changing the tension and position of the vocal folds. Such interactions may account for *tonogenesis*: the process by which tone contrasts arise over time. For example, F0 is always slightly higher following aspirated stops than following voiced stops, due to differences in vocal fold tension. Over several generations, that small effect may be reinterpreted as a tonal contrast.

In other languages, however, voice quality and pitch vary independently: in the Nambikwara language of Brazil, for example, any of three tones can occur on either a plain or laryngealized vowel, as shown in example (11). Vowel nasalization is also contrastive in this language, resulting in a plethora of diacritics, so tones are marked as superscripts: 1 = falling, 2 = rising, and 3 = level.

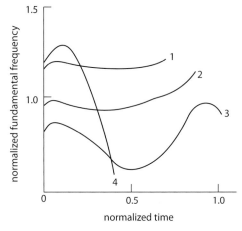

Figure 17.3   The tones of Mandarin Chinese.
Source: Gandour, J. 1978. The Perception of Tone. In V. Fromkin (ed.), *Tone: A Linguistic Survey.* New York: Academic Press. Reprinted with permission of Elsevier.

(11)   Contrastive tone, nasalization, and voice quality in Nambikwara. (Syllables illustrating the contrast are in bold.)

a.   Contrastive tone on plain vowels

ʔwã³**na**¹la²	I came
ʔwãn³**na**²la²	he came
ʔwãn²**na**³la²	he is coming

b. Constrastive tone on laryngealized vowels

ʔwḭ̃¹suʔ²	toad
waʔ³tṵtʔ²su²	frog
ʔwḭ̃³sʔu²	yam

An even more extensive systems of contrast is found in Mpi, spoken in Northern Thailand. This language contrasts six tones (three level, two rising, and one falling), any one of which can occur with either modal or creaky phonation, as shown in example (12).

(12) Tone and voice quality in Mpi:

	High	Mid	Low	Mid-Rising	Low-Rising	Falling
Modal voice	[siː] four	[siː] a color	[siː] blood	[siː] to roll rope	[siː] to be putrid	[siː] to die
Creaky voice	[sḭː] a name	[sḭː] classifier	[sḭː] seven	[sḭː] to smoke	[sḭː] to be dried up	[sḭː] a name

Contrasting with the rich tonal inventories of languages like Mpi or Cantonese are the sparsely specified *pitch accent* languages. In these languages, pitch is used to distinguish lexical meaning, but is not specified on every syllable. Rather, a particular tune, or *accent*, is associated to no more than one syllable in the word. It is the location of the pitch accent that creates the contrast. Pitch accent languages include Tokyo Japanese, Swedish, and Serbian/Croatian. In Japanese, for example, there is a three way contrast on disyllabic nouns (illustrated here with the unaccented nominative suffix "-ga"): accent and pitch fall on the first syllable [**ka**ki-ga] *oyster*, accent and pitch fall on the second syllable [ka**ki**-ga] *fence*, or no accent and no fall [kaki-ga] *persimmon*.

17.1.2 tonal representations

What phonological features best account for these systems? As was the case with segmental features (see Chapter 12), the question can be rephrased as "What is a possible tonal contrast?" What set of features is needed to account for all the attested contrasts, without predicting contrasts that do not occur? It is not the case that any random pitch shape can be a contrastive tone: while the set of contrasts in some languages may be large, it is not indefinitely large. Crucially, our set of features must account for up to five distinct levels (but not more), as well as the set of possible contours, which include simple rises and falls, falling-rising or rising-falling shapes, and rises and falls that move across only part of the pitch range, as in the high-rising vs. low-rising contours of Cantonese.

Here, an autosegmental representation will be assumed, in which contrastive tone features High (H) and Low (L) are linked via association lines to the units that realize them (the *tone-bearing unit* or *TBU*). As was discussed in Chapter 13.4, mostly with respect to two-tone Bantu languages, tone was the first kind of phonological contrast to be represented autosegmentally, and the representation offers many advantages. Here, we expand the discussion to account for a wider variety of tone languages and tone patterns.

The representation of a two- or three-tone register tone language, such as Setswana or Yoruba, is straightforward, as shown in example (13). In a three-tone language, any syllable may be associated with H (high tone), L (low tone) or no specification (realized as mid). In a two-tone language, the contrast may be analyzed as either H vs. L or H vs. Ø, depending on the alternations in which the non-high syllables participate or fail to participate. The TBU is usually assumed to be the syllable, because any syllable nucleus, whether a vowel or syllabic sonorant (as in Setswana [ńná] *many men* vs. [ǹná] *me*) can bear tone.

(13) Autosegmental representation of two and three levels in a register tone language:

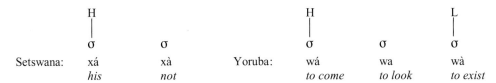

Setswana: xá   xà   Yoruba: wá   wa   wà
         his   *not*   *to come*   *to look*   *to exist*

For more than three levels, an elaboration of the tonal feature geometry is required. Several phonologists, beginning with Moira Yip in 1980, have argued for the addition of a **Register** feature, [+/− Upper], which distinguishes tones made in the upper half vs. the lower half of the pitch range. Thus, the five levels of Black Miao might be represented as in (14).

(14) Autosegmental representation of up to five levels:

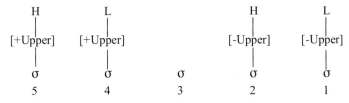

The mid tone, neither high nor low, remains unspecified. For simpler systems, the register feature may also be left unspecified, reducing the set of contrasts in example (14) to that in example (13).

Having accounted for up to five levels, we can now add contours to the mix. As was discussed in Chapter 13, an advantage of autosegmental representation is that associations between tones and TBUs are not necessarily one-to-one. Contours, therefore, can be represented as a sequence of tones associated to a single TBU: HL (Fall) or LH (Rise). One of the first languages analyzed with an autosegmental representation of tone contours was Mende, (Sierra Leone), analyzed by Will Leben in 1978. Mende contrasts five tones on monosyllables: High, Low, Rising, Falling, and a more complex Rise-Fall, which would be represented as shown in example (15).

(15) Autosegmental representation of levels and contours in Mende:

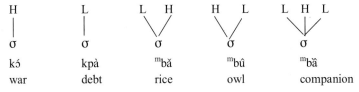

Such representations are particularly compelling when there is evidence that the forms with contour tones are related to or derived from forms where the H and L are realized on separate syllables. This was seen in Chapter 13 in Etsako (examples 18, 19, 20, 21, 22, and 23), where the rising tone in [ówǒwà] *every house*, is derived from the low – high sequence in /ówà # ówà/. When one of the vowels is deleted or becomes a glide, the two tones crowd onto a single syllable, creating a contour. Another example comes from Margi (Nigeria): /tì/ *morning* + /árì/ *definite suffix* becomes [tjǎrì] *the morning*.

Mende provides an example of tones spreading out when new vowels are added. Some Mende suffixes, such as [-hu] *in* and [-ma] *on*, have no inherent tone of their own. Instead, the tone or tones of the root spread out to cover the available syllables. Compare the forms in example (15) to those in example (16).

(16)   Toneless suffixes in Mende:

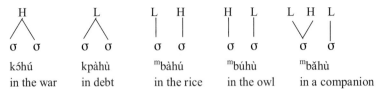

kɔ́hú	kpàhù	ᵐbàhú	ᵐbúhù	ᵐbǎhù
in the war	in debt	in the rice	in the owl	in a companion

Such alternations only make sense in a system where Rises and Falls are decomposed into sequences of H and L, with varying possibilities for association.

These kinds of alternations, however, while ubiquitous in Africa, are not often found in the contour tone languages of Asia. Thus, some linguists who study Asian tone languages argue that in contour tone languages like Thai, Mandarin, and Cantonese, the movement itself, the upward or downward pitch glide, is the non-compositional unit of contrast. Tone features proposed in this line of analysis might include direction, slope, and contour shape. Phonologists who argue for a non-compositional analysis rightly point out that actual contour shapes are more complex than a sequence of H + L or L + H.

Some of the details of contour complexity may be resolved, however, by reconsidering the TBU. In a number of languages, distributional facts suggest that the mora, rather than the syllable, is the tone-bearing unit. (See chapters 15 and 16 for more discussion of the mora as a sub-syllabic unit.) Hausa, for example, contrasts high, low, and falling tones. The falling tone, however, can occur only on heavy syllables, suggesting the representations in example (17).

(17)   The mora as the TBU in Hausa:

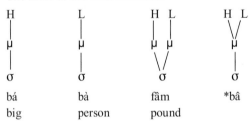

bá	bà	fâm	*bâ
big	person	pound	

The situation is similar in Thai. All five tones occur on syllables with long vowels or with a sonorant coda (as was shown above in example (8)), but no contours are permitted on open syllables with short vowels. This distribution suggests that, like Hausa, Thai allows only one tone per mora.

If tones associate to moras, more complex shapes can be represented. One can account, for example, for the fact that that High and Low tones in Thai begin in the middle of the pitch range and reach a high or low peak only at the end of the syllable (Figure 17.2) by assuming that the H or L specification is associated only to the second mora, as shown in example (18).

(18)   The mora as the TBU in Thai:

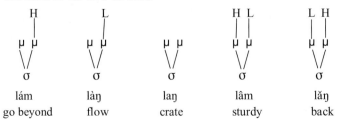

lám	làŋ	laŋ	lâm	lǎŋ
go beyond	flow	crate	sturdy	back

Many specialists in Asian tone languages remain skeptical of representations such as those in example (18), however.

How exactly a given tonal inventory is featurally represented depends not only on the inventory itself but on the tone alternations found in a language. It is to tone alternations that the next sections now turn. Tonal alternations in African (17.1.3) and Asian (17.1.4) systems have been the most extensively discussed in the literature. Similar rules do occur in tone languages on other continents, but the tonal phonology of the languages of the Americas and of Papua New Guinea have been less extensively studied.

17.1.3 tone alternations: the evidence from Africa and the Americas

Like segmental features, tones often change when morphemes or words are concatenated. Tones may assimilate or dissimilate, be simplified, inserted, or deleted. In addition, especially in African languages, tones show a striking *mobility*. As Yip (2002, p. 132) notes "[W]e have, time and again, seen tone that starts life on one morpheme, but either spreads to a chain of adjacent morphemes or surfaces on a different morpheme altogether." The mobility of tone, along with the many-to-one and one-to-many mappings illustrated in the previous section, strongly suggest its autosegmental representation.

We have already noted the example of tone spreading in Shona (Chapter 13, examples (24) and (25)), whereby the H of a high-toned verb spreads rightward over a string of suffixes. An example in which both H and L spread comes from Barasana, a language spoken in Colombia. In this language, rightward spread is triggered by compounding: the lexical tones of the second member of the compound are deleted, and the rightmost tone of the first word then spreads rightward, as shown in examples (19) and (20). (Nasalization also spreads rightward from a nasal consonant, but is not shown to limit notational complexity.) In Barasana, the evidence that Low tones can actively displace High, as in the word for *shaman*, argues for specification of both H and L.

(19) H and L spreading in Barasana:

    a. High tone spreads rightward

        héá + ŋìtáà –> héá- ŋìtáá
        fire   *stone*   *flint*

        cìtá + ùtía –> cìtá-útía
        earth   *wasps*   *species of wasp*

        wàí + kúbà –> wàí-kúbá
        fish   *stew*   *wai stew*
        species

    b. Low tone spreads rightward

        héè + jáí   –> héè-jàì
        ancestor *jaguar*   *shaman*

        ŋìtáà + hídò –> ŋìtáà-hìdò
        stone   *anaconda* *rock anaconda*

        újù + kúbà –> újù kùbà
        fish   *stew*   *uju stew*
        species

(20)   Autosegmental representation of Barasana tone spreading:

```
L H   H L          L H              L H
| |   | |          | |              | |⟍
w a i + k u b a  → w a i + k u b a → w a i + k ù b a      wai stew
```

```
H L   H L          H L              H L
| |   | |          | |              | |⟍
u j u + k u b a  → u j u + k u b a → u j u + k ù b a      uju stew
```

In both Shona and Barasana, the rightward spreading is long-distance: the spreading continues from syllable to syllable all the way to the right edge of the word. Other cases of tone spreading are local, with the tone spreading just one syllable over. If the spreading tone displaces the original tone of the next syllable, the process is known as *tone doubling*. Example (21) shows High tone doubling in Bade and example (22) shows Low tone doubling in Ngizim. (The languages are related; both are spoken in Nigeria. The exact pronunciation of the Bade tone sequence is discussed in example (29) below.)

(21)   High tone doubling in Bade:

```
H   L H              H   L H
|   | |              ⟍  ⧣ |
n ə n  k a t a w  →  n ə n  k a t a w      I returned
```

(22)   Low tone doubling in Ngizim:

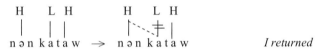

```
L   H              L   H
|   ∧              ⟍  ⤬∖
a  ga fi      →    a  ga fi      à gàfì  catch!
```

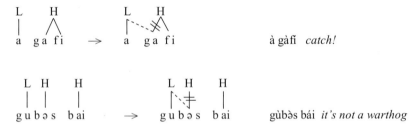

```
L H   H              L H   H
| |   |              ⟍ ⧣  |
g u b ə s  b ai  →  g u b ə s  b ai      gùbə̀s bái  it's not a warthog
```

As was noted in Chapter 13, the double strike-through indicates *delinking* of the association line: the underlying tone is no longer associated with that syllable. In other cases, spreading takes place without delinking, resulting in a contour, as is the case in Nupe (Nigeria), where Low + High sequences are realized as Low + Rising (example 23), and Lama (Togo) where High + Low is realized as High + Falling (example 24).

(23)   Low tone spreading without delinking in Nupe:

```
L   H              L   H
|   |              ⟍  ⟍|
e  b e      →      e  b e      èbě  pumpkin
```

(24)   High tone spreading without delinking in Lama:

```
H   L              H   L
|   |              ⟍  ⟍|
jo  ri      →      jo  ri      jó child + rì mother → jó rî  child's mother
```

Another example of tone mobility is *tone shift*, found in many Bantu languages. In tone shift, a tone surfaces on a syllable different from the one with which it is lexically associated. In Chizigula (Tanzania), for example, a verb root may be either high-toned or toneless, and it is this lexical specification that determines whether or not there will be a High tone in the word or not. The actual pitch peak, however, will always surface on the second-to-last syllable, as illustrated in example (25). In this example, the verb root /lómbez/, *to request*, contributes a high tone to the representation. The H does not appear on its "sponsoring morpheme," however. The tone shifts rightward, appearing on the second-to-last syllable, whatever that may be. Other verbs, such as /damaɲ/, *to choose*, are toneless. With toneless verbs, there is no H anywhere in the word. (The fact that verbs without High tone are inert, showing no change at all, supports an analysis of the language as contrasting H vs. Ø, rather than H vs. L.)

(25)   Chizigula tone shift:

High-toned verb		Toneless verb	
ku-lombéz-a	to request	ku-damaɲ-a	to do
ku-lombez-éz-a	to request for	ku-damaɲ-iz-	to do for
ku-lombez-ez-án-a	to request for each other	ku-damaɲ-iz-an-a	to do for each other

In languages that show tone shift, the movement is generally to a syllable at or near the word edge. The positional nature of the shift indicates an association with stress: pitch peaks, which make a syllable perceptually prominent, are attracted to syllables that are already made prominent due to stress. (See Chapter 16.)

In other cases, tone may shift *away* from a word edge. In Somali, for example, the last syllable of a phrase may not bear High tone. If a word that ends in a High tone occurs in phrase-final position, the tone shifts back one syllable: /tukéé/ *crow* becomes [túke] when it occurs at the end of a sentence. This sort of shift is likely an interaction with intonation (see 17.2).

Tone alternations illustrate mobility (spread and shift) and stability (sticking around when the TBU to which they were originally associated disappears, as in Etsako – Chapter 13, examples 18, 19, 20. 21, 22, 23). Tone alternations also show effects of the Obligatory Contour Principle (OCP). As was noted in Chapter 13, the OCP states that "adjacent identical elements are prohibited." Thus OCP effects are a type of dissimilation. The classic example of an OCP effect is Meeusen's Rule (H –> Ø / ___ H), which was illustrated in Chapter 13 (examples 26, 27, 28, and 29) with data from Shona. Another example is from the Bantu language Vai (Liberia). In this language, the first H in a sequence is deleted, with subsequent doubling of a preceding L.

(26)   OCP effects in Vai:

A further type of dissimilation and possible OCP effect is *downstep*. Sometimes, in a sequence of High tones, the second is realized a step down – not as low as a Low tone, but lower than the previous High. An example is seen in the contrastive tones of Efik (Nigeria). In this language, nouns are typically bisyllabic, and they exhibit five possible tone patterns, as shown in example (27). (The example follows the source, Welmers 1973, in indicating relative pitch height with horizontal lines. The autosegmental representations are added.) Traditionally, the downstepped tone is transcribed with a High-tone diacritic, but with an exclamation point preceding the syllable.

(27)   Contrastive tones of Efik:

Sequence	Example	Pitch levels	Representation
High-High	íják *fish*	(− −)	H / σ σ
Low-Low	èsò *pot*	(− −)	L / σ σ
High-Low	úfɔk *house*	(− −)	H L / σ σ
Low-High	ìwá *cassava*	(− −)	L H / σ σ
High-Downstep	ó!bóŋ *chief*	(− −)	H ? / σ σ

How should the downstepped tone be represented? One obvious approach would be to call this a mid tone, and leave the syllable unspecified. This fails to account, however, for why this mid-level tone occurs only after H, never in initial position, and never after L. The restricted distribution can be contrasted with true three-tone languages, like Yoruba, where Mid tones can occur in any position.

Further information comes from languages where downstep of High tones occurs in phrasal contexts. In many tone languages, High tones are downstepped after every Low tone. An example comes from Bimoba (Ghana). As shown in example (28), a sequence of High tones is realized with level high pitch (here indicated as 5). If a Low tone (1) interrupts the sequence, all following Highs are stepped down in pitch (3).

(28)   Downstep in Bimoba:

All High tones:
5 5   5 5   5 5
gbátúk   ŋmítí   gbátúk
a bushbaby is cutting a bushbaby

A Low tone interrupts: 5   5   1   3   3   3
                              gbátúk   gòtí   gbátúk
                              a bushbaby is looking at a bushbaby

In longer sentences, where H and L are interspersed, the effect is that High tones step down after every L, like a staircase.

In many cases, downstep can be traced to an underlying Low that has been delinked. This is the case in Bade. Recall, from example (21), that a Low between two Highs is delinked, with H doubling. The final H of the sequence, however, is realized a step down from the first, suggesting that the delinked L is still present and exerting a lowering effect, even if not associated to a syllable. Its *floating* status may be emphasized by enclosing it in a circle.

(29)   Delinked L causes downstep in Bade:

nɔnká!táw *I returned*

Assuming the generality of the principle that downstep of H is caused by a preceding L, whether or not it is overtly realized, floating Ls can be posited in lexical representations, to account for patterns of contrast such as those found in Efik.

(30)   Post-high contrasts in Efik (revised):

Sequence	Example	Pitch levels	Representation
High-High	íják *fish*	(– –)	H over σ σ
High-Low	úfɔk *house*	(– , –)	H L over σ σ
High-Downstep	ɔ́!bɔ́ŋ *chief*	(– , –)	H Ⓛ H over σ σ

On this account, downstep can be seen as an OCP effect, with the floating Low inserted to break up the sequence of identical H tones.

Tonal alternations can also signal syntactic and morphological changes. Information such as verbal tense and aspect, or nominal inflection, which are usually signaled in non-tone languages with segmental affixes, can in tone languages be indicated by tone changes without the addition of any segments. We've already seen an example of the tonal "associative morpheme" in Igbo in Chapter 13 (example 30). In Igbo, "jaw" is [àgbà] and "monkey" is [ènʷè] (all low tones), but "jaw of a monkey" is [àgbá ènwè], with the meaning "of" indicated by changing the tone of the second syllable from low to high. Another example is seen in Vai. In this language, verbs can bear a variety of underlying tone patterns, as illustrated in example (31a). The verb root is shown in bold. Some morphemes do have segmental content, as in the future suffix [-ʔá]. The imperative form, however, is indicated by a change in tone alone, with no segmental suffix, as in example (31b).

(31)   A tonal morpheme in Vai: L = imperative:

    a.   Future suffix: add [-ʔà], no change to underlying tone of the verb

        àì mú **kúné** - ʔà   he will wake us up
        àì kɔ̌ŋ **tǐé** - ʔà   he will cut sticks
        àì kɔ̌ŋě **lésì** - ʔà   he will catch the stick

    b.   Imperative: tone change with no segmental content

        mú **kùnè**   wake us up!
        kɔ̌ŋ **tìè**   cut sticks!
        kɔ̌ŋɛ **lèsì**   catch the stick!

The analysis is that the imperative morpheme consists of a Low tone, which replaces the underlying tones of the verb.

17.1.4 tone alternations: the evidence from Asia

The examples in the previous section have mostly been from African languages: tone mobility, stability, OCP effects, and tonal morphemes are highly salient characteristics of the phonology of these languages, and have been extensively discussed in the phonological literature. There are both similarities and differences between typical African and typical Asian tone systems. In Asian tone languages, complex contour tones are more common, and tone alternations are less so. Syllable structures tend to be more complex as well, but words tend to be monosyllabic, so there is less opportunity for the kinds of tonal alternations seen in languages like those of the Bantu family, with their concatenation of numerous morphemes. In many or most cases, syllables in Asian systems retain their underlying tones. When changes do occur, they are commonly referred to as *tone sandhi*. Several examples of tone sandhi in Asian languages will be discussed in this section, illustrating both similarities to and differences from African languages. (In the absence of phonetic data, transcriptions cited here follow those of the sources.)

> 17.1   *Sandhi* is originally a Sanskrit term, meaning *juncture*; phonologists borrowed it to refer to alternations that occur over a word boundary; tonal phonologists may use it more generally to refer to any contextually-determined phonological tone change.

A case of single-feature spreading, very similar to that seen in Barasana (examples 19 and 20) is found in Shanghai. As was the case in Barasana, non-initial syllables in a phrase lose their lexical tones, and the tones of the initial syllable spread over the phrase. In example (32), the word /mǎ/ *buy* has a rising tone. When the verb takes an object, the underlying tone of the object is deleted, and the LH pattern of the verb is distributed over the two words in the phrase. The loss of the underlying tone of the object can sometimes lead to loss of contrast, for which (as noted by Chen 2000) "presumably linguistic and pragmatic contexts more than compensate."

(32)   Tone deletion and spreading in Shanghai:

        ma-LH   buy
        mɔ-HM   cat
        mɔ-LM   hat

        ma-L mɔ-H   buy a cat
        ma-L mɔ-H   buy a hat

In other cases, contours can spread or be copied as a whole. One example is from Changzhi (central China). Like Mende (example 15), this language also has suffixes (such as [-tə(ʔ)] *diminutive*) that receive their tone from the root, but in this case the whole contour is copied, as in example (33).

(33) Changzhi tone copy:

tsə²¹³-tə²¹³   cart
paŋ⁵³⁵-tə⁵³⁵   board
xæ²⁴-tə?²⁴   child
çiaŋ⁵³-tə?⁵³   fillings

Whole tone copy can be represented as spreading of the register node, as in example (34), where the 535 tone is represented as HLH within the upper register. This is comparable to the representation of complete segmental assimilation, which involves spreading of the root node, vs. single-feature assimilation. As with segments, different models of tone feature geometry make different predictions about the sets of features that may or may not spread together: see Yip (2002) and Chen (2000) for further discussion.

(34) Tone copy as register node spreading:

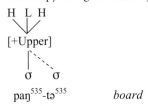

paŋ⁵³⁵-tə⁵³⁵   *board*

An example of an OCP effect is found in Tianjin, a language in the Mandarin family. In this language, two identical tones cannot occur on the two morphemes of a compound, as shown in example (35).

(35) The OCP targets the whole tone in Tianjin:

L.L –> LH.L	fei-L + ji-L –>	fei-LH.ji-L airplane
LH.LH –> H.LH	xi-LH + lain-LH –>	xi-H.lain-LH wash one's face
HL.HL –> L.HL	jing-HL + zhong-HL –>	jing-L.zhong-HL net weight

This is clearly a dissimilatory effect, ruling out identical tones on adjacent syllables, but the identical elements here are whole contours, not the terminal autosegments. Thus a sequence of Falling-Falling is ruled out, even though the H and L autosegments alternate. While it might be argued that this sort of whole-tone effect is evidence against an autosegmental account, the repairs to the violation, such as the creation of a Rising tone from a Low and a Low from a Falling, are consistent with a compositional representation for contours. The domain of the OCP must be broadened, however, to include adjacent syllables with identical specifications, not just immediately adjacent autosegments on the tonal tier. (In general, the domains and targets of OCP effects, both tonal and segmental, have been the subject of much discussion and debate.)

The change in Tianjin from L.L to LH.L can be modeled as insertion of an H to break up a sequence of two L tones, exactly parallel to the African cases of insertion of a L to break up a sequence of two Hs, as in Efik (example 30). Yip argues for essentially the same analysis in Beijing Mandarin "third tone sandhi," a well-known alternation. As was illustrated in

Figure 7.3 above, Mandarin contrasts four tones, phonetically 55 (Tone 1), 35 (Tone 2), 214 (Tone 3) and 51 (Tone 4). Yip argues that the details of contour shape, particularly the rise from 1 to 4 at the end of Tone 3) are contextually determined, and that the contrast is basically H (Tone 1), LH (Tone 2), L (Tone 3), and HL (Tone 4). In general, tones in Beijing Mandarin retain their underlying specifications, with one exception: if two adjacent syllables in a phrase are both Tone 3, the first changes to Tone 2. As shown in example (36), this can be modeled as an OCP effect: Tone 3 (L) becomes Tone 2 (LH) when another L follows.

(36)   "Third-tone sandhi" in Beijing as an OCP effect:

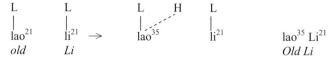

Asian languages also evidence an interaction between tone and prominence. In African languages such as Chizigula (example 25), we saw that tones were attracted to prominent syllables. The converse may be seen in Asian languages: tones in *non*-prominent syllables may be deleted or simplified. This was seen in the loss of distinctive tone on the object of the verb in Shanghai (example 32).

A different interaction between tone and stress is seen in Thai. In Thai, stress falls on the final syllable of a phrase, and contour tones are simplified in non-final position. An example is shown in Figure 17.4. Each of the six syllables in the phrase, /pʰɨ̀: nâ:t, nân klâj klâj nîm/,

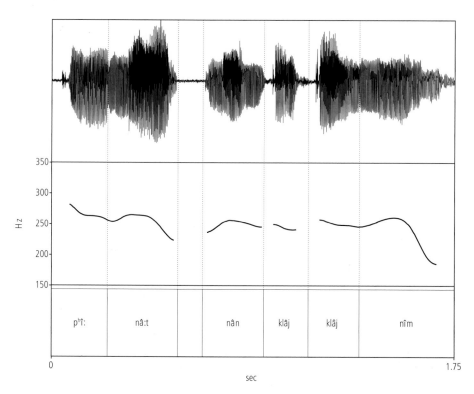

Figure 17.4   Thai falling tones only fall in phrase-final position: /pʰɨ̀: nâ:t, nân klâj klâj nîm / *Brother Nart, sit near Nim.* Source: Data courtesy of Peter Vail, based on a figure in Kallayanamit, S. 2004. The Phonetics and Phonology of Thai Intonation. Doctoral dissertation, Georgetown University, 2004.

Brother Nart, sit near Nim, carries a lexical Falling tone, and would be pronounced with steeply falling pitch in isolation. In the phrasal context, however, there is a pitch fall only on the two phrase-final syllables; the other Falling syllables are realized as a high plateau. (The elevated pitch at the beginning of the first syllable is due to the effect of the initial aspirated consonant.)

Thai falling tone simplification can be analyzed as the loss of the L in the HL specification, as shown in example (37): unstressed syllables in Thai can bear at most one tonal specification.

(37)   Tone simplification in Thai unstressed syllables:

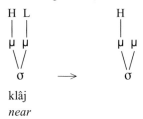

klâj

near

Finally, no discussion of tone sandhi would be complete without mention of an alternation known as the *Min Tone Circle*. In the Min languages of China, including Taiwanese, every tone has two different realizations: an isolation form (also used phrase-finally), and a sandhi form (used in non-final position). So far, this is similar to the pattern described for Thai. The fascinating aspect, however, is that the changes cannot be described in terms of simplification, because the changes are circular: 22 changes into 21, for example, but 44 changes into 22 under the exact same conditions. The circle is diagrammed in (38), and examples are given in (39).

(38)   The Min tone circle:

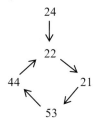

(39)   The Min tone circle: examples from Taiwanese:

24 –> 22	we^{24}	shoes	we^{22} tua^{21}	shoe laces
22 –> 21	pĩ^{22}	sick	pĩ^{21} lang^{24}	sick person (patient)
21 –> 53	ts'u^{21}	house	ts'u^{53} ting^{53}	house top (roof)
53 –> 44	hai^{53}	ocean	hai^{44} kĩ^{24}	ocean front
44 –> 22	p'ang^{44}	fragrant	p'ang^{22} tsui^{53}	frag. water (perfume)

The problem, clearly, is finding any general expression or phonetic grounding for such an alternation. Whatever grounding might be found for the fact that 22 changes into 21 (lowering, for example), would not cover the fact that 21 changes into 53. Chen (2000) pursues a comparative historical analysis of the tone circle in related languages, and concludes that the alternation originated centuries ago, and that its original phonetic motivation has now been lost due to subsequent phonetic changes. Some recent studies (cited by Yip 2002) suggest that the alternation is no longer really productive: Taiwanese speakers have memorized the sandhi forms of different lexical items, but do not apply the rules to new forms. Such factors – a once-productive and phonetically-grounded alternation now becoming more and more opaque and lexicalized – make this tonal alternation similar to lexically-conditioned segmental alternations, such that which gave rise to voicing alternations in words such as "loaf/loaves" or "gift/give" in English. Centuries ago the English alternation was simple, phonetically-grounded intervocalic voicing, but over time the vowels that conditioned the change (the now-silent "e"s) were lost, and what was once an exceptionless allophonic alternation has become a non-grounded phonemic substitution linked to certain lexical items. (It's "loafers," not "loavers," for example.) The similar historical trajectories of this rule in English and the substitutions in the Min tone circle thus support Welmers' point quoted at the beginning of this chapter: that the problems of tonal analysis are "simply typical problems of linguistic analysis" – no more difficult, but not in the end any easier, either.

17.2 intonation

17.2.1 what is intonation?

Intonation can be defined as the use of pitch and other suprasegmental features to convey discourse-level meaning. Intonation is similar to tone in that the same variable, pitch, is manipulated. It is different from tone, however, in the type of meaning that is conveyed. In intonation, a word's lexical reference is not changed by the pitch pattern, but the status of the item in the discourse is changed: the lexical referent may be asserted, queried, questioned with incredulity, brought into focus, or backgrounded, depending on the pitch pattern used. The sentences in example (40), modified from the example from Chapter 4 in order to include more sonorant sounds, illustrate three different intonational contours in English.

(40)   Intonation in English:

    a.   "You're a werewolf?"
    b.   "I'm a werewolf."
    c.   "A *werewolf*? I thought you were a vampire!"

In each case, the word "werewolf" receives a distinctive pitch pattern. Figures 17.5, 17.6, and 17.7 show pitch tracks for the word "werewolf" extracted from each of these utterances.

In example (40a) and Figure 17.5, rising pitch indicates a yes/no question; in example (40b) and Figure 17.6, falling pitch indicates a statement; and in example (40c) and Figure 17.7, a complex rise-fall-rise pattern signals surprise. In each case, however, the lexical item referred to remains the same: a lycanthrope. This can be compared to tone languages like Thai, where [na:] with falling pitch means *face*, but [na:] with rising pitch means *thick*.

Intonation is like tone, however, in that the relationship between pitch and meaning is linguistically structured and language specific. Intonation is not the direct expression of emotion in the voice (though such expression does of course occur). There do seem to be some universal, non-accidental properties to intonation: cross-linguistically, low or falling pitch is associated with assertion and finality, while higher pitch is associated with non-finality, uncertainty, a topic that

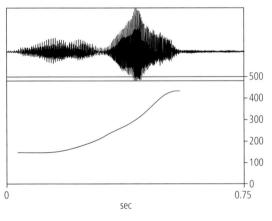

Figure 17.5   Pitch track for *werewolf?* (example 40a).

remains "up in the air." Languages differ, however, in how these tendencies are implemented. In Thai and Yoruba, for example, questions have higher pitch over the whole course of the utterance, the entire tone pattern raised a notch, instead of an English-like rise at the end. All languages, including tone languages, use intonation.

Within a language, specific syntactic patterns may receive specific intonational realizations. In English, for example, yes/no questions have rising intonation, but wh-questions have falling intonation. Positive tag questions, such as "You're not a werewolf, are you?" (Figure 17.8), have rising intonation on the tag; while negative tag questions, such as "You're a werewolf, aren't you?" (Figure 17.9), have falling intonation on the tag.

If language-specific and construction-specific intonational patterns must be learned, then intonation must be linguistic, not just emotional. There must be a level of abstraction, a phonological representation, that mediates between the continuously varying production and perception of pitch and the linguistic meaning. (This point is further elaborated by Ladd 2008). The next question is, of what does that representation consist?

17.2.2 intonational representations

How are intonational patterns to be represented? One school of thought follows linguists such as J.C. Wells and Dwight Bolinger, who discuss different *profiles*, or *tunes* that can be associated to texts in different ways, thereby conveying different meanings. Bolinger defines *Profile A*, for example, as a "jump up followed by a fall," usually used for simple statements such as those in Figure 17.6 or the main clause in Figure 17.9: "You're a werewolf." *Profile B* is a rise without a fall, as in yes/no questions and positive tags (Figures 17.5 and 17.8). More complicated patterns are analyzed as combinations of the simpler profiles. Another tradition defines a dozen or so different tunes, including Wells' "high fall," "low fall," "high rise," and "low rise," and associate a particular set of meanings or set of felicitous uses for each one. Like the non-compositional analysis of Asian tone languages, these approaches emphasize the unity of the whole contour, and the importance of movement up or down in carrying a particular tune.

The other representational approach follows Janet Pierrehumbert (1980) in assuming that intonation, like tone, is compositional. On this analysis, the tunes described by Bolinger and Wells can be decomposed into a sequence of H and L autosegments. This approach has the advantage of integrating the linguistic analysis of tone and intonation: the primitives of both are the same H and L features. This is the approach that will be followed here.

In an autosegmental approach, intonational contours can be broken down into two different kinds of markers, *pitch*

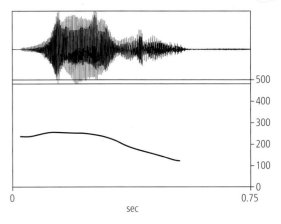

Figure 17.6   Pitch track for *werewolf* (example 40b).

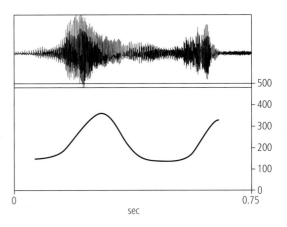

Figure 17.7   Pitch track for *werewolf?!?* (example 40c).

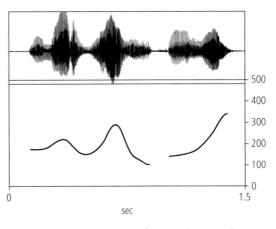

Figure 17.8   You're not a werewolf, are you? (positive tag).

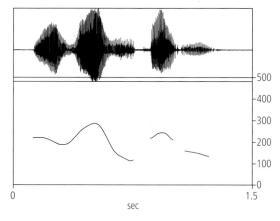

500
400
300
200
100
0

0

sec

1.5

Figure 17.9   You're a werewolf, aren't you? (negative tag).

accents and *boundary tones*, both consisting of H and L autosegments. Pitch accents associate to salient syllables in salient words, and boundary tones associate to phrase edges. Note that in a *pitch accent language*, as discussed in Section 17.1, an accent is associated to a salient syllable in a word for the purpose of creating lexical contrast, while in intonation, a pitch accent is associated to a salient syllable in a word for the purpose of conveying discourse information.) Following the typographical convention suggested by Pierrehumbert, intonational pitch accents are marked with an asterisk (H*, L*), and boundary tones with a raised dash or percent-sign (H⁻, H%), depending on the type of phrase edge they attach to.

   17.2   In Focus

To date, the patterns of English intonation have been the most thoroughly analyzed, and will be our focus here. Other languages for which an extensive literature exists include Dutch, German, Greek, Japanese, and Korean (perhaps mostly as a result of the native languages of linguists who happened to become interested in intonational phonology). In order to work toward standardizing the transcription of intonation in different languages, a group of linguists working on intonation have been developing a system of transcription called *Tone and Break Indices (ToBI)*. ToBI conventions for several languages have been or are being developed: links are on the companion website.

Intonational pitch accents associate to the primary stressed syllable of words that are salient in a phrase. The default, in English, is that words that are asserted in a simple statement receive an H* accent, and words that are queried in a yes/no question receive a L* accent. The final fall of a statement and rise of a question are the result of boundary tones: L% for a fall and H% for a rise. Thus the typical English intonational contours for simple statements and questions can be transcribed as in example (41).

(41)   Autosegmental transcription of intonation in English:

          *L   H%
          |

   a.   You're a werewolf?

          *H   L%
          |

   b.   I'm a werewolf.

Note that the phonologically-specified features are the same as in tone languages – H and L autosegments – but in intonational systems they are much more sparsely specified. English allows as few as one pitch accent and one boundary tone per phrase, compared to one pitch accent per word in pitch accent languages, and one tone per syllable or mora in more typical tone languages.

In between specified syllables, the pitch is interpolated: moving smoothly from one target to the next. An example from English is shown in example (42) and Figure 17.10. The utterance is "*Marion* mowed the lawn?" a question with contrastive focus on "Marion" (i.e., "I thought that it was Kim's job"). There is a L* pitch accent on the stressed syllable of Marion, and an H% boundary tone at the end of the utterance. In between, pitch rises smoothly between the two targets (notwithstanding a slight dip over the voiced obstruents).

(42)   Sparse specification of H and L in English:

L*   H%

Marion mowed the lawn?

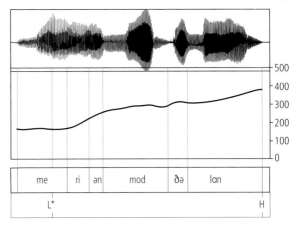

Figure 17.10   *Marion* mowed the lawn?

In order to get a single pitch accent very early in the utterance and no others, the reading must be a contrastive one. We've been talking about mowing the lawn, and I'm surprised that it was Marion, not Kim, who did it. In a non-contrastive reading, the default accent placement is on the last word of the phrase, as in example (43):

(43)   Default pitch accent on the final content word of the phrase:

H* L%

Marion bought me some flowers.

Because placement on the final word is the English default, the utterance in example (43) could be the answer to a general question ("What happened today?") with *broad focus* on the whole phrase. The same pattern could also indicate *narrow focus* on the word "flowers," as in answering the question "What did Marion bring you?" If the pitch accent moves away from the final word, however, as in examples (42) or (44), only the narrow focus reading is available. The pitch accent placement in example (44) would only be used if Marion usually gives flowers to someone else.

(44)   An earlier accent indicates narrow contrastive focus:

H*   L%

Marion bought me some flowers.

It is not always the case that only one word in an utterance is salient. The utterance pictured in Figure 17.8, "You're not a werewolf, are you?" might be represented as in example (45):

(45)   Multiple pitch accents and two boundary tones:

H*   H*   L⁻   L*   H%

You're not a werewolf,   are you?

Not and *werewolf* are both salient, and both accented, as can be seen by the separate pitch peaks in Figure 17.8. This example also serves to illustrate the two different levels of boundary tone. There is a phrase break after "wolf," indicated by falling pitch, lengthening of the

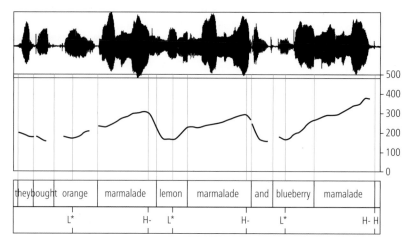

Figure 17.11   They bought orange marmalade, lemon marmalade, and blueberry marmalade?

final syllable, and perhaps a slight pause. The break is not as strong and definitive as at the end of an utterance, however: the two phrases still form a single sentence. This *intermediate phrase* break is indicated with the superscripted bar after the accent, while the full *intonational phrase* break is indicated with the percent sign. The intermediate phrase may be equivalent to, or one level up from, the *phonological phrase* discussed in Chapter 15. Researchers disagree on the number and type of phrases, if any, that may intervene between the phonological phrase and full intonational phrase. Here, we will use the term intermediate for any intonationally-marked phrase that is smaller than a full intonational phrase.

Intermediate phrases are also found in a multi-part statement or question, is shown in example (46), Figure 17.11.

(46)   A multi-part question:

(Varieties of marmalade, a monomorphemic multisyllabic word with initial stress and almost all sonorant segments, are a favorite with intonational researchers). The L* pitch accents are on the contrastive flavors of orange, lemon, and blueberry. Each questioned item, delimited by commas, constitutes its own intermediate phrase. Each phrase ends with a rise, with the final rise, indicating the end of the larger intonational phrase, being the greatest. Note again the smooth rise from the final pitch accent on "blue" to the boundary tone at the end of the utterance.

We have not yet dealt with more complex intonational contours, as in Figure 17.7: "A werewolf?!?" Following the analysis that was proposed for contour tones, complex intonational contours are also analyzed as combinations of H and L. Pierrehumbert (1980) proposed a set of *bitonal pitch accents*: two-way combinations of H and L, with either the first or second accent associated to the stressed syllable of the salient word. Thus H*+L indicates a high pitch on the stressed syllable followed by an immediate fall. This could possibly contrast with H+L* (a *fall to* the stressed syllable), L*+H (a *rise from* the stressed syllable), and L+H* (a *rise to* the stressed syllable). The exact inventory of accents needed, and the contexts in which each may be appropriate, remains a matter of debate. To give just one example, the complex contour in 17.7 might be represented as in (47).

(47)   A bitonal pitch accent:

H*+L   L⁻ H%

A werewolf?

The H*+L gives the steep fall at the end of the accented syllable, and the distinct L⁻ and H% give the low plateau and steep ending rise.

One may speculate about a compositional interpretation for complex pitch accents: the H of assertion plus the L of uncertainty add up to surprise. There needs to be room for cross-linguistic variation and conventionalization, however: intonation is not the direct expression of emotion. In some languages, for example, complex pitch accents are the default, and carry no particular emotional investment. Or, to take an example with boundary tones, it has been noted that young women are more likely to use rising intonation at the end of their sentences than are older women or men of any age. (This pattern reaches an extreme in the "Valley girl" speech of Southern California, though it is not exclusive to that area.) Should this pattern necessarily be interpreted as meaning that young women lack assertiveness? Or have they just conventionalized a different default? (Chapter 19 further discusses the role of phonological variation in expressing personal and regional identity.)

chapter summary

- Tone is the use of pitch to convey lexical contrast. Intonation is the use of pitch to convey discourse-level meaning.
- Register tone languages distinguish 2 to 5 relative levels. Contour tone languages distinguish levels as well as more complex rises and falls.
- In autosegmental representation, tone patterns are represented by H and L autosegments linked to one or more tone-bearing units.
- Tonal alternations include spreading, delinking, and OCP effects.
- In autosegmental representations of intonation, H and L autosegments link to salient words (pitch accents) and the ends of phrases (boundary tones).
- Combinations of pitch accents and boundary tones create complex intonational contours, which may be both language-specific and construction-specific.

further reading

Fromkin, V. (ed.), 1978. *Tone: A Linguistic Survey*. New York: Academic Press. The issues raised in this volume are still timely.

Gussenhoven, C. 2004. *The Phonology of Tone and Intonation*. Cambridge: Cambridge University Press.

Ladd, D.R. 2008. *Intonational Phonology*. Cambridge: Cambridge University Press. Lays out the motivations for the compositional approach, followed with numerous detailed examples.

Wells, J.C. 2006. *English Intonation: An Introduction*. Cambridge: Cambridge University Press. Up-to-date discussion from a non-compositional point of view.

Yip, M. 2002. *Tone*. Cambridge: Cambridge University Press. Survey of tone patterns and alternations in the languages of the world, with analyses from an OT perspective.

review exercises

1. How are tone and intonation different? How are they similar?
2. How are typical African and Asian tone languages different? How are they similar?
3. Define the following terms:

    register tone language
    contour tone language
    tonogenesis
    pitch accent language
    TBU
    tone doubling
    tone shift
    downstep
    tone sandhi
    pitch accent
    boundary tone

4. What is meant by "tone mobility" and "tone stability"?
5. Draw autosegmental representations for the seven tones of Cantonese, example (10), using the a register node as in example (14).
6. Review the discussion of Mende, examples (15) and (16). Some disyllabic words of Mende are given here. How would they be pronounced with the suffix [-ma] *on*? Draw autosegmental representations.

pélé	bèlè	ŋgílà	fàndé	ɲàhâ
house	trousers	dog	cotton	woman

7. Consider the intonational annotations on the English sentences below. Which is a broad focus statement, narrow focus statement, yes-no question, surprised question?

                                        L* H%
                                         |
    a. MaryAnne will nominate the mayor

              L*+H   H%
               |
    b. MaryAnne will nominate the mayor

              H*   L%
               |
    c. MaryAnne will nominate the mayor

                                    H* L%
                                     |
    d. MaryAnne will nominate the mayor

further analysis and discussion

8. More Mende. Write an autosegmental rule to account for the following tone alternations in Mende.

	X	matter of X	ugly X
matter	hìndà		
ugly	ɲàmù		
war	kɔ́	kɔ́-híndà	kɔ́-ɲámù
owl	ᵐbû	ᵐbú-hìndà	ᵐbú-ɲàmù
rice	ᵐbǎ	ᵐbà-híndà	ᵐbà-ɲámù
house	pélé	pélé-híndà	péle-ɲámù
trousers	bèlè	bèlè-hìndà	bèlè- ɲàmù
dog	ŋgílà	ŋgílà-hìndà	ŋgílà- ɲàmù
woman	ɲàhâ	ɲàhá-hìndà	ɲàhá- ɲàmù

9. Review the analysis of downstep in Bade, examples (21) and (29). Give an autosegmental derivation of the following Bade phrases.

/jə̀	gàfá	ə̀klán/ →	[jə̀ gà fə́k !lán]
we	caught	cow	we caught a cow
/jə̀	màsú	ə̀fcá:n/ →	[jə̀ mà sə́f !cá:n]
we	bought	mat	we bought a mat

10. In Digo (Tanzania), the verbal suffix [-a] surfaces with a high tone after certain verbs and with a non-high tone after other verbs. Assuming that high tones are marked with H and non-high tones are unspecified, propose an autosegmental analysis. (Data from Goldsmith, J. 1990. *Autosegmental and Metrical Phonology.* Oxford: Blackwell.)

all non-high tones:

ku-rim-a	to cultivate
ku-guz-a	to sell
ku-ambir-a	to tell
ku-vugir-a	to untie
ku-dezek-a	to spoil someone

high tone on the suffix:

ku-reh-á	to bring
ku-nen-á	to speak
ku-aruk-á	to begin
ku-puput-á	to beat
ku-bombor-á	to demolish

further research

11. Find a grammar of a tone language not mentioned in this chapter, and describe the system. How many contrasts? Is it a register or contour system? Any alternations? Propose an autosegmental representation.

12. Record the utterances in (7), and make pitch tracks for them. Can you see the pitch inflections that correspond to the pitch accents and boundary tones?

Go online Visit the book's companion website for additional resources relating to this chapter at: http://www.wiley.com/go/zsiga.

references

Bade, Ngizim, and Nupe
Schuh, R. 1978. Tone rules. In Fromkin, V. (ed.). *Tone: A Linguistic Survey*. New York: Academic Press.

Barasana
Gomez-Imbert, E. and M. Kenstowicz. 2000. Barasana tone and accent. *International Journal of American Linguistics* 66;4: 419–463.

Bimoba
Snider, K. 1998. Phonetic realisation of downstep in Bimoba. *Phonology* 15: 77–101.

Black Miao
Anderson, S. 1978. Tone features. In Fromkin, V. (ed.). *Tone: A Linguistic Survey*. New York: Academic Press.

Cantonese, Grebo, Mandarin, Mazatec, and Somali
Yip, M. 2002. *Tone*. Cambridge University Press.

Chizigula
Kenstowicz, M. and C. Kisseberth 1990. Chizigula tonology. In S. Inkelas and D. Zec *The Phonology/Syntax Connection*. Chicago: University of Chicago Press.

Efik
Welmers, W. 1973. *African Language Structures*. Berkeley: University of California Press.

English Intonation
Bolinger, D. 1986. *Intonation and Its Parts: Melody in Spoken English*. Stanford: Stanford University Press.
Pierrehumbert, J. 1980. *The Phonology and Phonetics of English Intonation*. Doctoral dissertation, Massachusetts Institute of Technology.

Lama
Kenstowicz, M., E. Nikiema, and M. Ourso, 1988. Tonal polarity in two Gur languages. *Studies in the Linguistic Sciences* 18: 77–103.

Mpi
Ladefoged, P. http://www.phonetics.ucla.edu/vowels/chapter12/mpi.html.

Munduruku
Picanço, G. 2005. *Munduruku: Phonetics, Phonology, Synchrony, Diachrony*. Doctoral dissertation, University of British Columbia.

Nambikwara
Kroeker, M. 2001. A descriptive grammar of Nambikwara. *International Journal of American Linguistics* 67;1: 1–87.

Navajo
McDonough, J. 1999. Navajo Tone. *Anthropological Linguistics* 41: 503–540.

Punjabi
Bhatia, T.K. 1993. *Punjabi: A Cognitive-Descriptive Grammar*. London: Routledge.

Setswana
Tlale, One. 2006. *The Phonetics and Phonology of Sengwato, a Dialect of Setswana*. Doctoral dissertation, Georgetown University.

Shanghai and Taiwanese
Chen, M. 2000. *Tone Sandhi*. Cambridge University Press.

Thai
Kallayanamit, S. 2004. *The Phonetics and Phonology of Thai Intonation*. Doctoral dissertation, Georgetown University.
Morén, B. and E. Zsiga. 2006. The lexical and post-lexical phonology of Thai tones. *Natural Language and Linguistic Theory* 24;1: 113–178.

18 Diachronic Change

When we see men grow old and die at a certain time one after another, from century to century, we laugh at the elixir that promises to prolong life to a thousand years; and with equal justice may the lexicographer be derided, who, being able to produce no example of a nation that has preserved their words and phrases from mutability, shall imagine that his dictionary can embalm his language, and secure it from corruption and decay . . . [S]ounds are too volatile and subtile for legal restraints; to enchain syllables and to lash the wind are equally the undertakings of pride unwilling to measure its desires by its strength.

Samuel Johnson, (Preface to *Dictionary of the English Language*, xxii, 1755)

The only constant is change.

Heraclitus (c. 500 BCE)

The Sounds of Language: An Introduction to Phonetics and Phonology, First Edition. Elizabeth C. Zsiga.
© 2013 Elizabeth C. Zsiga. Published 2013 by Blackwell Publishing Ltd.

As Heraclitus states, and Johnson laments, languages change. They change despite the best efforts of lexicographers, grammar mavens, elementary school teachers, and writers of letters to the editor. Grandparents find the speech of their grandchildren sloppy and full of slang; grandchildren find the speech of their grandparents quaint.

The study of how languages change over time is termed *diachronic linguistics* (dia *across*, chronos *time*), as contrasted with *synchronic linguistics*, which examines a language variety at a single point in time (syn *together*, (in) chronos *time*).

There is a tendency to see all language change as degradation, as many letters to the editor attest. Samuel Johnson, though he admits that language change is inevitable in the quote cited above, characterizes all change as "corruption and decay." In a more well-known quote, he opines that "Tongues, like governments, have a natural tendency to degeneration." As was noted in Chapter 1, such fears and charges are not new, to either the eighteenth century or the twenty-first. Sanskrit grammarians, writing perhaps 2500 years ago (the ones to whom we owe detailed descriptions of Sanskrit pronunciation as well as descriptions of general phonetics) were motivated in their work by a desire to correct the pronunciation of a younger, slangier, sloppier generation who couldn't read the scriptures correctly.

In this chapter, we'll look at sound change primarily through an extended case study of the history of English. Section 18.1 begins with an overview of sound change, as exemplified in English in the past thousand years. Section 18.2 goes back to the discovery of the earliest known ancestor of English, proto-Indo-European, and Section 18.3 traces in more detail the history of English to the present day. Along the way we'll investigate types of sound change, historical reconstruction and the comparative method, the Neogrammarian Hypothesis and the famous Great Vowel Shift.

18.1 languages change

18.1.1 English in the last millennium

Over time, changes accumulate. Eye-rolling on both parts aside, grandparents and grandchildren can generally understand each other, but the farther apart in time, the greater the difference. Consider the following, perhaps familiar, text.

(1) Version A, approximately 1000 CE:

Ēac swelċe sēo nǣdre wæs ġēappre þonne ealle þā ōðre nīetenu þe God ġeworhte ofer eorðan; and sēo nǣdre cwæð tō þām wīfe: Hwȳ forbēad God ēow þæt ġē ne ǣten of ǣlcum trēowe binnan Paradīsum?

Þæt wīf andwyrde: Of þāra trēowa wæstme þe sind on Paradīsum wē etað: And of þæs trēowes wæstme, þe is onmiddan neorxenawange, God bebēad ūs þæt wē ne ǣten, ne wē þæt trēow ne hrepoden þȳ lǣs þe wē swulten.

Þā cwæð sēo nǣdre eft tō þām wīfe: Ne bēo ġē nāteshwon dēade.

(2) Version B, approximately 1390 CE:

But and the serpent was feller than alle lyuynge beestis of erthe, whiche the Lord God hadde maad. Which serpent seide to the womman, Why comaundide God to you, that ye schulden not ete of ech tre of paradis?

To whom the womman answerde, We eten of the fruyt of trees that ben in paradis; sothely God commaundide to vs, that we schulden not eate of the fruyt of the tre, which is in the myddis of paradijs, and that we schulden not touche it, lest perauenture we dien.

Forsothe the serpent seide to the womman, ye schulen not die bi deeth.

(3) Version C, 1611:

Now the serpent was more subtill then any beast of the field which the Lord God had made. And he said vnto the woman, Yea, hath God said, Ye shall not eat of euery tree of the garden?

And the woman said vnto the serpent, Wee may eate of the fruite of the trees of the garden: But of the fruit of the tree, which is in the midst of the garden, God hath said, Ye shal not eate of it, neither shall ye touch it, lest ye die.

And the Serpent said vnto the woman, Ye shall not surely die.

(4) Version D, 1995:

The snake was sneakier than any of the other wild animals that the Lord God had made. One day it came to the woman and asked, "Did God tell you not to eat fruit from any tree in the garden?"

The woman answered, "God said we could eat fruit from any tree in the garden, except the one in the middle. He told us not to eat fruit from that tree or even to touch it. If we do, we will die."

"No, you won't!" the snake replied.

The passage is the third chapter of Genesis, verses 1–4. Religious texts in general are excellent vehicles for studying language change, as the content remains stable even as the words in which it is expressed change radically. This particular passage was chosen for the ready availability of the different versions.

Version A is *Old English*, translated from the Latin by Aelfric, Abbott of Eynsham. Once you know what the text is, many of the words can be figured out: "eorðan" for *earth*, "cwæð" (surviving in "quote" and marginally in "quoth") for *said*, "hwy" for *why*, "andwyrde" for *answered*, etc. Other words, however, could be from a different language: "wæstme" is *fruit*, "nientenu" are *animals*, "neorxenawange" means *garden*. Chances are that without knowing the context or having the translation, and apart from a few unchanged words like "God" and the Latin transliteration "Paradisum," this "English" would be completely incomprehensible.

Version B is *Middle English*, from Wycliffe's Bible, another translation from Latin, made approximately 1390. This text is understandable, if strange. There are unusual spellings, but you can probably recognize almost all of the words, though some are only familiar because characters in fairy tales or medieval-themed romances use them: words like "forsooth" or "peradventure." An immediately noticeable characteristic is all the final "e"s, which were really pronounced at that time: "alle, erthe, whiche, hadde, seide," etc.

Version C is from the King James Bible, written around 1611, in *Early Modern English*. This English is like ours, but sprinkled with spelling variations, as well as words and phrases we understand but never use, like "yea," "ye," "hath," "lest" and "said unto." It was, in fact, even a little old fashioned for the time. The committee that wrote the King James Version deliberately chose older forms, such as "hath" rather than "has" and "ye" rather than "you," forms that were already falling out of use in other contemporary writing, such as Shakespeare's plays. The committee thought the more conservative forms would be more appropriate for the public reading of scripture.

Version D (*Contemporary English*) takes the opposite approach, deliberately choosing modern, informal words in order to make its subject matter more accessible. (Specifically, the quotation is from the Contemporary English Version (copyright © 1991, 1992, 1995 by the American Bible Society) and used by permission.) Those of us who grew up with Version C may find the Contemporary English version shockingly informal and slangy. "The snake was *sneaky*?" "Ye shall not surely die" sounds so much more dignified than "No you won't!" Nonetheless, the difference between C and D represents not degeneration, but real changes that have taken place in English over the past 400 years.

It wasn't that a group of kids woke up one morning in 1300 and said "Let's confuse our parents and speak *Middle* English from now on." The differences between Version A and Version D result from the slow accretion of multiple gradual changes over a millennium.

One of the most obvious ways languages change is in vocabulary: words for new objects have to be invented, and words for obsolete objects become obsolete themselves. The word "blog" did not exist 20 years ago because the thing it denotes did not exist; while the word "hod" (a shovel for carrying coal, and a very useful member of a minimal set illustrating the contrastive English vowels) now has to be explained, because few English-speaking 20-year-olds have ever had to carry coal. When we appropriate a new object or activity from another culture, we often appropriate its name as well: we borrowed "sushi" and "futon" from Japanese, and they borrowed /besubaru/ and /komputa:/ from English.

New words are invented or borrowed, and old ones, like "forsooth," die out. More commonly, however, words stay in the language but undergo *semantic drift*: their meanings change gradually over time. (You can surely call to mind numerous terms that mean different things among your friends than among your parents' friends.) Several examples of *semantic narrowing* are found in the passages above. In Old English "nædre" was the general word for a snake; in Modern English "adder" is a specific kind of snake. (The "n" was lost in Middle English due to misparsing: "a næddre" was mistakenly reanalyzed as "an æddre." The same thing happened to "a napron.") The word "cwæð," meant just *said*; today "to quote" is a more specific kind of saying. In Old English, "wif" meant *woman*; "wife" now means a woman in a specific relationship. (Semantic *broadening* happens as well. The word "gifte," for example, originally meant "dowry," a very specific kind of gift.)

18.1 The Old English meaning of "man," by the way, was gender-neutral, and meant just *person*. Texts have sentences like "His daughter was a rich man." A female person was a "wif-man" (eventually "woman"), and a male person was a "wer-man" (related to words like "virile"). "Wer-man" fell out of use, however, and unmodified "man" came to be used for both *male person* and *person in general*, presumably on the assumption that being male is the unmarked human state. Despite the similarity in sound and meaning, "werewolf" probably comes from a different word, Germanic "warulf," though the similarity may have encouraged the borrowing.

Syntax and morphology also change. Old English was a fully-inflected language, with every noun taking a suffix indicating gender, grammatical function, and number. For example, four different forms of "tree" occur in the Old English passage above, as listed in example (5).

(5)   Some Old English nominal endings:

"trēow-e"   tree-neuter.dative.singular
"trēow-a"   tree-neuter.genitive.plural
"trēow-es"   tree-neuter.genitive.singular
"trēow"   tree-neuter.accusative.singular

These endings were already beginning to weaken by the time Old English was written down, however, and by Middle English they occur only as unstressed final vowels ("erthe"), and are now unpronounced in Contemporary English (though still spelled in some words).

A syntactic change evident in the passages above has been in how questions are formed. Old and Middle English mark questions by inverting subject and main verb: Old English "Hwȳ forbēad God ēow?"; Middle English "Why comaundide God to you?" Contemporary English inserts and inverts an auxiliary verb: "Did God tell you?" rather than "Told God you?"

The suggested readings at the end of the chapter provide much more information about diachronic change in general. Here, we turn our attention to sound change.

18.1.2 types of sound change

The kinds of changes that occur diachronically are much the same as those that occur synchronically, and which we have been studying all along. Over time, languages show the effects of assimilation, dissimilation, deletion, insertion, lenition, fortition, lengthening, shortening, metathesis: the whole catalog of alternations that were discussed in Chapter 11. The data in examples (6) to (12), comparing words in Old English with Contemporary English, serve as illustrations. Old English words are spelled as they were pronounced.

(6)   Intervocalic voicing assimilation, final vowel deletion, consonant deletion in clusters. (Compare Korean intervocalic voicing, Chapter 15, example 24.)

Old English   Contemporary English
gif - te   gift
dowry
gif - an —> givan   give
to give a dowry

knif	knife
knif - es –> knives	knives
xlaf	loaf
bread	
xlaf - as –> xlavas	loaves
bread-plural	

(7)   Intervocalic lenition of [d] to [ð]. (Compare intervocalic lenition of voiced stops in Spanish, Chapter 10.)

Old English	Contemporary English
fæder	father
gaderian	gather
weder	weather

(8)   Fortition of /ð/ after continuant consonants. (Compare Ancient Greek fricative dissimilation, Chapter 11, example 31.)

Old English	Contemporary English
byrðen	burden
morðor	murder
geforðian	afford
ðeofð	theft

(9)   Epenthesis of plosives after nasals. (Compare Contemporary English [hæmpstɚ] and [warmpθ], also the change from Latin "hominem" to Spanish "hombre.")

Old English	Contemporary English
ðunrian	thunder
æmtig	empty
nemel	nimble

(10)   Nasal deletion followed by compensatory vowel lengthening. (Compare lengthening after /l/-deletion in Komi, Chapter 11, example 42. Also note how English and Norse took different repair strategies to deal with the difficult [-nr-] cluster: epenthesis in English (9) and deletion in Norse.)

a. (pre-) Old English	Old English	Contemporary English
gans	go:s	goose (compare "gander")
tons	to:ð	tooth

b. (pre-) Old Norse	Norse	
ðunra	ðo:r	Thor
thunder		

(11)   Vowel shortening preceding a consonant cluster. (Compare vowel shortening in Yowlumne, Chapter 11, example 43.)

Old English	Contemporary English
ke:p / ke:p-t	keep / kept
sle:p / sle:p-t	sleep / slept

dre:m / dre:m-t	dream / dreamt
we:p / we:p-t	weep / wept
me:n / me:n-t/	mean / meant

(12)   Metathesis of /r/ (Compare Hanunoo, Chapter 11, example 44.)

Old English	Contemporary English
bridde	bird
frist	first
ðridde	third
hros	horse

As is the case with synchronic alternations, and as the above examples show, most sound changes are *conditioned*, taking place only in a specific environment, though unconditioned change, where sounds are affected across the board, is also possible.

18.1.3 causes and effects

Sound changes get started in different ways. Sound change can start in misperception, especially in the process of language acquisition. If a child perceives, and thus learns, a different sound pattern than the parent intends, diachronic change has begun. Reduced vowels or lenited consonants, for example, may simply be missed by the learner, leading to diachronic deletion. A slight tendency to reduce laryngeal opening in intervocalic position can be misinterpreted as the intention to produce a voiced consonant.

New alternations can then lead to changes in phonemic inventories. If synchronic assimilations or lenitions make sounds too similar, children may learn one sound category instead of two, resulting in *merger*. Alternatively, children can misinterpret an allophonic distribution (such as intervocalic voicing) as phonemic, creating two categories out of one, a *split*.

Social forces also play an important role. Changes spread as speakers consciously or unconsciously model their speech on others in the social group that they belong to, or wish to belong to. (See Chapter 19.) External social forces such as conquest, migration, and trade may introduce new sounds and sound alternations. (See Section 18.3.)

There are internal, systemic factors as well. Sound changes generalize across categories: if lenition begins with a labial, maybe a change of intervocalic [p] to [f], then intervocalic [t] to [θ] and [k] to [x] are likely to follow. Phonemic inventories tend toward symmetry, and equal distribution in the acoustic space. If [e] merges with [i], creating a gap where [e] used to be, then [ɛ] may move up to fill the space. Alternatively, if [e] moves down toward [ɛ], [ɛ] may move lower to maintain some distance. This kind of cascading move – where sounds move like the tiles in a puzzle, but the number of categories stays the same – is called a *chain shift*.

All of these forces, working together and against each other, keep sound systems constantly changing.

Because of diachronic change, as groups of people diverge, so do languages. As speakers of a single language split off from one another, sound and other changes affect the different groups differently, and their speech patterns become distinct. Over time, what started as one "mother" language develops into distinct daughters. (As with nodes in the syntactic tree, languages are female.) Working back in time, to figure out the characteristics of the mother based on the inherited characteristics of her various daughters, is the process of *historical reconstruction*.

18.2 historical reconstruction

18.2.1 Proto-Indo-European

In eighteenth-century Europe, there was a general scholarly interest in language origins, though progress in these studies was hampered by a desire on the part of some scholars to trace all languages back to Biblical Hebrew, a parentage that they assumed must follow from the story of the Tower of Babel in Genesis 11.

That focus changed after the publications of William "Oriental" Jones, an English jurist trained in classical languages who was sent to Calcutta in 1783 to serve in the British court system. While in India, he catalogued many hundreds of words in Sanskrit that were strikingly similar to words in Latin and Greek. Jones was not the first to notice these correspondences. As far back as 1585, Filippo Sassetti, a Florentine merchant who traveled to Goa, wrote letters home remarking on similarities he noticed between Sanskrit and Italian words. Jones, however, was the first to really grab the attention of the European scholarly community. Some examples of the words Jones listed are given in example (13).

(13)   Correspondences between Greek, Latin, and Sanskrit:

Greek	Latin	Sanskrit	English
mater	mater	matar	mother
pate:r	pater	pitar	father
treis	tre:s	trajas	three
deus	divus	devas	divinity
okto	octo	aʃta	eight
hekaton	centum	ʃata	hundred
deka	decem	daʃa	ten
genos	genus	ʤanas	race/tribe
	regem	raʤa	king
agros	agra	aʤra	field (compare "acre")
gon	genu	ʤanu	knee

Jones emphasized not just overall similarity, but the *regularity* of the correspondence.

In many cases, the sounds are the same across the three languages. Where there are differences, however, they are predictable: every time Latin has "c" (that is, /k/), Sanskrit has /ʃ/ ("octo, centum, decem" correspond to /aʃta, ʃata, daʃa/); every time Latin has /g/, Sanskrit has /ʤ/ ("genus, regem, agra, genu" correspond to /ʤanas, raʤa, aʤra, ʤanu/). These correspondences, Jones concluded, could not have come about by chance. Latin and Sanskrit must both be descended from the same language, and have split off from one another in prehistory.

Jones presented his findings to the Royal Asiatick Society of Calcutta in 1786, including a now-famous statement of this proposed relationship:

> The Sanskrit language . . . is of a wonderful structure; more perfect than the Greek, more copious than the Latin, and more exquisitely refined than either, yet bearing to both of them a stronger affinity, both in the roots of verbs and in the forms of grammar, than could possibly have been produced by accident; so strong, indeed, that no philologer [lover of words, linguist] could examine them all three, without believing them to have sprung from some common source.

This "common source" of Sanskrit, Latin, and Greek, as well as most of the other languages of Europe, became known as *Proto-Indo-European (PIE)*. The prefix "proto-" is used to refer to a parent language whose existence and structure has been hypothesized based on comparisons among descendant languages, but for which there is no direct written evidence. Jones hypothesized that a wider set of languages, including Germanic languages like English, and Celtic languages like Irish, might also be descendants of PIE. During the next century, linguists inspired by Jones applied the *comparative method* of historical reconstruction to test for these possible family relationships, and to deduce the structure of PIE.

The comparative method is very similar to the technique used to determine the UR in a synchronic phonological analysis. In a phoneme/allophone problem, we use the predictable distribution of surface allophones to deduce the underlying phoneme. In a historical reconstruction problem, we use the predictable distribution of sounds in different languages to deduce the original sound of the parent language.

The first step is to collect a set of possible *cognates* across a set of potentially related languages: words such as those in example (13) that have the same or similar meanings and that evidence regular sound correspondences. Another potential set of cognates is shown in example (14).

(14)   A set of potential cognates

	father	foot	five	two	ten	tooth
Spanish	padre	pie		dos	dies	diente
French	per	pie		deux	dis	dent
Greek	patros	podi	pente	duo	deka	donti
Slovenian		peʃ	pet	dva	deset	
Hindi	pita:	paira	pantʃa	do:	dasa	dante
English	faðɚ	fʊt	faɪv	tu	tɛn	tuθ
Icelandic	faðir	fotar	fim	tvier	tiu	tœn
PIE	*pater	*ped	*penkwe	*duwo	*dekm	*dont
Basque	aita	oin	bost	bi	hamar	hortz

Our example set has only four to six lexical items from each language. (Blanks indicate words that do not exactly fit the pattern, either because a non-cognate word has taken over that meaning through either borrowing or semantic drift, or because some other sound change has obscured the pattern.) A real historical reconstruction would use many hundreds of words, to more clearly reveal patterns despite exceptions, as well as to exclude the possibility of accidental correspondences. With a limited number of phonemes available to encode millions of words in thousands of languages, accidental matches are bound to occur, but one word does not a cognate set make. For example, the word for "mess" in Kaqchikel Mayan happens to be [mes] (Campbell, 2004, p. 113), but this does not mean that English and Mayan are closely related. Exactly how many words are needed to establish a "regular" correspondence, and thus a historical relationship, is a question for the statisticians; historical linguists working today often employ statistical models to support or refute the claim of a relationship.

Also, note that the words in example (14) and most of the words in example (13) are kinship terms, parts of the body, and numbers. Using "core vocabulary" items such as these minimizes the risk of accidentally including borrowings. The fact that the word for "coffee" in Japanese is [koːhiː] does not mean that English and Japanese are closely related. Languages often borrow words for food and technology, but no language is likely to need to borrow the word for "tooth."

Once we have a potential cognate set, we determine the sound correspondences. Across the first five languages in our table – Spanish, French, Greek, Slovenian, and Hindi – the initial sounds of the words in question are the same: Sp [p] = Fr [p] = Gr [p] = Sl [p] = H [p], and Sp [d] = Fr [d] = Gr [d] = Sl [d] = H [d]. In the next two languages, English and Icelandic, the initial sounds are not identical to those of the other languages, but a regular relationship is seen: [p] in each of the other languages corresponds to English and Icelandic [f]; and [d] corresponds to English and Icelandic [t]. From the regularity of the correspondence, we can conclude that a historical relationship exists between all of the first seven languages: they are all descendants of Proto-Indo-European.

Further, we can reconstruct the initial sound of these words in the parent language. For the set p/p/p/p/p/f/f/ we reconstruct *p, and for the set d/d/d/d/d/t/t we reconstruct *d. (The asterisk indicates the reconstructed proto-form.) As in an allophone problem, we can use the general principle that the sound that is found in the elsewhere case – the most diverse set of environments, or most diverse set of languages – is the basic, or proto, form. Phonetic naturalness of the sound change can also come into play, though the predictability of the correspondence is the most important consideration. We might state the historical sound change the same way as an allophonic distribution: PIE *p became /f/ in English and Icelandic, and /p/ elsewhere. The full reconstructed PIE forms for each word, based on numerous applications of the comparative method across numerous cognate sets, are shown in the table.

That leaves the final row of the table in example (14): Basque. This language is spoken in a region that straddles the border between France and Spain, so it would be a good guess that it would be related to French and Spanish. The table shows, however, that there is no regular sound correspondence with the other languages. Initial [p/f] in the other languages corresponds to [a, o, b] in Basque, in no particular pattern. Initial [t/d] corresponds to either [b] or [h]. The conclusion follows that, despite its geographical location, Basque is not a member of the Indo-European family. Basque is in fact an *isolate*, one of the few languages for which no family relationship can be established. It must be a remnant of a language spoken by the people who lived in Iberia before the Indo-Europeans moved in.

Over time, using the comparative method, linguists worked out the complete phonemic inventory of Proto-Indo-European, and the family tree shown in Figure 18.1.

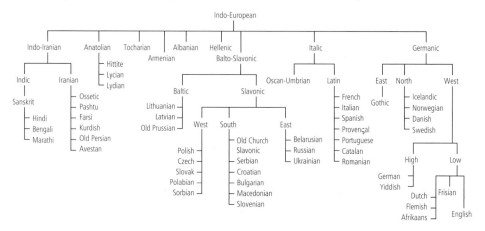

Figure 18.1   Proto-Indo-European family tree.
Source: Fennel, p. 22.

18.2 In Focus

The people who spoke Proto-Indo-European left no written record, so everything that we know or hypothesize about them comes from linguistic reconstruction, hypotheses about the rate of language change and thus language diversification, and archeological evidence from sites whose time and place are consistent with what the linguistic research tells us. There has also been some preliminary research on DNA diversification among the speakers of descendant languages. The different lines of evidence are not always in agreement, but the speakers of Proto-Indo-European probably lived about 6000 years ago (give or take a millennium) in North-Eastern Europe or Western Asia, from which they spread out to the East, West, and South. From the vocabulary items that have been reconstructed, we can infer that they had domestic animals (words for *cow, sheep, horse, dog*), agriculture (words for *grain, field*), technology (words for weapons, wheeled vehicles, watercraft, textiles), and a structured political and religious system (words for *king, god*). Beyond that we know very little. The Indo-Europeans dominated whatever languages were spoken in the places to which they migrated, and this fact leads some scholars to guess that they were formidable warriors, but others argue for a more peaceful cultural expansion. Diversification into the major branches shown in 18.1 had probably occurred by 3000 BCE, by which time inscriptions in distinct daughter languages (Old Indian, Old Persian, and Hittite) were beginning to appear. Inscriptions in Latin, Greek, and Sanskrit can be dated back only to about 500 BCE, but diversification must have begun long before that date.

The Indo-European family tree has been the most extensively studied, and was the main focus of work in the nineteenth century, but the comparative method has been applied to language families around the world, including Proto-Bantu, Proto-Algonquian, and Proto-Polynesian. Attempts have been made to go further back in time, and to relate Indo-European to other language families spoken around the world. If it is indeed the case that language arose in the human population just once (perhaps in Africa 50,000 years ago), an original "mother tongue" from which all human languages are descended must have existed. No scientifically-based and widely-accepted reconstruction to that depth of time has been possible, however.

18.2.2 Grimm's Law, Verner's Law, and the Neo-grammarian hypothesis

The correspondences of *p to /f/ and *d to /t/ shown in the table in example (14) are just a few examples of a more general pattern found in not only English and Icelandic, but also in Dutch, German, Danish, Norwegian and Swedish – languages that are grouped under the Germanic branch of the family tree in Figure 18.1. (The words for "tooth" in these languages are /tand/, /tsan/, /tand/, /tann/ and /tann/, respectively.) The parent language of this family is known as *Proto-Germanic (PG)*, spoken by the descendants of a group of Indo-Europeans who must have moved into Northwest Europe about four thousand years ago. The correspondences that mark the divergence of Proto-Germanic from the other Indo-European languages were first noticed by the Danish linguist Rasmus Rask (1787–1832), but they were popularized by Jacob Grimm (1785–1863), in his 1822 book, *Deutsche Grammatik* (*Germanic Grammar*). They have thus come to be known as *Grimm's Law*.

18.3   Jacob and his younger brother Wilhelm were the "Brothers Grimm" of fairy tale fame. Grimm's motivations in both studying linguistics and collecting folk tales were at least in part the same: to document close affinities among the Germanic peoples of central Europe, in order to promote the political unification of Germany.

The correspondence between the consonants of PIE and of PG, worked out by Rask and Grimm, are shown in example (15).

(15)   Grimm's Law:

Proto-Indo-European				Proto-Germanic		
p	t	k	->	f	θ	x/h
b	d	g	->	p	t	k
bʰ	dʰ	gʰ	->	b/β	d/ð	g/ɣ

To generalize the relationship between PIE and PG: voiceless stops became voiceless fricatives, voiced stops became voiceless stops, and voiced aspirated stops became plain voiced stops (which later changed to voiced fricatives in some positions). Some examples of the results of each change are shown in example (16). If you know any Latin or Latin roots, you can probably think of many others yourself.

(16)   Examples of Grimm's Law:

p -> f
Latin "**p**ater", English "**f**ather", from PIE *pater, *father*
Latin "**p**iscis", English "**f**ish", from PIE *peisk, *fish*

t -> θ
Latin "**t**ri-", English "**th**ree", from PIE *trejas, *3*
Latin "**t**enuis", English "**th**in", from PIE *ten *stretch*

k -> x -> h
Latin "**c**entum", English "**h**undred", from PIE *kmtom, *100*
Latin "**qu**od", English "**wh**at" (Old English **hw**æt), from PIE *kwos *who*

b -> p
few examples exist; one is
Latin "ver**b**er" *whip*, English "war**p**", from PIE *wer**b**, *to bend*

d -> t
Latin "**d**ent", English "**t**ooth", from PIE *dont, *tooth*
Latin "se**d**", English "si**t**", from PIE *sed, *sit*

g -> k
Latin "**g**enu", English "**k**nee", from PIE *genu, *knee*
Greek "**g**no-", English "**k**now", from PIE *gno, *to know*

b^h –> b
Sanskrit /**b**^{h}ar/, English "**bear**", from PIE *b^{h}er, *brown*
Sanskrit /**b**^{h}ratar/, English "**brother**", from PIE *b^{h}rater, *brother*

d^h –> d
Sanskrit /**d**^{h}a/ *put*, English "**do**", from PIE *d^{h}e, *put*
Greek /**t**^{h}ygater/, English "**daughter**", from PIE *d^{h}ug^{h}eter

g^h –> g
Sanskrit /**h**amsa/ *swan*, German "**g**ans" *goose*, from PIE *g^{h}ans, *water bird*
Latin /**h**ostis/ *enemy*, English "**g**uest", from PIE *g^{h}ostis, *strange*

Grimm's Law accounted for a very large set of correspondences. Linguists were challenged, however, by some seeming exceptions. PIE *pater became PG *fadar. Why did Grimm's Law apply to the first consonant but not the second? Similarly, PIE *septm, "7," became PG *sebun, not *sefun. Such seemingly random exceptions challenged the hypothesis of the regularity of sound change, on which the validity of historical reconstruction rested.

The hypothesis that "sound change is without exception," came to be known as the *Neogrammarian hypothesis*, after a group of German or German-trained historical linguists working in and around Leipzig in the mid to late nineteenth century. (The original German term, *Jung-grammatiker*, may have been intended to be derogatory.) The goal of the Neogrammarians was to put historical linguistics on a scientific footing. They expected that the properties of linguistic sound change would be as regular and amenable to precise statement as were physical laws. Just as a physicist would not expect Newton's laws to have unexplained exceptions, with the apple occasionally flying up from the tree, so the Neogrammarians expected that Grimm's Law would apply without exception.

The solution was found by another Danish linguist, Karl Verner (1846–1896), who figured out that the exceptions to Grimm's Law were not random, but followed their own rule. There was, as he wrote, "a rule for the irregularity." Grimm's Law applied in initial position and at the end of stressed syllables, but when a voiceless PIE stop followed an *unstressed* syllable, it became voiced instead. This stressed-based voicing rule is now called *Verner's Law*. Verner figured out, for example, that PIE *pa'ter was stressed on the second syllable: thus Grimm's Law applied to the initial *p but Verner's Law applied to the medial *t, resulting in OE [fadar]. PIE *sep'tm had the same stress pattern, thus its medial *p became *b. The words subject to Verner's Law only looked like exceptions because a later rule, the *Germanic Stress Shift*, realigned stress to root-initial position in Germanic words, obscuring the original PIE conditioning environment.

> 18.4 Verner was apparently a very modest person, who preferred his position as a librarian to seeking a prestigious professorship. Verner published his 1876 paper, *An exception to the first sound shift*, only at the urging of friends and colleagues who realized how important it was.

The real significance of Verner's discovery went beyond solving a little problem in Germanic morphology, though we certainly have to admire the care and ingenuity that went into reconstructing an opaque interaction in a 5000-year-old stress system for which there are no written records. By demonstrating that there was a pattern to the exceptions to Grimm's Law, Verner was able to show that sound change really was completely regular.

One of the most dramatic confirmations of the Neogrammarian hypothesis was in work by Ferdinand de Saussure (1857–1913), the same linguist who wrote about "the arbitrariness of the sign," (see Chapter 10). By the time Saussure joined the discussion, the reconstruction of PIE was well-established, to the level of reconstructing different verb forms, but certain aspects remained unexplained. Saussure tackled the problem of a certain set of verb roots, which he argued exhibited compensatory vowel lengthening, which required a word-final consonant in the proto-form.

The difficulty was that Saussure had to argue that these final consonants were later lost in *all* the daughter languages. He thus had no data from which to reconstruct the actual phonetic content of these consonants, and substituted an algebraic variable, *A*. For the ancestor of Sanskrit /pa:/ and Latin /po:tare/ *drink* (note the long vowels), Saussure reconstructed PIE *peA. Some of Saussure's contemporaries guessed that *A* might have been a laryngeal (/h/ or /ʔ/), but there was no real evidence. Others were skeptical of the abstract, theory-internal nature of the argument: there was no data from an actual language to suggest the existence of *A*. Saussure only argued that *A* existed because the theory said such a consonant *had* to exist, because sound change *had* to be regular.

Meanwhile, archeologists had been working on translating cuneiform tablets that had been uncovered in Turkey, and that were associated with the ancient Hittite culture. As the translations were published in the early twentieth century, it was discovered that Hittite was Indo-European. The correspondences were as clear as they had been for Sanskrit. For example, "foot" in Hittite is /pata/.

Then, to everyone's surprise, Hittite was found to have /h/ in exactly those contexts where Saussure had hypothesized *A*. For example, Saussure's hypothesized PIE *peA, corresponded to Hittite /pahs/. The consonant had not been lost in *every* daughter language after all. While linguists still debate what the exact quality of these proto-consonants must have been, regularity of sound change, and thus the survival of linguistics as a scientific discipline, was confirmed.

18.2.3 limits to the tree model

While praising the successes of the Neogrammarian hypothesis and the genetic model of language change, we also need to acknowledge their limitations. One clear limitation is that the family-tree model of genetic relationships between languages is overly simplistic. Groups seldom split off from one another absolutely. There is usually at least some continued interaction for a long period of time, even after relative separation, with continued linguistic influence. Languages can also borrow large chunks of vocabulary and even syntax from neighboring languages to which they are not related. Such lateral influences are not shown in a family tree such as the one in Figure 18.1.

Another caveat is that the hypothesis that sound change is regular does not mean that sound change instantaneously affects every word in the language. Sound change is regular and relentless in its final effect, but it takes time to get started and to propagate through a language. Frequency and familiarity of use play a role in how fast sound change propagates. Lenitions, for example, often begin in very frequent words: speakers are just not as careful with them, and listeners need less specific information to make the right guess about the intended content. Regularizations, on the other hand, begin most often with infrequent words: users may just not remember what the irregular form is supposed to be if they do not use it often. Similarity among words plays a role, too. Sound change spreads more quickly among words that are otherwise similar, while it might be retarded in words that are similar to sets outside the targeted context.

More sophisticated *wave models* of diachronic change take into account the uneven and gradual (if still inevitable) spread of sound change, the importance of both historical and lateral influence, and the crucial role of social factors. We now turn to the question of how all these factors played out in the history of English.

18.3 history of English

18.3.1 Old English

We do not know what language the original inhabitants of England spoke. Archeological evidence shows that there have been people living in Britain for at least the past 15,000 years. These earliest inhabitants left carved drawings, burial mounds, and monuments such as the ones at Stonehenge and Avebury, but no evidence of their language has survived.

Sometime in the first millennium BCE, the first waves of Indo-European settlers, the Celts, began arriving from mainland Europe. By 100 BCE, the Celtic tribes had completely taken over: Picts and Caledonians in the north; Britons, who gave their name to the island, in the south. The Celts left written inscriptions, but their language had surprisingly little influence on what was to become English, other than place names. "London," "Lincoln," "Thames," and "Severn," for example, are all of Celtic origin.

In 55 BCE, Julius Ceasar conquered the Celtic tribes, and Romans controlled the land that is now England for the next 400 years. The north (current Scotland) remained in Celtic control. The Romans introduced Christianity to England, and the Latin language was pre-served in monasteries, churches, and religious writing throughout all the social changes of the next millennia, contributing to English words including "angel," "martyr," and "shrine."

After the fall of Rome in CE 410, the Roman army withdrew, and in the ensuing power vacuum the northern Picts attacked the southern Britons. Desperate, the Britons called on Germanic mercenaries to help repel the invaders. According to The Venerable Bede, a monk who wrote a history of England about three hundred years later, the first Germanic warriors arrived in 449, landing in Kent in "three long ships." The combined efforts of the Britons and the mercenaries, Angles and Jutes from Denmark as well as Saxons from Germany, beat back the Pictish invasions.

Once invited in, however, the Germanic tribes didn't leave, and more kept coming. Within two hundred years, Germanic newcomers had pushed the Celts out of England to the far north and west, into Scotland, Ireland, Wales, and Cornwall, where Celtic languages are still spoken (Figure 18.2). Scots Gaelic and Cornish are now highly endangered, however, and the last native speaker of Manx, a Celtic language that survived on the Isle of Man in the Irish Sea, died in 1974. School-based efforts to revive these languages are underway; the revival of Irish, which nearly also died out, is a rare success story.

In England, Anglo-Saxon chieftains established numerous small kingdoms, and the languages spoken in these kingdoms became the basis of the language now called *Old English*.

It was not long, however, before new invaders/settlers came from across the North Sea. Viking raids from Denmark into the northeast of England, especially around York, began in 792, and intermittent battles between Danes and Anglo-Saxons continued over the next several hundred years. The Vikings eventually gained control of most of Northeast England, and there was extensive trade and intermarriage between the groups. Old English borrowed many now-basic words from the Norse (Viking) language, including "hit, skin, sick, want, wrong" and the pronouns "they" and "them."

Surviving manuscripts written in Old English include codes of law, Biblical passages (such as the one cited at the beginning of this chapter), and Bede's history. Many manuscripts were ordered by King Alfred "The Great," who was king of Wessex (near Winchester) from 871–899. The epic poem *Beowulf*, portraying the adventures of a Scandinavian hero-king, also dates from this time.

A few lines from Beowulf, along with a translation by Ben Slade, are given in example (17). The lines illustrate the repetition and alliteration typical of Old English poetry.

Figure 18.2   The arrival of the Anglo-Saxons in England.
Source: David Crystal, *The Stories of English.* Harmondworth: Penguin Books. Reprinted with permission of Penguin Books UK.

(17)   An example from Beowulf, lines 118–125.

Fand þá ðaér inne æþelinga gedriht	he found then therein the nobles' company
swefan æfter symble· sorge ne cúðon	slumbering after the feast; they did not know sorrow,
wonsceaft wera· wiht unhaélo	misery of men; that damned creature,
grim ond graédig gearo sóna wæs	grim and greedy, soon was ready,
réoc ond réþe ond on ræste genam	savage and cruel and from their rest seized
þrítig þegna· þanon eft gewát	thirty thanes; thence back he went
húðe hrémig tó hám faran	proud in plunder to his home, faring
mid þaére wælfylle wíca néosan.	with the banquet of bodies to seek his shelter.

Various characteristics of Old English have already been described. Like PIE, Old English was an inflected language, with many diverse word endings. These endings, however, were already beginning to weaken by the time the time the Saxons reached England. The inventory of Old English vowels and consonants (based primarily on the Wessex dialect and discerned both from historical reconstruction and manuscript evidence) are given in examples (18) and (19).

(18)   Old English vowels:

i, i: y, y: u, u:
e, e: o, o:
æ, æ: ɑ, ɑ:

(19)   Old English consonants:

	Labial	Dental	Alveolar	Post-alveolar	Velar
Stops	p, p:, b, b:		t, t:, d, d:	ʧ, ʧ:, ʤ, ʤ:	k, k:, g, g:
Fricatives	f, f:	θ, θ:	s, s:	ʃ	x, x:
Nasals	m, m:	n, n:			
Liquids			l, l:, r, r:		
Glides	w		j		

Old English had only seven different vowel qualities, including front round [y], but vowel length was contrastive. Long vowels are indicated with an accent in the transliteration above: note, for example, "són" for "soon." Length was also contrastive for most consonants. In the original Anglo-Saxon there was no phonemic /h/ or /ŋ/, but there were velar fricatives, which became [h] in some positions. Old English also allowed initial clusters that contemporary English does not, such as /kn/, /gn/, /wl/, /xl/, and /xw/. Note that all fricatives were underlyingly voiceless, but they became voiced intervocalically, as was shown in example (6), above.

The split of the English fricatives into voiced and voiceless phonemic categories was helped along by contact with Norse, which had phonemic voiced fricatives. As borrowed words such as "they" and "them" became accepted, the connection between voicing and intervocalic position was obscured and then lost entirely.

18.3.2 Middle English

In the century after Alfred's death, the kingdom of Wessex expanded until it encompassed all of the territory of modern England, though the kingship changed hands several times between Saxons and Danes. In 1066, when King Alfred's descendant, Edward the Confessor, died childless, the succession to the throne was muddled. Duke William of Normandy, Edward's distant cousin, believed he had a claim to the throne, and arrived from France with an army to prove it. At the battle of Hastings in September 1066, William defeated the Saxon claimant, King Harold of Wessex, whose forces had been weakened repelling the advance of the Norse claimant, King Harald of Norway. Thus "William of Normandy" became "William the Conqueror" and set in place Norman rule of England for the next 400 years.

William placed French-speaking nobles in positions of power throughout the kingdom, and French thus became the language of government, law, and the aristocracy. (England and Normandy were essentially administered as a single kingdom for 150 years. It was not until around 1200 that the Norman kings lost their connections to and holdings in mainland France, and began to consider themselves English, and the French their enemy.) The common people, who vastly outnumbered the Norman ruling class, continued to use English; Norse and Celtic languages were still spoken in border communities; and Latin was used in churches and schools. This multi-lingual situation ushered in *Middle English*.

One of the biggest changes from Old to Middle English was the influx of French words. Some examples are shown in (20). Typically, the words refer to the concerns of the upper class, such as government, art, learning, and fashion.

(20)   Borrowings from French into Middle English:

    a.   Law and government: government, state, court, crime
    b.   Art: music, color, paint, poet
    c.   Learning: student, grammar, logic, chapter, letter
    d.   Religion: religion, chapel, sermon, divine
    e.   Food: pork, beef, pastry, spice
    f.   Fashion: fashion, dress, lace, beauty

The French loans also kept much of their native phonology (notably stress) and morphology, with the result that Contemporary English often needs to be analyzed as having two strata with different sets of rules, one for Germanic words and one for French/Latinate words.

Other important changes from Old English were continued simplifications and lenitions. The inflectional endings continued to weaken. In addition, consonant clusters were simplified; [x] weakened to [h] or in some cases [f] (thus the spelling of "cough" and "tough"). Intervocalic [g] weakened to [ɣ] weakened to [j]: thus OE [dæge] "day" became ME [daj]; OE [wege] "way" became ME [wej].

The length distinction was lost for consonants, and was beginning to become allophonic for vowels. Long vowels were shortened before consonant clusters, as was shown in (11) above, resulting in alternations such as [ke:p / kept] and [sle:p / slept]. (The fact that this alternation is no longer synchronically active is seen in the regular plurals, which show no vowel change: "beeped, heaped, seeped," etc.) At the same time, Middle English short vowels lengthened in open syllables, as shown in example (21).

(21)   Open syllable lengthening; together with fricative voicing and loss of final vowels:

[nosu] –> [noː.su] –> [nɔː.zu] –> [nɔː.zə] –> [nɔːz] (eventually [noːz]), compare [nas.tril]

[læfan] –> [læː.fan] –> [lɛː.van] –> [lɛː.və] –> [lɛːv] (eventually [liːv]), compare [lɛft].

Vowel quality was also changing. Front round [y] simplified to [u], [i], or [e] depending on context. The long low vowels raised (the first step in an upward trip that would continue in the next few centuries). The vowel [æː] raised to [ɛː], as illustrated for "leave" in (21), and the vowel [ɑː] raised to [ɔː], so that OE [gɑːst] is on the way to [goːst], [stɑːn] is on the way to [stoːn], and [hɑːlig] is on the way to [hoːlij], with weakening of post-vocalic [g]. The remaining short [ɑ] and [æ] merged in a more central position, and the resulting [a] developed a long allophone due to open syllable lengthening: OE [nɑma] "name" became ME [naːmə]. By the fourteenth century, the vowel system was approximately that of example (22). There are now four heights, no front round vowels, and only two low vowels.

(22)   Middle English vowels (circa 1300):

i, iː		u, uː
e, eː		o, oː
ɛː		ɔː
	a aː	

By the end of the period, the Middle English consonant system had become basically identical to Contemporary English, with loss of [x] and development of [h], loss of the length distinction, and phonemic voicing of fricatives.

Thousands of texts – poems. letters, legal documents, Bible translations – survive from the Middle English period. The Wycliffe Bible cited in Section 18.1 was written in 1380. Geoffrey Chaucer's *Canterbury Tales* (example 23) offer further examples of Middle English, as well as an insightful and comic view of the social situation at the time.

(23)   From Chaucer's *Canterbury Tales*:

> Whan that Aprille, with hise shoures soote,
> The droghte of March hath perced to the roote
> And bathed every veyne in swich licour,
> Of which vertu engendred is the flour;
> Whan Zephirus eek with his swete breeth
> Inspired hath in every holt and heath
> The tendre croppes, and the yonge sonne
> Hath in the Ram his halfe cours yronne,
> And smale foweles maken melodye,
> That slepen al the nyght with open eye-
> So priketh hem Nature in hir corages-
> Thanne longen folk to goon on pilgrimages

In general, the words should be pronounced as they are spelled: every vowel and consonant is pronounced, "y" represents a high front vowel or glide, doubled vowels are long, and the final "e"s are [ə]. Note "hise" for *his*: the lost final vowel is where the voiced fricative comes from.

18.3.3 Modern English

The transition from Middle English to Modern English began with the re-establishment of English as an official language. In 1362, Parliament passed a law making English rather than French the official language of the criminal courts, accepting the argument that defendants could not understand what was being argued either for or against them (though the verdict was still to be recorded in Latin). Some decades later, King Henry V (1413–1422), fighting the Hundred Years' War with France (and nicely book-ending the battle of Hastings by re-annexing Normandy at the battle of Agincourt), continued the trend by instructing his civil servants to use English rather than French for all official business. The emergence of a written literature, including the Wycliffe Bible and the *Canterbury Tales*, also helped to raise the status of English.

The period of Modern English is often held to have begun in 1474, when William Caxton set up the first printing press in England. Early Modern English is the English of Shakespeare (1564–1616) and the King James Bible (1611). These works are familiar, so there is little need to copy them here. Some differences in vocabulary and syntax between Early Modern and Contemporary English were mentioned in Section 18.1 We seldom say "yea," "hath," or "said unto," and "subtle" no longer means "sneaky."

As far as pronunciation is concerned, the huge change that took place in the Modern English period was the *Great Vowel Shift (GVS)*. The GVS was a chain shift that affected the pronunciation of all the long vowels in English, moving them in a circular pattern: the high vowels diphthongized, and the mid and low vowels all moved up a step. It did not happen overnight: the GVS began in the mid-1500s and was not complete until the 1800s. The eventual effect of the GVS is schematized in the diagram in (24); its more gradual application is shown in Table 18.1.

Table 18.1   The Great Vowel Shift as a gradual change: From Lass, R. 2006. Phonology and Morphology. In Richard Hogg and David Denison (eds), *A History of the English Language*. Cambridge: Cambridge University Press, p. 83. Reprinted with permission.

	ME	1569	1653	1687	Nineteenth century
bite	iː	ɛi	əi	ʌi	ai
meet	eː	iː	iː	iː	iː
meat	ɛː	ɛː	eː	eː	iː
name	aː	aː	ɛː	eː	eː
house	uː	ɔuː	əu	ʌu	au
food	oː	uː	uː	uː	uː
bone	ɔː	ɔː	oː	oː	oː

(24)   The Great Vowel Shift

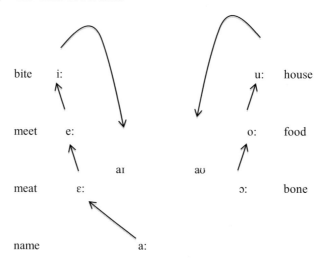

(In the late 1600s some original [ɛː] words, such as "break," merged with the "name" class and ended up as [e]. Most words in this class, however, merged with "meet" instead.)

In the meantime, the short counterparts of the long vowels moved in the opposite direction. Glossing over some complicating factors (as do examples (24) and Table 18.1), short [i] and [e] lowered and laxed to [ɪ] and [ɛ], [u] became either [ʊ] "put" or [ʌ] "cut," [o] lowered to [ɑ], and [a] fronted (again) to [æ]. Lass (2006) provides further details, additional examples, and numerous sub-regularities beyond the scope of what can be covered here.

The GVS began *after* the spelling of many words had been standardized. Thus English "long i" ("bite") is pronounced [aɪ], "long e" ("cede" or "meet") is pronounced [i], and "long a" ("name") is pronounced [e]. The spelling correspondences for the back vowels are a little more complicated, because of some additional mergers and splits, but "oo" ("food") is (usually) pronounced [u], and "short o" ("pot") is pronounced [ɑ].

Additionally, pairs that were originally the same vowel, and that were first affected by rules of open syllable lengthening and closed syllable shortening, were further affected by the GVS. The long vowel of the pair moved up or diphthongized, the short vowel of the pair moved down. Further complicating the situation, the context for open syllable lengthening was obscured by the loss of final endings, a process that was finally completed in Early

Modern English with the loss of word-final reduced vowels, all that was left of the Old English inflections. As a result of this whole series of changes, Contemporary Modern English is left with alternations such as those shown in example (25).

(25) Contemporary English tri-syllabic laxing

Middle English before the GVS	Modern English after the GVS	Examples
iː ~ i	aɪ ~ ɪ	divine / divinity sublime / subliminal derive / derivative
eː ~ e	i ~ ɛ	serene / serenity please / pleasure impede / impediment feet / fetters
aː ~ a	e ~ æ	grade / gradual grave / gravity profane / profanity
uː ~ u	aʊ ~ ʌ	profound / profundity abound / abundance pronounce / pronunciation
oː ~ o	u ~ ɑ	goose / gosling food / fodder school / scholar
ɔː ~ ɔ	o ~ ɑ	mode / modify sole / solitude close / closet provoke / provocative

These alternations are known in the phonology of Contemporary English as *tri-syllabic laxing* (a term introduced by Chomsky and Halle 1968), because the alternating vowel is often found in the antepenultimate syllable. This rule has lost the phonological conditioning it had in Early Modern English: closed syllable shortening makes phonetic sense and is widely found cross-linguistically, but an alternation where [aɪ, i, e, aʊ, u, o] become [ɪ, ɛ, æ, ʌ, ɑ] makes reference to no natural class: the features that change [aɪ] to [ɪ] are not the same as those that change [u] to [ʌ]. Today, the alternation is lexically conditioned, occurring only with certain suffixes, which must be memorized: "divine/divinity" shows the alternation, but "pirate/ piracy" does not. Some words that ought to undergo change do not ("obesity" is not pronounced [obɛsɪɾi]), and others vary (the first vowel of "penalize" can be [i] or [ɛ], the first vowel of "codify" can be either [o] or [ɑ]). In many cases, in fact, the native speaker has no sense that an alternation or derivation has applied: does a speaker without training in etymology or linguistics think of "modify" as derived from "mode," or "gravity" as derived from "grave"?

Trisyllabic laxing thus serves as an illustration of how phonological rules both arise and die. It arose in Old English as a phonetic tendency to shorten vowels in closed syllables, making room for the final consonant. In Middle English, shortening became a categorical change, just as weakening of final vowels became categorical deletion. The loss of the final vowels then obscured the original conditioning of the alternation, and the shift in vowel quality moved the long and short vowels in opposite directions and obscured the clear relation between long and short. In the meantime, semantic drift, such as loss of the close semantic tie between "grave" and "gravity," further obscured the relationship. What was once a real and active alternation becomes in Contemporary English a fossilized lexical relationship. Different vowel qualities are memorized when different forms of a word are learned: [i] in "serene", [ɛ] in "serenity," [i] in "obese," [i] in "obesity." Finally, the "rule" drops entirely below the notice of the language user, and becomes a curiosity to be found in an etymological dictionary, no more real to the modern speaker than the relationship between "nædre" and "adder." It is not clear if tri-syllabic laxing has reached a completely fossilized state yet, but it is close to it.

chapter summary

- Diachronic linguistics studies language change over time.
- The kinds of sound changes that occur diachronically are the same as those that occur synchronically: assimilation, dissimilation, deletion, insertion, lenition, fortition, lengthening, shortening, and metathesis. As groups of people diverge, sound change affects the different groups differently, and their languages diverge as well.
- The comparative method of historical reconstruction uses regular sound correspondences among descendant languages to deduce the structure of the proto-language.
- Historical linguists in the eighteenth and nineteenth centuries, including Jones, Rask, Grimm, and Verner, used the comparative method to reconstruct Proto-Indo-European, and to deduce a "family tree" of the Indo-European languages.
- Grimm's Law and Verner's Law describe a set of changes in the consonants of PIE to Proto-Germanic, and demonstrate the validity of the Neogrammarian hypothesis: sound change is without exception.
- Wave models of diachronic change take into account not only historical relationships, but also the gradual spread of sound change, the importance of lateral influence, and the crucial role of social factors.
- Important events in the history of the English language include: Anglo-Saxon displacement of the Celts in the fifth century, Viking invasions in the ninth century, Norman conquest in 1066, and the re-establishment of English as an official language in the fourteenth century.
- Old English had many word endings. The phonology included front round vowels, length distinctions for both vowels and consonants, and allophonic voicing of fricatives.
- Middle English was inundated with French borrowings. Its phonology included allophonic vowel lengthening and shortening, and weakening of final vowels.
- The Great Vowel Shift was a chain shift that affected the long vowels of Early Modern English: high vowels diphthongized, and non-high vowels raised. At the same time, short vowels laxed and lowered. English spelling was standardized before the shift began.
- Phonological alternations may arise as gradient phonetic tendencies that are misperceived as categorical. They become non-productive when their phonological conditioning is lost due to further sound change, and they become permanently associated with specific morphemes. Tri-syllabic laxing is an example of this process.

further reading

Hogg, R. (series ed.), 2001. *The Cambridge History of the English Language*. Cambridge: Cambridge University Press (6 big volumes).

For a more condensed version, see:

van Gelderen, E. 2006. *A History of the English Language*. Amsterdam: John Benjamins.

See also the companion website: http://www.historyofenglish.net/.

Campbell, L. 2004. *Historical Linguistics: An Introduction.* Cambridge, MA: MIT Press.
Hock, H. 1991. *Principles of Historical Linguistics.* Berlin: Mouton.
Robins, R.H. 1997. *A Short History of Linguistics.* Harlow: Longmans.

review exercises

1. Define the following terms:

   diachronic vs. synchronic linguistics
   semantic drift
   merger
   split
   chain shift
   conditioned sound change
   cognate set
   proto-language

2. List an example from the history of English of diachronic

   assimilation
   dissimilation
   lenition
   fortition
   epenthesis
   deletion
   lengthening
   shortening
   metathesis

3. What is the Neogrammarian hypothesis? Why were the exceptions to Grimm's Law a challenge to the hypothesis, and how did Verner's Law save it?

4. Give approximate date ranges for Old English, Middle English, and Modern English. What historical event marks the beginning of each stage?

5. List three more examples of tri-syllabic laxing.

further analysis and discussion

6. List three ways that your speech is different from your grandparents. (Try to find something more insightful than the fact that you have words for things that did not exist when Grandma was your age.) Are the differences semantic, syntactic, or phonological?

7. Choose any book in your possession, and find the first (content) word on pp. 100, 200, 300, 400, and 500 (or use some other random selection of pages). Then, look up each word in the *Oxford English Dictionary* (which your library should have in hard copy), or the Online Etymology Dictionary at: http://www.etymonline.com/. For each of your five words, answer the following questions:
   a. Is it a PIE root, a borrowing, or both?
   b. If a borrowing, when did it enter English and from what language?

(Continued)

c.   Describe in general terms any sound changes that the word has undergone. (You'll have to infer the sound changes by comparing the original and current forms, with reference to the changes described in the text.)

d.   Describe in general terms any semantic drift the word has undergone.

8.   Catalan is spoken in the border region between Spain and France, and the Catalans, like the Basques, seek political independence. Look up the Catalan words for the cognate set in the table in example (12). What can you conclude?

9.   Do the same for Albanian. Is it Indo-European?

10. Latin [k] was subject to conditioned sound change as it evolved into French. Based on the data below, describe the sound change.

Latin		French		
centum	[kentum]	cent	[sɑ̃]	100
celer	[keler]	célérité	[selerite]	quickness
certus	[kertus]	certain	[sɛrtɛ̃]	settled
cantare	[kantare]	chanter	[ʃɑ̃te]	sing
calor	[kalor]	chaleur	[ʃalœːr]	heat
cappa	[kappa]	chapeau	[ʃapo]	hat
campus	[kampus]	champ	[ʃɑ̃]	field
cor	[kor]	cœur	[kœːr]	heart
cura	[kura]	cure	[kyr]	cure/care for
clarum	[klarum]	claire	[kler]	bright/clear

11. Consider the cognate words in the table below, from languages spoken on six different Pacific islands. Reconstruct the Proto-Polynesian sound for the initial sound in each row. (Some rows have the same initial consonant.) Write the rules for any sound changes. Data from the Polynesian Lexicon Project Online at: http://pollex.org.nz/.

	Tuvalu	Tokelau	Samoa	Tikopia	Futuna (Eastern)	Renell	Proto-Polynesian
dry/empty	masa	maha	masa	masa	masa	masa	
night	poo	poo	poo	poo	poo	poo	
drag	toso	toho	toso	tosi	toso	toso	
split	tosi	tohi			tosi	tosi	
breast	susu	huhu	susu			susu	
different	kese		ʔese	kese	kese	kese	
digging stick	koso	koho	ʔoso	koso	koso	koso	
day	aso	aho	aso	aso	ʔaso	ʔaso	
cloud			ao	ao	ʔao	ʔao	
gather up	ao		ao	ao	ao	ao	
termite	ane	ane	ane	ane		ane	
Dawn	ata	ata	ata		ata		

12. Choose any three sound changes described in the chapter, and rewrite using SPE, autosegmental, or OT formalism.

Go online Visit the book's companion website for additional resources relating to this chapter at: http://www.wiley.com/go/zsiga.

references

On the origins of sound change:

Ohala, J. 1981. The listener as a source of sound change. *Proceedings of the Chicago Linguistics Society*, 178–203.

Old English vowel alternations are from:

Campbell, L. 2004. *Historical Linguistics: An Introduction*. Cambridge, MA: MIT Press.

Other examples of Old English and Middle English phonology, as well as description of the Great Vowel Shift, are from:

Lass, R. 2006. Phonology and Morphology. In R. Hogg and D. Denison (eds.), *A History of the English Language*. Cambridge: Cambridge University Press.

Proto-Germanic and PIE roots:

The Oxford Etymological Dictionary
The Oxford English Dictionary
Dictionary of Indo-European roots

19 Variation

Col. Pickering: How do you do it, if I may I ask?

Prof. Higgins: Simple phonetics. The science of speech. That's my profession, also my hobby. Anyone can spot an Irishman or a Yorkshireman by his brogue, but I can place a man within six miles. I can place him within two miles in London. Sometimes within two streets . . .

My Fair Lady, Act I, Scene 1

Prof. Higgins: What could possibly matter more than to take a human being and change her into a different human being by creating a new speech for her?

My Fair Lady, Act 1, Scene 9, script by Alan Jay Lerner, 1956

Chapter outline

The Sounds of Language: An Introduction to Phonetics and Phonology, First Edition. Elizabeth C. Zsiga.
© 2013 Elizabeth C. Zsiga. Published 2013 by Blackwell Publishing Ltd.

In the play (and later movie) *My Fair Lady*, Professor Henry Higgins is introduced as an expert in dialects: on the basis of hearing a few words, he identifies the exact neighborhood where a person was born and where he or she has lived. His friend, Colonel Pickering (himself an expert in Sanskrit), suggests this skill would make a lucrative sideshow act. The plot thickens when Higgins agrees to take on a poor, young woman, Eliza Doolittle, as a student. When Higgins first meets Doolittle, he quickly transcribes a few words of her speech, identifies her neighborhood of origin and then comments condescendingly that her "kerbstone English . . . will keep her in the gutter to the end of her days. . . . It's 'aooow' and 'garn' that keep her in her place, not her wretched clothes and dirty face." In effect, Doolittle's speech not only reveals where she was born, but that she belongs to the lowest classes of society, where she is destined to stay, until Higgins intervenes. The theme of how language shapes perception and creates identity runs through the play. By giving Doolittle a new set of vowels, and teaching her to pronounce word-initial [h], Higgins indeed creates "a different human being."

Previous chapters of this book have discussed the phonetic properties and phonological rules of English and other languages as though speech production was uniform, and the rules consistently applied always and everywhere. When the point is to study differences between languages and commonalities across speakers, such simplifications are useful, but they are not strictly true. There is always some variation in pronunciation, at both the phonetic and phonological levels.

Speech variation comes from many sources. Some of it is purely physical, due to the size of the speaker's vocal folds, the shape of his nose, or a missing tooth. Some of it is idiosyncratic habit: an individual may tend to speak quickly, or softly, or more or less clearly, as a personality trait. Such unpredictable, individual differences are of little interest to linguists, however (excepting, perhaps, those concerned with forensic voice identification.) Linguists, particularly *sociolinguists*, are interested in *patterns* of variation, patterns that reveal the interaction between linguistic and social systems. Sociolinguists may be interested in variation that is correlated with place (*dialect*), with situation (*register*), or with social affiliation and identification, including class, race, gender, sexuality, age, and membership in different communities.

In this chapter, Section 19.1 discusses phonological and phonetic variation by place, including a general overview of dialectology, and some consideration of dialects of English around the world. Section 19.2 discusses variation influenced by social factors such as those named above. Section 19.3 turns to a discussion of the interaction of variation with formal phonological representations.

> 19.1　George Bernard Shaw, author of *Pygmalion* (the original, darker, non-musical version of *My Fair Lady*), based the character of Henry Higgins on the real-life phonetician Daniel Jones, of cardinal vowel and IPA fame. Pickering may have been modeled on Sanskrit expert William Jones. Later, when the play was being made into a movie, the actor Rex Harrison, who played Higgins, found he couldn't pronounce all the unusual vowel sounds required. An assistant professor of phonetics from UCLA was brought in to help. The voice actually pronouncing [aaaaa ooooo yyyyy œœœœœœ] in the movie is not Rex Harrison but Peter Ladefoged.

19.1　variation by place

19.1.1　what is a dialect?

A *regional dialect* is a language variety spoken by a group of people who live in a particular place. We thus talk about the Australian dialect of English, the Florentine dialect of Italian, the Shoshong dialect of Setswana. Dialects may differ from one another in lexical items, such as "soda" vs. "pop," and in syntax. To take just one syntactic example, "he might could do it" is grammatical in some parts of Virginia but not others. With respect to sound patterns, dialects often differ in the way certain segments are pronounced: Australians says [ʌɪ] while Californians say [eɪ] (as in "mate"); Brooklynites say [d] while their neighbors in Connecticut say [ð] (as in "dis" vs. "this"); speakers of the Shoshong dialect have [pʃ] in many words where relatives further south in Gaborone say [tʃ]. Dialects may also differ in whether or not phonological rules apply. Most speakers of English in America pronounce an intervocalic, post-stress /t/ as [ɾ]; most speakers of English in England will not. Italian speakers in Florence apply a rule of debuccalization to intervocalic [k], while speakers of other dialects do not: a Roman who wants a carbonated beverage might order [una koka kola], while a Florentine will ask for [una hoha hola]. A cluster of such place-specific lexical, syntactic, phonetic, and phonological features constitutes a dialect.

Prof. Higgins' claim to be able to place a person within two streets notwithstanding, dialect boundaries are blurred, not sharp. A community member may exhibit dialectal characteristics to a greater or lesser extent. We recognize different dialects in Albany and in New York City, but there is not a particular exit on the New York State Thruway where one dialect turns suddenly into the other.

There is no linguistic definition for when two dialects become different enough to count as two different languages. It is often the case that what we call two dialects of a single language are mutually intelligible (that is, people can understand each other even if they do not speak alike), while what we call distinct languages are not mutually intelligible. This doesn't always hold, however. Speakers of "Chinese" in Beijing and Hong Kong would not understand one another at all, while speakers of "Norwegian" and "Swedish" understand one another perfectly. The decision about what is a "language" and what is a "dialect" is more political and cultural than it is linguistic. "A shpracht iz a dialekt mit ein army," said Max Weinrich in 1945. The fact that you can probably understand his Yiddish just emphasizes that German and English are very nearly mutually intelligible. (You might need to be told that "shpracht" means "language"; the word is related to English "speech.")

Because every person was born someplace and lives somewhere, everyone speaks a dialect; everyone has an "accent." It is the case, however, that in all languages some dialects hold a higher social status than others. A particular variety is elevated as the "standard," and this will be the variety taught in school, used by news announcers, and expected from applicants for high-paying jobs. Being able to speak and write the standard dialect thus confers a social advantage. From the point of view of linguistics, however, every dialect is equally systematic and rule-governed, and each has the same potential for logical and nuanced communication. The rules will not necessarily be the same, and the nuances might be conveyed in different ways, but no one dialect is intrinsically better than any other.

The following sections review some of the characteristics of the larger dialects of English, first in America, then around the world.

As it happens, the dialects of English differ mostly, though not exclusively, in their vowel systems, having undergone different mergers, splits, and shifts (see Chapter 18). Because vowel qualities vary so much, linguists studying English dialects face a challenge in clearly and accurately describing similarities and differences in vowel systems without denigrating any particular system to a derivative status. It can be confusing and misleading to make statements like "In dialect A, the vowel [ɪ] is pronounced as [ʌ]," for example. In this dialect, the vowel isn't really [ɪ] at all. What is actually meant by such statements is "words that have the vowel [ɪ] in some standard reference such as General American are pronounced with [ʌ] in this dialect." As shorthand for "words that have the vowel X in some standard reference such as General American," the linguist J.C. Wells proposed the set of 24 words shown in Table 19.1. Following Wells' example, dialectologists will typically refer to the key word ("the KIT vowel" or "the DRESS vowel"), thus unambiguously pegging the intended sound without implying anything about what the "real" pronunciation is or should be. In this section, we'll follow this practice. Because sound change is regular (see Chapter 18), pronunciation of words within the set remains consistent within the dialect: whatever vowel is used, the words "dress, step, neck, edge, friend, ready" will all have the same one.

The literature and resources on English dialect variation is rich, and none of the major dialects is completely uniform. Every locale has its own way of speech. Some, like Cajun in New Orleans or Gullah in South Carolina, are very distinct from the larger dialects surrounding them. Here, we can only touch on some major areas and widely shared characteristics. As you read through the dialect sections, try out the different key words, and see how you sound.

19.1.2 dialects of North American English

Sociolinguists Bill Labov, Sharon Ash, and Charles Boberg, in their comprehensive 2006 study, *The Atlas of North American English*, divide the United States into six major dialect areas, as shown in the map in Figure 19.1: West, North Central, Inland North, Midland, South, and Northeast, with Canada making a seventh. Of the six major American dialects, Labov *et al.* claim that three are both expanding in territory and diverging from one another: South, Inland North, and West. The other dialect areas remain distinct, but seem to be losing ground to these three.

A "Southern drawl" is widely recognized as a regional variant. Linguists have noted two particularly salient characteristics of the Southern dialect. First is the *pin/pen merger*: mid vowels are raised before nasal consonants, so that "pen" becomes homophonous with "pin." Also homophonous are "bomb" and "bum." Various stories circulate on the web, of federal agents descending on a location prepared to defuse an incendiary device, only to find a homeless person innocent of nefarious intent, and a confused caller with a Southern accent.

Table 19.1   Wells' lexical sets, with General American and BBC English phonetic equivalents. Transcriptions are modified to be consistent with the system followed in this book.

Key word	General American	BBC English	Examples
FLEECE	i	i	creep, speak, key, leave
KIT	ɪ	ɪ	ship, sick, bridge, myth, busy
FACE	eɪ	eɪ	tape, cake, steak, day
DRESS	ɛ	ɛ	step, neck, edge, friend, ready
TRAP	æ	æ	tap, back, hand, cancel
BATH	æ	ɑ	staff, ask, dance, calf
LOT	ɑ	ɒ	stop, sock, dodge, quality
PALM	ɑ	ɑ	father, spa, lager
THOUGHT	ɔ	ɔ	taught, sauce, jaw, hawk
CLOTH	ɔ	ɒ	cough, broth, cross
GOAT	oʊ	əʊ	soap, joke, home, know
FOOT	ʊ	ʊ	put, bush, full, look
GOOSE	u	u	loop, shoot, tomb
STRUT	ʌ	ʌ	cup, suck, pulse, trunk
NURSE	ɝ	ɜ	hurt, urge, jerk, term
PRICE	aɪ	aɪ	try, buy, ripe, high
CHOICE	ɔɪ	ɔɪ	toy, noise, royal, join
MOUTH	aʊ	aʊ	out, house, loud, cow
NEAR	ir	iə	beer, fear, sincere
SQUARE	er	e	care, fair, pear, where
START	ɑr	ɑ	far, sharp, bark, heart
NORTH	ɔr	ɔ	for, war, short, born
FORCE	or	ɔ	four, wore, sport, borne
CURE	u	uə	poor, tourist, plural
(schwa)	ə	ə	comma

Another characteristic of a Southern accent is the pattern known as the *Southern Vowel Shift*, diagrammed in Figure 19.2. The most noticeable part of this shift affects the PRICE diphthong (GA /aɪ/), which is pronounced as long [aː]: PRICE is pronounced [pɹaːs]. But other vowels have shifted as well, as shown in the figure. The back vowels in GOOSE and GOAT are fronted. The front tense vowels move down and back, while the lax vowels move up to take their places. Thus FACE is [fʌɪs], but DRESS is [dɹeɪs].

Parts, but not all, of the American South are *r-dropping*: post-vocalic [ɹ] is not pronounced (unless another vowel follows). In the coastal plain from South Carolina to Louisiana, as well as parts of Virginia, NEAR, SQUARE, START, NORTH, CURE, NURSE are pronounced as [niə, skwæə, staːt, noːθ, kjuə, nɜs]. In the inland and mountain regions, [ɹ] is pronounced in these words. Scarlett [skaːlɪt] O'Hara of Georgia dropped her post-vocalic [ɹ]s; Dolly Parton [pʰaɹtən] of Tennessee does not. But both would pronounce "my" as [maː] and "Rhett" as [reɪt]; and both would have homophonous "pin" and "pen."

A different pattern in the vowel space, the *Northern Cities Shift*, characterizes the Inland North dialect (Figure 19.3). This dialect area is concentrated in the cities around the southern edge of the Great Lakes, including Chicago, Detroit, Cleveland, and Buffalo, but it is spreading southward, and into more rural areas. In the Northern Cities Shift, the vowel in TRAP is

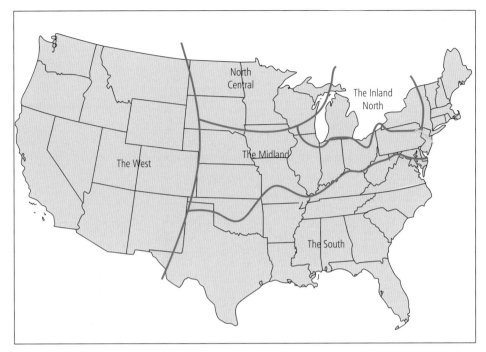

Figure 19.1 Major dialect boundaries in the United States.
Source: William Labov, Sharon Ash, and Charles Boberg. 2006. *The Atlas of North American English*. Reprinted with permission of De Gruyter.

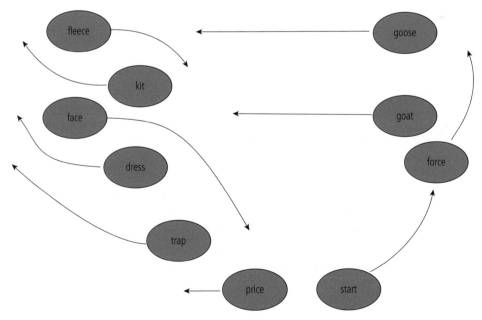

Figure 19.2 The Southern Vowel Shift.
Source: Following Labov *et al.*, 2006.

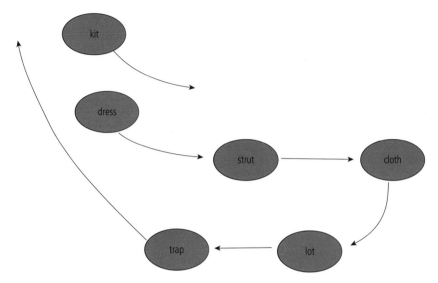

Figure 19.3   The Northern Cities Shift.
Source: Following Labov *et al.*, 2006.

diphthongized to [ɪə] (like the second syllable of "idea"). With /æ/ up and out of the way, low back /ɑ/ moves forward (LOT is close to [læt], and "sock" sounds like GA "sack,"), /ɔ/ moves down, and /ʌ/ moves back. In [ʃɪkʰægo], people in charge are [bɑsɨz], and [bɔsɨz] are a type of public transportation. The vowels /ɪ/ and /ɛ/ move toward the center of the vowel space (DRESS is [drʌs], "bed" sounds like GA "bud.") Note that in the South, the vowel in DRESS is moving forward and up, while in the Northern Cities, it is moving back and down.

The third expanding American dialect is the West, which covers any part of the United States west of a line running from Texas to the Dakotas. A major feature of Western speech is the merger of LOT, CLOTH, and THOUGHT: "cot" and "caught" are homophones. A second feature is fronting and unrounding of back vowels, so that "dude" is [dɨːd].

Between North and South lies the Midland, which Labov *et al.* characterize as a "buffer zone" between the three expanding dialects. Speakers in this area vary as to which, if any, dialect features they exhibit. This area most closely matches the American English vowel charts printed in textbooks (including this one), and if any area can be characterized as "General American," it is the Midland.

The North Central region, comprised of the Dakotas, Minnesota, Wisconsin, and Northern Michigan, has a distinct dialect. Its most noticeable characteristic is that the mid tense vowels are not diphthongized, as they are in other dialects: GOAT is [goːt], not [goʊt], "Minnesota" is [mɪnɛsoːrə]. This dialect has also resisted any of the other shifts and mergers found in other parts of America. If you're a fan of the movie *Fargo*, this is the dialect portrayed there.

The final major American dialect area is the North East. Unlike the Western part of the country, where speech is relatively uniform across thousands of miles, dialects in the North East are densely packed, with each city exhibiting distinct characteristics. Boston is known for alternations involving [ɹ]: [ɹ] is inserted between two vowels ("Cuba[ɹ] is an island"), and deleted preceding a consonant ("President [karə] followed President [fɔd]"). Instead of pronouncing START with [ɑɹ] or [ɑː], Boston has a unique central [a], famously illustrated in the phrase "park the car in Harvard Yard" [pʰak ðə kʰa ɪn havad jad].

Moving south from Boston, New York City is another dialect known for r-dropping, as well as for a particularly back, round [ɔ] (thus, "New Yawk"). It is also known for fortition of /θ/ and /ð/ to [t] and [d]. Philadelphia is unusual in America in preserving the tense/lax distinction before [ɹ]: Mary [meɹi] is distinct from "merry" [mɛɹi] is distinct from "marry" [mæɹi]; and "war" [wɔɹ] is distinct from "wore" [woɹ]. Baltimore (which the natives call [bɔlmɚ]) exhibits "Canadian" raising: PRICE is pronounced [pɹʌɪs], and MOUTH is [mʌʊθ].

As the term "Canadian raising" implies, raising of the nucleus of the diphthongs in PRICE and MOUTH is one of the most identifiable characteristics of Canadian English speech. (The other is the tag question, "eh?") In general, the pronunciation Canadian English is very similar to General American English, though its lexicon and spelling are more British. Canadian English merges LOT, CLOTH, and THOUGHT, and exhibits fronting of back vowels, both characteristics shared with the Western US As in America, speech is fairly uniform across the West, with dialects more dense in the East. Newfoundland and Prince Edward Island have distinct dialects, characterized by merger of KIT and DRESS, and pronunciation of NEAR and SQUARE as [nɛɹ] and [skwɛɹ]. It should also be remembered that English and French share equal status as official languages of Canada. According to the 2001 census, 23 percent of Canadians, concentrated in the province of Quebec, speak French as a first language.

Interestingly, the Northern Cities shift, characteristic of the southern side of the Great Lakes, is not moving across the border to Canada. Preliminary studies indicate that, if anything, the vowel in BATH is moving back and down in Canadian, not forward and up as in the Northern Cities.

19.1.3 dialects of British English

The standard, prestige dialect of Contemporary English spoken in England is often called *Received Pronunciation* (RP), a term coined in the nineteenth century, but popularized by Daniel Jones, who used it as the basis of his *English Pronouncing Dictionary* in 1924. RP is also variously called "The Queen's English," "Oxford English," "Public School English," or "BBC English," all of which connote the status of this variety as conferring social prestige on those who use it. (The term "received" was probably just intended to mean "generally accepted," but it has the pleasant connotation of "having been handed down from on high.") The vowels of RP were shown in Table 19.1. Noticeable differences from GA include GOAT as [gəʊt], and differences among the low vowels. RP has a rare three-way distinction among the low vowels: front unround [æ] as in TRAP [tɹæp], back unround [ɑ] in PALM [pɑm], and back round [ɒ] in CLOTH [klɒθ], all of which are distinct from mid, back, round [ɔ] in THOUGHT [θɔt]. RP is also r-dropping; continued reference to things English as conferring social prestige contributed to the preservation of r-dropping among English émigrés in American cities along the Atlantic coast.

RP is more of a social dialect than a regional dialect (see section 19.2). It is typical of a particular social class, not a particular place. There are, however, many, many regional dialects in the British Isles. Even more so than in the American North East, each city has its own typical pronunciation. Recognized experts on British dialectology include J.C. Wells (*Accents of English*, 1982), and Peter Trudgill (*The Dialects of English*, 1990), whose works can be consulted for further details. Within England, dialectal characteristics often follow a north/south division.

In Northern England (including areas around Leeds, Liverpool, and Manchester) FOOT and STRUT have merged into [ʊ], so "put" and "putt" are homophones, as are "look" and "luck." (In the far north, however, in areas influenced by Scots, "look" may instead be homophonous with "Luke.") These words remain distinct in the south, including London. Another north/south distinction is the vowel in BATH: in the north BATH and its lexical set are pronounced with a front vowel, more like GA [bæθ]; in the south the vowel is more like RP [bɑθ].

Several characteristics of consonant pronunciation are particularly associated with London, but can be found throughout the south of England: these include l-vocalization, t-glottalization, and h-dropping. In l-vocalization, syllable-final /l/ has a backed tongue position but no alveolar contact, sounding more like [w] or [o]: thus "old" is [owd] and "child" is [ʧɒɪowd]. Glottalization of /t/ occurs in the same environments in which GA speakers produce a tap: "pretty" is [pɹɪtɪ] in RP, [pɹɪɾi] in GA, and [pɹɪʔi] in London English. Across most of southern England, syllable-initial /h/ is not pronounced: "happy" is [æpi]. Each of these characteristics has in the past been stigmatized as lower-class, in contradistinction to RP, especially h-dropping. In *My Fair Lady*, Higgins (whose name may well have been chosen to give Eliza Doolittle ample opportunity to say [ɛnri ɪgɪnz]), spends a great deal of effort teaching Doolittle to say "In Hertford, Hereford, and Hampshire, hurricanes hardly ever happen."

The stigmatization of h-dropping often leads to *hyper-correction*: speakers who want to sound "correct" will insert initial [h] in words that are vowel-initial for RP speakers. "Ask" can be pronounced [hæsk], for example, with h-insertion particularly common in emphasized words. For many speakers across various English dialects, the letter "h" is, not unreasonably, [heɪʧ]. Note that all English speakers drop initial [h] from unstressed syllables: "We like him" is generally [wi laɪk ɪm], for example, unless the pronoun is stressed; or compare "vehicle" ['vi.ɪk.əl] and "vehicular" [vɪ.'hɪk.jə.lɚ] (The Middle English form of "its" was "hits.")

In Scotland and Ireland, Celtic languages were spoken by a majority of the population from the first millennium CE until the mid-eighteenth century, but due to continued social and sometimes legal pressure to adopt English, English is now the first language of almost all children in Scotland and Ireland. Though many people consider themselves bilingual, English is the dominant language used for most social interactions, and the monolingual Scots or Irish speaker is vanishingly rare. The influence of the Celtic languages on English pronunciation in these areas is still strong, however.

Both Irish English and Scottish English stand out from most other dialects of the British Isles in *not* dropping post-vocalic [ɹ], though their pronunciation of the rhotic and rhotacized vowels will differ. In Ireland, both NURSE and SQUARE are pronounced [ɛɹ]. In addition, there is fortition of /θ/ and /ð/, so a typical Irish pronunciation of "third" is [tɛɹd] and "there" is [dɛɹ]. In Scottish English, post-vocalic /r/ may be trilled, or more commonly tapped, so that the Scottish pronunciation of "pearl" is like the American pronunciation of "pedal": [pɛɾəl]. Scottish English has fewer vowel qualities than other varieties, and exhibits a number of mergers. Both TRAP and BATH are pronounced with [a], FOOT and GOOSE are both [u], and LOT and THOUGHT are both [ɔ]. The vowels [e] and [o] are not diphthongized; more saliently, MOUTH is also monopthongal: "cow" is [ku] and "house" is [hus].

19.1.4 Australia, New Zealand, South Africa

The first English speakers in Australia were convicts: prisoners sent to the penal colony of New South Wales in the late eighteenth century to ease overcrowding in London jails. They were soon followed by free settlers in search of land, adventure, or gold. The first English speakers in New Zealand came from whaling ships. There are few regional differences across Australia and New Zealand despite the size of the country/continent: probably because the introduction of English is relatively recent in linguistic time.

Australian and New Zealand English, like the London English of most of their first settlers, are r-dropping, and distinguish the vowels in BATH and TRAP. The BATH vowel is more fronted than in RP, however, and the vowels in TRAP and DRESS are raised: [baθ], [tɹɛp], [dɹes]. The vowel in FACE (as well as "day" and "mate") has mid-central rather than front starting point, thus the stereotypical [gədʌɪ mʌɪt]. The low diphthongs are distinct as well. PRICE

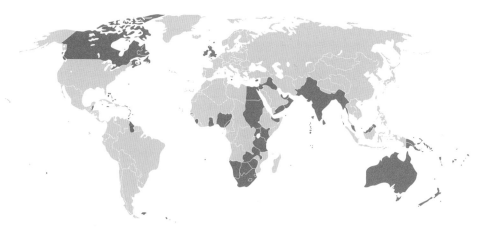

Figure 19.4 Extent of the British Empire in 1921.

[pɹɒɪs] starts with a round back vowel, and MOUTH [mæɐθ] starts from a front vowel: they cross in the middle. In other dialects, both PRICE and MOUTH start with a central [a]. Like GA and unlike RP, these dialects have a tap for /t/ and /d/ in "pretty" and "ready." One salient difference between Australia and New Zealand is the KIT vowel, which is fronted in Australian [kit] and backed in New Zealand [kɨt]. The KIT vowel is also a distinguishing feature of South African English, where it is undergoing a split: [ɪ] adjacent to velars and alveopalatals, [ɨ] in most other environments.

19.1.5 World Englishes

From the seventeenth to the twentieth centuries, representatives of Great Britain colonized broad swaths of the world, taking their language with them. (Spanish is also widespread because representatives of Spain did the same thing.) The map in Figure 19.4 shows the extent of the British Empire in 1921.

In some countries, including Australia, Canada, New Zealand, and the United States, the English established themselves as the majority culture, relegating the prior inhabitants and their languages to minority (often endangered) status, much as the Anglo-Saxons did to the Celts in the fifth century. In other countries, the native majority remained strong and eventually regained independence, but continued to use English as a language of education and government. Countries in this second group include India, many countries of Africa, and many Pacific and Caribbean islands. Although it is beyond the scope of this introduction to detail every variety of English spoken around the world, any survey of the dialects of English cannot neglect the millions of English speakers in these countries. In every place where English is spoken but is not the majority native language, the interaction of English with the local language produces a unique variety. These varieties are sometimes known as *World Englishes.*

Each former colony also has a unique history, but in general British rule began in the seventeenth or eighteenth century with the government stepping in (sometimes invited, sometimes by force) to protect English economic interests. A long period of English rule then established English as the language of government, law, education, and commerce. The situation is parallel to the French conquest of England in 1066: foreigners hold the positions of power in state institutions, and those who wish to deal with them must speak their language. In Medieval England, the French upper class eventually became Anglicized, and adopted the language of the common people. In the former British colonies, in contrast, English rule was eventually thrown off, but the linguistic situation remained complex. Factors that led to the continued use of English as a national language included national unity, tradition and social prestige, and economic issues.

Once Indian independence was won, for example, many Indians wanted to declare linguistic independence as well, abolishing the use of English as an official language and replacing it with a local language instead. But which one? The 48 million speakers of Urdu and the 35 million speakers of Malayalam were not eager for Hindi to be adopted as the sole standard for all of India. The use of English was at least equally unfair to everyone. The same situation holds in Nigeria, where speakers of Igbo, Yoruba, and Hausa (each about 20 million strong) agree to use English as a national language.

Across the former colonies, post-elementary education is conducted almost entirely in English, because advanced textbooks are not available in the local language, and it would not be cost-effective to produce them. Government business is often conducted in English, both as a matter of national unity and of tradition. Businesses want to hire English speakers, so that they can connect to global markets. For all these reasons, being fluent in English confers social prestige, and English remains an official, widely-used, high-prestige language throughout the former colonies.

The English dialects spoken in the former British colonies are generally based on RP, but show the influence of the local language as well. Vowel categories are often merged, resulting in a smaller inventory more similar to the local language. (RP has, after all, one of the most complex vowel inventories in the world.) Other marked structures of English are also often simplified, including deletion or epenthesis in consonant clusters, devoicing of voiced obstruents, especially fricatives, and fortition of /θ/ and /ð/. Most World Englishes are r-dropping, though some, such as Indian English, are not. Segment substitutions, such as retroflexes for alveolars in India, also reflect the influence of the local language. When the local language is tonal, as in much of Africa, English intonation often has a unique rhythm, blending elements of a stress system and a tonal system.

In the islands of the Caribbean and the Pacific, English may be used alongside an English-based *creole*. A creole develops from a rudimentary system of communication, called a *pidgin*, that arises when speakers of different languages are thrown together. In Jamaica, for example, native islanders, enslaved workers from different African cultures, and English-speaking overseers had to communicate. In Singapore, traders from England, Malaysia, and China had to make deals. In each case, speakers created a pidgin that borrowed basic words and short phrases from the different native languages in use. A pidgin has only a small vocabulary and simplified syntax, but when children learn the pidgin as a native language, they fill in the missing elements, and the pidgin develops into a creole, a full-fledged language with no deficit of syntax, phonology, morphology, or expressive range. The creole will show characteristics of the different languages from which it sprang. Jamaican creole combines elements of English with elements from different African languages; "Singlish" (the creole spoken in Singapore), combines elements of English with Malay and different varieties of Chinese. In many cases, creole will likely be learned at home as a first language, with English learned in school.

19.2   Most people in Singapore are at least bilingual, and many children grow up speaking English as one of the languages in their home (estimates vary from 25–50 percent native English speakers). The government strongly encourages English rather than creole, through education and publicity campaigns. In 2002, an otherwise unobjectionable movie about Singlish creole was given an NC-17 rating by the government, because it was judged to be a bad influence, unsuitable for children.

19.1.6 place and identity

While the goal of this section has been to describe regional variation, the discussion of English around the world has demonstrated that a dialect is never just about place: it is also about the pride that speakers take in the place that they are from, and how they see that place as integrated into, or separate from, other places. Whether one speaks the official standard or the local norm, social judgments ensue, both positive and negative.

The International Dialects of English Archive (see reference section on p. 445) contains an unscripted clip from a speaker of Boston English. This speaker begins by describing with pride his job as a member of the Harvard University campus police, and then goes on to talk about dialects:

> When you go to other parts of the country, people want to hear you talk . . . Like me, from being from Boston, I love the southern accent. It's respectful and it's quiet and it's, it's polished. I think, when you get away from Boston, that people pick up on that, and they like the accent. 'Cause you can't go anywhere. Like if I go to California, and I go through the drive-through, and I'll say, "Listen, I want a large coffee with cream and sugar ([laːʤ kɔːfi wɪt krim n ʃʊgə]). So the box'll come off, and it'll say "Uh, could you please repeat your order?" And I'll say, "Yes, I'd like a [laːʤ kɔːfi wɪt krim n ʃʊgə]." Then I'll hear like a little giggling from the box, and then they'll say "Sir, can you come to the window?" And then when I come to the window it'll be like, you know, a couple of people at the window just to look at me and see what this accent's all about."

This Boston police officer ascribes certain positive attributes to Southern American speech. He judges it to be genteel; others might judge it differently. What clearly comes through in his story, however, is the pleasure he takes in performing his Boston identity for the benefit of admiring California teens.

19.2 other sources of variation

Variation associated with place is important, but there are many other sources of variation. Variation can arise due to the specifics of a social situation, to affinity or affiliation with an ethnic or other social group, and other projections of personal identity.

19.2.1 register

Variation depending on social situation is termed *register*. The same person will speak differently when delivering a speech than when passing time with friends. Variation depending on situation can in some ways be indexed by *formality*: the extent to which the situation is structured and planned, that is, "scripted." Addressee also matters. We use more formal registers with those who are socially more distant or of higher status, and less formal registers with those who are closer or of lower status. In more formal situations (giving a speech, reading out loud, trying to impress a potential client or boss), talkers are likely to pay more attention to the act of speaking itself, so that speech tends to be more careful, with fewer mergers and reductions, and often exhibits more of the characteristics that are considered standard or high prestige. Lexical choice and syntactic complexity will also change with register: "It's a pleasure to see you again, sir," and "Hey, dude, what's up?" each have their place, but only one should be used in a job interview.

> 19.3   Phoneticians need to be aware of register differences when making recordings. Vowels that are distinct in a list read from a script might not be distinct in a spontaneous narrative. On the other hand, without a script, the speaker might not produce all the sounds and contexts you would hope to study. Sometimes this drawback can be overcome by using a very large corpus (collection) of spontaneous speech samples, increasing the chances that the desired context will occur. Sociolinguists also often address register issues by trying to record varying styles: often beginning with more formal read speech, and moving on to less formal storytelling as the speaker warms up. The effect of knowing that you're being recorded, however, is never entirely removed – though it is still never ethical to record speakers without their knowledge.

In some parts of the world, a change in social situation means using a different dialect or even a whole different language. In Tanzania, a boy may speak Chizigula with his family and neighborhood friends, Swahili when he goes to the market town, English at school, and Classical Arabic for his religious instruction. A Swiss-German girl will speak the Swiss dialect with her friends and Standard German with her teachers. A Jamaican banker will speak English at work and creole at home with his family. In these cases, which are found around the world, the language varieties are *stratified*: one variety, considered *high*, is used in formal situations, and is usually associated with a prestigious written literature, and another variety, *low*, is used in informal situations. When stratification is widespread and stable across the society, linguists refer to the situation as *diglossia*.

In the absence of society-wide linguistic stratification, bilingual individuals will still often *code-switch*: switching back and forth between their two languages, sometimes depending on the situation or addressee, sometimes in the middle of a sentence, if a particular meaning is more aptly expressed in one language or the other.

19.2.2 socioeconomic distinctions

Your speech will vary depending on where you grew up and where you live (regional dialect), as well as what you're doing and to whom you're speaking (register). Another important factor is socioeconomic class. Exactly what "class" means is hard to define: it's not just income, not just education, not just employment (or your parents' employment), not just "status" (whatever that means), but some combination of all of the above; and different factors may be weighted differently in different parts of the world. The fact remains, however, that how we speak is partly determined by how we fit into a stratified society (and the completely egalitarian society has yet to be discovered).

Sociolinguistic studies will often compare trends among "working class," "middle class," and "upper class" speakers, variously defined. But it is important to remember that no particular linguistic variable is inherently associated with higher vs. lower status. In London, r-dropping is associated with higher socioeconomic status; in New York, it is associated with lower.

In his 1966 book, *The Social Stratification of English in New York City* (re-issued in 2006), William Labov described an ingenious experiment. Labov chose three local department stores: Saks Fifth Avenue, catering to a more affluent clientele, Macy's, considered to be more middle class, and S. Klein, a discount chain. Labov spent time in each store, asking various employees where to find items that he knew in advance were to be found on the fourth floor. Having elicited that response, he pretended to misunderstand the answer, so that the employee would repeat "fourth floor" more carefully. He then quickly moved out of sight and noted down how many post-vocalic [ɹ]s the employee had pronounced. (He doesn't

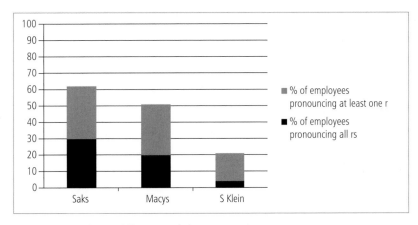

Figure 19.5 Social stratification of [ɹ] in New York department stores.
Source: Data from Labov, 2006.

report on whether the salespeople later compared notes on the strange guy who couldn't find the shoe department.)

The results of the study are shown in Figure 19.5. In each case, the regional feature of r-dropping was present to some extent, but the higher the status of the department store, the more likely the employee would be to say [fɔɹθ floɹ] rather than [fɔθ flɔə]. Labov also found that supervisors were more likely than stockboys and elevator operators to pronounce [ɹ]; women were more likely than men; and Whites were more likely than Blacks. In all groups, rates of [ɹ] pronunciation went up on the second repetition, where clearer speech was expected. Labov also looked at substitution of [t] for /θ/ in "fourth." In this case, the trend went the other way: rates of substitution were 0 percent at Saks, 4 percent at Macy's, and 15 percent at S. Klein. For both variables, higher socioeconomic status was associated with a higher percentage of standard pronunciations.

19.2.3 ethnicity

Ethnicity also matters. For social and cultural reasons, ethnicity is not independent of place and socioeconomic status, but some ways of speaking are characteristic of specific ethnic groups across places and socioeconomic lines.

A case in point is *African American Vernacular English (AAVE)*. Many features of AAVE are consistent across different geographic regions. The speech of a black woman in Detroit will probably be more similar to that of a black woman in New York than either will be to the speech of their white neighbors. AAVE is characterized by a cluster of lexical, morphological, syntactic, and phonological variables. Many of these are shared with other regional and social dialects, but the variety is defined by this particular combination, and the rates with which the different variants are used.

Phonological characteristics of AAVE include fortition of /ð/ to [d] and pronunciation of /θ/ as [f], especially in word-final position: "mouth" is pronounced [mauf]. Word-final consonant clusters are often simplified, especially when the final consonant is an alveolar: /t/ and /d/ are usually deleted in words like "most" and "hand." AAVE is r-dropping, and as in Southern England, coda /l/ and syllabic /l/ are vocalized, especially after back vowels: "cold" is [kowd] or (with both cluster simplification and l-vocalization) [kow], "bottle" is [bɑɾə]. Word-final voiced obstruents are also often devoiced. Like Southern American, AAVE, even in the North, exhibits the pin/pen merger, and has [a:] rather than [aɪ] in PRICE and "my."

Chicano English refers to the dialect of English spoken by Americans of Mexican ethnicity. Though the influence of Spanish is clear, Chicano English is a stable dialect of a group of native speakers of English, not learners of English whose first language is Spanish. It is similar to, but not identical to, other Spanish-influenced ethnic dialects, such as Cuban English in Florida or Puerto Rican English in New York City. Like Spanish, Chicano English merges tense and lax vowels (so that "live" and "leave," for example, are homophonous). The post-alveolars /ʃ/ and /tʃ/ are also merged: "ship" and "chip" are both [tʃip] (as are "sheep" and "cheap"). The glide /j/ merges with /d/, so that "you" is [ʤu] and "yes" is [ʤɛs]. The distribution of /d/ and /ð/ follow Spanish rules rather than English (see Chapter 10): "addition" is [aðiʃn̩], while "this" is pronounced [dis].

19.4   In Focus

As with regional dialects, ethnic varieties of English are associated with stereotypes, many of them negative. AAVE in particular has been stigmatized as a deficient form of English, and sociolinguists have worked hard to bring its equal linguistic status and rule-governed nature to the attention of the public.

19.2.4 gender, age, sexuality

From the sound of a person's voice, a listener can usually tell if a speaker is a man or a woman. As was discussed in more detail in Chapter 5, some of the variation between women's and men's voices, including pitch, breathiness, and different resonance patterns, is given biologically. Much remains under the speaker's control, however, and men and women may choose to accentuate or downplay gender-marked characteristics, depending on the situation in which they find themselves.

Age-related differences are also to some extent biological. The small bodies of young children are evident in their high-pitched voices and correlated high resonance patterns. In older adult voices, stiffening of the vocal folds and laryngeal cartilages, along with the rest of the body, results in lower pitch and a creakier voice quality, with more cycle-to-cycle variation.

Many other linguistic variables distinguish the speech of men and women. Word choice can be gender-marked, as is often noted with words referring to colors. (Word choice is also age-marked. Parents who attempt to use their children's slang terms generally sound ridiculous.) The typical intonation patterns of women and men differ, such that women tend to use more rising intonational patterns. These intonational patterns have been variously associated with negative traits such as uncertainty or indecisiveness, or with positive traits such as desire to seek consensus, though a number of linguists have argued that attaching any such psychological meaning to this conventionalized pattern is incorrect. Many sociolinguistic studies (including the Labov r-dropping study discussed above) have found that women tend to use pronunciations associated with the prestige dialect more often than men do (and again, this trend can be seen to be either a positive, negative, or neutral characteristic). Women, especially young women, have also often been found to be at the leading edge of sound changes: when a merger or split is taking place in a regional or ethnic dialect, young women will be the most likely to use the innovative pattern.

Speech can be a marker of sexuality as well as gender. Acoustic studies of the speech of gay men have found correlations with voice quality and pitch patterns, as well as distinctive segmental articulations, including an expanded vowel space, more fronting of back vowels, and distinct fricative productions. In perceptual studies, listeners can identify speakers as gay or straight at greater than chance levels. Introductions to the large and growing literature on the interactions of language with gender and sexuality include Eckert and McConnell-Ginet (2003) *Language and Gender*.

19.2.5 variation and identity

Previous sections have discussed how various linguistic variables are associated with social categories: Australian vs. American, Northerner vs. Southerner, upper vs. lower class, Black vs. White, gay vs. straight, female vs. male. In every society, there are characteristics and roles associated with the categories of place, class, ethnicity, gender, age, and sexuality: people in a given social category are expected to behave in a certain way. Individuals, however, may to varying degrees embrace or reject the behavior expected of them, sometimes consciously, consistently, and across-the-board, but more often in a more nuanced way. Recent studies have shown that speakers actively (if not always consciously) adjust their speech in order to accentuate or downplay different characteristics depending on the identity or persona they wish to express. Linguistic identity is not given; it is something that speakers construct.

When people relocate, for example, some effect on regional accent is inevitable, but the strength of the effect varies. Speakers who have a strong desire to fit in to a new place may lose their original accents more quickly, while those who continue to identify with their place of origin may retain their regional accents indefinitely. It is not that they are unable to learn to fit in; they are at some level choosing to remain distinctive. A 1990 study by Natalie Schilling-Estes and Walt Wolfram examined the local dialect of Smith Island, Maryland: a small island in the Chesapeake Bay that is losing both population and area. Traditional jobs working on the water are becoming less and less economically viable, and the land itself is literally sinking into the Bay. As there is growing realization that the community will not be able to sustain itself and that young people will have no choice but to leave, younger speakers are using *more* local dialect features than their parents, not fewer: an expression of solidarity with their dying community.

The expression of linguistic identity is not even fixed for a given individual, but may vary according to situation, in ways much more complicated than can be indexed by formality alone. Another recent study (by Robert Podesva) analyzed the speech of one individual, a gay man living in California, as he moved across different social situations: work, dinner at home, and a night out with a group of friends. Podesva found that numerous aspects of the subject's speech varied by situation, including voice quality and intonation patterns. Even the subject's vowel quality changed: the speaker's [u] as in "boot" and [o] as in "boat" varied significantly. These vowels were most fronted in the party situation; least fronted at work. Podesva suggests that back-vowel fronting, because of its association with California, has taken on the social meaning of a youthful, fun, and carefree lifestyle. Expressing this particular persona is appropriate at a party, inappropriate in a conversation with one's boss. The speaker adjusts his vowel quality accordingly. Even at this level of detail, the speaker is using speech variation to situate himself in a web of social categories: American, Californian, middle-class, professional, gay man, employee, friend.

19.3 formalizing variation

Where does this picture of variation leave us with respect to phonological theory as explicated in Chapters 11 through 14? In the past, there has been an unfortunate tendency for formal phonologists and sociolinguists to ignore one another. Traditional sociolinguistic analyses have not attempted to connect with formal theories, and traditional phonological analyses do not take any kind of variation into account. More recently, however, formal accounts of phonological variation have been offered, with benefits for both traditions.

19.3.1 traditional sociolinguistic analyses

A classic example of phonological variation is the rule of final t/d deletion in American English: if the second consonant in a word-final cluster is [t] or [d], it is deleted. Several examples are given in (1).

(1) Examples of t/d deletion:

left	[lɛf]
hand	[hæn]
planned	[plæn]
walked	[wɑk]
mist	[mɪs]
missed	[mɪs]

Numerous sociolinguistic studies have shown that this rule is variable, and that variation depends on a range of factors: phonological, morphological, and sociological. Some factors are listed in (2).

(2) Factors affecting final t/d deletion:
  a. Phonological
   i.   Preceding context: Deletion is most likely if the preceding sound is a sibilant ([s]), and least likely if the preceding sound is a liquid ([l]).
   ii. Following context: Deletion is most likely if the next word begins with a consonant and least likely if the target word is phrase-final.
   iii. Voicing: deletion is more likely with [d] than with [t].
  b. Morphological
   i.   Deletion is most likely in monomorphemes ("mist"), and least likely if the word has a regular past tense suffix ("missed").
   ii. Irregular past tense words ("left") have an intermediate status.
  c. Social
   i.   Gender: Men delete more often than women.
   ii. Race: Black Americans delete more often than White Americans.
   iii. Regional dialect: Deletion rates differ in different parts of the country.

Sociolinguistics have for several decades employed statistical programs using *logistic regression* to capture the systematic influence of different variables. Logistic regression measures the extent to which one variable predicts another, factoring out the influence of different interacting variables. A logistic regression program that was specifically written for analyses of sociolinguistic variation is *Varbrul* (Cedergren and Sankoff, 1974). The program has been improved and updated in the years since, and other regression programs tailored to linguistic analysis have been proposed (see the suggested readings at the end of the chapter).

In a logistic regression, the linguist collects a corpus of data, and inputs to the program information about every instance in the corpus where the rule could have applied, coding both dependent and independent variables. In any statistical analysis, the *dependent variable* is the thing that needs to be explained (here, whether or not deletion applies). The *independent variables* are the factors that the linguist hypothesizes affect the probability of application: phonological environment, morphological endings, gender, race, regional dialect, etc. The program then computes which independent variables have a significant effect and provides a quantitative measure of how strong the effect is. A factor weight of greater than .5 (50/50 chance) means that that factor makes the effect more likely, and a factor weight of less than .5 makes the effect less likely. For example, in a recent (unpublished) study of t/d deletion in Washington D.C., R. Podesva found that being African American contributed a factor weight of .716, and being Asian American contributed a factor weight of .372. Gender had a weaker effect than race: male gender slightly raised the chance of deletion (.559), female gender slightly lowered the chance (.441).

Such analyses provide a detailed, quantitative picture of variation within a community but do not address the concerns of more traditional phonologists, who have focused on the grammars of individual speakers. How can such quantitative information be incorporated into a grammatical formalism?

19.3.2 traditional phonological analyses

A traditional phonologist can account for the *fact* of variation in several different ways. To begin with, one might just say that different speakers have different grammars: some dialects have a rule of t/d deletion, and others do not. This is surely true, but does not account for variation *within* a grammar: the same speaker will sometimes delete and sometimes not.

To account for variation within an individual grammar, one might hypothesize that certain rules are just marked "optional" as in example (3).

(3)   Optional rule for t/d deletion:

[coronal, +anterior, -continuant] → Ø / C ____ # (optional)

In OT, variation could arise from tied constraints. If the constraint against complex codas and the constraint against deletion are tied, as in tableau (4), variation results.

(4)   Tied constraint ranking results in variation:

lɛft	*COMPLEXCODA	MAX
→ lɛf		*
→ lɛft	*	

See Chapters 13 and 14 for explication of the formalism. (If I've lost you already, you probably should read those chapters before proceeding with this section.)

Another idea is to assume that each speaker has multiple grammars, among which they choose depending on social situation. The "informal" grammar, for example, might require deletion, and the "formal" grammar would not. It becomes difficult, however, to answer questions such as, "How many grammars does a person have?" and "How different can those grammars be?" In many cases, a complete grammar switch seems like overkill. The New York store employees were just somewhat more likely to pronounce [ɹ] on the second repetition; they didn't start suddenly speaking Spanish.

None of these analyses, however, captures any of the complexity of the factors listed in (2), let alone the quantitative precision of a regression analysis. For that kind of precision, what is required is a *stochastic grammar*: a grammar that incorporates statistical distributions directly. This is a big step, but not an unprecedented or isolated one: recall the discussion of gradient grammaticality judgments in Chapter 11. Analyses that allow for quantitative as well as categorical differences turn out to be required in many areas of phonology.

19.3.3 stochastic grammars

Varying approaches to incorporating statistical distributions into phonological grammars have been taken; here we will briefly describe the approach of Paul Boersma and Bruce Hayes (2001), in their version of *Stochastic OT*.

The "classic" version of OT assumes ranking of constraints is fixed and linear: A >> B >> C >> D (where >> means "outranks"). In stochastic OT, constraint ranking is variable and probabilistic. Constraint ranking can change from instance to instance (resulting in variation), and the changes follow certain statistical patterns (accounting for fine-grained quantitative differences). The diagram in example (5) shows a hypothetical stochastic ranking for t/d deletion in English.

(5)   Stochastic constraint ranking

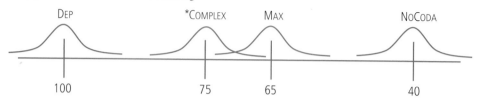

Each constraint is associated with a range of numerical ranking values, distributed about a certain mean. The means are shown on the scale in (5), the ranges are shown by the bell-shaped curves. For any given instance, some value within the range is chosen, with the likelihood of any particular value proportional to the height of the curve at that value. With bell-shaped curves, values are most likely to be close to the mean, but occasionally may be further out.

Constraint ranking is still determined by strict domination: If *COMPLEX is assigned a higher ranking value than MAX, deletion will occur; if MAX is assigned a higher ranking value than *COMPLEX, deletion will not occur. Given the distributions shown in (5), this grammar will result in deletion most of the time. But crucially, the ranges of the constraints overlap: some (small) percentage of the time, MAX will happen to be assigned a value at the top of its range and *COMPLEX will happen to be assigned a value at the bottom of its range, and the rankings will reverse.

The rankings and distributions can be adjusted to match the actual data, and thus can model exact degrees of variation. Depending on how much overlap there is in the constraint ranges, ranking may switch more or less often. If the rankings do not overlap at all, there will be no variation. Social variables might enter the mix by influencing either initial ranking values or distributions. Different individuals might have ranking variables slightly closer together or slightly further apart, depending on social characteristics. Different social situations might then skew the distributions in predictable ways: a more formal situation might add a positive value to all the faithfulness constraints, for example. Much more research remains to be done to flesh out the possibilities of the model.

In these programs, the analyst does not set the constraint rankings by fiat. Rather, the programs "learn" what the rankings need to be, based on the distributions of forms in the data. Thus, they offer the opportunity to model not only phonological variation, but phonological learning.

It is to the issue of learning phonological grammars that Chapter 20 now turns.

chapter summary

- Speech variation comes from many sources. Sociolinguists are interested in patterns of variation that reveal the interaction between linguistic and social systems.
- A regional dialect is a language variety spoken by a group of people who live in a particular place. Specific characteristics of some of the varieties of English spoken around the world are described in Section 19.1.
- Other important influences on variation include situation, socioeconomic class, ethnicity, gender, age, and sexuality (Section 19.2).
- Though certain speech styles are associated with social categories, speakers may (consciously or unconsciously) accentuate or downplay particular characteristics, depending on the situation in which they find themselves and the identity they wish to project.
- Stochastic analysis incorporates statistical information into the grammar.

further reading

on regional dialects

Melchers, G. and P. Shaw. 2003. *World Englishes*. Oxford: Oxford University Press.

Wells, J.C. 1982. *Accents of English*. Cambridge: Cambridge University Press.

Wolfram, W. and N. Schilling-Estes. 2006. *American English: Dialects and Variation*. Second Edition. Oxford: Blackwell.

on other sources of variation

Eckert, P. 2000. *Linguistic Variation as Social Practice*. Oxford: Blackwell.

Eckert, P. and S. McConnell-Ginet. 2003. *Language and Gender*. Cambridge: Cambridge University Press.

Green, L. 2002. *African American English: A Linguistic Introduction*, Cambridge: Cambridge University Press.

Labov, W. 1966/2006. *The Social Stratification of English in New York City*. CAL/Cambridge: Cambridge University Press.

Tagliamonte, S. 2006. *Analyzing Sociolinguistic Variation*. Cambridge: Cambridge University Press.

review exercises

1. Define the following terms:

   regional dialect
   World English
   hypercorrection
   formality
   register
   r-dropping
   logistic regression
   Varbrul
   stochastic grammar

2. Why did J.C. Wells develop the "lexical sets" in Table 19.1?

3. Name the six major American dialects. Which three are expanding?

4. Spell out the following abbreviations:

   GA
   RP
   AAVE

5. Which factors led to the continued use of English in the former British colonies?

6. Explain the difference between:
   a. diglossia and code-switching
   b. pidgin and creole
   c. dependent variable and independent variable

7. Describe Labov's department store study. What did he do and what did he find?

8. List three non-biological differences between the speech of women and men.

(Continued)

further analysis and discussion

9. Write an SPE-style rule for the "pin/pen" merger. What problems do you encounter if you try to write the rule in autosegmental formalism? What about OT? Can you propose a (grounded) markedness constraint that might be driving the alternation?

10. Transcribe the following sentences in each of the dialects listed. If you're unsure of how a segment would be realized in that dialect, choose the appropriate GA or RP realization.

    My new red car was pretty fast, and the engine was loud, too. When you saw a stop sign, you really had to hit the brakes hard.

    GA
    RP
    New York
    Chicago
    Atlanta
    Los Angeles
    London
    Perth
    AAVE
    any other dialect described in the chapter

11. Read your transcriptions, in random order, to a partner in your class. Can your partner guess which dialect is which?

further research

12. Transcribe a non-native speaker of English reading the sentences in 9. What influences of the speaker's L1 do you notice?

Go online Visit the book's companion website for additional resources relating to this chapter aat: http://www.wiley.com/go/zsiga.

references

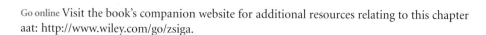

Boersma, P. and B. Hayes. 2001. Empirical tests of the Gradual Learning Algorithm. *Linguistic Inquiry* 32: 45–86.

Cedergren, H. and D. Sankoff. 1974. Variable rules: performance as a statistical reflection of competence. *Language* 50(2): 333–355.

Guy, G. 1991. Contextual conditioning in variable lexical phonology. *Language Variation and Change* 3: 223–239.

Labov, W., S. Ash and C. Boberg. 2006. Atlas of *North American English*. Berlin: Walter de Gruyter.

Ladefoged, P. 2002. *Phonetic Data Analysis*. (Reminiscence of *My Fair Lady*.)

Munson, B. 2007. The acoustic correlates of perceived masculinity, perceived femininity, and perceived sexual orientation. *Language and Speech* 50: 125–142.

Podesva, R. 2011. The California vowel shift and gay identity. *American Speech* 86: 1.

Schilling-Estes, N. and W. Wolfram. 1999. Alternative models of dialect death: dissipation vs. concentration, *Language*, 75(3): 486–521.

Schneider, E.W. *et al.* (eds), 2004. *A Handbook of Varieties of English: Phonology*. Berlin: Mouton de Gruyter.

The speech sample from the speaker of the Boston dialect quoted in Section 19.1.6 is from the International Dialects of English Archive: http://web.ku.edu/~idea/northamerica/usa/massachusetts/massachusetts3.mp.3

20 Acquisition and Learning

To think is to forget a difference, to generalize, to abstract.

Jorge Luis Borges, *Funes the Memorious*, 1942

The Sounds of Language: An Introduction to Phonetics and Phonology, First Edition. Elizabeth C. Zsiga.
© 2013 Elizabeth C. Zsiga. Published 2013 by Blackwell Publishing Ltd.

The task of learning the sound system of a language is, essentially, to figure out everything that we've been talking about in this book. As has been noted in previous chapters, many scholars over the past 50 years have framed the central question of linguistics as "What does it mean to *know* a language? " Other scholars have focused on the question "How do people *use* language to communicate?" In this chapter, we ask, "How is that knowledge and ability attained? What does the process of becoming a proficient language user look like? And what can it teach us about the systematic aspects of language in general?"

After a brief overview (Section 20.1), we begin with language acquisition in babies (Sections 20.2, 20.3), and then turn to adult language learning (Section 20.4). For both children and adults, we examine the tools used to study the phenomena, typical data for both speech perception and speech production, and the theories that are proposed to account for the data. Finally (Section 20.5), we end with a consideration of what the study of phonological acquisition and learning can teach us about linguistic theory.

20.1 language acquisition and language learning

The goal of the linguist is to propose an explicit analysis; the goal of the learner is to gain the knowledge needed to become a proficient language user.

When we speak of the process of gaining language proficiency as it applies to babies and children, we refer to *language acquisition*, and we call a native language acquired in childhood the *L1*. To say that language is "acquired" emphasizes the seeming effortlessness of the task. All babies, unless they have severe physical or cognitive disabilities, become competent (if not perfect) users of their native language by age 4.

The process is not nearly so effortless for an adult learning a non-native language. (Linguists may call any non-native language an *L2*, even if it is the third or fourth in the speaker's repertoire.) Most adults find the process of learning an L2 to be difficult, even with explicit instruction, and the results vary considerably. Differences in aptitude, motivation, type of instruction, and amount of social interaction play important roles in language learning for adults. Some adults have an aptitude for learning languages and are quite successful: some L2 speakers become so proficient that their speech is indistinguishable from that of a native. For most adult learners, however, a foreign accent of varying severity persists, even when the learner has been surrounded by native language users for many years. This is the case even for speakers who are otherwise highly intelligent: think of the thickly-accented English of Albert Einstein or Henry Kissinger, both native speakers of German.

If we wish to emphasize the differences, we may speak of L2 *language learning* (which is effortful, variable, and often noticeably unsuccessful even in the presence of genius) as opposed to L1 language acquisition (which is apparently effortless and is consistently successful except in the presence of severe disability). While there are differences, however, there are also similarities between language acquisition as it is experienced by children and language learning as it is experienced by adults.

20.2 child language acquisition: the data

20.2.1 tools

To study the process of language acquisition, we have to begin with infants. The trouble with studying babies, however, is that they can't talk. They don't sit still, they don't follow instructions, and they don't answer questions. In general, all an investigator can do is observe a baby's behavior in controlled conditions, and make inferences from that. Older children are more communicative, but not necessarily more cooperative.

If the focus is child speech production, the investigator simply needs to record what the child says. Numerous linguist parents have kept detailed diaries or made lengthy recordings of their children's language productions. While young children generally can't or won't sit still and read a word list, they can be engaged in structured play and question–answer games that elicit the kinds of words and sentences the linguist is looking for. An example is the *wug-test* that was described in Chapter 10.

In order to study infant speech perception, the investigator needs to be more ingenious. You cannot just ask babies, "Did that sound the same or different to you?" Two experimental approaches to studying infant speech perception are the *high-amplitude sucking (HAS)* paradigm, and the *head-turn preference (HT)* paradigm. These paradigms can be implemented in different ways, but essentially, both measure a baby's response to a stimulus perceived as different. A newborn infant will increase her rate of sucking on a pacifier when she hears a new sound, and a six-month-old will turn her head toward a sound she perceives as different and therefore interesting. By playing different sequences of sounds and carefully noting how the babies respond, an investigator can discover what differences babies can perceive, and what they can't. A problem with both the HAS and HT paradigms is that a large percentage of babies fuss, cry, look around randomly, or fall asleep in the middle of the experiment. An investigator has to plan on testing many more children than she'll need, knowing that a lot of the data will be unusable because the child could not finish the study. (Parents, who are usually excited to have their little scientist participate, are never told that their baby failed. The babies get sent home with a cute t-shirt no matter what.)

A third methodology gets around the attention and behavior problem by using direct measures of electrophysiological brain activity. In the brain of either an adult or child, neurons in specific areas of the brain activate in response to a stimulus, producing a specific pattern of electrical activity known as *event-related potentials (ERP)*. ERP responses are measured from a set of electrodes set in a cap placed on the baby's head. Different stimuli are played, and responses to the stimuli are compared: if the baby's brain detects the change, there is a corresponding change in the ERP output. The brain is an electrically noisy place, so many trials must be recorded in order for a statistically significant pattern to emerge. Happily, however, the ERP response works whether the listener is paying attention or not. The experiment can proceed while the baby is distracted with a quiet toy or silent video, with the sound stimuli playing in the background.

Any of these types of studies can be either *longitudinal* or *cross-sectional*. A longitudinal study tracks an individual over time: the same child or group of children is studied repeatedly, at different ages. A cross-sectional study examines distinct populations of children of different ages. A group of nine-month-olds might be tested one week, and a different group of six-month-olds the next week.

The next two sections of this chapter examine what studies of child language have told us about the process of language acquisition, first regarding perception, then production.

20.2.2 perception in the first year

Babies can hear even in the womb. The structures of the ear have developed by six months' gestation, and sound travels through the amniotic fluid. The prosodic characteristics of speech – pitch, stress, and timing – are especially clear. Because of this pre-natal exposure, babies recognize their own mother's voice at birth, and can distinguish their native language from other languages. One study has found that newborns can even recognize specific stories that their mother has read aloud during pregnancy. In each of these cases, babies are recognizing and responding to familiar prosodic patterns.

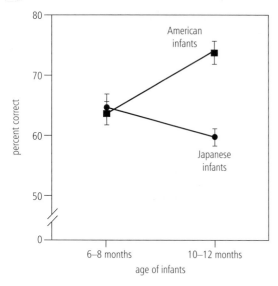

Figure 20.1   Discrimination of [ɹ] and [l] by American and Japanese infants.

Source: Kuhl, P.K., Stevens, E., Hayashi, A., Deguchi, T., Kiritani, S. and Iverson, P. 2006. Infants show a facilitation effect for native language phonetic perception between 6 and 12 months. *Developmental Science* 9 (2) March 2006, F13–F21. Reprinted with permission of John Wiley & Sons Ltd.

Numerous perception studies have established that babies are born with the ability to distinguish any and all speech sounds. American newborns and Thai newborns are equally good at distinguishing [ba] vs. [pa]; American newborns and Japanese newborns are equally good at distinguishing [ɹa] vs. [la]. This is an important first stage of language acquisition: a baby is born ready to acquire any language that will be spoken around him. There is no genetic predisposition to any particular language: babies adopted interculturally, for example, have no problems acquiring the language of their adoptive families.

Between the ages of six and twelve months, however, a change occurs. Babies begin to specialize in the particular sounds that are contrastive in their ambient language, and become less sensitive to other contrasts. This is an aspect of the phenomenon of *categorical perception*, which was discussed in Chapter 9. Results of one study showing this effect are shown in Figure 20.1, which graphs the ability of Japanese and American infants to distinguish syllables containing [ɹ] and [l].

At six months of age, the two groups of infants respond identically: 65% of the time, a six-month-old baby, either American or Japanese, will notice when a stimulus changes from [ɹa] to [la], and respond by turning her head. (65% is not extremely high, but as noted above, babies are not particularly well-behaved experimental subjects.) At ten months of age, however, the groups diverge. The American infants have become better at hearing the distinction, but the Japanese infants have become worse. Similar studies on non-English contrasts show similar results: at 6 months of age, Taiwanese (Mandarin-learning) and American (English-learning) infants are equally able to distinguish the syllables [tɕi] and [ɕi], which are contrastive in Mandarin, but do not occur in English. At 12 months of age, the Taiwanese babies have become better at hearing the distinction, and the American babies have become worse. Studies such as these show that babies at around one year old are learning to pay attention to sound differences that are important in their native language, and learning to ignore sound differences that are not.

20.1   In Focus

Figuring out what to pay attention to and what to ignore is a crucial aspect of speech perception. As Jorge Luis Borges put it in the quote that heads this chapter, "to think is to forget a difference." Borges' imagined character, Funes, perfectly remembers every single detail of every single experience, and gives all the details equal importance. As a result, Borges concludes, Funes is incapable of generalization, the basis of rational thought. He cannot even recognize the same dog seen on two different days. If Borges were a speech scientist, he would have further concluded that Funes would be unable to understand language, because he could not "forget" the details that distinguish messages that count as the same.

While learning to pay attention to differences that will pay off in distinguishing the L1's segmental categories, babies between six and twelve months old are also learning to recognize words. Discovering word boundaries is a crucial and difficult task. In order to learn a word, a baby must associate a chunk of sound to a particular meaning. In order to do that, the baby has to be able to pick out from the continuous stream of speech the particular chunk that bears that particular semantic content. For example, to learn "daddy," a baby has to figure out that in the phrase [sidædiwev], she needs to group together the syllable string [dædi] and assign a meaning to that, not the syllable strings [sidæ] or [diwev]. In speech, there are no pauses between words the way there are white spaces between words on a page. For proficient adult language users, our brains essentially insert word boundaries between chunks that we recognize as corresponding to different meanings; thus we cannot hear word boundaries in a language we do not understand. Babies are essentially constantly in that position: listening to a language they don't (yet) understand. How can babies learn the meanings if they can't separate the pieces they have to attach meaning to? How do they "bootstrap" their way into the system?

Babies sometimes get one-word utterances to learn from, but not often: one study estimated that only 10 percent of speech directed to infants consists of one-word utterances, and most of the speech that babies hear isn't directed to them but to the adults around them, and will be correspondingly more complex. Further, the words in these one-word utterances are not typical of the rest of the vocabulary, so they may not be much help. (I'm guessing here, but I would think that a pretty large percentage of the one-word utterances a baby hears consists of the lexical item "no-no.")

Babies, however, are *statistical learners*, as has been shown in numerous studies on infant word learning, many carried out by the psycholinguist Peter Jusczyk and colleagues. Babies notice that the syllable [dæ] is often followed by the syllable [di], and they remember that those two syllables go together (that is, the *transitional probability* of [dæ] + [di] is high). The syllable [si], on the other hand, can be followed by all sorts of syllables, according to the many different people and things to which the baby's attention is directed. Thus in the phrase [sidædiwev], infants pick out [dædi], not [sidæ] as a recurring sequence worth paying attention to, and likely to have a meaning attached.

Babies can also make use of transitional probabilities at the segment level. Common segmental sequences like [tr] and [pl] are likely to belong to a single word ("train," "play"), while infrequent sequences like [tʃm] and [lg] are likely to belong to different words ("watch me," "call Grandma"). So babies can guess that low-probability sequences indicate a word boundary. The correlations are not perfect, but they don't have to be. Relative frequency information at least gives babies a place to start in figuring out the system.

From this beginning, babies begin to notice and make use of other characteristics of the high-probability sequences, which they guess correspond to words. Predictable stress is often an important cue. In English, for example, bi-syllabic nouns are usually stressed on the initial syllable (['dæ.di], ['ma.mi], ['dɑ.gi] ['dɑ.li]), while in French, stress is usually final ([pa.'pa], [ma.'mã], [ʃi.'ɛ̃], [pu.'pe]). English-learning infants guess that word breaks come before the stressed syllable (helping them home in on ['dæ.di] rather than [di.'wev]). French-learning infants guess that word breaks come after the stressed syllable.

Finally, some infants also get help from the kind of speech their caregivers use to talk to them. *Motherese* is characterized by high pitch with exaggerated contours, slow tempo, repetition, and hyper-articulation of segmental contrasts. "Look at the doggy! See the doggy? What a *nice* doggy!" Babies prefer listening to speech that has the characteristics of motherese, and it is likely that slowing down, repeating, and exaggerating contrast helps babies notice important information. Motherese is not necessary to language acquisition, however. There are cultures where caregivers do not talk to their babies much at all while caring for them, let alone in motherese. Why carry on such a one-sided conversation? It's obvious the baby isn't going to answer. Children in these cultures learn language just as well, however, picking it up from the adult conversations they hear around them.

> 20.2   Motherese may not be necessary to language acquisition, but human interaction is. You can't acquire language from watching TV. To test this hypothesis, Patricia Kuhl and colleagues studied three groups of English-learning nine-month-olds. One group interacted with a Mandarin-speaking adult for twelve 25-minute sessions over several weeks. The second group watched the same adult on TV doing and saying the same things for the same amount of time, the third group just heard the audio. At the end of these sessions the infants were tested on the Mandarin [tɕ]/[ɕ] contrast. Those English babies who had interacted with a real Mandarin-speaking person performed just as well in the test as Taiwanese babies who had heard nothing but Mandarin their whole lives. Those few hours of live exposure were sufficient for them to remain sensitive to the Mandarin contrast. The babies who got only TV or audio input, however, were no better at distinguishing [tɕi] and [ɕi] than babies who had never heard Mandarin at all. (The study is published in Tsao et al. 2006; see references on p.464.)

20.2.3 child language production

Not all children begin talking at exactly the same age. The average age for first words is around one year old, but an individual child may be several months earlier or later. Whether a child is an early talker or late talker is not correlated with intelligence, but may have to do with personality: some kids are risk takers, others wait and see, some are social, others are reserved. Across individuals and languages, however, all babies follow basically the same progression, though the exact schedule for reaching each milestone will differ.

Babies are born with the ability to vocalize, and their first vocalization is crying, which healthy infants generally do with great energy and volume. By three months, they are starting to "coo," making vowel-like sounds. The sounds will not be adult-like, however, largely due to anatomical differences. Recall from Chapter 1 that infants have very limited movement in the pharynx, because of the high position of the larynx. Because their vocal tracts are shaped differently, the resonance patterns an infant is able to produce are not much like those of an adult. The larynx descends slowly over the first few months of life, as the baby learns to control her neck muscles, to sit up, and to swallow solid food. While the larynx won't descend to its approximate adult position until the child is five or six years old, it is low enough to be out of the way of the tongue by six months of age.

Even very young infants are imitators: smiling when they're smiled at, for instance. Between three and six months of age, infants begin to try to imitate speech sounds. At this stage, there is no meaning associated to any particular sound. Babies are practicing with their articulators, learning how to get tongue and lips under control, and figuring out the acoustic consequences of different articulatory gestures. At this age, babies may also engage in vocal play, producing sounds that don't occur in their native language, like clicks and bilabial trills for English-learning infants, apparently just for the fun of it.

Around six months of age, babies begin *reduplicative babbling*. They'll focus on producing one syllable, usually of CV structure, and practice repeating it: [ma.ma.ma.ma.ma.ma]. This is followed by *variegated babbling*, in which the child puts different syllables together. From six to twelve months, the baby's productions sound more and more like the language they hear spoken around them: French babies babble with French vowels and consonants, Mandarin babies with Mandarin vowels and consonants, etc. At the same time the perceptual system is tuning in to language-specific contrasts, the production system is homing in on making them.

20.3   Deaf babies being raised by deaf parents don't babble (much) with their mouths: they do not have the sensation of hearing what their mouths can do. Instead, they "babble" with their hands, trying out random combinations of the manual signs they see their parents using, in the same way that hearing infants try out random combinations of syllables.

From about 12 months of age, when babies are becoming secure in perceiving word-sized chunks of speech and assigning meaning to them (as described above), they begin to try out words of their own: not random sound practice, but real words with communicative intent. By 18 months of age, kids are usually producing meaningful two-word combinations (in the correct order for their language): "mommy eat," "hit ball," "me up," etc. Between ages two and three utterances get longer and more complex, and vocabulary takes off: toddlers have to be learning at the rate of dozens of words a day. By three or four years old, kids are sophisticated language users, knowing thousands of vocabulary items, correctly applying phonological rules, and producing complex sentences like my friend Johnny (in Chapter 10).

While children may produce recognizable words from age one, it takes several years for their pronunciations to become adult-like. A baby's first words may not have any consistent phonological structure, demonstrating that the child is producing a "vocal whole" that isn't yet analyzed into its parts. As vocabulary increases, however, with an increasing ability to combine different segments in different ways to make different items, some typical phonological patterns emerge.

Simplifications are very common in child speech. Unmarked CV structure is preferred, and children may either delete or insert segments to make syllables conform to this pattern. Consonant clusters are usually simplified through deletion: "play" will typically be pronounced [pe], for example, or "gramma" as [gæmə]. Final vowels may be inserted to turn a coda into an onset, as in "doggy." Consonants may also be inserted to break up a sequence of vowels, so that "hyena" becomes [haɪninə]. Devoicing is another kind of simplification: "big" is pronounced as [bɪk].

Unstressed syllables are often deleted, especially in word-initial position: giraffe becomes [ræf], "banana" is [nænə], "elephant" is [ɛfʌn]. It is not clear if loss of initial syllables is an effect of immature perception or immature production. Reduced syllables may be more difficult to pronounce, but it may also be the case that, due to the preference for figuring out word boundaries based on stress, kids do not realize that these syllables are part of the word at all. Teasing out *why* something is missing from child speech is actually a difficult problem. For example, kids will often leave off third person verb endings, producing phrases such as "Dolly talk" for "Dolly talks." But is the ending missing because the child has not acquired verb agreement, or because she cannot pronounce clusters? It may not be possible for the linguist to know for sure.

Children often substitute sounds for one another. One common pattern is *velar fronting*: [k] is pronounced as [t], and [g] as [d], so that "key" becomes [ti] and "go" becomes [do]. Glides are often substituted for approximants: "rabbit" is [wæbɪt], "Lisa" is [jisə]. Fricatives are often pronounced as stops, especially in onset position: "see" is [ti] and "sister" is [titə].

Another typical pattern, particularly in the earlier stages of child speech, is repetition, of either a consonant or a syllable. As in reduplicative babbling, it's easier to repeat a successful action a second time than it is to switch to a new one. It's no accident that words like "mommy," "daddy," and "baby" are reduplicative in language after language. Other examples of repetition in child English include "bottle" as [bɑ.bɑ], "tub" as [bʌb], "duck" as [gʌk], and "doggy" as [gɑ.gi]. Note that in the latter two examples, reduplication overrides velar fronting: velars are apparently easier if you can do two of them in a row.

> 20.4 Kids who exhibit patterns of segment substitution can perceive the difference between segments, but have trouble producing them. They'll get frustrated when adults repeat back to them their own productions, which they know are incorrect:
>
> *Child*: [tar pis] (= "May I have the car, please.")
> *Adult*: "You want a tar piece?"
> *Child*: [no, tar, pis!]
> *Adult*: "A tar?"
> *Child*: [no! tar! tar!]
>
> I was once quite confused when my two-year-old son kept pointing to his baby sister and vehemently insisting "Baby tan! Baby tan!" It took a while to figure out he wasn't commenting on her complexion, but was complaining, subject to cluster simplification and velar fronting, that she had grabbed his crayon.

Most children will outgrow these patterns by age three or four, and are speaking perfectly understandably by the time they start pre-school. Really marked sounds, like [ɹ] and [ð], may take a little longer. Only rarely is intervention required. Another aspect of child speech that takes a few more years to grow out of is the overgeneralization of regular patterns, as in the rule for forming plural and past tense: once a child learns a phonological alternation (usually between the ages of 3 and 4), she will apply it consistently, and will take some time to mark particular vocabulary items as exceptions.

20.3 theories of L1 acquisition

20.3.1 innateness vs. environmental effects

A major issue in L1 acquisition research is sorting out which aspects of the process are genetically determined and which are learned from the environment. What are kids born knowing? How much of language acquisition is attributable to general learning abilities, and how much to neural specialization unique to language?

Some theories emphasize the role of a genetic endowment specific to human language: *Universal Grammar (UG)*. (See Chapter 12.) UG is invoked to explain why language acquisition is so effortless. The child has a head start, in that much of the structure of language is known innately and doesn't have to be learned. The child doesn't have to learn what the phonological features are by listening to the language around her, she just needs to learn which ones her language uses contrastively. Similarly, she doesn't need to learn the constraints, she just needs to learn which way her language ranks them.

A specific argument in favor of innateness is the *poverty of the stimulus*. The argument is that some aspects of language *could not* have been learned by generalizing from examples, because the examples the child hears do not contain enough information for the child to make the right generalizations. If the child knows something that cannot be learned, it must be innate. Although most of the examples used to argue for poverty of the stimulus are syntactic, phonologists note that adult speakers have very definite knowledge about what *cannot* occur in their language. Setswana speakers, for example, know that no word can contain [g]. If they happen to want to borrow from another language a word that has a [g] in it, they change it to [k]. But how did they learn that? No-one ever told a Setswana-learning child "Don't pronounce [g]!" the same way his parents told him "Don't run into the street!" He would have to learn the prohibition from *negative evidence*: noticing that he *doesn't* hear [g] in any words. But how many times would the child have to not hear [g] before he concludes he's never going to hear it and that it is in fact prohibited?

A proponent of Universal Grammar would say that the child does not need to *learn* a constraint against [g], he's born with it, as part of a full set of universal markedness and faithfulness constraints. Further, proponents may argue that the initial state of the grammar (the way the grammar is innately structured, before the child starts learning anything) is to have markedness constraints dominate faithfulness constraints (see Chapter 14). This would explain why a child's early utterances generally contain only unmarked structures like CV syllables. If the child is innately provided with a grammar in which a constraint against [g] (*[g]) dominates a constraint against changing a voiced sound to voiceless (IDENT-VOICE), then [g] will never be pronounced, but will map to [k], as in fact happens in Setswana. The Setswana-speaking child has nothing to learn, he just retains his initial innate ranking. It is the English-speaking child who has to learn, based on the positive evidence of hearing people around him say words like [go], that his initial ranking has to be adjusted.

Other linguists, however, remain unconvinced of the innateness of features and con-straints. These linguists argue that the human brain is a powerful learner and generalizer, and that everything that needs to be known about language *can* be learned from what the child experiences. In the realm of phonology, one can argue that distinctive features and markedness constraints are learned during babbling. As the baby experiments with the acoustic consequences of different articulatory positions, she figures out for herself the dimensions that have to be varied to make the sounds of her language, and she learns through experience that [g] is a difficult sound best avoided unless there is positive evidence that her language requires her to use it.

The debate between models of acquisition based on UG and models based on general learning is far from resolved. The debate, after all, revolves around the profound question of the relative contributions of nature and nurture in creating the human personality. Obvi-ously, environment matters hugely: if a child hears Mandarin, he learns Mandarin. Just as obviously, a human brain is required: the family cat may hear just as much Mandarin speech as the baby does (see Figure 9.7), but learns nothing. The crucial questions lie in which aspects of human neuro-biology are most critical to language acquisition, whether these aspects are specific to language or are more general, and the mechanisms by which innate predispositions (whatever they may be) are shaped by language experience.

20.3.2 acquiring language-specific contrasts

The shaping of the brain by language experience has been extensively investigated by researchers interested in the acquisition of language-specific perceptual systems. These researchers seek to account for what is happening in the brain of the nine-month old English learner, for example, such that he is getting better at hearing native contrasts like [ɹ] vs. [l], and worse at hearing non-native contrasts like [tɕ] vs. [ɕ]. In general, the task of segmental learning is to divide up the *perceptual space* in a way that corresponds to language-specific categories. The perceptual space can be thought of as multi-dimensional, with each axis corresponding to an acoustic continuum that might distinguish speech sounds. Vowels, for example, occupy different parts of the space defined by F1 and F2: vowel charts, such as the ones in Chapter 4, can be thought of as maps of this part of the perceptual space. Consonants can be distinguished in part by the dimension of voice onset time (VOT), the amount of time between the release of the stop and the onset of voicing: aspirated stops have long VOT, unaspirated stops short VOT, pre-voiced stops (that is, those with voicing before the burst) have negative VOT. The child needs to learn where to make cuts in the F1 and F2 continua, or the VOT continuum, to get the right categories for her language.

One model of how this occurs is Patricia Kuhl's *Native Language Magnet (NLM)* model. Kuhl argues that as children compile language experience, individual instances (*exemplars*) of different segments form clusters in the perceptual space. Different instances of [i], for example, will not be identical, but they will all cluster in the "low F1 high F2" quadrant of the F1/F2 space, separated from the cluster of exemplars of [ɑ] in the "high F1 low F2" quadrant. Clusters will form in different places, depending on the language experienced: Spanish-learning babies will form five clusters corresponding to [i, e, a, o, u]; English-learning babies have to deal with 16 or so clusters. Instances in the centers of the clusters, the best exemplars, will begin to exert what Kuhl calls a *magnet effect*, pulling more marginal examples into the category, making it easier to distinguish between categories but harder to distinguish within-category sounds.

Another metaphor might be the warping of space-time caused by the mass of a planet, resulting in gravity. A dense cluster of exemplars warps the perceptual space, making "valleys" into which new instances will inevitably be drawn, as a ball rolls downhill. As a new random stimulus enters the warped space, the stimulus will inevitably roll downhill into one valley or the other (or be drawn into the field of one or another magnet).

It may be easiest to give an example using VOT, which is one-dimensional. Consider VOT in English and Spanish (for simplicity, assume syllable-initial position). Spanish [b] is usually prevoiced, and Spanish [p] is unaspirated. English [b], on the other hand, usually has no prevoicing, and English initial [p] is aspirated. Thus tokens of [p] and [b] in the two languages will warp the perceptual space in different ways, as shown in Figure 20.2.

In Figure 20.2, the orange line represents Spanish and the black line represents English. The dotted lines indicate the initial state of the perceptual space for Spanish and English infants. It is the same for both, presumably flat. Thus speech sounds are distinguished equally well or equally poorly by both babies. As the babies experience language, however, exemplars of [b] and [p], indicated in the figure by lower-case letters, form clusters in different places: centered around -30 ms VOT for Spanish [b] and +30 ms VOT for Spanish [p], compared to 0 ms VOT for English [b] and +60 ms for English [p]. (This distribution is consistent with the data that was presented in Figure 9.10 for these languages.) The density distributions of the clusters begin to warp the perceptual space in characteristic ways (solid lines), creating the magnet effect. New incoming stimuli (solid orange circles) now produce different responses in the warped space. For Spanish children, stimuli at -15 ms VOT will be drawn into the [b] cluster and stimuli at +15 ms VOT will be drawn into the [p] cluster (as though

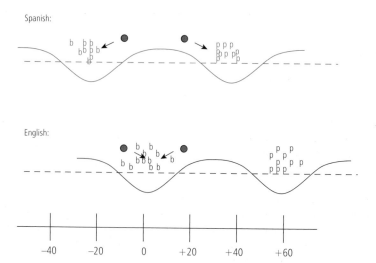

Figure 20.2   The VOT space for Spanish-learning (top) and English-learning (bottom) children.
Notes: Dotted lines = initial state, solid lines = perceptual space warped by experience.

they were rolling downhill in opposite directions), thus the sounds will be easily distinguished. For English children, both the +15 ms and -15 ms stimuli will be drawn into the [b] cluster (as though they were rolling downhill toward each other), and the sounds will not be easily distinguished.

This language-particular perceptual warping, it is argued, takes place between 6 and 12 months of age, thus accounting for the language-particular improvement in native categories, but worsening in non-native categories, that was shown in Figure 20.1. The +15 and -15 ms stimuli will sound *more* different to Spanish babies at 12 months (solid orange line) than at 6 months (dotted orange line), but *less* different to English babies at 12 months (solid black line) than at 6 months (dotted black line). Once the warping takes place, it is permanent.

Crucial to models of learning such as the NLM is the concept of *neural plasticity*, the ability of the brain to change the way it processes information. Because babies have so much to learn so fast, their neural circuitry for both perception and production is easily affected by experience, as in Figure 20.2. Over time, however, as certain patterns are learned and consistently reinforced, the learned patterns become more and more automatic, and the ability to change decreases. Just how fast and how completely is a matter of debate. Adults do not lose all ability to learn, but the more ingrained the habit is, the harder it is to change it.

Some researchers argue for a *critical period* of language acquisition: a window of opportunity in which language is easily acquired. Sometime in late childhood (maybe as early as seven years old, maybe as late as 15) the window closes (maybe because access to UG shuts down, maybe because crucial neural plasticity is lost), and acquisition becomes impossible. Language *learning* can still take place, in that a motivated and talented adult can learn the vocabulary and syntax of a non-native language, but it will be hard work, will use different, more explicit, cognitive capabilities, and will seldom if ever be completely successful. Other researchers argue that learning language as an adult is indeed more difficult, due to a decrease in plasticity, but that the same mechanisms available to children are still available to the adult.

Section 20.4 now turns to the data on adult language learning.

20.4 L2 learning

20.4.1 tools

Techniques for studying the speech of adult L2 speakers are basically the same as those used in studying adult L1 speakers, but one point is worth noting. While putting a microphone in front of a talker always has some effect, the effect on L2 learners is always going to be greater. They will often feel they are being "tested" in the L2, and their speech may be that much more self-conscious. To minimize the effect, L2 researchers may have the learners play a game or engage in a task, such as instructing an interlocutor to move pieces on a game board or on a map, that distracts the speaker from concentrating on pronunciation or syntax per se.

In investigating L2 perception, researchers may use naming, discrimination or similarity judgment tasks. The listener may hear a stimulus and be asked to name the word. In an AX discrimination task, the listener has to tell whether the second stimulus, *X*, is the same as or different from the first, *A*. In an AXB task, the listener has to tell whether *X* is more similar to *A* or to *B*. Similarity and discrimination tasks are useful in that they separate sensitivity to sound differences from knowledge of actual lexical items: the participant does not have to know what any of the words mean in order to say which sounds are most similar. That very separation may be problematic, however, in that it distances the experimental task from real-life language situations, where mapping sounds to meanings is the whole point.

20.4.2 L2 perception

Linguists generally assume that the initial state of L2 learning is the final state of L1 acquisition. Unlike babies, who begin the acquisition process equally ready to learn any language they hear, adults don't start with an even playing field. Their systems of perception and production have been indelibly shaped by years of exposure to and use of the L1. The adult L2 learner, therefore, begins with a warped perceptual space, as in Figure 20.2.

The trouble this causes should be clear. Adults have particular difficulty in perceiving differences that are categorical in the L2 but not in the L1. Adult English learners of Thai, for example have trouble distinguishing Thai pre-voiced [b] from unaspirated [p], tokens of which would correspond roughly to the two orange circles in Figure 20.2. In the English perceptual space, these two sounds have a strong tendency to roll into the same bin, and the task of keeping them separate involves reshaping the perceptual landscape. For the same reason, Japanese learners of English have trouble with [ɹ] vs. [l]; and Spanish learners of English have trouble with [i] vs. [ɪ].

In trying to learn the new distinction, adults may make the mistake of paying attention to the wrong cues, which may not turn out to be reliable. For these learners, the perceptual space may be adjusted, but along dimensions different from that of a native speaker. For example, Mandarin-speaking adults working on the English tense/lax distinction may focus on vowel length rather than quality: [i] is longer than [ɪ]. Native English speakers, however, pay more attention to quality ([i] is higher and fronter than [ɪ]). Because native speakers are focusing on quality, their production of length will vary more, so a non-native speaker who pays attention to length alone will make more mistakes in perception. The mismatch will also lead to problems in production: [ɪ] pronounced as short version of [i] will never sound quite right. Similarly, it has been shown that Japanese speakers learning [l] vs. [ɹ] tend to focus on F2 differences (which work for the sonorants of Japanese but are unreliable for English), rather than the F3 differences that native English speakers pay attention to, exacerbating their difficulties in both perception and production. In a different domain, English speakers trying to learn Thai tones pay attention to the wrong parts of the pitch contours.

Interestingly, distinctions among non-native sounds that are very different from anything in the native inventory are *not* hard to perceive. Catherine Best has shown, for example, that adult English speakers have no problem distinguishing place of articulation among the Zulu clicks. Essentially, such sounds are distant enough in the perceptual space from any English sounds to be able to avoid the influence of any of the native categories. It's the sounds that are close enough to the native sounds to be drawn into their influence that cause the trouble. Best's theory of the interaction of L1 and L2 in perception is called the *Perceptual Assimilation Model (PAM)*, and focuses on predicting when L1 and L2 categories will interact. PAM emphasizes the importance of articulatory gestures as units of both perception and production (see the discussion in Sections 5.4 and 9.3.5), so makes the specific prediction that sound categories that share gestures but differ in the details of specification, such as [i] vs. [ɪ] or [d] vs. [ð], will be most difficult to distinguish.

Adults *can* get better at perceiving non-native contrasts. Lots of exposure to the L2, and intensive training if it's available, will help. As in first language acquisition, slower and more-carefully-articulated speech may help learners distinguish the contrasts they need. Studies have found that when native speakers interact with a non-native speaker, native speakers do slow down and speak more clearly, though they do not use the exaggerated pitch contours typical of Motherese. Over time, continued exposure to L2 stimuli will eventually cause the perceptual categories of a learner to shift toward L2 norms, though the effects of the L1 may never be completely erased.

20.4.3 L2 production

Speakers who have learned an L2 as an adult almost always speak with an accent. In one study, James Flege and colleagues recorded English sentences from 240 adult native speakers of Italian who had immigrated to Canada between the ages of 2 and 23. Native English speakers rated the sentences for degree of accentedness. The results are graphed in Figure 20.3.

The results show a great deal of individual variation, but every speaker who arrived in Canada after the age of 15 was rated as having at least some accent. The older the immigrant was when he or she arrived, the stronger the accent tended to be rated. All the speakers were adults when they were recorded, and they had lived in Canada for an *average of 32 years*. Nonetheless, for many of the speakers, a strong accent persisted. A subsequent study, with 240 Korean speakers of English, found nearly identical results.

Flege argues, however, that these results should not be interpreted as supporting the Critical Period Hypothesis. Rather, the opposite: while age of arrival does have a significant effect, it is gradual, linear, and begins in young childhood. There is no "cutoff age" before which L2 learning is perfect and after which it is impossible. Many of the immigrants who came to Canada as young children were rated as "accent-free," but others were not.

Flege's *Speech Learning Model (SLM)* hypothesizes that a learner's perception and production are influenced by both L1 and L2, in proportion to the amount of exposure over the lifetime. Exposure is counted both in number of years spent in the L2-speaking country and number of hours per day spent in interacting with L2 speakers. The number of years accounts for the age-of-arrival effect in Figure 20.3: more years (that is, earlier age of arrival) correlates with less accent. The number of hours per day accounts for a lot of intersubject variability, and for the retention of an accent even for some speakers who arrived as children. Immigrants who use the L2 at school or work, but return to the L1 at home (Flege argues), never make a consistent change in their production habits or perceptual maps, and thus make little progress. A corollary hypothesis of the SLM is that speakers who get better at the L2 will necessarily get worse at the L1, as the categories shift in the L2 direction.

In what, exactly, does a "foreign accent" consist? To a large extent, an accent consists of the *transfer* of phonetic and phonological patterns from the L1 to the L2. Phonetic patterns include perceptual categories as illustrated above, as well as articulatory habits, routines, and settings, such as differences in the duration of VOT, exact place of articulation, or specific vowel quality. Phonological patterns include allophonic distributions, contextually-determined alternations, and prosody. When the patterns from the L1 and L2 do not match, and a learner uses an L1 pattern to pronounce an L2 sentence, the difference is heard as an accent. From a rule-based point of view (Chapter 13), phonological transfer consists of inappropriately applying the L1 rules in the L2. From a constraint-based point of view (Chapter 14), transfer involves running the L2 lexical items through the L1 constraint hierarchy.

Because the patterns of different L1s are distinct, accents arising from different L1s can be discerned. English learners of French will tend to say [kʰæfeɪ oʊ leɪ] when they want [kafe o lɛ], using English vowel qualities, and transferring their English habits of aspiration and vowel diphthongization to French. Hindi learners of English will use retroflex stops instead of alveolars. Spanish

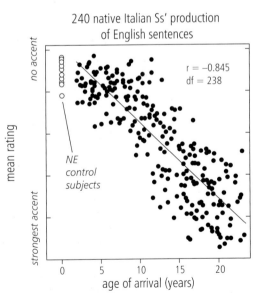

Figure 20.3 Accentedness of the speech of Italian speakers of English.
Source: Flege, J., Munro, M., & MacKay, I. 1995. Factors affecting degree of perceived foreign accent in a second language. *Journal of the Acoustical Society of America*, 97: 3125–3134. Reprinted with permission.

learners of English will tend to say [liv] instead of [lɪv], using the closest Spanish equivalent to the English lax vowel. They will also tend to say [aðiʃn̩] rather than [ədɪʃn̩], using the allophone of /d/ required by Spanish phonotactic constraints. Korean learners of English may say [ɹaɪt] for "light" and [pul] for "poor," transferring the Korean allophonic distribution of [l] and [ɹ] ([ɹ] in onsets, [l] in codas) to English words. They may also say [piŋ mi] for "pick me," using the Korean pattern of nasalization at word boundaries.

Suprasegmental patterns – syllable structure, stress, and tone – also transfer, and may in fact cause more difficulty in communication than using an incorrect segmental allophone, because suprasegmentals distort the expected shape of a whole word or sentence. Differences in syllable structure constraints cause many difficulties for L2 learners. Typically, learners will insert vowels to break up clusters or resyllabify codas that are allowed in the L2 but not the L1: English learners of Polish will call the city [gədænsk], Korean learners of English will request [aisi kiɹim] for dessert, and Spanish learners of English will ask about the local [eskul] for their children. Stress-based errors are also very persistent. Japanese learners of English have trouble learning to reduce the unstressed vowels of English; while English learners of Japanese have trouble learning *not* to reduce every second or third syllable. Speakers of tone languages may produce English intonation contours to match a tonal contrast in their native language, while English learners of tone languages despair of ever controlling pitch on a syllable-by-syllable basis.

The role of transfer was first seriously investigated by Robert Lado, in his 1957 book, *Linguistics Across Cultures*. Lado was one of the first scholars to bring linguistic analysis to bear on language teaching, by arguing that language teachers should engage in *contrastive analysis*, not just drill students in rote repetition. Contrastive analysis is the systematic comparison of the phonology, morphology, and syntax of the L1 and L2: *Linguistics Across Cultures* consisted of a contrastive analysis of English and Spanish. Lado argued that points where the L1 and L2 turned out to be the same would be easy for students, but points where the L1 and L2 differed would be difficult, and should therefore be given extra time and attention in the classroom.

The predictions of contrastive analysis turned out to be useful, but somewhat too simplistic: not everything that is different is hard. German and English differ, for example, in their treatment of coda obstruents: German devoices final obstruents while English does not. Despite this difference, English learners can learn German devoicing pretty easily, while Germans have a much harder time learning to preserve voicing in English codas. A refinement of the predictions of contrastive analysis that takes such asymmetries into account is the *Markedness Differential Hypothesis* (Eckman 1981): aspects of an L2 that are different from the L1 will be difficult only if the L2 structures are more marked.

Markedness plays an important role in both learner speech and child speech: markedness effects in L2 may also be called *developmental effects*. The simplifications that are typical of child speech often occur in learners' speech as well. As was noted above, L2 speech, like child speech, often shows a preference for CV syllables. (Markedness and transfer may both play a role in this L2 preference.) A difference, however, is that in child speech marked syllable structures are more likely to be repaired via deletion, while in L2 speech marked structures are more likely to be repaired by epenthesis. For example, a child may ask for [ai kim], while an L2 speaker is more likely to ask for [aisi kiɹim]. While deletion in L2 speech and epenthesis in child speech are not unknown, L2 speakers show a much greater commitment than children to faithfully producing all the segments of a word, at the expense of syllable count and prosody. It may be that children are more sensitive to prosody, since it plays such an important role in their acquisition process. However, orthography may also have an effect. Adults are usually exposed to written materials in the language they're learning, so they may just be more aware of what the segments are supposed to be because they can see the letters.

Sometimes, markedness effects arise in the speech of learners for whom neither the L1 nor the L2 provides evidence for the pattern. A case in point is coda devoicing. Mandarin, for example, allows no coda obstruents, so Mandarin learners of English have trouble pronouncing English obstruent-final words. However, they have an easier time pronouncing "pick" than "pig," and will sometimes pronounce "pig" *as* [pʰɪk] (Broselow, Chen, and Wang, 2006). The question is, why? Neither the L1 nor the L2 has a process of coda devoicing: Mandarin has no obstruent codas at all and English allows codas to remain voiced. The preference for voiceless codas in L2 must emerge, not as a transfer effect, but as an effect of universal markedness. The fact that Mandarin speakers apparently have a constraint against voiced codas, which they could not have learned from exposure to either Mandarin or English, argues in favor of the innateness (or at least universal learning) of constraints.

20.5 acquisition, learning, and linguistic theory

This last observation brings us to the role that the study of acquisition and learning can play in the more general study of linguistic sound patterns (and with this question, to the end of this book). In the same way that an engineer who wants to really understand a car or a TV must see how it is put together, a linguist who wants to really understand language must watch how it is acquired. Numerous inner workings that are not obvious in the finished product are revealed in the stages of its creation. Also, in the same way that physicists can learn about the structure of atoms by seeing what happens when atoms crash into each other, linguists can learn about phonological structure by examining the way phonological systems interact when a speaker of one language begins to learn another. Child languages and learner languages are linguistic systems, too – special cases whose special circumstances reveal the inner workings of language in new ways. (Although it has not been a focus in this book, language loss due to old age or injury is equally worthy of study: in many ways, language loss is like child language acquisition in reverse.)

We have mentioned above how child language data is crucial in debates on Universal Grammar. Linguists studying the perceptions and productions of children can investigate what can be learned and how; and what, it seems, that children must be born knowing. Both child and learner languages teach us about markedness. Everything seems "easy" to the competent adult language user: the clicks of Zulu, the rhotics of English, the tones of Cantonese. But for children and L2 learners, some patterns are harder than others; and in these difficulties linguists find confirmation of, or challenge to, theories of what counts as marked and unmarked cross-linguistically.

We have asked, "How are speech sounds made? How are they perceived and distinguished? How many different sounds do languages use?" In this chapter, we've seen that babies are born ready to learn any sound in the IPA chart, and they practice any and all of them in vocal play. It may be that babies learn the limits of human phonetic capabilities based on the feedback they get from their own vocal tract muscles and their own ears.

We have asked, "How do languages organize sounds, both to distinguish words and to create larger prosodic structures? What are the constraints on licit sequences? What sorts of alternations arise to repair what is illicit?" Child language and learner language data have informed, and must continue to inform, models of phonology. Models of phonemic categorization, including the Native Language Magnet and Perceptual Assimilation Model, crucially rely on child and learner data to predict processes of category formation and change. Models of phonological alternation, be they rule- or constraint-based, must address the question: "Is it learnable?" If you posit an adult system you must also propose a path by which the learner can attain it. Phonological theories must include in the space of their predicted possible languages not only the 6000-plus phonologies of the adults of the world, but the phonological systems of children, and the "interlanguage" phonologies of learners. To the extent that a theory accounts not only for stable systems, but systems undergoing change, that theory is to be valued.

In writing these twenty chapters and almost 500 or so pages, I have emphasized areas of agreement and historical context, so that the student will be able to command a body of knowledge shared by working phoneticians and phonologists. But, more often than I can count, I have also pointed to open questions, to areas of "research and debate." Not one of the questions raised in the introduction has been thoroughly and completely answered. We have a lot left to learn. As my mother used to say, "I've taught you everything I know, and you still don't know nothin'." Well, maybe you now know enough to begin.

chapter summary

- L1 acquisition by babies is apparently effortless, and is consistently successful except in the presence of severe disability. In contrast, L2 learning by adults is effortful, variable, and often noticeably unsuccessful.
- Babies are born with the ability to perceive distinctions between any and all speech sounds, but by the age of 12 months they become particularly attuned to the contrasts that are important for their native language. This attunement may be seen as a language-particular warping of the perceptual space.
- Babies are statistical learners, using transitional probabilities between syllables and segments to discern the recurring patterns that correspond to words. They are sensitive to prosodic patterns from birth, and by the age of one year are using prosodic patterns to aid in word recognition.
- Once language-specific articulatory routines and topographies of the perceptual space are learned, they stay learned, allowing automatic and easy processing of the L1, but causing difficulty in switching to an L2. Some linguists argue for a critical period in which language acquisition can take place, but after which the cognitive mechanisms that make acquisition effortless are no longer available.
- The speech of L2 learners shows both transfer effects from L1 to L2, and developmental effects that reflect universal markedness.
- Theories that address the interaction of L1 and L2 categories in perception and production include the Native Language Magnet model, the Perceptual Assimilation Model and the Speech Learning Model.
- Phonological and phonetic theory has benefited from the study of L1 and L2 learners, and should take into account for linguistic systems that are undergoing change.

further reading

Edwards, J.G.H. and M. Zampini (eds), 2008. *Phonology and Second Language Acquisition.* Amsterdam: John Benjamins.

Kuhl, P. 2004. Early language acquisition: Cracking the speech code. *Nature Reviews* 5: 831–843.

review exercises

1. Explain the difference between:

    language acquisition and language learning
    a longitudinal study and a cross-sectional study

reduplicated babbling and variegated babbling

AX and AXB perception tests

2. Define:

L1

L2

motherese

neural plasticity

critical period

velar fronting

transfer

developmental effects in L2

3. Describe three techniques used to study infant speech perception.

4. Describe typical speech production for a child at:

birth

3 months

6 months

12 months

18 months

4 years

5. How does child speech perception change between 6 and 12 months of age?

6. Match the name of the theory or approach with the name of its principal proponent/founder.

    a.   Contrastive Analysis

    b.   Markedness Differential Hypothesis

    c.   Infant Statistical Learning

    d.   Native Language Magnet

    e.   Perceptual Assimilation Model

    f.   Speech Learning Model

____ Catherine Best

____ Fred Eckman

____ James Flege

____ Peter Jusczyk

____ Patricia Kuhl

____ Robert Lado

7. Match each of the statements below with one of the theories in (6) above.

____ Babies keep track of word and sound sequences that are more and less frequent.

____ Clusters of exemplars warp the perceptual space.

____ Developmental effects are as important as transfer effects in predicting what learners will find difficult.

____ Time spent in exposure to the L2 is an important factor in predicting learner success.

____ It is important to compare patterns of L1 and L2 contrast and allophony in predicting what learners will find difficult.

(Continued)

____ Sound categories that share articulatory gestures but differ in the details of constriction location and degree will be most difficult for language learners.

further analysis and discussion

8. What is meant by "poverty of the stimulus," and how is this idea used to argue in favor of an innate universal grammar?
9. How would a ninth-month-old English-learning child use transitional probabilities and stress patterns to extract the word boundaries in the phrase "Wave bye-bye to Gramma."?
10. You've probably heard the joke where the parent says to the child, "Behave!" and the child replies "I *am* being [hev]!" How would transitional probabilities and stress patterns mislead the child into thinking that "behave" consists of two words?
11. Which is harder for a native English speaker – perceiving the difference between Zulu [ǂ] and [ǁ] or Thai [pa] and [ba]? Explain why this should be so.

further research

12. Record or transcribe the speech of a young child. What differences from adult speech do you notice?

Go online Visit the book's companion website for additional resources relating to this chapter at: http://www.wiley.com/go/zsiga.

references

Aoyama, K., J. Flege, S. Guion, R. Akahane-Yamada, and T. Yamada, 2004. Perceived phonetic dissimilarity and L2 speech learning: The case of Japanese /r/ and English /l/ and /r/. *Journal of Phonetics* 32: 233–250.

Brent, M.R. and J. Siskind, 2001. The role of exposure to isolated words in early vocabulary development. *Cognition* 81: B33–B44.

Broselow, E., S.-I. Chen, and C. Wang. 2006. The emergence of the unmarked in L2 phonology. *Studies in Second Language Acquisition* 20: 261–280.

Eckman, F.R. 1981. On predicting phonological difficulty in second language acquisition. *Studies in Second Language Acquisition* 4: 18–30.

Flege, J., M. Munro, and I. MacKay 1995. Factors affecting degree of perceived foreign accent in a second language. *Journal of the Acoustical Society of America* 97: 3125–3134.

Jusczyk, P.W. 1997. *The Discovery of Spoken Language*. Cambridge, MA: MIT Press.

Kuhl, P.K., E. Stevens, A. Hayashi, T. Deguchi, S. Kiritani, and P. Iverson. 2006. Infants show a facilitation effect for native language phonetic perception between 6 and 12 months. *Developmental Science* 9: F13–F21

Lado, R. 1957. *Linguistics Across Cultures*. Ann Arbor, MI: University of Michigan Press.

Tsao, F.-M., H.-M. Liu, and P.K. Kuhl. 2006. Perception of native and non-native affricate-fricative contrasts: Cross-language tests on adults and infants. *Journal of the Acoustical Society of America* 120: 2285–2294.

Uther, M., M.A. Knoll, and D. Burnham. 2007. Do you speak E-NG-L-I-SH? A comparison of foreigner- and infant-directed speech. *Speech Communication* 49: 2–7.

Index

References to figures and tables are indicated by a lower-case f or t after the page reference (e.g., 15f or 15t).